Immigrants
in American History

Immigrants in American History

ARRIVAL, ADAPTATION, AND INTEGRATION

VOLUME 4

ELLIOTT ROBERT BARKAN, EDITOR

 ABC-CLIO

Santa Barbara, California • Denver, Colorado • Oxford, England

Library of Congress Cataloging-in-Publication Data

Immigrants in American history / Elliott Robert Barkan, editor.
   p. cm.
Includes bibliographical references and index.
   ISBN 978–1–59884–219–7 (hardcopy : alk. paper) — ISBN 978–1–59884–220–3 (ebook)
1. United States—Emigration and immigration—History. 2. Immigrants—United States—
History. 3. United States—Ethnic relations—History. 4. Minorities—United States—History.
I. Barkan, Elliott Robert.
JV6450.I5536   2013
305.9′069120973—dc23   2012034665

ISBN: 978–1–59884–219–7
EISBN: 978–1–59884–220–3

17 16 15 14 13   1 2 3 4 5

This book is also available on the World Wide Web as an eBook.
Visit www.abc-clio.com for details.

ABC-CLIO, LLC
130 Cremona Drive, P.O. Box 1911
Santa Barbara, California 93116-1911

This book is printed on acid-free paper ∞

Manufactured in the United States of America

Contents

VOLUME 4

PART 4   ISSUES IN U.S. IMMIGRATION

PART 4

ISSUES IN U.S. IMMIGRATION

Introduction: Issues in U.S. Immigration

Elliott Robert Barkan

Parts 1–3 of *Immigrants in American History: Arrival, Adaptation, and Integration* were designed to describe three distinct periods in American history with respect to immigration. We seek to understand who came, where they settled, how well they adapted, and what critical issues they faced. Clear-cut differences set the three eras apart, even though some lines of consistency ran through them. Just what were those lines is a key issue for Part 4. That we find both distinctive group experiences, even in one era only, and a fair number of groups sharing common experiences in the same or different eras underscores the need to include both aspects of immigrant experiences.

The United States is a vast country, and it has received migrants from many countries (approximately 200), migrating in from all directions. But, to what extent do they represent 200 stories? Rather than including short entries on many dozens of groups, we opted for longer, better developed chapters—163 to be exact—concentrating on a few dozen key communities—a number of which are covered in two and even all three time periods. In the process of identifying which groups fall into one or more eras—and notwithstanding the group differences—we recognized that there have existed thematic lines of thought and experiences cutting across the time periods and the separate group accounts to warrant the discussions of multiple groups in the chapters in this volume. These chapters provide the links, the parallels, the comparable encounters and responses binding the cohorts' histories. At the same time, enough variations emerged so that, while in this part of the book we are compelled to move beyond the single group encounters, we must

also examine those groups' histories that do establish the singularities as well as the commonalities, especially when covering more than one era. To appreciate the extensive group coverage in Parts 1–3, one must explore the comparative chapters in Part 4 in order to define the context for the individual groups we encountered in Parts 1–3.

The thematic chapters provide the foundation of shared experiences in the array of similarities among immigrant accounts, especially those groups found in more than one time period. At the same time we must give due acknowledgment to those noteworthy episodes whose distinctive experiences set apart the many dozens of individual groups.

The 30 chapters in Part 4 offer related themes and issues analyzed from a variety of perspectives and disciplines. The themes include:

1. Departure from Homelands

Most groups initially, however, held onto an array of persisting ties binding migrants with their origins, ranging from family to community to country. The ties are not uniform, nor do they extend to all members of a group. Moreover, some of the ties are of considerable strength and of multiple and quite durable strands (transnationalism), while others weaken or begin to fade and become intermittent links (translocalism). And then there are people whose migration motives were marked by fear and the quest to escape their homeland. For them, the homeland bonds are much more in doubt at the outset.

2. Categories of Admission and Deportation

These categories hardly existed at state or federal levels prior to 1875 and the enactment of the first significant federal legislation. Gradually, laws and policies were enacted and developed, creating limitations, guidelines, and eventually new categories of persons regarded as marginal and unacceptable, versus individuals seeking admission who did pass scrutiny and some who were newly identified types—such as refugees, asylees, and displaced persons. At the same time, categories of persons considered unfit, unsuitable, or undocumented were also created and expanded, providing grounds for denial of admission or their subsequent deportation—a considerable change from the *laissez faire* situation before 1875.

As the legal complexities of federal laws intensified, three additional dimensions displayed the challenges presented by the evolving policies. First, the line between foreign policies and immigration laws blurred, requiring additional perspectives, or considerations, in the formulation of federal immigration laws. Second, periodically states contested (and continue to contest) federal supremacy involving immigration and citizenship laws, and here, too, lines blurred and challenges have to be resolved. And, third, on still another level, lines were not always clear between temporary migrants and lawful permanent residents, especially as individuals sought to move from the former to the latter status. As the dual categories were developed, similar ones were needed for those not acquiring permanent residence. Many thousands were soon being designated temporary visitors—tourists, students, religious figures, businessmen, temporary workers, scientists, and engineers, as well as theatrical performers. Gradually, more and more temporary migrants eagerly sought to change their status to lawful permanent residents. Currently, half of those persons "admitted" to the United States have already been living in it.

3. Conditions upon Arrival

At first, entry ports for immigrants were unregulated and quite lax, reflecting an optimism regarding the absorption of newcomers. In addition, over time, immigrants were able to make use of several key ports of entry, including Boston, New York, Philadelphia, New Orleans, Galveston, San Francisco, and Seattle, along with many crossing points on both the Canadian and Mexican borders. Immigration stations abounded, but the principal processing centers were established on Ellis Island, in New York City's harbor (principally 1892–1924), and on Angel Island, in San Francisco Bay (1910–1940). In recent years, with technological advances, many key airports have become the important ports of entry. Even Los Angeles over the past several decades has come to be viewed as the Ellis Island of the West. However, at times, ambivalence overshadowed optimism, and fears regarding the unprecedented waves of immigrants troubled Americans.

At the same time, laws and policies began to take shape, providing the framework for screening admissions: physical and mental acceptability, cultural compatibility (regarding unfamiliar cultures, races, and religions), and ideological or philosophical concerns. (What does America represent; what is its manifest destiny for the peoples arriving every day from so many parts of the world, and how will the immigrants contribute to that manifest destiny?) In sum, beginning in 1875, open doors periodically have given way to partially closed ones, and at times, nativist responses have favored closing the nation's gateways entirely.

4. International Events and Upheavals

Mass population movements from homelands in the face of crop failures and widespread starvation, civil wars, revolutions, and invasions have ignited emigration, including from Cuba, Haiti, eastern and southern Europe, the Soviet Union, Yugoslavia, Southeast Asia, and Africa. The United States was forced (for strategic reasons) to modify policies in order to admit some of the worldwide tide of refugees. Federal responses were more generous where U.S. policies had played a role in the foreign events (e.g., via military intervention) or where humanitarian considerations were added objectives for diplomatic considerations. Prior to the development of policies in the last quarter of the nineteenth century, persons fleeing starvation and/or revolution faced few obstacles to admission to the United States. As those policies became more elaborate, the conditions for admission became more complex and conditional.

5. Enclaves of Newcomers

Whether new immigrants stayed with their homeland's communities in the United States or dispersed, involved decisions often determined by the resources newcomers brought with them, or not, and how much they needed the support of their ethnic community compared with those with advanced skills and capital who frequently lived away from the enclaves, even in early years. Institutional as opposed to economic components came into play, as did family and communal bonds. The extent of adaptation and accommodation of the newcomers also became relevant in terms of the attitudes of the immigrants and of Americans, the new host society. Group identities evolved as immigrants and their children sought to demonstrate who were most receptive to the American culture and who were more resistant, who were well received by Americans, and who despaired (or never planned to remain) and emigrated or returned home. In all three eras, such considerations became apparent.

6. The Impact of Accommodation on Domestic Conditions

Most notable was the status of women immigrants, the degree of Americanization among second-generation men and women, the extent of racial and ethnic intermarriage, and the role of religious institutions in family and communal affairs. Many changes took more than a generation to realize, and in some cases, resistance to changes came from within the immigrant community and sometimes from the broader American society. The more varied newcomers were, or the more exceptional from the norm that their cultures were, the more complex their process of gaining acceptance became. Wartime crises made responses even more uncertain and contested.

7. The Impact of Accommodation on Livelihoods

Newcomers, from enclave networks to professional associations to entrepreneurialism, have had to adjust to pursue work. Other aspects have involved the hiring of ethnic kinsmen or the fostering of ethnic business links for credit, wholesaling, and marketing. Ethnic businesses have usually played important multiple, intermediary roles within ethnic communities in addition to providing various goods and supplies, such as assisting with money transfers, letter writing to families in the homeland, and helping newcomers find employment. Even presently, ethnic community businesses are considered vital, both where the communities have dispersed and where they remain concentrated.

More trained and more educated newcomers have usually been drawn to related educational or professional organizations (especially if they had already been living and studying or working in America); and their cultural adjustment has preceded the adjustment of status. Semiskilled and unskilled workers tend to hold on to traditional associations and memberships (including unions), and, therefore, social ties are more strongly maintained with individuals of the same group (especially if they are kin or from the same village or area). In fact, in light of the ethnic members, many immigrants either bring experiences with unions from their homelands or prior residence or become acquainted with unions in the United States and are often quick to join compatriots.

8. Settlements in Various Environments

Well into the nineteenth century, most immigrants chose to live in rural communities, engaging in agricultural livelihoods, or in small towns and villages where they employed various trade skills or operated businesses for members of the community, especially where it had been founded to foster a specific ethnic community. Others, such as the Catholic Irish, Germans, and Jews more often settled in urban (or mining) communities, or commercial centers. As cities became more complex, with more factories and innovations in urban transportation, more immigrants—who frequently envisioned themselves as temporary migrants in the United

States or simply wished to bypass farming (or good land was less available)—moved into the cities.

This transition was most conspicuous in the 1800s and up to World War I. On the one hand, many immigrants and refugees since World War II had often studied, lived, and worked in homeland urban settings—quite unlike most pre–World War I migrants. On the other hand, during the past half century, many refugees have come from rural backgrounds yet opted to live in metropolitan areas and locate entirely new kinds of employment. VOLAGs (VOLunteer aid AGencies) and ethnic associations frequently assisted them in the adjustment process.

9. Religion as a Provider of Key Community Institutions

Religions, a major agency for both cultural retention and Americanization—in terms of languages, rituals, social services, and the ethnic origins of church leaders—are all modified or shifted by exposure to American culture and society. In addition, with the arrival of religious groups hitherto scarcely present—or visible only in small numbers, religious tolerance, even in the early years, did not come easily, and challenges came from both small groups and major ones, such as during World War I and shortly thereafter. During that period, the insistent concerns about the loyalty of immigrants and churches conducting services and distributing newsletters in foreign languages disturbed many Americans, especially in small towns that tended to be heavily white and Protestant. In other words, religious institutions helped immigrants to define and identify themselves at the same time that they sought acceptance from mainstream society. And yet, one important aspiration was the hope that the ethnic church would remain relevant (and appealing) to second- and third-generation offspring.

Religions have been powerful unifying institutions, and loyalty issues and cultural resistance have continued along with the Americanization of mainstream churches. Among the groups caught up in these struggles at various times have been the Quakers, Catholics, Greek and Russian Orthodox, the Armenian Apostolic Orthodox Church and the Armenian Church in America, Zoroastrians, Hasidic Jews, Baha'i, Atheists,

and, most recently, Muslims (including Sunni, Shiites, Salafi, and Sufi). Anti-Catholicism marked the years when German and Irish Catholics were arriving prior to the Civil War. It took decades for Catholics to gain some acceptance, especially in schools and politics. Indeed, the hostility against Catholicism flared up in the 1928 presidential election and even in that of 1960. The ostracism encountered by Japanese and Japanese-American Presbyterians in Los Angeles during the 1920s well illustrates the dilemma even Protestant Christians faced in overcoming hostilities based on racial differences—even in times of peace. The extensive presence of anti-Semitism during the 1920s and 1930s and that against Muslims following 9/11 likewise illustrated obstacles facing certain religious groups. Although immigrant communities frequently turned to their religious institutions as a shield against discrimination and for the preservation of group solidarity.

10. Encounters on Many Levels: Involving Cultural and Economic Clashes

Such encounters often took place near the borderlands and involving Native Americans and other American-born workers. In addition, job competition close to the borders was often acute between immigrants and native populations—even where the same ethnic origins in the Southwest (mostly Mexicans) were involved. Conflicts in various dimensions periodically exposed American nativism (and such organizations as the Know Nothings, the American Protective Association, the Ku Klux Klan, and, more recently, the now-defunct Arizona Minuteman). The clashes have also involved issues of Americanization and eligibility for citizenship along with women's rights to seek citizenship without their husbands and the right of children born in the United States to claim U.S. citizenship, even where the parents were undocumented persons.

11. Impact of Immigration on American Culture and Society

In many spheres of American life, immigrants and the children of immigrants have made profound contributions, including foods, clothing, fashions, marketing strategies (e.g., department stores), popular and classical music, art, fiction and nonfiction literature, theaters, vaudeville, cinema (in all aspects), sports, medicine, information technology, and architecture. Among the many other spheres where immigrant cultural influences have been considerable three are vital, past and present.

First, the military contributions and services as seen in the American Revolution, Mexican-American War, the Civil War, World Wars I and II, and all those wars fought during the past six decades. Second, immigrants and their children seeking roles in American politics, which may have taken time, but from Hawai'i to California to New York and Massachusetts, there immigrants learned about democracy and political action. And, third, the vital role immigrants have performed (unskilled, semiskilled, and skilled) in taking on jobs many Americans have shunned—in mines, on farms and plantations, railroad construction and maintenance, laying cobblestone city streets, construction of newer urban buildings, and especially in recent years, food processing plants, among many others.

12. Assimilation of Immigrants Is Rare

Few immigrants have gone through the stages of acculturation, adaptation, integration and, finally, assimilation. Ethnic/national identities and ties to homelands (especially families and communities)

were regarded as traditions that were viewed as essential to maintain. Indeed, the cultural demands of Americanization, and the resistance of newcomers on the basis of religion and/or race, are among the factors that slow the process of individuals' full incorporation in the host society. Immigrant individuals and ethnic communities were therefore confronted with important decisions determining what to retain (as essential and relevant) and what to change (as amenable to compromise). Moreover, individuals, not groups, assimilate; and therefore the pace of assimilation not only runs unevenly in communities, but the movement toward assimilation occurs more clearly by the time that second and third generations reach adulthood.

At whatever level or generation such contestations take place, religious institutions remain a key cultural and identificational borderline, intersecting the collective and individual decisions of community members (that is, to insist on traditions or adapt to changes, or join new churches or merged churches). Furthermore, at the most personal levels, social ties and marriage choices frequently involve determinations that have a direct bearing on choices that eventually shape assimilation outcomes and the receptivity of mainstream individuals and communities to those seeking to join. In the final analysis, while not all groups assimilate—by choice or circumstances—American society has become *relatively* more accessible to many populations of newcomers.

Immigrants and Native American Populations

Roger L. Nichols

When American Indians, or Native Americans, reached North America, they had the land to themselves. Immigrants who came after 1500 had the opposite experience. They found the continent already occupied by the descendants of the first arrivals 12,000–15,000 years earlier. From their earliest meetings to the present, both groups encountered widely differing circumstances within what became the United States. Indians saw the land and its resources as belonging to them. European newcomers, however, thought of the natural environment as almost vacant and available for their uses. Often, those opposing views brought competition, displacement, and then violence. At the same time, both natives and newcomers worked together for their mutual benefit repeatedly. Clearly, immigrants and Indians faced similar challenges, usually but not always from opposite sides.

Ideas about how to deal with each other affected everyone. At times, early arrivals from Britain, France, and Spain sought to incorporate indigenous people into their societies. Native communities, however, strove to remain separate from and unencumbered by the social and legal practices of their troublesome neighbors. As waves of immigrants continued for more than four centuries, they joined American society. Because of this long time span, their experiences with the indigenous people varied widely. The most general pattern of the changing relations between the two groups went from cooperation and coexistence to competition and then conflict, although no one model describes the many interactions accurately. Like the vast majority of the Anglo-American society, most immigrants had little direct contact with Indians. However, no matter what their origins or time of arrival, the newcomers participated fully in the nation's actions toward Indians throughout its history.

Nonnative people reaching America during the seventeenth century had several roles. Some came as invaders and, if successful, assumed being able to extract wealth from the tribal people they met. Generally not far behind and usually less violent, others saw themselves as traders and businessmen, not soldiers. They, too, expected to profit, but from trade rather than conflict. The bulk of immigrants for at least the first 200 years became average colonists. Farmers, fishermen, tradesmen, and day laborers, they comprised the largest part of colonial populations. They came from many parts of Europe and Africa, too. For example, by the mid-1600s, people in the Dutch settlement of Nieu Amsterdam (present New York City) spoke at least 17 different languages, and while other settlements had less variety, they did include a motley assortment of people. After the first few decades, those living farthest from the Atlantic coast encountered Indians far more often than their fellow colonists who lived in the more developed settlements. When thinking about how the newcomers dealt with their tribal neighbors, one needs to keep in mind the variety of Europeans and their differing positions in the structures of the colonial societies.

Upon arrival, these immigrants encountered a dizzying array of Indian groups, even before they moved far inland. For example, in Virginia, the Powhatan Confederacy included some 30 bands and tribes, only a small part of the 600 or more distinct native societies in America at the time of early settlement efforts. These indigenous groups or their ancestors had inhabited North America for thousands of years by the time Columbus "discovered" the Western Hemisphere. Complex societies such as Cahokia in Illinois had included at least 20,000 inhabitants, while Mississippian and related groups had spread over much of the territory east of the Mississippi River. Most recent estimates suggest that these and other groups numbered between 3.5 million and 5 million people when they first met the invading Europeans. They had dealt successfully with their local environments; fed, clothed, and housed themselves; and carried out diplomacy, trade, and warfare with other native peoples.

The development of what became American society placed enormous challenges before the indigenous people and their European neighbors. Gradually, over generations and probably without their recognition, natives and newcomers began to share experiences. Both moved from their traditional homes either by choice or necessity. In their new locations, they lacked earlier connections to place, to religious or historical sites, to long-accustomed social and economic traditions. They had to establish new ties with the land and the people they met, and to fill gaps in their knowledge resulting from relocation. By the nineteenth century, both had to adapt to a rapidly developing market economy that was substantially different from anything they had experienced in rural European villages or Native American camps. So the multigenerational process of Americanization proved difficult, even wrenching, for immigrants and Indians alike.

Early Challenges

Often the early immigrants lacked essential skills needed for survival. At the same time, they either feared or despised the nearby indigenous groups. In either case, that inhibited peaceful relations. Early European intruders had a variety of objectives for dealing with the Indians, which divided them

Trade relations involving natives and Europeans were begun early on and in some cases polarized the stances of existing enemy tribes, and, with others, strengthened alliances. (The Print Collector/StockPhotoPro)

repeatedly. These included carrying out successful trade, gaining access to the land and its resources, and establishing their power and control over the local situation. Almost from their first landings along the coast, some colonists traded with the villagers for everything from basic foodstuffs to valuable furs and the hides of larger animals. For such exchanges to continue, two things had to happen. First, the intruding people had to remain at peace with their indigenous neighbors. Trade and warfare did not mix. Second, the exchanges depended on isolation, and the authorities had to limit the immigrant settlers' efforts to encroach on Indian land. When they could or would not do that, the traders' native partners either moved away or fought to retain their homes. In some ways, would-be missionaries and educators shared the traders' views, hoping to keep the native groups sheltered from contacts with the rest of their countrymen. They complained repeatedly that lower-class whites cheated and debauched the villagers, so the clerics sought to limit such exchanges.

At the same time, the general immigrant population, mostly would-be farmers, sought tribal land and showed little concern about disrupting the fur trade or the modest missionary efforts nearby. Thus, the intruding population remained divided over when, where, and how much land they dared take. Those internal debates continued for generations and to some extent shaped later American policies and actions toward Indians for a century or more. While similar divisions developed among most of the competing international powers, they proved far less important among the Spanish, French, and Swedish settlements than among the English. The latter relied most heavily on settler occupation of the land, which, in turn, brought those immigrants into more frequent competition and conflict with the tribal groups.

New Netherlands

The little-known Dutch experiences with the nearby indigenous groups offer a clear example of these complexities. By the early 1620s, the Dutch West Indian Company brought a few settlers to the Hudson River Valley in present New York. There they built what became Fort Orange at Albany and opened a profitable trade with the nearby Iroquoian people. For a decade, the two groups traded peaceably. During the mid-1630s, however, company authorities wanted to increase business and profits, and they sent hundreds of people to the colony. Once these newcomers came, relations between the immigrants and the nearby Indians changed abruptly. The settlers wanted land, and to them the native villagers' cleared and well-tended fields appeared irresistible. As the Dutch encroached on their land, native anger and fear grew. Unfenced European livestock caused other difficulties, too, as cattle and swine trampled and ate the Indians' crops while frightening away the wild game the villagers depended on for food. When they killed the wandering domestic animals, Dutch authorities armed the farmers and ordered them to clear the natives from the region. Beginning in the 1640s, bitter fighting swept through the region as the invaders destroyed most of their close neighbors. Settlements of the other colonial powers provide similar examples.

Pilgrims

Yet, not all immigrants followed this path to rapid violence and warfare. For some groups, cooperation and coexistence lasted for generations. The frequently mentioned Pilgrims of Plymouth Colony experienced far more peaceful relations than had the Dutch during their early settlement. Although originally terrified of the people they described as "cruel, barbarous and most treacherous" savages (Bradford, as quoted in Nichols 2003, 47), in March 1621, their views changed when Wampanoag chief Massasoit visited Plymouth. Accompanied by English-speaking Tisquantum (Squanto), he proposed a defensive military alliance between the English and his people. Both the villagers, who feared their powerful Narragansett neighbors, and the Pilgrims, desperate over having lost nearly half of their tiny settlement the preceding year, agreed quickly. The resulting treaty benefited both groups. Although the English at Plymouth and the Wampanoags often had disagreements, they needed to cooperate for mutual survival. So the 1621 agreement helped ensure peace between them for the next 50 years.

Puritan New England

Nearby, in the Massachusetts Bay Colony based at Boston, the invading English proved arrogant and ethnocentric as they pushed the small coastal tribes aside quickly. Like the small Pilgrim settlement to the south, the Puritans came to stay, and during the 1630s, thousands of immigrants poured into their colony. This flood of newcomers strained peaceful dealings with the nearby indigenous groups, but at least briefly the religious scruples of colonial leaders helped avoid major incidents. They sought to protect Indian property and to settle disputes over the destruction of the villagers' crops by white-owned livestock. However, Puritan theology and numbers led to a long-term effort to control all aspects of life in the region. English laws and courts provided the avenue for resolving interracial issues. Protestant clergymen worked to convert the villagers to Christianity and to turn them into small-time farmers within the colony's precapitalist economy. Operating with the heavy hand of those who believed that God was on their side, they fought a war of near-extermination against the Pequot tribe whose leaders had refused Puritan demands. Their 1637 wanton killing of hundreds of Indian men, women, and children appalled some observers. One wrote that "it was a fearful sight to see them [the Pequots] thus frying in the fire ... and horrible was the stinck & sente thereof" (quoted in Nichols 2003, 49–50). At the same time, the English military tactics so terrorized many of the local tribes that no other serious war erupted for nearly 40 years.

Another aspect of the Puritans' determination to dominate all aspects of life in the colony may be seen through the tactics several ministers used to convert their tribal neighbors to Christianity. To do this, they had to destroy the influence of the village shamans, whom they labeled as spokesmen for the devil. Working with colonial authorities, they got laws passed outlawing work on the Sabbath and conducting native healing and other cultural ceremonies. During the middle of the seventeenth century, John Eliot in Massachusetts and Thomas Mayhew (father and son) working on the nearby offshore islands had established Christian Indian congregations there.

By the 1660s, Eliot had persuaded colonial authorities to establish a dozen so-called praying towns, populated by converts whose societies or villages had collapsed under the cultural pounding they had experienced from the English. There, living under the watchful eye of Puritan magistrates, they had to avoid such actions as drunkenness, Sabbath breaking, swearing, and polygamy and to participate in Christian worship services. Despite having accepted virtually all aspects of English culture and life, these converts almost never received full membership in the Puritan churches, and during the 1676 King Philip's War, the authorities feared that they might join the hostile groups and so exiled them to a few rocky islands off the coast. By then the colonial leaders had achieved their long-sought goal, near total control of all aspects of life for most of the indigenous people still living within their colony.

Virginia

At first the invaders' actions in colonial Virginia resembled those in New England. In 1607, the English built their tiny settlement at Jamestown well within the region dominated by the Powhatan Confederacy. After several minor incidents they reached a tenuous peace, but when the starving colonists stole corn from nearby villagers at gunpoint, war followed. When the fighting ended, the invaders assumed they had won and acted as though they controlled the region. The Pamunkey leader Opechcancanough reinforced this idea by appearing to allow English missionary work to continue and by agreeing to let Indian families move into or near to Jamestown. In 1622, he responded to the murder of a prominent shaman by leading a devastating surprise attack on the immigrants. The war that followed continued sporadically for much of the next decade, but in the end, the indigenous people sued for peace. In the 1620s and 1630s, hundreds of new immigrants poured into the colony, and in 1644, when the tribesmen made a second effort to drive out the hated English, it failed, too.

After that second victory over the villagers, the Virginians shifted most of their attention to other matters. Instead of using their strength to dominate the Indians, they quarreled bitterly among themselves. Several issues divided the immigrant society. They argued over who should control the fur trade and which frontier defense policies needed to be implemented. Because the governor and his tidewater political allies dominated the fur trade, they wanted peaceful Indian relations. The frontier pioneers who lived nearest the indigenous people demanded that the government carry out vigorous military operations to acquire tribal lands for their use. In 1676, these opposing goals led to open conflict. When a frontier farmer refused to pay a small band of Doeg Indians for work they had done for him, they took several of his hogs. An argument over the pigs led to a shooting that soon brought out frontier militiamen, who attacked nearby Indian settlements against the direct orders of the colonial governor. After killing many peaceful villagers, the pioneers launched an attack, now called Bacon's Rebellion, on the Virginia colonial government. Clearly by this time, immigrant pioneers in Virginia had come to fear and hate their indigenous neighbors enough to engage in aggressive warfare against them and each other.

French

Immigrants from other European nations developed similar patterns of interracial contacts. Early Spanish actions in the Southwest focused on controlling the indigenous groups there, and that narrative appears in "Borderlands and the American Southwest" in Part 4. However, the French actions, as they moved south from Québec and north from tiny settlements near the mouth of the Mississippi River, offer other examples of early colonial era contacts with the native people. In 1608 Samuel Champlain founded the village of Québec. Yet for most of the next century, few people emigrated to the struggling settlement on the St. Lawrence River. Necessity forced its inhabitants to open what became a major fur-trading network that extended into the northern colonies. Because few of the French farmers needed land and because of the settlers' heavy reliance on economic exchange with the Indians, they fought with their immediate neighbors less often than did the British colonists. In Louisiana, far to the south, the situation differed as French immigrants turned quickly to agriculture, encroaching on tribal lands and setting off a series of brutal wars in the early decades of the eighteenth century.

Later Colonial Actions

So the encounters of each intruding European group followed similar patterns despite their occurring at different times, in different places, and with different indigenous groups. That resulted from shared motivations for actions toward Indian people. Leaders of each early immigrant group sought to dominate their local circumstances. They expected to wield power, to gain wealth and resources, and, hopefully, to remain at peace. As they worked to achieve the first two of those goals, their actions led to repeated violence and warfare. At times tribal actions triggered conflict, but more often those of the invaders did. International competition and intertribal conflicts further complicated affairs. Gradually as immigrants populated the many small colonies, the leaders became hopelessly involved in Indian trade, diplomacy, and military actions. From the 1680s to the 1760s four major international wars—King William's, Queen Anne's, King George's, and the French and Indian War—kept tribes fighting other tribes, colonists attacking other colonists, and immigrants and Indians battling each other repeatedly.

Between 1700 and 1750, immigration from Europe increased sharply as nearly a half million Germans and Scots Irish flooded into the English colonies. The surge of new colonists persuaded local authorities to seek more land from their tribal neighbors. By this time, tribal leaders had encountered frequent pressure to surrender land to the intruders. Usually the requests went to leaders of groups allied with local governments and asked for only modest-sized areas. This time Pennsylvania leaders, sensing a chance for solid profits, cheated their Indian neighbors. They persuaded James Logan to "find" a misplaced 1686 treaty with the Delaware Indians. Supposedly in the treaty, they had agreed to sell a tract between the Delaware and Lehigh Rivers that included land as far as a man could walk in a day and a half. The colonists sent workers to clear a trail through the forest and hired three runners to do the "walking." When they finished their run, the "Walking Purchase" included more than twice the land the Indians had expected to surrender. While the new arrivals from Europe had no part in the swindle, their presence gave colonial leaders a strong motivation for the action.

The large mid-eighteenth-century migrations of immigrants to the British colonies brought ever more newcomers, mostly from Europe, to the frontier areas. Would-be farmers, once here, had few chances to get land except in the newly opened frontier areas. As they traveled to western regions of the Carolinas, Virginia, and Pennsylvania, they met Indians frequently. Before long, they came to despise the tribal people. The intruders had plenty of reasons for their feelings, some legitimate, others not. They saw the indigenous people as standing between themselves and their dreams of land ownership. An inability to talk to or understand most of what the tribal people said contributed to frequent misunderstandings. Heavy drinking among both the pioneers and the nearby Indians did little to ensure peace. Indian participation in the imperial wars during the 1740s and 1750s–1760s fanned existing tensions and bitterness against all native groups among many newcomers who were living in some of the frontier villages.

Particularly during the 1755–1763 French and Indian War, the Scots-Irish immigrants in western Pennsylvania became involved in a cycle of raids and counterraids with nearby Indians. When, in the summer of 1763, the pioneers' demands for help in defending themselves from raids during Pontiac's War brought no response from colonial authorities, the frontiersmen took matters in their own hands. Suspicious of Indians living nearby in the Moravian mission towns, these immigrants responded angrily to rumors that the peaceful native villagers spied for the warring bands. By December 1763, pioneers decided to attack, and about 50 armed men rode into the small settlement at Conestoga, murdered the 6 Indians they found, and burned their cabins. Two weeks later, they decided to kill the others who had been moved to Lancaster for their protection, and they slaughtered another 14 Moravian converts. Consequently, in this case, the two immigrant groups took opposite actions toward the

indigenous people. The German Moravian missionaries offered peaceful conversion to Christianity; the Scots Irish brought death and destruction.

During the 1760s–1780s, the repeated violence and warfare between the colonists and the nearby tribes persisted to such an extent that, when the colonists gained independence in 1783, many of the long-term patterns of immigrant-Indian relationships had been set. Unsettled conditions in the United States and the European conflict following the French Revolution reduced emigration to America drastically for a time. Yet, the continuing need for laborers and harsh conditions in their homelands persuaded people to cross the Atlantic seeking opportunity. In 1819, the federal government established a system to keep statistics on the newcomers, and it became clear that more than 80 percent of the immigrants came from either Germany or Britain and Ireland. At least until the end of the 1840s, the population base of American society had changed only minimally.

Mormons

While the vast majority of immigrants to America before the 1870s continued to come from those three areas, overseas missionary efforts and the California Gold Rush attracted thousands of people from other countries, even other parts of the world. Some early Mormon converts from both the eastern United States and Western Europe arrived earlier than the gold seekers. Others continued to enter the country long after the mining booms had ended. Both groups had substantial contacts with Native Americans in nineteenth-century America, but they often differed substantially in their responses. In 1830, Joseph Smith finished translating and transcribing *The Book of Mormon*, and the next year he founded the Church of Jesus Christ of Latter-day Saints. From the start, he claimed that the book was a direct revelation from God and fully equal to the Bible. Many Americans considered this to be preposterous, while others viewed Smith's assertions as heresy, and soon his followers became the objects of derision and suspicion. During the 1830s, the group moved to Kirtland, Ohio, and then on to western Missouri, but trouble dogged their movements repeatedly. When a new revelation told Smith about plural marriage, the announcement split the Mormon community and further antagonized their neighbors. In 1844, a hostile mob killed Joseph and his brother, and within two years, Brigham Young led the believers west to present-day Utah. From there, church officials established a highly successful foreign mission program that brought thousands of converts, particularly from Scandinavia, to the United States.

In several ways, Indians played a significant role in these immigrants' lives because of their place in church doctrine, which named the indigenous people Lamanites and called for their conversion. So Mormons established a continuing mission program that focused on nearby Indian groups. Actually, the earliest church members had preached their beliefs to the Seneca tribe near Buffalo, New York, and the later efforts in Utah merely followed that previous practice. The missionaries hoped that native groups would respond positively to their teachings because only Mormon doctrine included Indians as a central part of its theology. During the 1850s, church leaders sent more than 130 men on missions to tribal groups from Idaho south to Arizona and New Mexico.

Their efforts to convert and incorporate indigenous people into their society proved difficult. Despite church teachings, many of the Latter-day Saints held the same anti-Indian views as did their Gentile countrymen. Still, many of them and their immigrant converts followed church directives. Yet they found it difficult to avoid repeated difficulties because of actions taken by gold seekers and other migrants moving west. In 1857, Brigham Young complained that the overland travelers attacked and robbed the nearby Shoshone, Bannock, and Paiute peoples so often that the Indians considered all whites as enemies. A series of retaliatory raids that followed targeted the nearby Mormons as the only permanent white residents nearby. The violence severely curtailed missionary efforts for a time. Despite that, church authorities encouraged a program to buy enslaved Indian children and adopt and incorporate them into white families. Meanwhile, its mission program in Europe succeeded, and a continuing stream of immigrants came into the Mountain West, where some of them had to deal with Native Americans.

Miners

As Brigham Young and his followers began to settle in the Mountain and Desert West, another large stream of immigrants poured into that region. The discovery of readily available gold by laborers working for John Sutter while American and Mexican negotiators haggled over terms for ending hostilities between the two governments triggered the famous California Gold Rush. The figures vary widely, but it seems likely that in 1848–1849, at least 80,000 newcomers hurried west to get their share of the gold. Whereas most of these people were not new entrants into the United States, thousands of men came to the California mines from Australia and China, from many nations in Europe, and at least from Chile and northern Mexico. Once in America, their presence altered local ethnic and racial populations substantially as they joined others in moving from place to place with news of each new mineral find. Frequently, their mining occurred in the heart of already Indian-occupied areas, putting stress on indigenous societies and at times bringing tension and violence to interethnic relations.

From the start, as Americans and immigrants rushed into the gold fields, they encountered Indians already there. Having previously labored for the Californios, many now worked for the newcomers or for themselves. The early guidebooks published to inform would-be miners suggested that hiring Indians would lead to success. It appears certain that at the end of the 1840s, hundreds of California tribesmen toiled in mines. In late 1848, one observer claimed that about 2,000 whites "and more than double that number of Indians" sought gold (Rawls 1984, 119). Earlier that year, Colonel Richard Mason had reported that indigenous people made up more than half of the 4,000 men then at the mines. Apparently, newcomers adapted the existing Hispanic labor system, often hiring the native people directly from nearby ranches. One account noted that in California, ranchers considered Indians almost as livestock and sold their services to incoming miners. Local reports suggest that groups ranging from 20 to 100 Indians worked in the mining areas for the newcomers. Other natives located large gold deposits on

Carson's Creek and Wood's Creek in the area soon called the Southern Mines. During 1848, in almost all cases, peaceful indigenous men and women earned food, clothing, and perhaps small wages helping their employers gain large profits. Small numbers of the tribal people mined on their own, but most served as wage earners working for others.

These exploitive but peaceful relations faded within a single year. During 1849, tens of thousands of outsiders poured into the mining regions, and most of the newcomers had no knowledge of, or experience with, the Hispanic labor system then in operation. Having crossed the plains, many of the forty-niners feared or hated Indians. Thus, when they encountered natives as gang-laborers helping other miners to profit, they objected bitterly. They raised the same complaints when a few southern slave-owners brought their workers to the mines. Those who could exploit either Indian or black slave labor held an advantage in the race for gold. At first these protests came from miners rushing south from Oregon, but during 1849, they became far more widespread, and violence followed. Newcomers threatened Californians who dared employ Indians in the mines, raped native women, attacked the men when they objected, and began a campaign to destroy many of the nearby indigenous villages.

It is difficult to know exactly what roles immigrants had in these events, but there is little doubt that some of them took part in the slaughter. Army Captain Edward Townsend described these civilian vigilante actions as "a picture of cruelty, injustice and horror scarcely to be surpassed by that of the Peruvians in the time of Pizarro" (Tate 2006, 221). Widespread disease and starvation accompanied the raids, and together they reduced the indigenous population of California drastically. According to demographer Sherburne Cook, the number of Indians there dropped from about 150,000 in 1845, to 100,000 in 1850, to 50,000 in 1855, and to 35,000 by 1860.

At the same time, many immigrants in early gold rush California faced the discrimination and antagonism from American miners as did the Indians. Large numbers of Chileans with considerable experience as miners or suppliers came quickly. Their obvious early success triggered the same "the gold is for Americans" feelings, and native-born miners organized their traditional mining associations to exclude foreigners from the diggings. In the summer of 1849, armed gangs attacked several Chilean camps, driving these foreign miners out of the hills. When the angry immigrants reached San Francisco, rioting broke out. When the violence ended, the shops of many well-to-do Chilean merchants lay in smoldering ruins, and those merchants had to stand by helplessly while the criminals held public auctions of their goods. In December that year, the violence extended into the mining camps themselves. There, Americans attacked the Hispanics again, and when the Chileans defended themselves, mobs overwhelmed them. Rioters forced them to surrender their claims, seized their tools, and arrested, tried, and executed some of those who dared to fight back. Sonorans from northern Mexico and the Chinese suffered equally violent treatment. When California gained statehood in 1850, its legislators enacted a foreign miners' tax, essentially a fine on non-Americans who remained in the diggings. Consequently, in the early mining areas, even when immigrants had little direct contact with indigenous people, they suffered from the same greed and hatred that nearly destroyed the Indians in the mining regions.

Overland Trail Encounters

While would-be miners continued to drift west, reports of hardship, danger, and failure ended the frenzied 1849 rush within a year. However, they did little to halt the continuing movement of Americans, immigrants and others, to the West. Most of this took place between 1845 and 1860, but some continued until 1870 when the completed transcontinental railroad curtailed overland wagon-train travel. In 1854, Congress had established the Kansas and Nebraska Territories, bringing the last western land areas outside Indian Territory within the reach of some governmental authority. During the decades preceding and following the Civil War, the United States sought to push the tribal groups onto reservations, usually far removed from the major overland trails. Large, mobile groups, such as the Comanche, Cheyenne, and Sioux, all resisted, and bitter Indian wars kept the nation focused on them. As much danger as these conflicts represented, it is clear that the vast majority of people moving west across the plains at the time never encountered hostile natives.

Nevertheless, interracial relations on the western trails proved anything but easy for the Plains groups and the migrants passing through. Among the latter, both resident Americans and Europeans in the wagon-train parties carried with them often exaggerated fears of Indians. Long-time American dwellers had heard and read tales of Indian savagery and violence that stretched back for 250 years. While after the War of 1812 few pioneers faced the threat of tribal violence, the telling and retelling of the earlier stories only magnified the cruelty and destruction indigenous people represented in the national history. Apparently, many people traveling west never escaped the fear that grew out of those narratives. Often they had only negative ideas about any indigenous people they might encounter. Hearing tales of danger, newly arrived immigrants had little reason to discount them, so it seems likely that they would become equally nervous about meeting native people.

Even while increasing contacts with whites moving through their country made some Indians living near the trails nervous, many sought out the strangers as possible trade partners. For them, barter offered possibilities to get manufactured goods and varieties of food not readily available most of the time. On the northern Plains, the Lakota Sioux visited wagon trains repeatedly seeking items such as flour, sugar, or coffee. Metal items of all sorts, fishhooks, pots, and pans as well as knives caught their attention. They wanted to trade for almost any fabric items, including blankets, clothing, or simple cloth. What the travelers considered as routine household or personal articles like matches, tobacco, mirrors, or jewelry, all found eager takers when exchanges took place. Trading guns, powder, and lead as well as alcohol raised tensions on both sides. Native men wanted these items, while the travelers feared violence might follow. Despite some uneasiness about these items, the repeated trading had direct impacts on people of both races. Indians made their lives easier through access to items not part of their own economies, while those moving overland got food, buffalo robe blankets, and Indian footwear they wanted. When successful,

trading along the trail may have lessened both the newcomers' fears about being attacked, and the Sioux's curiosity and distress at the continuing presence of whites passing through their country.

Nevertheless, at the same time, the continuing flood of pioneers moving through regions the Indians considered to be their homeland led to a gradual worsening of relations between the races. Near the Platte River, indigenous people asked repeatedly for a few head of cattle because the animals accompanying the wagon trains ate the grass and drank from and fouled the water holes. Often travelers thought nothing of killing the wild animals they saw along the trail, obviously reducing the game left for the hunting peoples' subsistence. Their movement across the central trails also disrupted the migrations of the bison, a central part of Plains tribes' diet. When young hunters found no buffalo and killed the whites' cattle or horses for food, violence followed. Most of the time whites, either native or immigrant, failed to understand the deeply held Indian ideas about exchange and sharing.

In these circumstances, few people of either group had any idea what the other was saying, so tensions remained high. The whites' real fears meant that the Plains dwellers often faced equal or more danger from their meetings than did the pioneers. Even when Indians tried to help the strangers traveling through their homelands, they worried about how the whites might react. In the early twentieth century, Lakota Sioux elders reported an incident that demonstrated this. In their version, a small group of hunters found a single wagon containing a woman and her two young children abandoned by her traveling companions. The men tried to calm the terrified family, bringing them food, and, after helping them for two days, bringing them into contact with another wagon train (Tate 2006, xii–xiii). Another group of hunters found a small boy hiding in the bushes. After feeding him, they took him back to the trail ahead of another caravan so that the travelers would find him. The Sioux reported that they feared riding up to the wagons with the child because they spoke no English and pioneers might misunderstand their motives. These incidents illustrate Indian worries about possible trouble if they met the travelers. Such fears extended to all whites, not only those just entering the country for the first time.

Contact and Conflict

While thousands of newcomers reached Utah or California, many settled in the upper Mississippi River Valley. During the middle decades of the nineteenth century, authorities in states and territories from Indiana west to Iowa and from Illinois north to Wisconsin and Minnesota sought to lure immigrants from Western Europe to their communities. For example, only a few years after gaining statehood in 1848, Wisconsin established an office to seek out possible immigrants and to help them get across the Atlantic. Not every state and territory followed suit, but most welcomed new residents when they arrived. Within the next two or three decades, easily identifiable ethnic communities dotted the countryside of states from Wisconsin west to the Rocky Mountains. Swiss, Finns, Scandinavians, Dutch, Russians, and Germans all settled on the rolling prairies and plains. In this process, they occupied land long used by native people, replacing Indian villages with their European communities.

Some of the new settlers sought actively to avoid conflict over land with the indigenous people. This happened in the Republic of Texas when authorities there tried to enlarge their population. The Texas government issued a grant to the Society for the Protection of German Immigrants, under the direction of Prince Carl of Solms-Braunfels for land used by the Comanche tribe. The award called for survey work before the end of 1847; so early that year, John Muesebach, accompanied by Robert Neighbors, who was already well known to Comanche leaders, led a well-armed party to contact and negotiate with the Indians. They met peacefully and, after several days of talks, signed the Muesebach-Treaty, which promised both the immigrants' and native people's safety in each other's territory. It provided for a survey and a payment of $1,000 in return for just over three million acres of land. This agreement resembled the 1622 treaty between the Pilgrims and Massasoit, promising cooperation against criminal activities toward either group. There are questions about the

document's effectiveness, but later the U.S. government accepted it as a legitimate treaty, the only privately negotiated one in American history.

Like the Germans in Texas, many immigrant groups had quiet, even beneficial contacts with native groups. As hunting declined and the government forced the tribes onto reservations, Indian men sought work in the nearby rural areas. On ranches they worked as cowboys, fence builders, and general laborers. In farming settlements they hauled crops and freight and helped with crop harvests as they sought to keep their families from abject poverty. Near reservations, both ranchers and farmers leased land from tribal members who lacked the capital or skills to use the acres themselves (following the allotment of tribal lands beginning in 1887). Most of the time, immigrants and native-born Americans welcomed Indian workers or access to their land, keeping relations peaceful. By 1890, when the government implemented the allotment policy, Western ranchers and farmers enlarged their holdings through access to newly opened Indian lands.

Despite that, bitter wars did break out, bringing tragedy for everyone involved. The so-called Santee Sioux War of 1862 provides a good example. By the early 1850s, the rolling prairie lands of southern Minnesota attracted German migrants fleeing their homes after the failed 1848 revolutions and the upheavals that followed. Many of these people joined Americans as they moved into the new state. Their presence disrupted the Dakota Sioux's annual round of farming, hunting, trapping, and gathering. The whites' hunting reduced game available to the Indians, who depended on it for food and as a source of hides and pelts for trade. Far more concerned with the Civil War than with Indian affairs at the time, federal officials had difficulties in getting the promised annuity goods to the native camps on time. This upset village leaders, and when local traders refused to provide food on credit because of the delays, a crisis ensued, and an isolated incident set off a wave of terror and warfare. In August 1862, what might have been only a minor incident resulted in the murder of five pioneers by a few young Dakota hunters. This set off an immediate frontier war in which Dakota attackers caught the hundreds of German settlers along the Minnesota River by surprise. A major Sioux attack on August 19, 1862, brought the German immigrants at New Ulm face to face with the horrors of an all-out Indian war. Fierce house-to-house fighting destroyed much of the community.

Other raiding parties threatened several small Swedish communities as well. The next day, August 20, Indians attacked farms near New London, Minnesota, killing some 20 men, women and children there. A lurid report of torture and killings there circulated quickly among nearby Swedish settlers, and some of these pioneers fled to St. Cloud. A few days, later the same observer noted that some of the reputed victims had, in fact, survived, but were all homeless and nearly destitute. When the immediate terror passed, a second correspondent offered a more dispassionate view. He noted that while some prospective settlers might avoid Minnesota, in the long run the uprising would have good results for the state. This proved correct on two counts. The actual settlers in the Swedish Lutheran congregation near New London fled. At the same time, the government moved to expel the Indians, and that opened "enormous tracts of land" for almost immediate settlement. When the conflict ended a few months later, somewhere between 400 and 800 settlers had been killed. The Dakota Sioux lost fewer than 100 men, but on December 26, federal authorities hanged 38 of the Indian men convicted of having killed some of the settlers. This brief and bloody conflict demonstrated that even though fears of Indian violence may have been overstated, immigrants living in pioneer communities shared whatever danger events might bring.

Building the Transcontinental Railroads

Other than the California Gold Rush, no single event in the last half of the nineteenth century attracted as many immigrants as the building of the first transcontinental railroad and the competing lines that soon followed. At the end of the Civil War, the Union Pacific hired as many as 10,000 Irish and Germans to lay its track west from Omaha. At the same time, the Central Pacific employed about 8,000 Chinese laborers to build their line east from Sacramento. Certainly not all of the workers arrived on the job directly from their home countries, but many did, and others had entered the country years earlier. If they stayed close to the temporary housing the corporations provided, usually their large numbers insulated them from Indian attacks. However, by the late 1860s, tribal leaders realized that the ever-increasing number of whites in the West limited their freedom to travel and hunt in many areas on the Plains. As the Union Pacific work crews extended the tracks ever farther west, small war parties carried out sporadic raids on them. Both Sioux and Cheyenne warriors harassed the laborers, but they lacked the numbers needed to delay construction seriously.

Still, the government and corporation leaders worried about delays and extra costs the Native Americans entailed. The army enlisted a force of Pawnee men—traditional enemies of the Sioux and Cheyenne—to help defend the workers. Despite this, even after the 1869 completion of the first line west, San Arc Sioux leader Spotted Eagle threatened that "he would fight the rail road people as long as he lived [and] would tear up the road and kill its builders" (quoted in Utley 1993, 107). If carried out, his pledge threatened immigrant workers directly. Occasionally, Indians tried to destroy part of the main line track, but that proved difficult. So at times, young men climbed the telegraph poles that stood along the route, cut the wires, and filled the gaps with strands made of buffalo hide. This disrupted communication and delayed needed repairs because of the difficulty of seeing where the lines had been cut. Yet, the indigenous people lacked not only the numbers to seriously disrupt the transcontinental railroad, but also the technological skills to inflict permanent or even serious long-term damage. Chief Red Cloud recognized this when he said that "the white children [of the Great Father] have surrounded me and have left me nothing but an island" (quoted in Nadeau 1967, 250).

Immigrant Soldiers and Indians

When crises in Indian affairs arose, the United States called on the army to settle them. In much of the nineteenth century, many Americans believed that the ranks of enlisted men in uniform consisted of "the scum of the population of the older states, or . . . the worthless

German, English, or Irish emigrants" (quoted in Coffman 1986, 137). Echoing that characterization one veteran described his former companions as "foreigners, generally of the lowest and most ignorant class" (quoted in Coffman 1986, 137). While not particularly accurate, these labels demonstrated that often young male immigrants arrived in the country both destitute and speaking little English. For many of them, the army offered temporary stability while they learned the language. Although recruiting officers had orders not to accept non-English-speakers, during the 1840s and 1850s, Irish and German immigrants together comprised 66 percent of the troops. Their numbers and percentages fell after the Civil War, but foreigners remained an important component among the enlisted men.

Few of these soldiers had any knowledge of the tribal societies they had to oversee. It seems likely that they brought whatever ideas had circulated in their home communities before they emigrated. Once in the United States, after spending months with native-born Americans, they could not have avoided learning what their peers thought about indigenous people. For most of them, this represented little more than shared ignorance until they met real Indians. Then, despite the lurid stories of the repeated wars in the West, most soldiers spent far more of their time carrying out boring garrison duties than they did campaigning against the indigenous people. That meant that many soldiers visited nearby Indian camps, held horse and foot races, traded for personal items, hunted together, learned each other's languages, and occasionally enjoyed sexual exchanges.

For many these peaceful experiences shaped their ideas about Native Americans, but the soldiers could not ignore the possibility that sometime they might have to fight against the tribesmen. Therefore, the enlisted men held no one set of ideas about Indians. For example, when two men in the Second Cavalry heard that a wagon master had been killed in an Indian raid, they reacted in two opposing ways. One wanted to attack and wipe out the attackers. His friend demurred. Perhaps "that would be right," he responded, "but you see . . . they are here and were here before we came . . . and they have the absurd notion that this country belongs to them" (quoted in Coffman 1986, 392). Few

immigrant soldiers left written accounts that clarify their attitudes toward the tribal people, but it seems likely that most of them shared the popular thinking of their day.

Individual Experiences

Beginning with the earliest European landings in North America to the twentieth century, thousands of immigrants met Indians repeatedly. Certainly, from the days of John Rolfe and Pocahontas in colonial Virginia, if not before, individuals shared intimate contacts. Fur traders and other merchants married into the village societies with whom they did business, and gradually their descendants gained leadership positions within many tribes. A brief glance at the number of English and French names of many indigenous leaders in American history illustrates how often interracial sexual relations occurred. Cherokee leader John Ross, Potawatomi chief Billy Caldwell, and Comanche spokesman Quanah Parker were among the many mixed-race native leaders. Occasionally these men could use their background and connections to shield their tribes successfully from American demands for land and cultural change.

The immigrants' experiences in coming to terms with American society varied as much as those of the Indians. A few, such as Andrew Carnegie, rose to corporate wealth and power. Most achieved less economic success even though they contributed. A couple of examples can illustrate this. The first, a German immigrant named Carl Schurz, entered politics. He reached the United States in 1852, held offices in Wisconsin and Missouri, served as a general in the Civil War, and in 1876 became secretary of the interior. In that position he supervised the commissioner of Indian affairs, which gave him direct contact with the growing reservation system, reform groups, tribal leaders, and the political wrangling related to the indigenous people. While he occupied that cabinet office, he opposed the groups working to move the Office of Indian Affairs from the Interior to the War Department and also launched a widespread investigation of both the personnel and practices of the Indian service. He met visiting delegations of tribal leaders in Washington and listened to their concerns, but usually upheld existing reservation and acculturative policies. In his cabinet position, it is likely that Schurz exercised as much authority in Indian affairs as any immigrant did.

Another newcomer, the German artist Winold Reiss, migrated to New York City in 1913, two generations after his fellow countryman Schurz, and had different experiences. When he came west, he followed the steps of earlier European artists from Karl Bodmer in the 1830s to Alfred Bierstadt later in the nineteenth century. Before participating successfully in the Harlem Renaissance in New York, Reiss traveled west to the Blackfoot Reservation in 1919, where he produced 35 portraits of individuals there. Eight years later, in 1927, the Great Northern Railroad invited him back to Montana to paint scenes in Glacier National Park. The corporation used much of his work in their "See America First" campaign to encourage tourists to travel to the West on its trains. Although better known for his art-deco style paintings at the Cincinnati Union (RR) Terminal, during his career, the artist completed 181 portraits of Montana Indians. His experiences in executing those paintings brought him into far closer contact with the native people than most of his New York contemporaries, and certainly more than most other immigrants.

Conclusion

By the late nineteenth century, the sources of immigration to America shifted dramatically. Often referred to as the "New Immigration," millions of people from southern and eastern Europe poured into the nation's East Coast and Midwestern cities. Italians, Greeks, Poles, Russians, and a host of others entered the country until World War I, which cut off most migration across the Atlantic. Even considering the modest numbers of people who came from Asia and Latin America, only a few newcomers moved directly into the rural West or had much direct contact with Indians then mostly living on isolated reservations. For the twentieth century, it becomes much more difficult to narrate relations between immigrants and the indigenous people. That fact reinforces the central themes of this essay. First, during much of

the nation's history, foreigners who joined American society had the same variety of experiences with American Indians as did citizens born here. Second, as outsiders, both immigrants and indigenous people faced discrimination and pressure to assimilate into the general society. How each group responded varied widely throughout the generations considered here.

Bibliography

Anderson, Nels. 1966. *Desert Saints: The Mormon Frontier in Utah*. Chicago: University of Chicago Press.

Barkan, Elliott Robert. 2007. *From All Points: America's Immigrant West, 1870–1952*. Bloomington: Indiana University Press.

Bean, Frank, and Gillian Stevens. 2003. *America's Newcomers and the Dynamics of Diversity*. New York: Russell Sage Foundation.

Bradford, William. 1952. *History of Plymouth Plantation, 1620–1647*. Edited by Samuel Eliot Morrison. New York: Knopf.

Coffman, Edward M. 1986. *The Old Army: A Portrait of the American Army in Peacetime, 1784–1898*. New York: Oxford University Press.

Deloria, Philip J., and Neal Salisbury, eds. 2002. *A Companion to American Indian History*. Malden, MA: Blackwell.

Dinnerstein, Leonard, Roger L. Nichols, and David M. Reimers. 2010. *Natives and Strangers: A History of Ethnic Americans*. 5th ed. New York: Oxford University Press.

Fogleman, Aaron Spencer. 1996. *Hopeful Journeys: German Immigration, Settlement, and Political Culture in Colonial America, 1717–1775*. Philadelphia: University of Pennsylvania Press.

Griffin, Patrick. 2001. *The People with No Name: Irelands' Ulster Scots, America's Scots Irish, and the Creation of a British Atlantic World, 1689–1764*. Princeton, NJ: Princeton University Press.

Holmes, Kenneth L., ed. 1983. *Covered Wagon Women: Diaries and Letters from the Western Trails, 1840–1849*. 11 vols. Glendale, CA: Arthur H. Clark.

Luebke, Frederick. 1980. *Ethnicity on the Great Plains*. Lincoln: University of Nebraska Press.

Nadeau, Remi. 1967. *Fort Laramie and the Sioux Indians.* Englewood Cliffs, NJ: Prentice-Hall.

Nichols, Roger L. 2003. *American Indians in U.S. History.* Norman: University of Oklahoma Press.

Rawls, James J. 1984. *Indians of California: The Changing Image.* Norman: University of Oklahoma Press.

Tate, Michael L. 2006. *Indians and Immigrants: Encounters on the Overland Trails.* Norman: University of Oklahoma Press.

Utley, Robert. 1993. *The Lance and the Shield: The Life and Times of Sitting Bull.* New York: Henry Holt.

Indigenous Peoples and Borderlands

Yuka Mizutani

Before the coming of European settlers, there were no international borders on the North American continent. Many different indigenous peoples (called *Native American* or *American Indian* in the United States, *First Nation* or *Aboriginal people* in Canada, and also *Indígena* in Mexico) lived on this continent, and their cultures flourished. Even after the division of the continent by international borders among Canada, the United States, and Mexico, indigenous peoples still survive and thrive there. Also, some indigenous peoples have come to live in borderlands and deal with many different problems.

In Canada, there are 615 communities of indigenous peoples, and in 2006, 976,305 people identified themselves as either indigenous, Métis (people with indigenous and nonindigenous heritage), or non-status indigenous (people who practically are indigenous but are not indigenous in legal terms). In the United States, there are 561 federally recognized indigenous peoples and around 200 federally non-recognized peoples. In 2000, 4,315,865 people identified themselves as indigenous alone or in combination with another race. There are 62 indigenous linguistic groups in Mexico; their population is estimated as 103,263,388. Although each country has its own way of counting the number of indigenous people, and the range of people covered by the definition of *indigenous* is not standardized; these numbers convey an idea of how many people are associated with this issue. Just as with many other peoples in other parts of the world, these indigenous people had traveled and migrated for a considerable distance in search of better living conditions, due to environmental and other changes. Many indigenous peoples built communities in different places, traded goods, and allied with other indigenous peoples. The character of indigenous peoples has been more dynamic than many people think today.

Currently, indigenous peoples in borderlands have to face many problems caused by the existence of international borders. Some of these problems happen equally to anyone who crosses a border, while others are unique to indigenous peoples. This chapter will take up several cases to introduce indigenous peoples' histories in relation to international borders and current struggles unique to indigenous peoples. Examining these will enable the reader to more readily and more deeply understand immigrants working and settling on the North American continent, as well as in the historical and modern North American borderlands.

Indigenous Peoples' Political Uniqueness

Being indigenous is more than just being born or living in a particular land for a long time. Rather, indigenous people have had their lands, human rights, languages, histories, and many other aspects taken away by settlers, mainly from Europe. In order to politically identify who are indigenous peoples, blood quanta are used in the United States and Canada, while fluency in an indigenous language is used in Mexico. In terms of blood quantum, each indigenous people possess a right to regulate the level of acceptance, although the widespread standard to qualify for membership is a one-fourth blood quantum requirement. Many people identify themselves as indigenous even if their blood quantum is lower than the regulation or they do not speak any indigenous languages. Additionally, although people may have more than two different indigenous traditions, but very often they are allowed to be enrolled in only one tribe.

With the establishment of nation-states, indigenous peoples in North America have come under the control of governments of nation-states according to their geographical location. Currently, all recognized indigenous peoples receive nationalities from one of the nation-states. Therefore, within statistics, indigenous people appear just as Canadian, U.S. American, or Mexican. The reasons indigenous people cross international borders would be the same as other immigrants, such as for wage labor and education. However, in some cases, problems happen specifically to indigenous peoples, because of their histories and traditions. Each nation-state has its own policy on indigenous peoples; therefore, the rights indigenous peoples possess vary depending on the nation-state to which they belong. Additionally, the rights given to each indigenous people may differ in the same country, based on treaties made between the people and the federal government, or other factors. Therefore, it is hard to generalize about the experiences of indigenous peoples with international borders. Accordingly, I take specific cases of several different peoples in this chapter to introduce various issues.

In the United States, Canada, and sometimes in Mexico, some indigenous peoples have received lands (*reservations* in the United States, *reserves* in Canada, *zonas indígenas* in Mexico). For them, having these lands matters, and it is not because of their monetary value. Although they are under control of one of the nation-states, indigenous peoples have stronger rights on their indigenous lands to govern themselves. There, indigenous people feel much safer to conduct their ways of life. In many cases, these lands are not large enough to accommodate all members of an indigenous group, and people live outside of these lands. Yet important rituals and ceremonies tend to be held on their lands. For indigenous people, having their own land, and their land not being divided by an international border, are both crucial for social and cultural survival. Many indigenous peoples have their own governments, including their own police and judicial system, which take care of certain issues happening on their lands. Indigenous governments deal with issues with the federal governments, too.

In the case of the United States, several indigenous peoples have already had their governments for a long time. However, many created one only after Congress's enactment of the Indian Reorganization Act of 1934, which is the basic structure of modern indigenous society as decided by the U.S. government. Owning a political structure that is recognized by the federal government is one of the biggest differences between indigenous peoples and immigrants and ethnic groups.

Compared with the indigenous governmental organizations, which are relatively artificial, the traditional social structure of many indigenous peoples consists of sections often based on family systems, which may be called *bands* or *clans*. When a part of an indigenous people moves and constructs a new community, they may move together as one section. In this chapter, the Akwesasne Mohawk, the Chippewa-Cree, the Aroostook Band of the Micmacs and the Kickapoo Traditional Tribe of Texas follow this criterion, while the Pascua Yaqui and the Tohono O'odham do not. Finally, in the United States or Canada, indigenous people must prove their historical existence to be officially recognized as indigenous. As a result, not all indigenous peoples have been recognized by their respective national governments. Without the recognition of those federal governments, the indigenous peoples are not eligible for any political rights as indigenous entities, including land tenure or rights related to border crossing. Sometimes recognition is done by the state government, and state-recognized indigenous people receive partial benefits. The problems of federally unrecognized people are not well known. In the following sections, we examine the histories of several indigenous peoples and their modern problems associated with international borders. It is only a part of a huge issue; more serious cases have not even been given attention by scholars.

U.S.–Mexican Border

Along the 1,969 miles of the U.S.-Mexican international border, there are many indigenous peoples whose lives have been affected by it. Through the Bracero Program back in the 1940s (1942–1964), and since the establishment of the North American

Free Trade Agreement (1994), many people from Mexico, including indigenous people, have come to the United States as laborers. However, there are also indigenous people who had to come to the United States for reasons unique to indigenous peoples. Also, some indigenous peoples have been commuting across the current international borders for more than a century and a half. Very roughly, the relationship between the border and these peoples can be categorized into three different types. The first is typified by the Yaqui (also known as Yoeme or Hiaki). Yaqui people crossed the border from the Mexican side. The second is that of the Tohono O'odham. Tohono O'odham traditional land is located on the border,

and their land was literally cut by it. The third is that of the Kickapoo Traditional Tribe of Texas. These Kickapoo people first moved southward and then came back to the United States.

Following are three histories and modern border issues.

Pascua Yaqui

Pascua Yaqui are part of the Yaqui people. Yaqui people lived in the state of Sonora in Mexico as well as the southwestern United States, especially the states of Arizona and California. The majority of the Yaqui people in the United States now live around the cities

A member of the Pascua Yaqui tribe enacts a ceremonial victory blessing in front of the Arizona state capitol in Phoenix, July 2010. A federal judge had decided to enjoin parts of Arizona's controversial SB1070 law. (Rick D'Elia/Corbis)

of Tucson and Phoenix in Arizona. The Native American tribe, the Pascua Yaqui, federally recognized in 1978, holds a reservation of 202 acres in Tucson. According to the Pascua Yaqui tribal government's official website, the number of enrolled members is around 14,300 as of the year 2005. As explained in the preceding section, the reservation is not large enough to hold the entire Pascua Yaqui population, and most people live outside of it. However, buildings of the Pascua Yaqui tribal government stand on this land, as well as their ceremonial place, and it has been a symbol of their existence in the United States. On the Mexican side, along the Yaqui River in southern Sonora, seven mission towns (Belen, Huirivis, Raum, Potam, Vicam, Torim, Bacum, and Cocorit) were established back in the sixteenth century by Jesuit priests.

Although the locations of these towns have changed from time to time, many Yaqui people today live in or close to these mission towns. In 1938, land around the Yaqui River was reserved as indigenous land, the Yaqui Zone. Yet, this land does not function as a typical U.S. reservation. The distance between the Yaqui River in Mexico and Tucson is approximately 310 miles, and there are no big communities of Yaqui people between them. Therefore, in practice, their land in modern times is not on the border. However, when we examine their history, the border was set within their traditional territory.

While the traditional lands of the Yaqui people are in southern Sonora, historical documents left by missionaries show that a part of their ancestors lived in another mission town, Tumacacori, which is in the current territory of the United States. Today, Tumacacori is registered as a National Historical Park by the U.S. Department of the Interior. The Tumacacori mission was built by a Jesuit missionary from Italy, Father Eusebio Francisco Kino, in 1683. According to documents, Tumacacori, which was a small village at that time, asked Kino to send missionaries to its residents in 1691. Thus, Tumacacori was occasionally a stopping place for missionaries. After the deportation of the Jesuits in 1767, the Franciscans took over the mission. Many different indigenous peoples resided in this mission, such as Yaqui, Tohono O'odham, and Apache. However, the Tumacacori mission was abandoned before 1861. The reason is not clear, although it may be because of an attack by Apache people in 1848. Thereafter, indigenous peoples' existence in the U.S. territory, including the Yaqui's, was forgotten for a long time. Yet, this historical fact of Yaqui residence in the United States is the reason many people think that Pascua Yaqui people should not be considered as immigrants from Mexico.

At the same time, many people have regarded them as immigrants. While some Yaqui people lived in Tumacacori, the majority of the Yaqui lived in Sonora, Mexico. Then, a big change occurred with Porfirio Diaz's two regimes (from 1876 to 1880 and from 1884 to 1911), Yaquis were persecuted with force by the Mexican government. The exact number is not clear, but it is estimated that around 40,000 Yaqui died in this period. Therefore, some Yaqui people moved northward and crossed the international border in order to protect their lives. This mass international migration of the Yaqui people started around 1890; the peak was around 1910. Yet, even before this mass migration, many Yaqui people had crossed the border in search of gold in California. In the United States, Yaqui people settled down and constructed their own communities on "unused" land as political refugees. Yaqui people worked as wage laborers at farming, mining, and railroad construction sites to earn their living. At the point when the Yaqui entered the United States, they were treated as Mexican refugees, not as Native Americans. In sum, the ancestors of current Pascua Yaqui people came from Mexico and settled down in the United States.

Whether considering Pascua Yaqui as a part of Mexican immigrants or not depends on one's political perspective. At the same time, some Pascua Yaqui people regard them as Mexican. In fact, some Pascua Yaqui communities, especially the ones in the Phoenix area, became ethnically mixed communities with Mexican-American people. Due to frequent contacts with Mexican-American people, in addition to contacts with Yaqui people in Mexico, many Pascua Yaqui people are fluent in Spanish. On the other hand, other Pascua Yaqui people wish to be recognized just as Yaqui, not as Mexican American or Latino. The Yaqui regard themselves as a people having a distinct identity apart from mainstream Mexican people. Also, many Yaqui people were killed by mainstream Mexican people, and their descendants have negative feelings toward being seen as Mexican American. However, this does not mean that Pascua Yaqui and Mexican Americans have had a bad relationship. After settling down in Arizona, the Pascua Yaqui have had contacts with many people of different ethnicities, including Mexican Americans. Pascua Yaqui worked among other laborers, mainly at construction sites and agricultural fields. Their contribution was indispensable for the development of Arizona.

Nonetheless, being indigenous people did not mean they were automatically eligible for all benefits defined by federal laws. Not having a federally recognized Native American status prevented Yaquis from receiving any legal and social support for their survival, and they struggled for a long time to overcome social and economic disadvantage. Finally, in the 1960s, the Pascua Yaqui Association, a club organized for community improvement, claimed land and rights as Native Americans in the United States. After discussions in Congress in 1978, the Yaqui in the United States gained federal recognition by the U.S. government as the Pascua Yaqui tribe. They received all rights as Native Americans and their reservation in Tucson. Still, other communities remain in Tucson, Phoenix, and other areas where they either rent or own the land. After the second generation, most Pascua Yaqui people had been born in the United States and had U.S. citizenship. (Peoples indigenous to the Western Hemisphere had become eligible for U.S. citizenship by the Nationality Act of October 14, 1940.) However, it was 1978 when their existence as an ethnic group was recognized by the government. Today, the Pascua Yaqui live in the United States as Native Americans. They own casinos, an amphitheater, and other sources of revenue in order to afford the costs of all the social needs of their people, such as education, housing, health care, and cultural maintenance.

The biggest problem the Yaqui and other peoples are facing today is associated with the customs officials on the border. From time to time, indigenous people have to bring material goods for ceremonial use in their communities into the United States. Very often, the goods contain such materials as animal fur

and hooves. Also, they may bring some meat for ceremonial food from wild animals that may not be available in their current residential locations. Yaqui and many other indigenous peoples claim that U.S. Customs and Border Patrol do not treat these goods properly and sometimes destroy them. Indigenous peoples insist that these goods are to be transported not for profit. Some kinds of meat and fur are prohibited, yet it is crucial for them to keep their traditions alive. Furthermore, some indigenous people, including some Yaqui, think they need to be free to cross the border without a passport issued by one of the nation-states (see below, the Kickapoo Traditional Tribe of Texas). At the same time, people committed to the traditional part of indigenous cultures have to conduct a part of their practice on the other side of the border. For them, passport and visa issues cause many inconveniences. Particularly in the case of the Yaqui, obtaining a Mexican passport is problematic. Because of their history of persecution by Mexico, Yaqui men often do not register for the Mexican military, which prevents them from obtaining a passport and crossing the border. In May 2009, Pascua Yaqui and the U.S. Department of Homeland Security reached an agreement to issue a special ID card, which can replace the passport, for the time being solving this problem.

Tohono O'odham

The Tohono O'odham reservation, located on part of their traditional land, is right on the border in Arizona. Although their reservation is next to the Pascua Yaqui's, the Tohono O'odham have a different relationship with the international border than do the Yaquis. At the same time, the Tohono O'odham's and Yaqui's histories share many aspects. Just as the Yaqui people did, the Tohono O'odham lived in a Jesuit mission. Father Kino, who built the Tumacacori mission, arrived on Tohono O'odham land in 1687. He built a church and mission headquarters at Cosari on the San Miguel River on Tohono O'odham land, and in 1697, he completed a mission called San Xavier del Bac, located in Tucson. Today, San Xavier del Bac is a national historic landmark, attracting many tourists, as well as being used by the Tohono

O'odham people for rituals. Both the Yaqui and the Tohono O'odham lived in Tumacacori, and even today, these peoples work together for many cultural events. As do the Pascua Yaquis, the Tohono O'odham live in both the United States and Mexico. The only difference between them is that Tohono O'odham's traditional land is connected across the international border, while there is a geographical blank between Yaqui lands. Therefore, different from Pascua Yaqui, Tohono O'odham is considered to be, without any doubt, a U.S. Native American people.

Europeans met the Tohono O'odham by the end of the 1540s, when the Coronado expedition moved north from New Spain into North America. Because Spaniards were not interested in Tohono O'odham desert land, the latter were left as they were. In 1852, the Tohono O'odham people were officially "discovered" by John R. Bartlett. He was exploring land newly gained by the United States in the Gadsden Purchase of 1854. Via the Gadsden Purchase, almost two-thirds of traditional Tohono O'odham land came to be in U.S. territory. However, this change did not affect the daily lives of the Tohono O'odham people right away. After the Gadsden Purchase, many nonindigenous settlers came to Tohono O'odham land. As their land is located in the desert, the Tohono O'odham people constructed their communities around wells and springs. The European-American settlers stole these wells and springs from the Tohono O'odham. These wells and springs as well as the land around them, including water rights and claims to underground minerals, were finally returned to the Tohono O'odham in 1955.

In 1865, the United States had selected Many Skirts, a Tohono O'odham leader, as the head chief of the tribe, and the U.S. government and the Tohono O'odham started to have political contact. Then, in 1874, a reservation of 69,200 acres was set aside around San Xavier del Bac. A decade later, the small Gila Band Reservation was established. In 1916, 2.75 million acres of land adjacent to the U.S.-Mexican border was set aside as the Papago (former name of Tohono O'odham) reservation. The size of the Papago reservation changed several times, but it was fixed at the current size in 1940 as a place where they can safely conduct their rituals and other traditional activities.

As noted above, Tohono O'odham people have had many conflicts with nonindigenous people, since European settlers had come to their traditional land. Pascua Yaqui communities and their small reservation are within or very close to a city, and for them, it is almost impossible to live without contacts with people of other ethnicities. To the contrary, Tohono O'odham's main reservation is big, and it is possible to spend a day without seeing outsiders. Still, Tohono O'odham men have worked with nonindigenous people since the 1850s, at mines and railroad construction sites, and later in the cotton fields. Very often, they were paid less than were nonindigenous workers. At the same time, Tohono O'odham women worked in Tucson, the closest big city, as maids or cooks in households, thereby supporting their families. After World War II, the Bureau of Indian Affairs of the U.S. government tried to send Native-American people from their reservations to big cities as wage laborers. Due to this program, more Tohono O'odham people, among many other Native-American peoples, came to work at cities and places outside of their reservation. At these places, Native Americans, Mexican Americans, African Americans, and progressive Caucasians allied and fought for their rights as workers.

Today, many Tohono O'odham people on the Mexican side come to the U.S. side to live, due to the better opportunities for employment on the U.S. side. Also, many Tohono O'odham people feel that their traditional culture is more respected in the United States than in Mexico. Tohono O'odham are the only Native American people in the United States who are allowed to grant full enrollment to their members in Mexico as U.S. Native Americans. Therefore, Tohono O'odham in Mexico cross the border to the U.S. side to receive social welfare, such as medical treatment. At the same time, the U.S. Border Patrol does not know this special law for Tohono O'odham people, often forcing sick people and elders to return to Mexico, although their stays in the United States are legal. Additionally, some drug dealers try to recruit Tohono O'odham to transport drugs across the border, using Tohono O'odham land. Even away from international borders, drug abuse is one of the biggest problems in Native American lands.

Kickapoo Traditional Tribe of Texas

The Kickapoo's traditional land is located in the current state of Michigan. Due to the U.S. Indian removal policy, which started at the beginning of the nineteenth century and which was codified in the Removal Act in 1830, Kickapoo people were forced to migrate for quite a long distance and reside in many different places, such as Illinois, Indiana, Iowa, Missouri, Kansas, Oklahoma, and Texas. Before the U.S.-Mexican border between Texas (then still Spanish territory) and Oklahoma was finally set in 1819, some Kickapoo people were invited by governmental officials of Texas to defend Texas from the United States. Soon after, in 1821, Mexico gained independence from Spain. Texas was governed by Mexico from 1821 to 1836. The Texas Republic was then established in 1836, continuing up to 1846. During this time, villages of Kickapoo peoples and other indigenous peoples in Texas were attacked by the Texas army. The Kickapoo either fled to Indian Territory (currently the state of Oklahoma) or to Mexico. People who fled to Mexico were integrated into the Mexican army, and they became Kickapoo pioneers in Mexico.

In 1877, the Northern Frontier Investigation Commission (*Comisión Pesquisidora de la Frontera del Norte*) in Mexico reported that many European settlers in the U.S.-Mexican border area had been attacked by indigenous peoples, such as the Comanche and Mescalero. The commission invited "civilized" indigenous peoples, such as Kickapoo and Seminole, to Mexico in order to pit them against these "barbarous" indigenous peoples for the protection of settlers. Another group of Kickapoo people in Texas responded to this invitation. They crossed the border southward and settled in the village of Nacimiento, in the state of Coahuila, Mexico. While living in Nacimiento, Kickapoo men seasonally commuted to the United States as migrant farm labors to harvest crops. Kickapoo women and children remained in Nacimiento.

The Kickapoo people were given land in Mexico that was not in good condition. At first the Kickapoo cultivated it, planted crops, and sold harvested wheat and corn to Mexican people. Then, a major drought began, and the land became unsuitable for agriculture. The Kickapoo could also not obtain enough water in Nacimiento for rituals and for survival. At the same time, the number of animals, which Kickapoo people relied on for food, decreased in that area. These conditions made it difficult for them to stay in Nacimiento. In the 1940s, the Kickapoos in Nacimiento started to return to Texas and then to other parts of the United States, such as Arizona, Oklahoma, California, and even as far away as New York, mainly as agricultural labors among workers of other ethnic groups. Although legally they were already Mexican citizens and needed passports to cross the border, the border control at that time allowed Kickapoo people from Mexico to enter the United States without any restriction. It was a group migration rather than a number of individual ones. Many contractors for farms and factories were sent in advance to either Eagle Pass or Nacimiento to look for Kickapoo workers. As the employment of *braceros* (predominantly Mexican farm laborers under a contract between the United States and Mexico) was increasingly restricted, the Kickapoo were more and more welcomed.

The Kickapoo constructed a camp under a bridge over the Rio Grande, between two cities divided by the border, Eagle Pass (United States) and Piedras Negras (Mexico). While other members of families stayed in the camp, Kickapoo men commuted to farms to work. Along with the changes of season, they moved to other parts of the United States to seek employment. Life under the international bridge between Eagle Pass and Piedras Negras appears to have been a difficult one. Their shelters, made of cardboard, cane, deerskin, and wood, were affected by flood, fire caused by cigarettes, and trash thrown from the bridge. Among these Kickapoo, a few had U.S. citizenship due to their birth in U.S. territory, while others were recognized as Mexican citizens. Those with U.S. citizenship moved to Eagle Pass and started to negotiate with the U.S. government to ask for their recognition as Native American people of the United States. The Immigration and Nationality Act of 1952 allowed them to receive parole, in order to be able to cross the border freely. The Kickapoo in Mexico were the only indigenous people (see the preceding section

An elderly Kickapoo woman hangs washing in her village near Eagle Pass, Texas, 1980. The Kickapoo, trying to acquire full citizenship and tribal recognition, live in poverty and without rights to own land they once owned. (AP Photo/John P. Filo)

about Pascua Yaqui) who could receive such recognition, which could enhance their migration to Texas. The Texas Indian Commission asked the U.S. Department of Housing and Urban Development to provide them some land so they could move out from under the international bridge. Yet, in order to receive U.S. citizenship and other rights as Native Americans, the Kickapoo in Mexico needed to be recognized by the U.S. government.

Between 1981 and 1982, the legal status of these Kickapoo people was discussed. In 1982, they were recognized as Native American people in the United States, called the Texas Band of the Kickapoo. Currently, they call themselves the Kickapoo Traditional Tribe of Texas. The decision was made based on these two points: the ancestors of the Texas Band were of U.S. origin, and the majority of other Kickapoo

people resided in U.S. territory. In 1983, the Texas Band of Kickapoo Act was established. By this act, U.S. citizenship was provided to the people who were already in the United States. Also, Kickapoo people who were still in Mexico received all rights except the vote. The reservation was established south of Eagle Pass. Today, the Texas Band of Kickapoo is widely called the Texas Traditional Tribe of Kickapoo. Because of the Texas Band of Kickapoo Act of 1983, Kickapoo Traditional Tribe of Texas people are in a better situation than other indigenous peoples, who have no way to be united with a segment of their people on the other side of the border. However, even with the conditions granted to them, some in the Kickapoo Traditional Tribe of Texas are interested in improving their rights on transborder issues, with the cooperation of other indigenous peoples.

Other Indigenous Peoples on the U.S.-Mexican Border

Besides the Pascua Yaqui, Tohono O'odham, and Kickapoo Traditional Tribe of Texas, there are many other indigenous peoples who live in the U.S.-Mexican borderland. Apaches living across the border are well known. The Seminoles are another interesting case. Originally from Florida, they had moved to Texas and then to Mexico. Another segment of the Seminole people came from the Bahamas, and an interethnic group was created. The Cocopah's land is also on the border; and they have issues with border control, just as Tohono O'odham people do. The Kumeyaay's border crossing has been disrupted by the many nonindigenous people trying to cross the border and claiming that they were Kumeyaay. At the same time, many other indigenous peoples from Oaxaca and other parts of Mexico also cross the border to work. Still other indigenous peoples from Latin America—further south than Mexico—come to the United States as well. These indigenous peoples from Mexico and Latin America live and work with people with other ethnicities in the United States, as is the case with the three principal peoples examined here.

U.S.-Canadian Border

On the 3,987-mile-long U.S.-Canadian border, there are also many indigenous peoples whose histories and lives have been affected by the border. There are several types of relationships along this borderland. The case of the Akwesasne Mohawk people, who were divided by the border, seems very similar to Tohono O'odham people's situation on the U.S.-Mexican border. The Chippewa-Cree people's case is close to that of the Yaqui. In fact, the Chippewa-Cree history and federal recognition process was used as a reference for Pascua Yaqui seeking federal recognition. The Aroostook Band of the Micmacs illustrate the unique topic of indigenous peoples and sovereignty. Because their federal recognition is relatively recent, their case shows a new trend in borderland indigenous issues.

Akwesasne Mohawk

The Akwesasne Mohawk are a part of the Mohawk (also known as Kahniakehaka) people who traditionally lived on lands extending from the current state of New York to the St. Lawrence River area along the New York–Québec border. The Mohawk people are members of the historic Iroquois confederation, which is a political unit consisting of the Mohawk, Seneca, Onondaga, Oneida, Cayuga, and Tuscarora peoples. After the coming of French settlers in the sixteenth century to what is currently Québec, the Mohawk's lands began to be eroded by Europeans. The first Mohawk encounter with the French was in 1609 in a battle at Ticonderoga. Then, Mohawks met Jesuit missionaries, and they settled at a French Jesuit settlement called La Prairie, near Montréal. After taking up in the mission, Mohawk people became active in trade between Montréal and Albany, using their relationship with other peoples in the Iroquois confederacy. With the help of the Mohawk people, French and English merchants profited by trading fur and other goods. This development convinced the colonial governments to provide the Mohawk with a special status, a degree of independence, and the right of free travel. During the Prohibition era of the 1920s and early 1930s, smuggling of alcohol beverages was conducted using the Mohawk land. Some made a profit, while others lost their lives by committing to the smuggling. Many Mohawk were crossing the border daily for their business and family affairs without much problem. However, changes began for the Mohawks in the 1920s.

U.S. law started restricting Mohawk people's transborder activities. In the United States, the Indian Citizenship Act of 1924 gave the remaining indigenous people (who did not yet have it) citizenship, and having that citizenship certainly benefited many of these indigenous peoples. On the other hand, it prevented Canadian indigenous people from freely crossing the border. Obviously, the Mohawk were affected by the passage of this 1924 act. Before the Indian Citizenship Act, indigenous peoples along the U.S.-Canadian border could freely cross because of the Treaty of Amity, Commerce, and Navigation of 1794, also known as the Jay Treaty or Jay's Treaty. In 1814, the Jay Treaty's ideas about indigenous policy were incorporated in the Treaty of Peace and Amity, also known as the Treaty of Ghent.

The Jay Treaty had established the right of free passage across the border to indigenous peoples on either side of the border and enabled them to freely engage in trade or commerce with other indigenous nations. At the same time, it eliminated the assessment of custom duties on the indigenous peoples upon border crossing and trading. However, the United States and Canada treated the Jay Treaty differently, thus causing this confusion for indigenous borderland peoples. The Mohawk and the other peoples in the Iroquois confederation understood the Jay Treaty to be a new threat to their sovereignty, although it had not been agreed upon to trouble indigenous peoples. This trouble happened specifically for indigenous people and not to other immigrants in general.

In the same year as the establishment of the Indian Citizenship Act, the Immigration Act of 1924 was enacted. In this act, the U.S. government decided on quotas, or the number of immigrants each country could annually send to the United States. Indigenous peoples on the borderlands, including Akwesasne Mohawk, were affected because they were counted as immigrants from Canada to the United States, although their border crossing right had been assured by the Jay Treaty. In 1925, a Kahnawake (a Mohawk community on the Canadian side) Mohawk person called Paul Diabo was arrested in the United States as an illegal alien. Diabo insisted that he was a Mohawk and that indigenous people were supposed to be able to cross the U.S.-Canadian border freely, due to the Jay Treaty. Diabo's individual case was expanded to include all peoples in the Iroquois confederacy, and this case went to the U.S. Supreme Court. In the 1927 decision, *United States ex Rel. Diabo v. McCandless*, Diabo won the case, for it was determined that Article 3 of the 1794 Jay Treaty exempted indigenous people from the U.S. immigration law.

Today, the Akwesasne-Mohawk reservation in the United States, called the St. Regis Mohawk Reservation, functions as a duty-free shopping place on the U.S.-Canadian border, especially for tobacco and alcohol. The U.S. Citizenship and Immigration Services has been entering the St. Regis Mohawk Reservation to prevent smuggling as well as to find undocumented immigrants. This is perceived as questionable by the Akwasasne Mohawk people. Additionally, as of July 2009, Canadian and U.S. authorities had been blocking a bridge called Seaway International Bridge (also known as Three Nations Bridge) and, for two months, preventing Mohawk people from crossing the border. The Canadian government was asking the Akwasasne Mohawk to accept armed agents of Canada Border Service staying in the Akwasasne nation. The Mohawk were not willing to accept them, and, due to this political conflict between the Canadian government and Akwasasne-Mohawk government, the bridge was closed. As many Mohawk people work or go to school across the border, they were taking charter boats to cross the border. It symbolized the conflicts and problems happening specifically to border-crossing indigenous peoples that continue until today.

Chippewa-Cree

The Chippewa-Cree live in Montana. Due to an interesting history, two different bands of the Chippewa (also known as Oijbwe, Ojibwa, or Anishinabe) and Cree (also known as Iyiniwok, Nehiyawok, and other names) came to live together and to construct a new identity. The Chippewa people traditionally lived in the Great Lakes area on the U.S.-Canadian border. The Cree were the Chippewa's neighbor, who traditionally lived in Canada's current states of Saskatchewan and Alberta. Little Bear's Band of Cree was exiled from Canada due to the Frog Lake Massacre in 1885. That was a small battle at the European settlers' village of Frog Lake, in which European settlers were killed by Cree. Meanwhile, there was a group of Chippewa led by Chief Rocky Boy. Not much information is available about him today. Some claim he was born in Canada or Montana, whereas others contend he was born in Wisconsin.

Little Bear's Band of Cree and Chief Rocky Boy's Band of Chippewa fought together in the Riel Rebellion between 1869 and 1884. The Riel Rebellion was a series of two rebellions led by a Métis person, Lois Riel, against the Dominion of Canada (Canada before independence). The aim of the series of rebellions was to request land ownership by Métis people, just as for other European settlers. The first rebellion, the Red River Rebellion, happened in 1869 in Manitoba. In 1884, the Saskatchewan Valley Rebellion (also known as North-West Rebellion) happened in Saskatchewan.

After these rebellions, Little Bear's Band of Cree and Chief Rocky Boy's Band of Chippewa had come across as a group and lived together in Montana. Although they were not considered refugees (cf. Pascua Yaqui), they were wandering around northern Montana without having a place to stay together.

However, in 1916, the two groups were finally able to obtain a home by being recognized as one Native-American people, "Chief Rocky Boy's Band." The decision was made because the U.S.-Canadian border had not been precisely determined until 1873; therefore, it was difficult to establish which country they were traditionally from. At the same time, most of the Chippewa people lived in U.S. territory. Moreover, Chippewa and Cree had been allied and lived close together, and the U.S. government thought that providing these Cree with rights to stay in the United States was adequate. Along with the federal recognition as a Native-American people, Chippewa-Cree people were given a reservation in Montana, formally called the Fort Assiniboine Military reservation. They settled there and continued their way of life. Today, Chippewa-Cree people strive and survive on this given land. The tribal government's website indicates they own their own accredited two-year college, a ski resort, a clinic, and some enterprises.

Aroostook Band of Micmacs

The Micmac (also spelled as M'ikmaq) people traditionally live in southeastern Canada and in the U.S. state of Maine. In the United States, they were recognized in 1991 as a Native American people, the "Aroostook Band of Micmacs." U.S. federal recognition came because a document by European settlers was found that showed that the ancestors of the Micmac had lived in Maine. The Micmac constructed many communities along the U.S.-Canadian border area as migrant labor camps. Each community had special housing in addition to residents' housing, which enabled members from other communities to stay and go to work from there. Micmac men traveled across the U.S.-Canadian border, stayed in many different Micmac communities to work among people with other ethnicities, and earned wages in agriculture. Women, children, elders, and sick people stayed

in their community and lived off the money coming from either the U.S. or Canadian government. Micmac traditional land is right on the current international border; they have been traveling around the land for many centuries. Their transborder migration was further enhanced by the development of railroads. In 1870, the railroad arrived in Maine. The potato starch industry was connected to the railroad system, and starch from Maine was exported across the United States and Canada. Therefore, more labor came to be needed in the industry, and Micmac men took up that opportunity. Furthermore, trains helped Micmac people travel across the borderland more easily.

The Micmac are a part of the Wabanaki Confederacy, which consists of the Penobscot, Passamaquoddy, Maliseet, Micmac, and Abenaki peoples, currently in New England and the Canadian Maritimes. They maintain strong ties and hold conferences and festivals. After federal recognition in 1991, one legal issue arose. Three people working on Aroostook Band of Micmac land were fired in 2001. These individuals complained that the Aroostook Band of Micmacs violated the Maine Whistleblower Protection Act, which protects employees in Maine. The case was taken to the Maine Human Rights Commission, then to court. The Aroostook Band of Micmacs insisted that they were given sovereignty within their tribal boundaries, which includes determining employment. In fact, three other indigenous peoples in Maine have had to follow most state laws in Maine since 1980. At that time, the Aroostook Band of Micmacs was not yet recognized by the U.S. federal government. Therefore, from the standpoint of Aroostook Micmac people, they were not covered by the decision to follow laws in Maine. As a result, the court ruled that the Aroostook Band of Micmacs is not under state law, and they won the case. The judge decreed that besides the Aroostook Band of Micmacs, other indigenous peoples in Maine should not be regulated by the 1980 decision. This means that indigenous sovereignty came to be more valued than the state law. Generally, immigrants to the United States are under the laws of the state and the federal government. However, the Aroostook Band of Micmac case shows that an exception applies to transborder indigenous peoples. Also, establishing sovereign lands on both sides of the

U.S.-Canadian border draws a clear line between other Canadian immigrants to the United States and the borderland indigenous people.

Other Indigenous Peoples on the U.S.-Canadian Border

Many more indigenous peoples in the U.S.-Canadian border area are having problems, mainly because they cannot cross the border to see another segment of their people. Nor can they transport sacred items or reach culturally important sites beyond the border. Dakota (or Lakota, also known as Sioux) and other peoples struggle with transporting eagle feathers to the USA. Eagle feather is important to many indigenous peoples, but its transportation is prohibited for the purpose of protecting this species. Many indigenous peoples are claiming that a small number of feathers for ritual use should be exempt from the regulation. The Blackfoot tribe is a big indigenous confederacy divided by the border. The existence of the border is eroding their unity and identity. Although it is not addressed in this article, there is another U.S.-Canadian border, that between Canada and Alaska. The U.S. indigenous policy applies to indigenous peoples in Alaska, and border-crossing problems can occur in that location, too.

Conclusion

Various kinds of problems exist among borderland indigenous peoples, including border-crossing and custom issues. Some problems are associated with legal matters, whereas others are associated with social, economic, and historical ones. As was shown in the Pascua Yaqui and Chippewa-Cree cases, some indigenous peoples had to cross the border to physically protect themselves. The traditional land of both the Pascua Yaqui and the Chippewa-Cree transcended the border, so for them it was natural to move across the border to seek safety. Also, it is difficult to determine the exact range of indigenous peoples' traditional lands, because traditionally their geographical territories had been more dynamic (less explicitly defined) than today's national territories. Therefore, indigenous border crossing is not a modern political

phenomenon. Rather, it should be understood in relation with indigenous peoples' histories and cultures, in addition to current political issues. Just as perspective toward indigenous territories, the way to determine the membership of indigenous people differs between nation-states and indigenous peoples. As noted, indigenous membership today is determined by a combination of recognition by the nation-state, blood quantum, language, and other factors. There are people who are practically indigenous but cannot receive special rights because they do not meet a part of these requirements. As a result, people who are not legally indigenous but are practically indigenous can be prevented from having rights to cross the border. This point needs to be understood by nonindigenous people as well. In cases of Akwesasne-Mohawk and Tohono O'odham people, although their border-crossing rights are assured by nation-states, in fact these rights do not seem to operate well in practice.

Efforts by the nation-states to notify border control, customs, and other authorities about indigenous border-crossing rights and other legal issues are crucial. Kickapoo history shows that indigenous migration has been led and conducted by nation-states, while most nonindigenous people migrate according to their own free will. This is probably the biggest difference between borderland indigenous peoples and other immigrants to North America. Many immigrants have arrived voluntarily to North America to pursue their dreams, opportunities, and safety. In contrast, after the arrival of European settlers, indigenous peoples in North America were forced to migrate domestically and internationally. In most cases, indigenous peoples' migration benefited only the European settlers, not the indigenous peoples themselves. This type of indigenous migration has to be distinguished from their ancient history of migration to follow a herd or crop.

The political difference between borderland indigenous peoples and nonindigenous people after settling down in the United States is, first, having sovereignty, which mostly comes with historic (aboriginal) land claims as a group. The case of the Aroostook Band of Micmacs shows that indigenous people would rather construct "a nation within a nation" in the United States than be governed by the U.S. federal government. Yet, this condition applies only when that indigenous people's traditional land was proved to be a part of the United States. This situation is quite different from other immigrants, who either assimilate themselves into the dominant society, or construct a new identity as an ethnic group within the United States. Besides the right to possess land, indigenous people have received the right to benefit from trading as a group. From the perspective of indigenous peoples, such as the Akwesasne Mohawk, it is a way of keeping their tradition of trading and taking advantage of their sovereignty.

However, in modern society, tobacco and alcohol, or even drugs and arms, can be traded in such situations, just as with the problem the Tohono O'odham people are facing. They may make a big profit out of it, but handling these products can endanger the indigenous people themselves. A part of trafficking in risky items seems to be deeply related to economic poverty among indigenous peoples. As a result of their history of persecution, indigenous peoples are still disadvantaged politically, socially, and economically. In order to gain enough money to govern themselves as an independent people, they need supplemental income in addition to federal assistance. Yet, most of the land given to indigenous peoples is poor in natural resources and often very small.

Thus, many peoples have to rely on casino operations, which bring them instant money. In the case of Akwesasne Mohawk's trading, alcohol and tobacco are associated, too. Trading has been the Mohawk's tradition. Meanwhile, trading does not require many resources or space and would be the most suitable industry for the current Akwesasne Mohawk people. However, suitability of handling alcohol and tobacco is debatable, as these can cause negative effects on young people. However, trading might be one of a few ways to support themselves economically. Although both nonindigenous and indigenous cross the border, these aspects and problems are unique to indigenous border crossing as groups.

Indigenous and nonindigenous peoples who migrate beyond the international borders on the North American continent partially share the same experience. At the same time, some experiences are very unique to indigenous peoples. Yet, transborder indigenous peoples have worked among other immigrants, and there have been many contacts between them. Including experiences unique to indigenous migration in borderland history and society would enhance a deeper understanding of issues concerning the United States and immigration.

Bibliography
Erickson, Winston P. 1994. *Sharing the Desert: The Tohono O'odham in History.* Tucson: University of Arizona Press.
Ewers, John C. 1974. "Ethnological Report on the Chippewa Cree Tribe of the Rocky Boy Reservation and the Little Shell Band of Indians." In *Chippewa Indians VI*, 9–182. New York and London: Garland Publishing.
Gibson, Arrell Morgan. 1963. *The Kickapoos: Lords of the Middle Border.* Norman: University of Oklahoma Press.
Horr, David Agee, ed. 1974. *American Indian Ethnohistory: North, Central and Northeastern Indians. Chippewa Indians I.* New York and London: Garland Publishing.
Horr, David Agee, ed. 1974. *American Indian Ethnohistory: North, Central and Northeastern Indians. Papago Indians III.* New York and London: Garland Publishing.
Latorre, Felipe A., and Dolores L. Latorre. 1976. *The Mexican Kickapoo Indians.* Austin and London: University of Texas Press.
Luna-Firebaugh, Eileen M. 2002. "The Border Crossed US: Border Crossing of the Indigenous Peoples of the Americas." *Wicazo Sa Review* 17, no. 1: 159–81.
Mandelbaum, David G. 1979. *The Plains Cree: An Ethnographic, Historical, and Comparative Study.* Regina, Saskatchewan, Canada: Research Center, University of Regina.
Meeks, Eric V. 2007. *Border Citizens: The Making of Indians, Mexicans, and Anglos in Arizona.* Austin: University of Texas Press.

Miller, Tom. 1981. *On the Border: Portraits of America's Southwestern Frontier.* New York: Harper & Row.

Prins, Harald E. L. 1996. "Tribal Network and Migrant Labor: Mi'kmaq Indians as Seasonal Workers in Aroostook's Potato Fields, 1870–1980." In *Native Americans and Wage Labor: Ethnohistorical Perspectives*, edited by Alice Littlefield and Martha C. Knack, 45–65. Norman and London: University of Oklahoma Press.

Slowe, Peter M. 1991. "The Geography of Borderlands: The Case of the Quebec-US Borderlands." *Geographical Journal* 157, no. 2: 191–98.

Spicer, Edward H. 1980. *The Yaquis: A Cultural History.* Tucson: University of Arizona Press.

Taliman, Valerie. 2001. "Borders and Native Peoples: Divided, but Not Conquered." *Native Americas*, March 31.

Borderlands and the American Southwest

Manuel G. Gonzales

By the early twenty-first century, the U.S.-Mexico border region, the Greater Southwest, had become the subject of intense scrutiny by scholars on both sides of the international divide. Incompletely integrated into the life of the two nations, the residents of this region, the borderlanders, had much in common with one another. In fact, as political scientist Robert A. Pastor has justly noted, "New Mexico and Sonora have more in common ... than New Mexico has with Pennsylvania or Sonora has with Jalisco" (Pastor and Castañeda 1988, 285). Consequently, there arose a unique way of life that came to be embraced on both sides of the border. The full emergence of this binational culture after World War II is the focus of this chapter. In an age of globalization, with increasing economic interdependency, the regional identity that has emerged there, though disparaged by cultural nationalists on both sides of the international boundary, promises to grow stronger rather than weaker as time goes by.

Geography

The Greater Southwest consists of Texas, New Mexico, Arizona, and California on the U.S. side, and, on the Mexican side, from east to west, the states of Tamaulipas, Nuevo León, Coahuila, Chihuahua, Sonora, and Baja California. Straddling the 1,952-mile international border, these 10 states encompass an area of 960,000 square miles. The "core borderlands," the heart of this binational region, is a corridor consisting of the 25 U.S. counties and thirty-eight Mexican *municipios*—roughly the equivalent of U.S. counties—that abut against the international border. (See Anderson and Gerber [2008, 39] for a complete list of counties and municipios.) Although vast stretches of land are virtually uninhabited, the entire core region is overwhelmingly urban, with 90 percent of the region's inhabitants residing in 14 twin cities along the border. The major pairs of these binational urban centers, from east to west, are Brownsville, Texas–Matamoros, Tamaulipas; Laredo, Texas–Nuevo Laredo, Tamaulipas; El Paso, Texas–Ciudad Juárez, Chihuahua; Nogales, Arizona–Nogales, Sonora; and San Diego, California–Tijuana, Baja California. Ciudad Juárez and Tijuana, the two largest cities, had populations in excess of 1.5 million in 2010. Altogether, the total population of the immediate border area, the binational corridor—which numbered 12.2 million in 2000—exceeded well over 13 million inhabitants by this time, with roughly half living on either side of the divide.

The outstanding natural feature of the Greater Southwest is aridity. Throughout most of the interior border area, the Chihuahua and Sonoran deserts dominate the Mexican side, much of which encompasses the northern *altiplano* (high plain) bounded on the west by the Sierra Madre Occidental and on the east by the Sierra Madre Oriental. On the American side, this desert province extends deep into New Mexico and Arizona, where the Rocky Mountains and the Colorado Plateau, with its distinctive buttes and mesas, form its northern limits. To the west, these arid lands can be found well beyond the heart of the Southwest. The Mojave Desert covers extensive portions of southern California, as well as Nevada and Utah in the Great Basin.

The only major rivers are the Colorado, the Rio Grande, and the Conchos, which originates in the Sierra Madre Oriental and flows into the Rio Grande. Given the chronic shortage of water, typical vegetation consists of mesquite and a wide variety of cacti, including the famous saguaro in the Arizona-Sonora Desert; and agaves, yuccas, creosote bushes, and the ocotillo in the Chihuahua Desert. Arid landscape is also typical of the western borderlands running from the coastal plain along the Gulf of California, through the Mexicali Valley, across the Sierra de San Pedro Mártir, and on to the Pacific Coast above the mountainous peninsula of Baja California. To the east, the Rio Grande—known as the Río Bravo del Norte to Mexicans—forms the boundary between Texas and Mexico and flows southeastward from the twin cities of El Paso and Ciudad Juárez, situated on the edge of the Chihuahua Desert. The river makes the big bend and gradually snakes its way across hilly, undulating country into the subtropical lowlands of the Gulf of Mexico, a vast grassland area now transformed into rich farmland on both sides of the international divide. Grasslands can also be found here and there in other parts of the borderlands, particularly in the coastal plains of the Gulf of California and the river basins of both Sonora and Arizona.

Historical Origins

The present-day boundary separating Mexico and the United States is a product of the Treaty of Guadalupe Hidalgo of 1848, which ended the Mexican-American War, and the Gadsden Purchase five years later. Inhabited by both sedentary and nomadic tribes, the region had belonged to Spain before 1821 and thereafter to a newly independent Mexico. *Norteamericanos* (American citizens), who began to enter the area about 1800, established a significant presence, especially in California and Texas, only after 1821, when the Mexicans terminated imperial Spain's mercantilist policies.

The rapid expansion of Americans into Texas in the 1820s and 1830s soon threatened the Mexican government's hold over the territory. Moreover, a cultural conflict quickly became evident between these new arrivals and the resident *tejanos* (Mexican Texans). Staunch Protestants, these immigrants were loath to adopt Catholicism, a requirement for land ownership. Moreover, the newcomers, predominantly from America's southern frontier, brought with them deep-seated racist sentiments; many of them were

slaveholders. Nonetheless, these recent immigrants, led by Sam Houston, initiated the Texas revolt against the central government in Mexico in 1835–1836. As its chief architects, they dominated the short-lived Lone Star Republic.

The loss of Texas—annexed by the United States in 1845—outraged Mexican nationalists and strained the relations between the two nations. War was in the air. The predominant cause of the looming conflict, however, was the U.S. desire to expand to the west. By now Manifest Destiny had won the hearts and minds of many Americans, especially on the southern and western frontiers. Their leading spokesman was James K. Polk, a slaveholding planter from Tennessee who won the presidency in 1844 running on an expansionist platform. Intent on war, Polk used a border dispute in South Texas to lure the Mexicans into an attack on "American territory" in April 1846, and the U.S. Senate declared war on May 13. Given the vast discrepancies in wealth and numbers between the two nations—Mexico, with a population of 7 million, mostly Indians, faced a formidable adversary whose population numbered 17 million—the war was virtually inevitable, as were the results.

The Treaty of Guadalupe Hidalgo, signed on February 2, 1848, and ratified by the U.S. Senate on March 10, transferred Mexico's vast northern frontier to the United States, 947,570 square miles of land. The richest prize was the province of Alta California (present-day California), the gateway to the Orient. The vanquished nation received $15 million in compensation. The treaty also guaranteed the civil and land rights of those Mexicans choosing to remain in the alienated territory—anywhere between 50,000 and 80,000 settlers, mostly along the Rio Grande. The few thousand repatriates generally settled immediately across the redrawn border, where they founded several communities, including Nuevo Laredo and Nogales.

It was not too long before expansion-minded Americans found the newly created boundary unsatisfactory. Anxious to build a railroad line from El Paso to southern California via northern Sonora, the Franklin Pierce administration sent an agent, James Gadsden, in 1853 to negotiate the purchase of additional land. The mission was a resounding success: the Mexicans were coaxed into surrendering 29,142,000 acres south

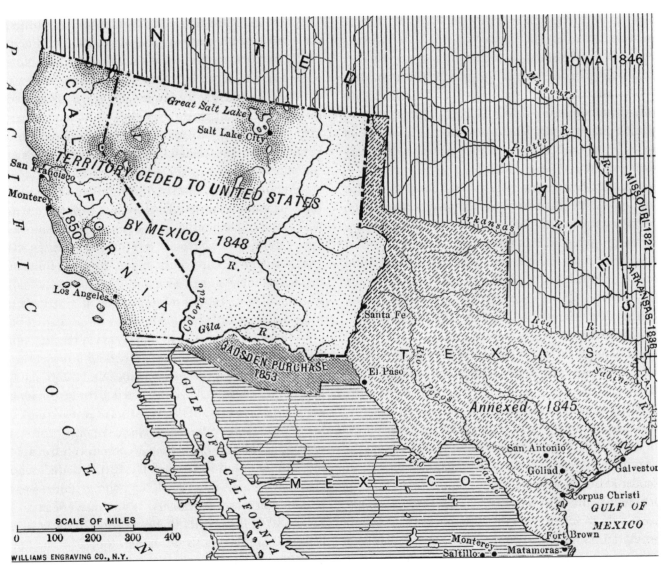

The U.S. took possession of the territory north of the Gila River (shown on map) according to the Treaty of Guadalupe Hidalgo following the Mexican-American War in 1848. In 1853, the Gadsden Purchase added the territory south of the Gila River. (North Wind Picture Archives)

of the Gila River for another $10 million. The Gadsden Purchase, which went into effect in 1854, rounded out the southern U.S. boundary, the present-day divide between the two nations.

The aftermath of the war found Mexican Americans facing a bleak future in a conquered land. The Texas Revolt and the Mexican-American War left a legacy of bitterness for decades. Anglo Texans were particularly outraged by the stinging humiliation suffered at the Alamo on March 6, 1836. The race issue, too, fanned anti-Mexican sentiment. The attitudes toward Mexicans in the United States mirrored American contempt for their defeated homeland, which was plagued by chronic political instability and economic collapse, an easy prey for the French, who foisted an Austrian archduke on the unhappy republic in the 1860s. Mexico's troubles in the immediate aftermath of the 1848 war also encouraged a series of filibustering expeditions by American adventurers, which together with banditry and Indian problems kept tension high on the border until the 1880s. The best known of these incursions were led by William Walker into Baja California in 1853–1854 and Henry Alexander Crabb into Sonora in 1857.

Throughout this confused period, the U.S. government was unwilling or unable to rein in its unruly citizens. Indeed, there was continual talk of further annexations of Mexican territory in Washington, D.C. It was only with the establishment of the Porfiriato (the dictatorship of Porfirio Díaz) in 1876–1911 that the border was stabilized and threats to Mexican sovereignty faded, though they never completely disappeared until after 1920.

In the Southwest, however, at the hands of Anglos throughout the last decades of the nineteenth century, Mexican Americans continued to suffer ill treatment, based primarily on racial prejudice. One of the most damaging blows, despite the 1848 treaty guaranteeing Mexican residents "all the rights of citizens of the United States," was the loss of land, which began practically before the ink was dry. In 1851, the U.S. Congress passed a Land Act that called for the validation of land titles in California, thus initiating the process of Hispanic dispossession throughout the conquered region. In no time at all, Mexicans in the Southwest were reduced to a landless and marginalized proletariat, increasingly forced into menial jobs in agriculture, railroad maintenance, and particularly mining, which greatly expanded on both sides of the border by the turn of the century.

Many of these *obreros* (workers) were immigrants. Beginning with the California Gold Rush, when 10,000 miners from Sonora arrived in the Mother Lode country, Mexican immigration gradually swelled. These numbers, however, were miniscule compared to the tide of eastern immigration that commenced with the gold rush in 1849 and reached flood proportions with the proliferation of railroads throughout the border region following the completion of the construction of the first transcontinental railway in 1869. Two lines, the Atchison, Topeka, and Santa Fe Railroad and the Southern Pacific Railroad, arrived in El Paso, the Queen City of the Southwest, in 1881. Anglos poured into the borderlands, particularly into southern California. The population of Los Angeles leaped from 6,000 in 1870 to more than 100,000 by 1900.

Hopelessly outnumbered, most U.S. Mexicans, both immigrants and native-born, resigned themselves to their fate. A few, particularly members of the Hispanic political and economic elite, even allied themselves with the Anglo newcomers. Prominent collaborators included Donaciano Vigil in New Mexico and Mariano Vallejo in California. Other members of this privileged class, though, championed the cause of their oppressed compatriots, gaining their respect and political support, among them Mariano Samaniego in Tucson and Pablo de la Guerra in Santa Barbara.

Accommodation was not a realistic option for lower-class *mexicanos*. Occasionally, resistance was their only viable alternative. A popular reaction was the establishment of *mutualistas* (mutual-benefit societies) throughout the border region, the most influential being the Alianza Hispano-Americana, which was founded in Tucson in 1894 in the aftermath of a local nativist upsurge. "Mexican immigrants," a prominent Mexican-American historian has argued, "did not see themselves as members of a proletariat class but as Mexicans temporarily in a foreign land; hence, they organized and protected themselves along ethnic lines" (García 1981, 108–9). A few disgruntled *mexicanos*, on the other hand, chose the path of armed resistance, among them Juan Nepomuceno Cortina, the famous "Red Robber of the Rio Grande," who operated in South Texas and neighboring Tamaulipas beginning in the late 1850s. In the late 1880s and early 1890s, *las Gorras Blancas* (the White Caps) in New Mexico turned to violence, too, as Hispanos found themselves increasingly dispossessed of their ancestral lands, a process that took longer there than elsewhere given the slow Anglo penetration of the territory.

The hostility between *gringos* and "greasers" was most intense in Texas, especially along the border. Given the persistence of widespread transborder banditry, which prompted endless retaliatory strikes, particularly on the part of Anglos, violence came to be endemic on both sides of the international boundary. The lynching of *tejanos* and *mexicanos* in some Texas border communities came to be commonplace. The Texas Rangers were particularly brutal, gaining the hatred of Spanish-speaking border residents well into the twentieth century.

Like their conquered brethren in the north, the *fronterizos* (borderlanders) on the Mexican side also experienced myriad problems during the late nineteenth century. As before, they continued to be neglected by the central government in Mexico City. Indeed, given the chronic instability in the core area, their situation was dire throughout most of this troubled period. However, the gradual imposition of the rule of law after about 1880 by Porfirio Díaz, who delivered on his promise of *orden y progreso* (Order and Progress), brought about a general amelioration in the quality of life of *norteños* (Northerners).

As Don Porfirio consolidated his regime, American entrepreneurs found fabulous opportunities for profit south of the border, where they were welcomed with open arms. U.S. investors flocked to Mexico and invested $1 billion during the Porfiriato (the period of Díaz's rule). Railroad construction was particularly lucrative. In no time at all, beginning with the construction in 1884 of the Mexican Central Railroad—linking Ciudad Juárez and Mexico City— virtually the entire national railway system came to be controlled by New York bankers. Mining, ranching, and agriculture offered foreign investors other attractive alternatives for hefty profits. Allied with Díaz and the native elites, American businessmen struck a bonanza. By 1910, on the eve of the Mexican Revolution, some 15,000 Americans controlled 130 million acres of land, almost 27 percent of the national patrimony.

The expansion of capitalism into Mexico benefited both native and foreign entrepreneurs and investors, but it created a multitude of problems for the country's lower classes and particularly for its indigenous population, who were seen by Díaz's economic advisors as a major barrier to modernization. Indian villages in central Mexico paid a heavy price as their *ejidos* were broken up. On the northern border region, the Yaquis of Sonora suffered many atrocities after the 1880s at the hands of the dictator and his local henchmen. Many were exiled to the henequen plantations of Yucatán, though some escaped into southern Arizona, eventually establishing a binational identity.

On the more positive side, Mexicans on the northern rim found unprecedented economic opportunities in railroad construction, agriculture, and mining. The expansion of U.S. capitalism into northern Mexico, especially Chihuahua and Sonora where the mining industry boomed, encouraged a growing migration from the interior, a trickle that became a flood during the Mexican Revolution. Though the labor force was heavily exploited by local white elites and their Yankee allies, wages in the North were sufficiently high that a few modest desert communities along the border began a slow transformation into significant manufacturing and commercial centers by the last days of the Porfiriato.

The Twentieth Century

The decade of the Mexican Revolution (1911– 1920) introduced momentous changes along the U.S.-Mexican border. The most consequential was an acceleration of immigration from the south. Some newcomers were political refugees. Their main destinations were El Paso and San Antonio. Though the overwhelming majority of these conservative *émigrés* intended to go into exile temporarily, many eventually settled in the Southwest.

The greatest number of immigrants, however, entered the United States for economic reasons. These constituted the bulk of what Mexican-American scholars later labeled "the Great Migration"—the entry of over one million Mexicans into the United States in 1900–1930. There were a plethora of jobs for these uprooted newcomers during World War I and its immediate aftermath as the southwestern economy grew by leaps and bounds. This was especially the case in agriculture, for America's Newlands Reclamation Act in 1902, creating irrigation projects throughout the West, resulted in the widespread expansion of factory farms in the rich agricultural valleys of the Southwest. Many of these desert oases were immediately adjacent to the border and thus readily accessible, particularly the Lower Rio Grande Valley. The Mesilla, Salt River, and Imperial Valleys were also major recipients of federal water and served as magnets for armies of desperate *campesinos* (farmworkers). The termination of World War I did little to slow down the exodus from the south, in part because the Cristero Rebellion (1926–1929), centered in Jalisco, Michoacán, and Guanajuato, stimulated a fresh supply of disillusioned migrants looking to improve their lot by moving *al norte* ("to the north," meaning to the United States). The creation of the Border Patrol in 1924 did little to stem the tide. This migration was largely confined to the American borderland—89 percent of Mexicans in the United States resided in the Southwest in 1920—with immigrants moving primarily to Texas in the early years and gradually shifting to California, where they formed the bulk of the labor force in agriculture by the onset of the Great Depression. Indeed, it was *mexicanos* who transformed California and the Southwest into the nation's breadbasket. Aside from farm labor, Mexicans also came to dominate railroad maintenance and mining in the Southwest.

Unfortunately, the massive influx of destitute and undereducated immigrants into the United States during the first decades of the twentieth century sparked powerful nativist sentiments, which along the southwestern border centered on *mexicanos*. While major immigration acts in 1917, 1921, and 1924 effectively reduced the entry of southern and East Europeans, it was only the dire need for cheap labor in the Southwest that saved Mexicans from suffering the same fate.

Anti-Mexican sentiment, however, remained pronounced, and as in previous periods, it mirrored the troubled relationship between the two nations. Following a dispute with President Victoriano Huerta, for example, the United States invaded and occupied the port city of Vera Cruz in 1914. The troubled U.S.-Mexican border also continued to strain relations. In 1915–1916, the discovery of a Mexican plot to raise an insurrection in South Texas, announced in the mysterious *Plan de San Diego*, resulted in massive and bloody Anglo reprisals against *mexicanos* living on both sides of the border. Another well-known instance of cross-border tension in this period resulted from the General John J. Pershing–led punitive expedition into Mexico in search of Pancho Villa, following his raid on the New Mexican border town of Columbus on March 9, 1916. These violations of national sovereignty, on both sides, were not unique.

The movement of *mexicanos* into the United States in the late nineteenth and early twentieth centuries has been well documented. Few scholars, though, are aware that there was a concurrent migration by

U.S. citizens into Mexico. While a sizable contingent set up residence in Mexico City during this period, the turn of the century, most of these "boomers," as they came to be called, settled down in northern Mexico. Thousands of Americans, many of them members of colonization societies, established homes in the fertile valleys of Sonora, Chihuahua, and particularly Tamaulipas. The majority of these newcomers came from Texas and the Midwest. Among the most intrepid of these Yankee arrivals were some 4,000 Mormons who established nine small farming communities in Chihuahua and Sonora beginning in 1885. Altogether, some 40,000 Americans resided in Mexico by 1910.

Mexicans were ambivalent in their attitudes toward these English-speaking immigrants, especially given their devotion to Protestantism and their propensity to live in isolated communities outside the Mexican mainstream. The popular animosity directed at U.S. entrepreneurs favored by the Díaz administration also poisoned their relations with the boomers, resulting in the expropriation of lands belonging to both businessmen and settlers during and after the revolution, when anti-Americanism ran rampant. Many Americans were forced to abandon their homes in Mexico, particularly during the agrarian reforms of the 1920s. Faced with expropriation, U.S. land and mine owners were forced to sell their holdings at bargain-basement prices. This process of land alienation accelerated during the presidency of Lázaro Cárdenas (1934–1940), whose sweeping reforms included the nationalization of both the railroads and the oil industry. American companies and stockholders were outraged, but there was little to be done; President Franklin D. Roosevelt, fearing a looming global war and anxious to maintain the loyalty of neighbors in the Western Hemisphere, did something U.S. administrations rarely do in such instances—he refused to intervene. It would take years for American investors to regain lost ground south of the border.

In the boom years of the 1920s, communities on both sides of the international divide experienced rapid growth and—for some residents, at least—a measure of prosperity. These communities benefited considerably from the nascent tourist industry stimulated by the mass production of inexpensive automobiles. On the American side, Phoenix, Tucson, and San Diego were particularly favored, given their reputations as health havens. Tourism became just as vital to the economy on the southern side of the border. Mexican border communities became attractive destinations once political stability was restored after the revolution. These towns were aided, too, by the passage of the 1919 Volstead Act, which made it illegal to produce or consume liquor in the United States. Throngs of Americans now eagerly descended on Mexico, both to consume alcoholic beverages and to smuggle them back home. U.S. and Mexican businessmen, often working in tandem, were quick to seize the opportunities to supply drinks and entertainment, including gambling and prostitution. Before too long, casinos, hotels, dance halls, and bordellos lined the entire length of the border, as modest Mexican villages were transformed into thriving tourist meccas. By the 1930s, the most popular of these destinations were to be found in Ciudad Juárez and in Baja California, particularly the border towns of Mexicali and Tijuana. The latter, a village of about 250 inhabitants in 1900, grew to more than 16,000 residents in 1940.

The Depression was particularly hard on Mexican border communities, especially after the repeal of the Volstead Act in 1933. Moreover, the repatriation from the United States, both voluntary and coerced, of some 425,500 *mexicanos* (with estimates ranging from significantly lower than that near half million to well above it) and their Mexican-American children during the early 1930s resulted in the unwelcome arrival of thousands of destitute repatriates, a major burden on limited municipal resources.

Good times returned to the borderlands during World War II as the global conflict stimulated both industrial and agricultural production. Mexican labor was now indispensable in the Southwest. The Mexican government was called upon to aid its northern ally by supplying temporary workers, mainly as agricultural laborers. The Bracero Program (1942–1964), a wartime expedient, proved to be so lucrative that the agreement was repeatedly extended into the Korean conflict and beyond. Altogether, close to one-half million Mexican nationals participated in this managed migration (4.4 million contracts, but involving approximately one-half million individuals, many of whom were repeaters). Braceros were a mixed blessing, however, for in border areas like South Texas they displaced Mexican-American workers in droves. In the meantime, Mexican border communities again began to experience rapid growth, many of the newcomers being either ex-braceros or would-be braceros who failed recruitment requirements.

One unforeseen consequence of the Bracero Program was an unprecedented surge of undocumented Mexican workers into the United States—initiating transnational migration circuits that continued to function into the twenty-first century. The sheer volume of illegal entrants led, in turn, to Operation Wetback, a massive U.S. campaign in 1953–1955 to apprehend and repatriate them. Although scholarly estimates vary greatly with respect to the number of undocumented persons (mostly Mexicans) apprehended or pressured to depart voluntarily, some compute a high end guesstimate of one million sent across the border, usually to communities just across it. *Barrios* (Mexican neighborhoods) in U.S. border towns were especially vulnerable. In one week in July 1954, 35,000 illegal aliens were rounded up in El Paso. Although the Immigration and Naturalization Service (INS) achieved some success in stemming the tide, changing conditions in both Mexico and the United States soon led to a revival of the immigrant flow, both legal and illegal.

The 1950s witnessed an economic boom throughout Mexico, but particularly in the North where the rural sector flourished. Even before the war, a series of Mexican presidents who hailed from northern states—Álvaro Obregón, Plutarco Elías Calles, Emilio Portes Gil, Pascual Ortiz Rubio, and Abelardo Rodríguez—had provided generous federal subsidies for agricultural development throughout the northern border region. During and after the war, major irrigation projects in both the Northeast and the Northwest created even greater opportunities for the region's large farmers. As jobs opened up in the agrarian sector, immigration from the interior swelled, drawn to border communities as well as to factory farms. From 1950 to 1980, the population of Tijuana went from 59,950 to 461,257, and that of Ciudad Juárez from 122,566 to 567,365. The Mexican border economy was aided, too, by an unprecedented growth in the number of American tourists. Since so many U.S. military facilities were now scattered throughout the Sunbelt, large numbers of these northern visitors were servicemen looking for a good time in the free-wheeling "sin cities" across the border.

By the mid-1960s, however, Mexico's postwar economic boom was beginning to wane. Overpopulation loomed as an acute problem. The end of the Bracero Program, moreover, contributed to massive unemployment. The problems were especially severe along the border, where the population had mushroomed in recent years. In 1965, this dire state of affairs prompted the initiation of the Border Industrialization Program (BIP), a cooperative economic venture undertaken by the U.S. and Mexican governments. Under the terms of this binational agreement, Mexico would permit foreign corporations to set up a series of assembly plants called *maquiladoras*, or *maquilas*, on its territory. Located predominantly across the border from the United States in order to facilitate transportation from the United States to American factories in Mexico, these industrial plants, mostly American-owned, would import raw materials from the north duty free and send back finished products, paying U.S. taxes only on the value added. Mexican citizens would gain much-needed jobs; and Americans, both businessmen and consumers, would reap the benefits of low-wage labor and cheap commodities. Though the program got off to a modest start, it soon proved to be a huge success in generating jobs. Workers poured into Ciudad Juárez, Tijuana, and other border communities from the southern interior. Some disillusioned migrants, those unable to find employment locally, would often continue their journey northward, surreptitiously across the border.

A product of dire economic times in Mexico caused largely by overpopulation and a chronic debt crisis, on the one hand, and burgeoning U.S. labor needs, on the other, immigration to the north, both legal and illegal, would continue practically unabated for the rest of the twentieth century. Between 1961 and 2000, more than 20 percent of all immigrants legally admitted into the United States came from Mexico. These included some two million *mexicanos*

who were legalized under the Immigration Reform and Control Act (IRCA) of 1986, which sought to bring order to the United States' chaotic immigration policy. During this same period, Mexicans also constituted the vast majority of undocumented aliens, who represented a massive exodus of people that IRCA targeted but failed to curtail. By the early twenty-first century, Mexican immigration had actually swelled rather than diminished. By 2006, immigrant remittances, totaling $24 billion, had surpassed tourism and ranked second only to oil exports as Mexico's greatest source of income. Many of these remittances were collective projects of over 600 Mexican home-town associations (HTAs), popularly known as *clubes de oriundos*, linking immigrant communities in the United States with friends and relatives back home.

Together with continuing U.S. tourism and the expansion of the *maquiladora* industries, which received a huge boost in the mid-1990s thanks to the North American Free Trade Agreement (NAFTA), the unprecedented numbers of illegal aliens who used Mexican border communities as staging areas served as a major stimulus to the regional economy. This was especially true of the underground economy, for illegal immigration gave rise to a thriving business centered on transporting undocumented workers across the border, as well as providing them with forged documents. Concurrently, there was a major upswing in transborder drug smuggling, particularly in Nuevo Laredo, Ciudad Juárez, and Tijuana. The illegal transport of people and narcotics were among the primary causes of the widespread political corruption and violence—most of it drug-related—which became endemic by the turn of the twenty-first century all along the border, from Matamoros to Tijuana.

By this time, too, border communities were beginning to feel the full impact of free trade. A product of the neoliberal philosophy fostered by globalization, NAFTA had a far-reaching influence on the borderlands. Business elites in Mexico, Canada, and the United States had sold the idea of a free-trade zone as a solution to a variety of problems. The controversial pact was signed on December 17, 1992, by U.S. President George H. W. Bush, Mexican President Carlos Salinas de Gortari, and Canadian Prime Minister Brian Mulroney. Buoyed by commerce, both legal and illegal, with the United States, Mexico's borderland, especially the western half, had long enjoyed a higher standard of living than the rest of the country. The trilateral pact, which went into effect in January 1994, succeeded in increasing this socioeconomic disparity with the interior.

The economies of many Mexican border communities boomed. Nuevo Laredo, which witnessed a huge increase in truck traffic from Monterrey to the port of Houston, was the most extreme example; by 2008, 40 percent of Mexico's imports to the U.S. entered via the Interstate 35 corridor. These cities paid a heavy price, though. Wealth was distributed very unevenly, a socioeconomic imbalance reminiscent of the Porfiriato. Ecological problems proliferated along the border, where 75 percent of the *maquiladoras* were located. Moreover, NAFTA had a devastating impact on the economy of many states in the Mexican interior, notably those with large indigenous populations south of Mexico City, small-scale farmers who could not compete with cheap U.S. imports.

The chief beneficiaries of the trilateral program were U.S. businessmen, who took advantage of low-wage labor to accumulate healthy profits at home. And thanks to NAFTA, American firms like Monsanto, Cargill, and Anderson Clayton achieved domination over both Mexican agricultural imports and exports. The international agreement also enabled U.S. companies to take full advantage of Mexico's race to privatize its major industries, a process initiated during the administrations of Presidents Miguel de la Madrid (1982–1988) and Carlos Salinas de Gortari (1988–1994). Then, too, the devaluation of the peso in 1994, a catastrophe for the national economy even more disastrous than the one following the 1982 devaluation, encouraged wealthy investors, further intensifying U.S. engagement in the country's economy.

If Mexican political and economic elites generally profited from free trade, workers in the *maquiladoras* barely got by on their meager wages, especially female employees, who represented 58 percent of the total workforce in 2000. *Mexicanos* were critical, too, of the alienation of their national resources. Moreover, loans by the U.S. government, the World Bank, and private financiers were all advanced with the understanding

not only that privatization would be expanded, but also that social welfare programs would be reduced —a heavy burden on the Mexican masses, who led a difficult existence in even the best of times but who grew increasingly desperate after the economic debacle of the mid-1990s.

Borderlanders: The People and Their Culture

Recent scholarship has indicated that a convergence of peoples and cultures are typical of borderlands. This is particularly true of the U.S.-Mexico borderlands, where society was very diverse at the beginning of the twenty-first century and included significant numbers of African Americans, Asians, and Native Americans. The three major residents of these communities, however, continued to be Mexicans, Mexican Americans, and Anglo Americans. Most borderlanders were Mexicans, who dominated the southern side of the divide but who were also prominent on the U.S. side, as immigrants, legal and illegal, and as commuters. North of the border, there were a growing number of Mexican Americans. Some of them traced their roots on the border back decades or even centuries. Most were products of twentieth-century immigration. Living next to the motherland, these Mexican-origin residents retained many native traditions and values, but the influence of American culture was now pervasive, resulting in a thoroughly bicultural population. Most Anglos, too, were recent arrivals, generally entering the Sunbelt after 1940. However, they tended to live outside the narrow border strip, in places like Los Angeles and Phoenix, and consequently, most of them had only a passing acquaintance with their neighbors across the border. The most obvious exception was South Texas, where interethnic relations were reasonably cordial.

Generally, however, relations between Anglos and Spanish-speakers in the borderlands remained ambivalent. Historically, there had been much animosity, which continued to surface periodically, especially on the part of U.S. citizens. Anti-Mexican sentiments were more pronounced among new arrivals; long-time Anglo residents were more accommodating to their Spanish-speaking neighbors, particularly if their

A street in El Paso, Texas, 2006. Many links have existed across boundaries—social, economic, and cultural, especially in the Southwest where the same peoples exist on both sides, sometimes with ties preceding 1848. (Hector Mata/AFP/Getty Images)

economic interests were served by catering to a Hispanic market. Occasionally, intermarriage occurred between Anglos and Mexican Americans, rarely between Anglos and Mexicans.

Tension also typified the relations between Mexicans and Mexican Americans. The latter were often disdainful of recent arrivals, sometimes labeled *cholos*, who tended to come from the lower classes, thus lacking both job and language skills. At times there was also competition for jobs, though immigrants, especially the undocumented, were stuck in the lowest rung of the economic ladder. For their part, many Mexican nationals, on both sides of the border, resented Mexican Americans, who were seen as

arrogant and ill-mannered. Alluded to by the derogatory term *pochos*, they were perceived as shallow turncoats who had lost touch with their ethnic roots—who were ignorant of Mexican history and culture as well as the Spanish language. Relations between native-born and immigrant Mexicans tended to be considerably better in South Texas than in other parts of the borderlands; many *tejanos* had extended family networks just across the border.

The culture of the borderlands was as vibrant as its society. In the Southwest, most Mexican-American residents were bilingual, as were many Anglo Americans. Also common on the U.S. side was Spanglish, that odd mixture of words taken from both languages; and south of the border, the English language had made significant inroads in its own right but also influenced the native language in the form of anglicisms. However, a high percentage of Mexican-American residents north of the border spoke only Spanish, its popularity ensured by continuing migration from the homeland. The best example was the Lower Rio Grande Valley. "Nowhere in the Hispanic American borderland is the Spanish language as geographically resilient as it is along the South Texas borderland" (Arreola 2002, 198). Eighteen counties in the Lone Star State were predominantly Spanish-speaking at the beginning of the twenty-first century. The Spanish spoken throughout the region, on both sides of the international divide, was characterized by only subtle variations from one border state to another, both in vocabulary and dialect.

The Mexican food of the Southwest, a variation of the cuisine that evolved in northern Mexico, became immensely popular throughout the region and indeed across the United States; in fact, by now salsa had replaced ketchup as the country's favorite condiment. Food remained a crucial component of Mexican and Mexican-American identity. While there were significant variations in this cuisine from state to state, there were certain commonalities throughout the border region. The widespread popularity of the flour tortilla—in contrast to the corn tortilla that was preferred in the Mexican interior—was one of them. On the other hand, corn tortillas were used for enchiladas; and, of course, tamales were also made of maize. Rice and beans continued to be the most common elements of the border diet. Dishes were usually spicy. *Chiles rellenos* were on most menus. *Barbacoa* was a staple of home cooking along the Texas border, particularly on weekends and days of celebration. Beer, often imported from Mexico, remained the beverage of choice. In the 1980s, fajitas, a *tejano* dish, became the rage throughout the entire border region. Concurrently, seafood became much more common in Mexican-American restaurants, as it had long been along both Mexican coasts. Still another emerging trend, notably in urban California, was the fusion of Mexican dishes with exotic influences, resulting in the creation of a haute cuisine.

Another important component of borderlands culture was music. One of the most admired musical forms along the border since the nineteenth century was the *corrido*, a folk ballad generally celebrating the deeds of local heroes. Of these, "perhaps the most memorable" was "El corrido de Gregorio Cortez," commemorating the life of a *tejano* who killed an Anglo sheriff in the Lower Rio Grande Valley in self-defense at the turn of the century and became the object of the largest manhunt in Texas history (Peña and Burr 1994, 567). This musical genre reached the height of its popularity, both on the border and in the Mexican interior, at the time of the revolution.

By the beginning of the twentieth century, music along the borderlands had achieved a distinctive style. Called *norteño*, it centered on the *mexicano* communities along the Texas-Mexican border. Its trademark instrument from the very outset was the diatonic button accordion, a nineteenth-century German contribution that came to be as influential in Texas as it was in northern Mexico. Exclusively instrumental in the beginning, *norteño* music incorporated vocalists soon after World War I. The most successful of these early singers was Lydia Mendoza, the legendary "Songbird of the Border." Selena (Quintanilla), another *tejana* interpreter of *norteño* music, also achieved iconic status before her premature death in 1995. A later manifestation of *norteño* music was *banda*, which began in Sinaloa and gradually spread north, gaining immense popularity throughout the *barrios* on both sides of the border, especially among the immigrant population in the Southwest.

Bridging two powerful musical traditions, borderlanders have benefited from a wide variety of styles emanating from both south and north. Arguably, the music of the Mexican interior was and remained the most pervasive into the twenty-first century. These musical favorites included mariachis, as well as various forms of *música tropical*. Truly binational, Mexican borderlands music was powerfully impacted, too, by American musical styles. These included country and western, which produced at least one major Mexican-American star, the *tejano* Freddy Fender. The swing music of the Big Bands was another weighty influence on borderlands musicians, notably the Tucson-born singer and composer Lalo Guerrero. More far-reaching in its impact, however, was rock 'n' roll. From its very inception in the 1950s, rock made steady inroads not only north of the border, but also among audiences in Mexico, especially in the Far North—much to the chagrin of Mexican nationalists, who saw in this fascination the most egregious example of American cultural imperialism. Carlos Santana, a native of Tijuana, ranks among the most successful borderlands representatives of this popular musical style.

Catholicism remained the dominant religion in Spanish-speaking border communities at the turn of the century. In most places, however, especially in rural areas, a folk variation distinctly at odds with that of the institutional church had emerged since the late nineteenth century. It was a syncretic tradition that developed initially in central Mexico, where it incorporated many pagan beliefs and practices. At the center of this belief system was the veneration of the Virgin Mary, the brown-skinned Virgen de Guadalupe, Mexico's patron saint. In fact, as in medieval Catholicism, the cult of the saints was pervasive in the religious life of Hispanic Catholics. It follows that pilgrimages to sacred sites continued to be much more popular among Mexican Catholics than among their Anglo counterparts. Along the border, the most popular shrines were Chimayò in northern New Mexico and the crypt of the Jesuit priest Eusebio Kino, the renowned "Padre on Horseback," in Magdalena, Sonora. Home altars, too, were a crucial component of this folk Catholicism, as were *descansos*, roadside shrines to commemorate loved ones killed in auto accidents.

The heavy-handed efforts of the institutional church to eradicate objectionable folk practices and to reinforce orthodoxy gradually gave way after the 1960s to accommodation. This more relaxed attitude by Catholic bishops was, in part, a response to the pressure for church reform that emerged during the Chicano civil rights movement. However, there was a more pressing consideration—the advent of Hispanic Protestantism.

Protestantism made sizable inroads into Mexican border communities throughout the course of the twentieth century, especially in South Texas. It was only after World War II, however, that Protestant denominations began to win over large numbers of Mexicanos, both native-born and immigrant, as well as other Hispanics. Presbyterians, Baptists, Mormons, and Jehovah's Witnesses, in particular, made proselytizing Spanish-speakers a top priority at this time. During the last decades of the twentieth century, however, the most successful missionary efforts were launched by Pentecostals. Disillusioned with a Catholic Church that was slow to meet their psychic needs, many Spanish-speaking border residents were attracted to Protestant denominations, like the Pentecostal churches, that also stressed strong family values but provided greater emotional involvement than they found in mainstream Catholicism. Then, too, the strong emphasis on individualism of Protestant denominations in general and Pentecostals in particular was more consistent with the spirit of capitalism, which many Mexicans came to espouse as they gradually integrated into U.S. society. Finally, particularly gratifying to immigrant communities, these denominations displayed a willingness to train Spanish-speaking members for the ministry and to encourage the use of the Spanish language in church services, whereas the Catholic Church seemed reluctant to meet these needs.

The disaffection with the Catholic Church was not limited to Mexicans residing north of the border. In fact, by 2000, according to one estimate, more than 10 percent of Mexico's population embraced some form of evangelical Protestantism. These numbers were a direct result of missionary activity emanating from the north. "In recent years," observed one scholar in 2002, "the number of American Christian sects in Mexico has multiplied to over 300, with the northern border area playing host to at least 250 separate Protestant groups and missionaries from the United States" (Hart 2002, 496). As is true north of the border, below it, too, the most successful proselytizing efforts have been made by Mormons and by evangelicals, and for some of the same reasons.

Although the cultural elements delineated above were common throughout the border region, significant local variations occurred from one end of the international divide to the other. Among historians, the most thorough and insightful studies of these patterns were made by borderlands scholar Oscar J. Martínez, who argues persuasively (1994) for four major cultural subregions: the southern California–Baja California borderlands, centering on San Diego–Tijuana; the Arizona-Sonora borderlands, centering on the Nogales communities; the New Mexico–West Texas–Chihuahua borderlands, focusing on El Paso–Ciudad Juárez; and the southern Texas–northeastern Mexico borderlands, the most distinctive subregion of all, concentrating along the Rio Grande from Laredo–Nuevo Laredo to Brownsville-Matamoros.

Borderlands Problems

Hardworking and energetic, the residents of the borderlands made huge strides after World War II. Living in a binational and bicultural environment, borderlanders succeeded in creating a unique way of life. However, socioeconomic progress was not easy. Borderlanders had to struggle against many obstacles. The most serious of these related to urbanization, the environment, drugs, immigration, and an array of international relations.

Urbanization

Large-scale urbanization in the Greater Southwest was a product of World War II, when both sides of the border witnessed a spectacular population increase. On the U.S. side, for example, during the war, the population of El Paso jumped from 99,000 to 277,000; Phoenix from 65,000 to 439,000; and San Diego from 202,000 to 510,000. Americans flocked to cities looking for better wages, particularly in defense industries. Populations continued to soar during the postwar economic boom, when the Cold War served as a powerful stimulus to the southwestern economy.

This unprecedented growth also had important ramifications south of the border, among them the creation of many new jobs. As one historian put it, "Wartime conditions in the United States generated a considerable demand, particularly along the border, for Mexican raw materials, goods, and workers" (Timmons 1990, 242). The Mexican tourist industry on the border benefited as well, fed in part by the proliferation of military bases throughout the Sunbelt.

Thus, the spectacular growth of Mexican border communities was also swelled by workers from throughout the country. They had been attracted to the newly irrigated factory farms on the northern periphery but now yearned for the superior career opportunities available in cities. The population of Ciudad Juárez, for example, soared from 49,000 in 1940 to 122,000 in 1950. The construction of *maquiladoras*, beginning in the mid-1960s and mainly along the border, ensured a continual influx of workers into these communities.

However, the sudden growth of border cities was largely unplanned, resulting in urban sprawl. Among the most massive problems in the mushrooming slums were unemployment, poverty, crime, housing shortages, understaffed and underfunded schools, disintegrating families, and inadequate municipal services—the same maladies that the anthropologist Oscar Lewis described in Mexico City in this period in his 1961 classic, *The Children of Sanchez*. Unfortunately, all of these social ills continued to plague border communities into the twenty-first century.

Environment

Urbanization and rapid industrialization also contributed to myriad ecological difficulties along the border. On the U.S. side, decades of mining activity had taken their toll on the landscape. In its rich agricultural valleys—notably, the Imperial Valley, the Salt River Valley, the Mesilla Valley, and the Lower Rio Grande Valley—the heavy reliance after the 1950s on insecticides, defoliants, and chemical fertilizers eventually threatened to create an ecological nightmare.

These environmental problems were much worse on the Mexican side of the divide, where the *maquiladoras* were located. Water pollution, in particular, was widespread. The Río Nuevo, an intermittent stream running north from Mexicali into the Imperial Valley, was probably the most polluted waterway in North America. The Rio Grande received thousands of gallons of untreated sewage from industrial plants lining the waterway from Ciudad Juárez to Matamoros. Hazardous waste was often dumped in municipal sewers and waste dumps. Air pollution, too, was rampant, primarily a product of industrial waste, vehicle emissions, and pesticides. Big Bend National Park on the Texas border, for example, was plagued most of the year by smog produced by nearby Mexican coal-fired power plants.

Environmental problems abounded in the countryside, as well. While soil destruction was endemic throughout Mexico, the problem was most pronounced on the northern border given excessive cattle-raising and the high levels of salinity resulting from large-scale irrigation. More than 60 percent of the lands in this region were in a state of complete or extreme erosion.

Mexico enacted many environmental laws, and NAFTA had its own regulations. But enforcement was lax, often nonexistent. Environmental groups on both sides of the border were assiduous in calling for reform, but the bottom line was that the political and economic elites who gained from NAFTA were perfectly content to maintain the status quo. Enforcement cost money, and they had other priorities.

Drugs

While drug smuggling on the U.S.-Mexican border began earlier, it only became a serious problem in the early 1970s, an inevitable development given Mexico's poverty and the existence of the world's largest market for drugs right next door. Before too long, the traffic in marijuana, cocaine, heroin, and methamphetamines flourished throughout the entire length of the U.S.-Mexican border. By the beginning of the twenty-first century, four major crime syndicates competed for hegemony along the border: the Sinaloa Cartel, the Tijuana Cartel, the Chihuahua Cartel, and the Gulf Cartel. So lucrative was this illicit trade, given the vast U.S. market, that police agencies, offered the choice between "plata o plomo" (silver or lead), were often co-opted by ruthless drug lords. Violence all along the border escalated as well-connected drug rings, using high-powered weapons, sought to collar a trade that yielded unimagined profits. In 2007, some 2,275 killings in Mexico were attributed to warring *narcotraficantes*. Most victims were "mules," lowly drug runners paid to make the hazardous crossing. Cartels were not above assassinating police and military authorities, which occurred with troubling frequency along the major drug routes, particularly in border cities.

Not all the violence on the border was directly connected to drugs. Beginning in 1993 and continuing through the next decade, more than 350 young women, most of them *maquiladora* workers, were tortured, raped, and murdered with impunity in Ciudad Juárez by unknown assailants. Mexican authorities seemed unwilling or unable to solve the crimes or combat the violence, further eroding public confidence in state institutions.

Immigration

Finally, border communities also continued to struggle with another seemingly intractable problem—large-scale illegal immigration. Except for the Depression era, illegal immigration from Mexico to the United States had been a fact of life along the border since at least 1917, given the vast disparity between the standards of living of the two nations. Beginning in the 1960s, however, the number of undocumented workers steadily increased until it reached floodtide proportions by the first decade of the twenty-first century. This increase reflected the continual economic crises occurring in Mexico throughout this period. So dire was the economic situation after the devaluation of the peso in 1982 that even Indians, the most traditional of Mexico's citizens, were forced to uproot themselves and head *al norte*. By 2005, it was estimated that the number of Mexican undocumented workers in the United States exceeded six million. Intended in part to stymie illegal immigration, NAFTA only succeeded in increasing it. "Arguably," it has been concluded, "the most significant impact of NAFTA has been the increase of immigration flows between Mexico and the U.S. since its implementation" (Romero 2008, 42).

As Mexican immigration ballooned, so too did anti-immigrant feeling. Opponents of a liberal immigration policy began to mobilize on an unprecedented scale, a populist movement that was largely the work of the radical political right, which had come to dominate the Republican Party. Anti-immigrant hysteria was perhaps most pronounced in Arizona and California, and in 1994, California voters passed Proposition 187, limiting illegal immigrant access to many public services (most provisions of which were subsequently struck down in federal court). The media, too, helped to heighten nativist sentiments, as mainstream journalists joined with right-wing talk show hosts to fan the flames. By the turn of the century, particularly after 9/11, fear of the "barbarians at the gate" proved to be so pronounced that the borderlands witnessed the advent of a massive vigilante movement intent on regaining control of the border. The best known of these initiatives was the Minuteman Project, founded in April 2005 and headquartered in Tombstone, Arizona. Sheriff Joseph Arpaio of Maricopa County (Phoenix) became known for his outspoken support of the militant anti-immigrant crusade.

Paralleling this popular response to "the silent invasion" were federal government efforts to prevent illegal entry. Beginning in the 1990s, a whole series of campaigns—or "operations," as they were called—were launched by the U.S. government, under both Republican and Democratic administrations, to seal off the most popular border crossings, such as the El Paso–Ciudad Juárez area and the Tijuana–San Ysidro sector. From 1995 to 2006, the number of U.S. Border Patrol agents was increased from 5,000 to more than 12,000. These strenuous efforts, according to polls, were supported by 60–70 percent of Americans. After the turn of the century, responding to an upsurge of border violations along its Sonora boundary and to the popular outcry that it provoked throughout Arizona, government police efforts centered on that state.

There were several noteworthy consequences of the increasing militarization of the border. One was that illegal border crossers, in an effort to avoid traditional routes, now well patrolled, began to switch to more isolated desert areas. Unfortunately, these new routes were also more dangerous, and scores of illegal aliens died on the Sonora Desert of heat stroke, dehydration, and hypothermia as well as homicide—the fate of over 3,000 individuals between 1995 and 2007. However, another important consequence was the rise of a nationwide immigrant rights movement. The year 2006 witnessed massive protests in defense of undocumented workers in Los Angeles, Chicago, and more than 100 other communities across the country. Even in Phoenix, possibly the most conservative city in the American Southwest, one rally drew 200,000 demonstrators, the largest protest march in Arizona history. For the first time, illegal immigrants themselves joined these public demonstrations. Along the border, many individuals and groups, including a large number of churches, came to the aid of the victims, sparking acrimonious confrontations among border residents.

Array of International Relations

It is clear from the foregoing that the problems borderlanders faced often created serious conflicts in their communities; but despite these tensions, it should be noted that there were just as many instances, if not more, of cross-cultural and binational cooperation. The international relations between Mexico and the United States after 1940 were characterized by cooperation—the Bracero Program; the restitution in 1964 of the Chamizal district, a 440-acre tract of land near El Paso, which Mexico had lost to the United States decades before when the Rio Grande changed its channel; the Border Industrialization Program; NAFTA; water projects on the Colorado and Rio Grande; the resolution of boundary disputes; and law enforcement efforts relating to drugs and immigration, just to name the most obvious examples.

In the same manner, binational border communities generally enjoyed positive relations during this time. The federal initiatives mentioned above were paralleled by a whole host of similar cross-border cooperative efforts at the local level, including sister-city organizations, business associations, and voluntary groups like the Rotary Clubs. The economies of communities on both sides of the international border, after all, were intertwined. This was especially the case in the twin cities. Moreover, far removed from their respective mainstream societies, borderlanders were forced to rely on one another in the absence of adequate resources from their central governments. Sanitation systems were often linked, as in Tijuana and San Diego. Institutions of high learning on both sides of the border regularly shared facilities, professors, and even students. This symbiotic relationship was even seen in the sports area. Since the 1970s, Laredo and Nuevo Laredo, for example, sponsored a single professional baseball team. And sports teams on both sides of the divide regularly competed against each other. Finally, the culture that had emerged on the borderlands, the transitional zone between two nations, was clearly an amalgam of influences emanating from both directions. As one historian rightly concludes: "The international boundary is a place where the English and Spanish languages are increasingly blended, where bilingualism flourishes, where multiculturalism is a fact of daily life" (Lorey 1999, 3).

Conclusion

Clearly, as this broad overview illustrates, Mexico and the United States are mutually dependent on one another in a variety of ways. As Oscar Martínez and other borderlands scholars have pointed out, the relations between the two nations continue to be highly unequal, given the great socioeconomic disparity between the two. This asymmetrical relationship is undoubtedly what most distinguishes the United States' southern border from its northern border. It is also true that, unlike the Canadian borderlands, this southern divide has all too often been an arena of bitter conflict. Despite continuing problems, however, cross-border tensions between Mexicans and Americans in the early twenty-first century are not nearly as pronounced as they have been in the past. Moreover, given growing economic interdependence and threats to international security, there is good reason to expect continued, and even growing, cooperation along the U.S.-Mexico borderlands.

Bibliography

Anderson, Joan B., and James Gerber. 2008. *Fifty Years of Change on the U.S.-Mexico Border: Growth, Development, and Quality of Life.* Austin: University of Texas Press.

Arreola, Daniel D. 2002. *Tejano South Texas: A Mexican American Cultural Province.* Austin: University of Texas Press.

Danelo, David J. 2008. *The Border: Exploring the U.S.-Mexican Divide.* Mechanicsburg, PA: Stackpole Books.

García, Mario T. 1981. *Desert Immigrants: The Mexicans of El Paso, 1880–1920.* New Haven, CT: Yale University Press.

González, Gilbert G. 2006. *Guest Workers or Colonized Labor? Mexican Labor Migration to the United States.* Boulder, CO: Paradigm Publishers.

Hart, John Mason. 2002. *Empire and Revolution: The Americans in Mexico since the Civil War.* Berkeley and Los Angeles: University of California Press.

Lorey, David E. 1999. *The U.S.-Mexican Border in the Twentieth Century.* Wilmington, DE: SR Books.

Martínez, Oscar J. 1994. *Border People: Life and Society in the U.S.-Mexico Borderlands.* Tucson: University of Arizona Press.

Martínez, Oscar J. 2006. *Troublesome Border.* Rev. ed. Tucson: University of Arizona Press.

Pastor, Robert A., and Jorge G. Castañeda. 1988. *Limits to Friendship: The United States and Mexico.* New York: Alfred A. Knopf.

Peña, Manuel, and Ramiro Burr. 1994. "Music." In *The Hispanic Almanac: From Columbus to Corporate America,* edited by Nicolás Kanellos, 561–602. Detroit, MI: Visible Ink Press.

Romero, Fernando. 2008. *Hyperborder: The Contemporary U.S.-Mexico Border and Its Future.* New York: Princeton Architectural Press.

Timmons, W. H. 1990. *El Paso: A Borderlands History.* El Paso: Texas Western Press.

Immigrant Ports of Entry

Robert Eric Barde

Immigrants have come to America through many ports of entry. The names of nearly 400 cities, towns, and border outposts have appeared in official immigration statistics since 1819, when federal law first mandated that records be kept. They range from Morse's Line, Vermont, and Machias, Maine, which claimed but a single immigrant each, to New York, which has admitted over 33 million immigrants. These ports of entry differed not only in the number of immigrants admitted through them, but also in how those numbers fluctuated over time, in the origins of the people arriving through those ports, how they were received upon arrival, and the extent to which immigrants remained in the port of arrival or moved on to other parts of the country.

"Ports of entry" once meant only those places accessible to oceangoing ships, but it has become more useful to think of "port" as meaning "gateway" or "portal." These places of entry have come to include the many land "ports" along the borders with Canada and Mexico—as well as numerous seaports—and, after World War II, the multitude of "air" ports where newcomers have arrived by plane. Several major trends in the nature of immigration through these various portals have played out since the early days of the republic:

- The overwhelming prominence of New York during the first century and a half
- Since World War II, a shift away from the "old immigration ports" (including New York, but also Boston, Philadelphia, Baltimore) and toward a more diversified number of entry points
- A corresponding rise of immigration through Miami and the ports of the West Coast
- An increase in the share of legal immigration coming through the Canadian and, especially, Mexican border areas

- Increases in the number of immigrants arriving by air, and thus arriving through cities in the interior of the country
- Increases in the volume of "immigration" that involves a change of status (from, say, student, tourist, or worker) to permanent resident (i.e., immigrant) rather than a new movement across a border
- A rise in the late twentieth century of the proportion of residents in these "ports" who are foreign-born
- A rise, also in the late twentieth century, of undocumented migrants, making it difficult to determine where and when these new residents have entered

These long-term trends are punctuated by short-term phenomena specific to individual ports—upward or downward spikes in arrivals, or abrupt changes in the ethno-racial composition of the arrivals. Examples might include the 20-year explosion in immigration through Providence, Rhode Island; immigration through New Orleans being totally cut off by the Civil War, or through Philadelphia by World War I; Chinese immigration drastically curtailed in 1882 by the Chinese Exclusion Act (followed by a long period of increasing numbers of "nonimmigrant" arrivals); or extreme peaks and valleys in Cuban migration through the port of Miami.

There have been significant changes in the mode of travel by which newcomers have arrived at the border or port. Prior to World War II, immigration levels through a particular port were intimately tied to the fortunes of shipping lines serving that port. World Wars I and II, for example, disrupted shipping and immigration at all the Atlantic and Gulf ports, while

San Francisco (whose trade ties were with Asia, rather than with war-torn Europe) was largely spared. With civilian travel by ship practically impossible during World War II, air travel became the only practical mode for reaching the United States. By 1951, arrivals by air were clearly and permanently in the ascendancy. Over time, this made it possible for relatively large numbers of immigrants to enter through such interior cities as Atlanta (11,995—based on 1997 data), Chicago (38,936), Dallas (13,198), and Washington, D.C. (18,838)—none of which have ready access to the sea.

For much of the period of mass immigration, two forms of "processing" took place at most ports. For arriving immigrants, it was important to get off the ship quickly and transition to the next stage of the journey—perhaps by train or boat to a destination in the interior, or perhaps simply to a lodging in the port city itself. This was nearly always the responsibility of the city or state where a particular port might be situated. Even when the federal government provided additional facilities—e.g., dredging a harbor to accommodate oceangoing ships—it was usually at the insistence of state and local politicians.

A second function was to make sure that the arriving immigrants were suitable additions to the American population—that is, that they could pass the immigration and health inspections. Most American cities have had long experience with quarantine procedures to protect the general population from acute, infectious diseases, and the experience included quarantining arriving ships. State governments, often dominated by smaller towns and rural areas of the interior, were frequently at odds with the coastal cities, where local business concerns saw declarations of quarantine as extremely bad for business, and frequently lobbied hard to avoid having the quarantine stigma attached to their city and their businesses. In the nineteenth century, federal health inspections for chronic conditions were added to existing local quarantine procedures, and by the early twentieth century, the federal government had largely taken over the quarantine system. Federal quarantine stations became part of the landscape at many immigrant ports, and by the end of the twentieth century, there were over 55 such stations.

The creation of federal immigration stations followed a similar path: sporadically evolving, beginning in the 1890s, from a hodge-podge of facilities that were often local-federal partnerships, to a system where, by the 1920s, most facilities were wholly federally owned. It is these immigration stations—especially those at Ellis Island and Angel Island—that have become symbolic representations of *all* immigration facilities and of the immigration ports where they were located—New York and San Francisco.

This chapter covers the years 1820 to 1997, from when official, national-level data were first collected and published to when the Immigration Service ceased providing reliable public data on port of entry. This chapter concludes with a brief discussion of trends in the decade after 1997, using official data that track the arrival of new legal residents somewhat differently. (An Excel file containing the published data for the period 1820–1998 is available at http://staff. haas.berkeley.edu/barde/_public.) Note that graphs in this chapter omit data for certain years: 1942–1944 (data not available), 1980–1982 (data are unreliable), and the "transition [fiscal year] quarters" for 1850 and 1976 (so that only annual data are used for purposes of comparison).

New York

Any discussion of American immigration ports must begin with New York, the "portal of portals." Since the beginning of the nineteenth century, New York has been the dominant port of arrival for persons coming to the United States. Its share of total arrivals to the United States peaked at 90 percent in 1864 and remained over 70 percent for most of the period ending with World War II. As a twentieth-century Italian immigrant was quoted as saying, "I did not choose America; I chose New York" (Barkan 1991, 215).

The history of New York as an immigrant port is as long as that of the city itself, dating back to 1614. New York grew substantially during colonial times, but it remained second to Philadelphia in total population, number of ships, and volume of cargo passing through its port. After the Revolution, New York began to assume a leading position in the economic life of the new nation, and by 1790, it was the republic's largest city. Immigration to the United States was still relatively small—estimated at less than 10,000 per year—with at most a dozen ports receiving more than 100 persons per year. Until the second decade of the nineteenth century, Philadelphia retained its lead in that regard.

New York's fine natural harbor had always been superior to Philadelphia's, with Long Island and Staten Island protecting the Upper Bay from the fury of Atlantic storms. By 1797, New York had captured much of the reexport trade and for the first time surpassed Philadelphia in the total tonnage of shipping through its port. With the end of the Napoleonic Wars and the conclusion of the War of 1812, maritime commerce resumed and grew, with New York being the prime beneficiary as the British began sending the bulk of their manufactured exports to New York. Another significant factor involved the cotton trade, for much of the South's cotton exports began to be channeled through New York. Nearly all immigrants in this period arrived on ships whose primary purpose was to carry freight, and even though the flow of immigrants was small compared to later years, it was an important complement to other cargoes.

The prospect of large volumes of both exports *and* imports made New York a supremely attractive port to shipowners. In 1817, New York merchants formed the Black Ball Line, the first New York–based packet line with fast ships sailing between New York and Liverpool (and, later, Le Havre) on a fixed schedule. Making travel faster and more reliable (by not having to wait for a ship to be ready to leave port) led to a shipbuilding boom and an increase in the number of ships operating between New York and Europe. Packet ships were most profitable if carrying "fine freight, cabin passengers, mail, and specie" (quoted in Cohn 2009, 62), and only 40 percent or so of their passengers traveled in "steerage." The majority of steerage passengers traveled on non-packet ships, still specializing in bulk freight but now much larger and more amenable to the immigrant trade—and cheaper for the individual immigrant because there were so many ships needing cargoes, human or otherwise. And the greatest numbers of both kinds of ships were destined for the New York trade.

New York became an even more attractive immigration port after the completion of the Erie Canal in 1825. The territories of the Old Northwest, from Ohio to Illinois, were being opened up for settlement, and immigrants bound for those parts would want to land at the port providing the easiest access to them. The opening of the Erie Canal made New York the port of choice. From there, immigrants could travel by boat up the Hudson River, cross New York State by the Erie Canal, and reach Buffalo on Lake Erie, the gateway to the West. Not only did the number of immigrants arriving at New York begin to grow after 1825, but New York's share of the immigrant trade also grew as well, with over half of all immigrants choosing New York as their port of entry.

New York was thus well positioned to take advantage of the great surges in immigration during the pre–Civil War period. The first surge occurred in 1830–1831, when total immigration more than doubled over the previous years as immigrants from Ulster and southwestern Germany began arriving. Most of this increase went through New York, beginning a long chain of "path dependent" migration: once a port had built up a network of international trade and shipping relationships—linked to either industrial jobs or easy transportation to the interior—and developed a sizable immigrant population to act as both greeters and promoters back in the old country, success in the immigration trade fed upon itself. By the time of the next large influx, New York's dominance as an immigrant port would become both overwhelming and enduring.

A second, much larger, surge in immigration through New York began in 1846 when the failure of Irish potato harvests and the resulting famine brought about an unprecedented emigration from Ireland. By 1847, immigration to the United States had nearly doubled from two years prior, and over 60 percent of that increase went through New York, cementing the city's position as the United States' foremost immigration port.

The arrival of immigrants brought many of the same problems that plagued other cities. Because many immigrants were poor, some were bound to become public charges. Such concerns dated back to colonial times, when various localities imposed taxes or bonds to pay for the upkeep of arriving poor. Throughout much of the nineteenth century, the "dumping" of "paupers" by European countries was central to the debate over the number and quality of immigrants to be admitted.

As the number of arriving immigrants grew, some were sent to private establishments, such as Tapscott's Poor-House and Hospital. Abuses of all sorts led to the state of New York creating a Board of Commissioners of Emigration in 1847, charged with investigating all the various frauds and abuses practiced upon immigrants, especially those by unscrupulous "runners," who steered arrivals to equally unscrupulous boardinghouses, forwarding companies, and passenger offices.

In response to the Commissioners of Emigration report, New York authorized the creation of a depot on Manhattan Island where all immigrants could land. In 1855, the commissioners leased Castle Garden, a circular sandstone building at the foot of the island that had been first a military installation (the West Battery), then a theater. When it opened on August 1, 1855, it became the country's first receiving station for immigrants. The services included registering immigrants, helping them with their baggage, exchanging money, and purchasing tickets to any onward destination. By the time it closed in 1890, over eight million people had entered the United States through Castle Garden, whose name for many years was synonymous with the immigrant receiving station at New York.

New York contained other facilities that regulated the flow of immigrants. Shortly after the country achieved its independence, the city established both a quarantine station on Bedloe's Island with a port-appointed physician, and a Marine Hospital on Staten Island. The federal government maintained a quarantine station at Red Hook, run by the Marine Hospital Service. The State Emigrant Refuge was opened on Ward's Island in 1847, and during the 1850s, it became the biggest hospital complex in the world.

The Commissioners of Emigration attempted to require steamship companies to pay various head taxes or bonds that would be used to underwrite state and local services for processing immigrants or providing services to them. Most such efforts were rebuffed by the courts. Only a head tax of 50 cents, imposed in 1882 through federal legislation, was

available to fund local facilities. The explosive growth in immigration in the 1880s led to overcrowding at Castle Garden and at many other immigration ports, so much so that congressional investigations in 1887 found the local facilities to be totally inadequate. Castle Garden was the poster child for the federal government moving to assume responsibility for providing the buildings in which immigrants would be processed.

After making do for two years with temporary (and grossly insufficient) facilities at the Barge Office and a landing space in Battery Park, the federal government created a new facility on Ellis Island. What commended the site was its isolation and that it would be completely under federal control. Ellis Island became the first federal immigration station, and because it was located in New York, it would process more arriving immigrants than any other immigration station: during its operational existence from 1892 to 1954, over 12 million arrivals passed through its doors.

Ellis Island went through several phases, each of which mirrored the changing legal framework of immigration. From 1892 to 1924, it served as a mass processing center for arriving immigrants. The peak year at Ellis Island was 1907, when 1,004,756 immigrants arrived, including a record daily high of 11,747 on April 17. At the end of World War I, during the "Red Scare," it also became a center for *expelling* aliens suspected of being political radicals. With the Immigration Act of 1924 and the end of mass immigration to the United States and, of course, to New York, Ellis Island ceased being chiefly an immigrant processing station and became a center for the assembly, detention, and deportation of aliens who had entered the United States illegally or had violated the terms of admittance. In 1949, the Immigration Service noted that: "Ellis Island . . . is used solely as a detention and deportation center by the U.S. Immigration Service. Once a general reception center for all aliens entering the United States, it has not been used for that purpose for 30 years. No immigrant or visitor whose passport and entry papers are in order now goes to the island. More than 99 percent of all immigrants and visitors arrive with documents and papers in order" (quoted in Pitkin 1975, 171).

Emigrants came up this boardwalk from a barge which had taken them from the steamship's docks and transported them to Ellis Island. The big building in the background is the new hospital, 1902. (Library of Congress)

When Ellis Island closed in 1954, any "processing" of immigrants moved to the Immigration Service's new facilities at 70 Columbus Avenue in Manhattan and, increasingly, to new portals: New York's international airports. Even though the total number of immigrants coming through New York increased, and New York remained the largest immigrant port of entry, less than 20 percent of total immigration flowed through its port and airports at the end of the twentieth century. Nonetheless, New York remained *the* immigrant destination, the city with the largest foreign-born population (nearly double that of Los Angeles) and a percentage of foreign-born (35.9 percent in 2000) surpassed only by Miami.

New York's role as the "portal of portals" expressed more than just a numeric primacy. With a larger immigrant population than any other city, and with powerful immigrant-aid societies, New York was long able to influence immigration policy and practice in ways that most other cities could not. The post of commissioner of immigration at New York was an important patronage position, one that was perforce responsive to local political demands for humane enforcement, as well as to national policy pressures for vigilance at the border. Immigrants at the port of New York were long regarded as central to the debates over *national* policy and practice, especially where and how it was to be principally carried out.

Baltimore

Early-nineteenth-century immigration through Baltimore was heavily influenced by commercial relationships that the city's commercial elite established with firms in Europe. Numerous cotton mills had sprung up in Baltimore, and along with Maryland tobacco, they needed export markets in Europe.

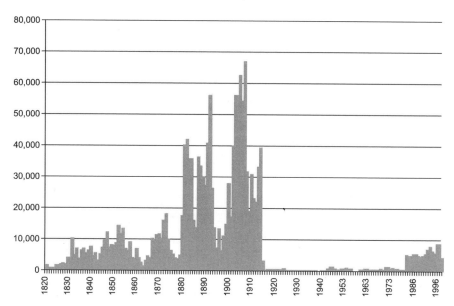

Figure 1.   Immigration through Baltimore.

Baltimore merchants developed firm trade links with Liverpool and Bremen, and by the 1830s, these patterns of trade began to influence the flow of immigrants through the city. Ships whose holds were filled with tobacco or cotton goods going east needed a cargo to make the return trip profitable, and "human cargoes" of Irish and German emigrants met the need.

Immigration picked up again after the Civil War hiatus. In 1867, the North German Lloyd Steamship Line signed an agreement with the Baltimore and Ohio Railroad, enabling an immigrant to buy a "through" ticket from Europe to Baltimore (by ship) and on to some western point (by train). Other steamship lines soon followed, enabling Baltimore to nearly double its share from 2 percent to 4–6 percent of the immigrant "market"—a market that grew by staggering proportions in the last third of the nineteenth century.

These trade patterns were interrupted by World War I: immigrant arrivals fell from a high of over 66,000 in 1907 to just 124 in 1916. Baltimore's commercial links with Europe were irreparably severed and, coupled with the effects of the Quota Acts that affected most other ports, Baltimore declined as an immigrant port of entry. The foreign-born population of Baltimore also decreased precipitously, from 21.1 percent in 1870 to 11.6 percent in 1910 and, despite the nationwide surge in immigration in the late twentieth century, to a mere 4.6 percent in 2000.

Boston

Since comprehensive immigration data began being kept in 1819, only New York has received more immigrants than Boston. Between 1819 and 1998, over 2.5 million immigrants first arrived through the port of Boston. Despite being one of the oldest places where European arrivals set foot on American shores, Boston was not an important immigration port before the 1840s. Despite its many cultural amenities, its hinterland offered neither good soil to attract farmers nor water access to the interior, and laborers and craftsmen found more opportunities elsewhere.

Only with the failure of Ireland's potato crop in 1845, and the subsequent exodus of Irish fleeing famine, did Boston begin receiving large numbers of immigrants. Its rise as an immigrant port was facilitated by being the North American terminus of Britain's Cunard Line, founded in 1840. Cheap, subsidized fares and some of the earliest transatlantic steamships made it possible for large numbers of impoverished Irish to make the crossing via Liverpool on Cunard ships. For the next 100 years, it was generally the second-most popular immigrant port (after New York, of course),

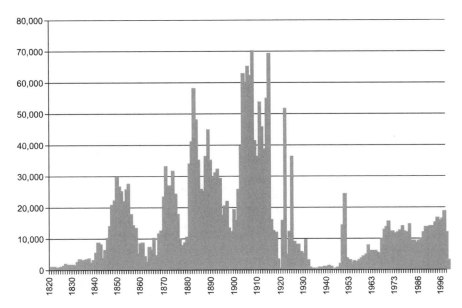

Figure 2. Immigration through Boston.

only occasionally surpassed by New Orleans and Philadelphia. Like New York, Boston experienced great surges in immigration immediately after the Civil War, from 1880 to 1888, and finally from 1902 until World War I. In some years during the Great Depression, more people emigrated via Boston than immigrated through it.

In 1847, an immigration station was opened on the Long Wharf, where arriving immigrants were greeted. A temporary quarantine hospital was set up on Deer Island, with a more permanent one established two years later. The Long Wharf immigration station, even though long considered inadequate, was not replaced until 1920, when the graceless East Boston immigration station was opened at 287 Marginal Street.

Many of the early Irish stayed in Boston and its industrial environs, working at unskilled jobs and comprising a large majority of the city's foreign-born population. Immigrants came from other countries, especially Germany and Sweden, but they tended to move west rather than settle in Boston. This movement into and out of Boston was neatly captured in 1909 by an immigration official comparing the ease of entry at Boston to the more cumbersome process at Ellis Island:

Upon the arrival of a vessel at Boston the steerage passengers are landed at the dock, inspected, and those detained given a hearing before the Board of Special Inquiry. Those still detained by the board are conveyed to the Immigration Station at Long Wharf, while those admitted either at the primary inspection or at the first board hearing, walk out into another part of the steamship dock where they receive their baggage and directly proceed to the city proper or suburbs, excepting those passengers bound for the West. These, right there on the dock are placed aboard special trains, or cars, as the occasion demands, regulated by the number of people, and proceed directly to the West. (Letter from George B. Billings, Department of Commerce and Labor, Immigration Service, Boston to the Commissioner-General of Immigration, Washington, D.C., on May 11, 1909, accessed NARA, Northeast Region, Waltham, MA, August 2008.)

After World War II, Boston was definitively overtaken by ports on the southern and western coasts. Perhaps the biggest change in immigration at the port (or airport) of Boston stemmed from the 1965 Hart-Celler Act, which changed the sources of immigrants coming to Boston, with many arrivals coming from the new sending countries in Asia and the

Caribbean. Boston again became a heavily immigrant city: in 2000, over a quarter of the city's population was foreign-born, nearly double the low of 13.1 percent in 1970 and approaching the high of 35 percent a century earlier. Perhaps high levels of immigration through a city like Boston were not necessary to make it a desirable city for immigrants to settle it.

Philadelphia

Philadelphia was the leading commercial city and immigrant port during colonial times. William Penn's city was the beneficiary of an early "marketing campaign" in Europe, designed to attract settlers to the colony. Such advertising bore fruit, especially after 1717 when there were significant migrations of Germans and Scotch-Irish who settled in Philadelphia's immediate environs. It maintained this preeminence in the early days of the republic, ceding primacy to New York only at the very end of the eighteenth century, when the latter's many advantages as a port made it, rather than Philadelphia, the place where the largest number of arrivals first set foot on American soil.

The number of immigrants arriving directly in Philadelphia reflected the varying fortunes of the city's transportation links. Located some 110 miles up the Delaware River from the Atlantic Ocean,

Philadelphia's access to the sea was impeded by winter ice on its river, the necessity of navigating a meandering river channel, and the disadvantage of being some 200 miles farther from Europe than New York was. Only when shipping lines were specifically committed to Philadelphia did the city thrive as an immigrant port. When the first great Irish migration began in 1847, the Cope Line's sailing ships serviced Philadelphia, to be joined by William Inman's line of steamships in the 1850s. When Inman pulled out of the Philadelphia market in 1857, following several tragic accidents, the city's share of total arrivals fell to around 2 percent and stayed there for nearly 20 years.

Even as immigration to Philadelphia declined to almost nothing during the Civil War, it was still becoming one of the United States' great immigrant cities. The nineteenth century saw the transformation of Philadelphia from a mercantile city to a modern, industrial one, with many businesses relying on skilled trades, and with a large foreign-born population of Irish, Germans, and others. Those two groups were at the core of a resurgence in immigration in 1873, when the American Line was launched and provided direct service from Liverpool, and the Red Star Line (with backing from the Pennsylvania Railroad) provided service to Antwerp. Philadelphia briefly

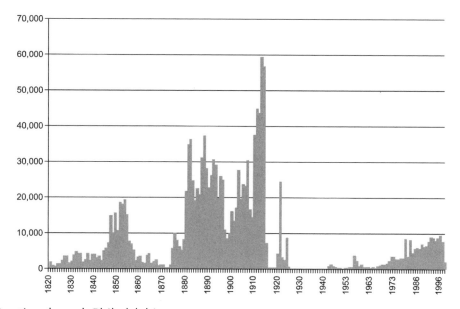

Figure 3.   Immigration through Philadelphia.

overtook Boston as the second-leading immigrant port and remained a major port of arrival until World War I and the Quota Act of 1924, which virtually destroyed the city's immigration business. Only after 1965 did Philadelphia again become an important immigrant port of entry, though greatly eclipsed by Miami, Los Angeles, and others. As an immigrant destination, the share of its populations that was foreign-born shrank from a high of 27 percent in 1870 to a mere 6.4 percent in 1980, with only a slight rebound over the next two decades.

New Orleans

New Orleans has been an immigration outlier in many ways: A Catholic, French- and Spanish-speaking city in a nation that was largely Protestant and English-speaking, and the only southern city among the major early immigration ports. Unlike the large East Coast immigration ports, it never industrialized (a trait it shared with San Francisco).

The boom years for immigration through New Orleans were the three decades preceding the Civil War. The cotton trade with Europe made low fares possible on the return voyage, attracting poor Irish, Germans, and French immigrants. From 1820 to 1860, New Orleans was the second-largest immigration port,

with the number of arrivals nearly as large as those of Boston and Philadelphia combined. Accessible by both blue-water ships and Mississippi steamers, it was the gateway to the western interior. This fact helped overcome some of the city's disadvantages: an insalubrious climate and a reputation for such diseases as yellow fever and cholera, a longer sailing time from Europe compared to East Coast ports, and few employment opportunities that might encourage immigrants to linger and settle.

The first boom in immigration through New Orleans began to wane in 1857, when the railroad finally reached St. Louis and negated the city's advantage of closer proximity to farmland being opened west of the Mississippi. That boom came to an end when the Union Navy blockaded New Orleans during the Civil War.

The city itself, rather than the federal government, attempted to deal with the public health issues that dampened immigration. In 1818 and 1820, local leaders made feeble attempts to regulate the health of incoming vessels, undone by a presumption that the city was a healthy place put at risk by immigrants. Yellow fever epidemics in 1853 and 1854 finally moved the state of Louisiana to establish quarantine stations outside the city and have ships inspected well before they reached it. Not until 1859 did New

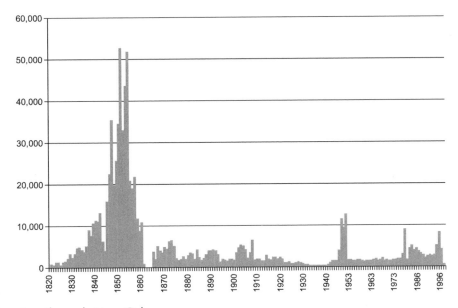

Figure 4.   Immigration through New Orleans.

Orleans create a shore-side facility for inspecting arrivals—just as the boom was ending.

After the Civil War, Louisiana, like many other states, created an "immigration bureau" to encourage white immigration. New Orleans received a steady but modest flow of newcomers, remaining a second-tier immigration port with around 1 percent of the national total. The absence of an immigration station and generally poor conditions for medical inspections were typical of many Gulf Coast ports. Nonetheless, in 1911 the city successfully lobbied Washington to become one of the ports to which immigration would be diverted from New York. The federal government did provide a modest immigration station in 1913, but it closed in 1934 for lack of activity. By then, New Orleans had long ceased to be a city with a large immigrant population: the foreign-born component of the city's population steadily dwindled from a high of 25 percent in 1870 to around 4 percent in 2000, a decline impervious to the modest increase in immigration through New Orleans in the late twentieth century.

Miami

Immigration at the port of Miami, Florida, has been reported since 1897, although a regular flow of immigrants reported through Key West stretches back to 1836. As an immigrant port, Miami has always been associated with arrivals from Latin America and the Caribbean. As a twentieth-century city, it had a unique economic base as a resort community and as a thriving financial center serving commercial networks connecting to regions to the south from which so many of its foreign-born residents had come.

Incorporated in 1896, the city's earliest immigrant flow was from the Bahamas. Since at least 1870, Bahamians had been coming to South Florida for jobs in construction, fishing, agriculture and, early in the twentieth century, tourism. In 1908 and 1909, the first "boatlift" of Bahamian immigrants reached Miami, as hundreds of seasonal farm workers arrived on small sailing ships of every description. Even then, immigration authorities were vigilant, preventing some 10 percent of them from entering. Bahamians remained the heart of a modest flow of 1,000–1,500 arrivals that continued until the Quota Act was enacted in 1924.

The next period of Miami's immigration history centered on Cuba. Cuban political exiles had been coming to Florida—especially to Tampa and Key West—since the 1870s. In the late 1930s, Cuban exiles began coming to Miami in increasing numbers. This flow picked up steam after World War II during

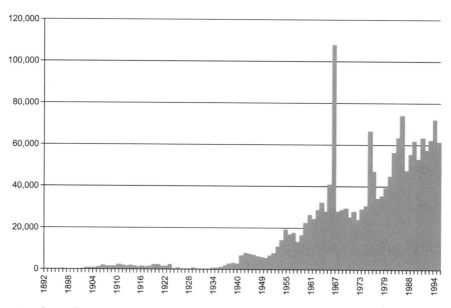

Figure 5.   Immigration through Miami.

the Batista dictatorship. After 1959, and the victory of Fidel Castro and the establishment of a socialist state, Cuban immigration was soon based on the political upheavals and shifts in Cuban-American relations. A graph of immigration through Miami shows a series of spikes, evidence of those upheavals: the "freedom flights" airlift of the late 1960s, the 1980 Mariel boatlift, and the continuing exodus by boat and air that began in the late 1980s. Cubans were different from most other Hispanics in income, education, and fertility rates—and, of course, in that they were fleeing Communism. Such preferential treatment as the U.S. government's Cuban Refugee Program made it easy for Cubans to enter as political refugees. Most ended up in Miami, even if they entered through other ports or borders.

A third wave of migration through Miami also came from the Caribbean, this one from Haiti. Beginning in the 1960s, with Haitians fleeing the dictatorship of Francois "Papa Doc" Duvalier, Haitian professionals were soon joined by emigrants of all classes. The exodus continued even after the fall of the Duvalier regime, as thousands of Haitians fled the seemingly endless political instability and poverty. Those who survived harrowing sea journeys in rickety boats were given a welcome very different from that given to Cubans fleeing Castro: rather than being welcomed at the "Freedom Tower," where arriving Cubans were processed, many Haitians' appeals for political asylum were rejected and the arrivals imprisoned in refugee camps.

During the decades of the 1960s and 1970s, Miami was second only to New York as an immigrant port. And no city exceeded Miami in its large percentage of foreign-born residents, with nearly 60 percent of its population in the year 2000 having been born abroad.

San Francisco

San Francisco was the first major immigration port on the West Coast, and between 1850 and 1997 it ranked fourth (after New York, Boston, and Los Angeles) in the total number of immigrants admitted. Issues associated with immigration long dominated the city's politics.

Shortly before California was acquired from Mexico in 1848, gold was discovered, and San Francisco became the maritime portal to the gold fields. The Gold Rush brought people from all over the world to San Francisco—native-born Americans, Europeans, South Americans, and Chinese. The explosive growth in the city that accompanied the Gold Rush immediately made it the largest city on the West Coast and gave it a large immigrant population that defined its cultural and political character for generations. It instantly became both an immigrant city and an immigrant depot. By 1870, nearly half (49.3 percent) of its residents were foreign-born, and for the next 20 years, it had the highest proportion of immigrants of any major American city. By the 1880s, the Irish were the largest immigrant group in San Francisco, dominating its politics. The "new immigration" of the late nineteenth century brought Italians and others from southern and eastern Europe.

The chaotic scene at the port, where both passengers and crew often abandoned their ships in their haste to reach the gold fields, was not conducive to the collection of immigration statistics. The federal government recorded 43,615 arrivals in 1850, but none in the previous year and in the three succeeding years. Many of those who arrived in California through the port of San Francisco were Europeans who had previously entered the United States through an East Coast port, making San Francisco a significant secondary-migration destination.

The vast majority of Chinese who entered the United States during the last half of the nineteenth century did so through San Francisco. A steady flow of Chinese immigration contributed to an average of 10,000 immigrant arrivals through San Francisco per year during the 1860s. That flow turned into a wave in the late 1870s as Congress debated laws that would exclude the Chinese. The passage of the Chinese Exclusion Act in 1882 was preceded by a surge of 32,000 arrivals at San Francisco, many of whom were Chinese attempting to enter before the door was barred. San Francisco then saw official immigration nearly disappear but then averaged less than 5,000 for the next 85 years. Even repeal of the Chinese exclusion laws in 1943 was not sufficient to revive immigration patterns disrupted by World War II.

Official immigration statistics during the exclusion period (1882–1943) concealed a large flow of Chinese and other Asians who came to stay. They were listed in the statistics not as "immigrants"—because the Chinese Exclusion Act and, later, the Immigration Act of 1917, expressly prohibited most Asians from becoming citizens— but as "nonimmigrants." They entered through the few loopholes in the exclusion acts, if they could establish that they were merchants, American-born Chinese, students, or their dependents. In many years, the number of "nonimmigrants" (including returning nonimmigrants) at San Francisco exceeded the number of official "immigrants," a pattern found at few other ports.

San Francisco developed facilities similar to New York's for the control of immigration. The first was the Quarantine Station, authorized by Congress in 1888 and opened by the Marine Hospital Service on Angel Island in 1891. It was the result of a series of requests by the state of California going back to 1883, an indication of long-standing local perception that diseased immigrants—especially those from Asia—were a threat to the public's health. Although established by the federal government, and ostensibly subject to legislation establishing federal supremacy in matters related to immigration and to the health of immigrants, the Quarantine Station's role in public health crises illustrated the struggle between the national government and the state of California for control of the port of San Francisco and of the authority to regulate immigration through it. Not until the bubonic plague outbreaks of 1900–1908 did the federal government definitively establish its primacy.

Whereas New York eventually developed an iconic federal immigration facility at Ellis Island, it took nearly 20 years longer for a similar facility to be opened in San Francisco. In fact, for the first 15 years of the Chinese exclusion era, there was no one place of enforcement: arrivals were inspected aboard ship. Those not admitted on the spot stayed on the ship; when it came time for the ship to leave, they were simply transferred to another ship—a sort of floating, virtual detention center.

In 1898, with the Spanish-American War, this system was disrupted and the Pacific Mail Steamship Company, with the consent of the Immigration Service, started using its Shed on Pier 40, at First and Brannan Streets, to house passengers who were not being admitted. Pier 40 became, over the next 12 years, the place where immigrants entering through San Francisco first touched American soil as they descended from the great ships that brought them from Asia, South America, and beyond.

The Detention Shed came to symbolize the process of exclusion and detention. It was simply a 5,000-square-foot area on the second floor of the Pacific Mail's warehouse-office, built over the water on the wood-piling pier. Its crowded, wretched conditions were deplored by the public in general and the Chinese in particular. When the new Immigration Station on Angel Island opened on January 22, 1910, all 102 detainees in the Shed were transferred to Angel Island—to what the *San Francisco Chronicle* called a "summer resort which the Immigration Bureau has provided"—but which soon came to have an unsavory reputation of its own.

The Angel Island Immigration Station (AIIS) operated from 1910 until its administration building burned in August 1940. Two features distinguish Angel Island from its more famous New York counterpart: the high concentration of one group (Asians) among its detainees, and the relatively long periods of time during which they were held in detention. It is believed that nearly 90 percent of those detained at AIIS were Chinese or Japanese and that about 75 percent of Chinese and 90 percent of Japanese entering through San Francisco were detained. The average length of detention at Angel Island was four days, but this conceals a great difference between Japanese, who were rarely kept more than a day, and Chinese, some of whom were kept for extraordinarily long periods—in one case, over 600 nights.

It is often said that "Ellis Island was built to let Europeans in, while Angel Island was built to keep Asians out" (Barde 2008, 13). The greeting given to the first person to pass through Ellis Island was, if not typical, at least symbolic of the difference. Annie Moore, an Irish girl from County Cork, was personally welcomed to Ellis Island by the commissioner of immigration and given a $10 gold piece. A similar welcome for any of the aliens who passed through San Francisco's Angel Island is unimaginable.

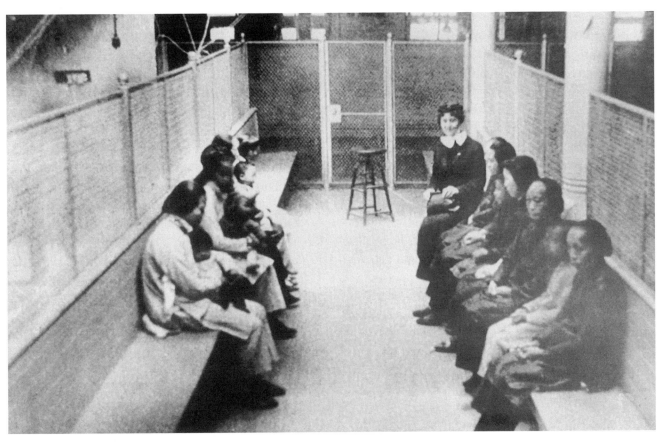

Angel Island was opened in 1910 as the principal station for processing Chinese migrants (and others) and it remained active until 1940. New screening procedures were developed in this San Francisco Bay facility. (AP/Wide World Photos)

These differences flowed from the existence of the Chinese Exclusion Act and its successors, which affected San Francisco and Angel Island disproportionately as, indeed, they were intended to do. Racist attitudes, and a not-unfounded suspicion that many Chinese were lying about their identity, led immigration officials to conduct extensive interrogations of Asian arrivals. Assembling evidence, calling witnesses, filing appeals—all took time and led to long stays on Angel Island while one's case played out.

More than any other port, San Francisco was one where class and racial differences mattered. At the Quarantine Station, the Oceanic and Oriental Navigation Company constructed separate barracks for first-class cabin passengers, those in second-class cabins, and for Chinese and Japanese steerage passengers. The immigration facilities—both the Detention Shed on the Pacific Mail docks and the Immigration Station on Angel Island—separated passengers by race, although not by class. In fact, there were many complaints from the Chinese community that class was *not* taken into account and that many "respectable" wives of merchants were detained in the same room with prostitutes or servants.

As at the port of New York, immigrant-aid organizations helped newcomers upon arrival. Some were ethnic-based, such as the Chinese Consolidated Benevolent Association (known as the "Chinese Six Companies"), while others sprang from religious roots, for example the Hebrew Immigrant Aid Society, whose representative on Angel Island helped Jews from many countries who had been detained there. The Methodist Episcopal Church's Deaconess Katharine Maurer ministered to those detained (especially women) on Angel Island, and Donaldina Cameron, of the Presbyterian Church, "rescued" young Asian women from houses of prostitution.

The processing of immigrants moved back to the Appraisers Building on the mainland in 1940, and many immigrants from Asia arriving by ship were processed there. Beginning in the mid-1960s, the big increase in immigration saw most new immigrants arrive by plane at San Francisco International Airport. Even though the proportion of San Francisco's population that was foreign-born had declined after its early days, among large cities at the end of the twentieth century, it was surpassed only by Miami and Los Angeles in the percentage of its population that was foreign-born (35.8 percent).

Because the history of immigration at San Francisco is so closely associated with the Chinese Exclusion Act, it is worth recalling how that act affected American immigration history more broadly. As one historian particularly emphasized, "Chinese exclusion also introduced a 'gatekeeping' ideology, politics, law, and culture that transformed the ways in which Americans viewed and thought about race, immigration and the United States' identity as a nation of immigration. . . . Precursors to the United States Immigration and Naturalization Service, United States passports, 'green cards,' illegal migration and deportation policies can all be traced back to the Chinese Exclusion Act itself" (Lee 2002, 37).

Honolulu

Honolulu, capital of the westernmost U.S. state, has a unique position in American immigration history. Not only is Hawai'i the only state that was once an independent kingdom, it is closer to Asia than any other major American city. For many years, both immigration to Hawai'i *and* emigration to the mainland were restricted by the federal government. These facts account for Hawai'i's ethno-racial make-up and for Honolulu's singular history as an immigration port.

Hawai'i's annexation by the United States in 1898 brought with it a history of immigration not reflected in the official *American* statistics. Data kept by the Kingdom of Hawai'i for the years 1852–1893, and the Republic of Hawai'i for 1894–1898, track a significant stream of Asian immigration as well as a smaller, more episodic inflow of Germans,

Portuguese, and other European groups. During the pre-annexation period, over 72,000 Chinese and, beginning in 1885, over 68,000 Japanese, were admitted to Hawai'i as immigrants—the vast bulk of them through the port of Honolulu. Many came as agricultural laborers and immediately went to other islands or other parts of Oahu. All became Americans when Hawai'i was annexed in 1898, a sort of "immigration d'état" that is not captured by official immigration data. (The formal extension of U.S. citizenship to citizens of Hawai'i was enacted two years later.)

Once the United States assumed formal responsibility for the Hawai'ian Islands, it set about exercising control over immigration to them. In 1900, the U.S. Marine-Hospital Service (forerunner of the Public Health Service) took over operations of the Quarantine Station on Mauliola Island at Honolulu. In 1903, the federal government opened an immigration station on the mud flats at Kaka'ako: an imposing stone structure connected to the shore by two foot bridges—one (the "China Bridge") for immigrants, and the other for officials and visitors. This facility was replaced by a new one of pseudo-tropical design in 1934—when fewer than 100 immigrants were admitted through the port, a level that characterized the years between 1925 and 1947, when first the Quota Act, then the Depression, and finally World War II combined to severely limit immigration through Honolulu.

A significant increase in immigration during the 1950s turned into a flood after the enactment of new immigration legislation in 1965. The city was a major beneficiary of subsequent growth in immigration to the United States, particularly of people coming from East and Southeast Asia. A spike in immigration through Honolulu in the mid-1970s reached as high as 55,732 in 1976, due largely to surges in immigration from Korea (18,897) and the Philippines (22,866). By the end of the 1990s, ultra-long-range aircraft made it possible for most immigrants from Asia to bypass Honolulu in favor of Los Angeles, San Francisco, and even Seattle. Nonetheless, the city retains visible signs of immigration from many parts of Asia, reflected in a city where the foreign-born percentage of the population has risen from a mere 10 percent in 1960 to over 25 percent in the year 2000.

Los Angeles

Los Angeles might never have become an important immigration port had it relied on its maritime connections. Without a significant natural harbor, early arrivals coming to Los Angeles were obliged to take a lighter to shore at San Pedro and then a stage to the city. Even the federal government's improvements to the harbor in 1911 did not encourage significant immigration. The city's expanding industrial base and mild climate—vigorously promoted by the railroads and other real estate developers—did attract many newcomers, although until the 1930s, those who were foreign-born had generally entered through some other port. If they entered through a West Coast port, in all likelihood it was through San Francisco.

The first published data for immigration at the port of Los Angeles (as distinct from the Los Angeles border district) are from 1933, when a mere 273 persons were shown as entering through that port. Prior to 1922, immigration had been sufficiently small and episodic that arrivals were processed through the customs building. In that year, a two-story immigration station, constructed by the Los Angeles Harbor Department—and based very much on the model of Ellis Island—was opened in San Pedro. Despite

extremely low levels of immigration due to the Depression and the quota law of 1924, the federal government in 1938 finally opened its own, three-story facility at the harbor. Not until 1952 would annual admissions exceed 1,000 persons.

Los Angeles did not become a serious immigration port until mass air travel came of age after World War II. In 1946, the immigration service opened its first offices at the Los Angeles airport when Pan American Airways began its first international flights. Mexicana Airlines soon followed, and the age of international air travel began reshaping immigration at Los Angeles. In 1957, it overtook San Francisco, and in 1981, it definitively surpassed Honolulu in the number of immigrants admitted. The annual totals grew from 3,895 in 1957 to 56,528 in 1981. Throughout the 1990s, Los Angeles averaged more than 100,000 immigrants per year, making it the second-leading port of arrival after New York, with roughly 14 percent of total immigration passing through it. By the end of the twentieth century, the city had changed from being simply an immigrant destination to a major immigration portal as well.

In addition to technological change in the mode of arrival, another factor behind the large increase in arrivals through Los Angeles was the change in the

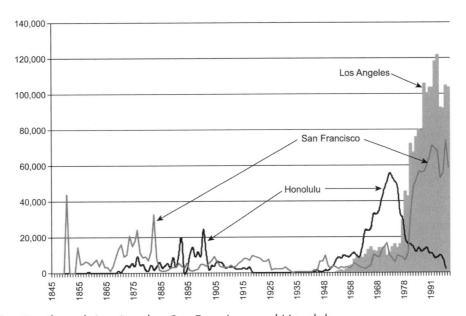

Figure 6. Immigration through Los Angeles, San Francisco, and Honolulu.

sources of that influx. After 1965, immigrants from Pacific Rim countries in East Asia and Central America constituted the bulk of arrivals, having profound effects on the ethno-racial makeup of the city. Los Angeles had the largest increase in minority population of any major city during the 1990s, turning a metropolitan area that was two-thirds non-Hispanic white in 1960 into one where over two-thirds are members of a nonwhite ethnic minority and the foreign-born made up 40 percent of the city's population.

Other Ports

Several cities had short periods when, for various reasons, they experienced surges in the number of immigrants coming through their ports. Two examples of this were a direct result of a 1909–1911 effort to divert immigrants away from "overcrowded" New York and other eastern metropolises and toward newer destinations.

Providence

Providence, Rhode Island, figured in early statistics on immigration, but with rarely more than several dozen arrivals. In 1909, however, the state of Rhode Island floated construction bonds in response to the federal initiative, enabling Providence to purchase land and build large piers to handle both freight and human cargoes. In 1911, the city successfully wooed the French-owned Fabre Line, which set up routes from its base in Marseille, through the western Mediterranean and on to Providence. Briefly interrupted by World War I, Fabre's service to Providence withstood the drastic decreases in immigration brought about by the Quota Acts of the 1920s, only to be brought down by the Depression. Between 1911, when the *Madonna* first visited Providence (and ran aground), and the last visit by the *Sinaia* in 1934, over 83,000 immigrants arrived through the port of Providence—a flow that completely stopped when the Fabre Line pulled out. Though the influx of passengers recruited from the eastern Mediterranean was short-lived, the cultural and social makeup of Providence and its environs was completely changed by 20 years of immigration through this one port.

Galveston

Galveston, Texas, also experienced several short, sharp episodes of heavy immigration (although official data do not capture an important secondary migration via coastwise shipping). The earliest period was from 1846 to 1860, when the migration of Germans as part of an average annual inflow of 2,000 immigrants gave Texas's principal city a distinctive character. After the Civil War, a modest boom in immigration led by local railroad and real estate interests, consciously trying to make Galveston an immigration "funnel," brought in an average of 750 people a year. Until 1913, there was no federal immigration station to accommodate immigrant arrivals; they most frequently stepped right onto a train bound for another city, or spent the night in a waterfront warehouse.

But the most pronounced boom was, like that in Providence, a direct result of restrictionist pressure to deflect arrivals away from the big East Coast ports and toward smaller ones. Having recently convinced the federal government to provide Galveston with a deep-water port, city elites cooperated with the Jewish Immigrants' Information Bureau to bring thousands of East European Jews to the United States. Known as the Galveston Movement, between 1907 and 1914, it brought more than 10,000 Jews to Galveston (over 20 percent of total immigration through the port), largely on ships of the North German Lloyd line. Nearly all of them had prearranged jobs in states in the interior, with few staying in Galveston. With the outbreak of World War I, this unique—and successful—instance of sponsored migration through a minor port came to an end.

Borders

Very large numbers of immigrants have reached the United States by crossing the long and, until recently, undefended borders with Canada and with Mexico. Nonetheless, it is tempting to think of ports or "portals" as places *facilitating* immigrants' entry into the United States and borders as geared to their *exclusion*. Borders are clearly the domain of the federal government, while ports have often been under the control of municipal or state governments. In another sense, of course, all ports are "at the border" when it comes to international travel if they can be reached directly by ship or airplane from a foreign country.

During the nineteenth century, many immigrants came to the United States by way of Canada. However, until 1894, their entry would have been "undocumented," as there were no immigration stations or immigration officers along the border. But as immigration surged in the last decade of the century, and as immigrants were subjected to increasing levels of scrutiny at American ports, many saw Canada as a way of evading such inspection. Thus, Halifax and St. John, Québec City and Montréal became "American immigration ports," and the Immigration Service posted inspectors to collect information about immigrants bound for the United States. Other inspectors monitored immigrants at the actual U.S.-Canadian border, at such remote stations as Malone, New York, and ones as large as Buffalo, Port Huron, or Detroit. At the end of the twentieth century, American immigration inspectors operated out of Canadian international airports, registering those with immigrant visas on their way to the United States.

The early system of data collection produced anomalous results: some immigrants were counted twice (once at the Canadian port, again at the border), while many others were not counted at all. The graph in Figure 7 combines official U.S. data showing various places on the Canadian border with data on immigration through U.S. cities and towns that are on the Mexican border. After 1965, the two border regions together accounted for 15–20 percent of all legal immigration into the United States.

Migration across the border with Mexico has been problematic since the border first jumped over the inhabitants of territories conquered during the Mexican War. The earliest attempts at controlling travel across the southern border involved not Mexicans, but Chinese: the Chinese Exclusion Act forced many Chinese to try subterfuges to enter the United States, and entry by way of Mexico (or Canada) was an oft-tried tactic. The various programs to admit Mexican workers during World Wars I and II may have stimulated travel and led indirectly to chain migration, but the large numbers of legal workers involved also translated into increases in *immigration* across the border.

As the accompanying graph shows, it was not until 1955 that legal, documented immigration across the border with Mexico exceeded that through the Canadian border posts and cities. Throughout much of the twentieth century, the Immigration Service

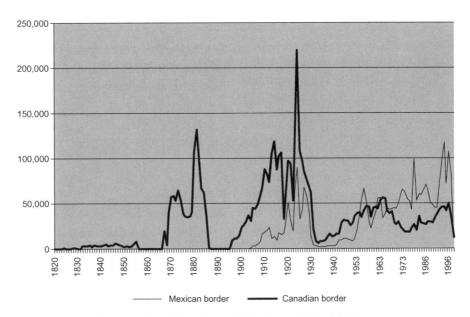

Figure 7.   Immigration through the Borders: Canada and Mexico, 1820–1997.

was viewed as treating the two borders quite differently. Along the Canadian border, the stations were small and scattered, lightly staffed, with irregular hours. As one scholar recently noted, "There is no evidence that the inspection along the Canadian border resembled that along the Mexican border, where immigrants arriving by train, foot, or other means were relatively intensely inspected en masse" (Fairchild 2008).

At the major portals on the Mexican border (El Paso, Laredo, Calexico, Nogales), plus the large cities close to the border (San Diego, Dallas, Phoenix, San Antonio), the flow of legal immigrants has been dwarfed by two other streams: illegal immigrants and "nonimmigrants," the latter being the huge daily flow of workers, shoppers, and tourists back and forth across the border.

The counting of "immigrants" through a particular port is fraught with uncertainty. For many years, official immigration statistics differentiated between "immigrant" and "nonimmigrant" aliens. The latter included bona fide tourists who might or might not settle in the United States, immigrants returning from a visit abroad, and "aliens ineligible for citizenship," such as the Chinese during the period of the Chinese exclusion acts. These "nonimmigrants" were often long-term residents and represented a substantial portion of the foreign-born traveling into and out of the United States. In some years of the late nineteenth and early twentieth centuries, nonimmigrants formed a majority of alien arrivals at San Francisco, whereas they were but 10 or 15 percent in New York and perhaps 4 or 5 percent in Boston or Philadelphia.

In 1930, nonimmigrants began to exceed immigrants among alien arrivals, and in the post–World War II era, the difference became extraordinarily large. What this meant for the various immigration ports is that "immigrating" no longer signified just stepping off a ship or a plane, or even walking over the border. It could mean stepping into an immigration office to have one's status "adjusted" from, say, "student" or "tourist" to "permanent resident"; by the first decade of the twenty-first century, such adjustments annually made up 60 percent of those admitted to legal permanent resident status (64.7 percent in 2008). As nonimmigrant data were not as assiduously reported early on, and are many times larger than modern-day

immigration (legal or otherwise), it is perhaps fair to say that the data used here give us a sketch of the relative size of immigrant flows through various ports rather than a precise count of the true volume of the flow of foreigners through those ports.

In the data published since 1997, the Immigration Service (part of the Department of Homeland Security since 2002) has emphasized the state or metropolitan area of residence (Core Based Statistical Area) of those obtaining legal permanent resident status. While not strictly equivalent to "port of entry data," they are sufficiently analogous (if we think of "entry" as where immigrants reside when they achieve legal permanent resident status) to allow us to extend the comparisons and inferences discussed above.

In general, the post-1997 data confirm the continuation of the major secular trends witnessed over the last quarter of the twentieth century. New York City's share of new immigrants (16.3 percent in 2008), while still the largest of any American metropolis, has diminished substantially from nineteenth-century highs. In large part, this corresponds to the displacement of the population center of gravity westward and southward. Los Angeles and Miami (8.7 percent and 7.9 percent, respectively) compare favorably with New York as entry points, and the four major metropolitan areas of California combined receive more immigrants than New York. The top four receiving *states* account for fully 55 percent of LPRs between 2000 and 2008, as well as 40 percent of the estimated increase in *illegal* residents. That California, Florida, and Texas are in both groups is a further indication of the continued dispersion of the immigrant flow away from the ports of entry that dominated the "old immigration," when most immigrants came from Europe and arrived by ship.

Bibliography

Barde, Robert Eric. 2008. *Immigration at the Golden Gate: Passenger Ships, Exclusion, and Angel Island.* Westport, CT: Praeger.

Barde, Robert Eric, Susan B. Carter, and Richard Sutch. 2006. "International Migration." In *Historical Statistics of the United States, From the Earliest Times to the Present: Millennial Edition,* edited by Susan B. Carter, Scott Sigmund Gartner, Michael R. Haines, Alan L. Olmstead, Richard Sutch, and Gavin Wright, 523–657. New York: Cambridge University Press.

Barkan, Elliott. 1991. "Portal of Portals: Speaking of the United States 'As Though it Were New York'—And Vice Versa." In *Immigration to New York*, edited by William Pencak, Selma Berrol, and Randall M. Miller, 215–42. Philadelphia: Balch Institute Press.

Cohn, Raymond L. 2009. *Mass Migration under Sail: European Immigration to the Antebellum United States*. New York: Cambridge University Press.

Fairchild, Amy L. 2003. *Science at the Borders: Immigrant Medical Inspection and the Shaping of the Modern Industrial Labor Force*. Baltimore: Johns Hopkins University Press, 2003.

Gibson, Campbell, and Kay Jung. 2006. Table 23: Nativity of the Population for the 50 Largest Urban Places: 1870 to 2000. In "Historical Census Statistics on the Foreign-Born Population of the United States: 1850–2000," Working Paper No. 81, U.S. Census Bureau, Washington, DC. February.

Immigration and Naturalization Service (and predecessors). Yearbooks, Annual Reports, Statistical and Public Use Tapes.

Kapp, Friedrich. 1870. *Immigration, and the Commissioners of Emigration of the State of New York*. New York: The Nation Press, 1870.

Klebaner, Benjamin J. 1958. "State and Local Immigration Regulation in the United States Before 1882." *International Review of Social History* 3: 269–95.

Lee, Erika. 2002. "The Chinese Exclusion Example: Race, Immigration, and American Gatekeeping, 1882–1924." *Journal of American Ethnic History* 21, no. 3.

Novotny, Ann. 1971. *Strangers at the Door: Ellis Island, Castle Garden, and the Great Migration to America*. Riverside, CT: Chatham Press.

Pencak, William, Selma Berrol, and Randall J. Miller, eds. 1991. *Immigration to New York*. Philadelphia: Balch Institute Press.

Pitkin, Thomas M. 1975. *Keepers of the Gate: A History of Ellis Island*. New York: New York University Press.

Rozek, Barbara J. 2003. *Come to Texas: Attracting Immigrants, 1865–1915*. College Station, TX: Texas A&M University Press.

Smith, Marian. 2000. "By Way of Canada: U.S. Records of Immigration across the U.S.-Canadian Border, 1895–1954." *Prologue* 32, no. 3 (Fall).

Solarik, M. Mark, ed. 1988. *Forgotten Doors: The Other Ports of Entry to the United States*. Philadelphia: Balch Institute Press.

Stern, Gail F., ed. 1986. *Freedom's Doors: Immigrant Ports of Entry to the United States*. Philadelphia: Balch Institute.

U.S. Office of Immigration Statistics. 2008. "U.S. Legal Permanent Residents: 2008" and "Estimates of the Unauthorized Immigrant Population Residing in the United States: January 2008."

Williams, Ralph C. 1951. *The United States Public Health Service, 1798–1950*. Washington, DC: Commissioned Officers Association of the United States Public Health Service.

Zolberg, Aristide R. 2006. *A Nation by Design: Immigration Policy in the Fashioning of America*. New York: Russell Sage Foundation.

U.S. Immigration Laws and Policies, 1870–1980

Diane C. Vecchio

Give me your tired, your poor, your huddled masses yearning to breathe free . . . Send these, the homeless, tempest-tost to me.

These words, immortalized by Emma Lazarus in her famous poem, are etched into one of the most important symbols of America: the Statue of Liberty. Was there ever an immigrant who passed "Lady Liberty" who did not tear up, even weep, at the first welcome they received in America?

While the United States has welcomed millions of immigrants during its short history, it has also denied and limited entrance to other would-be immigrants. During the late nineteenth century, in particular, Americans began to question the impact of immigration on the country. Who were the immigrants, and where did they come from? What impact did immigrants have on the economy, urban life, and politics? Should the United States impose limits on what sort of people it accepted as immigrants and citizens? Since the nineteenth century, when immigration laws began to be codified, policies regarding immigration and the naturalization of immigrants have reflected Americans' views on foreign policy and economics, as well as race and national identity.

Federal Regulation of Immigration

For roughly the first 200 years of American history, immigration law was designed primarily to promote immigration. At the same time, however, individual colonies (and later, individual states) penned their own immigration laws governing who might enter the colony and under what terms. A key concern from the time of colonial and state regulation of immigration was those persons who might become a burden or a "public charge." Massachusetts enacted the

earliest American public charge laws in 1645. The arrival in the colonies of "undesirables," such as criminals and paupers, spurred other colonies to enact similar laws. Many colonies, and later states, protected themselves against public charges through such measures as mandatory reporting of ship passengers, immigrant screening and, upon arrival, exclusion of designated "undesirables." For much of the nineteenth century, the job of regulating such immigration was left to individual states by a relatively unobtrusive federal government.

On August 1, 1855, the state of New York (which had replaced Philadelphia as the nation's chief port of entry for immigrants) opened the first immigration station, Castle Garden, located on an island off the southwest tip of Manhattan. Castle Garden was designated as a "reception place for new arrivals, a place where immigrants would be processed, their needs met and their interests protected" (Cannato 2009, 36). Receiving stations such as Castle Garden prevented people with contagious diseases from entering the United States. It also helped immigrants who were victims of deceit and robbery. Over the 37 years it remained in operation, more than seven million immigrants entered America through its doors.

Increasingly, however, Castle Garden, an institution run by New York machine politicians, was badly administered, and immigrants were exploited. Inevitably, the federal government became increasingly involved in the regulation of immigration, making Castle Garden obsolete. A desire to provide consistent laws "which govern the right to land passengers in the U. S. from other countries [were] to be the same in New York, Boston, New Orleans, and San Francisco," declared the Supreme Court following a ruling in *Henderson v. Mayor of New York*. The decision "stated that state laws requiring immigrant head taxes were unconstitutional because they usurped Congress' constitutional powers to regulate immigration" (Cannato 2009, 42).

On August 3, 1882, Congress passed the first comprehensive national immigration law. The Regulation of Immigration Act empowered Congress to levy a 50-cent head tax on all immigrants, blocked the entry of idiots, lunatics, convicts, and persons likely to become public charges, and made the regulation of immigration a duty of the federal government.

Expanding federal power over immigration resulted in a joint House and Senate Committee decision that selected Ellis Island in New York Harbor for the home of a new federal immigration station. On March 3, 1891, Congress passed an act establishing the office of superintendent of immigration. Ellis Island consequently became the nation's leading immigrant port of entry, processing largely European immigrants. On the West Coast, conversely, the Gold Rush and post–Civil War railroad building drew tens of thousands of Chinese, mainly male laborers, through the port of San Francisco. From 1870 to 1880, a total of 138,941 Chinese immigrants entered the country, 4.3 percent of the total number of immigrants (3,199,394) who entered the country during the same decade.

Exclusion and Restrictions: The Chinese Exclusion Act

While Chinese immigrants made up a miniscule percentage of the total number of immigrants in the United States, they were, nonetheless, soon targets of racial hostility, discriminatory laws, and violence. During the 1870s, massive population growth and an economic downturn in California provoked fierce hostility against the Chinese. Anti-Chinese leaders charged that the Chinese were brought to the United States under servile conditions as "coolies" and were engaged in a new system of slavery that degraded American labor. West Coast laborers claimed that the Chinese depressed wages and created unfair competition for the "white man." In addition, opponents of Chinese immigration cited the heavy use of opium among some Chinese and the importation of Chinese women for prostitution as evidence of their lack of morals and degraded living standards.

Consequently, the first efforts of the United States to control immigration and deport "undesirables" began in 1875 in response to the California lobby to exclude Asian contract labor and women suspected of entering the country for "lewd or immoral purposes." The resulting Page Law, enacted in 1875, represented the country's first regulation of immigration on the federal level.

In 1882, three months before the first general immigration act was signed, unrelenting lobbying by anti-Chinese groups resulted in a revision of the Burlingame Treaty that had protected Chinese immigration since 1868. Congress succumbed to racial fears and passed the Chinese Exclusion Act (May 6, 1882), which marked the beginning of U.S. immigration restrictions for ten years by prohibiting the admission of laborers from China.

Furthermore, in an effort to crack down on illegal entry and residence, San Franciscans clamored for more laws and officials outlined a registration policy for all Chinese immigrants. The Chinese exclusion laws were amended to require all Chinese already in the country to possess "certificates of residence" and "certificates of identity" that served as proof of their legal entry into and lawful right to remain in the country (the registration provisions were later adopted by the federal government as part of the Geary Act of 1892). The Chinese Exclusion Act also set other precedents by defining illegal immigration as a criminal offense, by disqualifying Chinese from applying for U.S. citizenship, and by providing the basis for declaring the spouses of Chinese laborers as equally of that class of persons and therefore equally barred from entering the country. It declared that an individual who secured certificates of identity fraudulently would be guilty of a misdemeanor, and could be fined $1,000 and imprisoned for up to five years. Defining and punishing illegal immigration directly led to the establishment of the country's first modern deportation laws as well. More importantly, however, the Chinese Exclusion Act reflected a racial version of nativism that soared in the late nineteenth century in the West and soon became a national phenomenon.

The first immigration regulations were directed at the Chinese (1875 and 1882), seen as a threat to America, and shown here in this *Puck* cartoon, 1888. The 1882 law also banned Chinese from American citizenship—the first such law. (Library of Congress)

In 1888, the Chinese Exclusion Act was refined by Congress and prohibited all Chinese from entering the country except "teachers, students, merchants, or travelers for pleasure or curiosity." The law also prohibited any returning Chinese laborer from entering the country unless he had a lawful wife, child, or parent in the United States, or had property or debts due him worth at least $1,000. Chinese exclusion helped redefine American politics, race, class, and gender relations; national identity; and the role of the federal government in controlling immigration. "The result was a nation that embraced the notion of building and guarding America's gates against 'undesirable' foreigners in order to protect white Americans" (Lee 2003, 46).

Nativism and the "New Immigrants"

While the Chinese Exclusion Acts (1882, 1892, and 1904) effectively curtailed the immigration of Chinese to the United States, it was not long before native-born Americans felt threatened by another group of immigrants. In the early nineteenth century, European immigration had been dominated by persons from the United Kingdom, Ireland, and Germany. During the late nineteenth century, however, a flood of southern and East Europeans escaping religious persecution and economic adversity landed on American shores. The sheer numbers of Russians (predominantly Jews), Greeks, Italians, and Austro-Hungarians were staggering and revealed a new trend in immigration patterns. In the 1880s, nearly 3.8 million immigrants from northern and western Europe had entered the United States, compared to 956,000 from southern and eastern Europe. By the 1890s, however, among the nearly 3.7 million Europeans who immigrated to the United States, those from southern and eastern Europe outnumbered those from northern and western Europe by 1.9 million to 1.6 million. In the first decade of the twentieth century, there were three southern and eastern European immigrants for every one immigrant from northern and western Europe.

Like the Chinese before them, the "new immigrants" aroused fears among nativists that they would never assimilate. Because most immigrants worked in a variety of laboring jobs, they were paid low wages and often lived in congested urban areas identified with poverty. Their tendency to live in ethnic enclaves where they spoke their native language and maintained their culture and traditions was viewed with disdain by many Americans. Unlike the largely Protestant northern European immigrants who preceded them to the United States, the "new immigrants" were overwhelmingly Catholics and Jews.

The Immigration Restriction League, composed of New England's leading Anglo-Saxons, lobbied Congress for a literacy test as a means to keep out the "illiterate rabble" from southern and eastern Europe. In 1891, three years before the League was formed, Henry Cabot Lodge, a Republican member of the House from Massachusetts, introduced an

unsuccessful bill to institute a literacy test as a qualifi-
cation for admission to the United States. During the
next 25 years, Congress continued introducing
literacy-test bills to exclude from entry into the
United States immigrants who could neither read nor
write. In 1896, Congress passed a literacy-test bill
but President Cleveland vetoed it, characterizing the
bill as "illiberal, narrow and un-American."

While subsequent Congresses reintroduced
literacy-test bills, one president after another, from
McKinley to Wilson, for political or economic reasons, vetoed them. Finally, the Immigration Act of
February 5, 1917, was passed over President Wilson's
veto, codifying all previous law and adding a literacy
test in hopes of restricting immigration by those from
"undesirable" nations.

Exclusion and Removal

While late-nineteenth-century immigration law served
to increase the federal government's role in regulating
immigration, later laws expanded or increased the
number of "excludable classes," as well as those immigrants who could be deported after entry. Deportation
became a powerful tool for controlling immigration.
According to Daniel Kanstroom, there were two basic
types of deportation laws according to "extended
border control" and "post-entry social control"
(Kanstroom 2007, 5). The former was a basic feature
of a sovereign nation: the control of territory by the
state and the legal distinction between citizens and
noncitizens. Historically, such "extended border
control" deportation laws have mandated the deportation of persons who evade border controls either by
"illegal" entry or by fraud or misrepresentation.

Following the assassination of President
McKinley on September 6, 1901, by anarchist Leon
Czolgosz, the federal government moved swiftly to
enact exclusion and deportation laws. In 1903, a new
law prohibited the entry of any person who is opposed
to all organized government (anarchist), or who was a
member of, or affiliated with, any organization that
opposes all governments. As part of a major codification of immigration law, the Act of March 3, 1903,
"was the first such ban on the entry or the naturalization of persons based upon their political or

ideological beliefs" (LeMay and Barkan 1999, 90),
and it paved the way for the later exclusion of members of Communist organizations (1940, 1950,
1952). The other form of oversight, the "post-entry
social control" deportation statute, provided in 1907
that "any alien woman or girl [found to be a prosti-
tute] . . . within three years after she shall have entered
the United States, shall be deemed to be unlawfully
within the United States and shall be deported"
(Kanstroom 2007, 125).

The need for exclusion and deportation control
was addressed by President Theodore Roosevelt in a
1905 message to Congress, in which he sought "an
increase in the stringency of laws to keep out insane,
idiotic, epileptic and pauper immigrants. And not just
the anarchist, but every man of anarchistic tendencies,
all violent and disorderly people, all people of bad
character, the incompetent, the lazy, the vicious, and
physically unfit, defective, or degenerate should be
kept out" (Kanstroom 2007, 132).

While individuals with specific negative characteristics as described above were to be barred from
entry, race was also an important element of exclusion. It was the major motivation in the 1882 Chinese
Exclusion Act, and in 1917, a "barred Asiatic zone"
similarly expanded the Chinese laws to most Asians.
Deportation for "post-entry" criminal conduct was
also contained in the 1917 Immigration Act. That
1917 legislation strengthened the antiradical provisions of immigrant law and made immoral or criminal
behavior or espousal of certain kinds of radicalism by
immigrants within five years after they came to the
United States could be grounds for deportation. In
addition, the time limit for retroactive deportation
was extended from three to five years.

In 1917, Russian-born Emma Goldman, a self-
professed anarchist, and her former lover, Alexander
Berkman, who had served 14 years in jail for the
attempted murder of industrialist Henry Clay Frick,
were arrested under the Espionage Act for speaking
out against the draft and sentenced to two years in jail.
When Goldman was released from jail, she was
stripped of her citizenship for a decade. She was
ordered to appear at Ellis Island for a hearing on
October 27 to answer charges that she was actively
advocating anarchy and the violent overthrow of the

government. To each question posed, Goldman responded, "I refuse to answer." A subsequent hearing in November produced much the same result, and officials recommended deportation. On December 21, 1919, Goldman, Berkman, and 246 other radicals were escorted to the *Soviet Ark* bound for Russia.

Closing the Golden Door: The Dillingham Commission and the Immigration Acts of 1921, 1924, and 1929

Between 1905 and 1914, nearly 9.9 million immigrants were enumerated entering the United States. Ellis Island processed over a million people in 1907 alone. The growing fear of the "new immigrants" had led Congress to create a joint congressional/presidential commission to study the impact of this latest wave of immigrants. Begun in 1909, the Dillingham Commission, named after its chair, Senator William Dillingham, issued a 42-volume report in 1911. Its main conclusion was that the newer immigrants from southern and eastern Europe were more ignorant, more unskilled, more prone to crime, and more willing to accept a lower standard of living than previous immigrants from northern and western Europe. The data gathered by the commission were used to substantiate its prejudged conclusion, namely that the immigrants then coming to the United States were inferior in education, ability, and genetic makeup when compared to most of those who had come previously. Therefore, the commission recommended that a new and generally restrictive and ethnically discriminating immigration policy be instituted. Dillingham introduced a plan to limit immigration by establishing national quotas on Europeans that would reflect the percentages of all foreign-born Europeans who were counted in the most recent census. The law would also reinforce the need for a literacy test as a means to control immigration.

Intense nativism during the 1920s, fueled in part by World War I and Americans' disdain for Germans as well as a growing fear of European-born labor radicals, led to a broad consensus favoring restriction. In 1921, Congress established the principle of restriction based on nationality and placed a ceiling on immigration from Europe. For a one-year period (but renewed), the 1921 Emergency Quota Act limited the number of entrants of each nationality to 3 percent of the foreign-born of that group in the United States based on the 1910 census. It imposed a ceiling of 357,800 immigrants annually from outside the Western Hemisphere, with more than half set aside for northern and western Europeans. Congress extended the law before passing the Johnson-Reed Immigration Act of 1924. That act continued the prior qualifications, such as the exclusion of anarchists, prostitutes, illiterates, and those likely to become public charges; increased the head tax; and tightened the quotas established three years earlier. It cut the number of immigrants to 2 percent of the foreign-born of each group based on the 1890 census, further discriminating against southern and eastern European nations, which was exactly what Congress wanted to do (along with the general exclusion of migrants ineligible for U.S. citizenship—first enacted in 1882 and now most notably, but inconsistently, applied generally to Asians).

Furthermore, on March 22, 1929, President Hoover issued a presidential proclamation that stipulated the new and permanent quotas for each fiscal year thereafter. Identified as the national origins system, it was based on the proportion of each nationality in the total U.S. population determined by an analysis of the 1920 census. The new National Origins Act lowered the overall immigration ceiling to 150,000 per year and granted immigrants from the United Kingdom almost half of the yearly quota.

The Johnson-Reed Act of 1924 and the National Origins Act of 1929 marked the end of an era in American history. Asians had already been excluded for the most part (e.g., the Chinese Exclusion Acts, and the 1907–1908 Gentleman's Agreement regarding Japanese and Korean laborers) but for most Europeans, America had been an open door. The act ended the virtually free immigration policy, reflecting the fears of a society experiencing dramatic social, economic, and cultural changes. Although the United States modified its restrictions after World War II, it never again opened its gates to unlimited numbers of newcomers.

Regrettably, the quota laws of the 1920s caused more people to attempt to enter the United States illegally. Chinese and European emigrants, for example, traveled first to Canada or Mexico, then illegally crossed the border by land. Many others went to Cuba, and smugglers brought them from there into the United States by water.

In a further attempt to enforce immigration laws and to regulate the control of illegal aliens the Congress established the Border Patrol in 1924. Its purpose was to monitor the land border and stop smuggling. The Bureau of Immigration was given the power to arrest any alien without a warrant who was entering or attempting to enter the United States in violation of any law or regulation. In 1929, Congress made unlawful entry a misdemeanor, punishable by one year of imprisonment or a $1,000 fine, or both. It defined a second entry as a felony, punishable by two years' imprisonment or a $2,000 fine, or both.

Illegal immigration in the 1920s was exacerbated by Prohibition, the rise of organized crime, smuggling and liquor-running. The California Joint Immigration Committee described illegal aliens as "vicious and criminal," comprised of "bootleggers, gangsters, and racketeers of large cities" (Ngai 2003, 7). Edwin Reeves, a Border Patrol officer in El Paso during the 1920s, recalled that "Every fellow you caught with a load of liquor on his back . . . was a wetback." In these instances "aliens were not only subjects—that is, the smugglers—they were also the objects, the human goods illegally trafficked across the border" (Ngai 2003, 7). In 1927, the Immigration Bureau reported that the "bootlegging of aliens was a lucrative industry second only to smuggling of liquor." While authorized to apprehend illegal aliens without warrants, the Border Patrol also seized goods it believed were "obviously contraband or smuggled" (Ngai 2003, 7).

The Great Depression and Immigration

While quotas dramatically restricted European immigration, a back door to relatively unrestricted Mexican and Canadian immigration was kept open. Demand for Mexican workers, who had long provided an alternative source of cheap labor for American employers, came from the massive agricultural expansion that took place in the southwestern United States in the early twentieth century. Mexicans were often seen as less threatening than Chinese and other foreign workers and considered by many to be the most preferred of all the cheap labor available across the Southwest. During the 1930s, however, American attitudes regarding Mexican workers became more resentful as the United States reeled from the effects of the Great Depression.

The 1930s was a decade of economic hardship. Immigration policies and practices of the 1930s were shaped by reactions to the Great Depression as well as the restrictionist notions of the 1920s. Naturally, fewer immigrants chose to come to the United States in the 1930s, given that nearly 25 percent of the working population was unemployed. Indeed, "in 1931 just 97,100 newcomers arrived and 61,900 left. The next five years, between July 1931 and June 1936, marked the lowest level for that length of time in American immigration since record keeping began in 1820: only 159,400 persons were admitted, whereas 297,800 emigrated, a net out-migration of 138,400 persons" (Barkan 1995, 45).

The Depression years were particularly threatening for Mexican immigrants and their American-born children. Over 459,000 Mexicans had entered the United States during the 1920s, many of whom had fled the political and civil strife of the Mexican Revolution and then the Cristero Rebellion. Northern industrialists and farmers in the central states had begun hiring Mexicans to replace Europeans. By 1927, some 58,000 Mexicans worked in the sugar beet farmlands extending from Colorado to Ohio. Mexicans also worked in mining industries in Colorado and in the Chicago metropolitan areas, where there were almost 20,000 Mexicans on the eve of the Depression. The hub of the nation's railroad network attracted a significant number of Mexicans working in the packing plants and steel mills of the city and its suburbs.

The collapse of the economy in the 1930s increased racial tensions between native-born Americans and Mexicans that had been brewing since the 1920s when nativist groups as well as organized labor led an anti-Mexican campaign on economic grounds, contending that immigrants depressed wages and took jobs from white Americans. The leading spokesman for labor in the fight to exclude Mexicans was Samuel Gompers, president of the American Federation of Labor (AFL) until 1924. In Congress, the campaign to restrict Mexican entry in the 1920s was led by Representatives John Box (D-TX), Albert Johnson (R-WA), and Senator William Harris (D-GA), all of whom sponsored bills to curtail immigration. Their opponents in Congress agreed that Mexicans were racially inferior, but they countered with the argument that Mexican labor was indispensable.

The campaign to restrict Mexican immigration did not end in the 1920s, but the Depression, in large part, solved the problem of Mexican labor. It has been estimated that about one-third of the Mexican population in the United States left the country during the Depression years. Between 1929 and 1935 (the numbers vary greatly), somewhere between 500,000 and 1,000,000 Mexicans were repatriated. Some Mexicans who were employed in agriculture in the Southwest left voluntarily after being pushed out of their jobs by the Okies (Oklahoma farm families) who had migrated to California as a result of the Dust Bowl.

Not all of the repatriations were voluntary, however. It has been argued that "as many as half of those who left did so against their will" (Gonzales 1999, 148). County, state, and federal government agencies were all involved in the coercion and deportation of Mexicans and their families. William Doak, secretary of labor from 1930 to 1933, believed that deportation enforcement was a good way to create jobs for unemployed Americans during the Depression. In fact, "to conduct full hearings [on deportation] in such a large number of cases would be prohibitively expensive, [and] thus many tens of thousands of these removals, were done 'voluntarily,' " with considerable coercion ranging from stepped-up federal enforcement with state and local practices designed to encourage, or compel, Mexicans to leave the United States (Kanstroom 2007, 216). In some instances, convicted criminals were offered reprieves if they accepted deportation. For example, in 1932, 90 prisoners at the McNeil Federal Penitentiary in Washington were freed and sent to Mexico after voluntarily accepting deportation.

Civil liberties were violated on a regular basis, as American-born children of immigrants (who were, of course U.S. citizens) often were denied the option to stay in the country when their alien parents were deported. "On February 26, 1931, U.S. immigration agents and Los Angeles Police surrounded some 400 men, women, and children in La Placita (the Alvera [sic] Street plaza near downtown Los Angeles). The police and immigration agents cordoned off with trucks an area in which many people were sitting on benches or resting from shopping. A mass round-up followed, and hundreds of captured people were shipped straight to Mexico with no word to their families" (Kanstroom 2007, 219).

While many repatriados agreed to leave, others were deported—with or without warrants—and still others were coerced into going. Raids such as these created a climate of fear and anxiety and prompted many Mexicans to leave voluntarily. The real tragedy is that while many Mexican aliens were "repatriated," thousands of American-born children of Mexican descent were also forced to leave the country of their birth.

Refugees, Resident Enemy Aliens, and World War II

The Great Depression, with its millions of unemployed, exacerbated the already widespread anti-immigrant, antialien, and often anti-Semitic mood of Americans in the 1930s. The United States chose strict adherence to restrictive quota laws that limited the number of German-Jews in the wake of Hitler's anti-Semitic decrees. Restrictionists in Congress, bent on quelling any new influx of immigrants, reflected the consensus of an American public that was opposed to refugee admissions.

From his first days in office, Franklin D. Roosevelt was made aware of the plight of the Jews in Germany. Because of the severe economic problems of the Depression, however, as well as the antialien climate in Congress and popular opposition to the possibility of a flood of Jewish newcomers, Roosevelt followed the advice of conservative officials in the State Department to whom he gave a free hand on immigration matters despite their harsh and sometimes even anti-Semitic attitudes concerning Jewish refugees.

The atrocities of *Kristallnacht*, on November 9, 1938, a night of terror and violence against German Jews and their property, convinced President Roosevelt to take at least some limited action to aid the refugees despite the objections of the State Department. Francis Perkins, secretary of labor, convinced Roosevelt to adopt a more flexible approach in extending visitor's visas to German Jews who could not be expected to return to Germany. Despite the objections of the State Department, the president announced in November 1938 that 12,000 to 15,000 visitor visas already granted to German Jewish visitors would be extended for at least six months. Since the law did not specify how many six-month extensions could be granted, there was no limit to the number of times such visitors' visas could be renewed.

Unfortunately, that was the only decision Roosevelt made that effectively helped the plight of some German Jews. In 1939, nearly two-thirds of Americans opposed special quotas for Jewish children from Europe. In February 1939, Roosevelt refused to endorse the Wagner-Rogers Bill, which proposed to admit 20,000 German refugee children without regard to the European quota, but it failed to reach the floor of the House. The United States missed another opportunity to aid Jewish refugees when it denied admitting 930 Jews aboard the ship SS *St. Louis*, docked in Havana in the spring of 1939, prior to sailing up along the American coast—within sight and sound of the mainland. Many of the refugees, forced to return to Europe, were eventually sent to extermination camps.

The failure to save Jewish refugees was a combination of antialien sentiment and anti-Semitism, which was pervasive in 1930s America. In March 1938, for example, "41 percent of the American people polled thought Jews had too much power. Two months later a poll showed that one-fifth wanted to drive the Jews out of the country in order to reduce their power; one fourth would keep them out of politics. During that spring another poll reported 82 percent opposed the admission of any large number of Jewish exiles" (Barkan 1996, 51). Ultimately, only two-fifths of European quotas were filled between 1933 and 1944, for the State Department intentionally hampered visa allocations by imposing administrative obstructions

and harsh security measures designed specifically for those who were most desperate to leave Germany and other Nazi-occupied lands.

World War II and the Forced Relocation of Japanese Americans

When World War II broke out in Europe in September 1939, the U.S. government increased security and instituted measures to deal with the five million foreign-born citizens, one-fourth of them nationals of the Axis powers, principally Germany, Italy, and Japan. The State Department controlled immigration by imposing severe restrictions on visas, while Congress enacted a program to monitor resident aliens. In August 1940, Congress approved the Alien Registration Act (also known as the Smith Act). All aliens age 14 and older (and not naturalized) were required to register annually with the government. The Smith Act also authorized the president to deport any alien where such action would be "in the interest of the United States."

When the Japanese bombed Pearl Harbor on December 7, 1941, the United States was forced into a war it had hoped to avoid. The antialien sentiments that kept the United States from providing refuge for German Jews grew even stronger toward enemy aliens residing in the United States. Almost immediately, there were demands for the imprisonment of West Coast Japanese Americans. These demands were fueled by decades of simmering anti-Asian racism and anxieties over the potential security threat that might be posed by people who shared a heritage with an enemy nation.

On February 19, 1942, President Roosevelt, in response to mounting calls for action, signed Executive Order 9066. In an atmosphere of World War II hysteria, Roosevelt, encouraged by officials at all levels of the federal government, issued the executive order eventually leading "to the evacuation and internment into what were called 'relocation camps' of all West Coast Japanese residents and Japanese-American citizens, some 70,000 native-born citizens of Japanese ancestry, for what was called military necessity" (LeMay and Barkan 1999, 192).

The same executive order (and other wartime orders and restrictions) were also applied to Italian and German aliens living in the western United States. A total of 3,200 resident aliens of Italian ancestry were arrested, and more than 300 of them were interned. About 11,000 German residents—including some naturalized citizens—were arrested, and more than 5,000 were interned. Yet, while these individuals suffered violations of their civil liberties, the wartime measures applied to Japanese Americans were worse, uprooting entire communities of citizens as well as resident aliens, based on a widely held belief that "the evil deeds of Hitler's Germany were the deeds of bad men, [whereas] the evil deeds of Tojo and Hirohito's Japan were the deeds of a bad race" (Daniels 2004, 396). The government brought no charges collectively against them, nor until 1944 were they able to appeal their incarceration. All lost personal liberties; most lost homes and property as well. Compensation ($20,000 for each survivor) would not be approved for 44 years.

On the other hand, the previously maligned Chinese now became the "good Asians." Because China was an ally of the United States, the government sought to reverse its previously discriminatory policies aimed at the Chinese. The Chinese Exclusion Repeal Act (December 17, 1943) repealed the Chinese Exclusion Acts and permitted Chinese nationals already in the country to become naturalized citizens.

The Postwar Years: Displaced Persons and Labor Policies

In the postwar years, the executive branch began to play a more active role in shaping immigration policy. When the war ended in the European theater in May 1945, there were anywhere from 7 million to 11 million displaced persons there. While large numbers of them were repatriated to their own countries, many no longer had a country. This was true for the survivors of the Holocaust as well as for those who fled west before the advance of the Red Army.

At the end of 1945, President Truman issued a formal directive reserving half of the quotas of European countries for displaced persons, which, he hoped would bring some 40,000 displaced persons a year to the United States. Despite the president's wishes, only about 5,000 displaced persons, not all of them Jews, entered the United States in the first nine months of 1946. Truman's announcement triggered years of intense discussion and debate over immigration policy, which led not only to special laws for refugee admissions but also to the first major revision in American immigration law since 1924, the McCarran-Walter Act of 1952.

First came the 1948 Displaced Persons Act, which called for the admission of 100,000 displaced persons over and above the quotas in each of four years. The bill required that the immigrants meet all of the other qualifications of American immigration law and gave preference to close relatives of American citizens and Allied war veterans. In its final form, the act of 1948 (renewed and extended in June 1950) provided for the admission of more than 409,700 displaced persons through mid-1952 by " 'mortgaging' their entry against their homelands' future quotas" (LeMay and Barkan 1999, xxxv). More than 70 percent of those admitted under the DP program were refugees from the Soviet Union and Eastern Europe. Only about 16 percent, or 63,000 persons, were Jewish; about 47 percent, or 187,000 persons were Roman Catholic; about 34 percent, or 136,000 persons were recorded as "of Protestant and Orthodox faith"; and 2 percent, or 8,000 persons, were classified as "other."

The postwar years also witnessed labor shortages within the United States that caused yet another reversal of policy toward Mexican immigration: not only were Mexican laborers again allowed to cross the border, at first sanctioned by Public Law 45 under a new agreement between Mexico and the United States (1942–1947) with the outbreak of World War II and then again, with the outbreak of the Korean War (1951–1964), under Public Law 78 (July 1951), but large numbers were actively recruited by the federal government. As had taken place during World War I, the Bracero Program was renewed during the next two wars and repeatedly funded from July 1942 to December 1964. Thus, authorized by Congress, the program endured and employed over 4.4 million workers.

The Bracero Program

A civilian labor shortage began to be recognized in the United States when the country mobilized for World War II. Though originally devised as a wartime expedient to resolve rising labor shortages within the agricultural sector of the American Southwest, the Bracero Program, a bilateral agreement reached between the United States and Mexico, regulated the managed migration of contract laborers from Mexico to the United States. This resumed, in many ways, a policy started as a result of wartime labor needs during World War I when the U.S. government first became systematically involved in the recruitment of Mexican workers. From 1917 to 1921, an estimated 50,000–80,000 Mexican farm workers entered the United States under this program.

To reiterate, in 1942, Mexico and United States had agreed to the Emergency Labor Program (funded in 1943 by Public Law 45). With the outbreak of the Korean War, Congress enacted P.L. 78 in July 1951, reauthorizing the Bracero Program and extending temporary visas to Mexican laborers willing to work seasonally on farms and railroads. They would arrive in the largest numbers in the summer and fall (particularly in California, Arizona, New Mexico, and Colorado, but not Texas until 1947) when crops were harvested and then they headed home for winter and early spring. The AFL-CIO, the Teamsters' Union, and the railroad brotherhoods vigorously protested the program, insisting that it would drive down wages and eliminate jobs for American workers. George Meany, head of the AFL-CIO, labeled the Bracero Program an "affront to every American working family." Meany charged that "the growers want to enrich themselves at the expense of the working poor." Commercial growers disagreed. One California grape farmer commented, "How can it take away American jobs when I can't get American workers to sign up. If I left my fields to American workers, my grapes would rot on the vine" (Olson 2003, 46).

In October 1949, Congress enacted the Agricultural Act of 1949, which codified prior laws and provisions for temporary agricultural workers and established the Bracero Program that permitted the legal immigration of temporary agricultural workers.

As noted, the program was regularly renewed until December 1964, bringing in overall close to five million Mexican workers to the United States.

In addition to a staggering refugee crisis and agricultural labor shortages, U.S. policy makers faced the prospect of reunifying American alien spouses and children with American husbands and fathers who had served in the armed forces. On December 28, 1945, Congress passed the War Brides Act, granting admission to the United States to alien spouses and alien children of U.S. citizens who served honorably during World War II. The act enabled 120,000 wives, husbands, and children of the armed forces to immigrate to the United States. The newcomers were mostly German and English, but Congress amended the act to include Asian women, and as a result, nearly 10,000 Chinese women came to the United States.

America Turns Inward: Cold War Fears and Immigration Policies

The post–World War II atmosphere in the United States ushered in an era characterized by Cold War fears and immigration restrictions that reflected those fears. The Cold War that evolved between the United States and the Soviet Union at the end of World War II impacted every aspect of American foreign and domestic policies. From the Soviet occupation of Berlin to the Berlin blockade and the growing sphere of Soviet influence in Eastern Europe, the United States viewed every Soviet action as an attempt to spread Communism and solidify its stranglehold over Europe. The fall of China to Communist revolutionaries and the onset of the Korean War further created a culture of fear in the United States exacerbated by the hysteria provoked by Senator Joseph McCarthy (R-WI) during the 1950s over potential Communist infiltration of the government.

Following the Chinese Exclusion Act of 1882, Chinese would-be immigrants had devised a strategy for side-stepping the restrictive law. Young Chinese immigrants claimed to be a son of a citizen (the law allowed exemption for merchants, students, diplomats and sons of American citizens) but were, in fact, sons on paper only. Because the San Francisco earthquake destroyed City Hall, which contained all birth records, their birthplace could not be verified. The "paper son" system thus instituted a chain migration pattern that allowed multiple generations of Chinese to enter the country using fraudulent papers" (Ngai 2003, 204).

By 1950, data from the U.S. Immigration and Naturalization Service revealed that at least 25 percent of the Chinese-American population was illegal. The Cold War, anti-Communism, and the continuing concern over illegal entries led the federal government to begin large-scale investigations in Chinese communities across the country. The goal was to end the admission of paper sons, which had continued after 1943. The result was the "Confession Program," established in 1956 to allow Chinese who had entered the country by fraudulent means to make voluntary confessions of their status. Confessors who were longtime residents would be granted amnesty while aliens who had served in the U.S. armed forces for at least 90 days could also become naturalized citizens. Altogether, some 30,530 Chinese immigrants confessed.

During this period, Congress passed the McCarran Internal Security Act of September 1950 over Truman's veto. The law was largely aimed at "domestic enemies" of the United States. Membership in any subversive organization could now constitute grounds for exclusion, deportation, denial of citizenship, and even the loss of citizenship. Furthermore, the Internal Security Act authorized the president, in a national emergency, to round up and detain persons suspected of threatening the national interests. Consequently, the 1950s were terrifying for large numbers of Chinese Americans. Indeed, "no immigrant group in America was more vulnerable than Chinese Americans because so many of them had either gained admission by fraud—chiefly by varieties of the 'paper sons' device—or by illegal entry" (Daniels 2004, 154).

The need to amend the quota system, instituted in 1924, led to the McCarran-Walter Immigration Act. The 1952 law represented the most complete codification of the immigration and naturalization laws up to that time. Furthermore, it meant to exclude certain groups from immigrating to the United States, particularly individuals who held certain political viewpoints deemed "un-American." Subversives and Communists were specifically denied eligibility, as were gays and lesbians. The 1952 act was not just about perpetuating old exclusions directed at southern and eastern Europeans. Now, persons whose political opinions or sexual identities did not mesh with "American values" were added to the list of undesirables.

The act set a numerical limit of 150,000 on immigration from the Eastern Hemisphere and retained an unlimited number for the Western Hemisphere. At the same time, however, it included a small quota for Asian immigrants not covered by specific national quota limits and removed all racial, gender, and nationality barriers to citizenship. Although the law preserved the quota system, it shifted the preferences according to which persons could be admitted. Importantly, a category of non-quota immigrants was specified and remains a major provision for the admission of spouses, minor children, and parents of U.S. citizens. Finally, the law provided an option that would ultimately constitute the backdoor of American immigration for almost three decades: it gave the attorney general, in emergencies, the power to "parole" temporarily into the country an individual lacking a visa.

President Truman, who actually favored broadening immigration laws, vetoed the 1952 bill, deeming it discriminatory, punitive, and distrustful of all aliens. Congress, however, overrode his veto. All immigration laws since the McCarran-Walter Act went into effect are technically amendments of the 1952 law.

Within a year after the McCarran-Walter Act became law, efforts were made to modify it. President Eisenhower wanted to admit more refugees, and, after the Displaced Persons Act expired in 1952, Congress enacted the Refugee Relief Act (August 1953), which provided 214,000 visas for immigrants without regard to national quotas. In addition, the act provided for the emergency immigration of an extra 186,000 political refugees from Communist countries. Between 1946 and 1960, a total of approximately 703,000 immigrants entered the United States as "displaced people" or refugees. Passed at the height of the Cold War, these measures were especially meant to aid refugees and escapees from Communist-dominated areas and those fleeing natural disasters. Thus, the 1953 act defined an "escapee" as any "refugee who, because of persecution or fear of persecution on account of race, religion, or political opinion fled from the U.S.S.R. or communist Eastern Europe and cannot return because of fear of persecution on account of race, religion, or political opinion" (Bon Tempo 2008, 67). The Refugee Acts of 1953, 1957, 1958, 1959, and 1960 provided non-quota visas for refugees from Communism (especially Hungarians) as well as from Italy and Greece, plus Dutch fleeing Indonesia, and for several thousand other persons from Asia and the Middle East.

In the post–World War II era, the admission of refugees created one of the greatest challenges to existing immigration policies. From the refugees fleeing Soviet-controlled Eastern Europe to Cubans escaping Castro's Communist regime and Vietnamese seeking refuge in the United States after the Communist takeover of South Vietnam, the result of American refugee policies is that some four million people have migrated to the United States since 1945.

The Hungarian Revolution and Cold War Immigration Policies

On November 4, 1956, Soviet forces launched a major attack on Hungary aimed at crushing a national uprising against Communist rule that had begun 12 days earlier. The "revolution" precipitated a flood of Hungarian refugees into Austria and Yugoslavia. In a matter of weeks, there was a serious Hungarian refugee problem.

In Washington, U.S. officials observed the events in Hungary with shock. The American decision to help Hungarian refugees was largely driven by foreign policy concerns and U.S. Cold War ideology. According to Bon Tempo, "the Eisenhower administration calculated that a commitment to Hungarians fleeing Soviet tanks was a strong and clear sign of support for the Hungarian Revolution that, at the same time, would not greatly damage delicate American-Soviet relations or lead to a larger superpower conflict" (Bon Tempo 2008, 60). The Eisenhower administration then approved a program that admitted approximately 38,000 refugees in about one year. Bon Tempo maintains that such "Hungarian refugee admissions were

remarkable for two reasons: First, the executive branch, to an unprecedented degree, assumed control of American refugee policy, especially with the utilization of a new process, called 'parole,' to admit refugees. Second, the admissions process focused on admitting Hungarians quickly without screening them. The Hungarian crisis bolstered and reinforced the association between 'refugee' and 'anticommunist' " (Ibid.).

In the United States, there was tremendous support for the Hungarian Revolution, in part, because of the development of an American identity in the 1950s that strongly opposed Communism. Because the annual Hungarian immigration quota of 865 visas could not accommodate the thousands of refugees, Hungarians were admitted to the United States with "escapee" visas.

In December 1956, Eisenhower ordered the "parole" of 15,000 more refugees into the United States. His directive took advantage of a little-known clause in the Immigration and Nationality Act that permitted the attorney general to admit (or "parole") an alien into the United States on an emergency basis if the admission served the public interest. The decision to parole the Hungarians significantly increased the Executive Branch's control of refugee policymaking and provided Eisenhower with the means to admit Hungarians almost immediately. The policy did not require either congressional approval or consultation, nor did Congress have a direct hand in overseeing its implementation. Nearly 38,000 Hungarian parolees who had been admitted to the United States during the late 1950s were put on the path to citizenship by the act of July 25, 1958, which adjusted their legal status and granted permanent residence to those already here by parole authority.

By January 1957, in addition to the Hungarians, both Yugoslavian and Chinese refugees were also admitted to the United States. In 1958, some 31,000 Dutch Indonesians expelled from the former Dutch colony of Indonesia, a non-Communist country, came in under a law passed by Congress. The same act of 1958 provided for the admission of nearly 4,000 Cape Verdeans from the Azores, following earthquakes and volcanic eruptions.

In 1953, President Eisenhower appointed a special commission to study immigration and naturalization policy. It recommended a more liberalized approach. In 1962, Congress enacted the Migration and Refugee Assistance Act to aid the president in these matters. Some of the commission's recommendations were finally enacted in the Immigration and Nationality Act of 1965, which ended the national-origins quota system and ushered in a new era of immigration policy.

Cold War Exiles: Cubans, Phase One

Between 1959 and 1980, some 700,000 Cuban refugees, primarily in three distinct waves, gained admission to the United States. Cuban refugees were regarded as political agents engaged in the combat against Communism as a result of fleeing Fidel Castro's revolutionary Cuba. Much like the Hungarian refugees of the late 1950s, they largely entered the United States under the parole power of the attorney general.

As American refugee policy was redesigned to fit Cold War foreign policy concerns and to admit first wave Cuban immigrants, it essentially circumvented U.S. immigration quotas set under the McCarran-Walter Act of 1952 and practically granted Cubans unlimited admission until 1965. Although a significant number of Cubans had not fled particular acts of persecution, they officially secured recognition as political refugees with Eisenhower's invocation of the Mutual Security Act in October 1960 justified by their blatant renunciation of, and victimization by, Communism. Under the auspices of U.S. foreign policy the admission of Cubans emerged to serve a political purpose within the Cold War; it undermined Castro's Communism. But even though the new legislation capped the number of annual refugee admissions at 17,400, approximately 297,318 second-wave Cuban refugees were paroled into the United States by the time the Freedom Flights, which commenced in December 1965, terminated on April 6, 1973.

After receiving parole or refugee status, Cuban migrants received benefits from the Cuban Refugee program, established by the Kennedy administration, which included monetary assistance for education, resettlement, job training, and relief. With the creation of the Cuban Adjustment Act of 1966, the U.S. government again dealt with Cuban refugees outside the existing policy provisions. It essentially streamlined the process for acquiring permanent residency and U.S. citizenship solely for the Cuban migrants. Under this 1966 act, Cuban refugees who had lived in the United States for at least two years were permitted to apply for permanent resident status without having to complete the expensive bureaucratic steps of traveling to a third country in order to acquire an immigrant visa and then reentering the United States. Additionally, unlike any other immigrant or refugee group, up to 30 months of the Cubans' stay in the United States counted toward the five-year residency requirement for citizenship. However, most strikingly for Cuban refugees, securing permanent resident status neither necessitated renouncing allegiance to Cuba nor demanded pledging to refrain from returning to a post-Castro Cuba.

Immigration Reform, 1965

The 1960s and early 1970s were a watershed in American history. The emergence of the civil rights movement and African Americans' demands for equal rights sparked similar movements by Latinos, Asians, and Native Americans. In addition, European Americans found a voice in American society and a sense of pride in their ethnic background. Italians, Greeks, Poles, and Portuguese, for example, spoke out against immigration quotas that discriminated against them in favor of western Europeans.

During the early 1960s, the inadequacies and discrimination inherent in the McCarran-Walter Act of 1952 led to demands for immigration policy reform. The rush of displaced persons and political refugees had resulted in a reactive U.S. immigration policy, and many critics began to demand reform legislation. Because the McCarran-Walter Act had retained the old quota system, which had long been biased in favor of northern and western Europeans and against eastern and southern Europeans, Asians, and Africans, many civil rights activists considered the law an anachronism from the country's racist past. Democrats in Congress took up their cause with support from President Kennedy. In 1963, Kennedy sent a proposal to Congress eliminating the quota system.

After Kennedy's assassination, Congress passed and President Lyndon Baines Johnson signed the

President Lyndon B. Johnson (left) speaks after signing the Immigration and Naturalization Act of 1965 below the Statue of Liberty. Chief restrictions enacted in 1917, 1924, 1929, were gradually repealed until the 1965 overhaul. (Lyndon B. Johnson Library/Yoichi R. Okamoto)

Immigration and Nationality Act of 1965 (the Hart-Celler Act). At the signing of the bill at Liberty Island on October 3, 1965, President Johnson stated that "for over four decades the immigration policy of the United States has been distorted by the harsh injustice of the national origins system. This system violated the basic principle of American democracy—the principle that values and rewards each man on the basis of his merit as a man." The Immigration and Nationality Act of 1965 reflected changes in the political climate in the United States toward race and ethnic diversity and effectively leveled the playing field for immigrants, giving a nearly equal chance to newcomers from every corner of the globe.

Basically, the act scrapped completely the concept of national quotas and origins and substituted overall hemispheric limits on visas issued. It set an annual limitation of 290,000 visas for immigrants, including 170,000 from Eastern Hemisphere countries with no more than 20,000 per country, ending discrimination against Asians and Africans. The act emphasized family reunification, and preferences also went to refugees and professional and skilled workers. The act established an overall limit of 120,000 immigrants from the Western Hemisphere. As a result, while the rest of the world enjoyed an expansion in numerical limitations after 1965, Mexico and the Western Hemisphere for the first time were suddenly faced with numerical restrictions.

As a result of the 1965 act, the composition of new immigrants from non-European nations changed dramatically the ethnic makeup of the United States. Rising numbers of Asians, Africans, West Indians, and persons from the Americas created a shift in the regional origins of American immigrants. At the same time, however, American communities of Italians, Greeks, and Portuguese, among other European Americans, benefited from the act, which favored family reunification. Between 1960 and 1975, for example, 20,000 Italians arrived annually to reunite with extended family members who had immigrated earlier. Similarly, the vast majority of Filipino women and men entered the United States under the occupational and family unification provision. The occupational preferences for professionals in 1965 provided Filipinos with another opportunity to migrate. In the first five years of the new law, over 17,000 Filipino professionals immigrated to the United States, and in the first 20 years of the new law, 25,000 entered; among them were thousands of Filipino nurses.

Family-based reunification catapulted the number of immigrants who were admitted as a result of the 1965 act. Non-quota immigrants included parents, spouses, and minor children of American citizens. In addition, preferences of the 1965 law included (1) unmarried children of citizens and their children; (2) spouse and unmarried children of resident aliens; (3) members of professions and family; (4) married children of citizens and family; (5) siblings of citizens and their families; (6) needed skilled and unskilled workers and their families; and (7) refugees. The result was that immigration doubled between 1965 and 1970 and doubled again between 1970 and 1990. The Immigration and Nationality Act of 1965 defined the conditions under which 15.53 million immigrants were admitted to the United States between 1966 and 1991.

Cold-War Exiles: Cubans, Phase Two

After more than 10,000 Cubans sought refuge in the Peruvian embassy in Havana during March and April 1980, Castro opened the port of Mariel on April 21, 1980, and declared that any who wished to leave could do so. During the next five months, the dramatic "Freedom Flotilla" took place, bringing nearly 125,000 more Cubans to the United States by September 25, 1980. While the U.S. government generally supported the Mariel Cubans, the American media and many persons in the Cuban émigré community reacted adversely toward them. Discovering that Castro forced criminals and the mentally ill to leave the island, American correspondents irresponsibly focused disproportionate attention on the "undesirable" and "social deviants" arriving during the exodus. According to the Refugee Act of 1980, the Mariel Cubans failed to be classified as legitimate refugees—the first time during the Cold War the United States neglected to assign refugee status to emigrants from a Communist country. Although the Carter administration paroled the Mariel migrants into the United States and granted them an ambiguous status—"entrants"—they eventually received the same rights and benefits guaranteed to refugees under the Refugee Act of 1980.

Between 1932 and 1960, approximately 7,000 Haitian immigrants, many of them exiles from increasingly authoritarian Haitian regimes, immigrated to the United States. Between 1961 and 1980, some 90,000 came. The 1980 Refugee Act encouraged Haitians to apply for asylum. However, in almost all instances, the United States rejected Haitian asylum requests, arguing that Haitians were economic refugees and thus ineligible for asylum (thereby creating an environment ripe for illegal entry). Unfortunately for the Haitians, they were fleeing from right-wing tyrants; if the corrupt Haitian regime had been Communist, the American government would have, more than likely, provided the Haitians with asylum.

Southeast Asian Refugees

The Vietnam War and its aftermath during the 1960s and 1970s produced a wave of new Southeast Asian immigrants—Vietnamese, Cambodians (Khmer), and Laotians (Hmong)—to the United States. The war uprooted millions of people, and eventually more than one million of them made their way to the United States.

Ethnic Chinese in Saigon as well as ethnic Khmers in the Mekong Delta were targeted for discrimination, as were the mountain peoples of Laos and Cambodia who had come to Saigon in search of work. The discrimination they faced made all of them candidates for emigration. Politically suspect individuals were forced out into reeducation camps in rural areas where they engaged in forced hard labor and received political indoctrination. In Cambodia, the genocidal maniac Pol Pot instituted a bloody reign of terror that depopulated the country's major cities and towns and led to the deaths of as many as two million people.

In 1975, when Communist troops overran South Vietnam, Laos, and Cambodia, millions of Vietnamese, Khmers, and Laotians who had worked for the United States, fearing retaliation from the Communists, decided to flee their countries. Most of the Indochinese immigrants who got away after 1976 (approximately 1.3 million) were boat people who left by sea in small boats. Congress moved quickly to appropriate assistance to the refugees, and in October 1977, it permitted Vietnamese, Laotians, and Cambodians to be "paroled" into the country (as were the Cubans) and given permanent residence after two years. Congress passed the Indochinese Migration and Refugee Assistance Act of 1975 and renewed the law in 1977, which provided economic assistance to the refugees. Nearly 548,000 persons arrived within seven years. The United States arranged with Vietnam an Orderly Departure Program through which about 50,000 people annually came to the United States directly from Vietnam (1982–1987). Then, in 1987, arrangements were made between the United States and Vietnam for Amerasian children of American soldiers to leave Vietnam, enabling 18,600 children to enter the United States between 1988 and 1993.

Overall, between 1975 and 1993, approximately 1.3 million Indochinese were received by the United States.

At first, Americans welcomed the immigrants with open arms. They were systematically settled throughout the United States and not concentrated in one region. Thousands of small and large communities sponsored immigrant families, and the government often contracted the services of local churches and charitable organizations in settling the immigrant families into apartments, jobs, and schools. Most Americans, even those who had opposed the war, felt a certain responsibility toward the war's victims. The government paid their airfare to the United States, extended loans to those who wanted to open businesses of their own, and provided scholarships to Indochinese children wanting to attend college. The federal government also provided extra funding to local districts enrolling Indochinese immigrant children.

By 1973, the U.S. government had spent $1 billion assisting Cuban refugees. By 1978, after merely three years, it had already spent $1 billion aiding the resettlement of Southeast Asians. No immigrant group benefited from any comparable programs as did the Cubans and Southeast Asians who were given preferential treatment largely because of U.S. anti-Communist foreign policies. Seemingly, exceptions could be made to rigid American immigration policies when the immigrants were escaping Communist regimes.

Post-1965 Immigration Policies: The Refugee Act of 1980.

On March 4, 1980, after a year-and-a-half effort by Congress and the Executive Branch, President Carter signed the Refugee Act of 1980 into law. One of the most significant aspects of the 1980 refugee policy is that it incorporated the United Nations' definition of a refugee, "one who had a well-founded fear of persecution owing to race, religion, nationality, or membership in a social group or political movement" (LeMay and Barkan, 1999, 272).

Prior to the 1980 act, persons escaping from Communist-dominated or Communist-occupied states, or from countries in the Middle East, were considered eligible for refugee status. The Refugee Act raised the annual limitation on regular refugee admissions from 17,400 to 50,000 each fiscal year; set aside 5,000 slots for persons seeking asylum; replaced the use of the "parole authority" with new statutory language asserting congressional control over the process of admitting refugees, and provided a full range of federal programs to assist in the resettlement process.

According to Senator Edward Kennedy, (D-MA), a sponsor of the bill, "the political climate at the time the Refugee Act was introduced worked for and against it." On one hand, Kennedy wrote, "the dramatic plight of the 'boat people' captured the attention and concern of millions of Americans in 1979. But the same year also saw the greatest need for the resettlement of refugees from around the world . . . [dramatizing] the need for a new law to deal with refugee resettlement in a more efficient manner, but the numbers [of refugees] also alarmed many in Congress" (Kennedy 1981). Indeed, the 1960s and 1970s "evidenced flows in which refugees arrived in mass asylum movements: 400,000 from Cuba, 340,000 from Vietnam, 110,000 from Laos, nearly 70,000 from the Soviet Union and a like number from Cambodia, 30,000 from Yugoslavia, nearly 25,000 from mainland China and Taiwan, nearly 20,000 each from Rumania and Poland, and about 10,000 each from Czechoslovakia, Spain, and Hungary" (LeMay and Barkan, 1999, 272).

The 1980 Act recognized the federal government's responsibility to assist state and local communities and the voluntary agencies in resettling refugees. To administer these programs, provisions were made for a U.S. coordinator for refugee affairs but, while the nation was preoccupied with refugee policies, the problem of undocumented aliens was growing. The ending of the Bracero Program in 1964, coupled with a ceiling on Western Hemisphere immigration, led to a growing number of Mexicans and other Central Americans trying to cross the border illegally. Congress enacted the Simpson-Rodino Act of 1986 (also known as the Immigration Reform and Control Act, or IRCA) which legalized nearly three million undocumented workers, over one-half of whom were Mexicans. In the mid-1990s, the undocumented population rose again; experts estimate that nearly 11 million unauthorized persons lived in the United States in 2009. Again over one-half were from Mexico.

Conclusion

The "Open Door" symbolizes U.S. immigration policies that welcomed immigrants for nearly 200 years. However, the "Open Door" began to close on specific immigrants as a result of race and ethnic prejudice. Nowhere is this seen more clearly than in the Chinese Exclusion Act of 1882, which was inflamed by racism. In 1907, the assault on Asians shifted from Chinese to Japanese when President Theodore Roosevelt and the government of Japan curtailed Japanese immigration to the United States with the "Gentlemen's Agreement."

At the turn of the twentieth century, nativist attitudes were directed at southern and eastern Europeans who dominated the large numbers of immigrants to the United States. Opponents of immigration lamented that the national origins of the "new immigrants" were shifting steadily from northern and western to southern and eastern European sources. The "new immigrants" were portrayed as racially inferior, impoverished, crime ridden, illiterate, and overwhelmingly Catholic and Jewish. Defenders of Anglo-Saxon Protestant culture sought restriction of these persons through literacy tests and quotas. The result was the Quota Law of 1921, enacted as a temporary measure setting numerical limitations on immigration and the Immigration Act of 1924. That act dramatically limited the number of immigrants coming from southern and eastern Europe.

The passage of the 1952 Immigration Act also confirmed quotas based on national origins. But the act went much further: influenced by the Cold War atmosphere and anti-communist fervor of the post–World War II era the law restricted the immigration of individuals who held certain political viewpoints deemed "un-American."

In 1965, the U.S. door to immigrants began to open again, yet, there were still limitations as to just how far the doors would open. While the act abolished the national origins quota system and vestiges of Asian exclusion laws, it introduced an overall limit of 120,000 immigrants from the Western Hemisphere. As a result, while the rest of the world enjoyed greater opportunities to immigrate to the United States, Mexico and the Western Hemisphere for the first time were suddenly faced with numerical restrictions.

By the end of the 1970s, the desperate plight of refugees from Cubans to Southeast Asians was taken up by the Carter administration (1977–1981). The Refugee Act of 1980 provided the first permanent and systematic procedure for the admission and effective resettlement of refugees. Thus, immigration laws between 1870 and 1980 have also reflected American foreign policy considerations, most notably the Cold War. The Cold War that evolved between the United States and the Soviet Union following World War II led to laws, such as the Refugee Relief Act in 1953, which provided for the emergency immigration of an extra 186,000 political refugees from Communist countries. Further immigrations acts, including the Indochinese Migration and Refugee Assistance Act of 1975 and 1977, provided economic assistance to refugees. By 1973, the U.S. government had spent $1 billion assisting Cuban refugees, and by 1978, it had spent another $1 billion aiding the resettlement of Southeast Asians. Because of its zealous anti-Communist foreign policy, the United States was willing to take extraordinary measures to liberalize immigration laws and allocate money to support those persons who were political refugees of Communist regimes.

Tragically, the U.S. commitment to refugees had not taken the same liberal approach earlier to Jews seeking a safe haven in the United States in the late 1930s. The failure to save Jewish refugees reveals a combination of the antialien sentiment and anti-Semitism that was pervasive in American society prior to World War II.

Moreover, while deportation is part of the immigration control system, it also reflects American anxieties about immigrants who harbor "un-American" political beliefs, such as anarchists or Communists. Historically, deportation powers served to defend the public against crime or economic burden as occurs with criminal aliens or public charges; or it protects national security by removing subversive or disloyal aliens as it did in 1919, when 246 radicals were deported to Russia. However, deportation has also been used in times of economic crisis, such as the Depression when Mexicans and their American-born children were "repatriated" to Mexico.

Restrictions and opportunities often coincided and were linked to domestic conditions and foreign policy considerations. Given that, immigration doubled between 1965 and 1970 and doubled again between 1970 and 1990. In 1991, the United States witnessed its largest influx of immigrants ever (1.83 million), surpassing the previous record from 1907. During the 1990s, an average of just less than 1 million immigrants entered each year, a trend that would continue into the new century due to legislative changes.

The great migration of Europeans has largely run its course. In the 1990s, only 14 percent of immigrants came from Europe, while 22 percent came from just one country: Mexico. Another 22 percent came from the Caribbean and Central and South America, while 29 percent arrived from Asia. However, that does not include illegal or undocumented immigrants. The challenges that the United States faces with illegal immigration will surely impact the way Americans view immigration in general, which may well mean that the "open door" will once again, begin to close.

Bibliography

Barkan, Elliott Robert. 1996. *And Still They Come: Immigrants and American Society 1920 to the 1990s*. Wheeling, IL: Harlan Davidson Press.

Bon Tempo, Carl. 2008. *Americans at the Gate: The United States and Refugees during the Cold War*. Princeton, NJ: Princeton University Press.

Cannato, Vincent. 2009. *American Passage: The History of Ellis Island*. New York: HarperCollins.

Congressional Digest. 1977. "Evolution of U.S. Immigration Policy," 227–56.

Daniels, Roger. 2004. *Guarding the Golden Door*. New York: Hill and Wang.

Dinnerstein, Leonard, and David M. Reimers. 2009. *Ethnic Americans: A History of Immigration*. New York: Columbia University Press.

Dobkin, Donald S. 2009. "Race and the Shaping of U.S. Policy." *Chicana/o-Latina/o Law Review* 28, no. 19 (July): 19–42.

Feingold, Henry L. 1995. *Bearing Witness: How America and Its Jews Responded to the Holocaust*. Syracuse, NY: Syracuse University Press.

Gjerde, Jon. 1998. *Major Problems in American Immigration and Ethnic History*. Boston: Houghton Mifflin Company.

Gonzales, Manuel G. 1999, Mexicanos: A History of Mexicans in the United States. Bloomington, Ind.: Indiana University Press.

Kanstroom, Daniel. 2000. *Deportation Nation: Outsiders in American History*. Cambridge, MA: Harvard University Press.

Kennedy, Edward M. 1981. "The Refugee Act of 1980," *International Migration Review* 15, no. 1–2 (Spring–Summer): 141–56.

Lee, Erika. 2003. *At America's Gates: Chinese Immigration during the Exclusion Era, 1882–1943*. Chapel Hill: University of North Carolina Press.

LeMay, Michael, and Elliott Robert Barkan. 1981. *U.S. Immigration and Naturalization Laws and Issues*. Westport, CT: Greenwood Press.

Ngai, Mae M. 2003. "The Strange Career of the Illegal Alien: Immigration Restriction and Deportation Policy in the United States, 1921–1965." *Law and History Review* 21, no. 1 (Spring): 1–37.

Olson, James S. *2003. Equality Deferred. Race, Ethnicity, and Immigration in America since 1945*. Belmont, CA: Wadsworth Thompson Learning, Inc.

Shapiro, Edward S. 1992. *A Time for Healing: American Jewry since World War II*. Baltimore: Johns Hopkins University Press.

U.S. Department of Justice. Immigration and Naturalization Service. 1991. "An Immigration Nation: United States Regulation of Immigration, 1798–1991," 1–25.

U.S. Immigration Policies, 1986–2011

Christina Gerken

The Immigration Reform and Control Act of 1986

During the late 1960s and early 1970s—aside from Cuban refugees and their efforts to escape from Fidel Castro's Cuba and the concurrent struggles among middle-class Haitians to flee from the Duvalier father/son dictatorship—immigration policies remained relatively uncontroversial and, apart from a few relatively minor amendments that were passed with bipartisan consensus, there was little debate about immigration reform. In the late 1970s, however, the political climate began to change and immigration reform became, once again, a hotly debated topic. As a response to public concerns about a "broken" immigration system and the increasing number of undocumented immigrants, Public Law 95-412 established the Select Commission on Immigration and Refugee Policy "to study and evaluate . . . existing laws, policies, and procedures governing the admission of immigrants and refugees to the United States." The commission, which was appointed in 1978 and chaired by Notre Dame President Theodore Hesburgh, published its final report on March 1, 1981. The 453-page report, entitled "U.S. Immigration Policy and the National Interest," provided a moderate response to political pressures to limit and restrict the immigrant influx. Instead, the commission made clear distinctions between policies for documented/legal immigrants, undocumented/illegal immigrants, and refugees.

With regard to undocumented immigrants, the commission tried to correct irrational fears and emphasize that "most studies indicate that undocumented/illegal aliens do not place a substantial burden on social services" or on the labor market, the education system, or the health care system. They acknowledged that undocumented immigrants have made important social, cultural, and economic contributions despite their lack of legal status. Hence, the commission recommended a combined amnesty and enforcement approach that would allow undocumented immigrants who were already present in the United States to gain legal status, while making it harder for future generations to enter the United States without legal papers. The proposed interior enforcement included legislation making it illegal for employers to hire undocumented workers and the establishment of a fully automated system to track the departure of temporary visa holders. In addition, the report called for added border patrol measures (e.g., increasing the number of Border Patrol officers and providing them with planes, helicopters, and other equipment). Interestingly, the commission decided against the establishment of a large-scale "guestworker program" in a decisive 14–2 vote.

Contrary to the popular call for a reduction of immigration quotas, the commission wanted to increase the annual ceiling of immigrant visas by 100,000 for the next five years and continue to exempt immediate relatives of U.S. citizens from numerical restrictions. Throughout their report, they highlighted the positive contributions of immigrants to American society and underscored their belief that a generous legal immigration system is in the U.S. national interest.

This report as well as the ensuing debates during the 98th Congress (1983–1984) foreshadowed a lot of the issues and introduced many of the key players who continued to dominate the immigration reform discourse in the late twentieth and early twenty-first centuries. Following the report's call for a legalization program, Immigration Subcommittee chair Alan K. Simpson (R-WY) and ranking members Edward Kennedy (D-MA) and Strom Thurmond (R-SC) developed one of most groundbreaking reform proposals during the 98th Congress: they advocated an amnesty program for undocumented immigrants who had resided in the United States for an extended period of time. A few politicians expressed concerns that these legalized immigrants would immediately petition for additional family members and thus cause an already overburdened legal immigration system to collapse. Still others were worried that the amnesty provision might lead to increasing expenditures for social welfare programs. Generally speaking, though, the Immigration and Control bill of 1983 (S. 529) caused surprisingly little controversy and was approved by the Senate by a wide margin (76–18).

However, there were several amendments that are worth noting. Early on in the debate, Senator Jesse Helms (R-NC) introduced an amendment that would have allowed states to deny undocumented immigrants' access to public schools and other public benefits. Senators Simpson and Kennedy were both strongly opposed to this amendment, arguing that it was unfair to punish innocent children and deprive them of the right to get an education. In the end, the Helms Amendment was defeated on a 60–34 vote. On the following day, Senator Gordon Humphrey (R-NH) argued that newly legalized immigrants should be temporarily disqualified from receiving public assistance for a minimum of five years. Several members of Congress—including Senators Simpson and Kennedy—argued that, as tax-paying members of society, legalized immigrants should be eligible for public support. Even though the Humphrey Amendment was initially

President Reagan signs the Immigration Reform and Control Act of 1986. Other immigration laws were the Immigration Act (1990), and stricter regulatory/deportation measures in 1996 and in the USA Patriot Act (2001). Further reforms have remained in limbo. (Ronald Reagan Library)

rejected, it finally made its way into the Immigration Reform and Control Act of 1986 (IRCA).

Yet, in contrast to the relatively unanimous votes in the Senate, the House version of the bill (H.R. 1510) turned out to be much more controversial. Due to the increasing controversy about the amnesty provision and in anticipation of a highly competitive presidential primary season, Congress decided to delay further discussion until after the election. A full year after the legislation had been reported out of committee, the House finally held a general hearing on the Immigration and Control bill. In total, 69 amendments were offered and a lengthy debate followed.

There is evidence that suggests that most representatives actually favored an orderly legalization process for some undocumented workers. Yet there was much disagreement about the criteria that should be used to determine who was eligible and who should be forced to leave the United States. Because there were no reliable statistics about the number of undocumented immigrants, several representatives raised concerns that there might be millions of eligible candidates who were all eager to stay in the United States permanently. One possible solution to this perceived problem was to raise the residency requirement. E. Clay Shaw (R-FL), for example, offered an amendment that would have moved the eligibility date from January 1, 1982, to January 1, 1980, thus cutting off a significant number of newly arrived immigrants. Another popular suggestion expected potential amnesty candidates to fulfill additional requirements, such as passing an English-language proficiency exam or a test about American history and government.

After the House had passed a compromise version of the amnesty provision by a narrow 216–211 margin, conference meetings began in September 1984. While the conference committee members tried to resolve the differences between the House and Senate versions, another major stumbling block appeared: funding. Border state representatives, who were understandably concerned about this issue, insisted on full reimbursement of the anticipated increased costs for education, health care, and other public services. In the end, Congress was unable to reach a compromise, and action on immigration died in October 1984.

During the 99th Congress, politicians were more determined than ever to pass a substantial immigration reform measure that contained some kind of amnesty provision. In the Senate, Simpson was once again instrumental in the passage of this legislation. In May 1985, he introduced a slightly altered version of his bill (S. 1200). The House version of the bill (H.R. 3810) was sponsored by Peter Rodino (D-NJ) and Romano Mazzoli (D-KY). Even though several provisions turned out to be highly controversial—including the funding issue that had caused the stalemate in the 98th Congress—a compromise was reached, and both chambers approved the conference report in October 1986.

The Immigration Reform and Control Act of 1986 (P.L. 99-603) was by far the most extensive and influential immigration reform measure since the passage of the Immigration and Naturalization Act of 1965. In addition to the amnesty provision, which enabled approximately 2.7 million persons to legalize and gain legal permanent residency status, IRCA also contained a number of other remarkable provisions. Most notably, IRCA established a "Temporary Disqualification of Newly Legalized Aliens from Receiving Certain Public Welfare Assistance," which made newly legalized immigrants ineligible for public benefits for a period of five years. This provision and the general debates about immigrants' welfare eligibility foreshadowed some of the controversies that became even more pronounced during the 104th Congress (1995–1996). In addition, IRCA also established sanctions for employers who knowingly recruited and/or knowingly hired undocumented immigrants. Aware that this provision might lead to increased levels of discrimination of foreign-looking and foreign-sounding individuals on the job market, Congress added a section that prohibited employment discrimination based on national origin or citizenship status and established civil penalties for violations.

The Immigration and Nationality Act of 1990

After the groundbreaking effort to reform the treatment of undocumented immigrants, the 101st Congress turned toward the legal immigration system.

After the elections, some new central players emerged. On the Republican side, the Immigration Subcommittee chairmanship was given to Lamar Smith (R-TX). On the Democratic side, Bruce Morrison (D-CT) was awarded the position of chairman of the Subcommittee on Immigration, Border Security, and Claims. Meanwhile, Senators Kennedy and Simpson continued to work as a team and formulate bipartisan reform proposals. Kennedy, in particular, had become increasingly concerned with the effects of the 1965 INA on the national origins of immigrants. According to him, the undue emphasis on family reunification had all but shut out European immigrants. This situation, Kennedy argued, was untenable, in violation of the United States' historical commitments, and in dire need of reform. As a result, Kennedy and Simpson developed a bill that emphasized job skills and shifted visas away from family reunification. Their bill eliminated the preferential treatment of immediate relatives of U.S. citizens, who had been exempt from the numerical limits in the past, and capped the total number of immigrant visas at 600,000 per year—480,000 for family members and 120,000 for immigrants who possessed special skills.

The House was split between two entirely different reactions to the perceived legal immigration problem. On the one hand, Democrats, such as Morrison and Howard Berman (D-CA), introduced bills to increase the number of available visas and, in the case of Berman, exempt immediate relatives of legal permanent residents from numerical limitations. These suggestions were supposed to reduce the immigrant backlog and help reunite families who had been separated for an extended period of time. In reaction to the changing national origins of contemporary immigrants, Charles Schumer (D-NY) introduced a new "Diversity Category," which would reserve a number of visas for immigrants from underrepresented—i.e., European—nations. On the other hand, Smith and John Bryant (D-TX) advocated more restrictive policies, especially for unskilled family members. In the end, the more liberal proposals prevailed, and the House bill increased annual immigration quotas to 800,000.

On November 29, 1990, Congress passed the compromise version of the Senate and House bills. The Immigration and Nationality Act of 1990 (P.L. 101-649) increased the annual immigration level to 675,000 (a 37 percent increase), including 480,000 family-based immigrants, 140,000 employment-based immigrants (up from 54,000), and 55,000 "diversity" immigrants. Immediate relatives of U.S. citizens (i.e., their children, spouses, and parents) were still exempt from numerical limitations (Sec. 201 (2)(A)(i)). In addition, Section 111 of the INA of 1990 also reformed the family preference system and established the following four categories: (1) unmarried adult sons and daughters of U.S. citizens; (2) spouses and unmarried children of permanent residents; (3) married sons and daughters of U.S. citizens; and (4) brothers and sisters of adult U.S. citizens.

The Immigration Reform Discourse in the Mid-1990s

By the mid-1990s, it had become increasingly clear that the IRCA had failed to reach its purported goal of stopping illegal immigration. Quite the contrary, Americans were once again bombarded with media reports about a new "flood" of "illegal aliens," document fraud, crime, drug trafficking, welfare abuse, and rising expenditures for health care and education. These negative accounts, combined with an uncertain economic climate, lead to a rise in nativist sentiments and a barrage of anti-immigrant legislation. Such states as California passed their own restrictive and mean-spirited initiatives (Proposition 187) and Congress discussed more than a dozen original immigration bills with hundreds of amendments. While the final version of the immigration reform law—which was signed into law by President Bill Clinton on September 30, 1996—primarily focused on border enforcement, undocumented immigrants, and a reform of the sponsorship system, previous debates had contemplated much more far-reaching reform measures. In addition to these immigrant-specific provisions, the 104th Congress also passed a comprehensive welfare reform and a new antiterrorism law, both of which affected the rights and responsibilities of immigrants.

Proposition 187

Battling for reelection, Republican Governor Pete Wilson of California decided to make illegal immigration one of his cornerstone issues of the 1994 governor's race. Early on in his campaign, Wilson filed a highly publicized lawsuit against the federal government, trying to recoup at least some of the money that California had supposedly spent providing services, for example related to welfare, health care, and education for undocumented immigrants. A few months later, Governor Wilson endorsed Proposition 187—the so-called "Save our State" initiative—which declared that the people of California "have suffered and are suffering economic hardship" and "personal injury and damage caused by the criminal conduct of illegal aliens in this state." In order to remedy these perceived injustices and protect legal California residents from further harm, Proposition 187 intended to ban undocumented immigrants from publicly funded social services, including nonemergency health care and, most controversially, public elementary and secondary schools. Every publicly funded school, social services agency, or health care facility would also be required to cooperate fully with the INS and report anyone suspected of being an undocumented immigrant. In addition, manufacturing, distributing, or selling false citizenship or residence documents would become a felony.

California voters approved the initiative in the general election of November 8, 1994. Yet despite its popularity among voters, Proposition 187 was controversial from the very beginning, and legal scholars as well as civil and immigrant rights activists warned that some of the key provisions would not only be ineffective and overly punitive, but that they also violated immigrants' constitutional rights. As soon as Governor Wilson signed the proposition into law on November 9, 1994, the American Civil Liberties Union (ACLU), the Mexican-American Legal Defense/Education Fund (MALDEF), and the League of Latin American Citizens (LULAC) filed several lawsuits in California state court. On November 11, Judge Matthew Byrne issued a temporary restraining order to prevent the law from taking effect. Eventually, Judge Mariana Pfaelzer consolidated a number of the cases against Proposition 187 and declared the law unconstitutional in November 1997.

The Illegal Immigration Reform and Immigrant Responsibility Act of 1996

The Immigration and Nationality Act of 1990 mandated the formation of a bipartisan Commission on Immigration Reform to examine the accomplishments of earlier immigration policies and make recommendations for the future. President Clinton appointed former Congresswoman Barbara Jordan (D-TX) to chair this nine-member advisory commission. In September 1994, after numerous hearings, fact-finding missions, and expert testimony, the U.S. Commission on Immigration Reform released their first interim report, which focused solely on "illegal" immigration. This report, *U.S. Immigration Policy: Restoring Credibility*, found it to be self-evident that undocumented immigrants were undesirable. Since they had no legal right to join the U.S. labor market, it did not even matter whether their hard physical labor and their willingness to take temporary positions and accept minimal wages had had a positive impact on the U.S. market. Undocumented immigrants had disobeyed the rules of the game and should not be rewarded for their behavior.

The commission, therefore, recommended a threefold strategy to reduce the number of undocumented immigrants and decrease public expenditures on this population. First, and most important, the U.S. needed to prevent as many illegal entries as possible. In order to achieve this, the 1994 report advocated increased resources for border management, additional personnel to patrol the U.S.-Mexican border, the construction of additional barriers, tighter airport security with more INS officers, improved interagency cooperation (between INS and Customs), and the introduction of a land border-crossing fee that could help finance these costly endeavors. Second, the Jordan Commission called for the development and implementation of a fraud-resistant system for verifying work authorizations and a vigorous enforcement of sanctions against employers who knowingly hire undocumented workers. Third, the report proposed that undocumented immigrants should not be eligible for any publicly funded services except emergency care and programs necessary to protect public health and safety. At the same time, the commission explicitly and strongly opposed "any broad, categorical denial of public benefits to legal immigrants."

Soon after the Jordan-Commission released its interim report, the Democrats lost their majority in the House and the new Speaker, Newt Gingrich (R-GA), launched a new round of immigration reform debates. Gingrich advocated the formation of several influential congressional task forces, which were to develop specific policy recommendations. The Congressional Task Force on Immigration Reform, which was chaired by Elton Gallegly (R-CA), a keen supporter of California's Proposition 187, consisted of 54 members and was organized in six topic-oriented working groups. Taken together, the Jordan Commission and the congressional task force's recommendations—which, apart from some minor differences with regard to numbers, were basically identical—set the tone for the ensuing debate.

On January 24, 1995, Senator Simpson introduced the first comprehensive immigration reform bill to warrant significant debate during the 104th Congress: S. 269, the Immigrant Control and Financial Responsibility bill. Simpson's bill—which contained provisions to increase border patrols; improve the work authorization verification system, reform asylum, exclusion, and deportation procedures; and limit immigrants' welfare usage—was soon joined by two competing reform proposals. On March 21, 1995, Dianne Feinstein (D-CA) submitted S. 580, the Illegal Immigration Control and Enforcement bill. Six weeks later, Senator Edward M. Kennedy (D-MA) offered yet another comprehensive immigration reform bill (S. 754), which included measures to prevent "illegal" immigration and reduce employment opportunities for undocumented workers who were already present in the United States.

Simpson, who had taken over the position as chair of the Senate Subcommittee on Immigration, soon started to build bi-partisan alliances, and Senators Kennedy, Feinstein, and Simpson agreed to combine their bills. When the Subcommittee on Immigration voted on this combined bill, which was still called

S. 269, only Paul Simon (D-IL) and Kennedy voiced their opposition.

In June 1995, the U.S. Commission on Immigration Reform sent their second interim report, *Legal Immigration: Setting Priorities,* to Congress. According to the commission, the allocation of immigrant visas needed to reflect the demands of the U.S. labor market and make sure that newly arrived immigrants would be self-supporting. In the end, the report recommended a significant reduction of legal immigration levels, a reallocation of visas away from unskilled laborers and distant family members to skilled workers and the nuclear family, and an increased emphasis on the "effective Americanization of new immigrants, that is the cultivation of a shared commitment to the American values of liberty, democracy, and equal opportunity." On June 22, 1995, only days after the Jordan Commission's report was released, Representative Lamar Smith took up their recommendations on legal immigration reform and sponsored H.R. 1915 (Immigration in the National Interest bill). The first version of this bill cut the number of immigrants to about 200,000 a year, eliminated several family reunification categories (e.g., brothers and sisters of U.S. citizens) and introduced an income requirement for U.S. citizens and legal permanent residents who wished to sponsor a family member. Initially, this income requirement was set at 200 percent of the federal poverty line. In addition to these legal immigration reform proposals, Smith's bill also contained an assortment of provisions that would have affected refugees, asylum seekers, and undocumented immigrants. According to Smith, legal and "illegal" immigration were inextricably linked and could not be looked at separately. Throughout the debate, he strongly advocated reform proposals that tackled both issues in tandem.

Senator Simpson championed this comprehensive approach. When he suggested merging the Senate versions of the legal (S. 1394) and "illegal" immigration reform bills (S. 269) on November 3, 1995, he proclaimed that "curbing or even stopping illegal immigration is not enough. . . . The American people are increasingly troubled about the impact legal immigration is having on their country. Poll after poll shows us this. The people have made it so very clear they believe the level of immigration is too high." The new omnibus proposal (S. 1394) represented one of the harshest anti-immigration legislations in decades. Compared to the House version, however, Simpson's bill was slightly more generous. S. 1394 wanted to lower the annual level of non-refugee admissions from 675,000 to 540,000, reduce employment-based immigration, eliminate several family reunification categories, and establish income requirements for sponsors (at least 125 percent of the poverty line). On November 28, 1995, the Senate Immigration Subcommittee agreed to move S. 1394 out of the subcommittee.

Shortly afterward, various individuals and organizations started to question the logic behind these comprehensive reform proposals that combined legal and illegal immigration reform. Representatives of the American Immigration Lawyers Association (AILA), who served as expert witnesses in multiple committee hearings, voiced their concern that these bills seemed to conflate "legal" and "illegal" immigration. In addition, high-tech business executives lobbied Congress to remove the provisions concerning skilled workers. According to this influential business coalition, U.S. companies were dependent on their ability to recruit qualified foreigners if they wanted to survive in a highly competitive international market. In an attempt to strengthen their claims even further, these lobbyists formed an alliance with various minority and immigrant rights groups, who had long since criticized the claim that legal immigrants were just as much of a problem as undocumented workers.

In the end, this unlikely alliance proved successful. On March 14, 1996, Senator Spencer Abraham (R-MI) proposed an amendment to split S. 1394 into two different bills: a legal and an "illegal" immigration reform bill. After little debate, the Senate Judiciary Committee decided to split the bill. In the meantime, the House had decided to adopt the Chrysler-Berman-Brownback Amendment, which sought to eliminate the cuts in legal immigration. However, these successes came at a high price. While politicians from both parties had responded positively to the idea that legal immigrants were commendable

human beings who contributed to U.S. society in multiple ways, they were far less willing to acknowledge that undocumented workers deserved any kind of protection. Quite the contrary, the discourse about undocumented immigrants became increasingly hostile.

Much of the debate also focused on undocumented immigrants' use of public services. While most politicians agreed with the idea that undocumented immigrants should be ineligible for almost all forms of public support, there was much debate over the role that public education should play in this context. When Elton Gallegly originally proposed a Proposition 187–type amendment that allowed states to deny undocumented immigrants access to public schools, he was joined by most of his colleagues. Even though the Gallegly Amendment caused an emotional and divisive debate, the Amendment was passed (257–163) and integrated into the House version of the bill (H.R. 2202). On March 21, 1996, the House passed H.R. 2202 by a wide margin (333–87).

A few weeks later, the Senate began their debate on two separate bills. On April 10, 1996, Senator Orrin Hatch (R-UT) introduced S. 1664, the Illegal Immigration bill of 1996, and S. 1665, the Legal Immigration bill of 1996. Yet several senators were still dissatisfied with the decision to discuss these issues separately. Knowing that it would be much more difficult, if not impossible, to pass an immigration reform bill that solely focused on legal immigrants, Senator Simpson made several unsuccessful attempts to integrate legal immigration provisions back into S. 1664.

After much debate, the Senate invoked cloture and passed the bill almost unanimously. Only Senators Russ Feingold (D-WI), Bob Graham (D-FL), and Paul Simon cast no votes. Interestingly, there were a number of stipulations for legal immigrants that remained in both the Senate and the House bills. Both S. 1664 and H.R. 2202 contained provisions that made the affidavit of support, which had to be signed by U.S. citizens and legal permanent residents who wanted to sponsor a family member, legally enforceable. In addition, both versions of the "illegal" immigration bills established income requirements for potential sponsors and stipulated that a certain percentage of the sponsor's income should be "deemed" available to the immigrant if he or she applied for public services. Despite the rhetoric about splitting the bills and examining both issues separately, the 104th Congress had eventually come to the realization that the political climate would have made it impossible to pass a comprehensive legal immigration reform to reduce the numbers and change the priority categories. However, the affidavit of support and the deeming requirements had become entwined into a larger debate about welfare reform, personal responsibility, and self-sufficiency. As prime examples of cost-saving reform measures, these provisions had been endorsed by representatives from both parties as well as by minority and immigrant rights organizations. To ensure their ratification, these two issues were thus taken out of a controversial legal immigration reform bill and rejoined with the much more popular "illegal" immigration bill.

Following the passage of "illegal" immigration reform bills in the Senate and the House, a conference committee faced the daunting task of combining the two bills and reconciling the differences between them. While previous Congresses had always relied on bipartisan committees, the Republican majority decided to exclude Democrats from the decision-making process in 1996—a decision that would cause a lot of controversy in the end. Yet even the Republican committee members had a difficult time building a consensus among themselves. In particular, the conference committee struggled to reconcile three major differences between the House and Senate versions: First, S. 1664 expected future sponsors to prove that their annual income was at least 125 percent of the federal poverty line, whereas H.R. 2202 set the income requirement at 200 percent. Second, there was much disagreement about which types of public services should be included under the "deeming requirement." Whereas the House version made educational programs and student loans available to all recent immigrants regardless of their sponsor's income, the Senate version merely exempted current recipients from the deeming requirement, while applying it to future applicants for higher-education loans and grants. Third, the House version still contained the Gallegly Amendment, which gave states the option to deny undocumented immigrants the right to receive a public education.

In late July, the conference committee finally reached a compromise. After lengthy debates, they included the Gallegly Amendment in the bill. Knowing that this decision would be highly controversial among their colleagues, they added a provision that exempted all children who were already enrolled in public schools across the nation. However, this specification satisfied neither their Democratic colleagues, who were already irritated by the Republicans' decision to exclude them from the conference committee, nor President Clinton, who threatened to veto the bill if Congress included any version of the Gallegly Amendment. With the legislative period coming to an end, the Republican conference committee felt that they needed to make quick decisions. After all, they did not want to be blamed for jeopardizing a widely popular bill weeks before an important election. As a result, the conference committee eventually removed the Gallegly Amendment and presented their report to the House, which ratified the bill on September 25, 1996.

To the dismay of the conference committee, President Bill Clinton made a few additional requests. In addition to several relatively minor technical amendments, Clinton disagreed with the idea that employers could face discrimination charges only if the wronged person could provide proof that the employer had intended to discriminate against them. He also insisted that the deeming provisions and sponsor income requirements should be deleted from the bill. A furious Speaker Gingrich grudgingly lowered the income requirement to 125 percent of the federal poverty line and deleted the new public charge provision, which would have made immigrants subject to deportation if they received more than 12 months of public benefits during their first five years in the United States. However, Congress was unwilling to change the rules for discriminatory employment-practices lawsuits and to strike the popular deeming requirements from the bill. President Clinton accepted this as a valid compromise and included the immigration bill, which had passed the House on September 28, 1996, in the "Omnibus Consolidated Appropriations Act" (P.L. 104-208).

Compared to the original bills, the final version of the Illegal Immigration Reform and Immigrant Responsibility Act of 1996 (IIRIRA) was slightly more generous. As previously mentioned, the IIRIRA had lowered the income requirements for sponsors to 125 percent of the federal poverty line, protected legal immigrants from deportation as public charges, and restored undocumented immigrants' access to emergency medical care and public schools. However, the IIRIRA still contained a number of provisions that severely restricted the rights and protections of documented as well as undocumented immigrants. In particular, the IIRIRA changed the definition of an "aggravated felony" for immigrant offenders and made even those immigrants who had committed nonviolent crimes and crimes for which no sentence was served subject to deportation. In addition, the IIRIRA limited the opportunities for judicial review by inserting 3- and 10-year bars of entry for persons who had been unlawfully present in the United States for more than 180 days or one year, respectively; and it barred for life persons who misrepresented a material fact on a visa application. With regard to legal immigrants, the IIRIRA limited access to public benefits and turned the affidavit of support between sponsor and immigrants into a legally binding contract.

The Personal Responsibility and Work Opportunity Reconciliation Act of 1996

Parallel to the lengthy debate about immigration reform, the 104th Congress also deliberated a major welfare reform act. The Personal Responsibility and Work Opportunity Reconciliation Act of 1996 (PRWORA) was signed into law on August 22, 1996 (P.L. 104-193), a few weeks before President Clinton approved the immigration reform act. Taken together, these two acts represent a two-pronged attempt to limit immigrants' access to certain welfare programs.

Even though the act was not primarily focused on the special status of noncitizens, immigrants' welfare eligibility was central to this reform package. While some representatives preferred a solution that would simply eliminate immigrants' welfare eligibility, the

majority supported compromise measures that distinguished between citizens and immigrants, without banning immigrants completely from all welfare programs. Throughout the 104th Congress, the reform proposals affecting immigrants' welfare eligibility not only grew more complex but they also created a careful balance between these conflicting views. Compared to the final version of the bill, early reform proposals appear overly broad and unsympathetic to the effects blanket provisions would have had on an increasingly diverse immigrant population.

On January 4, 1995, Representative Steven C. LaTourette (R-OH) and 119 Republican co-sponsors had introduced the Family Self-Sufficiency bill of 1995 (H.R. 4), the first comprehensive welfare reform act in the 104th Congress. The original version of this act consisted of seven separate titles, one of which was entitled "Restricting Welfare for Aliens." Section 401(a) determined that no future immigrants, with the exception of refugees and, after five years, legal permanent residents who were older than 75 years of age, "shall be eligible for any program referred to in subsection (d)." Said subsection lists a total of 52 programs, ranging from emergency food and shelter grants to immunization programs and a wide variety of higher-education benefits. The only federally funded program for which all immigrants remained eligible was emergency medical care.

In August and September 1995, the Senate held their general debate on the Family Self-Sufficiency bill. During this debate, the Senate approved special provisions for victims of domestic abuse, restored eligibility for educational programs, and unanimously adopted the Boxer Amendment (No. 2529), which made sure that the immigrant-specific restrictions did not apply to foster care or adoption-assistance programs. In contrast, all of the more radical amendments, which would have either restored eligibility to large parts of the immigrant population or amended the list of programs to cash- and cash-like programs, were rejected by wide margins.

By January 1996, the conference committee had devised seven different versions of the Family Self-Sufficiency bill of 1995, each of which contained significant changes with regard to immigrants' welfare eligibility. Gradually, a straightforward two-section title had grown into a compromise that distinguished between different classes of immigrants and benefits and introduced additional requirements for immigrants' sponsors. The final version of the act was based on the following two imperatives: "It continues to be the immigration policy of the United States that (A) aliens within the nation's borders not depend on public resources to meet their needs, but rather rely on their own capabilities and the resources of their families, their sponsors, and private organizations, and (B) the availability of public benefits shall not constitute an incentive for immigration to the United States" (Section 400, H.R. 4, January 3, 1996). Accordingly, H.R. 4 declared all future immigrants—with the exception of veterans and soldiers on active duty—to be subject to sponsor deeming. During the first five years, the income and resources of the person who had signed an affidavit of support should be deemed available to the immigrant and taken into consideration when determining their eligibility for certain means-tested benefits. Significantly, the deeming provision no longer applied to emergency medical services; short-term non-cash emergency disaster relief; immunization programs; public health assistance for communicable diseases; all benefits under the "National School Lunch" bill and the "Child Nutrition" bill; programs of student assistance under Titles IV, V, IX, and X of the Higher Education Act of 1965; as well as local programs, such as soup kitchens, crisis counseling and intervention services, and short-term shelters. After a period of five years, immigrants would gain access to the entire list of public benefits, including the four major programs (TANF [Temporary Assistance for Needy Families], SSI [Supplementary Security Income], Medicaid, and food stamps).

Yet, shortly after both the House and the Senate agreed to this conference report, President Clinton vetoed the bill. On June 27, 1996, Representative John R. Kasich (R-OH) introduced H.R. 4's successor—the Personal Responsibility and Work Opportunity Reconciliation bill of 1996 (H.R. 3734). With regard to immigrants' welfare eligibility, the first version of this act was remarkably similar to its predecessor. After stressing the fact that everyone—including undocumented immigrants—remained eligible for emergency medical services, immunization programs, and public health assistance for testing and treatment of serious communicable diseases, H.R. 3734 established that newly arrived immigrants would be ineligible for most other federal benefits for a minimum of five years. In addition, H.R. 3734 reiterated the sponsor-deeming provisions that were already part of the final version of H.R. 4.

In the end, President Clinton signed the bill, which became Public Law 104-193, on August 21, 1996. The immigrant-specific regulations can be found in Title IV ("Restricting Welfare and Public Benefits for Aliens"). Most importantly, the final version of the bill declared new immigrants, who had not yet contributed to the system, ineligible for the major federal welfare programs but restored eligibility to pre-enactment immigrants and made exemptions for some of the aforementioned programs. In addition, the PRWORA also shifted responsibility toward state governments. Within certain limitations, states were now able to decide which groups of immigrants were particularly worthy of public support. At the same time, the PRWORA limited the overall availability of federal funds and earmarked these funds for specific groups and programs. In particular, states were allowed to attribute federal funds only to programs that provided TANF and Medicaid to immigrants who had arrived before August 22, 1996. If they wanted to provide the same services to post-enactment immigrants, the money would have to come out of the state budget. As a whole, the PRWORA ended an era of increasingly generous welfare benefits that had made no distinction between U.S. citizens and legal permanent residents.

The Antiterrorism and Effective Death Penalty Act of 1996

When Islamic terrorists planted a car bomb in the underground parking garage of the World Trade Center on February 26, 1993, they sent a shockwave through the United States. The bomb, which was meant to destroy the foundation of the north tower and trigger the collapse of both buildings, failed to achieve its proclaimed goal. The massive detonation killed six people, injured over 1,000, destroyed several electrical power lines, and cut off telephone service for much of lower Manhattan. Most importantly, the attack reminded U.S. citizens that terrorism was a reality and that the United States was not immune from terrorist attacks. Almost two years after the bombing, President Clinton introduced comprehensive antiterrorism legislation—the Omnibus Counterterrorism bill (S. 390). Yet at that point, Congress was no longer convinced that there was an imminent terrorist threat that warranted an immediate response. President Clinton's bill was thus quickly put on the back burner. Two months later, this general apathy came to a sudden end when Timothy McVeigh, a 26-year-old Gulf War veteran, loaded a rented Ryder truck with homemade explosives, drove up to the Alfred P. Murrah Federal Building in Oklahoma City, ignited a timed fuse and walked away. One hundred and sixty-seven persons were killed in the explosion.

Immediately after the attack, the media broadcasted interviews with people who had reportedly seen several Middle Eastern–looking suspects. Within a few hours, however, McVeigh was arrested for driving without a license plate and, while in jail, he confessed to the attack in Oklahoma City. McVeigh was soon put on trial, where a jury imposed the death penalty. Up until his death on June 11, 2001, McVeigh maintained that he had acted alone. The American public, however, had a very hard time believing that a young, white man with no criminal history could have committed such an atrocious act. Instead, investigators maintained that McVeigh must have had ties to Islamic terrorists. Some people even contended that McVeigh was linked directly to Ramzi Yousef, a member of Abu Sayaf, who had planned the 1993 bombing of the World Trade Center. Despite lengthy investigations, no one ever found sufficient evidence to connect McVeigh to a militant Islamic organization.

President Clinton and Senate Majority Leader Bob Dole shake hands as terrorism victims embrace after Clinton signs the Anti-Terrorism Bill into law at a White House ceremony on April 24, 1996. (AP Photo/Doug Mills)

Ironically, the acts of this white, native-born U.S. citizen were used to justify the passage of a comprehensive antiterrorism law that would have had little effect on terrorists like McVeigh. Instead, the Antiterrorism and Effective Death Penalty Act (AEDPA) was directed against all foreign-born criminals, not just terrorists. Knowing that Americans' desire for public safety and security represented a powerful argument, politicians were eager to portray the AEDPA as a direct reaction to the Oklahoma City bombing. Only eight days after the attack, on April 27, 1995, Senator Orrin Hatch and Senator Bob Dole (R-KS) introduced a bipartisan "bill to prevent and punish acts of terrorism," as the synopsis phrases it. This bill, the "Antiterrorism and Effective Death Penalty" bill (S. 735), was passed by the Senate after only four days of debates. In the House, Representative Henry J. Hyde's (R-IL) version of the antiterrorism bill (H.R. 1710) caused slightly more controversy. On the one-year anniversary of the Oklahoma City bombing, Congress passed the final conference report on both bills. A few days later, on April 24, 1996, President Clinton solemnly proclaimed that the AEDPA "stands as a tribute to the victims of terrorism and to the men and women in law enforcement who dedicate their lives to protecting all of us from the scourge of terrorist activity." At the same time, President Clinton was also acutely aware of the fact that "this bill also makes a number of major, ill-advised changes in our immigration laws having nothing to do with fighting terrorism." In an effort to ensure maximum national security, President Clinton eventually signed a law that sacrificed noncitizens' individual liberties and freedoms all too quickly.

Title IV of the Antiterrorism and Effective Death Penalty Act (AEDPA; P.L. 104-132), in particular, has had a direct effect on the legal rights and responsibilities of all legal permanent residents and future immigrants. The official purpose of this title can be summarized as follows: Title IV amends the mechanism to bar members of terrorist organizations and enables the U.S. government to devise a list of organizations with terrorist intentions, facilitates the removal procedures for alien terrorists who are already present in the United States, modifies the asylum procedures to ensure that terrorists cannot get political asylum, and expands the list of deportable

offenses. Taken together, these new procedures established a system that was supposed to protect U.S. citizens from dangerous terrorists and other criminal aliens. As such, these procedures were fairly uncontroversial. Yet these protective measures came at a high price for the entire immigrant community.

If we look at the same title from a defendant's perspective, the law's effect could be more accurately described like this: Title IV creates special removal procedures that allow the court to introduce "secret" evidence that had been obtained illegally, and it eliminates federal court review of these decisions by denying noncitizens access to habeas corpus examination. Throughout the debate, several politicians were highly critical of these strict limitations. In their opinion, these procedures were not just unethical, but they also stood in clear violation of a defendant's fundamental right to due process. Even after weighing the inherent dangers against the potential benefits, these representatives were unwilling to sacrifice fundamental individual liberties that had represented a cornerstone of the American legal system for generations. Jerrold Nadler (D-NY), for example, repeatedly stressed that "we cannot have a procedure for deporting aliens who are allegedly terrorists where they have no opportunity to cross-examine their accusers, no opportunity to see the evidence against them, no opportunity even to know the specific charges" (U.S. Congress, House, March 13, 1996). His opponents, on the other hand, were convinced that the end justified the means. For them, it was perfectly legitimate to limit a suspected terrorist's constitutional rights in order to protect the American public.

However, while the majority was willing to support these antiterrorist provisions, many politicians were much more reluctant to limit judicial review in cases involving other "criminal aliens." In the end, Congress basically agreed that the introduction of secret or classified evidence and evidence that had been obtained illegally should only be admissible if there was some kind of *national* security risk involved. "Alien criminals" who did not pose a national security risk were granted the right to have counsel and get a public hearing. In addition, their attorneys were granted the right to access all evidence, to introduce additional evidence, and to cross-examine all witnesses. Importantly, though, the AEDPA also mandated the creation of a special removal court. In all cases involving undocumented immigrants or temporary residents, this court's deportation order would be final, and the defendant would not get a chance to seek judicial review. Legal permanent residents were still able to appeal a deportation order to the Board of Immigration.

In addition, the AEDPA also increased the number of deportable offenses. With the passage of the Anti-Drug Abuse Act of 1988, the United States had introduced a new class of crimes: "aggravated felonies." Initially, this category consisted of a small number of crimes that were deemed serious enough to warrant the deportation of a noncitizen after he or she had completed their criminal sentence in a U.S. prison. Outside of immigration law, the term was completely meaningless. Shortly after the introduction of this new class of deportable offenses, the term "aggravated felony" underwent a rapid expansion. With the enactment of the Immigration Act of 1990, Congress added all violent crimes for which a court had imposed a minimum sentence of five years in prison. In 1996, the AEDPA extended this category even further. Section 435 lowered the "term of imprisonment" threshold from five years to one year in prison. As a result, shoplifting, fraud, bribery, and many other nonviolent crimes were turned into deportable offenses. Even more significantly, the AEDPA also ruled that it was no longer important whether the noncitizen had actually served a prison sentence. Instead, the language of the law included all cases in which the defendant had decided to settle, accept a plea bargain, or went on probation—the important factor was that a judge *could* have imposed a sentence of 12 months or more.

This provision, in and of itself, would have led to the deportation of thousands of relatively minor criminals who did not pose a threat to society at large. Yet to make an already over-inclusive provision even more broad, Congress decided that this new definition of aggravated felonies should be applied retroactively and that criminal offenders should no longer be granted discretionary relief (e.g. a "waiver of deportation" or a "suspension of deportation").

Unfortunately, subsequent events have shown that the AEDPA was only the first in a long line of overly invasive laws that, under the pretense of protecting Americans from terrorist attacks, severely limited the fundamental rights of all noncitizens and, increasingly, U.S. citizens as well.

Current Debates

After the rise in anti-immigrant feelings in the mid-1990s, public sentiments slowly started to change at the dawn of the twenty-first century. Low unemployment rates and a positive economic outlook provided an ideal climate for more generous immigration reform measures. In February 2000, the AFL-CIO Executive Council called for an overhaul of immigration policy to protect workers' rights, help reunite families, enforce worker protection laws, and hold those employers accountable who knowingly hire and exploit undocumented immigrant workers. Their resolution from February 16, 2000, also emphasized that "a new amnesty program is needed to provide permanent legal status for undocumented workers and their families, millions of whom have made and continue to make enormous contributions to their communities and workplaces." Congress endorsed the idea to protect immigrant workers and their families, but they were not quite ready for another debate about a potentially large-scale amnesty provision.

In the Senate, Edward Kennedy sponsored the Latino and Immigration Fairness bill (S. 3095), while Representatives Henry Bonilla (R-TX) and Lamar Smith introduced the Legal Immigration Family Equity Act (LIFE Act; H.R. 4942) in the House. Congress ultimately passed the House version of the bill. This legislation expands the use of "K" visas, which used to be restricted to fiancé(e)s of U.S. citizens, to spouses and minor children who have petitions for legal permanent residency pending. It also creates a new "V" visa category that grants employment authorization and protection from removal to spouses and minor children of legal permanent residents who have been waiting more than three years for an immigrant visa. Perhaps most importantly, the LIFE Act also reinstated Section 245(i) of the Immigration and Nationality Act. This section allows undocumented persons who qualify for permanent residency, but are ineligible to adjust status in the

United States because of an immigration status violation, to pay a $1,000 penalty to continue processing in the United States. On October 3, 2000, Congress also passed the American Competitiveness in the Twenty-first Century Act of 2000 (S. 2045), which added an additional 297,500 H-1B visas over the next three years; but senators eventually rejected the proposed measure to increase the number of H-2A visas for agricultural workers.

During his first presidential campaign, George W. Bush had made a clear commitment to further improve trade relations with Mexico, in particular, and develop a temporary worker program that would enable much-needed migrant laborers to enter the United States through legal channels. Shortly after he took office, President Bush began talks with newly elected Mexican president Vicente Fox, who had run on a decisive pro-migration platform and promised voters to protect the interests of Mexican workers abroad and prevent further deaths of illegal border crossers. This initial meeting in Guanajuato, Mexico, was not only of symbolic importance—it was Bush's first foreign visit—but it also led to the formation of the high-level Mexico-U.S. Migration Working Group, which was chaired by U.S. Attorney General John Ashcroft, U.S. Secretary of State Colin Powell, Mexico's Foreign Minister Jorge Castaneda, and Mexico's Interior Secretary Santiago Creel.

During their second meeting in September 2001, which took place in Washington D.C., Fox and Bush instructed the working group "to reach mutually satisfactory results on border safety, a temporary worker program and the status of undocumented Mexicans in the United States." At the time, the working group was in the process of exploring a variety of options, including a temporary "guestworker" program, a legalization program with a path to U.S. citizenship, or a possible combination of both. President Bush, however, maintained that he was vehemently opposed to a "blanket amnesty" but open to a limited legalization program—without specifying either one. He also continued to support plans for a new temporary worker program.

The terrorist attacks of September 11, 2001, put an abrupt end to the movement toward more generous immigration laws and instead turned immigration into a homeland security issue. As an immediate response to the attacks, Congress passed three highly restrictive laws that would significantly diminish the legal rights of current and future immigrants. The USA PATRIOT Act (PL 107-56; Uniting and Strengthening America by Providing Appropriate Tools Required to Intercept and Obstruct Terrorism Act), which was passed by a wide margin in both houses of Congress and signed into law on October 26, 2001, enabled law enforcement agencies to access personal information (including e-mail and phone conversations and financial records) of terrorism suspects and gave them more leeway in detaining, investigating, and deporting noncitizens suspected of terrorist activity. In addition, the PATRIOT Act broadened the definition of "terrorist" and "terrorist activity." On March 14, 2002, President Bush signed the Enhanced Border Security and Visa Entry Reform Act of 2002 (PL 107-113) into law. This act required the INS, which had been widely criticized for their inability to identify and deport those terrorists who were in the U.S. illegally, to develop a database that would allow federal law enforcement and intelligence agencies to share data with the INS and the State Department. On November 22, 2002, the Homeland Security Act (PL 107-296) finally disbanded the INS and created the Department of Homeland Security.

Ten months after the USA PATRIOT Act was passed, Attorney General John Ashcroft and the Department of Justice initiated the National Security Entry and Exit Registration System (NSEERS), which required citizens of 25 predominantly Muslim countries to go through a special registration process. Under special registration, new arrivals who were male, between the ages of 16 and 45, and citizens of one of these 25 countries had to register at a specially determined port of entry. Immigrants and visitors who were already present in the United States had to appear at a domestic registration center to be fingerprinted, photographed, interrogated, and, in many cases, detained. In a press release from December 3, 2003, the DHS reported that as of September 30, 2003, they had collected information on 93,741 persons at the Port of Entries and 83,519 individuals at the former INS offices. Of all these, 13,799 were placed in deportation proceedings due to a variety of immigration violations. Not a single one of these

177,260 boys and men were charged with terrorist activities.

While the government eventually suspended the special registration measure in December 2003, they maintained that they might decide to reinterview certain individuals at a later date. On June 28, 2005, Senators Richard Durbin (D-IL), Edward Kennedy, and Russ Feingold wrote a letter to the new secretary of the U.S. Department of Homeland Security, Michael Chertoff, stating their belief "that Special Registration was ill-conceived, badly executed, and ultimately counterproductive." Further, they urged Chertoff "to terminate the Special Registration program in its entirety and to take steps to remedy the damage it did." So far, the courts have upheld the program and ruled that the U.S. Justice Department had the authority to enforce NSEERS.

In addition to these terrorism and homeland security-related concerns, the declining economy had also diminished hopes for a liberal immigration reform and a significant increase in available green cards (conferring legal permanent residence). With the start of the 108th Congress, however, Republicans and Democrats once again started to discuss significant immigration legislation. The first in a long line of bills was the Agricultural Job Opportunity, Benefits, and Security bill of 2003 (S. 1645). This bipartisan bill proposed a business-friendly reform of the H-2A visa program for agricultural workers and an earned legalization program. On July 31, 2003, Senators Hatch and Durbin reintroduced the Development, Relief, and Education for Alien Minors (DREAM) bill (S. 1545), which was originally discussed in 2001 as H.R. 1918 and S. 1291, but quickly shelved after September 11, 2001. The DREAM bill wanted to make undocumented immigrant students eligible for in-state tuition and provide a path to legalization for immigrants who had entered the United States before the age of 16, had resided in the United States for a minimum of five years, and were of "good moral character." Even though both acts seemed to have bipartisan support in the beginning, they were soon criticized from both ends of the political spectrum, and discussion stalled.

On January 7, 2004, President George W. Bush thus asked Congress to join forces in an effort to pass a comprehensive immigration reform bill that would simultaneously protect our borders, American workers, American businesses, and legal immigrants. In his press release on "Fair and Secure Immigration Reform," Bush stated that he "does not support amnesty because individuals who violate America's laws should not be rewarded for illegal behavior and because amnesty perpetuates illegal immigration." Instead, he proposed a temporary worker program that would be open to prospective workers who were still abroad as well as to undocumented immigrants who were already present in the United States. He argued that these individuals should eventually be eligible for legalization as well as citizenship. His rhetoric was immediately dismissed by immigration opponents, who claimed that this was yet another amnesty provision, while pro-immigration activists criticized the idea that undocumented immigrants who came forward to apply for a temporary visa would face a significant risk of deportation (e.g., if no more temporary work permits were available). In light of this opposition, President Bush eventually abandoned his plans to introduce a formal immigration reform bill, and the 108th Congress ended without passing any immigration reform legislation.

Bush's second term in office was characterized by more controversy over immigration. This time, however, the debates were not limited to Congress, but millions of pro-immigration activists started to voice their dissatisfaction with restrictive enforcement-only bills. The first bill of the session—the REAL ID Act of 2005—was still relatively uncontroversial and was signed into law on May 11, 2005. The passage of the Border Protection, Antiterrorism, and Illegal Immigration Control bill of 2005 (H.R. 4437), on the other hand, drew a lot of public criticism. H.R. 4437, which was originally introduced by Representative F. James Sensenbrenner (R-WI) on December 6, 2005, contained a number of highly controversial provisions: Not only did the Sensenbrenner bill turn unlawful presence in the United States into a felony and propose a penalty of up to five years in prison for those individuals or organizations who assisted an undocumented immigrant in any way; but it also introduced new expedited removal procedures, mandated a 700-mile-long border fence and increased border patrol, and authorized state and local law enforcement to enforce federal immigration laws. The House passed the bill by a slim margin (239–182) on December 16, with 82 percent of Democrats opposed and 92 percent of Republicans in support of the bill.

The passage of the Sensenbrenner bill served as the catalyst for an unprecedented wave of pro-immigration activism, and a growing coalition of grassroots organizations and well-established immigrant and human rights groups spoke out against the proposal to criminalize and deport millions of undocumented workers. In the spring of 2006, millions of protesters rallied in favor of immigration, with more than 500,000 in Los Angeles alone. As a response to the growing unpopularity of this highly restrictive, enforcement-only approach, Senator Arlen Specter (D-PA) introduced the Comprehensive Immigration Reform bill of 2006 (S. 2611) which opposed mass deportations of undocumented workers and instead called for an orderly legalization process for deserving individuals. In addition, this act would establish a new visa category for "guest workers" (H-2C), increase the cap on H-1B visas from 65,000 to 115,000; and require the United States to build a 600-mile border fence and develop new border security initiatives. State and local law enforcement officers would be prohibited from helping the federal government enforce immigration violations. S. 2611 passed the Senate on May 25, 2006, by a comfortable margin (62–36). Due to the widely differing provisions in the two bills (H.R. 4437 and S. 2611) and the presidential election campaign, neither bill passed the conference committee, and eventually both the 109th and 110th Congresses failed to ratify a comprehensive immigration reform bill. And, in the next half dozen years (2006–2012), no significant federal immigration-related measures were enacted.

For example, a compromise bill was introduced on May 9, 2007, and the bill was debated on nine full days. During this time period, over 300 amendments were filed and 31 were voted on. On June 7, 2007, an initial vote to invoke cloture failed due to the lack of support by Republican senators (46 rejected the cloture motion, 1 abstained). After the second attempt to end debate failed (45–50, 15 votes short of the

required 60), Senate Majority Leader Harry Reid (D-NV) announced that "we are finished with this for the time being." Senator Arlen Specter (D-PA) was slightly more optimistic in his assessment that immigration reform "is on life support, but it is not dead." A few days later, President George W. Bush expressed his continued commitment to immigration reform and promised to lobby Republican senators in an effort to garner more support. In a bipartisan meeting on June 13, 2007, several key senators agreed on a deal to revive immigration legislation. Major aspects of their compromise involved increased funding for worksite enforcement and border security and a new rule that required all undocumented immigrants to return to their home country before they could adjust their status to legal permanent residency. Five days later, on June 18, Senators Kennedy (D-MA) and Specter (R-PA) introduced the new version of the bill as S. 1639—the Unaccompanied Alien Child Protection Act of 2007. After much disagreement and several postponements, the Senate passed a cloture motion on June 26, with 64 senators in support of the bill. On the same day, however, the House Republican Conference passed a resolution introduced by Pete Hoekstra (R-MI) that expressed opposition to the Senate immigration bill. On June 28, S. 1639 finally failed by a vote of 53–46, with 37 Republicans, 15 Democrats, and 1 independent voting against the cloture motion. After this second defeat, Congress agreed to postpone further discussion until after the presidential elections in 2008.

Soon after President Barack Obama took office, Congress once again started to discuss a variety of immigration reform bills, most of them focusing on a specific issue or group of immigrants. On February 12, 2009, for example, Representative Jerrold Nadler (D-NY) and Senator Patrick Leahy (D-VT) introduced the Uniting American Families Act (H.R. 1024 and S. 424), which opened up the family reunification category to permanent partners of U.S. citizens and legal permanent residents, thus ending the discrimination of gay and lesbian couples under immigration law. In addition, both houses of Congress addressed a new version of the DREAM Act (S. 729 and H.R. 1751) and legislation to make an electronic work authorization verification system mandatory for employers (S. 1196 and H.R. 1196). During the 112th Congress, Senator Robert Menendez (D-NJ) also introduced a comprehensive immigration reform bill (S. 1251) that contained both the DREAM Act and AgJOBS, which would provide agricultural employers with a legal labor force by revising the H-2A program and allowing undocumented farm workers to legalize their status.

In May 2011, President Obama reiterated his commitment to fixing our "broken" immigration system. In his blueprint for immigration reform, "Building a 21st Century Immigration System," the president urged Congress to develop an "immigration system that meets our economic and national security imperatives and that upholds America's proud tradition as a nation of laws and a nation of immigrants." The report emphasized the need to secure our borders, strengthen our economic competitiveness by fixing our legal immigration system, and hold illegal immigrants and their employers accountable when they break the law. Yet even though immigration reform continued to be a major concern, in the midst of a recession and historically high levels of unemployment, the 112th Congress did not even come close to agreeing on a path of action and passing a comprehensive immigration reform act.

Bibliography

Barkan, Elliott R., Hasia Diner, and Alan M. Kraut, eds. 2007. *From Arrival to Incorporation: Migrants to the U.S. in a Global Era*. New York: New York University Press.

Beasley, Vanessa B. 2006. *Who Belongs in America? Presidents, Rhetoric, and Immigration*. College Station: Texas A&M University Press.

Gimpel, James G., and James R. Edwards Jr. 1999. *The Congressional Politics of Immigration Reform*. Boston: Allyn and Bacon.

Hing, Bill Ong. 2003. *Defining America through Immigration Policy*. Philadelphia: Temple University Press.

Jacobson, Robin Dale. 2008. *The New Nativism: Proposition 187 and the Debate over Immigration*. Minneapolis: University of Minnesota Press.

Newton, Lina. 2008. *Illegal, Alien, or Immigrant: The Politics of Immigration Reform*. New York: New York University Press.

Perea, Juan F., ed. 1997. *Immigrants Out! The New Nativism and the Anti-Immigrant Impulse in the United States*. New York: New York University Press.

Romero, Victor C. 2004. *Alienated: Immigrant Rights, the Constitution, and Equality in America*. New York: New York University Press.

Tichenor, Daniel J. 2002. *Dividing Lines: The Politics of Immigration Control in America*. Princeton, NJ: Princeton University Press.

Wroe, Andrew. 2008. *The Republican Party and Immigration Politics: From Proposition 187 to George W. Bush*. New York: Palgrave Macmillan.

Refugees, Asylees, and Immigrants

Carl Bon Tempo

Many Americans believe that their nation historically has served as a place of refuge for those fleeing persecution and intolerable circumstances. To begin to understand this powerful and central aspect of American identity, one need only read the inscription on the Statue of Liberty—Emma Lazarus's "The New Colossus," Or read the words of George Washington: "The bosom of America is open to receive . . . the oppressed and persecuted of all nations and religions" (quoted in Daniels 2004, 7). Or Franklin D. Roosevelt: "For centuries this country has always been the traditional haven of refuge for countless victims of religious and political persecution" (quoted in Daniels 2004, 77). Or Ronald Reagan: "America's tradition . . . of welcoming and resettling those who flee oppression" (quoted in Woolley and Peters, The American Presidency Project). But does this deeply cherished memory accurately reflect the United States' history with refugees?

This chapter will illustrate how the American experience with refugees has been much more complex than national lore suggests. Part of this complicated history originates in the changing size and scope of the global refugee problem, which evolved through the twentieth century as nationalism reshaped the very idea of nationhood; as wars reshaped state boundaries; and as observers inside and outside of governments became more expert at identifying and counting refugees, especially outside of Europe. In 1965, a leading refugee organization alarmingly warned that the world's refugee population had grown to 7.9 million persons. Yet, between 1998 and 2006, the global refugee and asylee population reached a high of 14.9 million (in 2001) and never dipped below 11.5 million (in 2004). The figures attest to the lasting and growing problem of refugees.

While the United States has not welcomed each and every refugee seeking admission—nor has it sent considerable aid to every refugee camp overseas—it has played a role in alleviating global refugee problems. Moreover, the size and generosity of the American commitment to refugees has varied over time, depending upon a multitude of factors: partisan politics, economic conditions, cultural and social biases, foreign policy concerns, war, and immigration issues. In this sense, the United States' efforts to aid (or not aid) refugees are very much a part of larger historical currents and events.

Before exploring this history, two larger issues require attention. Most important, what is a "refugee," and how is a refugee different from an immigrant? Colloquially, an immigrant is a person who chooses to leave his or her homeland, while a refugee is a person who is forced to leave the homeland for fear of persecution and cannot return without endangering himself or herself. Such a distinction, however, only goes so far. In the American historical context, refugees typically have fled political persecution, though the nature of that persecution—its ideological sources, relationship to geopolitics, and the exact definition of persecutory acts—has evolved over time and in response to circumstances. Moreover, the distinction between refugee and immigrant raises the question of the relationship between U.S. policies toward these two groups of newcomers. In general, immigration affairs have greatly influenced, but not predetermined, American commitment to refugees. Refugees, like immigrants, were newcomers to the United States and thus subject to many of the same restrictionist, xenophobic, and nativist sentiments that greeted immigrants. But, because refugees were not traditional immigrants, at least in relation to the general definitions offered above, they were not always treated or greeted the same as immigrants.

The second issue is the type of aid that the United States has provided to refugees. In general, the United States has offered two kinds of help. One type, quite simply, involved admitting and resettling refugees in the United States. While straightforward in the abstract, the execution of refugee admissions and resettlement proved quite challenging because of immigration politics, the ramifications for foreign policy, and the difficult administrative tasks of admission and resettlement. The second type of aid centered on providing relief supplies and materials to refugees in their current place of residence. These two types of aid were not mutually exclusive, and often the United States pursued both in dealing with a refugee crisis. Moreover, both types of aid required, to varying degrees, that the United States work with other nations and international organizations, though American partnerships with other nations and international institutions were much more pronounced and extensive regarding the delivery of aid.

Refugees and the United States, 1776–1900

The arrival of refugees in the United States from the founding to the end of the nineteenth century occurred against the peculiar backdrop of the nation's policies toward newcomers in general. Through the nineteenth century, immigration grew slowly and steadily. In the 1820s, about 150,000 immigrants entered; but during the last 50 years of the century, no fewer than 2.3 million entered in any decade. Until the 1890s, Germany, Ireland, and the United Kingdom regularly sent the most immigrants to the United States. By the 1890s, more immigrants were arriving from southern and eastern Europe than from northwestern Europe, a trend that continued into the new century.

During these decades, the United States generally held an "open door" for immigrants, in part because of labor needs in an expanding economy, and in part because of electoral benefits to politicians courting ethnic constituencies. Just as important, immigrants were eager to come to the United States, especially because of the availability of land. The open door

did not preclude attempts to "construct a nation by design," and these efforts accelerated in the latter part of the century (Zolberg 2006, 1). For instance, the Chinese Exclusion Act of 1882 severely restricted the arrival of Chinese immigrants, while other statutes forbade the entry of certain types of individuals: prostitutes, persons "likely to become a public charge," felons, and persons with communicable diseases.

With immigration laws and regulation underdeveloped for most of the nineteenth century, it should come as little surprise that the federal government—and the state governments before it—had no organized, overarching set of refugee policies or laws. Instead, the U.S. government usually preferred not to adopt a position on the arrival of refugees, which generally had the effect of condoning their entry. State and local governments more actively commented on refugees, mainly by establishing programs of resettlement aid. As a result, refugees tended to enter the United States as part of the larger flow of immigrants rather than as a separate category of newcomers, as they would in the last half of the twentieth century. To be sure, though, the term "refugee" was in use, and it generally referred to persons fleeing political violence and upheaval or escaping religious persecution. And, just as surely, refugees arrived in the United States almost from the nation's founding.

The first substantial group of refugees to come to the United States comprised about 2000 French elites who fled the Revolution in France and settled in East Coast cities. Their arrival immediately became entangled with domestic politics, especially the formation of the first party system in the 1790s. The Federalists, generally suspicious of the French Revolution, worried that these refugees might bring radical revolutionary politics to the United States. Unable to restrict their entry because the Constitution did not allow Congress to halt immigration to the United States until 1807, the Federalists instead decided to toughen naturalization laws. The Federalists' chief opponents, the Democratic-Republicans, were generally supportive of the Revolution but also slightly suspicious of the newcomers, whom they feared might bring their aristocratic pretensions to the United States. As a result, the factions/parties agreed to more stringent naturalization laws in the

1790s, even as their disagreements over the Revolution and its meaning intensified.

Another two groups of refugees soon joined the French. Less important, in the short term, were Irish fleeing after their rebellion against Britain failed in the late 1790s. Their arrival immediately contributed to partisan differences between Federalists and Democratic-Republicans, with the former looking to align U.S. interests with the British, while the latter recruited the newcomers into their political camp. In the long term, of course, these Irish refugees were the first of many to come to the United States to escape British rule. The second group of refugees—French fleeing a slave insurrection in St. Dominique—was more important and more numerous. The insurrection began in 1791 and culminated in the establishment of an independent black state in 1804. About 20,000 refugees from Haiti—white French planters (and their slaves) and mulattoes—arrived in the United States, with large numbers settling in New Orleans. White southerners, sympathetic to the plight of their slaveholding brethren, generally welcomed these French planters, though they also worried that the slaves arriving with their masters (as well as the mulattoes) might spread the revolutionary contagion to American blacks. Sympathy with these refugees came not just from the South; the New York state government and the New York City Common Council provided relief funds for poor refugee families from Haiti, while Congress voted to suspend duties on French ships if they carried refugees.

The next notable wave of refugees landed in the United States in the 1840s and 1850s, fleeing the political upheaval unleashed by the Revolutions of 1848. Several thousand Germans and several hundred Hungarians arrived, the former part of a larger wave of nearly 1.4 million German immigrants who arrived between 1841 and 1860. As in the 1790s, the U.S. government maintained a neutral stance toward events in Europe that essentially allowed for refugee entry. The newcomers, though, did roil American politics. The famed Hungarian revolutionary Louis Kossuth undertook a national tour, creating a great stir but little in the way of concrete support for his cause. Likewise, the arrival of refugees from the 1848 Revolutions surely helped feed the anti-immigrant

backlash best represented by the Know-Nothing movement. But, in the rise of antebellum nativism, German refugees were a secondary factor, as compared to immigration more generally.

Immigration to the United States shifted decisively in the late nineteenth century in terms of both total numbers and origins. Among these newcomers were Jews from Eastern Europe, specifically Russia, Poland, Hungary, and Romania, who came in search of economic opportunity and to escape persecution that escalated in the years after 1880. In Russia, for instance, the government responded to the assassination of Tsar Alexander II in 1881 with a series of pogroms and anti-Jewish statutes. Because neither the immigration authorities nor census officials catalogued a person's religion, it is difficult to discern exactly how many East European Jews came to the United States. One estimate holds that the Jewish population in the United States grew from 250,000 in 1880 to nearly four million in 1920 (a figure that of course also includes the children and grandchildren of Jewish immigrants). Nonetheless, any accounting of refugee entry in the late nineteenth century must recognize the arrival of East European Jews.

The United States and Refugees, 1900–1933

Mass immigration reshaped the politics, economics, and culture of the United States in the early twentieth century. It also unleashed a nativist backlash that reformed immigration laws and policies in the 1910s and 1920s. The new national origins quota immigration system that emerged by the end of the 1920s did much to close the open door to the United States that immigrants, with certain exceptions, had enjoyed for most of the nation's history. The new system, though, was consistent with past practice in that it made no special efforts to help refugees or outline a comprehensive refugee policy. The failure to address the admission of refugees should not be surprising, though, when one considers the tone of immigration politics and policies in the 1920s.

During this same period, refugees ironically became a much more significant part of international life. The emergence of refugee "problems" can be traced to larger changes in geopolitics. Most important, the sprawling multiethnic empires of the nineteenth century collapsed. The Russian Empire fell apart in 1917 under the weight of revolution and world war. The Austro-Hungarian Empire disappeared after its defeat in World War I. Finally, the Ottoman Empire, long in decline, entered its death throes in the 1910s and finally dissolved in the early 1920s. In some cases the new states, like Turkey, that emerged in the imperial aftermath were driven by nationalism and a desire for ethno-national homogeneity. In other cases, as with the Soviet Union, political ideology was the core of the new state. Either way, the construction of the nation-state revolved around certain defining principles that necessarily included some of the population and excluded others, sometimes with violence. The results were the same: persons who could not return to their homes for fear of persecution. The two biggest refugee crises occurred in Turkey and the Soviet Union. In the USSR, the ouster of the tsarist government brought on a civil war that was slowly but surely won by Lenin's Bolsheviks. Millions of Russians chose to leave rather than stay. As the Ottoman Empire fell and the new state of Turkey emerged, Armenian Christians found themselves the targets of a campaign of persecution and genocide designed to force their departure (or death). In 1915–1916, an estimated one million Armenians perished and hundreds of thousands—if not more—fled.

The League of Nations took the lead in trying to help these refugees. Most important, the League appointed Dr. Fridtjof Nansen to head resettlement and relief efforts. One of Nansen's most important contributions was the development of the "Nansen passport," essentially a set of documents that identified refugees in the hopes of establishing and protecting some of their legal rights. With the League's work with Armenian and Russian refugees, a definition of the term refugee also came into being in international politics. The definition asserted that refugees lacked the protection of a government and suffered political persecution; League policy makers specified political persecution because they worried that a definition that addressed economic deprivation would be too inclusive. The League and Nansen were fairly effective,

so much so that the League predicted that its refugee work would be over by the end of the 1930s.

The United States worked in very minor ways to solve these refugee problems. The 1917 Immigration Act waived the literacy test for persons fleeing religious persecution. In the aftermath of World War I, the U.S. government appointed Herbert Hoover to head relief efforts to help the victims. Likewise, a few bills that would have admitted Armenian refugees made their way through Congress but none passed. Those bills, though, did define refugees as Armenians who fled their homes in fear of persecution by the Turkish government or people. Overall, American efforts to aid the world's refugees were not extensive for two sets of reasons. First, domestically, the restrictionism of the era meant that refugee admissions bringing newcomers to the United States would not be politically popular or expedient. Second, American policymakers did not view aiding refugees as a central concern of foreign affairs.

The United States, World War II, and Refugees

The United States' role in solving refugee problems began to change during the era of World War II. The war eventually brought on a substantial effort to help refugees, but only after the United States had failed miserably in the face of the European refugee crisis of the 1930s. Just as important, a more open door for refugees, even in the war's aftermath, was never assured, nor did those efforts come about as part of a comprehensive national refugee policy. Rather, the war began a new era in American refugee policies, one marked by ad hoc programs, intense political conflict over refugee policies, and limited admissions that while generous compared to the prewar years, still left hundreds of thousands in refugee camps.

The European refugee crisis unfolded in stages in the 1930s. Almost as soon as Hitler came to power in January 1933, Germans, especially Jews, began fleeing his regime. By the end of 1933, about 50,000 Jewish refugees had fled. Over the next few years, Nazi persecution of Jews increased—the best example being the Nuremburg laws of 1935—so that by the beginning of 1938, a total of 135,000 Jews had

8

emigrated. (Estimates held that another 15,000 non-Jewish Germans had also fled between 1933 and the end of 1937.) The year 1938, though, would prove a turning point. First, the *Anschluss*, or the German invasion of Austria, quickly brought that nation's 180,000 Jews under attack. In the year after the *Anschluss*, about 100,000 Austrian Jews left. This scene repeated itself in the fall of 1938 after the Nazi occupation of the Sudetenland in Czechoslovakia. A pattern had emerged: Jews living in the new territories controlled by the Nazis would be subject to persecution. Second, Jewish persecution intensified in Germany itself under a series of debilitating laws and then with the "Night of the Broken Glass" (*Kristallnacht*), a government-sponsored anti-Jewish pogrom in November. The violence of 1938 led another 140,000 Jews to depart Germany, including—hastily arranged by their parents—some 10,000 Jewish children whose escape, mostly to Britain on the *Kindertransport* (trains from expanding areas of Nazi-threatened Europe). While some Jews fled to Palestine and South America, many moved to other areas of Europe, where they would soon be in danger as the continent fell under the Nazis' control after the war broke out. By the war's beginning, about 200,000 Jews remained in Germany, almost all desperate to escape.

The United States, of course, did not confront the refugee problems of the 1930s alone. The League of Nations engaged in a number of efforts to ensure legal protection of refugees and to coordinate private aid efforts, but it plainly struggled in the face of the growing magnitude of the problem, the German government's recalcitrance, and the League's own institutional weaknesses. In 1938, at President Franklin Roosevelt's behest, a group of over 30 nations met in Evian, Switzerland, and formed the Intergovernmental Committee on Refugees. This organization did its best work before the German invasion of Poland in September 1939 but was hampered by the general reluctance of nations around the world to open their doors to those fleeing the Nazis. Indeed, one of the remarkable aspects of the 1930s European refugee crisis was the solidity of restrictionism around the globe.

In the United States, the political and cultural environment most certainly was not welcoming. The national origins quota immigration system embodied the desire to restrict immigration. The Great Depression only strengthened those sentiments, causing Americans to view newcomers as competitors for jobs in a tight employment market. Finally, of course, a strong and long-standing strain of anti-Semitism meant that a portion of the public would object to any efforts to bring in Jewish refugees. In Congress, conservatives from both parties stood ready to block efforts to admit refugees. They were buttressed by a vocal and influential collection of patriotic groups (the Daughters of the American Revolution) and veterans' organizations (the American Legion).

Of course, a strong pro-refugee bloc existed as well. Those urging aid to refugees were bipartisan, powerful, and potentially well placed: First Lady Eleanor Roosevelt, former President Herbert Hoover, and famed actress Helen Hayes, to name a few. Jewish organizations worked tirelessly to help their coreligionist refugees. They were joined by major labor unions like the CIO, ethnic organizations, Protestant and Catholic church groups, and American liberals; in fact, most of the Democratic New Deal coalition, with the important exception of southern Democrats, supported the admission of refugees. These two competing blocs battled over refugee admissions through the 1930s, with the restrictionists often emerging victorious.

Two paths to refugee admissions existed during the years before the United States entered the war in late 1941. The first path was via special legislation or programs, and the second path was via regular immigration laws. Special legislation was problematic because it required navigating Congress, which often seemed more intent on restricting the entry of newcomers in the 1930s. Indeed, several efforts by northeastern liberals in the 1930s to pass laws providing for refugee admissions failed. The story of the most important effort to craft legislation to bring refugees to the United States illustrates the difficulties. In early 1939, Democratic Senator Robert Wagner and Republican Representative Edith Nourse Rogers introduced identical bills to bring 20,000 German child refugees to the United States. The legislation benefited from a more-than-competent lobbying effort at the hands of a group of refugee advocates called the Non-Sectarian Committee for German Refugee

German-Jewish refugee children salute the American flag, in 1939, in Philadelphia. All entered under immigration quotas, a Philadelphia lawyer paying their way, but no refugee reforms were enacted before 1945, leaving huge numbers of Jews unable to leave Europe and dying in the Holocaust. (AP Photo)

Children. Wagner's and Rogers's legislation, however, never made it out of the Senate or the House. In committee, opponents of the bills—Democrats from the South and Republicans from the West—blasted the proposals as placing the interests of foreigners above Americans, and they did not want to see newcomers enter outside the quota system. The American Legion and other patriotic organizations only added to the attacks. As the legislation lay dying, President Roosevelt decided not to come out in support of the bill, even though the First Lady was a member of the Non-Sectarian Committee.

The other avenue by which refugees from Nazism might come to the United States was regular immigration procedures. The German quota allowed for about 26,000 visas annually, and from 1933 through 1940, two trends were clear. Each year, more visas were issued to Germans. In 1933, 1,919 Germans entered via the quota system. In 1935, 5,201 arrived. In 1937, 10,895 entered. And in 1940, 21,520 arrived—actually a dip in entry from the previous year. The second trend is just as important: each year, the immigration quota went unfilled. State Department consuls were charged with managing visas and immigrant admissions and historians have found that both at the upper levels of the State Department and among certain consular officers, anti-Semitism was rampant. These officials made it very difficult for German Jews to receive visas, often by enforcing each minute regulation in the law, which effectively created "paper walls" that kept refugees out (Wyman 1968). Moreover, by 1940, State Department officials played up fears that saboteurs and secret agents, posing as refugees, might enter via the immigration flow. Here, concerns about American national security in the face of world war served the restrictionist cause.

The number of Germans entering, though, managed to grow through the 1930s for a few reasons. First, not all American consuls were intent on keeping Germans out; some were heroically proactive, entering concentration camps to help prospective immigrants. Second, President Roosevelt pushed the State Department bureaucracy at the end of the 1930s to be more aggressive in admitting largely high-status refugees. Third, the sheer number of applicants trying to win a quota visa grew so that it was much more likely that the total numbers would increase. Nonetheless, one noted scholar of American immigration history declares the total record of the 1930s "dismal" (Daniels 2004, 78).

A special word must be reserved for the role of President Roosevelt. His friends, advisers, and political allies did keep him informed of the German government's persecution of Jews in the 1930s. Moreover, these same people urged FDR to take action and sometimes suggested specific efforts, such as sending a distinguished delegation to the 1936 League of Nations meeting on refugees. Roosevelt sometimes did listen, and sometimes he took action. For instance, in 1938, he set up a personal Advisory Committee on Political Refugees that later oversaw the admission of a few thousand eminent cultural and political figures from Europe. At times, FDR also saw fit to push the State Department to expedite the issuance of visas.

Yet, it also must be said that Roosevelt was head of a government that, by any measure, did not do all it could to try to ensure maximum entry. For all that he pushed the State Department to lower its barriers, he could have pushed harder. Finally, he made little or no effort to shift either congressional or public opinion on the issue; witness his reaction to the 1939 child refugee legislation. Thus, if the record is "dismal," FDR deserves part of the blame.

The United States' entry into the war did bring minor changes to American refugee policies. Roosevelt in June 1944 launched a small program that brought 987—mostly Jewish—refugees from Italy to a resettlement camp in Oswego, New York. Most U.S. efforts for refugees during the war, though, did not admit refugees to the United States but rather sent aid to them in camps around the world. In 1942, the State Department started funneling aid to refugees in North Africa. In 1943, this aid program was essentially transferred to the United Nations Relief and Rehabilitation Administration (UNRRA). In 1944, confronted with irrefutable details about the Nazis' "Final Solution," Roosevelt set up the War Refugee Board, which placed refugees in a variety of camps throughout Europe and North Africa.

World War II's greatest effect in refugee affairs was that the conflict left millions homeless, helpless, and stateless and left whole continents in such ruins that it was a severe challenge just to keep these persons alive. Estimates at the war's conclusion held that the number of displaced persons and refugees reached at least eight million, and perhaps more, in Europe. In the war's aftermath, the United States joined with a whole host of nations in efforts under the direction of UNRRA to relocate these refugees and displaced persons. The war's victims did not always acquiesce easily to these resettlement schemes, some of which saw persons being relocated to areas under Soviet control; but by 1946, about six million had been resettled. The refugee problem in Europe, though, was further compounded by outbreaks of anti-Semitism in Eastern Europe in 1946 and by growing Soviet repression, both of which sent East Europeans streaming west.

President Harry Truman met these challenges in a number of ways. In 1945, shortly after taking office,

he demanded that the State Department work to bring as many refugees to the United States as possible under regular immigration laws. In 1946, he went further, making public his support for a plan to admit European displaced persons to the United States. The usual alliances of immigration politics fought for the next two years over this proposal. Restrictionists claimed that it violated the quota system and would increase unemployment, while some darkly warned that mainly Jews would enter. But, unlike in the 1930s, refugee advocates won the day. Religious groups from all denominations underlined the plan's humanitarianism, while labor unions downplayed economic concerns, an easier task in the relatively prosperous late 1940s. Truman made clear he viewed the admissions as part of the country's World War II crusade against Nazism, whereas the State Department's leadership argued that refugee entry would help stabilize Europe economically and politically in the wake of the war and in the face of a growing Soviet threat. Finally, in 1948, Congress passed the Displaced Persons Act, providing for the entry of 202,000 persons over two years within the quota system, meaning that admissions would be charged against the future quotas from each country of origin.

The actual workings of the DP program, as it came to be called, were nearly as controversial as its origins. The program's supporters pushed for generous revisions to the law, some of which they received. Most importantly, another 200,000 displaced persons were granted entry over an additional two years. But restrictionists, led by Nevada Democratic Senator Patrick McCarran, counterattacked by harassing DP program officials and forcing them to share administration of the program with the more restrictionist-minded visa offices in the State Department. Likewise, while the program did admit European Jews, it also admitted a good number of Germans with ties to the Nazis, some of whom were recruited by American intelligence agencies. Ultimately, though, the DP program admitted about 400,000 Europeans over four years and, as compared to the 1930s, represented a substantial and strengthened commitment to refugees.

The Early Cold War

The development of the Cold War between the United States and the Soviet Union in the late 1940s was the dominant factor in shaping American involvement in refugee problems during the 1950s and, indeed, for the next 40 years. The Soviet Union's policies and the rule of Communist regimes in Eastern Europe annually compelled thousands of refugees to flee to the West, where they found themselves in camps awaiting resettlement. Even more important, politics, culture, and foreign policy in the United States quickly centered on anti-Communism and thwarting the Soviet threat. In the 1950s, all of these factors came to a head in American refugee policies.

In the early 1950s, American officials grew concerned that large refugee populations in Europe, especially in Germany and Italy, might destabilize those countries, producing unrest that would in turn weaken Western Europe in the face of the Communist and Soviet threats. The United States responded with the Refugee Relief Program of 1953 (RRP), which provided for the admission of just over 200,000 refugees over three years. President Dwight Eisenhower, Secretary of State John F. Dulles, and a whole host of church groups and ethnic organizations argued that the program would strengthen American allies and help Communism's victims; in addition, some saw it as a way to subvert the immigration quota laws without a politically costly battle to overturn them. Restrictionists in Congress objected, however. Senator McCarran and the American Legion, among others, complained that any refugee admission would endanger national security because the newcomers might be Communist agents or saboteurs. In the era of McCarthyism, this charge had real power.

After heated debate, the RRP passed Congress in the summer of 1953 but proved tricky in its implementation. Over the RRP's first 18 months, only a trickle of refugees entered the United States. The program, run out of the State Department by an ally of Senator McCarran, required extensive investigations into the backgrounds and political leanings of each potential entrant, grinding arrivals to a halt. It was as if the domestic Red Scare had come to the Refugee Relief Program. Worried that the RRP would utterly

fail, angering ethnic voters and allowing for Democratic counterattacks, Eisenhower and Dulles removed McCarran's ally, and the program picked up speed. By the end of 1956, almost all of the 210,000 visas had been issued to refugees. Ultimately, the RRP was important because it demonstrated the centrality of the Cold War to American refugee policies and the emerging tendency of the United States to privilege admission of refugees from Communism.

As the RRP wound down, another refugee crisis erupted when the Soviet Union crushed the fledgling Hungarian Revolution, sending tens of thousands of Hungarian refugees into Austria in November and December 1956. Eisenhower, who at the same time was dealing with the Suez Crisis in the Middle East, quickly ruled out military support for the Hungarians, fearing it would only escalate the crisis and provoke a broader Soviet military response. Rather, Eisenhower sought to condemn Soviet aggression, to demonstrate American compassion for the Hungarians, and to highlight the supposed failure of Communism. Thus, he ordered that any unused RRP visas go to Hungarians. When that proved insufficient, he authorized the attorney general to "parole" Hungarian refugees into the United States. The parole power, a little-used aspect of immigration law, allowed the attorney general to admit aliens to the United States without congressional approval.

While parole was intended to be used sparingly and in individual cases, the Eisenhower administration used it for mass admissions. Over the next eight months, about 38,000 Hungarian refugees entered and resettled in the United States. They faced almost none of the obstacles to entry that hindered the early RRP, as the Eisenhower administration desperately wanted speedy admissions. Moreover, the Hungarians' plight as victims of Soviet aggression, which the administration cleverly promoted through a sustained public relations campaign, tamped down opposition to their entry. As *Look* magazine reported, the Hungarians were "New Americans" (quoted in Bon Tempo 2008, 78).

Both the RRP and the Hungarian admissions were temporary programs that centered on the admission of European refugees from Communism and that viewed those refugees as weapons in the Cold War. Refugee advocates, an increasingly organized collection of NGOs (nongovernmental organizations), religious groups, and ethnic organizations began to argue that these programs were inadequate on two grounds. First, they believed that the United States needed a permanent refugee program, not a series of ad hoc admissions. Second, they believed that the focus on Europeans fleeing Communism or the Soviet Union was too limited in light of a world refugee problem that was growing in Africa and the Middle East and shrinking in Europe. Indeed, the U.S. response to the Palestinian refugee problem in the Middle East, which had numbered in the millions since the late 1940s, involved funding the United Nations Relief and Works Agency (UNRWA) rather than offering extensive admissions. To a small degree, Congress and the White House heeded these concerns. In 1960, the "Fair Share" refugee law provided for the entry of a small number of refugees annually. In 1965, the landmark revision of the immigration laws, which destroyed the national origins quotas, approved the annual admission of 10,200 refugees. As a result, by 1965, the United States had permanent annual admissions, but they were small (as compared to the size of the global refugee problem) and they confirmed the existing understanding that a refugee was a person, most often of European origins, fleeing Communism.

Cuba and Haiti

The next major refugee crisis erupted in the United States' own backyard: Cuba. The genesis of the Cuban refugee flow was Fidel Castro's ouster of the dictator Fulgencio Batista in early 1959. Upon Castro's triumph, Batista and several hundred of his followers fled. Shocked by the new Cuban government's revolutionary violence meted out to those Batista supporters who remained, President Eisenhower quickly allowed those first refugees from Cuba to enter the United States. In the following months, Castro took total control of the revolution. He began an ambitious program of economic nationalization, built deeper ties with Cuban Communists, and began forging a closer economic and diplomatic relationship with the Soviet Union. Concurrently, relations between the United States and Cuba deteriorated so

that by January 1961, the two nations broke diplomatic ties. Emblematic of the impasse, the U.S. government was at that time preparing for the Bay of Pigs invasion, manned in large part by Cuban exiles.

Cuban refugees came to the United States in roughly four phases between the Cuban Revolution and the early 1970s. Phase one lasted from January 1959 to January 1961 and saw about 100,000 enter the United States. (Other Cuban refugees went to Spain and countries in Latin America.) During phase two, from January 1961 to October 1962, nearly 150,000 refugees entered the United States. In phase three, which lasted from the fall of 1962 to early 1965, the number of refugees decreased as Castro shut off all travel between Cuba and the United States in the wake of the Missile Crisis; during these years, between 30,000 and 50,000 Cubans entered. Finally, in 1965, Castro declared that all who wanted to leave the island could do so. He hoped this open invitation both would strengthen the revolution and would place the U.S. government in a difficult position, which it did as Cubans began leaving en masse by boat. The U.S. and Cuban governments in fairly short order worked out a complicated agreement to govern refugee departure, and ultimately about 275,000 refugees entered the U.S. between 1965 and 1973 (when the Americans withdrew from this agreement).

The Eisenhower administration's decision to admit Cuban refugees, like previous decisions to accept European and Hungarian refugees, was based largely upon Cold War geopolitics. Accepting refugees from Castro was, according to Eisenhower and his successors, a way of demonstrating Communism's failures and of hopefully strengthening the anti-Cuban cause in Latin America. Of course, the United States' unique relationship with Cuba—a potent mix of economic colonialism, political hegemony, and extensive cultural contacts—helped ease admissions as many Americans felt a keen sense paternalism toward Cuba. The refugees themselves, who for the most part were white and middle or upper class in these years, made admissions easier as well. Finally, Eisenhower and his successors almost exclusively used the parole power to admit Cuban refugees (although some did enter via regular immigration procedures), which helped keep the issue out of Congress.

No refugee group has done more to assert themselves in American life than the Cubans, the vast majority of whom settled permanently in southern Florida. Almost immediately upon arrival, Cuban exiles set up vibrant communities that trumpeted many of the cultural traditions of their homeland. The concentration of Cubans in South Florida gave them political clout, which they exerted with growing vigor over the following decades. No national politician looking to succeed in Florida could overlook the Cuban community and its concerns, especially those relating to U.S. relations with Castro. Indeed, given its size, some have observed that the Cuban community has an oversized influence on American politics. To be sure, the integration of Cuban exiles into American life has not been seamless. In the 1960s, the U.S. government launched an extensive resettlement program that provided Cubans with economic aid. Such help angered native Floridians, especially in the African-American community, as did the strains that the hundreds of thousands of Cubans put on preexisting social services and schools. Nonetheless, no widespread opposition to Cuban refugee admissions emerged in the 1960s and early 1970s.

Perhaps no example better demonstrates the place of Cuban refugees than the contemporaneous case of Haitian refugees. Haiti buckled under the autocratic rule of François Duvalier in the 1950s and 1960s, with political repression and economic deprivation widespread. As a result, many upper- and middle-class Haitians began arriving in the United States. The American government largely acquiesced to their entry via regular immigration procedures in the 1960s, and did not deport those who overstayed their temporary visas. The Haitians, though, received none of the special treatment that Cubans did. Cubans were considered political refugees while Haitians were not, because Duvalier was closely allied with the United States, which considered him a valuable anti-Communist. Moreover, Haitians did not have the ease of entry that parole offered, nor did they have access to the government resources for resettlement that Cuban exiles did. In sum, the Haitian case made clear yet again the importance of the Cold War and geopolitics to American refugee policies.

Refugees and Human Rights in the 1970s

In the 1970s, the basic parameters of the American commitment to refugees shifted. For the first time, the United States admitted a significant number of refugees of color. Human rights concerns, along with the Cold War, justified refugee admissions. And, by the end of the decade, the United States had a law that provided for extensive annual refugee admissions and defined refugee in the most capacious manner yet.

Human rights ideas powerfully emerged in American politics and culture during the 1970s. On the liberal side of the political spectrum, such politicians as Ted Kennedy argued that human rights ought to be at the center of American foreign policy. They saw human rights as an alternative to Cold War anti-Communism that had led the nation into the Vietnam War and seemed bereft of any moral underpinnings. Groups like Amnesty International made a similar claim for the importance of human rights to international affairs generally. On the right, conservatives in the Republican and Democratic Parties embraced human rights as an alternative to what they saw as the amoral and ineffective policies of détente that accommodated the Soviet Union. In this view, an American foreign policy that stressed human rights would demonstrate the superiority of American ideals and the horrific nature of Soviet Communism.

The case of Russian Jews seeking to leave the Soviet Union was the first refugee issue to center on human rights. The Soviet government's mistreatment and persecution of Jews accelerated in the early 1970s, and the desire of Jews to leave only increased the mistreatment. American Jewish groups and conservative politicians, including Senator Henry "Scoop" Jackson—a Democrat from Washington State and an ardent anti-Communist—blasted the Soviets and pressured the Nixon administration to do more to help Soviet Jews. Their complaints framed the plight of Russian Jews as a human rights issue in which the Soviets denied the basic right of emigration. Such charges were particularly potent because, in the unstated rules of détente, the United States and the Soviet Union had agreed not to critique each other's conduct of domestic affairs.

Senator Jackson's ultimate gambit was his attempt in 1973 to scuttle Senate approval of an important Soviet-American trade agreement unless the Soviets agreed to speed the departure of Russian Jews. While neither the Nixon (and later, Ford) White House nor the Kremlin appreciated this maneuver, a series of complex negotiations in 1974 produced a vague Soviet acceptance of the emigration principle. Jackson claimed victory, which of course only angered the Soviets, who withdrew from the agreement anyway at the end of 1975. Soviet Jewish emigration to all destinations peaked in 1973 at 35,000 and began a slow decline afterward. About 30,000 of these Soviet Jews came to the United States in the 1970s.

With the Soviet Jewish emigration issue, refugee problems became human rights problems. This dynamic continued with the plight of Chilean refugees fleeing the government of Augusto Pinochet, which had ousted the leftist Salvador Allende in September 1973 and then launched a crackdown against its opponents. Pinochet's coup had been openly applauded and covertly supported by the Nixon administration, which saw him as a reliable anti-Communist. In this case, American liberals argued that Pinochet openly violated basic human rights and that the American government could protest his actions—and forward the cause of human rights—by helping those who sought to leave Chile. Under pressure, the Ford White House set up a small parole program for about 400 Chileans in 1975. Nonetheless, the dual cases of Soviet Jews and Chileans made two things clear. First, human rights principles had entered refugee politics and policies. Second, even with the rise of human rights, a double standard still existed in which Cold War foreign policy concerns privileged the admission of certain refugees.

The problem of refugees from Indochina, though, dwarfed the refugee flows from the Soviet Union and Chile in the 1970s. The Indochinese refugee crisis, which stretched from 1975 into the early 1980s, was a product of the Vietnam War and the instability it created in its neighbors Laos and Cambodia. Moreover, it actually consisted of several refugee problems. The first began in the spring of 1975 with the fall of Saigon and the collapse of South Vietnam. North Vietnam's victory raised fears, especially in

the State Department, that the United States' former allies in the South would be targeted and persecuted. While slow at first to act, President Ford agreed to parole up to 200,000 Vietnamese, arguing that the United States had a responsibility to those who had served loyally during the war. During evacuation operations, the U.S. military took custody of 130,000 refugees, who were then resettled.

The larger and longer Indochinese refugee crisis came to the fore in the late 1970s. It had several sources. Ethnic Chinese fled Vietnam because of persecution, while hundreds of thousands of Cambodians and Laotians sought escape from the genocidal mania that engulfed their nations. Some in the Western press referred to the events in Cambodia as the "Asian Holocaust," as if the only way to make sense of Pol Pot's destruction was to compare it to one of the other great mass murders of the twentieth century (Amiel 1979, 32). Refugees fled by land to camps in Thailand and elsewhere, but more memorably by sea in often flimsy crafts that gave the crisis its name: the "boat people." While the boat people had managed to escape persecution and genocide, they had hardly reached safety; an estimated one-fourth to one-half of all who departed in boats died at sea. By 1979, tens of thousands of refugees were entering sprawling and destitute refugee camps each month, which severely taxed their host nations despite the growing, but still insufficient, aid of the international community. In short, an immense humanitarian disaster had developed.

The American response was initially extremely paltry. In 1978, the Carter administration paroled 7,000 Indochinese refugees and announced plans for another parole of 25,000 the following year. (In fact, such small admissions were in line with those of other industrialized nations—with the exceptions of France and Australia, which took in 50,000 and 30,000, respectively, between 1975 and mid-1979.) But as the crisis deepened, Carter announced more extensive plans for parole so that in the summer of 1979, the United States began admitting 14,000 refugees a month. Carter, his aides, and his allies in the public, repeatedly justified these paroles by arguing that to help refugees was to protect and promote human rights. As one editorial put it, "The suffering of the

South Vietnamese refugees disembark from the first of ten refugee flights expected to arrive at Eglin Air Force base in Florida on May 9, 1975. (AP Photo)

boat people is an outrage to our common humanity" (quoted in Bon Tempo 2008, 152).

By the end of 1981, about 560,000 Indochinese had been resettled in the United States since 1975, roughly two-thirds of them refugees from the "Asian holocaust." The entry of Indochinese refugees continued through the early 1980s, though at a diminished pace. The area with the highest concentration of resettlement was California, but significant numbers of Indochinese found their way all around the United States. Like newcomers before them, the Indochinese refugees set about building communities, but their arrival also tested the preexisting social welfare net, already strained due to a generally weak economy. Large segments of the public deeply opposed the arrival of Indochinese refugees over the last half of the 1970s, though that opposition lessened slightly as the plight of the boat people earned more attention. It speaks to the general power of human rights

rhetoric and principles that even in the weak economy of the 1970s and the overriding desire to put Vietnam behind it, the United States admitted so many refugees from Southeast Asia.

A New Refugee Law and the Problem of Asylum

The apogee of human rights in refugee affairs occurred in 1980, with the passage of the Refugee Act. This landmark law, supported by President Carter, liberal Democrats, and refugee experts and NGOs, revised the foundations of American policies. Since 1965, annual regular refugee admissions, excluding the persistent paroles of refugees, had come under a section of immigration law. The new law established refugee admissions separate from immigration admissions. The Refugee Act contained a new definition of refugee that made no reference to the Cold War, specific political ideologies, or geography, but instead broadly defined refugees as victims of persecution. It provided for the annual admission of up to 50,000 refugees, although the law also empowered the White House— after consulting Congress—to admit more than 50,000 refugees if it believed circumstances warranted the increase. Moreover, under the Refugee Act, the White House and Congress would set regional ceilings on refugee entry, essentially dividing up the total annual refugee allotment into regional admissions. Finally, the law strengthened refugee resettlement efforts.

The Refugee Act of 1980 also addressed the challenge of asylum claims. The chief difference between an asylee and a refugee was that an alien in the United States fearing persecution in his homeland applied for asylee status, while an alien outside the United States fearing persecution in his homeland applied for refugee status. While the United States had agreed to several international conventions regarding asylum, the U.S. government in the 1970s had not developed a coherent set of asylum procedures. This failing was not really a problem in the 1970s because the number of asylum claims was very low and were often denied. The 1980 Refugee Act mandated that the government undertake this administrative task and allowed the government to reserve 5,000 of the 50,000 refugee admissions for asylees. In the wake of the Refugee Act, the number of asylum cases ballooned. Between 1973 and 1979, the most asylum cases filed in any year was 5,801 (in 1979). But between 1980 and 1990, the high was 101,679 (in 1989), and in no year did the number of cases filed shrink below 16,622 (in 1985). This surge led to a massive backlog of cases, and the approval rates during most years in the 1980s rested between 20 and 40 percent.

The first test of the new refugee law came quite quickly and from a familiar place: Cuba. Cubans began leaving from the port of Mariel in April 1980— which gave the episode its name, the Mariel Refugee Crisis. Over the next six months, about 130,000 arrived in the United States, a dramatic increase from the mid-1970s. At the same time, an upsurge in Haitian arrivals occurred as well. These refugees fled Jean-Claude "Baby Doc" Duvalier, the son of the Haitian dictator, who carried on his father's oppressive policies yet remained aligned with the United States

because of his staunch anti-Communism. The arrival of the Cubans and Haitians set off a political firestorm. Media coverage of the Marielitos, as the Cubans were known, suggested that the vast majority were black and criminals, drug users, and homosexuals; in fact, the vast majority of the Cubans arriving in 1980 were white (though more blacks entered in this group than in the 1960s) and only a very small minority were criminals, drug addicts, or gay. Meanwhile, the Haitians, who applied for asylum once they landed, were trumpeted by refugee advocates and black politicians as victims of both political persecution and a double standard that saw their claims denied merely because they fled an American ally.

The Carter administration, then, was in quite a political bind. The United States had a tradition of accepting Cuban refugees and, regarding the Haitians, some of the administration's strongest allies were making a case for Haitian entry. After flip-flopping, the Carter White House set on a policy of accepting Cuban refugees, but not under terms of the 1980 Refugee Act. Instead, the Mariel refugees were granted a special immigration status. Moreover, the American courts ruled that Haitian asylee claims had not been fairly adjudicated in the past and ordered the Immigration and Naturalization Service (INS) to revamp its procedures. The Carter administration decided, then, to allow any Haitians who entered the United States prior to October 1980 to stay, but again under a separate legal status not related to the 1980 Refugee Act. Any Haitians entering after October 1980 would be subject to the new asylum process. Thus, the Cuban and Haitian refugee flows of 1980 ultimately showed the limits of the Refugee Act.

The End of Cold War and Beyond

The true test of new refugee law lay in its implementation by the Reagan administration. Ronald Reagan came to the presidency as the leading man of the conservative revolution. An ardent anti-Communist who saw the Cold War as a struggle between good and evil, he advocated an aggressive anti-Soviet foreign policy based on military strength. Reagan tended to view refugees as a natural byproduct of Communism, once remarking that "of all the millions of refugees we've seen in the modern world, their flight is always away from, not toward the Communist world" (Woolley and Peters, *American Presidency Project*). Reagan, while a free-market conservative who favored the easy flow of labor into the United States, also was well aware of the growing power of restrictionist elements within his own Republican Party. Such conditions help explain his refugee policies and admissions.

Each year of Reagan's presidency, the total annual quota for refugee admissions exceeded the 50,000 mandated by the 1980 law, but by smaller amounts as his presidency wore on. (This trend did reverse itself at the end of the 1980s.) Unsurprisingly, the Reagan administration's refugee policies tended to favor those escaping Communism. While the new refugee law was less centered on the Cold War than previous refugee legislation, Reagan consistently abetted the entry of refugees from the Soviet Union, Eastern Europe, and Indochina, assigning them larger portions of the annual quota than he did refugees from other regions of the world. For instance, in 1982, the Reagan administration allotted 96,000 slots for refugees from East Asia, 20,000 slots for those from the Soviet Union, and 11,000 slots for those from Eastern Europe. In contrast, refugees from Africa received 3,500 slots, Latin America 3,000, and the Middle East 6,500. As the total quotas shrank, though, the Reagan administration did shrink the visas available to those previously favored regions.

Reagan's policies toward refugees from Central America were particularly controversial. Nicaragua, El Salvador, and Guatemala each experienced political and economic upheaval in the 1980s as factions in those nations—often funded by the United States, the Soviet Union, and Cuba—battled each other. The hot spots were Nicaragua, where Reagan worried that the leftist Sandinista government might lead a Communist takeover of the region, and El Salvador, where a rightist, American-backed government abused its opponents and allowed anti-Sandinista forces to operate with impunity. The result of the violence, terror, political repression, and economic stagnation was a massive refugee problem of two million persons, tens of thousands of whom entered the United States, many illegally. Reagan did little via the Refugee Act to bring these

refugees to the United States. Those who applied for asylum after landing in the United States—and many did, leading to the aforementioned surge in asylum cases in the 1980s—found that that government was much more likely to grant asylee status to those who fled Communist governments than to those who escaped American allies. Liberals and refugee advocates howled in protest, but to little avail.

The Cold War ended with a whimper rather than a bang, but the effect on the world's refugee problems was ambiguous. In southern Africa and Central America, the collapse of the superpower rivalry helped bring resolutions to regional conflicts, which allowed refugees to return home. But the demise of the Soviet Union and its empire in Eastern and Central Europe unleashed the centrifugal forces of ethnic nationalism that tore multiethnic nation-states apart and led to the forced movements of populations. Nowhere was this more apparent than during the bloody civil war in Yugoslavia, but it was a scene repeated in the countries birthed from the Soviet wreckage. In other instances, refugee crises developed that had no relation to the Cold War whatsoever. In Central Africa during the early 1990s, rivalries between Tutsis and Hutus in Rwanda and Burundi erupted into violence that spilled over into neighboring nations and lasted into the new century. The genocides and military campaigns in Rwanda killed at least a million and displaced more. By 1995, the global refugee and displaced-person population stood at around 15 million.

American policies were mixed in the face of these problems. U.S. participation in the peace processes in southern Africa and Central America helped bring about the end of those conflicts. But the Clinton administration largely stood aside in the face of the crisis in Central Africa. As genocide engulfed Rwanda, the United States refused to intervene and instead offered rather paltry material aid that could not keep pace with the human misery. Reflecting on this inaction, former President Clinton has expressed deep regrets. In the Balkans, the Clinton White House eventually adopted a more aggressive approach of limited military action—mainly through bombing—that halted the genocide. American and international troops then moved in to enforce the uneasy peace that allowed some of the displaced to return.

As it had since 1980, the Refugee Act remained the main vehicle for admissions. Here, the Clinton administration slowly shrank the annual ceiling on admissions. It had risen in the early 1990s under President George H. W. Bush to a high of 142,000 in 1992, but then fell to around 90,000 in the last half of the decade. Of those 90,000 potential admissions, Eastern Europe and the former Soviet Union received the most spots, although refugees from Africa saw an increasingly more generous allotment by the end of the 1990s. The other revolution in refugee affairs came with the INS decision in 1995 to consider gender-based persecution in asylum claims. This revision was the first major change to the definition of refugee since 1980.

Refugee Admissions in the Age of the "War on Terror"

The September 11, 2001, attacks ushered in another new era in American refugee policies. The George W. Bush administration had not yet announced publicly how it would oversee annual refugee admissions under the Refugee Act when the attacks occurred, so it is not clear whether they would have continued or departed from the Clinton administration's policies. Nonetheless, immediately after the attacks, the Bush White House suspended refugee admissions and pulled administrative personnel from around the world. While admissions restarted shortly thereafter, only just over 27,000 refugees entered the United States in fiscal year 2002, even though the Refugee Act provided for 70,000 admissions. Over the following three years, the 70,000-refugee ceiling remained and admissions crept upward, so that in 2005, an estimated 53,000 entered. Nonetheless, many refugee advocates and organizations have noted that the admissions standards and screening of refugees prior to admission have tightened in the post-9/11 years. These experts worry that such measures do little to protect against potential terrorists while doing much to delay aid and help to refugees. As Jana Mason of the U.S. Committee for Refugees put it, "You'd have to be a pretty dumb terrorist to decide that the way you're going to get to the U.S. is to go to Pakistan, sit in a refugee camp for six years and hope the U.S.

selects you for admission" (quoted in Bon Tempo 2008, 205).

The War on Terror, then, may yet reshape American refugee policies in the same way that the Cold War did in the 1940s. In any event, the United States faced a burgeoning refugee problem in Iraq as that country descended into near civil war in 2005 and 2006 with the United States and its allies impotent bystanders. By April 2007, UN officials reported that 50,000 refugees fled Iraq each month and that 2 million had fled since the U.S. invasion in March 2003. Syria held 1.2 million Iraqi refugees; 750,000 were in camps in Jordan; and 100,000 found their way to Egypt. Smaller but still significant Iraqi refugee populations were in Iran, Lebanon, and Turkey. Inside Iraq, another 1.9 million people had left their homes but not their country. The countries that hosted Iraqi refugees buckled under the growing commitment, and the international community spent most of its time furnishing relief as resettlement opportunities were sparse. Refugee advocates, such as Ken Bacon of Refugees International, a leading NGO, put the blame squarely on the United States for causing the problem and failing to address it: "This is a refugee crisis that we triggered and aren't doing enough to deal with" (Rosen 2007, 74). Indeed, between 2003 and April 2007, the United States admitted 701 Iraqi refugees. It does appear, though, that admissions picked up between October 2007 and September 2008, a period when the State Department asserted that over 13,800 Iraqi refugees were admitted to the United States.

Conclusion

Over the course of its history, the United States' commitment to refugees has evolved and grown stronger. Prior to World War II, the U.S. government had no official policies toward refugees—other than neutrality—and made very few efforts to help refugees or bring them to the United States. Emblematic of this stance, the United States failed miserably in the face of the European refugee crisis of the 1930s, failing to admit refugees either through regular immigration procedures or with the creation of special programs. While specific circumstances—potent anti-immigration sentiments expressed at the time the national origins quotas were originally enacted, along with the Great Depression, bureaucratic intransigence, political calculation, and anti-Semitism—explain this historical episode, the result was no less galling.

Yet, in the aftermath of World War II and, then more importantly, with the coming of the Cold War, the United States became more active in searching for solutions to refugee problems. From the 1940s through the early 1970s, these efforts were mainly ad hoc and targeted Europeans fleeing Communism or the Soviet Union. The desire to gain the upper hand in the Cold War struggle with the Soviets often provided the impetus for, and proved key in shaping, these programs. But also influential were domestic political and cultural conditions, including electoral politics, immigration concerns, and public opinion. By the 1970s, American refugee policies began another important shift, as the entry of the Indochinese brought the first mass admission of refugees of color. But the biggest change was the injection of human rights concerns and principles into refugee affairs, which did more to weaken than strengthen the Cold War's hold on refugee policies. Thus, the landmark 1980 refugee law provided for regularized and substantial annual admissions of refugees without—at least according to the letter of the law—reference to Cold War geopolitics or ideologies. That the Reagan administration largely subverted this intent testified to the lingering importance of Cold War concerns. The United States' refugee programs, of course, outlived the Cold War but continued to be applied somewhat less uniformly. Annual admissions of refugees shrank from the early 1990s, but more and more spots went to refugees from Africa. On the other hand, major refugee crises in Rwanda and Iraq elicited no or little American aid.

Thus, we return to the question that began this chapter: how generous has the United States been toward refugees? It seems that there are three possible approaches to answering this question. The first, outlined above, is to note that over the course of its history, the United States has most assuredly grown more welcoming to refugees, an interpretation based less in triumphalism than in the fact that the United States was so indifferent to refugees until the 1940s.

The second approach is comparative, looking at American efforts in contrast to other nations. Here, perhaps the most judicious conclusion is that the record is mixed. In some cases, like the Cuban refugee flow, the United States has taken the lead role. In other cases, notably the Indochinese crisis of the 1970s, the United States admitted hundreds of thousands of refugees, but other countries—like Thailand—bore an even greater weight by providing both refuge and resettlement opportunities. In the case of Iraqi refugees, the United States has done little in comparison with other nations. Statistics of recent refugee aid efforts are similarly mixed. According to the U.S. Committee for Refugee and Immigrants, in 2007, the United States resettled 48,281 refugees, the most of any single country in the world. Yet, in a ranking of the ratios of refugee resettlement to total population, the United States finished sixth, behind Australia, Canada, Norway, Sweden, and New Zealand. Similarly, the United States committed the most money in total dollars to international refugee aid organizations in 2007 but ranked 16th in terms of per capita spending.

Finally, a third approach examines the American commitment to refugees in light of the global refugee problem. Here, the American record seems most problematic. The global refugee population has numbered in the millions—if not tens of millions—since World War II. The United States admitted about 4.5 million between 1945 and 2000. The differential is immense, and perhaps even more so when one considers the American capacity, not to mention the rhetorical commitment, to absorb newcomers. Moreover, for a nation that held itself as a—and sometimes *the*—preeminent global political, military, and economic leader, one can reasonably conclude that more could and should have been done. But, perhaps this history suggests that the barriers to inaction were just as great as the spurs to action, and that one might reasonably ask how the United States, however limited, managed to accomplish what it did in refugee affairs.

Bibliography

Amiel, Barbara. 1979. "Now an Asian Holocaust?" *Macleans*, July 2.

Bon Tempo, Carl. 2008. *Americans at the Gate.* Princeton, NJ: Princeton University Press.

Daniels, Roger. 2002. *Coming to America*. 2nd ed. New York: HarperCollins.

Daniels, Roger. 2004. *Guarding the Golden Door*. New York: Hill and Wang.

Loescher, Gil, and John Scanlan. 1998. *Calculated Kindness*. New York: Free Press.

Markowitz, Arthur A. 1973. "Humanitarianism vs. Restrictionism: The United States and the Hungarian Refugees." *International Migration Review* 7, no. 1: 46–59.

Pedraza-Bailey, Sylvia. 1985. "Cuba's Exiles: Portrait of a Refugee Migration." *International Migration Review* 19: 4–34.

Power, Samantha. 2002. *A Problem from Hell*. New York: Basic Books.

Reimers, David. 1992. *Still the Golden Door*. 2nd ed. New York: Columbia University Press.

Rosen, Nir. 2007. "The Flight from Iraq." *New York Times Magazine*, May 13.

Tichenor, Daniel. 2002. *Dividing Lines*. Princeton, NJ: Princeton University Press.

U.S. Committee for Refugees and Immigrants. *World Refugee Survey, 2008*. http://www.refugees.org/resources/refugee-warehousing/archived-world-refugee-surveys/2008-world-refugee-survey.html (accessed May 18, 2012).

Woolley, John, and Gerhard Peters. The American Presidency Project, University of California, Santa Barbara. http://www.presidency.ucsb.edu/ws/?pid=44128 and http://www.presidency.ucsb.edu/ws/?pid=42614 (accessed February 29, 2012).

Wyman, David. 1968. *Paper Walls*. Amherst: University of Massachusetts Press.

Wyman, David. 1984. *The Abandonment of the Jews*. New York: Pantheon Books.

Zolberg, Aristide. 2006. *A Nation by Design*. Cambridge, MA: Harvard University Press.

Unauthorized Immigration to the United States

Shannon Gleeson

Definitional Issues

Unauthorized immigration to the United States has a long and varied history that has been shaped by historical shifts in immigration policy. Fifteen to 20 percent of the global immigrant stock is estimated to be undocumented (30 million to 40 million). Today, undocumented immigrants comprise roughly 40 percent of the immigrant flow to the United States. Formal estimates of unauthorized immigrants refer to "foreign-born individuals who entered without inspection or who violated the terms of a temporary admission and who have not acquired LPR [legal permanent residence] status or gained temporary protection against removal by applying for an immigration benefit" (U.S. Department of Homeland Security 2008).

Therefore, unauthorized immigration can be broadly understood as the flow of individuals into the country who do not fit into any of the authorized categories of admission. For a foreigner looking to work in the United States, there are two sanctioned options: become a legal permanent resident, or obtain a temporary work visa. Legal permanent residency is largely shaped by family reunification provisions, favoring relatives of U.S. citizens or immediate family members of legal U.S. residents. Skilled workers, as well as refugees and asylees, also have access to this route if sponsored by a U.S. citizen or legal resident. Voluntary agencies (also known as "VOLAGs") can initially sponsor new refugee arrivals, and have historically provided significant resettlement assistance through contracts with the U.S. Department of State. After five years (three if married to a U.S. citizen), legal permanent residents may apply for naturalization (U.S. citizenship.) Temporary visas are available to investors from countries with which the United States has a free-trade treaty (such as certain classes of Canadian and Mexican workers), intracompany transferees, students, fiancées, and other temporary workers (including the H1-B, H2-A, and H2-B programs.) The third alternative is to enter illegally.

In general, the technical meaning of the terms "undocumented," "unauthorized," and "illegal" are all the same. One leading analyst utilizes the term "unauthorized migrant" to include a person who *resides* in the United States, but who is *not* a U.S. citizen, has *not* been admitted for permanent residence, and is *not* in a set of specific authorized temporary statuses permitting longer-term residence and work. Undocumented immigrants may fall into one of two categories: (1) those who entered the country without valid documents, and (2) visa overstayers. The latter group accounts for roughly 10 percent of this population and is likely to become unauthorized at some point. They include those with "temporary protected status" and other unresolved asylum claims.

Though the bureaucratic definition of this population may seem clear, the use of these terms is certainly politically charged. Some immigrant advocates, for example, have discouraged the use of the term "illegals" or "illegal alien," which tend to be used pejoratively against these populations. Other terms refer to "immigrants without papers" or "unsanctioned immigrants."

Legal Framework

Unauthorized immigration is an outcome of national borders, an immigration policy that determines who is allowed entry, and a bureaucratic apparatus that ensures its enforcement. Both the maintenance of borders and the monitoring of documentation status are elements of modern bureaucracies. "Identification papers of various kinds [today] constitute the bureaucratic equivalent of money: they are the currency of the modern state administration" (Torpey 2000, 10). As modern societies transitioned from feudalism to capitalism, the authority for that administration shifted from the private to the public sphere. At the same time, as national borders became more clearly demarcated, the understanding of who was "foreign" shifted from the internal to the international migrant.

The Early Era

A review of the United States' official history of border enforcement reveals a fairly young institutional history. At the turn of the twentieth century, fewer than 100 "Mounted Guards" patrolled the southern borders, intermittently in conjunction with military troops and Texas Rangers, largely seeking out Chinese immigrants trying to avoid Chinese exclusion laws. Prior to 1882, there were no significant barriers to migrating to the United States. That year, the Chinese Exclusion Act excluded Chinese immigrant laborers for 10 years under penalty of imprisonment and deportation. The act was a culmination of decades of restrictions at state and local levels, spurred by hostility toward Chinese laborers, who were seen as undercutting the wages of white workers. Only teachers, students, merchants, and travelers were allowed to enter, and no Chinese immigrants were allowed to apply for naturalization. The act was renewed in 1892, then again in 1902, and finally repealed in 1943, amidst wartime hostilities with Japan and strategic alliances with the Republic of China. During this time, however, the Chinese population continued to increase for at least a decade.

These first significant barriers to entry came late to the country's history. The Immigration Act of 1917 erected the first general requirements by doubling the head tax and imposing a literacy test, requirements from which Mexicans were actually exempted until 1919. Until then, the Immigration Bureau "did not seriously consider Mexican immigration within its purview, but rather as something that was 'regulated by labor market demands in [the southwestern] border states' " (Ngai 2003, 7). In fact, it even described the Southwest as the "natural habitat" of Mexicans and, oddly enough, acknowledged Mexicans' claims of belonging in an area that had once been part of Mexico. Prior to World War I, the Canadian border was permeable and sparsely patrolled. Efforts on the northern border were largely focused on keeping out the Chinese and "undesirable" classes of European migrants.

Early on, following its establishment in 1924, the Border Patrol's agents had to furnish their own horse and saddle and were given only a badge, a revolver, oats and hay for the horses, and a $1,680 annual salary. Until 1928, they did not even have uniforms. By fiscal year 2009, there were over 18,000 Border Patrol agents, and the previous year, Immigration and Customs Enforcement had budgeted $250.4 million alone for "Detention Bedspace" and another $200 million for the "Comprehensive Removal and Detention of Aliens."

Anti-immigrant sentiment flourished behind the policy developments, playing a significant role among nativists (mostly toward southern and eastern Europeans) during the sharp post–World War I economic downturn. These economic pressures combined with the fears of "being swamped by 'abnormally twisted' and 'unassimilable' Jews, 'filthy, un-American and often dangerous in their habits' " (Daniels 2008). The result was the Immigration Acts of 1921 and 1924, which spurred illegal immigration in mass proportions and, as we shall see, made deportation a central feature of immigration policy through the provisions of the national quotas. Essentially, the acts allowed only two groups of immigrants to be admitted outside the quota system: the wives and unmarried children under age 18 of U.S. citizens, and immigrants from Western Hemisphere nations.

During this period, concerns mounted regarding the toll border enforcement was taking on military forces and the lack of a coordinated effort. Following the Immigration Acts of 1921 and 1924, and in the midst of the Prohibition era, Congress quickly dedicated more resources to the Border Patrol via the Labor Appropriation Act of 1924. This officially established the U.S. Border Patrol for the purpose of securing the borders between inspection stations and a year later expanded its duties to patrol the seacoast. At this time, Congress also largely removed the statute of limitation on deportation and, by 1929, had made unlawful entry a misdemeanor punishable by a fine. Unauthorized entry was no longer a civil, administrative procedure, and "legal status now rested on being in the right place in the queue—if a country has a quota of *N*, immigrant *N* is legal but immigrant *N + 1* is illegal" (Ngai 2003, 61).

By then, "voluntary departure" had also become an alternative and was promoted by an immigration bureaucracy that was starting to feel overwhelmed by this growing population. By 1932, the Border Patrol was directed by a Mexican border office in El Paso and a Canadian border office in Detroit. Though perhaps astonishing in today's context, during this time, the majority of Border Patrol officers were assigned to the Canadian border. A year later, President Franklin D. Roosevelt combined the Bureau of Immigration and the Bureau of Naturalization into the Immigration and Naturalization Service (a move that would be reversed 70 years later). By 1940, the INS had been moved from the Department of Labor to the Department of Justice, and it provided additional services during wartime. By 2006, per border miles guarded, there were 28 times more Border Patrol officers facing south rather than north.

Bracero Program (1942–1964)

In 1942, the flow of Mexican immigrants who were considered illegal entrants slowed substantially, not because they stopped coming, but because the United States instituted what evolved into a 22-year-long temporary guest program to bring in *braceros* to compensate for the labor shortage created by the war. This was a negotiated agreement principally between the American and Mexican governments that provided Mexican workers a relatively good standard of living compared to their conditions in Mexico, including housing, food, and medical care, and additional earnings that were often sent home as remittances. The initial group of Mexican workers was targeted for agricultural labor in California. Subsequently, further waves of temporary workers were sent to work on railroads and elsewhere. All told, approximately 4.4 million Mexicans were recruited under this program between 1942 and 1964.

One of the legacies of the Bracero Program is that workers during the first decade of the program had 10 percent of their wages withheld by the Mexican government as an incentive for the braceros to return to Mexico. The money was deposited in Wells Fargo and later transferred to the Mexican national bank. Most braceros never saw this money again. A class-action lawsuit was ultimately filed in 2001 (*Senorino Ramirez Cruz et al. v. United States et al.*), but due to the complex document requirements and the few living workers from that cohort remaining, only a small portion of workers have ever been able to recover their wages once a settlement was eventually reached in October 2008.

When the program was ultimately disbanded in late 1964, many of these men were unable to find work in the communities they had left behind and ultimately returned as illegal immigrants. The Bracero Program was significant for undocumented immigrants because, while it set working conditions for braceros, it also eventually increased overhead costs for growers who would ultimately turn to cheaper undocumented Mexican labor. The program also created a well-developed set of social norms and networks that would lay the groundwork for undocumented migration during the ensuing decades.

Immigration and Nationality Acts of 1952 and 1965

The Immigration and Nationality Act of 1952 (the McCarran-Walter Act) emerged during the Cold War era. Under the existing national origins quota system, the act allotted visas for "one-sixth of one percent" of each European nationality's population in the United States in 1920. At the time, this resulted in 85 percent of the 154,277 visas being annually made available to individuals of northern and western European descent. While the 1952 Immigration Act also broke down existing provisions barring Asian immigration and naturalization, it allowed each Asian nation a minimum quota of 100 visas each year (based on an applicant's *race*, not national origin.) The legislation also introduced an initial system of preferences based on skill sets and family reunification.

The Immigration and Nationality Act was amended in 1965 (the Hart-Celler Act), eliminating the long-standing national origin quota system and creating new criteria for immigration. The act instituted hemispheric caps in lieu of national origin quotas: 170,000 for the Eastern Hemisphere and 120,000 for the Western Hemisphere, with a limit of 20,000 annually from any nation. These caps seemed to set an annual limit of 290,000 on immigration, but that was an illusion. The act also expanded the categories of family members who could enter without numerical limit and provided for the immigration of the relatives of legal permanent residents, and more distant family members of citizens.

The 1965 act allotted 6 percent of the global immigration cap to refugees, while still allowing for the "presidential parole power" that would facilitate the movement of the landmark flows of refugees from Hungary, Cuba, Tibet, and, later on, Vietnam and Cambodia, and other politically charged countries of the time. This change revolutionized the migrant flow to the United States, opening up channels for legal migration for immigrants from Asia and Latin America. The Hart-Celler Act particularly spurred migrants from Asia, who were for the most part excluded before this time but constituted over a third of all legal migrants in the 1970s (compared to only 3.6 and 6.1 percent during the 1940s and 1950s, respectively). Women also began to migrate in greater numbers than before.

Immigration Reform and Control Act (1986)

The Immigration Reform and Control Act (IRCA) of 1986 defines the current context of immigration policy. This legislation made it illegal to knowingly employ undocumented workers, mandated monitoring of employers (under a largely unsuccessful policy of "employer sanctions"), and provided resources to expand border enforcement. In addition, and perhaps most significantly, IRCA responded to pressure from employers who rallied for immigrant labor by instituting a broad amnesty program. Eligible immigrants included those who had been continuously unlawfully present since January 1982, and certain agricultural workers ("SAW"—Special Agricultural Workers). Three million undocumented immigrants, out of an estimated five million residing in the United States at the time, applied for amnesty under IRCA. Ultimately, 2.7 million adjusted their status. Over 85 percent of these legalizations included Mexican and Central American workers. By 2001, one-third of legal permanent residents who adjusted under IRCA had naturalized.

IRCA required that all newly hired employees and their employers complete I-9 forms, and employees were required to submit specified documents to establish their identity and work authorization status. It is no secret that quickly following IRCA, a prolific industry emerged to provide undocumented workers with false documents. The law required employers only to verify that the documents seemed reasonably valid. Indeed, many immigrant advocates feared that employers would make assumptions about a worker's documentation status in efforts to avoid violating immigration law. As a result, the federal government dedicated specific resources to monitor the matter via the establishment of the Office of Special Counsel for Immigration Related to Unfair Employment Practices, which enforced prohibitions of national origin discrimination under Title VII of the 1964 Civil Rights Act and ensured that employer sanctions did not accelerate the exploitation of undocumented workers.

North American Free Trade Agreement (1994)

Less than a decade following IRCA, the United States signed a free-trade agreement with Mexico and Canada that many hoped would reduce the undocumented flow from Mexico. Proponents of the North American Free Trade Agreement (1994) would allow Mexico to be competitive in the global market, in turn spurring economic growth and job creation, thereby reducing the need for laborers to migrate. The popular argument for NAFTA was that the rising tide (economic health resulting from free trade) would "raise all boats." In campaigning for NAFTA, then Mexican President Salinas sold NAFTA to the U.S. Congress on the premise of a zero-sum trade off: "either NAFTA, or Mexican immigration." History has shown that this did not entirely occur.

Unauthorized Immigration to the United States   1543

In retrospect, there had been some opportunity for agricultural trade to substitute for migration, though very limited. The evidence suggests that some crops, such as broccoli, moved to Mexico; yet the continued subsidies that American farmers have received made the playing field uneven for their Mexican competitors. In fact, the removal of tariffs on merchandise imports created a flood of products, causing hundreds of Mexican engineering firms to go bankrupt. Many of the transnational factories eventually moved to Asia in search of cheaper labor costs as Mexican living standards began to increase. These massive job losses were a significant impetus to undocumented migration, but oftentimes they occurred through an initial process of urbanization, whereby migrants moved to the booming capital in search of work and eventually headed north when there was none to be found. Reflecting on these changes, analysts have argued that "International migration, in short, does not stem from a lack of economic development, but from development itself" (Massey 1998, 2). The likelihood of undocumented Mexican migration is positively related to the U.S.-Mexico wage ratio. The high rates of inflation and peso devaluation actually reduced the likelihood of an initial undocumented trip to the United States. However, the increase in the rate of U.S. employment growth tended to spur an increase in the likelihood of undocumented immigration.

In addition, noneconomic factors associated with free trade propel migration, including cultural exchanges and the proliferation of social networks created by a variety of factors, including (1) internationalized production sites (such as the *maquiladoras* along the U.S.-Mexico border), (2) the development of major nodal cities, such as Los Angeles and New York City, that manage these complex systems, and (3) the role of direct foreign investment in Mexico as a major push factor for migration.

Some scholars have also argued that export-led production in third-world countries induces migration (much of it undocumented) by creating goods that compete with local commodities, by feminizing the workforce without providing factory-based employment for the large number of under- and unemployed males, and by socializing women for industrial work

and modern consumption without providing needed job stability. Women are pushed into nontraditional wage-labor jobs that oftentimes distance them from their communities of origin. This, combined with the typically short tenure in transnational factories, can leave them economically vulnerable. After being "laid off and westernized," these women have few other options than to emigrate. The fact that they spent the previous years creating goods for people and firms in countries with higher levels of development than their own also means that displaced male and female workers identify with these new destinations. In effect, the increased liberalization of trade, which has led to the increasingly free movement of people, has also resulted in a decline in the control powers of states over population flows.

Border Militarization

There was a significant increase in border enforcement in the United States to deter undocumented migrant flows during the 1980s and 1990s. During this period, the Border Patrol instituted the use of various modern tools, including infrared night-vision scopes, seismic sensors, and a modern computer-processing system. Several concerted operations were launched in border states, such as Operation Hold the Line in 1993 in El Paso, Texas, and Operation Gatekeeper in San Diego, California, the following year. However, rather than causing a reduction in undocumented migration, analysts have found that this enforcement shifted previously temporary and circular migration flows toward a more permanent settlement pattern. Mexican migrants no longer embody the old image of the seasonal migrant laborer who often returns to Mexico. Instead, because of the increased costs and dangers of reentering the United States due to changes in immigration policy and increased border enforcement, Mexican immigrants are staying longer and returning to Mexico less frequently.

The Clinton Era

Additional hallmarks of President Clinton's tenure included the August 1996 Personal Responsibility and Work Opportunity Reconciliation Act, which not only placed a lifetime limit of five years on welfare-related benefits paid by federal funds and instituted a work requirement, but also restricted the access that legal permanent residents had to safety-net programs (such as food stamps and Supplementary Security Income) and excluded undocumented migrants from such resources. Some of these rights were subsequently restored under the new Temporary Assistance for Needy Families (TANF) block grant program now administered under the states.

The following month (September 1996), Congress also passed the Illegal Immigration Reform and Immigrant Responsibility Act of 1996 (IIRIRA), which was significant for undocumented migrants in several ways. The first was a massive influx of resources for border enforcement. Congress doubled the size of the U.S. Border Patrol to 10,000 agents (over five years) and authorized the construction of several fences in heavily trafficked areas along the U.S.-Mexican border. Through IIRIRA and the Antiterrorism and Effective Death Penalty Act (also passed in 1996), Congress streamlined and accelerated the removal of noncitizens with criminal records by restricting judicial review of administrative removal orders and limiting alternatives to deportation. This instituted an "expedited removal" procedure that largely withdrew the discretion previously available to immigration judges.

The IIRIRA also mandated that the Social Security Administration (SSA) implement and evaluate three employment verification pilot programs over a four-year period. In response to this legislation, the INS implemented the Basic Pilot, the Citizen Attestation Verification Pilot (CAVP), and the Machine-Readable Document Pilot (MRDP) programs, all of which were to be evaluated independently. The Basic Pilot (E-Verify) Program was deemed the most successful of the three and expanded voluntarily to all states. Employers participating in the Basic Pilot Program simply enter the I-9 form information about their newly hired employees into a computer and electronically transmit this information to the federal government for validation. Employers are informed if the information submitted is consistent or not with data held by the Social Security Administration (SSA). Initial evaluations found problems in the

program that were identified for correction. These largely stemmed from erroneous non-confirmation responses and data entry errors. The program, however, was appealing to some employers. Participants were protected from employer sanctions provisions, and also escaped liability under discrimination protections as long as they could demonstrate that they acted in "good faith." To participate, employers simply had to enter into a memorandum of understanding with the Department of Homeland Security and possibly the Social Security Administration.

In June 2005, the Social Security Number Verification Service (SSNVS) was also made available in all states. The SSNVS allowed employers to verify Social Security numbers (SSNs) via the Internet. The program was intended to reflect whether the employer's records match SSA records, but not whether an employee had valid authorization to work in the United States. Employers were not allowed to use the program to prescreen applicants, or as a punitive device. However, immigrant advocates were similarly critical of the system, which was subject to inaccuracies in SSA's records, employer misuse of the program, and lack of monitoring by the SSA and other labor-standards-enforcement agencies. Many businesses also opposed the program for what was seen as unfair targeting of high-profile employers.

Similar concerns surrounding the accuracy of SSA data were raised regarding the "No Match Letter" program, which sends employers a letter when the names or SSNs listed on an employer's Form W-2 do not match SSA records. New rules were intended to go into effect in September 2007 that would have required employers to terminate workers who were unable to resolve a discrepancy within 90 days of an SSA "no-match" letter being sent. A lawsuit challenging the proposed Department of Homeland Security (DHS) rule was filed on August 29, 2007, in the U.S. District Court for the Northern District of California, cosponsored by the American Federation of Labor and Congress of Industrial Organizations (AFL-CIO), the American Civil Liberties Union (ACLU), the National Immigration Law Center (NILC), and the Central Labor Council of Alameda County, along with other local labor movements. As of April 2009, President Obama's new appointee to head the DHS, Janet Napolitano (and previously by Michael Chertoff, under President Bush), had requested yet another extension, leaving in place the injunction against the implementation of the 90-day rule.

The Post-9/11 Era

Following the attacks of September 11, 2001, enforcement mechanisms shifted their attention toward national security concerns. This shift revolutionized the tenor of public debate toward a framework focused on a "War on Terrorism." Perhaps the largest bureaucratic effect of this set of changes was the movement of the Immigration and Naturalization Service (previously under the Department of Justice) to the newly created Department of Homeland Security. Former INS departments now became the U.S. Citizenship and Immigration Service, the U.S. Border Patrol, and the U.S. Immigration and Customs Enforcement. Under this new rubric, the Border Patrol restated its mission to focus on the "detection, apprehension and/or deterrence of terrorists and terrorist weapons." The grounds for inadmissibility and deportability were also broadened, and nationality became more important in deciding immigration law enforcement priorities.

The 2001 USA PATRIOT Act gave the federal government broad powers to detain suspected terrorists. During this period, thousands of South Asian and Middle Eastern men were detained without being charged or being given due process. Shortly following the PATRIOT Act, the 2002 Special Registration system required nonimmigrant males between the ages of 16 and 24 to report to a local immigration office to be fingerprinted. As a result of this process, an estimated 13,000 men (most from largely Muslim countries) were placed in deportation proceedings in 2002. In 2004, the Asian American Legal Defense and Education Fund surveyed 219 of the 800 immigrants who received assistance from AADLEF for Special Registration proceedings and were mostly undocumented working-class Muslim immigrants from Bangladesh, Pakistan, Indonesia, or the Middle East. The survey found that over half of those who registered were put into deportation proceedings, and 80 percent of these deportees were visa overstayers.

Unauthorized migrants in the United States have also been impacted by the recent addition of resources to the southern border in this post-9/11 era. The passage of the 2005 Real ID Act mandated uniform national standards for state identification cards, and created provisions to facilitate the completion of a border fence. The Secure Fence Act of 2006 allowed for 700 miles of fence to be built along the Mexican border, spanning California, Arizona, New Mexico, and Texas. It also provided resources for additional surveillance mechanisms and high-tech equipment. The stated purpose of the fence, as articulated by President Bush in October 2006, was to "help protect the American people" and "make our borders more secure." As of April 2009, the DHS had erected approximately 613 miles of new pedestrian fencing and vehicle barriers. President Obama vowed to review these priorities during his campaign, while incoming head of the Department of Homeland Security Janet Napolitano noted after her appointment in 2009 that she would review the fence policy as a part of a comprehensive review of all border-security programs. Critics charge that the creation of such a border fence would only follow previous examples, such as "Operation Gatekeeper," and simply reroute border crossers to "more remote border regions where their agents have a tactical advantage over border-crossers" (Nuñez-Neto and Viña 2006, 4). In April 2009, the Associated Press reported that illegal immigrant deaths along the U.S.-Mexican border had risen in the prior six months despite a nearly 25 percent drop in arrests by the Border Patrol.

Demographic and Socioeconomic Profile of the Undocumented Population
Demographic and Family Characteristics

The majority of the unauthorized population living in the United States in 2008 were men (an estimated 6.3 million), versus 4.1 million women. This represents an increase over the 4.5 million unauthorized men and 3.4 million unauthorized women in 2003. The number of unauthorized children during this same period remained steady, estimated at 1.5 million in 2008, compared with 1.6 million in 2003.

Compared to the U.S.-born and legal immigrant population, unauthorized immigrants in 2008 were more concentrated among the prime working ages. Lower proportions of unauthorized are children or elderly. Thirty-five percent of the undocumented population were men 18–29, compared to only 14 percent of the U.S.-born, and 18 percent of the legal immigrant population. Thirteen percent of unauthorized immigrants are children, as against 27 percent of U.S.-born and 6 percent of legal immigrants. However, according to 2008 estimates, close to three-quarters of the 5.5 million children of unauthorized immigrants (73 percent) were born in the United States. This signals the large proportion of "mixed status" families (i.e., families with unauthorized immigrants and their U.S.-citizen children).

Unauthorized-immigrant households are more likely than U.S.-born or legal-immigrant households to be comprised of couples (married or cohabiting) with children. (In 2008, 47 percent of unauthorized immigrant households included couples, versus 35 percent and 21 percent of legal immigrant and U.S.-born households, respectively.) A larger share of unauthorized immigrant women than among men (83 percent versus 53 percent) were living with a spouse or cohabiting partner. Nearly half (48 percent) of unauthorized immigrants live with their children, and this is true particularly for women. However, consistent percentages of unauthorized immigrants, particularly men, are classified as "unpartnered adults without children" (35 percent since 2005).

Education

Generally, unauthorized immigrants are significantly less educated than their native-born counterparts; close to half have less than a high school degree, compared to only 8 percent of all native-born residents in 2008. Moreover, the younger an unauthorized immigrant's age upon arrival, the more likely he or she is to pursue a higher educational level. Nearly half (49 percent) of unauthorized immigrant high school graduates, ages 18–24, are in college or have attended college. While this pales in comparison to the rates of legal immigrants and U.S.-born residents (76 percent and 71 percent, respectively), it is quite impressive,

given the restrictions this population is facing in accessing institutions of higher education.

The 1982 Supreme Court decision in *Plyler v. Doe* ruled that undocumented immigrants are "persons" under the Constitution and thus entitled to equal protection under the law according to the Fourteenth Amendment. This ruling prohibited states from discriminating against these students on the basis of their legal status in terms of their access to public elementary and secondary education. Undocumented students are also permitted to attend most colleges but for the most part are not entitled to in-state tuition or government aid. One significant exception is California, which, under Assembly Bill 540, made undocumented students exempt from paying out-of-state tuition if they have attended a California high school for three years and graduated from high school in California. These students, however, are still ineligible for state or federal aid.

Labor Force Experiences and Well-Being

In 2008, undocumented men were more likely to be in the labor force (94 percent) than are those who are legal immigrants (85 percent) or native-born (83 percent). However, the converse holds for undocumented women, who were significantly less likely to be in the labor force (58 percent) than those who are legal immigrants (66 percent) or U.S.-born (73 percent). This is largely due to the larger proportion (one-third) of these women who say they have opted out of the labor force to raise their children.

Despite the higher rates of labor force participation, undocumented men in 2008 were actually more likely to be unemployed (6.5 percent) than legal immigrants and native-born men (5.6 percent each). This represents a significant shift from data gathered three years earlier, which placed the unemployment rates of undocumented men (4.5 percent) at far lower than native-born men (5.9 percent) or legal immigrant workers (4.9 percent). This change likely represented the ensuing economic recession and the enhanced vulnerability these workers face in the low-wage sector.

Among all civilian workers in the United States, 5.4 percent (8.3 million) were estimated to be unauthorized in 2008, an increase of 2 million over the previous five years. By far, the occupation with the largest share of unauthorized immigrants is farming, though significant levels are also found in building grounds keeping and maintenance (19 percent), construction (17 percent), food preparation and serving (12 percent), and production (10 percent).

Likely largely stemming from their lower education profiles, undocumented workers earn far less than their native-born counterparts (a median household income of $36,000 versus $50,000) and do not experience the same income mobility over time as do other immigrants. As a result, a third of the children of unauthorized immigrants live in poverty, nearly double the rates for those with U.S.-born parents (18 percent).

In large part due to the young age structure, low socioeconomic status, and relatively more mobile patterns of unauthorized immigrants, they are significantly less likely than those in U.S.-born households to own their own home (35 percent). While long-time legal immigrants are just as likely as U.S.-born individuals to be homeowners, the same is not true of long-term unauthorized immigrants. Unauthorized immigrants are also at a high risk of being uninsured, with nearly 60 percent lacking health insurance in 2007 (nearly twice the proportion of legal immigrants and four times the proportion of U.S.-born adults). While the children of unauthorized immigrants fare better than their parents, they are still significantly disadvantaged compared with their U.S.-born and legal resident counterparts.

Geographic Distribution

Though an estimated half of the 11.9 million unauthorized immigrants in the United States lived in California, Texas, Florida, and New York in 2008, the unauthorized population is becoming increasingly dispersed throughout the country. While California was still home to the largest number of undocumented migrants, its share of this population had dropped from 42 percent in 1990 to 22 percent. This was in large part due to the dispersion of the undocumented population to states in the Mid-Atlantic, Midwest, Mountain and Southeast regions. These new destinations are now home to 32 percent of the unauthorized immigrant population, which is more than double

their 14 percent share in 1990. Unauthorized immigrants are now also overwhelmingly city dwellers. Approximately 94 percent live in metropolitan areas, as opposed to 80 percent of the U.S.-born population.

Contemporary Flows

Undocumented migration from Europe was rampant during the first half of the century. Welcomed at first by Canadian agricultural labor programs, Belgian, Dutch, Swiss, Russian, Bulgarian, Italian, and Polish migrants would soon thereafter attempt entry to the United States via an emerging smuggling route. In fact, the most heavily traveled route by undocumented European migrants was through Mexico. These flows declined by the end of the 1920s, not only because of the deterrent of more aggressive apprehensions, but also because of the availability of alternatives that facilitated legal entry.

According to estimates by the Department of Homeland Security, the unauthorized immigrant population living in the United States increased by 37 percent between 2000 and 2008. Thirty-seven percent of these migrants entered since 2000, 44 percent entered during the 1990s, and 19 percent arrived during the 1980s. Critical immigration scholars have noted that undocumented status today has become a central component of the racialization of all Latinos, and in particular Mexicans. Historically, the experience of Mexican immigrants today stands in stark contrast to that of northern crossers who were treated hospitably as tourists. Pew Hispanic Center estimates reveal that the lion's share of undocumented migration flows is from Mexico (7 of the 11.9 million by 2008). However, significant percentages also come from other Latin American regions, including Central America (11 percent), South America (7 percent), and the Caribbean (2 percent). Non-negligible flows also hail from Asia (11 percent) and the Middle East (2 percent). The country of origin of unauthorized immigrants also varies across different states, with significant concentrations of Mexicans, for example, in California and Texas in 2000. Conversely, only 15 percent of the unauthorized population in New York is from Mexico, while the majority are categorized as "Other Latin Americans" and Asians.

Central America

Historically, Central American migration began in earnest during the 1980s in the midst of civil wars in Nicaragua, El Salvador, and Guatemala. Natural disasters in the decades following accelerated this flow. While a quarter of all Nicaraguans were granted asylum in the aftermath of the war there, only 2.6 percent and 1.8 percent of applicants from El Salvador and Guatemala, respectively, were granted asylum. This discrepancy has been attributed to the anti-Communist context of the time, whereby the United States opposed the Nicaraguan government though supporting the Salvadoran administration, which was fighting a Marxist insurgency.

The undocumented population living in the United States at this time, many of whom were unsuccessful in their asylum cases, were granted relief in 1997 through the Nicaraguan Adjustment and Central American Relief Act, which prevented the deportation of Nicaraguans, Salvadorans, and Guatemalans as well as other national origin groups fleeing Communist regimes. The Victims of Trafficking and Violence Protection Act (2000) added additional categories of relief under NACARA. These individuals were eligible for lighter residency requirements than those imposed under the 1996 Illegal Immigration Reform and Immigrant Responsibility Act, in order to gain legal permanent residency status.

Relief had also been made available under the new "Temporary Protected Status" (TPS) provisions (1990) to undocumented Central Americans in 1990 and renewed in 1998, 2001, and 2010. Though TPS does not provide a path to permanent residency, it does authorize beneficiaries to remain in the United States and work. As of 2009, the countries covered under TPS include El Salvador, Honduras, and Nicaragua as well as the African countries of Liberia, Somalia, and Sudan. Once this status expired for beneficiaries, the migrants will revert to unlawful status (unless the TPS provision continues to be renewed). Asylum applicants, and those who have applied for TPS, are also considered unauthorized.

The Central American Free Trade Agreement (which covers Costa Rica, the Dominican Republic, El Salvador, Guatemala, Honduras, and Nicaragua) was passed in 2003 and renamed DR-CAFTA in 2004, when it incorporated the Dominican Republic. There is significant debate over how this free-trade agreement will impact unauthorized migration flows. Central American scholars point to the lessons of NAFTA as an instructive example of what the effects may be in Central America. If the treaty successfully stimulates the region's economy and social development, it is possible that additional jobs will be created, thus deterring out-migration and increasing the gross domestic product. However if the agreement is ultimately not successful in reducing poverty, and there continue to be no legal routes to migration to the United States for an economic migrant from the region, then the unauthorized migration flow might continue and possibly increase. Approximately 1.3 million unauthorized Central Americans were estimated to be in the United States as of March 2005.

Caribbean

Half a million unauthorized Caribbean immigrants were estimated to be in the United States in 2008. Political turmoil and natural disasters have driven Haitians to seek refuge in the United States for at least three decades. Following the 1980 Mariel boatlift, 25,000 of the 150,000 asylum seekers who arrived in South Florida were Haitian. Large flows of asylum seekers and refugees also entered from 1991 to 1994, following the military coup d'état ousting President Jean Bertrand Aristide. Thereafter, limited flows have entered via family-sponsored legal permanent residence, employment-based work visas, or the very few undocumented migrants who arrive on boats. These latter flows, however, are often intercepted by U.S. Coast Guard forces. The largest number of interdictions was recorded on July 4, 1993, when 3,247 were intercepted. When a boat of Haitian migrants is stopped by U.S. Coast Guard forces, individuals must proactively make an asylum claims but are most often returned without a hearing. Those Haitians who reach U.S. soil and are apprehended are uniquely put into "fast-track removal procedures," in which they are subject to mandatory detention and are not eligible for release on bond. This policy stems from a 1981 agreement between then U.S. President Reagan and the Haitian dictator Jean-Claude Duvalier. These fleeing Haitians were largely seen as economic migrants, versus political refugees fleeing Communist governments. Human rights advocates, however, have expressed concern over this differential treatment, relative to other refugees and asylum seekers (such as Cubans). In 2002, the then-named Immigration and Naturalization Service classified all illegal mass migration by sea as a national security risk. The largest destinations for Haitian migrants include Florida, New York, and Massachusetts.

Haiti's land neighbor, the Dominican Republic, witnesses a significant flow of undocumented migrants each year to the United States, particularly to Florida, the Northeast, and Puerto Rico. The first flows of Dominican migrants began in earnest during the political unrest of the 1960s. This period included the assassination of longtime dictator Rafael Leonidas Trujillo, a coup against the leftist President Juan Bosch, the Dominican Civil War in 1965, and a U.S. invasion that attempted to install a more conservative leader. Following these events, restrictions on Dominican migration were intermittently lifted during politically opportune times for the United States. In between these periods, undocumented migration flows continued. During the 1980s and 1990s, the Dominican Republic continued to send large numbers of immigrants to New York City and Puerto Rico, most driven by poverty and many lacking legal status. Those with additional resources have migrated to the mainland and may overstay visas, while a cheaper option, which women in particular take, is to make the deadly trip via boat to Puerto Rico. According to the 2000 census, there were over 687,000 Dominican immigrants in the United States.

Asia

Undocumented migration from Asia is often lost in the dominant discussion of skilled workers and entrepreneurs. In 2006, the Office of Immigration Statistics estimated that 2 percent of all unauthorized immigrants in the United States were from the Philippines. This is a 40 percent increase from 2000, rising from 200,000 to 280,000. These flows have contributed to a rich history of Filipino migration to the United States, which included early settlements in Louisiana (prior to the U.S. acquisition of the islands), labor flows to Hawai'i in the prewar period, migrant workers in California and Alaska, military service during World War II, and significant streams in the post-1965 era. Today, the largest concentrations of Filipinos are in California.

An additional 2 percent of all undocumented immigrants were also estimated to be from China in 2006 (190,000). Large flows of undocumented from Fujian (located on the southeast coast of China), for example, is central to the New York Chinatown. Reports in 2007 reveal that some Chinese citizens are using intricate routes, first entering South American countries as tourists, such as Colombia and Ecuador, from which they head to coastal areas in Central America via fishing boats, and on to the United States through well-traveled land routes.

Undocumented migrants from India formed an estimated 2.3 percent of the unauthorized population in 2006 (270,000), also a doubling from six years earlier. This represented the fastest growth of any group during this period. The majority of these unauthorized migrants are visa overstayers. The largest Indian-born population in 2006 is in Santa Clara County (Silicon Valley), where many are high-skilled workers on H1-B visas. Were they fired, they would fall out of status if they did not find another employer to sponsor them, or they must leave the country within 60 business days (or sometimes fewer at the U.S. Citizenship and Immigration Services' discretion).

Vietnamese immigrants entered the United States in large waves as refugees in the aftermath of the Vietnam War, and have since largely become legal permanent residents, or naturalized citizens. Nearly three-quarters of Vietnamese immigrants were naturalized U.S. citizens by 2006, compared to only 42 percent of the foreign-born overall. However, following the normalization of relations with Vietnam in 1995, many entered and overstayed visas. In 2008, the two countries signed a repatriation agreement, which set in motion the deportation proceedings of 7,300 undocumented immigrants with criminal convictions. Data from the 2000 census reveal that California and Texas were, at that time, home to over half of all Vietnamese immigrants in the United States.

The Rights of Undocumented Workers

Undocumented workers are somewhat of a legal paradox. On the one hand, they are not permitted to legally reside or work here, yet most of them find employers ready and willing to hire them. While their illegal residence bars them from formal membership in American society, undocumented workers are eligible for a wide array of labor protections at both the federal and state level, despite their immigration status (e.g., the National Labor Relations Act [NLRA, 1935], the Federal Labor Standards Act [FLSA, 1938], Title VII of the 1964 Civil Rights Act, and the Occupational Health and Safety Act [1970]).

In 2002, this access was challenged by the Supreme Court case *Hoffman Plastics v. National Labor Relations Board*. In this case, the NLRB awarded back pay to an undocumented immigrant that it again deemed had been wrongfully fired for union organizing. The employer, Hoffman Plastics, appealed the decision all the way up to the U.S. Supreme Court, which ultimately reversed the lower court's decision in a 5–4 decision lead by Chief Justice Rehnquist. The majority argued that in fact, the Immigration Reform and Control Act of 1986 now prevented the NLRB from awarding back pay to an undocumented individual who had never been legally authorized to work in the United States in the first place.

Though it spurred significant debates in subsequent cases, *Hoffman* ultimately left much of the workplace protections for undocumented workers intact. For example, in response to the landmark decision, the U.S. Department of Labor stated in 2002 that "The Supreme Court's decision does not mean that undocumented workers do not have rights under other U.S. labor laws . . . The Department's Wage and Hour Division will continue to enforce the FLSA [Fair Labor Standards Act] and MSWPA [Migrant and Seasonal Worker Protection Act] without regard to whether an employee is documented or undocumented." Similarly, in its press release following *Hoffman*, the Equal Employment Opportunity Commission reaffirmed both its commitment to "root out discrimination against undocumented workers," and their commitment to *not* "inquire into a worker's immigration status" or "consider an individual's immigration status when examining the underlying merits of a charge." Following the example set by these federal agencies, many state agencies also declared their "commitment to protecting the rights of all workers." On January 1, 2003, section 1171.5 was added to the California Labor Code, which made a person's immigration status irrelevant to the issue of liability with respect to the enforcement of labor, employment, civil rights, and employee housing laws. On November 18, 2008, the U.S. Supreme Court refused to hear *Agriprocessors v. NLRB*, maintaining a lower court's ruling that gives undocumented immigrants the right to organize labor unions.

A good deal of research has highlighted the progress that labor unions have made in organizing immigrants. Some of the most prominent union victories include the Service Employees International Union's *Justice for Janitors* campaign, which for two decades rallied for the rights of immigrant workers. Immigrants, who used to be thought of as the "unorganizeable," have arguably reinvigorated the labor movement. Yet, it was only in 2000 that the AFL-CIO passed a resolution to "stand in solidarity with immigrant workers" and went on record calling for an amnesty for all undocumented workers and their families (AFL-CIO 2001). The national Change-to-Win (CTW) coalition, which made a split from the AFL-CIO with a mission to increase union organizing efforts, also represents a large sector of the immigrant low-wage workforce. The seven CTW-affiliated unions include the International Brotherhood of Teamsters, the Laborers' International Union of North America, Service Employees International Union, the United Brotherhood of Carpenters and Joiners, the United Farm Workers of America, the United Food and Commercial Workers, and the hotel and restaurant union UNITE-HERE!

On April 14, 2009, the leaders of the CTW coalition and the AFL-CIO issued a "unified framework for comprehensive immigration reform legislation." This joint announcement was intended to ensure that immigration reform remained a priority for Congress and the Obama administration. The proposal contained the following key aspects: "1) an independent commission to assess and manage future flows, based on labor market shortages that are determined on the basis of actual need; 2) a secure and effective worker authorization mechanism; 3) rational operational control of the border; 4) adjustment of status for the current undocumented population; and 5) improvement, not expansion, of temporary worker programs, limited to temporary or seasonal, not permanent, jobs" (Change to Win 2009).

State and Local Enforcement of Immigration

In addition to facing key challenges that all noncitizen immigrants share in the United States, such as limited access to safety net services and benefits, the inability to vote, and increased scrutiny in a post-9/11 political climate, undocumented immigrants also face a wide array of unique barriers to integration into U.S. society. Many of these policies that either facilitate or hinder immigrant incorporation are set at the local level by states and cities.

According to the National Conference of State Legislatures' Immigrant Policy Project, state laws related to immigration (and in particular unauthorized immigration) increased tremendously in recent years. The top three areas of legislation included employment, identification/drivers licenses, and law enforcement. Other policy areas for state policies regarding immigrants include education, health, and benefits sectors. In the first quarter of 2009, 25 states enacted 35 laws and adopted 40 resolutions concerning immigrants.

However, if states were becoming an increasingly important area of policy innovation for immigrants, cities and other localities were following close behind. In 2007, the Migration Policy Institute found that cities in particular have become very active in providing and withholding rights from undocumented immigrants in such areas as regulating landlords concerning the renting of apartments to undocumented tenants (e.g., Hazleton, Pa. Ordinance No. 2006-18), enacting anti-loitering and anti-solicitation ordinances that impact informal industries composed of largely undocumented workers, such as day laborers (e.g., Glendale, Ca. Municipal Code § 9.17.030, 2004), and memoranda of agreement (MOA) between local police departments and federal immigration authorities (e.g., Prince William County, Va., MOA signed 2/26/2008).

The local enforcement of federal immigration law has been a particularly contested policy arena. These policies fall under Section 287(g) of the Immigrant and Nationality Act, which gives state agents the authority to carry out immigration enforcement. Local 287(g) agreements have been on the steady rise since the Department of Justice reversed its position in 2002 and announced that states have the "inherent authority" to enforce civil provisions of immigration law. The stated goal of the program is to deport unauthorized immigrants who pose a threat to national security and/or public safety. Memoranda of understanding provide resources to local agencies in order to train and certify officers in the investigation, as well as the detention, apprehension, and deportation of aliens.

Several other cities, such as San Francisco and New York, have eschewed local enforcement of federal immigration law and expanded rights to undocumented populations. In 2007, the National Immigration Law Center (NILC) cited over 70 jurisdictions that limited cooperation with immigration authorizes. Cities adopting such policies are often loosely referred to as "sanctuary cities." Advocates, including the NILC, discourage the use of this term, emphasizing that such policies are not out of compliance with federal law and still permit information sharing for the purposes of identifying criminal or terrorist activities. These cities often justify such policies by citing the need to garner trust amongst immigrant communities to establish effective community policing models and facilitate daily bureaucratic needs for residents. It is important to note, however, that these policies are often subject to political shifts, and some former "sanctuary cities" have gone on to enact 287(g) agreements, particularly following on the heels of high-profile crimes involving undocumented immigrants (e.g. City of Houston, MOA approved 7/11/09).

Local policies extending rights and benefits to undocumented immigrants also abound. For example, on April 15, 2009, San Francisco launched a municipal ID program designed not only to benefit unauthorized immigrants but also all city residents. This photo identification card is to serve as proof of identity and residency and provides a variety of other functions for city bureaucracies. The program, however, was viewed as largely connected to the city's sanctuary city policy (declared in 1989), and a response against the 2005 federal Real ID Act, which prohibited issuing drivers licenses to undocumented immigrants. New Haven, Connecticut, formally created a municipal ID law in 2006; yet only a handful of localities were considering—but had not passed—similar provisions as of 2012. They include New York; Miami; Los Angeles; Richmond, California; and Marin County.

Both sets of policies—287(g) agreements as well as sanctuary city policies—have been highly scrutinized by legal scholars assessing the principle of preemption of federal law.

Fiscal Effects and Public Debate

Based on various polls taken in the months leading up to the largest immigrant rights mobilizations in spring 2006, an estimated one-third to one-half of Americans feel that illegal immigrants should be required to go home, rather than provided a route to citizenship. Roughly a third also answered that they felt that illegal immigrants take jobs away from Americans. Yet, there is no clear consensus on the net fiscal effects of undocumented immigration, and conclusions have varied from state to state. Other reports have warned against continued border security that would stem illegal immigration and ultimately put a drain on the economy (e.g., Hanson 2007).

Bibliography

AFL-CIO. 2001. "A Nation of Immigrants." Presented at the AFL-CIO 24th Biennial Convention: Conventions, Revolutions, and Executive Council Statements, Las Vegas, NV, December 2–6. http://www.aflcio.org/content/download/6951/75037/file/res5.pdf (accessed May 18, 2012).

Change to Win. 2009. "Change to Win and AFL-CIO Unveil Unified Immigration Reform Framework" (Press release). Washington, DC. http://www.seiu.org/2009/04/change-to-win-and-afl-cio-unveil-unified-immigration-reform-framework.php (accessed March 1, 2012).

Daniels, Roger. 2008. "The Immigration Act of 1965: Intended and Unintended Consequences." In *Historians on America*. Washington, DC: U.S. State Department. http://www.america.gov/st/educ-english/2008/April/20080423214226eaifas0.9637982.html (accessed March 1, 2012). Accessed April 3, 2008).

Hanson, Gordon H. 2007. "The Economic Logic of Illegal Immigration." *The Bernard and Irene Schwartz Series on American Competitiveness*. Council on Foreign Relations, CSR No. 26 (April).

Massey, Douglas S. 1998. "March of Folly: US Immigration Policy after NAFTA." *American Prospect*, March–April, 22–33.

Ngai, Mae M. 2003. "The Strange Career of the Illegal Alien: Immigration Restriction and Deportation Policy in the United States, 1921–1965." *Law and History Review* 21: 69–107.

Nuñez-Neto, Blas, and Stephen R. Viña. 2006. "Border Security: Fences along the U.S. International Border." Congressional Research Service, Library of Congress, Order Code RS22026 (September 15).

Passel, Jeffrey, and D'Vera Cohn. 2009. "A Portrait of the Unauthorized Migrants in the United States" (Report). Washington, DC: Pew Hispanic Center. http://pewhispanic.org/files/reports/107.pdf (accessed March 1, 2012).

Reyes, Belinda I., Hans P. Johnson, and Richard Van Swearingen. 2002. *Holding the Line? The Effect of the Recent Border Build-Up on Unauthorized Immigration*. San Francisco: Public Policy Institute of California.

Torpey, John. 2000. *The Invention of the Passport: Surveillance, Citizenship and the State*. Cambridge: Cambridge University Press.

U.S. Department of Homeland Security. 2008. "Detailed Methodology for Annual Estimates of the Unauthorized Immigrant Population Residing in the United States: 1990 to 2000." Washington, DC: Office of Immigration Statistics. http://www.dhs.gov/xlibrary/assets/statistics/publications/Ill_Report_1211.pdf (accessed April 3, 2009).

Nativism and Immigrants, Past and Present

David M. Reimers

Nineteenth-Century Nativist Precedents

The historian John Higham, whose study *Strangers in the Land: Patterns of American Nativism, 1860–1925* remains a classic, noted that nativism was difficult to define. He said its meaning denotes a general fear and hostility to foreigners and a movement to bar immigrants. Along the way, nativism can be violence directed toward newcomers. The hostility to foreigners was often an expression of American nationalism, the belief that the United States did not need newcomers. Or should any negative feeling about foreigners be counted as nativism? If so, then practically all the forebears of native-born Americans would have been victims at one time or another. Used here, nativism follows Higham's approach that stresses hostility to immigrants, immigration restriction, and laws aimed at foreign-born groups.

Prior to 1875, the federal government was content to allow states to control immigration. When the U.S. Supreme Court ruled that immigration was a federal matter, Congress subsequently passed laws that established a system for immigrant regulation. In passing the Page Act in 1875 and the Chinese Exclusion Act seven years later, Congress was responding to the hostility about immigrants that had existed since colonial times. Before the Supreme Court ruled the immigration was a federal and not a state issue, many states had enacted laws to control or ban the influx of newcomers. Some of these state provisions were not controversial, among them the banning of convicts, beggars, and those with infectious or loathsome diseases.

But the list of those to be excluded was by no means limited to criminals and paupers. The fear of immigrants holding views deemed to be dangerous to republicanism or democracy also played a role. Before the Civil War, nativists insisted that the Roman Catholic Church was flooding the United States with immigrants who were under the thumb of the church and did not share dominant American values. Some extremists claimed that priests arriving to minister to the immigrants were agents of the papacy, intent upon conquering and destroying the United States. Offered "proof" of their beliefs was the politics of Europe, where the church was allied with antidemocratic and antirepublican forces. Much of the pre–Civil War nativism was directed at Irish immigrants, who had the misfortune to be both Catholic and poor. During the Civil War, nativism was overwhelmed by the war itself and by slavery. Then, too, immigration declined during the conflict. Congress even passed a law to encourage immigration by permitting persons to contract their part of their labor for both the cost of the passage and the employment in the United States.

As immigration increased in the late nineteenth century, nativism grew apace. However, old political fears assumed a new form. Now, nativists perceived a threat from the left and not European political reactionaries. The new menace was identified as radical immigrants, anarchists in particular, rather than the reactionary hierarchy of the Catholic Church in Europe. The labor violence of those decades was often blamed on foreign radicals who were out to destroy capitalist America. In 1886 in Chicago's Haymarket Square, a bomb exploded at a rally of those demonstrating for an eight-hour working day. While it was never proved precisely who threw the bomb when the police moved in to break up the rally, nativists singled out foreign-born anarchists, especially Germans, who were considered the scum of

Europe. On scant evidence several anarchists were prosecuted, convicted and hanged. Higham considered the Haymarket affair the most important single incident in late-nineteenth-century nativism. It also marked the beginning of the shift in labor unions' views to an anti-immigrant posture. The assassination of President William McKinley in 1901 only added to fears of foreign radicals. The assassin was a native-born American, but his name, Leon Czolgosz, brought up images of foreign radicalism. Congress responded in 1903 by barring anarchist immigrants.

World War I and Nativist Responses

Fears of disloyalty received added support during World War I. The American army fought Germany abroad, and at home, many Americans had little use for German Americans and even some Irish Americans, who were opposed to waging a war on the side of Great Britain, Ireland's oppressor for hundreds of years. The war demanded absolute "Americanism." German-American periodicals and newspapers switched to English, and German-speaking ministers who had preached in German now gave sermons in English. German-American organizations closed their doors, and prominent German Americans loudly proclaimed their loyalty to the United States by publicly purchasing Liberty Bonds to finance the war. States passed laws to outlaw the use of the German language in public, and the teaching of German in public schools virtually disappeared. After the war, the first laws making English the official language appeared in several states, although these statutes were not enforced.

The Russian Revolution of 1917 loomed large in the minds of those who wanted no part of European conflicts and affairs. Right after the end of hostilities, several bombs exploded at the homes and offices of judges and businessmen, which offered proof to those who saw a new threat in the form of anarchism and Communism inspired by the revolution. A bomb detonated in front of the Wall Street's House of Morgan proved to be especially alarming, even though officials never found individuals or groups responsible for the explosion. In 1919, amid the heighten fears of Communism, A. Mitchell Palmer, Woodrow Wilson's attorney general, authorized sweeping raids of radical

headquarters and arrested and deported several thousand aliens without proper hearings to determine whether or not they were connected to the violence.

The federal government's early laws banning groups, such as paupers or anarchists, did not halt the growing numbers of immigrants. Nor were they, except for the Palmer raids, particularly controversial. Furthermore, businesses and state politicians often held different views about immigrants; they wanted immigrants and the labor, skills, and purchasing power that the newcomers brought with them. Even in the South for many years, white southerners tried to promote immigrant laborers to replace their former slaves, but they had little success; white southerners did not turn against immigrant laborers until after 1900.

Asians, Catholics and Emerging Nativism

In the early nineteenth century anti-Catholicism was the driving force behind anti-immigrant fears. While tension still existed between Protestants and Catholics in the Gilded Age, there was a shift in emphasis. During the 1840s and 1850s, hysteria over growing Catholicism was often centered on the immigration of Irish Catholics. After the Civil War, those who worried about the increase of Catholicism did not always focus on immigration. The largest group with an anti-Catholic base was the American Protective Association (APA), founded in 1887 in Clinton, Iowa. While anti-Catholic, the APA was not necessarily opposed to immigration. The organization concerned itself with issues of church-and-state relations but, unlike the Know-Nothings of the pre–Civil War period, it did not form a political party. The APA struggled to win adherents, yet in the end it collapsed with no accomplishments.

The demise of the APA did not mean the end of anti-Catholicism. The anti-Catholic journal, the *Menace*, founded in 1912, claimed a circulation of over one million readers, and the reappearance of the Ku Klux Klan (KKK) in 1916 attested to the fears of many Protestants that their nation was being besieged by Roman Catholics. At one time in the mid-1920s, the Klan claimed four million members. The Klan of that era drew support from those nativists worried by immigrant Catholics, but the reborn KKK was a broader movement winning support from anti-Semites, antiblack racists, and many fundamentalist Protestants. The KKK was part of the intolerant era of the 1920s, but it alone cannot explain the passage of immigration restrictions, or even the defeat of Catholic Al Smith in the 1928 presidential election, although it clearly played a role.

While disputes over religion were prominent during the Gilded Age, it was racism that ultimately explains the growing limitation placed on immigration, which dated from the 1882 Chinese Exclusion Act and ended with the enactment of the immigration restrictions of the 1920s. It should not be surprising that racism played such an important role in nativism. During the colonial era, white racism had been directed toward blacks and Indians, who were perceived as different, inferior, and potentially dangerous. Except for the Irish, little thought was given to other groups of newcomers until the arrival of the Chinese on the West Coast following the discovery of gold in California. Chinese immigrants, like most others who rushed to California after 1848, had come in search of riches. They quickly confronted hostility from persons of European origin and were subjected to special laws to hinder their competition with whites. The Foreign Miners Tax was clearly aimed at the Chinese, although other immigrants were also subject to it. The Chinese miners also faced violence intended to drive them out and away from competing with white miners.

Forced from the mines, Chinese immigrants farmed to fill the plates of hungry miners. Others found jobs in the cities, but especially important was their role in building the transcontinental railroad. E. P. Crocker, builder and financer of railroads, loved the Chinese as employees, known as "Crocker's Pets," because they labored long hours for wages lower than for whites. But for white laborers engaging in railroad building and laborers competing with the Chinese in cities, these Asian immigrants were looked upon as unfair workers who debased the American standard of living. The California legislature in Sacramento heaped restrictions on the Chinese as did such cities as San Francisco. In the end, about the only

employment open to Chinese immigrants was as operators of laundries, restaurants, and small tourist shops.

While economics did play a role in the ultimate barring of Chinese laborers, the hostility was laced with racism. A congressional committee examining Chinese immigration insisted that these Asians were innately inferior to white men and women. Others also insisted that the Chinese were an inferior race. The outcome of the rising racism was the Chinese Exclusion Acts (1882, 1892, and 1904) that barred all Chinese laborers from entering the United States and declared them ineligible for American citizenship. Merchants and their wives could still come but under restricted conditions.

During the 1880s, while Congress was beginning the process of barring Chinese immigrants, Japan began to allow its citizens to travel abroad and to immigrate to the United States. Most Japanese immigrants settled on the West Coast or in Hawai'i. Usually making a living from agriculture or small enterprises, their numbers were not large. Nonetheless, they quickly prompted white Americans—who considered the Chinese to be racially inferior and bad for those who competed economically—to call for Chinese restrictions. In the first decade of the twentieth century, the Hearst press and California politicians began to agitate for ending this stream of immigration. Nativists claimed that a virtual "yellow peril" existed that, unchecked, would conquer the United States. San Francisco created a foreign policy crisis for the administration of President Theodore Roosevelt when its Board of Education announced its intension to segregate Japanese pupils (who numbered less than 100) in the public schools. When the Japanese government protested, the Roosevelt administration in 1908 worked out a "Gentlemen's Agreement" with Japan. In return for the ending of school segregation, Japan agreed to halt the migration of Japanese laborers to the United States (and Hawai'i). Wives were not included, and many Japanese men, in contrast to the Chinese, began to bring their spouses to the United States. Often the men married by proxy without the couples seeing or knowing one another; the women were called "picture brides." Congress and the government of Japan finally curtailed the immigration of Japanese women in the 1920s.

Blocking other Asians was simple. Asian Indians had entered in small numbers and often from Canada where they first sought employment. Subject to harassment, the "turban heads," as the Sikhs were called, were banned by federal legislation in 1917. Korean immigrants, numbering only a few thousand in Hawai'i and California, were covered by the restrictions placed on Japanese immigrants because Japan had imposed controls on Korea and Korean emigration.

Harassment of Chinese and Japanese immigrants did not end with the restrictions. Chinese laborers found themselves the victims of violence in the West, while Japanese immigrants were barred from owning land. The land restrictions were based on the federal naturalization law of 1870 that limited citizenship to "white persons" and persons of African descent. Two important Supreme Court decisions, *Ozawa v. United States* (1922) and *United States v. Bhagat Singh Thind* (1923), held that Japanese and Asian Indians were not "white" aliens within the meaning of the naturalization law. The land laws simply barred ownership of lands by persons ineligible to become American citizens. Moreover, Asians found themselves barred from marriage to whites. Bans on black-white marriages had begun in the South and were strictly enforced until declared unconstitutional by the Supreme Court in 1967 (*Loving v. Virginia*). Some northern states followed the southern practice on intermarriage legislation, but in the western states, lawmakers also barred intermarriage between whites and Asians. Among the particular groups included in the marriage barriers were "Mongolians," "Malays," Chinese, Japanese, "Hindus," "Coreans," and "Asiatic Indians." For purposes of the marriage, Mexicans were not included in the intermarriage laws, and, as a result, in California about one-half of the Indian Sikh men married Mexican women.

The naturalization cases also became a vehicle to restrict Asian immigration to the United States. Congress simply barred the immigration of persons ineligible for naturalization. After 1924, the largest group of Asians who could immigrate freely was Filipinos, who numbered barely 100,000 when the Great Depression began in 1929. Because the United States had annexed the Philippines following the Spanish-American War, Filipinos were considered "nationals," not aliens. They, too, were considered inferior and especially troublesome as they courted white women. Finally, in the throes of the Great Depression, Congress limited their migration to 50 annually until the Philippines acquired independence 10 years later. Then the Filipinos would be aliens who were not white and hence barred from immigration. Congress also voted funds for a few thousand who wished to return to the Philippines. Most declined the offer.

While economic competition explains much of the opposition to Asians, the growing racism of the late nineteenth and early twentieth centuries lies at the core of nativism and immigration restriction. But could similar attitudes towards Europeans exist, considering the fact that Europeans were considered "white" within the meaning of the naturalization law? Court cases indicated that some groups on the fringe of Europe, or actually Asia, were to be counted as white. Armenian and Syrian immigrants who applied for citizenship were allowed to do so as were other persons from the Middle East. In 1915, Syrian immigrant George Dow, in *Dow v. United States*, won his case for naturalization. The court held that Syrians were to "be considered white persons" and therefore eligible for naturalization. In 1925 in *United States v. Cartozian*, the court affirmed that Armenians were also white persons. Apparently being white stopped at the Kyber Pass.

While excluding East Asians by law and court decisions, many white Americans also became alarmed by the trends in European immigration. After the 1880s, a growing proportion of newcomers from Europe came from the southern and eastern nations. Italians were the largest of these groups. Poles, Russians, Slovaks, Greeks, and Jews also came to the United States in increasing numbers just at the time when immigration from northern and western Europe was declining. Alarmed by this trend, in 1907, President Roosevelt and Congress established the Dillingham Commission (called by the name of its chairman, Senator William Dillingham of Vermont) to examine immigration. The commission eventually produced over 40 volumes of material and made suggestions about the flow of immigration to the United States. When it reported in 1911, it recommended that the existing bans on Asians be maintained, which was hardly controversial. When Congress debated immigration in the 1920s, Asians found few American friends; not even giving Asian countries tiny quotas had much support.

Europeans versus Europeans: Escalating Nativism

The more controversial area of debate about immigration centered on Europe and in particular the most recent influx from that continent. When the commission examined immigration, it did so with a background of late-nineteenth- and early-twentieth-century racial theory and eugenic thought. This racism was buttressed by studies coming from Great Britain about the criminal population and from France's innovations in IQ testing. Americans quickly accepted these dogmas and added their own twist to the emerging racism. Several states forcibly sterilized thousands of persons considered to be of low intelligence or innate criminals. Moreover, in 1927, a famous case decided by the U.S. Supreme Court (*Buck v. Bell)* sanctioned the practices.

The emerging racial theory divided groups that would be seen today as nationality or religious or ethnic groups and called them distinct races. Thus, the Dillingham report said that Slovaks, Hebrews, Polish, French, among others, were Caucasians but were distinct races or people. Its summary noted that the term Caucasians embraced all of these peoples from Europe. Other European races included Aryans, Teutons, and Celts, Nordics, or Germanic peoples. As whites, they could naturalize under the law for "free white persons." Moreover, southern and East European immigrants were not subject to the Jim Crow laws of the American South. They could vote once they became citizens, they did not attend separate public schools, they could buy property, and they were not subject to other social indignities facing Asians or African Americans.

But were all Europeans equal in morals, intelligence, and social characteristics? The emerging racism answered categorically, no. The studies of criminals or the insane demonstrated to many social scientists that certain traits were innate and could not be changed. "Scientific" evidence came in the form of IQ testing, which received a big boost when used

during World War I to test the intelligence of army recruits. What these tests allegedly demonstrated was that persons of southern and eastern European background were less intelligent than those from northern and western areas of Europe. Little sophistication was employed by the test makers, so that education and language ability to speak to English were not taken into account. A later generation would discredit the validity of such tests, but these dissenters in the 1920s were a distinct minority.

By the time of World War I, the idea that certain Europeans were innately inferior to others had been widely accepted in American thought. Moreover, popularizers of these notions perceived a threat to American blood if immigrants kept coming in such large numbers. According to Lothrop Stoddard's *The Rising Tide of Color against White World Supremacy* (1920), diluting the blood and the mixing of whites with Asians, Hispanics, and Africans would end the superior white peoples' rule of the world. Madison Grant went further and included certain Europeans among the inferiors, even though they might be white legally. He insisted that the new immigrants from southern and eastern Europe lacked the intelligence of the English and Germans to the north. These sentiments were by no means minority viewpoints. President Theodore Roosevelt certainly believed that African Americans, Indians, and Asians were inferior to older generations of European-origin Americans. The president and others worried that too many of the old-stock white families were having too few children. If overwhelmed by the incoming tide, they proclaimed that nation faced a threat of race suicide.

Immigrants had their supporters. Social workers and settlement house workers labored in immigrant communities to be of service. Other friends could be found in the Americanization movement of the early twentieth century. The movement drew support from the Bureau of Naturalization of the Department of Labor and many cities that ran programs to aid immigrants in their adjustment to their new homes. Some Americanizers tried to teach English and inform immigrants about the workings of American society. Others in the Americanization movement were eager to teach the newcomers that radicalism and unionization were anti-American.

In the 1890s, alarmed by the new immigration, an elite group of Bostonians had formed the Immigration Restriction League. Its most prominent spokesman was Senator Henry Cabot Lodge of Massachusetts. The League's main proposal to restrict European immigration was a literacy test. The test would bar those potential immigrants over age 16 who were illiterate. Lodge and his fellow members of the League made no secret of their intentions because they noted publicly that many southern and East Europeans were illiterate. The obstacle for Lodge and other nativists existed in the White House. Congress passed several bills providing for literacy tests, but Presidents Grover Cleveland, William Taft, and Woodrow Wilson vetoed them, and Congress did not have the votes to override Wilson until 1917. Then, just before American entry into World War I, the legislators found the needed two-thirds of the vote to override Wilson's veto.

Principal Nativist Legislation, 1921–1929

During World War I, immigration dropped dramatically, but it resumed its upward path after the war. The gatekeeper, Ellis Island, where most of the immigrants were processed, rejected only 2 percent of those wishing to settle in the United States. By then it was also apparent that most of the immigrants from southern and eastern Europe were able to pass the literacy test. As a result, congressional leaders who wanted drastic cuts in immigration had to come up with a different scheme. They found it in quotas and eventually the national origins provisions. Eugenic leaders, especially Harry H. Laughlin of the Eugenics Record Office, provided Congress with a racist rationale in fashioning an immigration policy. The first law, passed in 1921, limited immigration from each nation to 3 percent of its foreign-born according to the 1910 census. The total to be admitted was approximately 364,000. Not satisfied, nativists extended it for two more years, and then, in 1924, Congress passed the Johnson-Reed Immigration Act, which reduced the total to 2 percent and based it on the 1890 census. The new quota drastically reduced immigration from southern and eastern Europe because few immigrants

from those areas had arrived before 1890. The Johnson-Reed Immigration Act finally replaced these quotas in 1929 with national origins quotas as the basis of the immigration system. Each nation was given a quota based on that country's share of the white population (foreign- and native-born) as it existed in 1920. The national origins quotas gave a few more slots to southern and East European nations than did the 2 percent quota, but not many. Great Britain, Germany, and Ireland retained nearly three-quarters of the places. The national origins system went into effect in 1929.

These new laws received overwhelming support in Congress. It is difficult to know American opinion in the 1920s, but most historians would say that immigration acts of that era had wide support. Certainly in Congress there was little opposition. The final Johnson-Reed Act passed the Senate by a vote of 62–6, with 28 not voting. The vote in the House of Representatives was equally one-sided. President Calvin Coolidge signed it, noting that America must remain American—in other words, keep the nation's ethnic mix as it was in the 1920s.

Most of the votes against the restrictions came from representatives of cities where large numbers of the newest immigrants lived. Proponents of quotas said that these were also centers of opposition to the amendment for the prohibition of alcohol, politically corrupt urban machines, and crowds of unwashed immigrants who would never assimilate into the mainstream of American culture. In the heat of World War I, prohibitionists had insisted that the foreign-born were large consumers of alcohol, and German brewers were unpatriotic. Thus, nativism joined forces with the Prohibitionist movement to make the nation dry and to curtail immigration. Behind the passage of immigration restriction and Prohibition was the mood of small-town white American Protestants who believed that the United States had enough newcomers who would destroy Protestant American culture. Among those Americans who professed a religion, 80 percent were Protestant in 1900; if immigration went unchecked, this percentage was certain to decline.

It must be noted that anti-Semitism also played a role in the anti-immigrant crusade, even though Jews were a small minority of incoming migrants. During the 1920s, Harvard restricted its Jewish enrollment, and soon other elite universities, medical schools, resorts, and social clubs began to bar Jews. While members of these elite institutions did not join the Klan, they harbored hostility to Jews, immigrant or native-born. Then, too, during the 1920s, Henry Ford's *Dearborn Independent* carried anti-Semitic articles, including the *Protocols of the Elders of Zion*, a forgery concocted by the Russian secret police about an alleged Jewish plot to dominate the world.

Ethnic organizations did speak out on behalf of the new immigrants, but others lined up on the side of restriction as well. Patriotic groups, such as the Daughters of the American Revolution, were among the proponents of restrictions. The largest labor group in the nation, the American Federation of Labor, under its leader Samuel Gompers, who was an immigrant from England, supported restriction. Furthermore, some business groups that once favored a liberal immigration policy feared labor violence and revolution. Southern representatives had long given up their hope that immigrants would come to the South and labor as cheap workers. Businesses, except for railroads and large farms, which had usually been pleased by the flow of low-wage immigrants, reversed their positions. They joined the chorus of those wanting to keep "Bohunks," "Kikes," and "Dagoes" from entering and threatening American culture. The U.S. Chamber of Commerce, for example, decided that restriction was necessary, although it did want a few more immigrants than Congress was willing to admit.

1930s: Latinos, Jews, and Nativist Resistance

In the first days of the Great Depression, from 1929 to 1934, few Europeans expressed a desire to come to the United States. President Herbert Hoover instructed the immigration authorities to tightly enforce the "likely to be a public charge" provision of immigration law. As the situation changed with the rise of the Nazism in Germany and its spread across Europe, Jews and political dissenters were eager to escape. But the quotas remained a barrier in the late 1930s, and it became difficult to procure an American visa.

Certainly, anti-Semitism played a role. When Edith Rogers and Robert Wagner sponsored a bill in Congress to admit 20,000 German children outside the normal channels of immigration, no Jewish organization supported it for fear of stirring up anti-Semitism.

The Roosevelt administration did not back the Rogers-Wagner bill, which never got out of committee. After all, some opponents of the measure said, these would be mainly Jewish children who would grow to become adults. Moreover, Father Francis Coughlin, the popular radio priest, and his vicious anti-Semitic broadcasts had several million followers during the 1930s. Overall, only about 520,000 persons came to the United States during the 1930s, an average of only 52,000 annually. By way of comparison, in 2009, over one million immigrants arrived. The 52,000 figure was passed within three weeks of 2009.

The Johnson-Reed Act did not establish immigration quotas or any new restrictions on people from the Western Hemisphere. Most Mexicans lived in California and Texas, where they were hardly seen as equals or as desirable neighbors. Mexicans found themselves living in segregated neighborhoods, laboring in low-wage and dirty jobs, and attending inferior schools. While this segregation may have been by custom rather than by law, the treatment of Mexicans, especially in Texas, was little different from that of African Americans. Eugenicists believed they were a mongrel race inferior to Nordics, Teutons, Anglo-Saxons, or any other term given to northern and western Europeans. Representative John Box of Texas, for example, said that Mexicans were below white Americans in character and intelligence.

Why, then, did Congress not limit immigration from the Western Hemisphere? Growers, facing a decline in European migration, urged that no quota be given to Mexicans who came to work in their fields. Besides, they insisted, Mexicans would return home after the growing season was over. In addition, railroad operators needed the cheap labor of Mexican immigrants to maintain their lines. In northern areas such as Chicago, Mexicans were often last in line for jobs, and, when a brief recession occurred in 1921, they along with African Americans were the first persons to be laid off, and many Mexicans had to return home rather than remain in the United States.

In the end, business interests carried the day. In what was the first temporary worker program, begun in 1917, the government had suspended some of the immigration laws to allow Mexicans to enter temporarily and work in agriculture. This program, which ended in 1923, eventually covered 90,000 Mexican nationals. About all that Congress did to control the southern U.S. border was to establish and finance the Border Patrol beginning in 1924. However, the patrol provided for only a few hundred agents to control the nearly 2,000-mile southern border. Moreover, the federal government was more interested in keeping Chinese illegal aliens and liquor (during the early of Prohibition) from crossing the southern border into the United States than in controlling Mexican immigration. Only during the late 1920s did the Border Patrol begin to see Mexican illegal immigrants as a matter for supervision. Nearly 500,000 Mexicans entered legally during the decade and thousands more without being approved by the immigration authorities.

California agricultural interests, which had welcomed Mexican laborers in the 1920s, turned to a new source of farm workers in the 1930s. These were the Dust Bowl refugees from Oklahoma and other Plains states who left their farms, headed to California by the thousands, and often replaced Mexican farm workers. Local or state officials were in no mood to grant Mexican workers relief. Thousands of Mexican immigrants and their children (who were often U.S. citizens) were sent home, forcibly by state and local governments. Faced with such a bleak state of affairs, many other Mexican immigrants and their families voluntarily went home. It made little matter to American officials whether or not the children were U.S. citizens. Estimates vary as to the numbers, but at least several hundred thousand Mexicans found themselves returned to Mexico. When labor shortages in American agriculture reappeared during World War II, the Mexican government and individual Mexicans were somewhat reluctant to journey north.

Post–World War II: Measures Challenging Nativism

Following the end of World War II, a remarkable change in immigration occurred. Beginning with the repeal of the Chinese Exclusion Acts in 1943, Congress as well as presidents from both political parties either passed new laws or used executive authority to undo the restrictions enacted between 1882 and the 1920s.

Many of the new laws had popular support in Congress, for they were linked to the Cold War and foreign policy considerations. In 1956, President Dwight D. Eisenhower allowed the entry of over 36,000 Hungarians who had escaped an abortive revolution crushed by Soviet tanks and troops. The Hungarians had to be admitted by special presidential fiat, called the parole power, because the quota for Hungary was low; however, Congress agreed after the fact. Just who could oppose the admission of these "freedom fighters" in the midst of the Cold War? A similar situation arose in Asia. When the American-backed South Vietnamese regime fell to the Communists in 1975, many soldiers and officials who had supported the United States were now at the mercy of Communist forces. To be sure, a few members of Congress were reluctant to dole out aid and funds to help the Vietnamese (and later Cambodians and Laotians) establish themselves in the United States, but eventually over one million refugees from Indochina came to the United States.

Yet, other factors help to explain the liberalization of American immigration policy. The 1930s' high unemployment was not fertile ground for the acceptance of immigrants. The fears of another great depression were considerably relaxed in the postwar era as the economy expanded and the United States became the dominant economic power in the world. The growth of the economy was by no means even, and periodic downturns halted some economic gains, at least temporarily. A recession in 1949 and another in 1953 checked economic growth for many months, but these recessions did not lead to deep depressions. Indeed, the 1960s were a decade of strong growth in wages. During the 1970s, inflation became a problem, and not until the 1980s did the Federal Reserve cool the economy. Still, the late 1990s witnessed another era of growth, only to slow in the first decade of the twenty-first century until what has been called the Great Recession, beginning in 2008, led to serious unemployment and a drop in wages.

However, one can go too far in using economics to explain nativism after World War II. After all, the restrictions of the 1920s were enacted during a period of relative prosperity. There has been a steady increase in immigration since 1945, sometimes with little relation to economic conditions. The declining importance of racism also played a significant role in changing immigration policy. At the end of the 1930s, blacks faced overwhelming racial hostility in both the North and South. The Jim Crow society established by white southerners in the late ninetieth century denied the blacks the ballot and limited African Americans to public segregation, inferior schools and the potential of violence. Conditions in the North were somewhat better, but even though blacks voted there, black Americans were often the last hired and the first fired. The emergence of the civil rights revolution in the 1960s significantly changed racial patterns, eventually leading to the election of Barack Obama as president in 2008. In many areas of American life, African Americans found positions that had seemed to be permanently closed.

Before the 1960s, the 1952 McCarran-Walter Immigration Act actually had decreased black immigration from the Caribbean. Then, when the Hart-Celler Act of 1965 was enacted, these restrictions were ended. The executive branch argued that lifting those restrictions of only 100 per nation of the newly freed former British Caribbean colonies would increase the migration of blacks to the United States, but a large-scale migration was not envisioned. Moreover, in ending the national origins system in 1965, little attention was directed at Africa, and few persons believed that large scale African immigration would occur. No one thought that in both 2008 and 2009, Africa would send to the United States over 20,500 more immigrants than did Europe.

More important for immigration policy was the declining significance of racism directed at southern and eastern Europeans and Asians. During World War II, an effective lobby convinced Congress in 1943 to repeal the Chinese Exclusion Acts. The measure was based on foreign policy, as the United States was fighting the war against Japan with Chinese allies. With the repeal, the right to acquire American citizenship was also established. After the war (1946), token immigration quotas of 100 and the right to apply for citizenship were granted to both Asian Indians and Filipinos. More difficult to remove was the restriction against Japanese immigrants. However, California for the first time voted down a continuation of the policy of denying Japanese immigrants the right to become land owners, and several years later, the U.S. Supreme Court declared the alien land acts to be unconstitutional. Finally, all immigration and related racial bans were repealed by the McCarran-Walter Act. A factor in finally giving Japan an immigrant quota (of only 185) and allowing Japanese immigrants in the United States to become citizens was the wartime heroic performance of the second-generation Japanese Americans in both Italy and Germany and as interpreters in the Pacific war.

These changes were being buttressed by new scholarly thinking about race. The Senate committee reporting the McCarran-Walter Act still talked in terms of "race or people," much like the Dillingham Report decades earlier; but social scientists and scientists were debunking notions of a huge number of distinct races and were concluding that race was a social construct with little basis in biological facts.

Also important were the perceptions of the Catholic Church and the role of Catholics in American society as well as the decline of anti-Semitism after 1945. As noted, much of the nineteenth-century nativism was rooted in anti-Catholicism, the belief that American institutions and the American people were threatened by an invasion of Catholics and their priests. While the Ku Klux Klan still existed after 1945, it was a far cry from the Klan of the 1920s. Those few who worried about Catholicism did not focus on immigration but rather on the role of the church and Catholics generally.

In the 1950s, Paul Blanshard's *American Freedom and Catholic Power* went through two editions and was a best seller. The book was praised by several prominent Americans, and Blanshard himself became one of the founders of Protestants and Other Americans for Separation of Church and State to question the religious views of John F. Kennedy when he ran for the presidency in 1960. Blanshard was building upon American intellectuals' and liberals' views of Catholics that were common in the 1930s and 1940s. Then, even liberals questioned the separatism of American Catholics, and issues such as the Spanish Civil War and governmental aid to religious schools provoked opposition to Catholicism. Many intellectuals wondered aloud whether Catholics could become democrats and believers in the American tradition of separation of church and state. Blanshard did make a distinction between Catholic leadership and Catholics themselves, but his tone sometimes resembled that of the nineteenth century. He believed that the building of a distinct culture based on religious schools, Catholic churches, and separate social organizations was a threat to American democracy.

1960s–1990s: The Challenge Endures, Part I

When Al Smith ran for the presidency in 1928, he was badly defeated. No doubt his Catholicism was a major factor in many southern states (and elsewhere). Yet, no Democrat could have defeated Herbert Hoover, given the prosperous years of the 1920s. When Catholic John F. Kennedy ran for the presidency, he had to address his religion and speak on such issues as a representative to the Vatican and governmental aid for parochial schools and tell Protestants that he did not take orders from Rome. Kennedy's narrow victory in 1960 demonstrated that religion still played an important role in national politics, When Catholic William Miller ran as vice president on the Republican ticket with Republican Barry Goldwater in 1964, religion was barely mentioned. John Kerry's Catholicism was scarcely an issue in 2004 when he lost to President George W. Bush. Indeed, because Kerry's views on abortion were pro-choice, he was denounced by several prominent Catholic clerics. There remained issues that divided religious groups, such as aid to private religious schools, gay rights, abortion, and birth control; but the issues crossed religious lines, and no one group could claim that all of its adherents were unified in thought. When social scientists reported on intermarriage in the first decade of the 2000s, they concentrated on marriage across ethnic, nationality, or so-called racial groups. A highly respected organization, the Pew Foundation, said nothing about religious intermarriage among

Protestants, Catholics, and Jews when it released a study of intermarriage in 2010. By then intermarriage among religions groups was common and no longer an issue of controversy.

The growing acceptance of Catholics can also be seen in the image of Catholics in television and the movies, with such stars as Bing Crosby and others playing sympathetic priests. Finally, it should be noted that the Cold War also influenced the acceptance of Catholicism as many prominent Catholics were strongly anti-Communist.

Anti-Semitism in the United States also declined during the same era of diminishing anti-Catholicism. The opening of American institutions to Jews was a vital part of a new social America after 1945. Elite Ivy League universities dropped their Jewish quotas, and housing and jobs barred to Jews gradually changed after World War II. Who would have thought in the 1940s that such universities as Princeton, with its tight Jewish quotas, would have a Jewish president in the 1990s? Princeton even established a kosher eating place for its Jewish students who wished to follow the dietary laws.

Jews also became prominent in politics, television, and American institutions generally. In 2000, President Al Gore picked an Orthodox Jew, Senator Joseph Lieberman, as his running mate. Moreover, Jewish groups became more outspoken in their attacks on bigotry, and many supported the civil rights movement of black Americans during the 1960s.

Hollywood had attracted many Jewish actors and producers long before the 1960s. Yet the owners of the major networks were reluctant to criticize anti-Semitism before World War II. Finally, in the 1940s, two movies about anti-Semitism, *The House I Live In* and *Gentlemen's Agreement*, attacked bigotry against American Jews. Perhaps nothing illustrated the change more as it relates to immigration policy than the Lautenberg Amendment, passed by a vote of 97–0 in the U.S. Senate in 1989. This amendment stated that, because of the long history of anti-Semitism in the Soviet Union, Russian Jews should be considered refugees, entitled to entrance into the United States. The law was renewed several times. Although Armenians and Pentecostal Christians were included, the vast majority of the 300,000 admitted from 1989 to 1993 were Jews. Bear in mind that no Jewish organization had spoken in favor of the Wagner-Rogers Bill to admit 20,000 German children during the 1930s.

While the signs of declining religious bigotry were many after the 1950s, it should be noted how cautious emerging immigration policy was. The Citizens Committee to Repeal Chinese Exclusion emphasized that repeal was a wartime issue; besides, China was granted a quota of only 105. Right after the war, the Citizens Committee for Displaced Persons (CCDP) also treaded lightly in putting forth its program. Largely financed by the American Jewish Committee, the CCDP pointed out that the majority of the 400,000 displaced persons in Europe to be admitted were Christians, and that this was not a Jewish issue.

The McCarran-Walter Immigration Act of 1952 reaffirmed the national origins system, but, as noted, it did open the door for all races to become U.S. citizens and provided for Asian immigration. However, the quota for most Asian nations was set at 100, and a total of 2,000 was the figure for an area called the Asia-Pacific Triangle. An important exemption was the provision that allowed spouses and minor children of U.S. citizens to enter above the limits of the national quotas. This particular provision was especially important for Asian women who married U.S. military personnel. The Hart-Celler Act of 1965 then ended the national origins provisions and gave each nation in the Eastern Hemisphere a limit of 20,000, not including the spouses, children, and parents of U.S. citizens. For the first time, legislators placed a ceiling of 120,000 for the Western Hemisphere. It was a victory for those who were alarmed by the increases in Hispanic immigration in the late 1950s and early 1960s. Although opponents of Latin-American immigration did not express the crude racism of the 1920s, they did see Hispanics as a threat to American culture. In 1978, Congress merged the two hemispheres into a uniform worldwide system.

Several other laws passed after 1965 also increased immigration; but some, like the 1986 Immigration and Reform Control Act (IRCA), were not expected to be radical. In that law, in exchange for an amnesty for nearly three million illegal immigrants, the government outlawed the employment of future illegal immigrants. The Immigration Act of 1990 was largely a victory for high-tech business, which wanted to allow more persons with skills into the United States, and for European nations, such as Poland and Ireland. The 1990 law also provided for a lottery for visas, which was intended for Europeans, but Asians and later Africans were quick to utilize it. It is not known how much the low estimates and unforeseen consequences used in the debate about immigration played a role in reforms. After 1945, public opinion polls did not support substantial increases in immigration. It is quite possible that nativist voices would have been more effective in capping the numbers permitted to enter if it had been realized that the new laws and policies would have enormous unintended consequences.

Moreover, the undocumented population resumed its sharp growth in the late 1990s. Because IRCA's employment restrictions were not enforced, undocumented immigrants continued to cross the U.S.-Mexican border or to enter with legal temporary visas and then remain beyond the time when the visa expired. The best estimates are that between 500,000 and 700,000 persons were annually overstaying visas or entering without authorization annually from 2000 to 2005. As a result, by 2009, officials estimated the illegal immigration population—after peaking at about 12.4 million in 2007—had declined to approximately 10.8 million (and even less in 2010), with over 60 percent being Mexican. But the fact remains that the growth of immigration, documented and undocumented, was now greeted with alarm by many Americans.

In the late 1970s, a form of nativism appeared and expanded, based on environmental issues, economics, terrorism, and cultural arguments. A group of persons connected with the environmental movement and population growth increase in the United States organized anew. The main leader of the new nativism was Dr. John Tauton, who had been head of Zero Population Growth before turning his hand to immigration. Tauton and other like-minded people organized the Federation of American Immigration Reform (FAIR), and they were joined by other smaller groups, the Carrying Capacity Network (CCN) and Population-Environment Balance. Nativists organized many smaller state organizations, all with the goal of reducing immigration.

FAIR also had a research program run by the Committee for Immigration Studies. Most of these groups warned their members about what they believed to be the perils of immigration and especially the impact of large numbers of immigrants on the American environment. After 2000, Roy Beck, who had written perhaps the best nativist book, *The Case against Immigration* (1996), organized NumbersUSA, which claimed to have one million members in 2010. Beck also emphasized what he considered the threat to the American environment; yet when these nativists took their concerns to the major environmental groups, they were not successful. On two occasions they tried to convince the Sierra Club, the nation's largest environmental organization, that immigration should be placed on the agenda for discussion of the impact of population growth on the environment. However, they could win over only one-third of the board of directors.

2000s: The Challenge Endures, Part II

The nativists also found friends on television, especially after the destruction of the World Trade Center in New York City on September 11, 2001. Lou Dobbs, formerly of CNN, and Bill O'Reilly of Fox News claimed that immigration was too high and that American borders were out of control, which meant that terrorists had easy access to the United States. Several congressmen were also worried about terrorism, such as J. D. Hayworth of Arizona, who published *Whatever It Takes: Illegal Immigration, Border Security, and the War on Terror* (2008). The book was a call for more controls on illegal immigration and supervision of the southern U.S. border. A leading opponent of immigration on cultural grounds was Patrick Buchanan, a prominent Republican politician for a few years in the 1990s. Buchanan, pointing to the large influx of Hispanic immigrants, insisted that current levels and sources of immigration threatened the nation's European heritage in his *State of Emergency: The Third World Invasion of America* (2006). Congressman Tom Tancredo, author of *In Mortal Danger: The Battle for America's Border and Security* (2006), a book similar to Hayworth's about what they saw as out-of-control illegal immigration, attempted to become the

Republican Party's presidential candidate in 2008, but his efforts failed to win support from his party.

While some of the publications about immigration are particularly harsh, the new nativism also had followers among more respectable persons. Historian Otis L. Graham Jr. published *Unguarded Gates: A History of America's Immigration Crisis* in 2004, which dealt with the history of immigration policy. Perhaps the most respectable anti-immigration book came from the late Samuel Huntington, of Harvard University, who argued in *Who Are We: The Challenges to America's National Identity* (2004) that the continued influx of Hispanics, and especially Mexicans, was undermining what he considered to be the nation's Anglo-Saxon culture. The labor historian Vernon Briggs, at Cornell University, used economics in his book *Mass Immigration and the Nation Interest* (1996). Briggs argued that the large-scale admission of poorly educated immigrants competed with native-born Americans who lacked skills and training and as a result drove down the wages of low-income American workers or replaced them in the marketplace.

Economist George Borjas, professor at Harvard's John F. Kennedy School of Government, has been critical of the family unification preferences that drive immigration policy. He wanted immigration to emphasize skills needed in the United States. He also said that too many immigrants were using various welfare programs that cost the taxpayers money to fund these. Another scholarly book by Professor Jacob L. Vigdor, *From Immigrants to Americans: the Rise and Fall of Fitting In* (2010), agreed with Borjas that immigration policy should be based more on skills and less on family unification. Thus, these two scholars were more concerned about economics than the number themselves. They wanted changes in policy and their enforcement. They were not alone, as a majority of Americans believed that enforcement of the nation's immigration laws was poor. One did not have to want large decreases in immigration to be critical of American policies and their enforcement.

In 1994, the Republican Party carried Congress, which gratified the advocates of a more limited immigration. In the same election, California passed Proposition 187, which blocked undocumented immigrants' utilization of California's public programs and institutions. Among its provisions, Proposition 187 denied undocumented immigrants the right to attend public schools, even though that policy had been declared unconstitutional 15 years before. When taken to the courts, the proposition was deemed unconstitutional. Nonetheless, the 1994 election heartened the opponents of immigration, who now hoped that Congress would overhaul immigration policy.

Congressional leaders wanting immigration cuts were also heartened by the report of the Commission on Immigration (CIR), established by Congress in 1990, that recommended cuts in the number of legal permanent residents. Chaired by Barbara Jordan of Texas, the CIR had a distinguished group of scholars and politicians. The CIR recommended that the "brothers and sisters" preference of the laws be abolished, which would have been an annual cut of 64,000 persons. President Bill Clinton endorsed the report and then backed off when subjected to intense lobbying. The president's action helped those in Congress who killed this particular recommendation of the CIR. The Senate did vote on a proposal by Senator Alan Simpson to cut immigration by 20 percent over a five-year period, but it garnered only 20 votes and was not voted upon by the House. Instead, Congress decided to deal with illegal and legal immigration separately. The legislators finally agreed in 1996 to cut welfare benefits for immigrants, especially for those without proper immigration papers. However, some states then covered the cuts for legal immigrants, and later Congress restored others. The new laws also made it easier to deport immigrants. Thus, for nativists wanting a substantial decrease in immigration, the election of 1994 produced little. Congress did later examine other parts of immigration law, but nothing resulted from these actions. In early 2010, the CIS reported that American asylum policy was being abused, but whether its recommendations would result in fewer asylum places was doubtful.

After severing legal and illegal immigration, Congress turned toward controlling those immigrants who lacked proper documents, especially those entering illegally across the southern U.S. border. Indeed, since 1995, illegal immigration has almost always been the center of debate at congressional, state, and community levels. It appeared as if the main structure of immigration would remain intact. During the era 1990–2010, immigration averaged over 900,000 annually, the highest in any 20-year period (including the highest decade ever, 2000–2009, with 10.3 million), yet the southern U.S. border received the most attention.

Nativists, trying to avoid religious and racist appeals, insisted that the large-scale undocumented immigration hurt American workers, either by reducing wages (especially for the unskilled Americans) or replacing American workers. Representative Lamar Smith of Texas insisted in 2010 that if illegal immigrants were deported, millions of jobs would be opened to Americans. Nativists also insisted that many immigrants hurt the economy by using welfare benefits. Local communities were under siege because so many immigrants prompted the building of new schools and other public facilities, yet local cities and towns lacked the tax base to finance new institutions. Moreover, nativists attacked the use of bilingual education in schools, which they said produced few results and cost money to hire new teachers. Some of those involved with the new opponents of immigration became allied with the movement to make English the official language of the United States at both the federal and state levels.

Not satisfied with what the nativists considered an economic cost, they also pointed to the social impact of illegal immigration. The new nativists avoided for the most part the crude racist comments that were common around the turn of the twentieth century and into the 1930s. Racism was no longer in fashion; instead, the new nativists insisted that American culture was being fragmented and that many of the newcomers did not wish to become Americans. It is hard to avoid the conclusion that at bottom, nativism had come to mean that Hispanics (especially Mexicans) were dividing the United States into two distinct societies, and unless the Latino flow of immigrants were stopped, the United States was in danger of permanent fragmentation.

A new fear arose from the events of September 11, 2001 (9/11), when terrorists destroyed New York City's World Trade Center and damaged the Pentagon. American officials responded by rounding up

Demonstrators in New York City in 2011 protest the proposed construction of a mosque (actually an Islamic community center) near the site of the World Trade Center terrorist attack. (AP/Wide World Photos)

newcomer Arabs for questioning and even incarcerating some without having a lawyer present. Hundreds of Muslims were deported, although eventually most of those who were brought in and detained for questioning were released. Still, the government did successfully prosecute some Muslims' violations of the law. In addition, the federal government placed restrictions and tight procedures on the admission of persons from Islamic nations and from the Middle East. For nativists, 9/11 proved that borders must be made secure, lest terrorists strike again. Tom Tancredo, in his book *In Mortal Danger*, declared that the Department of Homeland Security guidelines permitted terrorists easy access to the United States. The fact that some of the contingent of those who had engineered the disasters of September 11 had been illegal and that all came from Islamic countries alarmed many Americans. And, in fact, a variety of incidents occurred, targeting women wearing headscarves (hijabs) and men who had turbans (Asian Indian Sikhs). In 2010 in Staten Island, one of New York City's five boroughs, an angry crowd turned out at a hearing to oppose the building of a mosque in their midst. One woman asked, "Wouldn't you agree that every terrorist, past and present, has come out of a mosque?" Not surprisingly, a proposal in the summer of 2010 to build an Islamic community center two blocks from New York City's World Trade Center ("Ground Zero") site generated fierce emotional resistance.

Federal actions to increase border security did not satisfy a small group who called themselves the Minutemen. Under the leadership of Jim Gilchrist, the Minutemen gathered in 2005 in Arizona to assist the Border Patrol in finding and deporting illegal immigrants. Gilchrist claimed that he headed a movement of thousands of Americans, but in reality, only a few hundred persons were members of his organization.

Yet, the appearance of the Minutemen (some of whom carried weapons) highlighted the belief of many Americans that the nation was being overrun by an invasion of potential terrorists and Latinos to the south.

In the late 1990s, the federal government had stepped up deportation of immigrants. Overall, the number of deportations rose by 2009 to nearly 400,000. These were divided about evenly between illegal aliens and legal immigrants who had violated American law, some for very minor offenses. Most persons deported were not those from the interior of the United States but those apprehended at the border. With increased enforcement, the number of deportations at the border in the late 2000s rose to about 700,000 annually. It had been roughly one million around 2000. The federal government also detained thousands of others who were sent to detention centers awaiting the outcome of their cases (often for asylum) to remain in the United States. Some lived in the centers for months and even years. Moreover, between 2003 and 2010, 103 persons died in detention. Journalists found that many received little or no medical care.

Then, in 2006, Congress took up the issue of immigration again, but could not agree except for tougher provisions for supervising the border between the United States and Mexico. A beefed-up Border Patrol along the southern border was the main result of the fears of terrorism, the presence of a large illegal population, and a Hispanic invasion. The Border Patrol, which numbered 3,000 in 1986, was increased to 19,000 employees by early 2010. Congress voted funds for a 700-mile-long fence along the border and a similar "virtual fence" (consisting of lights, sensors, and more aircraft). However, in early 2010, construction of the fence was halted because of cost overruns, and the "virtual fence" was plagued by technical as well as financial problems. (Another federal act providing funding for 1,500 more Border Patrol officers was approved in August 2010.)

Ongoing Issues and Policy Debates

On the state level, both Arizona and New Mexico declared immigrant "emergencies" and President George W. Bush authorized the use of the National Guard to aid the Border Patrol. The soldiers were sent home after one year, but in early 2010, President Barack Obama announced his intention of sending 1,200 members of National Guard to the border. This time the main target of the Guard's work was the cross-border drug trade that had grown in recent years.

Also at the state level, several thousand immigration bills were introduced in the first decade of the twenty-first century. They dealt with driver's licenses, tuition for unauthorized immigrants at state universities, and the utilization of health care by illegal aliens. In May 2010, Massachusetts barred illegal aliens from attending state colleges, required contractors doing business with the state not to employ illegal aliens, and mandated public housing authorities to give legal residents priority over illegal aliens. The state law drawing the most attention was that of Arizona, passed in May 2010. Arizona authorized the police to ask for identification from persons whom the police believed might not be authorized to live in the United States. The law set off a large debate, with opponents saying it gave law enforcement officers the power to stop anyone who appeared to be Hispanic. However, polls indicated that a majority of Americans approved of the Arizona law. Its harshest measures were declared unconstitutional by a federal judge just before it went into effect in July 2010, but the U.S. Supreme Court ruled in June 2012 that that only one part of the law could stand, allowing police officers who have legally detained someone for law-breaking (including traffic laws) can then determine the immigration status of the person detained. In June 2011, Alabama had passed an even stricter version of Arizona's proposed law. The Obama administration challenged it, but in September 2011, a federal judge in Alabama upheld the law. As a result, many undocumented workers left the state, and Alabama farmers have had trouble filling their jobs.

The debates in Congress and in state legislatures indicated that there was a widespread unease about immigration, especially illegal ones. Those favoring tighter controls on the southern U.S. border pointed to the drop in the number of persons trying to enter without documents as the Border Patrol increased supervision. The growing Border Patrol and tougher state laws no doubt help explain why officials believed that the undocumented population dropped from an estimated 12 million in 2008 to approximately 11 million a year later. But the economy certainly played a major role, and especially important for Hispanic workers was construction, which experienced a severe recession after 2007. By 2010, there appeared to be little chance of cuts in legal immigration, partly because of the economic contributions of these newcomers, and partly because they were supported by a great variety of religious and ethnic organizations. Moreover, there was a huge backlog of persons waiting for an American visa, indicative of a great desire to come to the United States. Undocumented immigrants were another story. They lacked immigration papers and hence were vulnerable for deportation. A poor economy left them open to the charge that they took American jobs. Thus, economics appeared to be a major factor in the opposition by many Americans to their presence in the United States.

Nevertheless, in America so much historically was invested in the preservation and inculcation of Anglo-Saxon Protestant culture and values, and nativist policies were fiercely marked by anti-Catholicism and then by anti-Semitism as well. It is therefore ironic that in 2010, the American bastion of the nation's principles, the U.S. Supreme Court, has six Catholic and three Jewish justices—and no Protestants.

If tighter border controls, increasing deportations, and the economy help explain the drop in the number of Mexicans legally and illegally entering the United States, some experts noted that conditions in Mexico also prompted the number of Mexicans wanting to head north after 2009. The drop in the birthrate reduced those coming onto the workforce as did improved wages and educational opportunities in Mexico. Finally, too, the number of H-2A temporary agricultural workers from Mexico increased 75 percent from 2006, thus reducing the demand to enter illegally. In the five-year period from 2006 to 2010, 250,000 Mexicans received H-2A visas. It should also be noted that, if Mexican emigration dropped elsewhere, the desire to come to the United States remained strong. In 2011, the number of persons applying for the annual 50,000 diversity visas determined by a lottery, topped 15 million. Those wanting fewer immigrants had insisted that the diversity visa program be dropped. But in June 2012, President Barack Obama announced that he was issuing an executive order, bypassing Congress, ending the deportation of illegal immigrants under 30 years old who were brought to the U.S. by their parents. Certain conditions had to be met: The person must have arrived in the U.S. before the age of 16; have lived in the U.S. for five years; and be in school, or a high school graduate, or a military veteran in good standing; and have no criminal records.

Bibliography

Alden, Edward. 2008. *The Closing of the American Border: Terrorism, Immigration and Security since 9/11*. New York: Harper.

Bakalian, Anny, and Medhi Bozorgmehr. 2009. *Backlash 9/11: Middle Eastern and Muslim Americans Respond*. Berkeley: University of California Press.

Daniels, Roger. 2004. *Guarding the Golden Door: American Immigration Policy and Immigrants since 1882*. New York: Hill and Wang.

Hernandez, Kelly Lyte. 2010. *Migra! A History of the U.S. Border Patrol*. Berkeley: University of California Press.

Higham, John. (1955) 1988. *Strangers in the Land; Patterns of American Nativism, 1860–1925*. 2nd ed. New Brunswick, NJ: Rutgers University Press.

King, Desmond. 2000. *Making Americans: Immigration, Race and the Origins of Diverse Democracy*. Cambridge, MA: Harvard University Press.

López, Ian F. 1996. *White by Law: The Legal Construction of Race*. New York: New York University Press.

Ngai, Mae M. 2004. *Impossible Subjects: Illegal Aliens and the Making of Modern America*. Princeton, NJ: Princeton University Press.

Reimers, David M. 1998. *Unwelcome Strangers: American Identity and the Turn against Immigration*. New York: Columbia University Press.

Roediger, David R. 2005. *Working toward Whiteness: How America's Immigrants Became White: The Strange Journey from Ellis Island to the Suburbs*. New York: Basic Books.

Tempo, Carl J. 2008. *Americans at the Gate: The United States and Refugees during the Cold War*. Princeton, NJ: Princeton University Press.

Zolberg, Aristide R. 2006. *A Nation By Design: Immigration Policy in the Fashioning of America*. Cambridge, MA: Harvard University Press.

Immigration and Incorporation of New Americans: Citizenship Prior to 1980

Robin Harper

Conceptual and Historical Foundations

Born American or made American? This question of how, whether, and which people to bring into the state and the nation has bedeviled policy makers since the founding of the republic. In a settler state, immigration is essential to peopling the land. But how to assure that the immigrants share values and are dedicated to the state's purpose is complicated. What if the immigrants are not the people that the state wants as members? What rights and obligations should immigrant children have? What should be the criteria for acceptance or exclusion from full political membership: Birthright citizenship? Birthright citizenship with conditions? Bloodline citizenship? Residency? Income? Wealth? Group affiliation? Conquest and acquisition?

All of these policies have been used at different periods of American history as policies for inclusion and exclusion. The current American population is a direct reflection of the patchwork of policies, both progressive and regressive, for incorporating and excluding immigrants. The rich mixed-ethnic heritage we have is a reflection not just of the incomparably generous open door for some (voluntary immigrants and refugees) but also of slavery, to Mexican and indigenous land acquisition for others. The United States has traditionally offered relatively easily attainable naturalization for some and racial bars to naturalization and opportunity for others. All along this spectrum is the story of American immigrant incorporation and naturalization.

This chapter covers the American naturalization and incorporation policies from the founding of the republic until the middle of the 1900s, reflecting both

the political discussion of who should be and could be a member. First, let us define some terms. "Naturalization," "incorporation," and "Americanization" are related, but by no means the same or even contingent. Naturalization is the formal bureaucratic process by which foreigners are transformed into citizens. It is a state process that is performed exclusively by bureaucratic actors with the intention of determining membership into the political community and establishing a legal boundary between members and nonmembers. The conferring of naturalization cements a legal relationship between the state and the immigrant and in so doing almost mystically metamorphoses the subject into a citizen.

Under the contemporary prevailing definition, citizenship is based either on being born on American soil, regardless of parental immigration status, or through naturalization. The Fourteenth Amendment to the Constitution, through its citizenship and equal protection clause, asserts that once naturalization is conferred, the naturalized citizen is legally indistinguishable from the native-born one. By means of naturalization, the immigrant is classified as a formal member of the democratic ruling class. Incorporation is the current term of art to mean joining the receiving society as full members in more than just the formal sense but in all social, economic, civic, and political ways. Americanization, by contrast, has little to do with formal citizenship but rather with the transformation of the personal qualities of the immigrant, thus accepting the dominant customs, culture, language, laws, rights, and responsibilities.

Americanization is most closely related to the programs titled "Americanization programs" initiated in the early twentieth century, but it is by no means limited to those programs. Such efforts have been found throughout U.S. history, starting in colonial times and leading up to the present day, albeit by alternative names. Americanization may be performed by any state or non-state actors and has been undertaken by federal, state, and local governments, private voluntary and religious organizations, labor unions, employers, social clubs, and even through socialization in educational institutions and the military. In short, incorporation refers to interaction, participation, and acceptance of receiving state culture; Americanization refers to programs for teaching acceptance of the dominant culture; and naturalization refers to state-sponsored legal transformation resulting in political membership.

Whether formal or informal transformation from foreigner into civic member, three major issues have colored American naturalization policy and, by extension, the perceived need for and implementation of Americanization programs: being a new state, race, and federalism. Being a new state meant that the state had to invent the notion of an American citizen as well as what it was to be "an American." In the earliest days of the republic, there was no state and no nation, and leaders' focus was firmly on generating and consolidating institutions and in the process making Americans out of colonists, regardless of their background, rather than making Americans out of foreigners. In contrast to the history of European states, in which the state centered on the consolidation of homogenous ethnic nations, the development of the state in America was more a story of how it "arose from a democratic-cosmopolitan nation shaped largely by immigrants" (Ueda 1997, 39).

Of course, the European states were not as homogenous as in their myth, and the American state is more than a sum of its immigration. As J. Hector St. John de Crevecoeur so famously wrote of "the American" in 1782: "What then is the American, this new man? . . . He is an American, who, leaving behind him all his ancient prejudices and manners, receives new ones from the new mode of life he has embraced, the new government he obeys, and the new rank he holds. He has become an American by being received in the broad lap of our great Alma Mater. Here

individuals of all races are melted into a new race of man, whose labors and posterity will one day cause great changes in the world. Americans are the western pilgrims" (Letter III).

As a settlement country, immigration has always been a part of American life in securing and settling the land. Later, as a developing country, the United States needed immigrants to people the land, fuel the ranks of workers, and provide markets for goods. It needed citizens to build the local democracy and participate in the building of the republic. Immigration and naturalization were so important that their inhibition was a major complaint against King George III and part of the rationale for secession in the Declaration of Independence: "He has endeavored to prevent the population of these states; for that purpose obstructing the laws of naturalization of foreigners; refusing to pass others to encourage their migration hither, and raising the conditions of new appropriations of lands."

However, to the framers of the Constitution, it was not at all clear whether the immigrants coming to the new United States could be absorbed appropriately and made into Americans. They feared instant naturalization. The framers thought it prudent to naturalize only after a period of social and political acculturation. George Washington (as cited in Fitzpatrick 1970, 23) wrote in a letter to John Adams that immigrants could not be juxtaposed in the local community and expected to be full members that benefited the nation. Rather, they should be positively incorporated and learn the local ways in order to form one nation. He wrote: "the policy or advantage of [immigration] taking place in a body (I mean the settling of them in a body) may be much questioned; for, by so doing, they retain the language, habits, and principles (good or bad) which they bring with them. Whereas by an intermixture with our people, they, or their descendants, get assimilated to our customs, measures, and laws: in a word, soon become *one people*." Alexander Hamilton (1997, 497) concurred: "To admit foreigners indiscriminately to the rights of citizens, the moment they place a foot in our country would be nothing less than to admit the Grecian horse into the citadel of our liberty and sovereignty." Rather, he suggested gradual incorporation, "to enable aliens to get rid of foreign and acquire American attachments; to learn the principles and imbibe the spirit of our government; and to admit of a philosophy, at least, of their feeling a real interest in our affairs."

Policy that includes some by definition excludes others. Again, on both sides of the Federalist fence, the framers noted their concern that lacking that knowledge and commitment to the republic would render the immigrant an inappropriate citizen and endanger the very fabric of the republic. Madison stated in a 1790 speech to Congress that America should exclude the immigrant who cannot "incorporate himself into our society." In *Notes on the State of Virginia*, Jefferson, fearing the influx of those unwilling to learn the new methods of governance, stated (2002, 39):

> Every species of government has its specific principles. Ours . . . is a composition of the freest principles of the English constitution, with others derived from natural rights and natural reason. To these nothing can be more opposed than the maxims of absolute monarchies. Yet, from such, we are to expect the greatest number of emigrants. They will bring with them the principles of government they leave, imbibed in their early youth; or if able to throw them off, it will be in exchange for an unbounded licentiousness, passing, as is usual, from one extreme to another. It would be a miracle were they to stop precisely at the point of temperate liberty. These principles, with their language, they will transmit to their children. In proportion to their numbers, they will share with us the legislation. They will infuse into it their spirit, warp and bias its direction, and tender it a heterogeneous, incoherent, distracted mass.

Even his Federalist opponent, Hamilton, concurred in 1802 (1977, 496): "The safety of a republic depends essentially on the energy of a common national sentiment; on a uniformity of principles and habits; on the exemption of citizens from foreign bias and prejudice; and on the love of country which will almost invariably be found to be closely connected with birth, education, and family."

The framers considered naturalization important enough to assign designing a naturalization law as one of Congress's first obligations. Article I, Section 8, Clause 4 of the U.S. Constitution stipulates that the Congress is authorized to "establish a uniform law of Naturalization." Congress passed the first such Naturalization Act in 1790 (1 Stat. 103), one of the first major acts to emerge from the legislature. The act provided:

> that any alien, being a free white person, who shall have resided within the limits and under the jurisdiction of the United States for the term of two years, may be admitted to become a citizen thereof, on application to any common law court of record, in any one of the States wherein he shall have resided for the term of one year at least, and making proof to the satisfaction of such court, that he is a person of good character, and taking the oath or affirmation prescribed by law, to support the Constitution of the United States.

The eligibility requirements foreshadowed serious problems that plagued the entire nineteenth century: freedom, race, state versus national citizenship (with their concomitant uniform codes), and federalism. On the more minor points, the oaths were not standardized, and determinations of good moral character were made by fellow citizens' affirmation, meaning a great deal of disparity between who should and could become a citizen. The clause about "free white person" was central to the day because it shut out both indentured servants and slaves from citizenship and left open the question of what the state meant by "free," "white," and "person." All three terms would be under fierce contention throughout the nineteenth century. By requiring a period of residency, the act provided a policy response to the framers' concerns that citizenship upon arrival could bring all of the ills of the old world to the new state. The idea of time represents their liberal contentions that democracy and civic republicanism can be learned. The short time period represented a balance between the need to "make Americans" quickly and bring people into the fold, diluting those loyal to the Crown or unaffiliated with the new state and to underwrite the legitimacy of the new state by filling it with citizens and not subjects.

News of the French Revolution and its Reign of Terror came to the United States in the early 1790s and provoked backlashes against immigrant and the Federalist Congress raised the residency requirements from two to five years in 1795. Jefferson's Democratic-Republicans assumed that incoming European revolutionaries would support the Democratic-Republican Party but feared that fleeing merchants would likely support their rivals the Federalists and suppress the rights of the stalwart supporters of the Democratic-Republicans, the citizen-farmers. The Federalists imposed still harsher restrictions, including a 14-year residency requirement in the Naturalization Act of 1798 and, even more insidious, signed into the law the Alien and Sedition Acts, which, while intending to curtail the political power of people sympathetic to the Jeffersonian Democratic-Republicans, had the effect of placing all immigrants under suspicion and curtailing the civic engagement of any noncitizen. Further, the acts had the effect of implementing extra-constitutional measures for noncitizens and further deportation of those holding socially or politically unacceptable views. Once Jefferson's party controlled Congress in 1801, the residency requirement was reduced to five years. The shifting requirements and imposition of anti-immigrant policy reflected more serious nativist concerns and fear of foreign influences on the American experiment. The Naturalization Act of 1802 reflects these nativist concerns:

> And the children of such persons so naturalized, dwelling within the United States, being under the age of twenty-one years at the time of such naturalization, shall also be considered as citizens of the United States. And the children of citizens of the United States, that may be born beyond sea, or out of the limits of the United States, shall be considered as natural born citizens: Provided, that the right of citizenship shall not descend to persons whose fathers have never been resident in the United States.

By limiting naturalizations to "white" people, the act established a hierarchical structure in which

nonwhite people were legally subordinate. Here we see already the tension between the civic nationalism to which Americans aspire and the racialized nativism that has also plagued the country even before its founding. The term "white" may have been used in legal terminology but was (and remains until today) an ambiguous, malleable concept. In the early part of the nineteenth century, the critical determination with respect to citizenship was a white-black dichotomy. Africans were largely slaves, and even though slave importation ended after 1808 based on the U.S. Constitution, the question of the status of those of African descent (whether of pure African or mixed stock) remained an important legal and political question. Further complicating the issue was the arrival of dramatic waves of immigrants, predominantly from northern and central Europe, especially Germany and Scandinavia as well as later Ireland, then China and Japan, and eventually eastern and southern Europe. Over the next century, massive influxes of immigrants escaping political turmoil in Europe, famine in Ireland, economic dislocation from industrialization, and seeking opportunities through contract labor, made the United States a major immigration destination. Incorporation of these immigrants would prove complicated and divisive. At the earliest stages of immigration, when it was more homogenous, to an outside eye, America looked like it had found the solution to incorporation. In a letter to a French friend, Alexis de Tocqueville (as cited in Boesche 1985, 38) wrote: "Imagine, my dear friend, if you can, a society formed of all the nations of the world . . . people having different languages, beliefs, opinions: in a word, a society without roots, without memories, without prejudices, without routines, without common ideas, without a national character, yet a hundred times happier than our own."

In later waves, immigrants were greeted with suspicion for their language, customs, and religious practices that differed from the now-native Americans. Some have argued that many of the political debates of the nineteenth century were really a reflection and rejection of the new ideas, new cultures, and practices coming with the new immigrants. The determination of what constituted a white person would become a pressing issue later in the nineteenth and the early twentieth centuries, when racial "science" became en vogue and determining legal whiteness was the only way out of subjecthood.

The history of naturalization also reveals that citizenship discourses centered on men. While the 1790 act naturalized all "persons" and so included women, it also declared that "the right of citizenship shall not descend to persons whose fathers have never been resident in the United States." This prevented the automatic grant of citizenship to children born abroad whose mother but not father had resided in the United States. Citizenship was inherited exclusively through the father. Congress did not remove the inequity until 1934.

The Constitution's silence on the issues of immigration, naturalization, and citizenship became resolved in the years following the Civil War. The clarification came through the limited inclusions. Aside from the mentions that certain offices have eligibility requirements of citizenship (Article I, Sections 2 and 3; Article II, Section 1), the Constitution notes that Congress could levy a tax on the importation of each slave to $10 and that slaves could no longer be imported after 1808 (Article I, Section 9).

Following the Revolutionary War, the former colonies (and eventually, states as they joined the Union), granted state citizenship as a mechanism to encourage local settlement. That citizenship, or the denial of citizenship, was used as the criterion for certain property rights, professional licenses, and suffrage. Many states offered voting rights to noncitizens once they had filed "first papers" or a declaration of intent to file for naturalization. Other states used the citizenship laws as a way to deny certain non-citizens of access to rights, especially as a mechanism for imposing racial bars on economic activity, the professions, settlement, and property rights.

Further Conceptual and Policy Foundations: The Nineteenth Century

That the Constitution placed the responsibility and authority squarely with Congress would influence immigration and naturalization policy throughout the nineteenth century and beyond. In the first case, the assumption that Congress could levy a tax and

stop immigration also implies that it had the authority to permit immigration. As such, the Supreme Court has usually placed the authority to determine immigration laws and implementation in Congress's purview. Like many issues throughout the nineteenth century, federalism made it more complicated to determine which level of government maintained the authority over naturalization of foreigners and the nature of citizenship in the individual states and with the United States as a whole. The authority over naturalization and citizenship remained in contention between state and federal governments until the passage of the Fourteenth Amendment, which clarified the principles that the citizen of any state was also a citizen of the United States, that birth was the criterion for determining citizenship, and that naturalized and birth citizens should be considered on a par.

Because of the lack of clear definition, most issues have been settled by case law. The Supreme Court has given great discretion to both the legislature in immigration matters (pointing to the plenary power of Congress and its constitutional mandate concerning immigration and naturalization matters) and to the executive, categorizing immigration matters as also related to questions of sovereignty and foreign policy. In this context, Congress and the executive, through the Plenary Power Doctrine, were, in 1889, given the power to make immigration policy free from judicial review. That doctrine rested on the assumption that immigration is a question of national sovereignty, relating to a nation's right to define its own borders, both territorial and intangible.

But who actually could be a citizen? Did noncitizens have rights? Earlier, in the 1857 *Dred Scott* decision, the Supreme Court declared that the legal category of citizen created by the Constitution was permanently unavailable to some, and the title of "citizen" conveyed rights that were limited to the citizen class. (Dred Scott had posed the question—unsuccessfully—whether a slave brought into free territory can become a full member of the political community that was created by the Constitution and sue in court, i.e., become entitled to all the rights, privileges, and immunities guaranteed by the Constitution to citizens.) In a country of freed slaves and a growing number of immigrants, something had to be done to rectify the problems imposed by that decision. Eleven years later, the Fourteenth Amendment (ratified 1868) returned to the liberal ideas prevalent at the founding of the republic, asserting that there must be equality, due process, and consent within the framework of a political membership community. It emphasized that a citizen of one state was a citizen of the United States.

To further clarify this, Congress passed the Naturalization Act of 1870, which extended naturalization to people of African descent. This law reflected the flexing of the republican governmental power over one area of federal control: naturalization. Throughout the late nineteenth and the twentieth centuries, however, restrictions on immigration and naturalization based on countries of origin continued. Naturalization was limited for groups thought suspect, such as Chinese nationals, perpetuating a racial idea of citizenship. This tension—between the ideals of equality and freedom on one hand, and the realities of race, gender, and politics on the other—set the stage for the debates about immigration and immigration laws during the twentieth century.

The slow stream of immigrants in the earlier days of the republic became massive waves in the 1840s and 1850s. In 1820, the number of immigrants was around 14,000; by the 1850s, the numbers approached 260,000. As of the 1860 census, immigrants accounted for over 8 percent of the national population. These immigrants also came from different ethnic and religious backgrounds. The Irish, almost all of them Roman Catholic, introduced new diversity, as did the arriving Germans. Previously, German immigrants were predominantly Protestant with some Catholics; now the immigrants were also Jewish. This wave included, for the first time, large numbers of temporary migrants, coming for seasonal labor and then returning to their native Canada and even Europe or Asia. Some Mexican workers were also entering for temporary work during this period; others were miners in the West. Many of these European and Canadian immigrants tended to cluster in enclaves in the Northeast, altering the demographic composition and, through their presence and their religious and cultural practices, challenging the dominant culture. The U.S. government was sought to develop means to incorporate these disparate populations and to generate some stability. The federal government used the Homestead Act of 1862 among other means to lure immigrants to settle free land and simultaneously get them (and natives) out of the cities. This free land policy was also used to entice immigrants from abroad to come and settle the West. In this way, ironically, the federal government could use space as a mechanism for incorporation, by dividing disparate populations.

Cultural clashes between the native-born and longer-standing immigrant communities with the newer immigrants bubbled into the political sphere. Both progressive and nativist strains reacted to the new cultural ways of the recent immigrants. On the progressive side, temperance movements, yielding to women's rights and civil rights movements, would emerge from anti-Irish, anti-Catholic political actions. More conservatively, the American or Know-Nothing Party emerged in the 1850s, espousing anti-immigrant rhetoric, specifically containing the cultural differences introduced by the new immigrants. The Know-Nothings demanded that the waiting period between arrival and naturalization should be extended from 5 to 21 years, mirroring the age of majority in the new state. The party had little impact on national politics, in large part due to the splintered federal system. Its decline occurred not due to the lack of popular support for its ideas, but rather because the nation was worried about the destruction of the Union itself and then the transformation of national politics and the party system following the Civil War. During the war, Lincoln offered quick naturalization for noncitizen soldiers as an enticement to join the Union army and as a way of solidifying the allegiance of the disparate immigrant groups to the Union.

The northern victory in the Civil War marked both an acceptance of continued immigration and the consolidation of federal power over immigration and naturalization and clarification of the nature of citizenship. At the ratification of the Fourteenth Amendment, it was assumed that many of the issues of who is a citizen, how citizenship is attained, the equality among citizens, and the primacy of the federal government over the naturalization and immigration policy was settled. However, in all of these issues,

A U.S. Department of Labor naturalization class, about 1915. (Library of Congress)

the amendment opened more issues than it settled during the next century.

Concurrent with and following Reconstruction, the nation experienced the second large wave of immigration from 1870 to 1920. During this period, more than 26 million people immigrated to the United States. Many of our ideas about naturalization and incorporation are based on the mythology and the reality of these immigrants. It was in this time that the Statue of Liberty and Ellis Island and, to a lesser extent, Angel Island, welcoming new immigrants became part of the national story. These immigrants had a disproportionate impact on the United States not just because of their impressive numbers, but also because they settled throughout much of the country, thus bringing a new presence, ideas, and cultures and fueling the Industrial Revolution. They represented a more diverse array of cultures than the previous wave, for the new one now involved more immigrants from southern, central, and eastern Europe as well as from

parts of Asia, the Americas, and, to a limited degree, Africa. The federal government then asserted its primacy over immigration and naturalization, generating new policies for naturalization and creating a bureaucracy within the federal government to manage immigration and naturalization.

With the inclusion of Chinese (and later Japanese) laborers emerging from contract work, especially that which solicited laborers for the railroads, the United States confronted new racial issues beyond the black-white dichotomy. As the number of Chinese laborers swelled, the nativist opposition reacted to the cultural and racial differences by the enactment of the Chinese Exclusion Act. That act denied the admission of Chinese laborers and disqualified Chinese from naturalization (22 Stat. 58, enacted May 6, 1882). The first challenge to these nativist volleys was the Supreme Court's holding that the wives of laborers were considered laborers and therefore were ineligible for admission. The court also upheld the sovereign power of the federal government to exclude prospective immigrants. However, the court had a very different reaction to those born in the United States, asserting that the Fourteenth Amendment specifically trumped any legislation, and to that end birthright citizenship was the law of the land. The court held that parental immigration status or lack of citizenship was immaterial, as the Fourteenth Amendment conferred citizenship on all children born in the United States. In *United States v. Wong Kim Ark* (169 U.S. 649, 1898) the court held that children born on American territory, even to (unnaturalizable) Chinese nationals, were still U.S. citizens.

It was now clear: all those born in the United States, regardless of their parents' status, were at birth U.S. citizens. That did not preclude Congress and the courts from baring naturalization to Asians. Efforts to gain naturalization by them were requested with the contention that they were white. In *United States v. Bhagat Singh Thind* (261 U.S. 204) in 1923, the government argued that Thind was not eligible for naturalization as naturalization was limited to whites. Thind countered that his Brahmin ancestry was not Asian but Indo-European, making him racially white and thus eligible for naturalization. In the majority decision, Justice Sutherland countered that "Hindus" are "aliens ineligible to citizenship."

Nonetheless, unprecedented was that the United States still offered citizenship to naturalizing new immigrants as well as recognizing their citizen-born children. The American birthright citizenship policy put an end to questioning the status of the children and descendants for all time: children born in the United States were American citizens, as was anyone who naturalized. Many sending countries continued to maintain links to their emigrants and continued to claim them as citizens long after emigration, and they even conferred citizenship on the emigrants' children who had never known the sending country. On the other hand, those same countries did not offer citizenship to immigrants coming to settle in those countries.

Beyond naturalization, incorporation was taking place at local levels. It included local government and political machine action, religious institutions, labor unions and employer programs, schools and the military, and socialization programs intended for both the children of immigrants and the immigrants themselves.

Many of the cities where immigrants settled were controlled by urban political machines. These machines were controlled, not infrequently, by first- and second-generation immigrants as well. The machines provided a crude social welfare system for the co-nationals and the political supporters of the machine leaders. The machines provided an entrée into the local community: offering food and supplies for newcomers, information about jobs or offers of actual jobs, and connections to landlords, employers, and local service providers, in addition to serving as intermediaries between the new immigrants and the native or older immigrant communities. As neither the federal nor the state governments provided social welfare assistance—services that the machines provided—those machines served as a critical link for the immigrants. That they were corrupt in all senses, including organizing mass naturalizations, is clear: their goal was to amass and concentrate power even though their ability to provide benefits was limited. Immigrants learned the political system, were socialized into naturalization, and voted through the political machines. By 1886, almost 80 percent of New York's Irish, German, and other western European immigrants had naturalized through the machine. New York City's Tammany Hall had so perfected the naturalization process that its own "Naturalization Bureau" had by 1868 organized "[i]mmigrants fresh off the boat [who] were given red tickets, allowing them to get their citizenship papers free. Tammany paid the required court fees and provided false witnesses to testify that the immigrants had been in the country for the necessary five years" (Erie 1988, 51). Some have argued that the importance of the machines in immigrant incorporation is overblown, making the observation that the machines (and other labor-based incorporation mechanisms such as the labor unions and employers) had virtually no effect on women's incorporation as they were largely outside of those relationships.

The Twentieth Century: Citizenship and Americanization

The Americanization movement, which emerged in the early twentieth century, can be understood in two completely different lights. Clearly, the movement was embedded with racist streams, seeking to eradicate difference and to meld the newcomers into the American mold whenever possible. In this way, we can understand Israel Zangwill's 1909 theatrical script (1920) that described the United States as the "Melting Pot." With new immigrants, through incorporation and eliminating differences, a new nation is born.

> America is God's Crucible, the Great Melting-Pot where all the races of Europe are melting and re-forming! Here you stand . . . in your fifty groups, with your fifty languages and your fifty histories, and your fifty blood hatreds and rivalries. But you won't be long like that, brothers, for these are the fires of God you've come to— these are the fires of God. A fig for your feuds and vendettas! Germans and Frenchmen, Irishmen and Englishmen, Jews and Russians— into the Crucible with you all! God is making the American. (Zangwill 1920, 33)

It is clear that Zangwill was concerned about the future of the nation, as he dedicated the play to Theodore Roosevelt "in respectful recognition, of his strenuous struggle against the forces that threaten to shipwreck the great republic which carries mankind and its fortunes." Previous generations also wondered how the influx of foreigners would affect the American experiment and, as the numbers of foreigners rose, the fears increased about the nation's ability to incorporate the newcomers. Roosevelt (1915) stated that: "The one absolutely certain way of bringing this nation to ruin, of preventing all possibility of its continuing to be a nation at all, would be to permit it to become a tangle of squabbling nationalities, an intricate knot of German-Americans, Irish-Americans, English-Americans, French-Americans, Scandinavian-Americans, or Italian-Americans, each preserving its separate nationality."

It is clear that the understanding was that the foreign elements are intrinsically backward and unhealthy for the American republic. Those supporting this view believed that maintaining identities of origin was antithetical to the preservation of the republic and had to be eliminated. This attempt to standardize the kinds of citizens reflected not just nativist perspectives, but also an alternative to the contemporary discussions of cultural pluralism put forth by such luminaries as Horace Kallen and Randolph Bourne. These ideas would become the basis for what is now labeled "multiculturalism." Kallen and Bourne eschewed the melting-pot theory in favor of cultural pluralism and derided Americanization as domination by those of Anglo-Saxon ancestry. By permitting and fostering Americanization schemes, they returned to the founding concepts in a positive and progressive light, a belief in change, modernization, hope and progressivism: one can learn to be American. The assumption was that not only could naturalization transform the foreigner into a member, but the foreigner could transform himself into an American by accepting our central tenets—through our creed, through acculturation and language acquisition, and through discarding foreign ways. Individuals were not, in an ascriptive tribal sense, locked into the ethnicities that they bring, but through education, affiliation with essential ideas, and ideals and self-reformation, the individual could be reborn. Race, culture, and religion can and do still marginalize; and yet, for the majority of immigrants, acceptance was within reach. Eventually, such quests for conformity would be counterbalanced by periods of celebration of diversity, expressing that the nation's diversity is a source of pride and strength, not weakness.

The modern state, emerging in the early twentieth century, needed to create the modern citizen. In connection with the Supreme Court's affirmation in the previous century that immigration and naturalization were under federal authority—see cases such as *Chae Chan Ping v. United States* 130 U.S. 581 (1889) and *Fong Yue Ting v. United States*, 149 U.S. 698, 730 (1893)—and as part of the federal government taking more of an engaged role in the development of the nation-state, the federal government began to take control of the naturalization procedures. The degree of (especially, but not exclusively, local) political corruption of the naturalization system through the machines was a major reason for the introduction of a national naturalization bureaucracy. The Naturalization Act of 1906 established procedural safeguards for the naturalization process, including fixed fees and uniform naturalization rules, and introduced a test of English-language proficiency as a requirement for

1578 Part 4 Issues in U.S. Immigration

naturalization. Symbolically, these actions were the beginning of a definition of what was required to be an American, and a self-understanding of what America should become.

From a policy perspective, the establishment of the rules and oversight represents the emergence of the modern state, the progressive movement as well as a national assertion of need for some testable markers of incorporation. Citizenship was to be standardized and organized. That said, given the tenor of the times, citizen making would be understood as a national enterprise and might involve the federal government, local governments, unions, employers, and private voluntary organizations. Harkening back to the framers' ideas and concerns about large influxes of foreigners bringing foreign ideas and corrupting the American ideals that Americans were not just born but made, all sectors of society engaged in a patchwork of efforts to standardize and "Americanize." Their goals were to eliminate those ways that were not in concert with the dominant culture. The movement to Americanize the immigrant was simultaneously an effort to bring foreigners into the American fold and to "de-immigrantize" the American political scene, which, by their aspiration for acceptance, alternative cultural practices and political organization might "destabiliz[e]" the dominant political class. However, by making immigrants into Americans, the dominant class could secure its dominant status and assure its cultural hegemony.

Americanization also reflected the way that the imagination of the production process had taken hold of the United States. Industrialization and its standardization of process meant we could make many things better through a perfected process. Citizen making seemed one more way we could break the incorporation process into activities, and it could benefit from standardization. With that in mind, private industry began to promote Americanization programs. Probably the most famous of these programs was a program hosted by the Ford Motor Company, originally called the Ford Sociologic Department and, eventually, the Ford Educational Department. Following Ford's paternalistic vision, the aim of the school was to improve foreign workers by educating them body and mind in American ways. Ford believed

that his social engineering would benefit the company, the individuals, and the state. He even paid immigrants extra to participate. As Stephen Meyer (1980, 70) explains, the Ford profit-sharing plan—through which workers earned extra for participating in education programs and living wholesome lives—as defined by Ford, "captured the Progressive Era's contradictory attitude toward the unskilled immigrant workers. On the one hand, it attempted to assist the worker and to elevate him to a better standard of life. On the other hand, it sought to manipulate of coerce the worker to match a preconceived ideal of a better life." They offered courses in efficiency, money management, domestic relations, community relations, and industrial relations. S. S. Marquis, who headed the Ford school, explained its purpose: "This is the human product we seek to turn out, as we adapt the machinery in the shop to turning out the kind of automobile we have in mind, so we have constructed our educational system with a view to the producing the human product we have in mind" (quoted in Meyer 1980, 74).

The Military as an Americanizer

Beginning in the nineteenth century, but enhanced and used much more frequently in the twentieth century and beyond, the military has been an incorporating institution. Military service has constituted a core obligation of citizenship since the establishment of the nation-state. States have used military service as a mechanism to cultivate nationalism by collectivizing risk, identity, and loyalty. Here, service is a function of *being* a citizen, and not *becoming* a citizen. The United States has used service as a way to create citizens as well. Since the Civil War, presidents have used offers of naturalization for noncitizens as a recruitment enticement. President Lincoln, in the Act of July 17, 1862, permitted: "any alien, of the age of twenty-one years and upwards, who has enlisted, or may enlist in the armies of the United States, either the regulars or volunteer forces, and has been, or may be hereafter, honorably discharged, shall be admitted to become a citizen of the United States, upon his petition, without any previous declaration of intention to become such; and he shall not be

Immigrants attend an English class given by the U.S. Department of Labor in the Ford Motor Company factory in Detroit in the early twentieth century. (Library of Congress)

required to prove more than one year's residence" (Act of July 17, 1862, 12 Stat. 597, section 21).

The policy was extended in 1864 to veterans in the navy and marines who had five years of honorable service. Similar enlistment inducements were used in the Mexican, Indian, and Spanish-American wars. Immigrants applying for naturalization under the normal naturalization procedure would file a declaration of intent to naturalize. Soldiers were not required to submit such declarations but were required to prove residency, good moral character, and honorable discharge. However, it was assumed that during peacetime, there was no need for the extension of special naturalization provisions. Moreover, the act of August 1, 1894 provided that: "No person (except an Indian) who is not a citizen of the United States, or who has not made legal declaration of intent to become a citizen . . . shall be enlisted in the Army of the United States during

time of peace" (Act of August 1, 1894, 28 Stat. 215, section 2.)

Toward the end of World War I, on May 9, 1918, Congress passed an act (40 Stat. 542) allowing special naturalization benefits conferring expedited citizenship, waiving the five-year residency requirement for a three-year period of enlistment, and making military personnel exempt for filing declarations of intention. Congress amended the act to extend the privilege for service members in World War II and Korea. In the Vietnam War, special provisions for wartime service were generally enacted but they covered only service during that war. There was no provision for retrospective or prospective service. In 1968, Congress amended the Immigration and Nationality Act to allow the president to issue executive orders determining periods of hostility during which special benefits could be conferred. President Reagan declared the Grenada campaign as "a period of hostilities," but a federal court invalidated the declaration because the executive order attempted to delimit the expedited naturalization benefit only to servicepeople serving in Grenada rather than according to the statute, which offered a blanket designation for all servicepeople.

The Government as Americanizer

The federal, state, and local governments were involved in both formally structured positive Americanization programs as well as punitive measures that were nativist in content and designed to get immigrants to conform to local standards of behavior or thought or practices. On the formal side, two branches of the federal government were engaged in designing and implementing Americanization programs.

In making Americans, the role as the adjudicator of citizenship status cannot be underestimated. And yet, despite the fact that the Constitution gives Congress the mandate to devise a uniform law of naturalization, it does not say who is responsible for implementing it. Throughout the nineteenth century, sub-federal bodies were involved in naturalization, yielding much concern about who was coming in and who was being given the right to join the political community. In the 1906 act, Congress made clear that the federal government held sole authority to naturalize. This matched the decisions issued by the Supreme Court in the decades before when it asserted the primacy of the federal government and the plenary powers of Congress. Prior to the 1906 act, individual states had designed and set the procedures for both state and federal citizenship.

The 1907 Federal Commission on Immigration was established as a result of political pressures to restrict immigration; by 1913, Congress charged the Commissioner of Naturalization with the responsibility to administer naturalization laws and gave the Bureau of Naturalization complete authority to deal with naturalizations. By 1918, two branches of the federal government ran Americanization programs. Immigration laws changed the need for incorporation programs. The 1924 Reed-Johnson Act established a national origins quota system on the number of incoming immigrants, thus seriously limiting the

number of immigrants who could eventually naturalize and halting the diversity of immigrants for several decades. It was not until the 1965 Immigration and Nationality Act—which removed the national origins quotas and based U.S. immigration on family reunification, national economic need, and humanitarian purposes—that the diversity of immigrants changed radically. Over time, there was a national interest in rethinking how to incorporate immigrants. However, even in the earliest days after the passage, few believed that the act would have much effect.

This form of coercive Americanization used fear and exclusion to keep some immigrant groups outside of the American mainstream, maintaining that their participation threatened the nation's well-being. Socially undesirable immigrants, including those from enemy countries as well as those deemed politically or socially undesirable—like communists, socialists, and others involved in labor organization—were stripped of their rights and deported. The Justice Department was given expanded authority to arrest, detain, and deport socially undesirable aliens. Deportation was a real threat even for native-born American women who, under the prevailing law, lost their U.S. citizenship upon marriage to a foreigner. Widespread xenophobia and fear of communism continued after the war and fueled nativist sentiment and backlash against immigrants, including such events as the Red Scare or the Palmer Raids of 1919 and 1920. Nativist rhetoric returned, and a number of writers, notably Madison Grant, took up the popular racialist discourse to argue that eastern and southern Europeans were racially inferior to the previous northern European immigrants. These sentiments and fears of radical politics continued throughout the rest of the century, although sensed most strongly during the Great Depression, World War II, and the Cold War. The nativist discourse claimed the word "Americanization" for itself and transformed the concept from one in which the disparate forces in society—government, employers, private voluntary organizations, schools, military, etc.—could incorporate immigrants, to one in which immigrants should be excluded. The word did not return to mainstream political discourse until the 1990s, and even then, it had mixed success.

States as Americanizers

A state commission in New York was established after the political success of the federal commission. Its findings and the way they were used were quite different. The New York state commission discovered what social workers had been complaining all along: that the conditions of immigrant life were deplorable. The commission proposed establishing a state bureau to deal with immigrant issues to use human resources wisely and improve the living conditions. In 1910, New York State established the Bureau of Industry and Immigration, a model government agency, copied and modified in states as close as New Jersey and Massachusetts and as far away as California. The goal was to achieve rapid assimilation and fairness in the incorporation of immigrants. It also set up programs to protect immigrants from fraud and discrimination.

Nativist efforts existed alongside the progressive ones. Some were discriminatory and intended to punish immigrants for being poor, or to limit competition with natives (or other preferred immigrants), or even to force immigrants to comply with societal norms. By World War I, however, the concerns about immigrants forced out progressive and paternalist Americanization schemes in favor of the nativist ones. The foreigner became the symbol of subversion, which brought on waves of xenophobia. The nation was at war abroad with many of the homelands of the new immigrants and feared a war at home among native-born and immigrants, as the United States was at war. Native populations worried if immigrants could be trusted. About five million foreign-born Americans had previously been Central Powers subjects, with about half coming from Germany and the rest from Bulgaria, Austria-Hungary, and Turkey. The possibility of fighting a war in Europe was bad enough. Nativism, relatively dormant, reemerged as the dominant discourse, and mass-scale anti-Catholic nativist sentiment easily morphed into anti-German sentiment. Almost overnight, where schools had required German as the foreign language, the requirements were eliminated. German social clubs changed their names to Americanized versions.

Schools as Americanizers

Early in the twentieth century, much of the focus on Americanization came through the schools. In much the same vein as the framers presented, the immigrants would learn the American ways while unlearning their foreign ones; schools were seen as institutions of incorporation. President Woodrow Wilson's secretary of the interior, Franklin K. Lane (Lane 1918), who was responsible for the Bureau of Education, spoke of "Americanization as a war measure." Echoing the common themes of the day, he implored all levels of government to join in the fight against those behaviors, cultures, and persons that threatened the American way of life and to use the full educational apparatus to engage, shape, and mold immigrant adults and children into good Americans. The Bureau of Naturalization developed school curricula to be implemented throughout the country. The Bureau of Education also made many plans for Americanization education, but as school districts were not under federal responsibility, it had little success in implementing a national plan. Local school districts designed their own hodgepodge of Americanization, English-language, and adult education classes. As the century continued, Americanization efforts were aimed more at the general public than at immigrants themselves. With the Cold War and ongoing Red Scares, schools were used to generate an American identity for all Americans rather than to make immigrants into Americans. After the Vietnam War and Watergate, even insipid civics classes were removed from many curricula. Incorporation efforts changed from stressing assimilation into the dominant culture to finding spaces for ethnic history in the American paradigm, Incorporation now meant recognizing and finding space for difference rather than eliminating it. Ethnic-studies classes proliferated, and bilingual-education courses were incorporated as per local interest into the normal curriculum.

Private Voluntary Organizations as Americanizers

Americanization projects were perceived as transcending federal and state governments and as an opportunity and obligation of private voluntary organizations (PVO) and religious institutions. PVO actions flourished through the years of large immigrant waves. Settlement houses, like Hull House, sprung up in congested immigrant neighborhoods and provided education, health, and social programs to local residents and pressured governments to provide better conditions for low-income residents. The North American Civic League, an umbrella organization of philanthropists, social workers, industry leaders, writers, and other prominent people, researched immigrant life conditions and offered programs aiming to solve those problems and provide immigrants with a "better appreciation" of America. The League supported programs of assimilation, education, distribution (spreading out immigrants), naturalization, and protection of immigrants from discrimination. Churches, synagogues, and religiously based PVOs provided support, education, fellowship, and guidance in the Americanization process. These kinds of organizations were particularly important for women immigrants as they were frequently left out of the labor-based and often politically based Americanization and incorporation schemes. Religious institutions, experiences with the private voluntary sector, and relationships with public schools for their children often provided women with the link to the receiving society, and these institutions helped immigrants attain formal and informal incorporation.

The Media as Americanizers

When formal Americanization programs ended around the Great Depression (although some would argue that the deportation of socially undesirable immigrants continued long after that and became state policy), the government became less of a factor in immigrant incorporation, except for children in the public school systems. However, the media began to fill a role on a scale that face-to-face contacts in settlement houses and mediating institutions no longer did. As the media became more ubiquitous in people's lives, through radio and films and then television, the media itself served as a great incorporator, nationalizing culture, softening regional differences, and building a national repository of stories, heroes, political

understandings, and virtual experiences. During World War I and World War II, the government commissioned filmmakers and generated corps of actors, directors, and filmmakers to tell the national story and to inspire patriotism. Governments underwrote public radio and television stations as media to get their messages to the people.

Conclusion

Since the early days of the republic, the United States has struggled over whom to bring in as citizens, how to bring them in, and how to build a nation with such disparate populations. The mid-twentieth century was no different. The Nationality Act of 1940 revised naturalization requirements and engaged naturalization, citizenship, and deportation laws in the name of national security. The Internal Security Act invoked educational requirements for naturalization. The Immigration and Naturalization Act of 1952 combined all of the immigration and naturalization laws into one comprehensive statute. In addition to the more legally elegant approach, the law at last eliminated racial bars to naturalization and asserted its commitment to naturalization as national policy. The law advocated continued cooperation with all levels of government and the public schools to provide education and information, raise awareness of naturalization, and design and distribute educational materials.

The 1965 Immigration and Nationality Act amendments radically altered the immigration system by establishing the main goals for U.S. immigration as family reunification, national economic need, and humanitarian purposes. As such, by making these changes, the entire immigrant population changed, bringing in more people from non-European countries—specifically, the bulk of immigrants coming from Asia and Latin America. The changes in law rendered increasing diversity and new questions about how to incorporate these diverse peoples and secure a unified nation. The discourse remains contentious over who is and who can be an American and how to get them from foreigner to member. Nativist and progressive approaches have been tried, simultaneously and consecutively. By the end of the twentieth century, questions emerged about how to incorporate and whether the methods used at the beginning of the century with large-scale migrations would be reasonable guides for this new large-scale migration wave. Alternatively, the state needed to consider whether a whole new understanding of what it was to be an American was necessary, and whether this new immigration harmed or helped the development of the American experiment. Many of the questions were the same as at the founding of the republic and it is incumbent on the state and the full expanse of officials to consider the issues and develop new responses and solutions.

Bibliography

Bloemraad, Irene. 2006. *Becoming a Citizen: Incorporating Immigrants and Refugees in the United States and Canada*. Berkeley: University of California Press.

Boesche, Roger. 1985. *Alexis de Tocqueville 1805–1859: Selected Letters on Politics and Society*. Berkeley: University of California Press.

Erie, Steven. 1988. *Rainbow's End: Irish Americans and the Dilemma of Urban Machine Politics*. Berkeley: University of California Press.

Fitzpatrick, John C., ed. (1931–1944) 1970. *The Writings of Washington from the Original Manuscript Sources, 1745–1799*. 39 vols. Washington, DC: Government Printing Office; reprint, New York: Greenwood Press.

Gusfield, Joseph. 1986. *Symbolic Crusade: Status Politics and the American Temperance Movement*. Urbana: University of Illinois Press.

Hamilton, Alexander. 1977. *Papers of Alexander Hamilton*, vol. 25, July 1800–April 1802. Edited by Harold C. Syrett. New York: Columbia University Press.

Handlin, Oscar. 1951. *The Uprooted: The Epic Story of the Great Migrations That Made the American People*. Boston: Little, Brown & Co.

Hartmann, Edward G. 1948. *The Movement to Americanize the Immigrant*. New York.

Higham, John. 1963 (2002). *Strangers in the Land: Patterns of American Nativism, 1860–1925*. New Brunswick, NJ: Rutgers University Press.

Jefferson, Thomas. 2002. *Notes on the State of Virginia*. Edited by David Waldstreicher. New York: Palgrave MacMillan.

Kallen, Horace. 1924 (1997). *Culture and Democracy in the United States*. New Brunswick, NJ: Transaction Publishers.

Kanstroom, Daniel. 2007. *Deportation Nation: Outsiders in American History*. Cambridge, MA: Harvard University Press.

Lane, Francis. 1918. "Americanization as a War Message: Report of a Conference . . . Washington, April 3." Washington, DC: Bureau of Education.

Meyer, Stephen. 1980. "Adapting the Immigrant to the Line: Americanization in the Ford Factory, 1914–1921." *Journal of Social History* 14, no. 1 (Autumn): 67–82.

"Roosevelt Bars the Hyphenated." *New York Times*, October 13, 1915, 1, 5.

Sterne, Evelyn Savidge. 2001. "Beyond the Boss: Immigration and American Political Culture from 1880 to 1940." In *E Pluribus Unum? Contemporary and Historical Perspectives on Immigrant Political Incorporation*, edited by Gary Gerstle and John H. Mollenkopf. New York: Russell Sage.

Ueda, Reed. 1997. "An Immigration Country of Assimilative Pluralism: Immigrant Reception and Absorption in American History." In *Migration Past, Migration Future*, edited by Klaus Bade and Myron Wiener, 39–63. New York: Berghahn Books.

Zangwill, Israel. 1920. *The Melting Pot: A Drama in Four Acts*. New York: Macmillan.

Immigration and Incorporation of New Americans: Citizenship Post 1980

Karen A. Woodrow-Lafield

The American immigrant has held a powerful role from historical to modern times, and the share of Americans of foreign birth now approaches the epic levels of around 1900. After five decades of increasing migration, the U.S. population is multidimensional on nativity, generational statuses, legal status, citizenship status, and origin, as race and ethnicity are being redefined through the lens of origin. Social institutions are being reshaped with respect to inclusion, adaptation or assimilation, and socioeconomic progress rather than exclusion, enclaves, and social inequalities. The majority of contemporary foreign-born persons are post-1980 arrivals, emphasizing the dramatic reshaping of the foreign-born population.

The phrase "pathway to citizenship" frequently appears in media and policy debates. Many new settlers step directly onto a pathway to citizenship by virtue of having been admitted for lawful permanent residence. Whether or not they become citizens depends on their willingness to meet, and their successful fulfillment of, the various requirements for naturalizing. The ratio of naturalized citizens to noncitizens or aliens differs markedly now (two to three) from the peak in the mid-twentieth century (four to one). That 78.7 percent level reflected the presence of many naturalized Europeans who were more likely to have naturalized and would remain the majority regional origin (more than three-quarters) until 1970. Many came as pioneers, the first of their families, and others traced their arrival to chain migration with a relative sponsoring them for an immigrant visa. Many early immigrants were successfully incorporated into the political structure of American society, acquiring English-language proficiency and advancing socioeconomically as they found opportunities in thriving northeastern cities and expanding cities in the Midwest, West, and South. Low immigration in the 1930s and the 1940s and emigration in the 1930s—after economic conditions improved with wage convergence between Europe and the United States—may well have helped processes of assimilation among the smaller pool of those foreign-born who remained. Annual numbers of naturalizations increased in the 1930s and during World War II, with an historic high of 441,979 in 1944 that would remain a record for more than five decades.

Those early-twentieth-century European immigrants are disappearing, as their stories of migration, becoming naturalized citizens, their accomplishments, and family backgrounds appear in obituary columns. High immigration from Latin America and other recent new immigration sources altered the composition of those acquiring citizenship between 1980 and 2000. Some 25 million immigrants were admitted legally, and several million unauthorized migrants who became undocumented residents were without a pathway to citizenship, such as the 2–4 million undocumented in 1980, the 2–5 million in 1990, and the 8–10 million in 2000.

By 2000, following significant, unprecedented movement of immigrants toward taking the mantle of U.S. citizenship, the number of naturalized citizens (12.5 million) was greater than ever before, and this continued in the first decade of the twenty-first century. After the numbers of Mexican immigrants increased in the 1980s and 1990s, Mexico appeared as the most highly represented country of origin among newly naturalizing individuals annually, and more than a million Mexicans naturalized in the 1990s. This is a startling change from the pattern of more Filipinos, Vietnamese, and Chinese than Mexicans among the newly naturalizing in earlier years. Mexican and other Latino immigrants have traditionally been less inclined to become U.S. citizens because they were likely to return easily to communities of origin as well as sharing ambivalent feelings about America.

In a new era of immigration and citizenship, contemporary immigration scholars are carefully considering current contexts, institutional structures, and institutional and community responses in relation to contemporary processes for incorporating immigrants whose characteristics add more diversity to the linguistic, educational, and ethnic composition of American society. Social scientists have considerable statistical information on ethnic and racial change through international migration and are at last more engaged in naturalization studies. This chapter examines recent major immigration laws and the extent to which immigrants have become Americanized through naturalization. First is a brief examination of the framework for legal immigration. Next, the chapter reviews major legislation that has had an impact on immigrant incorporation as citizens, beginning with the Immigration Reform and Control Act of 1986 (IRCA), aimed at reducing unauthorized migration and providing a pathway to citizenship for many formerly unauthorized residents and workers. The Immigration Act of 1990 (IA1990) altered the structure for legal immigration. The Personal Responsibility and Work Opportunity Reconciliation Act of August 22, 1996 (PRWORA), and the Illegal Immigration Reform and Immigrant Responsibility Act of September 30, 1996 (IIRIRA), focusing on reducing benefits accorded to immigrants, lawfully and unlawfully resident, held implications for the transition to U.S. citizenship and composition of foreign-born by citizenship status. Discussion of other legislation is included where relevant for the changing composition of the foreign-born population based on citizenship status and trends in naturalization statistics. These include the Legal Immigration Family Equity Act (LIFE), settlements in class-action lawsuits, and the Nicaraguan Adjustment and Central American Relief

Act (NACARA) of November 19, 1997. The major portion of this chapter concentrates on patterns of naturalization and evidence regarding those patterns from recent national surveys and administrative data of the U.S. Immigration and Naturalization Service (INS) and the Department of Homeland Security (DHS).

Legal Immigration, the Immigration Reform and Control Act of 1986, and the Immigration Act of 1990

As established by the 1965 amendments to the Immigration and Nationality Act of 1952 (INA), the great majority of immigrants granted lawful permanent residence have been admitted under family-sponsored preference categories or as immediate relatives of U.S. citizens, while many others have come either under employment sponsorship as professional, skilled workers or unskilled workers, or based on humanitarian criteria (including asylum and refugee provisions). Only after Congress enacted IRCA on November 6, 1986, representing comprehensive immigration legislation with a program of amnesty, discussed below, did Congress seek to expand the legal immigration system and respond to various demands for increased legal immigration of workers and family members, allowing more diversity. The Immigration Act of 1990 added a lottery involving diversity criteria for immigrant visas allocated to countries underrepresented in the foreign-born population, including nations in Asia and Africa in addition to Ireland and Poland.

IRCA included enforcement provisions, legalization programs, and mandated assessment of outcomes. With escalating apprehensions of aliens attempting to cross the southern border during the 1970s and early 1980s and evidence of a considerable presence of unauthorized persons in the nation—particularly in California, Texas, Florida, New York, and Illinois, states with considerable labor demands—Congress enacted immigration reform legislation. IRCA was meant to solve the illegal immigration problem through provisions for granting legal status for unauthorized residents and, especially, agricultural workers, and by intensifying border enforcement and imposing sanctions to promote employer responsibilities.

This immigration reform measure would have huge consequences for the composition of the foreign-born population by immigration status and citizenship status, immediately creating more mixed-status households and entitling many formerly unauthorized residents and workers to have a pathway to citizenship, economic mobility, and family reunification. From other perspectives, IRCA policies for intensified border enforcement led to changes in migrant behavior in attempting to cross the border, staying for longer periods and bringing wives and children along, although some migrants still opted to leave them in home communities. Sanctions prohibiting employers from knowingly hiring, recruiting, or referring for a fee aliens not authorized to work in the United States have been regarded as ineffective.

IRCA's legalization programs were of considerable import with consequences for naturalization and family reunification. First, about 1.7 million aliens received temporary resident status under Section 245(a) of the INA if they had resided in the United States in an unlawful status since January 1, 1982, were not excludable or subject to deportation, and had applied for amnesty during the period of May 5, 1987, and May 4, 1988. [Editor's Note: The application period was actually extended beyond the original one year.] Having been legalized, they later were eligible for adjustment to permanent resident status so long as they had evidence of continuous residence for one year and met minimum requirements for an understanding of English and a knowledge of American history and government (or demonstrated satisfactory studies), exempting those aged 65 years or older. Most (1.4 million) had entered illegally, and about 300,000 applicants had been temporary visitors with their authorized stay expiring before that date or with the government's knowledge of their unlawful status before that date. Second, IRCA made provisions for legalization under Section 210 of the INA of special agricultural workers (SAW); eventually about one million individuals—primarily those qualifying as having worked at least 90 days in seasonal agricultural services for one year (Group II) with a smaller number having done so for three years (Group I). All of those granted SAW status were automatically granted permanent resident status no later than December 1, 1990. Through the legalization programs and creation of H-2A temporary visas for seasonal agricultural workers, the Mexican-born population (and three-quarters were Mexican) was transformed to a more permanent status with IRCA. After IRCA, the mostly Mexican migrant workers could be found in even very rural Midwestern areas with inadequate local labor force pools, and these workers could be included in survey counts of noncitizens.

Some individuals were able to obtain legal status through IRCA's extension of the registry date from which an alien who has resided illegally and continuously in the United States is regarded as qualified for adjustment to permanent resident status. The previous date was June 30, 1948, and IRCA implemented January 1, 1972, as the effective date. IRCA also authorized adjustment to permanent resident status for Cubans and Haitians who had entered without inspection and had continuously resided here since January 1, 1982. In addition, IRCA allocated 5,000 non-preference visas in 1987 and 1988 for aliens born in countries from which immigration was adversely affected by the 1965 act (principally the Irish).

Thus, the pool of potential new citizens was enlarged by legalization of undocumented residents (those who entered without inspection or overstayers), legalization of special agricultural workers, the adjustment of Cubans and Haitians, and the preliminary diversity program.

Many of those who were legalized after long-term residence in an undocumented status were living with family members in mixed-status households, but many other family members of legalized immigrants were living abroad and hoping to immigrate legally, especially spouses or partners, children, brothers, and sisters. [Editor's Note: In some cases, family ties to lawful permanent residents was sufficient and in others direct family ties to U.S. citizens.] Most of these IRCA immigrants indicated they would definitely (48 percent) or probably (27 percent) apply to naturalize, and responses were similar for Mexicans (43 percent and 30 percent, respectively). Whether these intentions would be fulfilled seemed likely given that these IRCA legalization beneficiaries demonstrated English proficiency and knowledge of U.S. history and government in their applications for lawful permanent resident status.

Combining information about intended naturalization and reported family members intending to immigrate, about 1.2 million relatives were expected to appear among future petitions for immigrant visas. By 2002, the INS reported the naturalization experience of IRCA-legalized immigrants was similar to that of the 1989–1991 cohorts, except that Mexican-origin immigrants were more highly represented in the IRCA-legalized group and thereby lowered the overall rate. By 2005, more than one million IRCA beneficiaries had become naturalized citizens, about one-half of whom were Mexicans.

The IA1990 represented a major overhaul of immigration law and, specifically, increased total immigration under an overall flexible or piercable cap of 675,000 immigrants beginning in fiscal year 1995 (preceded by a 700,000 level in 1992–1994). Reflecting higher numbers for workers, this level consisted of 480,000 family-sponsored immigrants, 140,000 employment-based immigrants, and 55,000 "diversity" immigrants, that is, the new category for immigration from underrepresented countries. The composition of family-sponsored immigration was altered to include more spouses and minor children of permanent resident aliens, as especially apparent in subsequent Mexican immigration.

The Refugee Act of March 17, 1980, provided the first permanent and systematic procedure for the admission and effective resettlement of refugees of special humanitarian concern to the United States, specifically providing for adjustment to permanent resident status of refugees after at least one year of U.S. residence and of asylees one year after asylum is granted. Prior to that legislation, refugees and asylees were without a pathway to citizenship and were able to change their status only by obtaining an unused visa through the non-preference category. The presumption was that these persons would ultimately return to their nation when conditions improved; but in reality, several hundred thousand persons were living here on a permanent basis with a limited status.

The 1996 Welfare Reform Act and Immigrants

Until PRWORA, citizens, legal immigrants, and refugees had been nearly equally eligible for food stamps and means-tested public benefits programs. Those legal immigrants (with certain exceptions) entering the United States after date of enactment were barred from most federal means-tested programs for five years. Whereas the equal protection clause of the Fourteenth Amendment to the U.S. Constitution had prevented states from distinguishing among legal immigrants, refugees, and citizens, the PRWORA gave states broad flexibility in setting public benefit eligibility rules for legal immigrants by allowing states discretionary powers in distinguishing among foreign-born residents. Making the affidavit of support enforceable—so that benefits agencies could seek reimbursement—PWRORA also made immigrants' sponsors responsible financially either until the immigrant naturalized, or for 10 years. The inducement to seek citizenship in order to secure eligibility for a variety of government-funded programs was clearly most evident.

Immigration Reform and Deportation-Driven Deterrence

As the 1996 legislation demonstrated, several key pieces of federal legislation during the 1990s and early 2000s made the noncitizen status potentially quite costly and left aliens vulnerable to harsh new enforcement provisions. Following the initial 1993 attack on the World Trade Center in New York City, attention to criminal aliens as posing a potential terrorist threat accelerated. The Violent Crime Control and Law Enforcement Act of September 13, 1994, and the Antiterrorism and Effective Death Penalty Act of April 24, 1996, included provisions relating to deportation procedures for certain criminal aliens who are not permanent residents; expanded special deportation proceedings for expeditious deportation of denied asylum applicants; expedited hearings and removal procedures for alien terrorists; added specific measures for the exclusion of alien terrorists; modified asylum procedures to improve identification and processing of alien terrorists; improved procedures for prosecuting criminal aliens, such as expanded deportation criteria for crimes of moral turpitude; as well as an interior repatriation program; deportation of nonviolent offenders prior to completion of sentence of imprisonment; and authorizing state and local law enforcement officials to arrest and detain certain illegal aliens.

The IIRIRA of September 30, 1996, established measures to control U.S. borders, protect legal workers through worksite enforcement, and remove criminal and other deportable aliens and placed added restrictions on benefits for aliens, along with miscellaneous provisions. Other IIRIRA provisions broadly reformed exclusion and deportation procedures, including consolidation into a single removal process as well as the institution of expedited removal to speed deportation and alien exclusion through more stringent grounds of admissibility, institution of 3- and 10-year bars to admissibility for aliens seeking to reenter after having been unlawfully present in the United States, and barring reentry of individuals who renounced their U.S. citizenship in order to avoid U.S. tax obligations.

IIRIRA brought further distinction among categories of citizen, legal immigrants, and refugees. First, individuals sponsoring family members for visas were required to demonstrate an income satisfying the public charge threshold of at least 125 percent of the federal poverty level applicable (that is, the number of persons in their household plus the sponsored members). IIRIRA also involved provisions establishing procedures for requiring proof of citizenship for federal public benefits, verification of immigration status for purposes of Social Security and higher educational assistance, tighter requirements for an affidavit of support for sponsored immigrants, making the affidavit a legally binding contract to make financial support available, and confer authority to states and political subdivisions of states to limit the amount of general cash public assistance provided to aliens.

Expectations were that IIRIRA reforms would result in increased applications for naturalization and decreased numbers of admissions of lawful permanent resident aliens whose incomes were at lower levels. The difference between noncitizens and citizens became starkly evident with these restrictions, public benefits, and self-protective behavior. Also, there were expectations of reduced legal immigration due to less immigration from those in countries disallowing dual citizenship and by those for whom access to public benefits might have been an incentive to come, plus less sponsorship of parents and others for whom would-be sponsors expected a financial burden and less sponsorship due to inability to meet the public charge thresholds. Because poverty levels are higher among families headed by foreign-born householders than for natives, especially for noncitizen householder families, imposing this threshold likely affected the capability to sponsor parents, spouses, children, siblings, and adult sons and daughters.

Before further discussing legal immigrants' access to benefits in the wake of PRWORA and IIRIRA, there were unique ways during the 1990s and 2000–2009 for unauthorized residents and persons of indefinite status to seek documentation and a pathway to citizenship. In 1994, effective as of fiscal year 1995, Congress added Section 245(i) to the Immigration and Nationality Act with a lapse date of September 30, 1997. This allowed illegal residents who were eligible to acquire immigrant status to apply at an INS office for adjustment of status to permanent residence by paying a $1,000 fine. These persons had become eligible to acquire immigrant status by having applied while abroad, and the policy allowed them the luxury of paying a fine and not having them to return to the U.S. consulate abroad through which their visa application had been filed. The largest impact of this procedural shift may have occurred in the categories exempt from numerical limitation, such as immediate relatives of U.S. citizens. The actual numbers could not be quantified, but adjustment of status applications more than doubled between 1994 (91,000) and 1995 (288,000), and rose to 403,000 at the end of 1996, especially for immediate relatives of citizens.

The Nicaraguan Adjustment and Central American Relief Act (NACARA) of November 19, 1997, pertained to certain Central American and other aliens who were long-term illegal residents in the United States when hardship relief rules were made more stringent by the IIRIRA. NACARA allowed approximately 150,000 Nicaraguans and 5,000 Cubans to adjust to permanent resident status without having to make any hardship showing. In addition, it allowed approximately 200,000 Salvadorans and 50,000 Guatemalans, as well as certain aliens from the former Soviet Union, to seek hardship relief under more lenient hardship rules than existed prior to IIRIRA amendments. These individuals were placed on a pathway to citizenship and might likely have become citizens.

The LIFE Act of 2000 applied to several categories, including those individuals physically present on December 21, 2000, who qualified for permanent residency but were ineligible to adjust because of an immigration status violation. It also was "a corrective policy response" to three "late amnesty" lawsuits (*CSS v. Meese*, *LULAC v. Reno*, and *INS v. Zambrano*) in regard to unauthorized aliens who had not been able to apply for IRCA legalization and were living in the United States in uncertainty, specifically applicable to persons who had filed for class membership before October 1, 2000. In addition to LIFE, settlements in those lawsuits allowed applications from those individuals who had traveled abroad. Even two decades after IRCA, others were able to apply as IRCA beneficiaries following a December 2008 settlement that opened up amnesty for tens of thousands who entered on valid visas and were without legal status between 1982 and 1988. That class-action lawsuit challenged the rule that applicants had to prove their shift to legal status was "known to the government." For individuals eligible under the LIFE legalization provisions with their approval dependent on demonstrating knowledge of English and civics and continuous studies, their spouses and unmarried children would also be protected against certain categories of removal and would be given work authorization if they showed having begun unlawful U.S. residence before December 1, 1988. According to the *2008 Yearbook for Immigration Statistics* (OIS), there were approximately 700,000 nonimmigrant admissions under LIFE over 1999–2008. These persons would have many years of residence upon becoming legal immigrants and might have begun to naturalize after 2005. Considering likely numbers adjusting status under 245(i) provisions over 1996–1998, the total

number benefiting from these various policies is likely to be one million, essentially augmenting the legalization impacts of IRCA.

Legal immigrants' access to federal aid programs was reinstated in legislation in 1997, in 1998, and again in the Farm Security and Rural Investment Act of 2002 (P.L. 107-171), known as the 2002 Farm Bill. The 1997–1998 changes meant PRWORA restrictions would not apply to "qualified aliens" who met 10-year work requirements, or are veterans or certain active-duty personnel, and their close family members. These included legal permanent residents, refugees, aliens granted asylum or similar relief, aliens paroled into the United States for at least one year, and certain battered family members, plus the 1997 legislation added Cuban and Haitian entrants. The alienage restrictions would not apply to aliens who become citizens through naturalization. This act continued eligibility both for aged and for disabled "qualified aliens" receiving Supplemental Security Income (SSI) benefits as of August 26, 1996, as well as those disabled after August 22, 1996. SSI recipients remained eligible for Medicaid; for others, Medicaid is a state option. Refugees and asylees (including Cuban/Haitian entrants and Amerasians) were exempted for seven years from the bar against SSI and Medicaid. Later, for refugees through 2009–2011, the seven-year exemption from the bar against SSI was extended to nine years, plus one additional year if a naturalization application was pending.

Immigration and the Transition to Citizen

An Independence Day naturalization ceremony has been held annually since 1963 at Thomas Jefferson's home Monticello in Charlottesville, Virginia, including among 74 new citizens in 2008 some from Iraq, China, Khartoum, and the Sudan. There have been dramatic changes in origins represented among new citizens. The legal structure for making the transition from lawful permanent resident alien, or immigrant in a legal sense, to naturalized citizen has altered little since the first Congress enacted rules about citizenship in 1790. The Naturalization Act of

June 29, 1906, which framed the basic rules for naturalization (forms, filing with court and federal agency, English-speaking ability, and signing the petition in one's own handwriting), remain in effect as of this writing. The act assigned federal responsibility for supervising the granting of citizenship that was later handled by the INS, holding dual missions of benefit provision and enforcement. As of March 1, 2003, that role was taken over by U.S. Citizenship and Immigration Services (USCIS) as one of three legacy INS components to join the DHS.

For legal immigrants, the general requirements for U.S. naturalization have long been to be at least 18 years old, to have had continuous lawful permanent residence for five years, to demonstrate English proficiency, to have knowledge of the U.S. government and U.S. history, and to possess good moral character. A prolonged absence from the United States may break the continuity of an alien's U.S. residence for naturalization purposes, although an absence of less than six months does not do so. For an absence of six months to one year, a reasonable explanation may be accepted for naturalization purposes, and an individual may seek approval when the absence is for more than one year under certain circumstances. An individual may file the Form N-400 "Application for Naturalization" as early as 90 days prior to the date of satisfying the residency requirement along with any necessary supporting documents and the appropriate filing fees—$650 in 2009, plus a biometrics fee of $80, if necessary—at the USCIS service center having jurisdiction over the place of one's residence. The waiting time for eligibility to apply for naturalization is a preparatory period, but, many immigrants were already going through anticipatory socialization, i.e., acquiring education and language proficiency, while awaiting their immigrant visas in such countries as the Philippines and China (where there are long waiting times for preference visas) or while living here as nonimmigrants (temporary workers, foreign students, or visitors) before adjusting one's status.

Some individuals, such as spouses of U.S. citizens and aliens fulfilling military service requirements, are eligible to naturalize under special procedures.

Generally, certain lawful permanent residents married to U.S. citizens may file for naturalization after continuous residence for three years immediately preceding the filing of the application if, first, the applicant has been married to and living in a valid marital union with the same U.S. citizen spouse for all three years; second, the U.S. spouse has been a citizen for all three years and meets all physical presence and residence requirements; and, third, the applicant meets all other naturalization requirements. Although the majority of naturalizations are under general provisions, naturalizations under the spouses of U.S. citizen provision accounted for an increasing share from 1996 to 2005. There are also exceptions for lawful permanent residents married to U.S. citizens stationed or employed abroad in that the U.S. residence or physical presence requirements may be waived when the U.S. citizen spouse is employed by the U.S. government (including the U.S. armed forces), by a recognized U.S. religious organizations, U.S. research institutions, an American firm engaged in the development of foreign trade and commerce of the United States, or certain public international organizations involving the United States.

Through the National Defense Authorization Act for Fiscal Year 2004, signed into law on November 24, 2003, naturalization became easier for members of the armed services (or selected reserve) and their families with reduction in the required period of service to one year from three years, and waiver of all fees relating to naturalization for military applicants. Executive agencies were directed to ensure that applications, interviews, oaths, and other proceedings relating to naturalization be made available to members of the armed forces through U.S. embassies, consulates, and overseas military installations.

For minor children of naturalizing immigrants, their own naturalization is derivative from their parental naturalization and automatic, meaning that citizenship is regarded as acquired by law without application. Their parents may request a certificate of citizenship by filing a Form N-600 "Application for Certification of Citizenship." The path to citizenship for children of immigrants, including adopted foreign-born children, was simplified, effective February 27, 2001, by the Child Citizenship Act of 2000 (P.L. 106-395), which altered the requirement for a child to only needing one parent who is a citizen or naturalizing.

An FBI criminal background check, including fingerprinting, is required, and both the INS/USCIS agency processing and the FBI check may take several months. Because naturalization processing is handled through field offices, waiting times may be many months longer for applicants in some localities than for others. Delays in naturalization processing, sometimes three or four years, were frequent even after changes to streamline naturalization after 1991. Prior to the IA1990 amendments, the courts had exclusive jurisdiction over naturalization, but the IA1990 gave the INS sole authority for naturalization, restricting the courts' role to any requested judicial review of a denial decision on an application. Lengthy processing delays developed after 1994 with rising numbers of applications—more than one million in 1997—despite more than one million approvals in 1996. The INS backlog increased to one year after it had shrunk considerably. Both immigration and naturalization services are provided on a fee basis, but these fees are not particularly well designed for maximizing efficiency as demonstrated by higher processing backlogs despite a fee increase on July 30, 2007. Delays in processing naturalization applications have seemed especially evident when applications increased as immigrants anticipated voting in presidential elections in 1996, 2000, 2004, and 2008.

Even as the USCIS has made some improvements in processing for naturalization applications, the routine FBI criminal background checks or "FBI name-checks," essential for avoiding granting admission visas to terrorists, were slow and inefficient, creating delays. Through a settlement in a 2007 class-action lawsuit between the USCIS and plaintiffs, the National Immigration Law Center, the ACLU of Southern California, the Asian Pacific American Legal Center, and the law firm of Munger, Tolles & Olson, the USCIS is required to adjudicate citizenship applications within six months, and the kinds of indefinite processing delays incurred by many applicants should be ended. With completion of these steps for the "examination" phase, written notification is sent to the applicant setting a naturalization interview date. At his or her discretion, the adjudication officer may ask questions about supporting evidence and information concerning the applicant's background and character as well as his or her commitment to the principles of the constitution and willingness to take an oath of allegiance to the United States.

In anticipation of millions of lawful permanent residents becoming eligible to naturalize in the mid-1990s, in addition to immigrants under regular provisions, the bipartisan U.S. Commission on Immigration Reform's 1997 Report to Congress, *Becoming an American: Immigration and Immigrant Policy*, made recommendations for maintaining the current statutory requirements of naturalization along with increasing the efficiency and integrity of the naturalization process. Questions for the naturalization examination to assess knowledge of civics and U.S. history were regarded as indicative of the factual orientation rather than substantive understanding of the basic concepts of civic participation. In 2008, the USCIS implemented the newly revised naturalization testing and procedures with goals of standardization, fairness, and encouraging civic learning and patriotism. The new exam for reading and writing is similar to the past exam, but more civics-based vocabulary is included. During the naturalization interview, applicants have up to three chances to read aloud a sentence selected by the test officer or to write a sentence that the officer has read. The new civics exam is administered with 10 questions chosen from a master list of 100 civics and U.S. history questions, and the applicant must answer correctly at least 6 of these questions. That master list of questions and answers, study guides, and reading and writing vocabulary lists are available online.

Certain applicants are exempt from the English requirements—applicants over 55 years of age who have resided in the United States as permanent residents for 15 years or more, applicants over 50 years of age with 20 years or more of permanent residence, or applicants who have a medically determinable physical or mental impairment that affects the ability to learn English. Applicants whose impairment affects the ability to learn U.S. history and government are also exempt from being required to demonstrate knowledge of civics and history, and special consideration is given to applicants who have been permanent residents for at least 20 years and are over the age of 65. Even with these special considerations, certain older immigrants face difficulties in understanding the importance of becoming naturalized and successfully navigating the process.

Within 120 days following the interview, the USCIS is required to let applicants know if their applications have been granted, continued, or denied. If USCIS does not act on a timely basis, applicants may file a Section 1447(b) petition in the U.S. District Court seeking a hearing and decision to either grant it or so instruct the USCIS. A ruling on a 2008 lawsuit over immigrants awaiting decisions for longer than 120 days held that USCIS no longer has jurisdiction, and the district court must exercise judicial review over such applications denied or remaining undecided beyond the 120-day period (*Bustamante v. Napolitano*, U.S. Court of Appeals for the Second Circuit, 08-0990-cv, September 28, 1990). If USCIS grants the application, the individual is sent a notice instructing him or her when and where to take the oath of allegiance and officially become a citizen, although he or she may be able to do so on the same day as the interview in some cases and locations. If the applicant does not pass the English and/or civics tests, or if USCIS requests additional documents, the case is "continued," and the applicant is asked to come back for a second interview or to provide additional information. If USCIS denies the application, the applicant receives a written explanation. Some applicants have not been aware that histories of felony crimes or some misdemeanor offenses, even shoplifting, may affect not only their naturalization application, but also their lawful permanent residence status. Upon the FBI identification of them as having criminal records, individuals have been deported because the law removed most rights to fight expulsion by showing

evidence of community ties or hardship to U.S. citizen relatives.

To complete the citizenship process, one must take the oath of allegiance and swear to support the Constitution and obey the laws of the United States, renounce any foreign allegiance and/or foreign title, and bear arms for the U.S. armed forces or perform services for the U.S. government when required. The Judicial Naturalization Ceremonies Amendments of 1991 provided that each applicant for naturalization could choose to have the oath of allegiance administered either by the INS/USCIS or by an eligible court. From another amendment, courts may retain exclusive jurisdiction on administering the oath for 45 days from notification of approval for naturalization. The court then notifies USCIS of scheduled naturalization ceremonies, and USCIS informs the applicant. The administrative and judicial naturalization process was altered again in 1995 to extend jurisdiction for administering the oath to immigration judges in locations where the federal or state courts have not elected to retain exclusive jurisdiction. In most locations, the federal court has elected to retain jurisdiction over the administration of the oath.

As a caveat, the United States has not enforced the requirement of renunciation of original nationality, and the stance of the country of nationality is more relevant from the immigrant's perspective. Several nations (including Colombia, Vietnam, and Jamaica) have long permitted their citizens to retain their original citizenship, but other countries (Cuba, China, and Korea) have policies against duality of citizenship. Recognizing the value of immigrant remittances to their economies, several nations— e.g., Brazil, Ecuador, Mexico, India, the Philippines, and the Dominican Republic—recently changed laws to recognize dual citizenship and nationality rights for their citizens abroad. After many years of debate, Mexico also passed legislation that permits their citizens to participate in elections by mail from the United States. Dominican naturalizations increased even before the policy changes were made, but the change facilitated high political engagement with home affairs of Dominicans living in New York City.

New citizens are assisted in registering to vote in Miami Beach in 2004. At the time, voter's rights groups had been granted legal permission to recruit new citizens for voting registration outside of naturalization ceremonies. (AP/ Wide World Photos)

Recent Patterns in Naturalizing

Immigrants have naturalized in different patterns, historically and recently, according to personal characteristics (education, language ability, income, age, gender, and marital status), origin (associated with social, political, and economic contexts of sending country), history of U.S. residence, and a visa class of admissions indicative of social and human capital levels. For immigrant cohorts of 1978–1991, linking records of naturalization with original immigrant record, excluding IRCA legalized immigrants, 42 percent, had naturalized by 1996 after periods of permanent residence from 10 to 18 years. Adults older at admission are less likely to naturalize than are younger immigrants, for whom seeking citizenship may yield advantages in the labor market or may afford sponsorship for relatives abroad for immigrant visas. Being

married means having a spouse as social capital for acquiring skills to naturalize and for understanding the importance of citizenship. With a split-portfolio strategy, one member of the couple can take on citizenship in the new country while the other retains original citizenship and nationality rights. Younger and married immigrants are likely to have foreign-born and U.S.-born children and may naturalize in order to achieve status consistency within the family.

In the 1980s and early 1990s, those immigrants who had already been living here as foreign students, temporary workers, visitors, refugees, or asylees naturalized more quickly than those admitted as "new" arrivals. The majority of immigrants who received their green cards through employment sponsorship naturalized faster than immigrants under family-sponsored categories. Thus, highly talented immigrants—educated, skilled, experienced in the labor market, and knowledgeable about living here—are likely and able to become citizens relatively easily. Spouses of citizens and spouses of permanent resident aliens also naturalized quickly, for their husbands or wives (who may be a source of social capital) could help them prepare the application and understand the steps as well as the importance of citizenship. The sisters- and brothers-in-law of citizens and the sons- and daughters-in-law of citizens naturalized faster than some other family members. Siblings of U.S. citizens would have lesser family reunification needs than many immigrants among the first in their families to come, such as employment-sponsored immigrants and the spouses of citizens, spouses of resident aliens, and spouses of citizens' brothers, sisters, married adult sons, and married adult daughters, because they arrived through chain migration and family members already live here.

Focusing on the 10 leading origins, nearly two-thirds of Vietnamese and Filipinos and one-half of Chinese immigrants were naturalized citizens after 10 to 18 years of residence; whereas only one in four or five of Colombians, Indians, Cubans, Koreans, Jamaicans, Dominicans, or Mexicans had become naturalized. Immigrants from the Philippines, Vietnam, and China not only were observed as having naturalized more, but also they were naturalizing more quickly than other immigrants from India, Korea, Cuba, Colombia, Jamaica, the Dominican Republic, and Mexico. Filipinos, Vietnamese, and Chinese immigrants were six to eight times as likely to naturalize as Mexican immigrants, consistent with findings that Filipino and Southeast Asian foreign-born in national surveys were most likely to naturalize in the 1990s. More recently admitted immigrant cohorts were naturalizing after shorter durations of residence than earlier immigrants, based on experiences as of 1996 for 1978–1991 cohorts. This behavioral shift in becoming American citizens occurred before passage of the 1996 Welfare Reform Act and IIRIRA and may reflect increasing naturalizations in 1994–1996 following the anti-immigrant climate in the early 1990s.

An unprecedented era of naturalization applications commenced just as IIRIRA passed, leading to remarkably high levels of naturalization approvals.

Micro-level explanations of economic motivation and the family reunification incentive are relevant, but the massive mobilization toward naturalizing also occurred in order to increase political incorporation in response to particular policies favoring citizens. The likely effect of PRWORA for naturalization patterns was to increase naturalization levels, and increased applications and approvals in the 1990s were attributed to concerns over access to public benefits for Medicaid, SSI, and food stamps in reaction to the anti-immigrant debate and legislation. The increase was in part due to other reasons—eligibility of nearly three million IRCA beneficiaries, decisions to naturalize instead of paying a similar fee for green card removal, and motivation to obtain more satisfactory proof of legal status.

The Welfare Reform Act was expected to have the most deleterious impact for poorer immigrants, those unable to naturalize, those who simply did not expect to need welfare and therefore did not naturalize, and those who naturalized and then fell into economic hardship and needed greater access to public benefits for longer periods. At low income levels, there is considerable crossover from not-in-poverty to in-poverty status, and changing circumstances of divorce, widowhood, loss of wage-earning parent, or migration can push individuals into economic distress. Certain refugee groups have experienced economic difficulties despite eligibility for program assistance because their skill levels are inadequate in the U.S. labor market or their locale.

Considering the most recent evidence from the American Community Survey of 2008, among 38 million foreign-born residents, about 43 percent, had become naturalized citizens; and, by inference, non-citizens were equally divided among lawful and unauthorized. By 2008, more than 16.3 million Americans were naturalized citizens. Most (about two-thirds) had completed the naturalization process before 2000, especially in 1996–2000 (20.9 percent). Naturalization approvals increased from slightly less than one million for 1981–1985 to 3.7 million for 1996–2000, after record applications were submitted from IRCA immigrants and immigrants seeking citizenship for self-protection from deportation, for political involvement, and for access to public

Table 1.   Period of Naturalization for Foreign-Born Population in 2008 and Administrative Data for Periods

Period of Naturalization	Estimate	Margin of Error (+/-)	Percent by Citizenship	Percent of Total Naturalized Citizens	Naturalizations	Ratio
Total	37,960,935	122,968	100.0%	—	—	—
Not a U.S. Citizen	21,631,026	118,223	57.0%	—	—	—
Naturalized Citizens	16,329,909	68,667	43.0%	100.0%	—	—
Naturalized 2006 or later	2,272,348	29,593	—	13.9%	2,233,958	0.983
Naturalized 2001 to 2005	3,098,150	32,545	—	19.0%	2,806,854	0.906
Naturalized 1996 to 2000	3,411,696	33,628	—	20.9%	3,712,931	1.088
Naturalized 1991 to 1995	1,844,192	22,584	—	11.3%	1,958,890	1.062
Naturalized 1986 to 1990	1,518,796	19,575	—	9.3%	1,250,736	0.824
Naturalized 1981 to 1985	1,084,481	19,681	—	6.6%	950,898	0.877
Naturalized before 1980	3,100,246	28,052	—	19.0%	3,876,146	—

Note: Administrative data on naturalization approvals are interpolated to approximate counts on a calendar-year basis; the total for naturalizations before 1980 is based on naturalizations 1950–1980.
Source: Data set, 2008 American Community Survey 1-Year Estimates, B05011: Period of Naturalization.

benefits, and remained high after 2000. Comparing the survey estimates with naturalization statistics, the foreign-born population that reported as having naturalized between 2001 and 2008 (about 5.4 million) was slightly more than the actual number of naturalization approvals (5.0 million) by INS and USCIS (see Table 1). This difference could be explained by the lack of official records for many of those acquiring citizenship as children through a parental naturalization. More than 10 million of the foreign-born population reported as having become naturalized during the period 1991–2008 (10.6 million), while official naturalization statistics showed 10.8 million. Although survey reports are higher for the periods in the 1980s and for post 2000—suggesting misreporting by aliens or new citizens mistakenly including of derivative citizenships—naturalization approvals were higher for 1991–1995 (1.062) and 1996–2000 (1.088) than the estimates based on survey data. The discrepancy may have been due to new citizens having left the country or partaking of dual residence patterns and, hence, were not present, or nonresponses to the surveys. For example, some Mexicans may have taken up residence in Mexico after the 1998 constitutional change allowed them to fully retain or regain their nationality, or some naturalized citizens with dual residences may have altered their patterns of living at their U.S. home due to heightened security measures for international travel.

Examining the foreign-born population and region-of-origin groups as to citizenship and period of entry, having naturalized citizenship was least likely for the most recent post-2000 arrivals, as only 10.2 percent reported that status by 2008 (see Table 2). About two in every five foreign-born persons who entered in 1990 to 1999 (38.1 percent) had naturalized by 2008. Particularly for the post-1990 period, those who have not naturalized include many categories of persons ineligible to naturalize—unauthorized residents, nonimmigrants, and persons with temporary protected status or extended voluntary departure. After two or more decades of residence, nearly three-fifths (59.6 percent) had become citizens. Among longtime residents, those saying they came before 1980, over three quarters (78.6 percent) are citizens.

Patterns of naturalized citizenship in 2008 for long-term residents by country or region closely resembled patterns for long-term residents in 1990 and 2000, with lower naturalization for Mexicans (22.1 percent) and other Central Americans (30.2 percent) than for Europeans (60.3 percent) and Asians (57.5 percent). By 2008, the majority of long resident foreign-born persons (pre-1980 entrants) had become naturalized citizens, with 91 percent naturalized of Asians, and similar levels for Europeans (83 percent), Caribbeans (84 percent), South Americans (84 percent), and non-Mexican Central Americans (75 percent). Among long-resident Mexicans, 59 percent

Table 2. Place of Birth, Period of Entry, and Citizenship: Foreign-Born Population, American Community Survey 2008

Place of Birth	Foreign-Born	Naturalized Citizens	Percent
Total	37,960,935	16,329,909	43.0%
Entered 2000 or later	11,212,889	1,142,038	10.2%
Entered 1990 to 1999	10,842,813	4,135,058	38.1%
Entered 1980 to 1989	7,618,988	4,540,510	59.6%
Entered before 1980	8,286,245	6,512,303	78.6%
Europe	4,969,090	2,998,346	60.3%
Entered 2000 or later	1,020,257	161,989	15.9%
Entered 1990 to 1999	1,251,755	720,663	57.6%
Entered 1980 to 1989	608,474	384,019	63.1%
Entered before 1980	2,088,604	1,731,675	82.9%
Asia	10,355,577	5,952,897	57.5%
Entered 2000 or later	3,120,318	449,982	14.4%
Entered 1990 to 1999	2,894,673	1,767,653	61.1%
Entered 1980 to 1989	2,382,809	1,950,301	81.8%
Entered before 1980	1,957,777	1,784,961	91.2%
Latin America	20,150,245	6,317,801	31.4%
Caribbean	3,407,909	1,853,058	54.4%
Entered 2000 or later	772,274	111,742	14.5%
Entered 1990 to 1999	898,533	424,658	47.3%
Entered 1980 to 1989	769,868	499,604	64.9%
Entered before 1980	967,234	817,054	84.5%
Central America	14,175,411	3,357,328	23.7%
Mexico	11,412,668	2,523,260	22.1%
Entered 2000 or later	3,582,476	151,862	4.2%
Entered 1990 to 1999	3,634,440	463,105	12.7%
Entered 1980 to 1989	2,285,345	783,126	34.3%
Entered before 1980	1,910,407	1,125,167	58.9%
Other Central America	2,762,743	834,068	30.2%
Entered 2000 or later	892,509	60,793	6.8%
Entered 1990 to 1999	783,252	160,291	20.5%
Entered 1980 to 1989	742,350	353,687	47.6%
Entered before 1980	344,632	259,297	75.2%
South America	2,566,925	1,107,415	43.1%
Entered 2000 or later	903,287	87,417	9.7%
Entered 1990 to 1999	714,856	287,174	40.2%
Entered 1980 to 1989	490,642	346,836	70.7%
Entered before 1980	458,140	385,988	84.3%
Other areas	2,486,023	1,060,865	42.7%
Entered 2000 or later	921,768	118,253	12.8%
Entered 1990 to 1999	665,304	311,514	46.8%
Entered 1980 to 1989	339,500	222,937	65.7%
Entered before 1980	559,451	408,161	73.0%

Note: See source for margins of error.
Source: Data Set, 2008 American Community Survey 1-Year Estimates, B05007: Place of Birth by Year of Entry by Citizenship Status for the Foreign-Born Population.

were naturalized. Those levels are indicative of substantial integration and acquisition of English and knowledge. Social institutions and communities may have helped those who arrived in the 1970s to adapt and take U.S. citizenship with time. More recent cohorts may benefit from the stronger networks for employment opportunities and matters of daily life that have evolved with higher migration prevalence.

Toward Immigration Reforms in the Twenty-first Century

As the 109th Congress considered immigration reform legislation, the Senate approach (Comprehensive Immigration Reform Act [Senate Bill S. 2611]) combined enforcement emphases, which had been the focus in H.R. 4437 in 2005, with increases to family-based and employment-based visas plus allowances for temporary or guest workers, benefit provisions for legal status to unauthorized residents, and specifying the pathway to regular status and eventual citizenship. Comprehensive immigration reform would probably benefit Mexicans and other Central Americans because these groups are highly represented among unauthorized residents now as they were prior to IRCA. The current immigration dilemma is complicated by the greater ramifications of again putting unauthorized residents on the pathway to citizenship because the unauthorized population is estimated at two to three times greater than at the time of IRCA's passage. The IRCA legalization program was regarded as large scale with substantial demographic impact.

An escalating litany is evident from various think-tank and advocacy organizations on the subject of comprehensive immigration reform. Future immigration would result as migrants or foreign-born residents become immigrants and make the transition to naturalization. They could then sponsor adult sons, adult daughters, and siblings for preference visas and immediate relatives without limitation. Nonprofit and community organizations have roles in promoting civic engagement and political incorporation of immigrants and refugees through programs for English-language and civics classes, native-language citizenship instruction, and application assistance. The emergence of citizenship and civic participation stem from personal contact and social interaction as well as mobilization efforts of community leaders within communities with intricate interethnic ties and social capital—friends, ethnic businesses, immigrant organizations, and community leaders. Recent activities typifying these efforts include the National Day of Citizenship (July 12, 2008, and July 11, 2009) and the We Are America Alliance, 400 nationwide institutions united for civic integration. Not only naturalization, but also participatory or substantive citizenship, being politically engaged, makes up political incorporation or full citizenship.

Comparative studies indicate different trajectories of political incorporation for immigrants of the United States and Canada, with quicker incorporation in Canada with an official policy of diversity and multiculturalism since the 1970s. (The Canadian government promotes the value of Canadian citizenship and engages community organizations as agents of political socialization and training.) Immigrants to the United States more easily retain hyphenated identities (Mexican-American, Indian-American, etc.), while they are also Mexican citizens, European citizens, or Indian citizens in American society without needing to assimilate into the melting pot. U.S. government policies relating to becoming Americanized are quite simply not as definitive as in the Canadian case, and whether or not individuals become naturalized depends more on individual motivations or characteristics.

As policy makers are weighing immigration reforms inclusive of legitimizing those of unauthorized status and giving a pathway to citizenship, one suspects current public policies relating to newcomer integration would not be sufficient to ensure timely progression to citizenship given the persisting differences with respect to naturalization. Incorporation would take place more quickly, with greater emphasis on civic involvement and political engagement, but it involves the need to place greater emphasis on citizenship and promoting immigrant integration—along with linguistic assimilation, economic adaptation, and family integration.

Bibliography

Bean, Frank D., R. Corona, R. Tuirán, K. A. Woodrow-Lafield, and J. Van Hook. 2001. "Circular, Invisible, and Ambiguous Migrants: Components of Difference in Estimates of the Number of Unauthorized Mexican Migrants in the United States." *Demography* 38, no. 3: 411–22.

Bloemraad, Irene. 2006. *Becoming a Citizen: Incorporating Immigrants and Refugees in the United States and Canada.* Berkeley: University of California Press.

Bueker, Catharine S. 2005. "Political Incorporation among Immigrants from Ten Areas of Origin: The Persistence of Source Country Effects." *International Migration Review* 39, no. 3: 103–40.

Espenshade, Thomas J., Jessica L. Baraka, and Gregory A. Huber. 1997. "Implications of the 1996 Welfare and Immigration Reform Acts for US Immigration." *Population and Development Review* 23, no. 4: 769–801.

Jasso, Guillermina, and Mark R. Rosenzweig. 1990. *The New Chosen People: Immigrants in the United States.* New York: Russell Sage Foundation.

Newton, Lina. 2008. *Illegal, Alien or Immigrant: The Politics of Immigration Reform.* New York and London: New York University Press.

Woodrow-Lafield, Karen A. 1995. *Potential Sponsorship by IRCA-Legalized Immigrants.* Washington, DC: U.S. Commission on Immigration Reform.

Woodrow-Lafield, Karen A. 2008. "Migration, Immigration, and Naturalization in America." In *From Arrival to Incorporation: Migrants to the U.S. in a Global Era*, edited by Elliott R. Barkan, Hasia R. Diner, and Allan Kraut, 60–79. New York: New York University Press.

Woodrow-Lafield, Karen A., Xiaohe Xu, Thomas Kersen, and Bunnak Poch. 2004. "Naturalization for U.S. Immigrants: Highlights from Ten Countries." *Population Research and Policy Review* 23, no. 3: 187–218.

Ethnic Groups and Ethnicity

Joseph F. Healey

The focus of this chapter is on the United States and American ethnic groups, but other nations and situations will be mentioned. In particular, we focus on the ethnic groups created by two mass immigrations to the United States, the first from the 1820s to the 1920s, and the second beginning in the 1960s and much more diverse.

What Is an Ethnic Group?

Five characteristics describe and define ethnic groups: They share (1) a distinct cultural heritage and (2) a common identity and a belief in a common ancestry or place of origin. Ethnic groups also (3) maintain a network of social relationships, groups, and organizations separate from the surrounding society. Membership in ethnic groups is (4) an ascribed status, or commonly (but not in all cases) determined by birth, and the members (5) tend to be endogamous—marrying within the group.

A Distinct Cultural Heritage

An ethnic group has a cultural heritage that is noticeably different from other groups in their society. It includes customs, values, language, religion, cuisine, traditions, folklore, and many other components. Examples of cultural traits that identify ethnic group membership include the celebration of Hanukkah for Jews; the Irish wake to mark the passing of a loved one; ranchera music for Mexican Americans; the Creole language for Haitians; West Indian Carnivale; the simple, homemade clothing of the Amish; and the Chinese New Year. The cultural heritage helps to mark the boundaries of the group, providing a focus of identity and making the group more visible to both members and the larger society. However, the cultural dimension is not alone sufficient to define ethnicity, and, conversely, not all groups that share a culture are ethnic groups. Surgeons, professional baseball players, Republicans, jazz fans, and labor union members each collectively share values, information, customs, and experiences that make them identifiable, but they are not "ethnic groups."

Moreover, culture, like all of the defining characteristics, is variable. It can change and, over time, its distinctiveness or uniqueness—the extent of the cultural differences between one group and others—can decline. Indeed, the cultural differences can disappear altogether. For example, the white ethnic groups created by the massive immigration from Europe between the 1820s and 1920s were often, upon their arrival, highly visible on virtually every aspect of culture. They spoke a cacophony of languages, honored an array of distinctive customs and traditions, and observed notably different religious practices. Over time, the descendants of these immigrants learned English and adopted many cultural values of the larger society. Today, the cultural heritages that were imported early on from Ireland, Italy, Germany, Russia, Greece, Ukraine, Portugal, and scores of other places are barely visible, lost during the complex process of Americanization and assimilation (except those aspects nurtured, or revitalized, by a more recent wave of newcomers).

And yet, the decline of uncommon cultural characteristics does not, by itself, signal the disappearance of the ethnic group. Although much attenuated, white ethnic groups maintain a presence in American society. For example, when asked in a 2008 census survey: "From what countries or part of the world did your ancestors come?" 76 percent of white American respondents named some place other than the United

States, including Germany, Ireland, Italy, Poland, and a score of other nations and regions. Thus, most white Americans continue to feel a connection—at some level (ranging from casual to fervent)—with an ancestral European home notwithstanding the minimal persistence of a separate cultural heritage. Asian and Latino communities, many of which have more recent origins, share those kinds of attachment to the homeland culture but do not yet have the prolonged attachment or the range of sustained ties that would characterize them as "transnational"—preserving bonds (and involvement) with family and community in homeland and sending regular remittances, especially to one's family.

A Common Identity

This quality is often described in terms of a sense of peoplehood, a "we-feeling," or a sense of community and a common fate. For members, their ethnic groups are "in-groups," distinguished from "out-groups" by boundaries that are often expressed in terms of culture. Members of ethnic groups believe they are linked together by a singular common ancestry and a shared connection with a place of origin, and they maintain a sense of ethnicity as part of their self-image or personal identity. Thus, when people say they are Italian American, for example, they are expressing a link to others who trace their ancestry to the same region and a sense that they share more with members of their ethnic in-group than with out-groups. These feelings of "rootedness" can (and do) persist even after distinct cultural traditions have grown weak or disappeared.

This sense of identity, of common roots, and a shared fate is what differentiates ethnic groups from other categories of people that share cultural elements. As noted, other types of groups may connect with particular customs and history, but they do not trace their origins to a single place or ancestry group, and it is this sense of a shared common status and shared historical memory that can make ethnicity a powerful and deep aspect of self-image.

As with culture, the strength of ethnic identity is variable, and there may be less to the claim of common ancestry than meets the eye. In fact, the claim of shared peoplehood may be exaggerated or even false; what is important is that people accept it and behave as if it were real. Thus, ethnicity and ethnic groups can be "social constructions" based on subjective perceptions and shared understandings that may have little or no basis in objective fact. Thus, on occasion, people can "feel" Irish or Mexican or Italian—and be accepted by others on those terms—even when they may have no ancestors from that group. The *belief* in a common descent and a shared identity can at times be more important than its objective reality.

A Network of Relationships

Ethnic groups have separate and distinct social networks, organizations, and groups that link the members to each other and provide the social framework for the practice of the common culture and the expression of community and ethnic identity. The infrastructure can extend from local to national (or even international) organizations, and groups and can focus on a variety of needs. Some ethnic organizations may have a religious function; others may devote themselves to the preservation of language, family-name associations, cuisine, or other customs, or the maintenance of homeland ties; and still others might be oriented particularly toward business, music and dance, or travel and recreation.

As with other defining characteristics, the strength and scope of ethnic organization is highly variable. At one extreme are ethnic communities that are elaborately and comprehensively organized, have strong boundaries that separate them from other groups, and serve virtually all the needs of their members from cradle to grave. These types of communities can be illustrated with "ethnic enclaves," such as Chinatown or "Little Havana," the Cuban neighborhoods in South Florida. Other well-known and densely organized ethnic communities of the past and present include the Jewish Lower East Side of New York City, Irish South Boston, Polish Hamtramck and Arabic Dearborn in or near Detroit, and Mexicans' East L.A. adjacent to downtown Los Angeles. The United States is dotted with neighborhoods (and, indeed, towns and cities) that have been associated with specific ethnic groups, the sites where the expression and practice of the ethnic culture have been most completely realized. Consider the extensive German communities in and around San Antonio; prior to World War I, Mexicans arriving there in search of work initially found it more useful to learn German than English.

Ethnic communities are sometimes so comprehensively organized that members only rarely need to venture across the boundaries into the larger society. Among other services, they may provide midwives, schools, jobs, restaurants and grocery stores, places of worship, funeral homes, and individuals who can read letters from the homeland and write replies. Virtually all immigrant groups establish enclaves to some degree, at least for the first generation.

For example, contemporary white ethnic groups can be used to illustrate the other extreme of ethnic organization. Now in their sixth, seventh, or later generation, these groups have long ago left the ethnic neighborhoods founded by the immigrant generation (e.g., Little Italy) and have merged into the larger society. They have lost most of the distinctive culture and language of their immigrant ancestors, and their needs are now served by the same groups, organizations, and institutions that serve the general society. Some white ethnic groups may maintain both local and national organizations and networks (e.g., the Ancient Order of Hibernians for Irish Americans or the National Italian American Foundation), but the majority of group members do not now belong to these groups and may not even be aware of their existence. For many members of these highly assimilated groups, ethnicity is not a part of their daily reality or an important feature of their lives or identities—except for those who more recently arrived and are newcomers among the multiple generations within their ethnic community.

The Issue of Ascribed Status

Ethnicity is generally inherited from parents, and its primacy in the life cycle can make it an important, fundamental basis for self-image, comparable to gender and racial identity. However, since the cultural and organizational lines that define ethnic groups are permeable and sometimes indeterminate, membership can also, under certain circumstances, be voluntary. For example, when the group has lost its visibility and cultural distinctiveness, its hold may weaken. Members may chose not to identify with their group at all, or emphasize their ethnicity less than other aspects of their self-identity (occupation, social class, education), or change their ethnic identity over time—even claiming membership in groups to which they do not, objectively, belong. Thus, ethnicity may be inherited from parents but is also a social construction whose influence on self-image and identity is highly variable.

Endogamy

People generally choose their friends and marriage partners from within their in-groups, as defined by such social categories as ethnicity, social class, race, and religion. The tendency to marry within one's ethnic group can reflect the preferences of the in-group, the prejudices of other groups, or both. As in so many characteristics of American ethnic groups formed by immigration, the strength of endogamy tends to weaken as the generations pass and length of residence in the new society increases. That is, endogamy is strongest for the actual immigrants, but succeeding generations tend to be much more eclectic in their choice of marriage partners, especially as the group becomes more integrated and less visible. For the more visible racial groups, endogamy tends to be much more persistent. Even today, black-white marriages are a tiny percentage (less than 1 percent) of all American marriages.

The Variability of Ethnicity

Each of these defining characteristics is highly variable: some ethnic groups have an elaborate and unique culture that is sharply different from that of other groups in their society, a strong sense of identity, a complex and comprehensive array of organizations and social networks, and a very strong tendency to marry within the group. Membership in these groups may be determined solely by birth and be involuntary and permanent. For other ethnic groups, cultural distinctiveness is minimal (even nonexistent), and the sense of identity and community is weak, as is their

A wedding ceremony in Santa Ana, California. Vietnamese-born immigrants, the couple's wedding features both western and traditional Vietnamese dresses. (David Butow/CORBIS SABA)

organizational infrastructure. The criteria that define membership are unclear and the boundary lines separating the group from other groups are blurred and can be crossed easily in any direction. While membership in "strong" ethnic groups may be permanent and relatively unchangeable over the course of a person's lifetime, the members of "weaker," less distinct groups have choices: Over time, or from situation to situation, they may stress their ethnic identity, or ignore it completely, or redirect it. The same variability applies to ties with the homeland, where, as noted, visits, frequent contact, and remittances range from intense and ongoing to shallow and infrequent.

Additional Distinctions: Racial and Minority Groups

Some further distinctions will clarify our definitions and the focus of this chapter. First, it is common to distinguish between ethnic groups and racial groups. Usually, the former, as noted previously, are defined in terms of cultural characteristics and membership that can be voluntary; while the latter are defined in terms of relative visibility and permanent physical criteria, such as skin color, and membership is more ascriptive and involuntary. Examples of racial groups include Caucasians, Asians, Africans, and Native Americans. This social distinction is important, if for no other reason than the fact that racial characteristics are usually more difficult to mask than cultural traits. While race mixing blurs racial lines for some, overall—and especially in the past—racial groups had clearer boundaries, and membership in them was more fixed and permanent, inescapable, than membership in ethnic groups.

The distinction between race and ethnicity may seem fundamental at first glance, but it is not as sharp as it appears. Many ethnic groups have (or are thought to have) distinct physical characteristics (e.g., blond hair and fair complexions for Scandinavians) and racial groups have (or are thought to have) distinct cultural characteristics (e.g., values, norms, dialect, and cuisine). This chapter will focus primarily on groups defined by their ethnicity; but, since there is considerable overlap between the two types of groups, many of our comments will also apply to racial groups, and these will be addressed more specifically at various points.

Second, we need to distinguish ethnic groups from minority groups: these categories overlap, but they are not synonymous. Minority groups are frequently the objects of discrimination and prejudice. Their members have less access to resources and opportunities and occupy a lower social class position in their society. These disadvantages are a function of group membership, not individual qualities.

Ethnic groups are frequently—but not always—also minority groups. Some ethnic groups enjoy dominant positions, high status, wealth, and power and are the beneficiaries of structures of oppression that limit and control minority groups. For example, the European groups that conquered and colonized much of the world beginning in the 1400s were (and often remain) clearly dominant in their respective societies. These groups included the Boers in South Africa, the Spanish and Portuguese throughout South and Central America, the English in India, and the French in Southeast Asia.

Note that minority status is changeable: some groups that were clearly minority groups in the past no longer occupy that status and have joined the dominant group. For example, many European immigrant groups to the United States were minority groups upon their arrival; they had a lower share of resources, opportunities, respect, and power and were the objects of widespread prejudice—even to the extent of being labeled nonwhites. Their minority status persisted for generations, but today, the descendants of even the most disparaged European immigrant groups are, on the average, equal to (or higher than) national indicators of affluence, education, and achievement. Prejudice does persist toward some of these groups, including Jews and Poles, but feelings and stereotypes are mild and amorphous compared with those in the past, and with those attached to racial groups.

Varieties of Ethnic Groups and Group Relationships

Ethnic groups vary in terms of the conditions under which they took form, their relationships with each other, and their relationships with the larger society. In this section, we examine these important dimensions of diversity and, in later sections, will use the terms and concepts introduced here to analyze American ethnic groups, past and present.

The Contact Situation: Immigrant versus Conquered Groups

This chapter will focus mainly on groups created by immigration, the more or less voluntary decision to move to a new society. Other groups, however, were created by conquest, colonization, and coercion, and their membership in their new society was involuntary. Both conquered and immigrant groups typically become minority groups during the contact situation. However, the disadvantaged status of immigrant groups tends to be less severe and of shorter duration, especially when they come to be viewed as racially similar to the dominant group in their society. The contact situation is crucial in shaping all aspects of group relationships, including the extent of discrimination and inequality and the likely permanence of the disadvantaged status.

Immigration

Over the history of human society, there are literally hundreds of examples of ethnic groups being created by immigration as people have been driven from one place to another by war, famine, poverty, and natural and man-made disasters. Immigration is a particularly relevant experience to the United States, for the entire population—except for American Indians—consists of either immigrants or their descendants. The story of people leaving their homeland and making their way to these shores has been repeated over and over in our past and continues to be experienced today.

During the contact situation, immigrant groups typically experience some degree of discrimination and exploitation by more powerful groups, especially if they have characteristics that make them physically visible (for example, racial differences, religious practices, dress standards, and physical markings that set them apart), or they are perceived to be threats to jobs, political stability, or cultural integrity. This rejection forces group members to turn to each other for support and comfort. It reinforces a sense of common identity and lays the basis for the organizational practice of a common culture. For example, many of the European immigrants that arrived in the century between the 1820s and 1920s were substantially comprised of uneducated peasants who identified mostly with their families and home villages. They brought little or no sense of a broader or national identity, and it was not until they were treated as a single entity—as Italians, Poles, or Irish—that they began to think of themselves in those terms. Thus, in many cases, ethnic groups, the sense of ethnicity, and a shared feeling of peoplehood were created in the United States, not imported from the old country (with some notable exceptions, such as Jews, Armenians, and Japanese).

For immigrant groups, opportunities for upward mobility and inclusion in the larger society will tend to increase as the generations pass, especially if their physical or "racial" differences with the principal groups are accepted as minimal. This is, in fact, the trajectory followed by white American ethnic groups, which, although rejected and marginalized upon arrival, eventually achieved inclusion and equality. Whether contemporary immigrants will also follow this trajectory is frequently debated.

Conquest or Coercion

Ethnic groups can also be created by group competition and wars of conquest. The key characteristic of the contact situation for these subordinated groups is that their membership in their new society is involuntary, a result of coercion. Again, these groups, including African Americans, Mexicans, and American Indians, have been prominent in the American experience.

As is the case with immigrant groups, conquered or coerced ethnic groups may not have shared a culture and a common sense of identity prior to the contact situation—or, at least, had not thought in those terms. The group that is called "African American" today, for example, was created by the slave trade, which kidnapped and captured people in Africa. The slave trade operated in many different areas of Africa and brought together peoples with different languages, cultures, and physical appearances. The characteristic ethnic traits—the shared culture and a common identity—of this group were largely created during slavery, as African Americans were forced to learn English and adapt to Anglo-American culture.

Groups created by conquest and coercion are, by definition, minority groups at the time of contact. Their subordination leads to disparagement from other groups, relative powerlessness, lower status, and a lower share of resources and opportunities. All this helps to account for their greater difficulties in improving their situation and achieving more favorable status. African Americans, for example, have been a part of American society since the 1620s; but unlike white ethnic groups, they still face sizable gaps with the larger society in terms of affluence, status, education, and political influence.

Goals and Relationships with the Larger Society

Ethnic groups vary in their goals and their desired relationship with other groups and with the larger society. Group goals are shaped by many factors, including the contact situation and its relative standing in the larger society as a dominant or minority group. Goals need not be shared unanimously by all members of the group. Ethnic groups are frequently large, complex, and diverse, and different factions or subgroups may pursue different—even mutually exclusive—goals.

More powerful ethnic groups often wish nothing more than the continuation of their dominance and advantage. Consider the efforts of the white plantation elites in the antebellum South to preserve slavery, the cornerstone of their wealth and advantage.

Additional examples of oppression and exploitation would include white South Africans who worked hard to maintain Apartheid and Protestants in Northern Ireland when they were defending their privileges against the Catholics. Conversely, less powerful groups will seek to ameliorate their disadvantage, although they often lack the resources to realize this objective. Thus, African-American slaves resisted their oppression even though their lack of resources most of the time limited their resistance to sabotage, subterfuge, and running away.

Assimilation (Acculturation and Integration)

Assimilation is a process by which two or more separate groups merge together culturally and structurally. Culturally, assimilation may include learning a new language, acquiring new values and customs, and a host of other changes. Cultural assimilation is also labeled *acculturation*, while the structural phase is *integration*. Groups integrate as they enter the organizations and institutions of other groups and the larger society and become acquaintances and friends with members of other groups. As ethnic groups integrate, opportunities for upward mobility and improved status increase and they become more equal to other groups in terms of embracing behavioral norms, prevailing values, and pursuing education, affluence, home ownership, membership in associations, and, finally, prospects for intermarriage.

Assimilation is fully accomplished when the formerly separate groups can no longer be distinguished from one another. A completely assimilated society would have a single dominant language and culture and, subject to class differences, members would be equally integrated into all groups and institutions of the larger society. Assimilation is therefore a complex, multistage process that takes decades and generations to complete. Assimilation can take a number of forms. Perhaps the most basic distinction is between coerced and permitted assimilation. Coerced assimilation is associated with conquered and coerced groups and occurs when the dominant group forces the minority group to adopt its culture in order to further control them. The former preserves its advantage over

such ethnic groups and stops assimilation at acculturation. Even members of these groups who are completely acculturated still face inequality and exclusion from the organizations and institutions of the larger society. In the antebellum South, completely Anglicized black slaves were still slaves, powerless and set apart from white society. This situation of "acculturation only" can last indefinitely.

"Permitted assimilation" is associated with ethnic groups formed by voluntary immigration. It may be mixed with very strong pressures to assimilate but is not directly forced or required. In the American experience, immigrant groups have been allowed more leeway than conquered and coerced groups and permitted to retain more of their old customs for a longer time. However, the Americanization efforts during and after World War I were the exceptions, for immigrants were coerced by popular movements for one-hundred-percentism. By and large, for white ethnic groups, acculturation was the first step in a process that eventually led to integration and intermarriage, although it took generations for the process to be completed. Many of the ethnic groups being formed by immigration today are, for the most part, following patterns established by the European immigrant groups in the past. Acculturation and the acquisition of English remain the prerequisite for integration and upward mobility.

Pluralism

Assimilation has been the dominant theme of American group relations, but pluralism has been a minor—although constant—theme as well. Pluralism exists to the extent that groups retain their separate cultures, identities, and institutional networks over time. Most immigrant groups in the past eventually went through a stage of pluralism. When they first arrived, the immigrants tended to establish separate neighborhoods or enclaves in which they could speak the old language and practice the familiar old ways. The descendants of the immigrants—their children and grandchildren—left the old neighborhoods and, armed with English fluency, found their way into the institutions of the larger society.

Some groups in the United States have been able to maintain pluralistic relationships with the larger society for extended periods of time. These groups are small in size and marginal to the larger society both geographically and economically, characteristics that abet their ability to maintain their separate traditions. Examples include the Amish or "Pennsylvania Dutch," Hasidic Jews, and many American Indian tribes.

Other Goals

Assimilation and pluralism have been the most important goals and relationships for American ethnic and racial groups; but this does not exhaust the possibilities, either in the American experience or across the long sweep of human history. Other goals that groups have pursued (and been the victims of) include:

Involuntary population transfer

This occurs when a group is forced out of an area, either as a result of harassment and persecution (e.g., the Mormons' migration to what became Utah beginning in the late 1840s) or as explicitly ordered by a dominant group. In the 1830s, for example, the U.S. federal government required all Native Americans living east of the Mississippi to move to the Indian Territory (which later became Oklahoma).

Secession

This goal goes beyond pluralism to a desire for complete severing of all ties. Examples include the efforts to separate the province of French-speaking Québec from the rest of English-speaking Canada; Israeli Palestinians who desire a separate state; Chechnya's attempt to secede from Russia; and many American Indian tribes in both North and South America.

Genocide

This is the attempt to eliminate an ethnic group, and tragically, examples are easily found. The best-known genocide is probably the attempt by German Nazis to eliminate the Jews, the Roma (gypsies), and other groups; but more recent examples can be found in Rwanda, the Darfur region in Somalia, and the former Yugoslavia. In the annals of American history, some argue that the treatment of American Indians amounted to genocide.

American Ethnic Groups: Case Studies—the Dominant Group and the American Creed

In this section we will describe the principal ethnic groups in American society, concentrating on immigrant groups but including colonized groups as well. We begin by considering the dominant group, or the ethnic group that has occupied the most favored and privileged position.

From the beginning, American society was dominated by modest, middle-class, and affluent British Protestants, even though the early settlers were diverse in ethnicity (including French, Dutch, Germans, Scots, Irish, and Welsh) and in social class backgrounds (including wealthy planters and merchants, powerless indentured servants, and every status in between). The dominant group established a privileged position for their religion, language, institutions, and traditions, and other groups had to adjust to these core realities.

In the cultural traditions established by the English were the seeds of what became the dominant American Creed, or value system: democracy, individualism, respect for human rights and the rule of law, religious freedom, and faith in hard work and self-reliance. These values resonated with some of the most powerful political and economic forces in the European world and helped guide the American Revolution, the French Revolution, and other movements of liberation throughout the world.

Alongside these progressive elements, the American Creed also incorporated—from its very founding—support for slavery, antiblack racism, and rejection and exclusion of American Indians. Thus was created the great internal American contradiction between egalitarianism, justice, discrimination, and racism, which continues to haunt the United States.

Conquered and Coerced Groups: African Americans and Mexican Americans

There have been several conquered and coerced groups in U.S. history. All are racial as well as ethnic groups, and none had sufficient power resources to prevent their consignment to minority status. We will cover two of them here.

Africans entered the colonial United States as a coerced, unfree labor force. The plantation economy that developed in colonies (particularly in Virginia) in the mid-1600s required a large, highly controlled work force, and the planters tapped into the slave trade that was already supplying labor to South and Central America and the Caribbean Islands. Potential slaves were captured in Africa, marched to the Atlantic Coast under dreadful conditions, and then transported to the New World in the hold of slave ships where they were chained to each other and supplied with minimal food and drink. Many died before reaching the New World, and those that survived had little capacity to resist induction into slavery. Black Africans had the labor power desired by the planters and even small farmers and, because of the conditions under which they were brought into colonial society, they lacked the power and resources to resist their fate of enslavement.

Slavery ended in 1865 but was followed by nearly a century of state-sponsored segregation and inequality. In the South, the Jim Crow era featured political disenfranchisement, job discrimination, and segregation in schools and neighborhoods. Nevertheless, African Americans took advantage of their relatively greater freedom and expanded and strengthened the organizations and institutions that served their needs. Many of these institutions, such as the African Methodist Episcopal Church, had been founded in the North during the dark days of slavery. Others—educational institutions, protest organizations, social, religious, and business groups—were created after the Civil War. The black middle class, which included teachers, preachers, professionals, small-business owners, and college students, was at the forefront of these organizational developments and eventually supplied the leadership and resources for the civil rights movement of the 1950s and 1960s.

African Americans have enjoyed relative freedom and opportunity only since the end of legalized segregation in the 1960s. The group was culturally assimilated during slavery but their centuries of exclusion, powerlessness, and impoverishment, combined with the continuing racism of the larger society, has created a distinct black subculture, a variation on the dominant Anglo culture, most visible perhaps in popular culture, slang, and music.

These cultural differences are reinforced by the continuing lack of full integration. Although conditions have improved since the dark days of segregation and African Americans and those of African descent were granted citizenship in 1870, large gaps remain between African Americans and national norms for income and poverty, and the group remains massively segregated in their residential patterns and in schools. These continuing inequalities fuel a culture of alienation and resentment among blacks and reinforce the strength of their group identity. In spite of the dazzling success of some group members, the group's overall status might be characterized as "acculturation without integration" and issues of urban poverty, poor schools, crime, and community disorganization continue to plague the group as a whole.

A second conquered ethnic group was established when the United States came into contact with Mexico and Mexicans as it expanded westward in the 1800s. The areas that became the West and Southwest were ceded to the United States after Mexico was defeated in war in the late 1840s. Land was expropriated by the Anglo-dominant group as their numbers swelled and the Mexicans living in the affected areas became a minority group without moving an inch from their villages and farms.

Like American Indians, Mexican Americans lost their land and, like African Americans in the South, they became a relatively powerless, cheap labor force for the development of the regional economy. Like other ethnic minority groups, Mexican Americans attempted to organize their communities and improve their collective position whenever possible. Local communities were often organized around the Catholic Church but it also supported an array of other groups, including labor unions, political parties, and protest groups. Among the more prominent organizations based upon—and providing services for—segments within the communities were the League of United Latin American Citizens (LULAC), founded in Texas in 1929, and, after World War II, the Community Service Organization in Los Angeles, the American GI Forum in Texas, the Alianza de Mercedes (Alliance of Land Grants) in 1963, and the La Raza Unida (People United) party. Without a doubt, the best-known Chicano protest leader and organizer was Cesar Chávez, who organized the United Farm Workers, the first union to successfully represent migrant workers.

Over the generations since first contact with Anglo America, many Mexican Americans have assimilated into the larger society. However, because of the group's proximity to Mexico, Mexican Americans have been able to preserve their language and much of their culture. Today, the strength of Mexican-American ethnicity has been powerfully reinforced by high rates of immigration during the 1920s and since the 1960s; thus, while Mexican Americans were created by conquest, their current status is strongly shaped by recent immigration (see below).

Ethnic Groups Formed by Immigration: The First Wave (1820s–1920s)

By the 1820s, the United States had been politically autonomous for 40 years. The society was still largely agricultural, and the population was concentrated along the Eastern seaboard. A century later, by the 1920s, the society stretched from the Atlantic to the Pacific, had industrialized, and was a rising economic and military world power.

This transformation took place side by side with, and was largely fueled by, a massive immigration from Europe and parts of Asia. Immigrants began arriving in large numbers from Europe in the 1820s, largely from northern and western Europe. Depending on conditions in both sending and receiving societies, the volume of immigration rose and fell for the next 60 years, along with the arrival of new groups, including the Chinese. Then, in the 1880s, the sources of immigration shifted to southern and eastern Europe and Japan, and the volume increased and continued at high levels until World War I, which brought it to a standstill. The flow resumed at the end of the war and continued at high levels until curtailed by restrictive U.S. policies in 1921, 1924, and 1929. By setting

no limits on immigration from countries in the Western Hemisphere, the new laws allowed for substantial increases from many of those nations, particularly Mexico and Canada. The ethnic groups formed by this immigration swelled the population; helped to populate the frontier; and provided labor for factories, mills and mines, railroads, and "factory farms" across the western United States. In the process most settled in the United States, built communities, and confronted the pressures of Americanization.

A smaller wave of immigration from Asia also began in this era. Chinese immigrants began to arrive in the late 1840s initially to mine for gold and then to take advantage of employment opportunities on the West Coast. Several decades later, immigration from Japan began. These groups followed fundamentally different pathways than did European immigrants into American society and provide important examples of the power of racial visibility in shaping group relationships.

The First Wave: Northern and Western European Groups

We distinguish between four groups: first, the largely Protestant, more affluent, and better-educated immigrants from northern and western Europe; second, the less educated and less skilled "peasant laborers" who came from southern and eastern Europe but also included the Irish; third, Jews from central and eastern Europe; and, finally, immigrants from Asia. The first cluster of immigrants included English, Germans, Norwegians, Swedes, Welsh, French, Dutch, and Danes. Although they included many peasants and small-scale farmers whose livelihoods had been disrupted by the Industrial Revolution, one also found among them many more educated and affluent immigrants. While the former tended to focus on economic survival, many among the latter tended to be motivated by a search for political or religious freedom.

At any rate, these groups were similar to the Anglo-dominant group in the young United States in their racial and religious characteristics and also shared many cultural values with the host society, including the Protestant ethic—which stressed hard work, success, and individualism—and support for the principles of democratic government. These similarities eased their acceptance into a society that was highly intolerant of religious and racial differences until well into the twentieth century, and these immigrant groups generally experienced a lower degree of rejection and racist disparagement than did the Irish and southern and eastern European peasant laborers.

Northern and western European immigrants came from nations that were just as developed as the United States. Thus, these immigrants often brought money and other resources with which to secure a comfortable place for themselves in their new society. Many settled in the sparsely populated Midwest and in other frontier areas, where they farmed the fertile land that had become available after the conquest and removal of American Indians and Mexican Americans. By dispersing throughout the midsection of the country, they lowered their visibility and their degree of competition with dominant-group members.

We can use German immigrants to illustrate some of these patterns (and particularly because of the high numbers of Protestants, Catholics, and Jews among them). This was one of the largest and most continual immigrant streams in the 1820–1920 period, and, today, more Americans (about 15 percent) trace their ancestry to Germany than to any other country.

The German immigrants who arrived earlier in the 1800s moved into the newly opened farmland and the rapidly growing cities of the Midwest, as did many other northern and western European immigrants. By 1850, large German communities could be found in Milwaukee, St. Louis, and Cincinnati. Some German immigrants followed the transatlantic route of the cotton trade between Europe and the southern United States and entered through the port of New Orleans, moving from there to the Midwest and Southwest.

German immigrants arriving later in the century were more likely to settle in urban areas, in part because fertile land was less available. Many of the city-bound German immigrants were skilled workers and artisans, and others found work as laborers in the rapidly expanding industrial sector. The double penetration of German immigrants into the rural economy and the higher sectors of the urban economy

is reflected in the fact that by 1870, most employed German Americans were involved in skilled labor (37 percent) or farming (25 percent).

In both the city and in their farming communities, German Americans established a rich web of organizations and institutions to serve their needs and preserve their culture. They founded schools and churches, German-language newspapers, mutual-aid societies, and musical and recreational groups. Urban German Americans tended to live in close proximity to each other, and they used their relatively high levels of education, skills, and resources to start businesses and develop their communities.

German immigrants took relatively high occupational positions in the U.S. labor force, and their sons and daughters were able to translate that relative affluence into economic mobility. By the dawn of the twentieth century, large numbers of second-generation German Americans were finding their way into white-collar and professional careers. Within a few generations, German Americans had achieved parity with national norms in education, income, and occupational prestige.

Compared to other groups, assimilation for the Protestant immigrant groups from northern and western Europe was relatively rapid and smooth. Although members of these groups felt the sting of rejection, prejudice, and discrimination, their movement from acculturation to integration and equality was relatively effortless and accomplished in three generations or less. The ease of the process can be attributed to their lower visibility, their relative affluence and higher levels of education, and their cultural and racial similarities with the dominant group.

The First Wave: Non-Protestant Peasant Laborers—Irish, Southern European, and East European Groups

The relative ease of assimilation for northern and western Europeans contrasted sharply with the experiences of non-Protestant, less educated and less skilled immigrants. These immigrant laborers came in two waves. The Irish were part of the Old Immigration that began in the 1820s, but the bulk of this group—Italians, Poles, Russians, Hungarians, Greeks, Serbs,

Ukrainians, Slovaks, Bulgarians, and scores of other southern and East European groups—made up the New Immigration that began in the 1880s. Most of the immigrants in these nationality groups (like many recent immigrants to the United States) were peasants or unskilled laborers, with few resources other than their willingness to work. Most were non-Protestants and came from rural, village-oriented cultures in which family and kin took precedence over individual needs or desires.

Family life for them tended to be autocratic and male-dominated, and children were expected to subordinate their personal desires and to work for the good of the family as a whole. Arranged marriages were common. This cultural background was much less consistent with the industrializing, capitalistic, individualistic, Protestant, Anglo-American culture of the United States and was a major reason that these immigrant laborers experienced a higher level of rejection and discrimination than did the immigrants from northern and western Europe.

The immigrant laborers were much less likely to enter the rural economy than were the northern and western European immigrants. Much of the better frontier land had already been claimed by the time most new immigrant groups began to arrive, and a large number of them had been permanently soured on farming by the oppressive and exploitative agrarian economies from which they were trying to escape. They settled in the cities of the industrializing Northeast and found work in plants, mills, mines, and factories. They supplied the armies of laborers needed to power the Industrial Revolution in the United States, although their view of this process was generally from the bottom looking up. They arrived during the decades in which the American industrial and urban infrastructure was being constructed. They built roads, canals, and railroads as well as the buildings that housed the machinery of industrialization.

For example, the first tunnels of the New York City subway system were dug, largely by hand, by laborers from Italy. Other immigrants found work in the coal fields of Pennsylvania and West Virginia and the steel mills of Pittsburgh, and they flocked by the millions to the factories of the Northeast. They tended to live in ethnically distinct neighborhoods and enclaves and to create or join a variety of ethnically based organizations and associations, including mutual-aid societies, religious congregations and related groups, cultural associations, labor unions, and political parties.

Like other low-skill immigrant groups, these newcomers took jobs in which strength and stamina were more important than literacy or skilled craftsmanship. In fact, the minimum level of skill required for employment actually declined as industrialization proceeded through its early phases. To keep wages low and take advantage of what seemed like an inexhaustible supply of cheap labor, industrialists and factory owners developed technologies and machines that required few skills and little knowledge of English to operate. As mechanization proceeded, unskilled workers replaced skilled workers in the workforce. Not infrequently, women and children replaced men because they could be hired for lower wages.

Eventually, as the generations passed, the prejudice, systematic discrimination, and other barriers to upward mobility for the immigrant laborer groups weakened, and their descendants began to rise out of the working class. Although the first and second (and, for some, the third and fourth) generations of these groups were largely limited to jobs at the unskilled or semiskilled level, later generations rose in the American social class system. The descendants of the immigrant laborers achieved parity with national norms by the latter half of the twentieth century, although for some groups, it took five or even six generations to achieve equality.

The First Wave: East European Jewish Immigrants and the Ethnic Enclave

Jewish immigrants from Russia and other parts of Eastern Europe followed a third pathway into U.S. society. They were a part of both the Old and the New Immigration, arriving in great numbers during the 1850s and then from the 1880s onward. Unlike the immigrant laborer groups, who were generally economic refugees and included many young, single males, East European Jews were fleeing religious persecution and generally arrived as family units intending to settle permanently and become citizens. They settled in the urban areas of the Northeast and Midwest. New York City was the most common destination, and the Lower East Side became the best-known Jewish American neighborhood. By 1920, about 60 percent of all Jewish Americans lived in the urban areas between Boston and Philadelphia, with almost 50 percent living in New York City alone. Another 30 percent lived in the urban areas of the Midwest, particularly in Chicago.

In Russia and other parts of Eastern Europe, Jews had been barred from agrarian occupations and had come to rely on the urban economy for their livelihoods. When they immigrated to the United States, they brought these urban skills and job experiences with them. For example, almost two-thirds of the immigrant Jewish men had been tailors and other skilled laborers in Eastern Europe. In the rapidly industrializing American economy of the early twentieth century, they were able to use these skills to find work.

Other Jewish immigrants joined the urban working class and took manual labor and unskilled jobs in the industrial sector. The garment industry in particular became the lifeblood of the Jewish community and provided jobs to about one-third of all East European Jews residing in the major cities. Women as well as men were involved in the garment industry. Jewish women, like the women of more recent immigrant laborer groups, found ways to combine their jobs and their domestic responsibilities. As young girls, they worked in factories and sweatshops, and after marriage they did the same work at home, sewing pre-cut garments together or doing other piecework such as wrapping cigars or making artificial flowers, often assisted by their children.

Unlike most of the peasant-laborer groups, Jewish Americans became heavily involved in commerce and often found ways to start their own businesses and become self-employed. Drawing on their experience in the Old Country, many started businesses and small independent enterprises and developed an enclave economy. The Jewish neighborhoods were densely populated and provided a ready market for services of all kinds. Some Jewish immigrants became street

peddlers or started bakeries, butcher or candy shops, or any number of other retail enterprises.

Capitalizing on their residential concentration and close proximity, Jewish immigrants created dense networks of commercial, financial, and social cooperation. The Jewish-American enclave survived because of the cohesiveness of the group; the willingness of wives, children, and other relatives to work for little or no monetary compensation; and the commercial savvy of the early immigrants. Also, a large pool of cheap labor and sources of credit and other financial services were available within the community. The Jewish-American enclave grew and provided a livelihood for many of the children and grandchildren of the immigrants. As has been the case with other enclave groups, including Chinese Americans and Cuban Americans, economic advancement preceded extensive acculturation, and Jewish Americans made significant strides toward economic equality before they became fluent in English or were otherwise Americanized.

One obvious way in which enclave immigrant groups have improved its position is to develop an educated and acculturated second generation. The Americanized, English-speaking children of the Jewish immigrants used their greater familiarity with the dominant society and their language facility to help preserve and expand the family enterprise. Furthermore, as the second generation appeared, the American public school system was expanding, and education through the college level was free or inexpensive in New York City and other cities. There was also a strong push for the second and third generations to enter professions, but as Jewish Americans excelled in school, resistance to and discrimination against them increased. By the 1920s, many elite colleges and universities, such as Dartmouth and Harvard, established quotas that limited the number of Jewish students they would admit. These quotas were not abolished until after World War II.

The enclave economy and the Jewish neighborhoods established by the immigrants proved to be an effective base from which to integrate into American society. The descendants of the East European Jewish immigrants gradually moved out of the ethnic neighborhoods, and their positions in the economy—their pushcarts, stores, and jobs in the garment industry—were taken over by more recent immigrants. When they left the enclave economy, many second- and third-generation eastern-European Jews did not enter the mainstream occupational structure at the bottom, as the immigrant laborer groups tended to do. They used the resources generated by the entrepreneurship of the early generations to gain access to prestigious and advantaged social class positions. As a group, studies show that Jewish Americans today surpass national averages in income, levels of education, and occupational prestige.

The First Wave: Immigrants from Asia—Chinese and Japanese

Immigrants from China began arriving in the 1840s, drawn by the Gold Rush and, 20 years later, job opportunities in the construction of the transcontinental railroad and other areas in the rapidly developing West Coast economy. They were largely less educated and skilled males or peasant laborers, like the Irish, Italians, and other groups originating in Europe.

At first, the Chinese were accepted and even praised for their willingness to work long hours for low wages. However, when the economy slowed and unemployment increased in the 1860s and 1870s, an anti-Chinese campaign began. These efforts focused on pushing the Chinese out of the workforce and eliminating the perceived threat to jobs. The campaign culminated in the Chinese Exclusion Act of 1882, the first significant successful legislative attempt to limit immigration to the United States. The act was directed solely at the Chinese and closed the doors of entry to most of them.

In response to the widespread attacks, the Chinese withdrew from the larger society and formed enclave communities, as Jewish immigrants did on the East Coast. These Chinatowns were established on small businesses (e.g., restaurants, laundries, groceries and produce markets) and provided the framework for the preservation of the Chinese culture and language. In response to their rejection by Anglo society, the Chinatowns became highly elaborate and densely organized subsocieties separate from and parallel to the institutions of the surrounding communities.

The relative isolation of Chinese Americans permitted the ethnic group to preserve much of their traditional culture, language, and identity. The second and third generations tended to be successful in schools and were able to achieve relatively high levels of integration in the workforce when anti-Chinese prejudice declined after World War II. Like Mexican Americans, the current status of the group is very much affected by high levels of immigration since the 1960s (see below).

Japanese Americans began to immigrate later in the 1890s, partly to take up the slack left by curtailment of Chinese immigration after 1882. They experienced similar rejection and disparagement and also established separate, extensively organized enclave communities on the West Coast. The vast majority of the group was incarcerated during World War II, an experience that devastated the Japanese American socially and economically. After the war, they were able to restart the assimilation process and, since that time, have become one of the most successful and affluent ethnic groups in American society. Well educated and highly skilled, they took advantage of declining employment barriers. Unlike other Asian-American groups, immigration from Japan has been low recently, and the group as a whole is largely acculturated and integrated, at least in the public sectors of schools and workplaces.

Summary

The distinct cultures imported by European and Asian immigrant groups have faded over the generations, as have their languages, distinct ethnic identities, and elaborate organizational infrastructures. The descendants of these groups may retain a sense of their ethnicity; but, if so, it tends to be a pale refection of that which characterized earlier generations. Today, ethnic identity for these groups tends to be more voluntary, symbolic, and changeable. That is, their sense of being Italian- or Irish- or Polish American and of sharing a fate and a common destiny with others can often be exchanged at will as circumstances have warranted, usually via intermarriage or resettlement outside the enclaves (or both). It tends to include relatively few unique cultural elements that differentiate the individual from others in the society and mark him or her as a member of a specific group or as associated with a certain tradition. For contemporary white ethnics and many well-acculturated Chinese and Japanese, membership in ethnic organizations is low, and they do not seek to fill their needs within the institutions and groups founded by their ancestors (with the partial exception of organizations based on religion).

After the third or fourth generation, intermarriage across the white ethnic groups has been extensive, and many members of these groups have only a vague knowledge of—and little interest in—their origins and the experiences of their ancestor immigrant progenitors. According to many analysts, the separate and distinct white ethnic identities have not only faded; they have merged, more or less, with the dominant Anglo or white national identity, and all that is left are loose links with an ancestral European places of origin. White ethnicity has not disappeared, as indicated by the survey results mentioned at the start of this chapter, but it seems clear that it is fading rapidly in strength.

The ethnic groups formed by immigration from Asia are more intact. Chinese-American culture, identity, and organizational infrastructure have been strengthened by recent immigration, and the traditional Chinatowns have been reinvigorated and even expanded by the multitude of newcomers, as it fulfills a variety of needs (jobs, assistance, welfare, companionship) in the present as it did in the past.

Immigration from Japan has been much lower than that from China, and the traditional Japanese-American enclave, which was weakened by the World War II internment, has not been similarly reinvigorated. Japanese Americans have been successful in both acculturation and integration, but the ethnic identity has been sustained partly by in-group preference and partly by their racial visibility and some continuing rejection from Anglo society. That, however, has been offset by very high ratios of exogamy—out-marriage—which, of course, has accelerated their integration and near assimilation.

Ethnic Groups Formed by Immigration: The Second Wave (1965–Present)

In 1965, the United States changed its immigration policy. The old policy had strongly favored northern and western Europeans and primarily limited immigrants from southern and eastern Europe. The new policy abolished the blatantly prejudicial preferential quota system, favored family reunification and immigrants with skills that were in short supply in the United States, and imposed the first ceiling on migration from countries in the Western Hemisphere.

The result of the new policy was an immigrant stream larger and much more diverse than the mostly European mass immigration from 1820s to the 1920s. The United States has received 30 million documented immigrants since the 1960s, a number approximately equal to the total immigration from Europe during the earlier 100-year period of mass immigration. The more recent wave is much more global than the first. In 2008 alone, immigrants arrived from over 200 separate nations, from Albania to Zimbabwe. Only about 11 percent of the newcomers were from Europe. A third were from North America (17 percent from Mexico alone), and another third were from Asian nations (most from China), while South America supplied 9 percent, and Africa nearly 10 percent. The new immigrants bring every conceivable combination of race, culture, and language with them and are making the United States less Anglo and more reflective of the world as a whole.

These recent immigrants have the usual wide array of motivations for their journey, but, aside from the great number of refugees fleeing persecution and war, the primary underlying dynamic is economic. Immigrants come in search of work and the means to support themselves and their families, now as in the past. Some are highly educated and skilled and seek opportunities to pursue their profession in one of the most advanced and affluent economies in the world. Others, like the peasant laborers of years past, bring very modest educational credentials and skills and seek the employment opportunities created by the seemingly insatiable American demand for cheap labor.

The Second Wave: Professional/Highly Educated Immigrants

Many contemporary immigrants are accomplished, highly educated professionals. This is especially true for newcomers from India, China, the Philippines, some parts of the Middle East, Nigeria, and a few other places of origin. These immigrants are fluent in English, often have advanced degrees from American universities, and they enter the labor force at high levels and compete for jobs at universities, research and science facilities, hospitals, multinational corporations, and other highly prestigious and lucrative sectors of the job market. While they bring their native culture and their language with them, they are also cosmopolitan and sophisticated, and they have the resources and understandings to deal with conflicts and inconsistencies between their ways and Anglo customs. They tend to be relatively affluent and very integrated into the larger society in their occupations, their residence, and in schools.

We can illustrate some of these dynamics by considering immigrants from India, the second-most populous nation in the world with a population of more than a billion people. The number of Indians in the United States more than quadrupled between 1980 and 2000 and these immigrants include a select, highly educated, and skilled group of men (disproportionately). According to the 2000 census, Asian Indians are very overrepresented in some of the most prestigious occupations, including computer engineering, medicine, and college instruction. These immigrants are part of a worldwide movement of educated peoples from less developed countries to more developed ones. One need not ponder the differences in career opportunities, technology, and compensation for long to get some insight into the reasons for this movement.

Given the cosmopolitan orientation of highly educated immigrants, ethnicity is less crucial in their lives. Even though they may experience their ethnicity and "otherness" strongly, they also identify with their professions and tend to be integrated into and satisfy many of their needs in the mainstream society, not just with their co-ethnics.

It is common for well-educated, affluent immigrants to respond to the needs of the family members left behind. Assistance can take the form of remittances sent to relatives in the old country but can also include sponsoring the immigration of family members. As mentioned previously, U.S. immigration

policy places a high priority on family reunification and, once the original immigrants become citizens, they can send for immediate relatives and close kinfolk. This second phase of immigration has typically not been as populated by as educated nor as skilled newcomers as the first, and the result is a bifurcation in the ethnic community based on social class. In fact, some groups—including Chinese and Indian Americans—are said to be "bipolar," or concentrated in higher and lower social class positions with relatively few people in the middle.

The Second Wave: Immigrant Laborers

Insofar as occupation is concerned, the bulk of recent immigration falls in this category of laborers, especially immigrants from Mexico, other Latin American nations, and some Asian countries (including China). As was the case with immigrant laborer groups of the past (e.g., the Irish and Italians), many among these groups have been relatively low in education and job skills. Most are motivated by hard times in their native country and the possibility of relatively high wages in the United States. Many intended to be sojourners, initially planning to return eventually to their home villages. They are very likely to be non-English-speakers and barely literate in their native language. A large percentage of these immigrants, especially Mexicans, have also entered the United States without legal documents or have overstayed their visas..

Mexican immigrants, the largest single stream of immigration, can serve as an illustration. Mexico's economy has been disrupted by globalization, by the trend of multinational corporations to move jobs to the cheapest available labor force, and by the importation of goods (especially agricultural) produced in more developed economies (especially the United States). This large population movement has revitalized Mexican-American culture and the Spanish language, as has the arrival of many from Central and South America. Traditionally, Mexican and Central Americans have been clustered in the Southwest, but the new immigrants, in search of jobs, have dispersed the group into new areas, including the Southeast (Virginia and Georgia) and the upper Midwest

(Minnesota and North Dakota). The new immigrants, as in the past, have established or reinvigorated communities (the barrio) where they can practice their traditional culture, speak Spanish, and satisfy their personal and family needs, although a new phenomenon has involved the migration of indigenous peoples from Mexico and Central America (notably Mayans) who lack education, job skills, and often speak little or no Spanish.

While some segments of the Mexican-American community (e.g., the fifth or greater generations) continue to assimilate, the high levels of recent immigration have increased the degree of pluralism for the group as a whole. Even as some move into the middle class of the larger society, others arrive from south of the border and contribute to the revitalization of the language and culture. Thus, among these groups, assimilation and pluralism are happening simultaneously, and Latino ethnicities are becoming a stronger element in American culture. With an estimated 48.8 million Latinos reported in 2008 by the U.S. Census Bureau, of whom 30.7 million were Mexican, the increasing prominence of Hispanic ethnicity will undoubtedly influence certain aspects of American society and culture. Some fear that the dominant culture will be swamped and "Hispanicized." Others argue that Anglo culture and the power of the dominant group have survived challenges from immigrant groups in the past and will survive this wave, although probably in altered form. The issue is complex because, with so many Latinos present and so many at different stages of acculturation, community development, and incorporation into American society, their actual overall impact is difficult to measure.

The Second Wave: Enclave Groups

Several immigrant groups have established or revitalized ethnic enclaves in the United States. These include Chinese, Cuban, Southeast Asian, Iranian, Armenian, and other Middle Eastern groups and can be illustrated with immigrants from Korea. Korean Americans are heavily involved in small businesses and retail stores, particularly fruit and vegetable retail stores, or green groceries. One study, based on the 2000 census, shows that Koreans had the highest rate of business ownership among 11 different minority groups. As is the case for other groups that have pursued this course, the enclave allows Korean Americans to avoid the discrimination and racism of the larger society yet survive in an economic niche in which lack of English fluency is not a particular problem. However, the enclave has its perils and its costs. For one thing, the success of Korean enterprises depends heavily on the mutual assistance and financial support of other Koreans, and on the willingness of family members and other newcomers to work long hours for little or no pay. These resources would be weakened or destroyed by acculturation, integration, and the resultant decline in ethnic solidarity. Only by maintaining a distance from the dominant culture and its pervasive appeal can the enclave infrastructure survive. Churches, schools, mutual-aid associations, hometown groups, and local, ethnically oriented businesses have been among the components of that infrastructure by which ethnic groups persist.

For enclave groups, now as in the past, ethnicity is a vital ingredient in their recipe for survival. They tend to have the most elaborate and densely organized infrastructures and the strongest sense of ethnicity.

The Second Wave: Refugees

Refugees are involuntary immigrants forced out of their old country by political or religious persecution, or by civil wars and extreme economic and natural calamities. Refugees apply for admission prior to arrival in America; those seeking asylum do so after arrival. In recent decades, the United States has admitted refugees from Cuba, the nations of Southeast Asia, Iraq, the former Soviet Union and the former Yugoslavia, Nicaragua, Liberia, the Azores, and a variety of other places. Between World War II and 1990, 2.6 million refugees and asylees were admitted to the United States. In the recent decade (1999–2008), 290,500 persons were granted asylum and almost 537,300 refugees arrived in the United States.

Some of the most recent refugees come from Southeast Asia as a direct result of the war fought by the United States in the region. In 1975, when Saigon (the capital of South Vietnam, a U.S. ally) fell and the U.S. military withdrew, many Vietnamese and other

Southeast Asians (including Cambodians, Laotians, and Hmong) who had collaborated with the United States and its allies fled in fear for their lives. The earliest refugees from South Vietnam included high-ranking officials and members of the region's educational and occupation elite. Later groups of refugees tended to be less well educated and more impoverished. Many were "boat people" who fled Vietnam clandestinely, often in craft that were extremely overcrowded and of doubtful seaworthiness.

Many more Vietnamese refugees waited in camps for months or years before being admitted to the United States (or elsewhere), and they often arrived with few resources or social networks to ease their transition to the new society. Some—especially in the first wave—may have been highly educated and well-trained professionals in their homeland; but their credentials generally failed to meet the necessary criteria and licensing requirements in the American job market, especially when compounded by a lack of fluency in English. Other Vietnamese—especially in the later waves—tended to bring less impressive credentials and scant resources.

The Vietnamese had had little or no history of immigration to the United States, and there was no established community—no equivalent of a Chinatown or Little Italy—to ease their transition. Their relative isolation was exacerbated by the U.S. policy of spreading them across the nation so as to lower their visibility and limit any negative impacts on or reactions from local communities. Predictably, the Vietnamese slowly managed to find each other and, through "secondary migration," eventually formed enclaves across the nation and especially on the West Coast—notably in San Jose, San Diego, and Orange County (Westminster).

The first-generation Vietnamese—the actual refugees from Southeast Asia—are still very much alive and remain in positions of power in their communities. Ethnicity and ethnic identity are still quite strong for this group, as is dependence on the ethnically based associations and institutions that they were eventually able to develop. The second generation, as usual, is more Americanized and fluent in English.

The Vietnamese illustrate several important features of the refugee experience in the United States.

Perhaps most importantly, refugee groups tend to arrive with few resources and very limited contacts with others who speak their language and are familiar with their native culture. They tend to have high rates of poverty and other problems and be more dependent on assistance from the larger society, at least among the first generation. Because of the myriad factors propelling diverse peoples to flee their homelands in search of refuge, and because the time limits for refugees to obtain direct governmental assistance have been reduced since the Cubans were the first helped during the 1960s, the extent of ethnic persistence among these populations has varied considerably.

Conclusion

The United States is a society of groups as well as individuals, and ethnic groups and ethnicity have been major forces in American life. White Anglo-Saxon Protestants have been the dominant ethnicity since the beginning, and they continue to set the tone for the rest of society today. Yet, American ethnicity has been an ever-changing array of values and customs as these separate groups, traditions, and varieties of lifestyles and interpretations of ways of being, or becoming, American have come and gone. Ethnic groups have provided a vital sense of identity in a bewildering and complex society and networks of help and support for their members on multiple levels, from the personal to business and the spiritual.

In view of the racial diversity and the extent of cultural, linguistic, and economic differences as well as the competition for jobs and public resources, relations between ethnic groups and between newcomers and mainstream Americans have ranged from cooperation and mutual tolerance to racism, rejection, competition, and deadly violence. Immigrant groups that are Caucasian and Protestant have generally had an easier time achieving equality and incorporating into American society, while conquered nonwhite groups or non-Protestant populations have faced more formidable barriers. However, the civil rights movement and the expanding scope of toleration during the past half century have blurred boundaries and expanded economic and educational opportunities for newcomers and their children.

Today, most contemporary immigrant groups are nonwhite. Will they assimilate like European groups? How will these ethnic groups shape and change American culture and American society? Whatever the answers to these questions, it is clear that ethnicity will remain a major factor in American life for the foreseeable future.

Bibliography

Alba, Richard. 1990. *Ethnic Identity: The Transformation of White America*. New Haven, CT: Yale University Press.

Alba, Richard, and Victor Nee, 2003. *Remaking the American Mainstream: Assimilation and Contemporary Immigration*. Cambridge, MA: Harvard University Press.

Bean, Frank, and Gillian Stevens. 2003. *America's Newcomers and the Dynamics of Diversity*. New York: Russell Sage Foundation.

Blauner, Robert. 1972. *Racial Oppression in America*. New York: Harper and Row.

Bodnar, John. 1985. *The Transplanted*. Bloomington: Indiana University Press.

Foner, Nancy. 2005. *In a New Land: A Comparative View of Immigration*. New York: New York University Press.

Glazer, Nathan, and Daniel Moynihan. 1970. *Beyond the Melting Pot*. Cambridge, MA: MIT Press.

Gordon, Milton. 1964. *Assimilation in American Life: The Role of Race, Religion and National Origin*. New York: Oxford University Press.

Handlin, Oscar. 1951. *The Uprooted*. New York: Grosset and Dunlap.

Kasnitz, Phillip, John Mollenkopf, and Mary Waters. 2008. *Inheriting the City: The Children of Immigrants Come of Age*. New York: Russell Sage Foundation.

Portes, Alejandro, and Rueben Rumbaut. 2001. *Ethnicities: Children of Immigrants in America*. New York: Russell Sage Foundation.

Portes, Alejandro, and Rueben Rumbaut. 2001. *Legacies: The Story of the Immigrant Second Generation*. New York: Russell Sage Foundation.

Reimers, David M. 2005. *Other Immigrants: The Global Origins of the American People*. New York: New York University Press.

Telles, Edward, and Vilma Ortiz. 2008. *Generations of Exclusion: Mexican Americans, Assimilation, and Race*. New York: Russell Sage Foundation.

Thernstrom, Stephan, Ann Orlov, and Oscar Handlin, eds. 1980. *Harvard Encyclopedia of American Ethnic Groups*. Cambridge, MA: Harvard University Press.

Integration and Assimilation: The Core Concept and Three Contemporary Developments

Peter Kivisto

Assimilation has long been the major theoretical concept associated with the ways in which immigrants become incorporated into American society. Its history dates from the late nineteenth century to the present, during which time it has been widely embraced, critiqued, rejected, ignored, and subsequently revived and revised. The focus of this chapter is on the current return to assimilation theory, with particular emphasis on two efforts to articulate what might be called neo-assimilationist theory. At the same time, it will explore the current consensus that is emerging regarding the relationship between this concept with a long history and the new concept of transnationalism. However, before discussing these new currents of thought, they need to be located in the longer tradition of assimilation theory, which begins with the canonical formulation that had a major influence on immigration studies for roughly the first three-quarters of the twentieth century.

The Canonical Formulation

Robert Ezra Park, in conjunction with key colleagues of his at the University of Chicago, such as W. I. Thomas and Ernest Burgess, is generally and appropriately considered to be the sociologist most responsible for the canonical formulation of assimilation theory. However, there is no consensus about both what Park had in mind when he described assimilation and to what extent he merely presented a summary of prevailing views or developed an original position. His perspective has been portrayed by some as a theoretical articulation of the melting pot, as a synonym for Americanization, the final outcome of a race relations cycle, and an expression of a straight-line process of incorporation. In these various interpretations, it has been assumed that his particular perspective on assimilation is incongruent with, if not antithetical to, cultural pluralism or its more recent parallel concept, multiculturalism.

Park rejected the view that assimilation was a theoretical expression of the melting pot, or what Park and Burgess ([1921] 1969, 735) disparagingly referred to as the "magic crucible" version of assimilation that they associated with theories of "like-mindedness." First, he emphasized the role of culture over biology, for Park understood migration to be a group phenomenon and not merely an individual one. Second, he disagreed with the Anglo-conformity view of assimilation. Third, Park granted agency to ethnics. Finally, he articulated his position in a manner that very consciously sought to divorce sociological analysis from moral preferences and ideology.

Park's is a "bumpy-line" version of assimilation, not, as some commentators have assumed, a "straight-line" approach. Assimilation is the product of interaction and thus has a reciprocal character, although Park understood that differences in group location and power and status differences would affect outcomes. Racial hostility (he leaves out of consideration religious hostility) was consistently described as the major impediment to assimilation.

Assimilation boiled down to finding a way to live together cooperatively, playing by common rules that define the parameters of intergroup conflict. It entailed the creation of a shared national identity, which of necessity required certain commonalities, such as a shared language and core cultural values. However, it also permitted the persistence of ethnic identities and affiliations. Assimilation is thus not considered to be antithetical to a multicultural society; it does not require cultural homogeneity.

The unappreciated aspect of Park's contribution to this dialogue is his explanation for why modern societies can tolerate diversity and his account of why assimilation propels so many individuals to exit —totally or partially—their ethnic groups. Park insisted that, due to the division of labor in modern societies, assimilation did not entail homogeneity and considerable individual and group differences can persist without impairing national unity. The reverse side of the coin involves the lure of assimilation. Park thought that assimilation was attractive because modern societies are individualistic. What this means is that people will seek to enhance their own opportunities and expand their life options, and that one way of doing so is to refuse to permit the parochial constraints of the ethnic group to limit self-realization. It means that individuals will seek to expand their social circles and will treat the ethnic group not as a community of fate, but as one of a variety of possible affiliations and sources of personal identity.

The Research Tradition's Zenith

The version of assimilation articulated by Park constituted the hegemonic theory in studies of ethnicity in the United States. The apogee of such work was W. Lloyd Warner and Leo Srole's *The Social Systems of American Ethnic Groups* (1945), which was a part of their Yankee City Series. They offered a complex conceptual scheme to account for the likely assimilative trajectories of a wide range of groups that they broadly distinguished into three categories: ethnic, racial, and ethno-racial (this is not well defined, but represents something of an interstitial category). The focus of their study was on the differential barriers to incorporation confronting various groups. Key to defining the strength of the barrier was the level and degree of subordination each group confronts, but factored into the equation was the impact of the relative strength of the group's communal bonds. Located in

the social distance tradition, the traits that made incorporation difficult for ethnic groups were cultural in nature and, therefore, subject to change. In contrast, the racial traits that worked against assimilation were rooted in biology, and thus would remain persistent handicaps for racial groups. The ethno-racial groups (the two examples in the study were "Spanish Americans" in the Southwest and "mixed bloods" from Latin America) had sufficiently ambiguous identities that their futures might look like either the futures of ethnic groups or the futures of racial groups.

In their "scale of subordination and assimilation," Warner and Srole combined racial and cultural types to form a grid in which they located each specific group. They offered both a prognosis of the length of time it would take to assimilate (ranging from "very short" to "very slow") and their predicted future social location. In the case of ethnic groups, the movement over time would be from the ethnic group into specific social class locations. At the other end of the spectrum, for blacks it would be a movement from the racial group to a "color caste" location. Asians were destined to enter a "semi-caste" condition, while Latinos would either end up in a class or color caste location. Thus, they concluded that "The future of American ethnic groups seems to be limited; it is likely that they will be quickly absorbed. When this happens one of the great epochs of American history will have ended and another, that of race, will begin" (Warner and Srole 1945, 295). This is a rather odd formulation given the prominent role race has played throughout American history, but it does serve to differentiate the future historical trajectories of white ethnics and people of color. Both methodologically and in terms of the theoretical assumptions shaping their work, Warner and Srole's study can be viewed as emblematic of a tradition of sociological research that extended into the 1960s.

Gordon's Typology of the Canonical Theory of Assimilation

These works are representative of the central orientation of the majority of sociologists and historians into the 1960s and a reflection of the hegemony exerted by assimilation theory decades after its canonical

A New York teacher, with six Chinese children, recent arrivals from Hong Kong and Formosa, who are holding up placards giving his or her Chinese name and the name to be entered in school records, 1964. (Library of Congress)

formulation. A half-century after Park's initial formulation, Milton Gordon's seminal study, *Assimilation in American Life* (1964), both codified and systematized the theory of assimilation. However valuable this work may be, critics have pointed out that it is chiefly a typology, not a theory. Gordon (1964, 71) identified seven types of assimilation: (1) cultural or behavioral —also known as acculturation; (2) structural; (3) marital—or amalgamation; (4) identificational, which means creating a shared sense of peoplehood at the societal level; (5) attitude receptional; (6) behavioral receptional; and (7) civic, where interethnic conflicts over values and power are overcome by the shared identity of citizenship. Two of these, in our estimation, do not refer to assimilation per se, but rather to preconditions for assimilation, which have to do with

the absence of various impediments to incorporation: attitude receptional assimilation refers to the lack of prejudice, while behavioral receptional assimilation concerns the related absence of discrimination.

One of the intriguing aspects of Gordon's thesis is that he located cultural pluralism within this schema. This is because he did not think that there was a straight and uniform path to assimilation, but rather assumed, as had others before him, that it would occur along a variety of different avenues and at differing speeds. Moreover, if persistent levels of prejudice and discrimination characterize interethnic relations, all or some types of assimilation would be stymied. Thus, assimilation did not necessarily mean that ethnic identities and affiliations would disappear or become irrelevant.

Gordon referred to these aspects of assimilation not simply as types, but also as stages, and thus he did have a sense that assimilation might in some circumstances signal the demise of ethnic allegiances. He hedged his bets on how the process of assimilation would occur, although he was clear about two things. First, he thought that marital assimilation would be the last to occur. Second, he contended that the type of assimilation most crucial to the process was structural assimilation. Once it occurs, he argued, all the others will inevitably follow: "Structural assimilation, then, rather than acculturation, is seen to be the keystone in the arch of assimilation" (Gordon 1964, 81). In this regard, what Gordon had done was to codify and add analytical rigor to Park's formulation. If acculturation can be seen as that aspect of assimilation that Park described as occurring spontaneously, structural assimilation entails volition on the part of ethnics and members of the larger society.

The point at which Gordon adds a significant dimension to the matrix missing in Park is when he separates out civic assimilation from structural assimilation. Park's discussion of assimilation had a curiously apolitical quality to it—one that ignored entirely the significance of the role of citizen. He did deal with the identificational side of this when discussing the significance of national identity as a unifying and thus assimilating force. However, the extent to which the idea of the citizen as actor might override or complicate the idea of the ethnic as actor is not advanced in his formulation. In Gordon's case, he laid it out but did not develop it. It should be stressed that for both, it was not an either/or proposition pitting ethnicity against citizenship. Rather, what they had in mind was the capacity of citizenship to reduce levels of interethnic hostility and conflict. The enhanced salience of citizenship did not mean that the memories of ancestors and the embracing of one's cultural roots would necessarily disappear.

Assimilation Abandoned?

Within a decade after the publication of Gordon's book, assimilation theory's hegemonic status came under attack. Given that difficulties associated with dissociating the theory of assimilation from assimilation as ideology and policy, this is not surprising. The civic nationalism that took hold during the Progressive Era and defined American national identity until the 1960s came under attack during that tumultuous decade in what amounted to a revolt against assimilation. This was due chiefly to the combined impact of the civil rights and the anti–Vietnam War movements. In the case of the former, ideas associated with black pride and with the critiques of white America offered by militant black nationalists signaled an end to the idea that stressed integration. Opposition to the Vietnam War furthered this trend, especially insofar as the "best and the brightest" who had led the nation into the quagmire were associated in the mind of many antiwar activists with the WASP elite.

Related to these developments, in part as a reaction to them in a context where the center did not hold, by the early 1970s there was considerable discussion about an ethnic revival among the southern and eastern European ethnics whose ancestors had arrived in the nation between 1880 and 1930. Part of the heightened sense of ethnicity among these ethnics entailed a benign search for roots. However, it also signaled a reaction to the perceived gains achieved by blacks in the immediate aftermath of the civil rights movement and a resistance to integration.

Assimilation Challenged

The cultural climate of this era, not surprisingly, filtered into scholarship on ethnicity. Within both sociology and history, there was a rather widespread abandonment of assimilationist theory in favor of variant versions of pluralism. The idea of ethnic persistence gained currency with the publication—at virtually the same time that Gordon's book appeared—of Nathan Glazer and Daniel Patrick Moynihan's *Beyond the Melting Pot* (1963), which examined five ethnic groups in New York City (Italians, Irish, Jews, blacks, and Puerto Ricans) and concluded, in a richly documented and nuanced thesis, that these groups functioned to a large extent as interest groups. One could draw the conclusion that the extent to which this instrumentalist *raison d'être* persisted, so would the saliency of ethnic identities and affiliations. Despite the book's provocative title, the authors did not offer an explicit pluralist alternative to assimilation at the theoretical level.

The sociologist most responsible for the promotion of a research agenda that sought to indicate the persistence of ethnicity, rather than its erosion, was Andrew Greeley (1974), who relied on National Opinion Research Center surveys to examine a wide array of attitudinal and behavioral topics, all of which were intended to ascertain the extent to which ethnicity still mattered. Greeley limited his subjects to European-origin ethnics, excluding from consideration racial minorities that had not been able to assimilate structurally due to externally imposed barriers. His findings did not lend much validation to the idea that assimilation theory was irrelevant. Indeed, his results about the persistence of ethnicity were mixed at best, and moreover, crucial issues that would call the thesis into question, such as intermarriage rates, were largely ignored. Greeley's findings pointed to little more than the obvious fact that assimilation had not yet reached its end stage, even though no serious sociologist actually made such a claim. Greeley, too, did not attempt to offer a theoretical alternative to assimilation.

Pluralists who did attempt to provide theoretical explanations were divided between two alternative accounts of ethnic persistence. Some theorists embraced what has been described as a primordialist perspective (though the current terminology that could be used to describe this camp is essentialist). Ethnicity from this perspective is considered to be deeply rooted in the psyche or from a sociobiological perspective in the genes and as such is an immutable and universal given. Ethnic attachments are the result of a little-understood but nonetheless extraordinarily powerful psychological attachment to the group. This position is problematic insofar as it devalues the role played by both historical events and social structural factors and because it fails to appreciate the mutability of human attachments and loyalties.

For this reason, most sociologists who embraced pluralist theory did so from what became known as a circumstantionalist or optionalist perspective, which provided a more compelling sociological basis for understanding ethnicity. This version of pluralist theory looked to those social, cultural, and political factors that created conditions that either sustained or undermined ethnic attachments for particular groups at particular times.

Assimilation Ignored

Pluralist theory either implicitly or explicitly informed the work of social historians of ethnicity during this time period, who by being sensitive to the distinctive features of specific groups—along with the particularities of time and place and the significance of complexity and contingency—added to the appreciation of the variability of possible outcomes. This generation of social historians to a large extent neglected assimilation. In their effort to write history from the bottom up, they gave voice to the ethnics, stressing the choices they made, the strategies they employed, the resources they mustered, the ambiguities they felt, the coalitions they formed, and the constraints they encountered. This is clearly the case in John Bodnar's (1985) "transplanted" thesis, which, like much of the best social history of this period, represents a fruitful interplay between ethnic history and labor history. His portrait of the immigrant generation—the "children of capitalism"—is one in which they reacted pragmatically to the larger society's institutions and values, creating a world as best they could that was "an amalgam of past and present, acceptance and resistance" (Bodnar 1985, 210). He did not raise the prospect that, as Warner and Srole predicted, European ethnics would shift from a primary identity rooted in ethnicity to one located in class but rather concentrated on the dialectical tension and mutual reinforcement of these two aspects of individual identity.

Perhaps because there is a tendency among historians to focus on the particular and to resist the temptation to generalize about larger social processes, social historians such as Bodnar did not offer a frontal rebuttal of assimilation theory. Nor did they explicitly embrace cultural pluralism or propose an alternative. Rather, they tended to simply ignore assimilation, thereby implicitly casting into question its utility as a concept for understanding the incorporation of immigrants and their offspring into the larger society.

Rethinking the Theoretical Legacy

By the 1990s, a growing number of sociologists and historians, reacting to the critiques and the neglect of assimilation theory, began to express their conviction that a reconsideration of its utility and validity was in order. This included some scholars who had remained supporters of assimilation theory throughout this period, such as Herbert Gans, Nathan Glazer, John Higham, and Stephen Steinberg, in addition to a younger generation that included Richard Alba, Elliott Barkan, Rogers Brubaker, Douglas Massey, Ewa Morawska, Victor Nee, Alejandro Portes, Rubén Rumbaut, Roger Waldinger, and Min Zhou. The idea of a return stimulated an effort to rethink and reappropriate a line of thought dating back to Park.

In part, this disparate group of thinkers was challenging the theoretical adequacy of cultural pluralism in accounting for the fate of ethnicity over time for European-origin groups. At some level, the argument advanced was quite simple: assimilation had proven to be a far more useful analytical tool for understanding the historical trajectories of these groups. The fact that blacks have not been successfully incorporated into the mainstream of American society accounts for much of the criticism of assimilation, but this does not undermine assimilation theory. Rather, it illustrates the fact that prejudice and discrimination stymie assimilation. In other words, assimilation is a powerful force but not inevitable.

Other defenses of assimilation were generally linked with calls for correcting what were seen as certain problematic features of the classical theory of assimilation. These included that it was too simplistic and ahistorical, that its efforts to understand the dominant group and what it is that groups are assimilating into were insufficient, and that it exhibited a lack of concern about the role of gender in the assimilation process. As scholars cast a sympathetic but simultaneously critical perspective on assimilation theory, they also attempted to make the concept more complex and less unidirectional. Herbert Gans (1999), responding to the claims made in the 1970s about an ethnic revival among European-origin ethnics, developed the idea of "symbolic ethnicity." It was intended to account for both the indicators of the persistence of

various manifestations of ethnicity and the simultaneous gradual decline of ethnic affiliations and behaviors. He thought it was especially apt in describing the significance of ethnicity for the third generation and beyond. In Gans's view, by the latter part of the twentieth century, the ethnicity of these offspring of immigrants could be characterized as manifesting a low-level intensity—occupying an individual's attention only periodically. The decline in ethnic organizations and cultures no longer permitted more substantive expressions of ethnic identity or affiliation. Rather than relying on community or culture, these latter generations used symbols, primarily out of a sense of nostalgia for the traditions of the immigrant generation. According to Gans (1999, 12–13):

> Most people look for easy and intermittent ways of expressing their identity, for ways that do not conflict with other ways of life. As a result, they refrain from ethnic behaviors that require an arduous or time-consuming commitment, either to a culture that must be practiced constantly, or to organizations that demand active membership. Second, because people's concern is with identity, rather than with cultural practices or group relationships, they are free to look for ways of expressing that identity which suit them best, thus opening up the possibility of voluntary, diverse, or individualistic ethnicity.

Mary Waters described such an ethnicity in terms of "ethnic options," whereby individuals pick and choose from their ancestral cultural traditions. Like Gans, her portrait is one of an ethnicity predicated on *feeling* (at least periodically) ethnic rather than having to permanently *be* ethnic. This emptying out of a once-robust ethnicity would appear innocuous except that it serves to create a sense of "us" versus "them," wherein the "us" includes all white European-origin groups while "them" includes blacks and new immigrants of color. Waters (1990, 147, 155) contends that "symbolic ethnicity persists because of its ideological 'fit' with racist beliefs," offering these ethnics "a community without cost and a specialness that comes to you just by virtue of being born [white]." In this regard, assimilation is seen in terms of boundary-drawing.

The most sustained attempt to offer a systematic rethinking of assimilation theory rooted in the tradition was that offered by historian Elliott Barkan (1995). On the surface, it appears to represent an effort to revive the race relations cycle that, as noted earlier, has been inappropriately associated with Park insofar as it involves a model consisting of six stages: contact, acculturation, adaptation, accommodation, integration, and assimilation into the core society/core culture. However, Barkan insisted that this model ought not to be construed as a cycle or a straight-line teleological process, writing that *"there has been no one pattern, no cycle, no one outcome that uniformly encompasses all ethnic experiences"* (Barkan 1995, 46; italics in the original).

The analytical purpose of the model is to identify those patterns that occur with a certain regularity as well as the exceptions to the patterns. By noting the exceptions and by being attuned to the impact of prejudice and discrimination as well as individual choices on the part of marginalized people to either seek incorporation or to resist it, the model is designed to link assimilation to pluralism. He saw assimilation as a two-way process, entailing both the level of openness on the part of the host society and the extent to which there is a desire to incorporate on the part of marginalized individuals. More than that, as an effort to remedy a particular shortcoming in the canonical model, he viewed assimilation as "a bidirectional phenomenon in that the general society and culture are affected by the heritages of those who assimilate," while recognizing that the interplay between newcomer and host is not an equal exchange (Barkan 1995, 49). Barkan paid less attention to the fact that the host society is multifarious and thus outsiders who assimilate do so into differing sectors of the society, thus making assimilation a far more complex and varied phenomenon, and one that does not necessarily signal a successful entry into the societal mainstream.

Critics have identified problematic features of Barkan's model. Its inattentiveness to class and gender has been noted. Likewise, its singular focus on the individual over the group has been criticized. Finally, the model appears to be intended primarily to account for the historical trajectories of voluntary immigrants. This raises concerns about whether or not it can be proven suitable in accounting for the historical experiences of nonvoluntary immigrants, such as blacks, indigenous peoples, or ethnonationalist minorities.

Nevertheless, the model served to amplify the argument that assimilation and pluralism were interrelated phenomena, and not either-or propositions. In a sense, it can be read as a culmination of a rethinking of conceptual frameworks dating from the early part of the twentieth century. It can also be seen as offering a theoretical account of the historical fates of European-origin ethnics in the United States, and in so doing provides a theoretical framework for locating such studies as Richard Alba's *Ethnic Identity* (1990). This study was perhaps the most influential research project that mounted compelling empirical evidence for the erosion of ethnic institutions and neighborhoods, the declining role of ethnic cultures, the progressive decline in ethnic identities and loyalties, the concurrent increase in intermarriage rates, and substantial evidence of social assimilation.

During the past several years, two projects aimed at building on a long history of work on assimilation while pushing it in new directions. We turn to them in what follows.

New Directions I: Segmented or Downward Assimilation

Segmented or downward assimilation is a concept developed by Alejandro Portes and various colleagues, including Patricia Fernandez-Kelly, Rubén Rumbaut, and Min Zhou. However, one can turn to a speculative essay by Herbert Gans (1992) for a precursor discussion about the potential differential occupational and socioeconomic outcomes of contemporary immigrants. This article was part of a growing body of work devoted to exploring the possibility of second-generation socioeconomic decline. Gans describes six potential scenarios, three positive and three negative. The positive, involving outcomes resulting in intergenerational upward mobility, can be: (1) education-driven; (2) succession-driven (moving up into more attractive jobs as the native-born exit them in their own quest for upward mobility);

and (3) due to niche improvement (remaining in the jobs occupied by parents and using it for economic advance). The possible negative scenarios are the reverse of the positive: (1) educational failure (such as high dropout rates); (2) the stalling of ethnic succession; and (3) niche shrinkage. The reason for concern about the prospects of decline had to do with a sense that the changes in the American economy that led to positive outcomes for the earlier wave of European immigrants no longer exist, and instead the emergence of a postindustrial economy called into question whether contemporary immigrants were likely to follow the upward mobility pattern of the past.

In the first articulation of the segmented assimilation thesis, Portes and Zhou point out that for the first time since Irving Child's work of a half century earlier, sociologists were turning their attention to the second generation. They contend that in contrast to the Italians that were the focus of his work, the situation for many contemporary immigrants differs in two ways. First, many of today's immigrants are defined as nonwhite, and thus race must be factored into the equation. Second, the economy has changed as a result of deindustrialization, which has drastically reduced the number of available jobs in the manufacturing sector. The idea of segmented assimilation was born of the idea that the incorporative trajectories of contemporary immigrant children might take three possible paths. As Portes and Zhou (1993, 82) put it, "One of them replicates the time-honored portrayal of growing acculturation and parallel integration into the white middle-class; a second leads straight in the opposite direction to permanent poverty and assimilation into the underclass; still a third associates rapid economic advancement with deliberate preservation of the immigrant community's values and tight solidarity." By being incorporated into different sectors of the American class structure, immigrants are being socialized into different subcultures.

In considering the factors that can be expected to yield different outcomes, Portes and Rumbaut point first to the relationship between the first and second generations. Immigrants arrive with differing stocks of human capital, and these differences serve to locate them both in terms of occupations and residency. Related to parental human capital is family structure, which in large part means whether or not the family is headed by one (usually female) or two parents. Put simply, those second-generation children living in families whose parents possess high levels of human capital are expected to do better than those with lower levels. Likewise, dual-parent families offer a stronger system of parental guidance than do single-parent families, and they provide a richer network of social ties. In terms of their location in different sorts of families, gender is also salient insofar as socialization differs for boys and girls. The third background variable they specify is modes of incorporation, which refers to the varied types of reception of immigrants by the state, the society at large, and the immigrant's pre-existing ethnic community. In terms of state and society, some immigrant groups are favored and others are not. Thus, during the Cold War, the earliest waves of Cuban refugees were greeted warmly; while since 9/11, immigrants from the Middle East have not been.

The acculturation of the second generation is viewed as the outcome of the complex interplay of the three background factors. Portes and Rumbaut stress the relationship between the two generations that results from this interplay, distinguishing three types of acculturation: dissonant, consonant, and selective. Dissonant refers to a situation in which the children rapidly acclimate to the language and ways of life of the new society and simultaneously experience a dramatic loss of their cultural heritage. At the same time, their parents find getting acclimated difficult and thus remain rooted in the pre-migration worldview. In this setting, parents become dependent on their children, thus establishing a "role reversal, especially where parents lack other means to maneuver in the host society without the help of their children" (Portes and Rumbaut 2001, 54). In such a context, the second generation confronts three primary external obstacles—racial discrimination, a bifurcated labor market, and inner-city subcultures—on its own, without sufficient support from parents because there is either a generational rupture or a lack of parental authority, and without support from the ethnic community. Thus, dissonant acculturation can lead to downward assimilation, particularly if the children embrace the adversarial lifestyle associated with the "code of the street." Downward assimilation contributes to gang involvement, drug activities, unplanned pregnancies, and dropping out of school.

In contrast, one version of consonant acculturation results when parents and children acclimate to their new setting in more-or-less parallel fashion, both managing to become culturally and socially competent in the new society and at the same time exiting the ethnic community together. In this scenario, parents and children are on the same page insofar as both generations are seeking integration into the American mainstream. This particular trajectory is most likely among families whose parents possess high levels of human capital and are thus from the outset poised to enter the middle class and to experience upward mobility. In the other form of consonant acculturation, parents and children are again coming to terms with the new society congruently. However, in this version, both are slow to make a language transition and to embrace the host society's values and lifestyle. At the same time, both remain embedded in the ethnic community. These immigrants and their offspring remain isolated from the larger society, dependent on the ethnic enclave. One outcome of such acculturation is that mobility and integration into the larger society are blocked. If the sense of isolation becomes sufficiently pronounced and unattractive, it can prove to be an incentive to return to the homeland.

Finally, selective acculturation entails a successful balancing act on the part of both immigrants and their children between embracing the cultural values

A boy photographs the Lake Worth Christmas parade in Lake Worth, Florida, December 2005. He and other Mayan children who live in Palm Beach County participate in a photography program run by the Guatemala Maya Center. (AP Photo/Lynne Sladky)

and language of the society and remaining embedded in the ethnic community. Thus, assimilation occurs gradually and without the anomic dislocations that can occur in consonant or dissonant acculturation. The ethnic community in this case serves as a decompression chamber that helps ease the transition into the larger society. In this scenario, there is very little intergenerational conflict, the second-generation children count many co-ethnics among their friends, and they tend to be genuinely bilingual.

The three obstacles identified above serve to establish what Portes and Rumbaut view as the novel features making contemporary immigrant incorporation different from what it was in the past. They contend that although assimilation should still be viewed as the master concept in the study of today's immigrants, it is important to avoid concluding that assimilation is a uniform and unidirectional path. In their Children of Immigrants Longitudinal Study, a study of second-generation students in Miami–Fort Lauderdale and San Diego, they found that a majority of these youth are poised to experience a successful entry into the mainstream. They are acquiring educations that can serve them well in that quest, and their early occupational experiences suggest they are moving in a positive direction. On the other hand, a substantial number, though a minority, is being left behind.

Whether or not these findings ought to be read optimistically or pessimistically is open to question. In a major research project on new immigrants in New York City—one of the nation's two primary gateway cities—Philip Kasinitz, John Mollenkopf, Mary Waters, and Jennifer Holdaway conclude that their evidence leads them to be "guardedly optimistic about the second generation" (2008, 16). They contend that the portrait of entry into an oppositional culture that can over time reproduce downward assimilation is too negative. It overstates the significance of an adversarial subculture among both native minorities, particularly blacks, and second-generation immigrants and conversely fails to appreciate the fact that native-born whites, likewise, can be found embracing an oppositional identity.

This leads to explorations by Joel Perlmann and Roger Waldinger that call into question the assumption that segmented assimilation is a novel phenomenon characteristic of today's immigrants versus the presumably more uniform assimilation that occurred several decades earlier and involved European-origin immigrants. They particularly question the assumption that the racial makeup of contemporary immigrants—defined as nonwhite—puts them at a distinct disadvantage compared to their white European predecessors. As whiteness studies research argues, eastern and southern European immigrants from the nineteenth and early twentieth centuries were often defined upon arrival as nonwhite. As such, they were treated as racial outsiders by the hegemonic culture, and the process over time of becoming assimilated meant in part "becoming white." The wide variety of racial categories a century ago—Nordic, Mediterranean, Slavic, Semitic, and the like—employed as the markers used to distinguish those who were white from those who were not reduced in significance. Increasingly, they were replaced by a perspective that treated all European-origin groups as white, with Jews probably entering that side of the racial divide last due to the more durable character of anti-Semitism.

Gans (1999) raises the possibility that something similar might be occurring at present in pondering whether or not a new racial hierarchy might be in the process of formation. Specifically, he speculates about the prospect of a new racial divide that no longer is framed in terms of white/nonwhite, but instead in terms of black/nonblack. If, for example, Asian immigrants—sometimes depicted as the "model minority"—find themselves labeled as "honorary whites," this would suggest that for them at least, the significance of race is a declining barrier to incorporation. They would not actually have to be defined as white: the key to their acceptance is that they are on the nonblack side of the divide. Though their situation is not the same, a similar process might be underway for Latinos, which if true would mean that for the new immigrants as a whole, race will prove to be less and less of an obstacle; while for their part, native-born blacks will end up being more socially isolated. Gans is not claiming that such a new racial formation already exists; merely that such a scenario is a realistic possibility.

Perlmann and Waldinger contend that if taken as a whole, today's immigrants show little evidence of being uniquely disadvantaged. However, if there is one stark difference between the old immigrants versus the new, it is that today, far more middle-class immigrants come poised for upward mobility. Thus, generalizations about the new immigrants must be made carefully and with this reality in mind. Given the fact that Mexican immigrants in the United States represent by far the largest component of the new immigration and that they are considerably poorer and possess far less human capital than the new immigrants overall, it is reasonable to raise the question of whether they might be uniquely disadvantaged and thus particularly likely to experience downward assimilation.

It is with this in mind that Perlmann engaged in a comparative study of the Italian second generation of the past and today's second-generation Mexicans. When Oscar Handlin created his ideal typical portrait of the "uprooted" immigrant, Italians constituted a paradigmatic example. So, too, do Mexicans. Thus, this is a particularly apt comparison in testing whether or not the chances for intergenerational upward mobility today have declined compared to those in the preceding migratory wave. Perlmann's study reveals two things. First, the progress made by Italians was slower and more difficult than is often seen in retrospect. Second, although Mexican progress has been slower than that of their Italian counterparts, the trend is in the same direction. Without discounting the fact that the society into which Mexicans have entered in recent years is in many ways different from the one Italians entered earlier, Perlmann's study calls into question the view that upward mobility is less likely today than in the past—and implicitly challenges the claim that segmented assimilation is only applicable to the present.

One of the key assumptions of segmented assimilation is that contemporary immigrants confront a major economic obstacle due to the economic restructuring that has been underway since the early 1970s. The portrait of an hourglass economy is central to this conviction, for the precipitous decline in manufacturing jobs is considered to be a major barrier to mobility. This particular assumption has been widely accepted by immigration scholars, though it has only recently been subjected to empirical investigation. The untested assumption underlying this view is that manufacturing jobs proved to be the route to upward mobility for earlier immigrants. Waldinger (2007) has raised the fundamental question: "Did manufacturing matter?" He observes that a key difference between traditional assimilation theory and segmental assimilation is that while the former does not, the latter offers an explanation for how the children and grandchildren of immigrants in the past improved their economic lot: it was as a result of obtaining jobs in the manufacturing sector, which, it is claimed, provided them with wage levels that served to narrow the economic gap between them and native-born whites. He points out that this focus on the role of factory work in heavy industry "has a muscularly proletarian feel," an account of male rather than female workers, other than during World War II (Waldinger 2007, 9).

Waldinger contrasts two of the largest immigrants groups from that era, Italians and Poles. He found a pronounced difference between the two in terms of their respective locations in the manufacturing sector. While second- and 2.5-generation Poles were twice as likely as native white, native parentage (NWNP) workers to be located in manufacturing, Italians were less likely (preferring outdoor jobs). This would imply, from the segmented assimilation perspective, that Poles should have had higher incomes than Italians. In fact, the reverse was the case. Moreover, Poles did not narrow the income gap between themselves and NWNP workers, while Italians did. Thus, while finding work in the manufacturing sector did not produce the expected results, it appears that Italians found an alternative route to economic advancement. Precisely what this finding means for contemporary immigrants inhabiting a society that has been transformed by deindustrialization is not clear. However, one reasonable conclusion to be drawn is that the relationship between manufacturing jobs and upward mobility has been overstated.

Despite these problems, segmented assimilation theory has the virtue of attempting to connect immigrant socioeconomic destinations to different social class locations. If the classical assimilation theory paid scant attention to class, even with

Gordon's (1964) call for consideration of what he called "ethclass," this is a salutary development—one that represents less of a break with the older theoretical tradition than an emendation of it.

One problematic feature of the idea of segmented assimilation is that, in offering a dichotomous description of entry into either the upwardly mobile middle class or the underclass, the model oversimplifies a more complex picture. Although it may be that the economy looks more like an hourglass than it did before, the metaphor can mislead insofar as immigrants are to be found in the working class as well as the underclass and the educated middle class. As Alba and Nee point out, the concept also carries the risk of treating the culture of the underclass as static and immune to outside cultural influences. Related to this point, it also carries with it a tendency to overlook the fact that not all members of the underclass are embedded in an adversarial culture. Nevertheless, the significance of segmented assimilation is that it calls attention to the fact that the location of immigrants in the class structure plays a significant role in shaping distinctive incorporative paths.

Assimilation and economic mobility are interrelated but distinct processes. During the earlier phase of immigration research, it was presumed that upward mobility would occur over time and across generations, and therefore there was a tendency to convolute assimilation and mobility. Stepping back from this tendency, one might suggest that one of the tasks today is to consider the extent to which assimilation leads to mobility and vice versa. In so doing, there is a call for analyses of the relationship between cultural and structural assimilation.

New Directions II: Boundaries and the Mainstream

In comparison to segmented assimilation's focus on the connection between assimilation and mobility, Richard Alba and Victor Nee have produced a revisionist theory of assimilation, an approach that they refer to simply as "new assimilation theory." Influenced by the new institutionalism in sociology and building on the "forms-of-capital" model, their theory is intended to link both agency to structure and the

micro level to the macro level. Furthermore, the theory is intended to be sensitive to historical and structural contexts.

Alba and Nee distinguish between proximate and distal causes, the former referring to factors operating at the individual and group network levels and the latter to the macro-structural level, focusing for instance on the role of major societal institutions, particularly the state and the economy. From the agency side of the equation, their framework calls for considering differentials in financial, human, and social capital among immigrants and the varied ways in which these resources are deployed, both by individuals and collectivities (an approach clearly shared with segmented assimilation theorists). From the structure side, they seek to locate these deployments in terms of the existing institutional mechanisms that either facilitate or inhibit assimilation. Of particular significance in post–civil rights America is the impact that the rights revolution has had on both the potential for and modes of incorporation of immigrants and other minorities. In this regard, the state plays a critical role in structuring and enforcing mechanisms for incorporation, and its impact has been profound in challenging discrimination, particularly in the workplace.

The central concept employed in the new assimilation theory is that of boundaries. The idea that boundaries are socially constructed rather than being givens has since become a taken-for-granted assumption in ethnic and racial studies. In this regard, this subfield is not so unique, for boundaries and the related concept of borders have increasingly been employed by social scientists in a wide range of fields, including social and collective identity, class, ethnic/racial, and gender/sexual identity inequalities, the professions, science, communities, and national identity.

Boundaries are central to Alba and Nee's *Remaking the American Mainstream*. In this work, they "distinguish among three boundary-related processes: boundary crossing, boundary blurring, and boundary shifting" (2003, 60). This is not an original formulation but rather builds on the work of Aristide Zolberg and Long Litt Woon (1999). They distinguish three types of boundary processes. The first of these—boundary crossing—occurs at the individual level and does not entail the altering of the boundary itself. It does not make a bright boundary blurry, nor does it either expand the boundary or shift its location. Rather, the boundary remains intact as an individual opts to exit one group and enter into another. Assimilation posed in terms of boundary crossing means that the individual departs the marginalized outside group and enters the mainstream. The second process is blurring, which is a group phenomenon brought about by situations in which the boundary demarcating "us" and "them" becomes less clear, and thus calls into question where people are located. The third is boundary shifting. Here, as the term implies, the boundary moves rather than individuals moving.

It is worth summarizing Zolberg and Woon (1999, 8–9) at length to understand these three processes and their implications for evolving relationships between immigrants and the host society:

1. Individual *boundary crossing* refers to a process in which the receiving society's basic structures remain unchanged. Individuals who leave their group of origin to become a part of the receiving society do so by exhibiting a willingness to give up aspects of their cultural background, which can include giving up their native language, religion, and so forth, adopting in their place the dominant cultural features of the society they are entering. This process is often referred to as acculturation. Such individual transformations leave untouched the existing boundaries between groups, which remain fixed and offer a clear distinction between in-group and out-group members.

2. In contrast, *boundary blurring* refers to a process that involves change at the structural, and not simply the individual, level. This constitutes a mode of inclusion that permits and even valorizes difference. Individuals are not expected to abandon entirely their past sociocultural memberships but are permitted to create overlapping and hyphenated identities, adapting aspects of personal identity derived from the receiving society while preserving aspects of their previous identities. Zolberg and Woon suggest that this amounts to "the taming or domestication of

what was once seen as 'alien' differences" (1999, 8). Insofar as this occurs, changes may transpire that do have consequences for the receiving society, such as moving from monolingualism to bilingualism, legitimating dual citizenship, and facilitating religious pluralism.

3. Finally, *boundary shifting* refers to a process that leads to the reconstitution of what it means to be a member of the group due to a relocating of the original boundaries. This particular process is considered to have potentially far-reaching structural impacts, for in contrast to boundary blurring, involved here are changes at the structural, but not the individual level. The example they use to describe this process is one that pits pro-immigration activists against their anti-immigration counterparts. The former are depicted as calling for a redrawing of boundaries in order to bring immigrants within them, while the latter are seen as promoting a further constriction of existing boundaries in order to exclude immigrants.

Alba and Nee accept this model, as well as Zolberg and Woon's claim that "Boundary shifting can occur only after substantial boundary crossing and boundary blurring have taken place" (1999, 9). Their empirical focus for the post-1965 immigrants is on boundary blurring, which they consider to be distinctly characteristic of the contemporary second generation, for they have entered a society more receptive to difference than in the past. In contrast, boundary shifting is little discussed.

Boundary crossing is perceived as having been far more characteristic of immigrants and their children during the last great migratory wave to the United States, and as being less common today. Alba and Nee cite as an example the attempts made in the past to make physical changes by resorting to cosmetic surgery in order to eliminate what was seen as a distinctly ethnic look. As a case in point, they refer to the popularity among Jews of "nose jobs." Another common form of boundary crossing occurred when individuals shed their ethnic-sounding names for WASP substitutes. While this was commonplace among movie stars and entertainers, it was not limited to this group.

Such boundary crossing was a likely option for Jews in an earlier era when they were seeking to assimilate in a context characterized by a "bright boundary"—in other words, a sharp ethnic boundary as distinguished from a blurred one. However, there is evidence to indicate that the bright boundary has in recent decades given way to boundary blurring, which leads to a situation in which ethnic distinctions come to play a less significant role in shaping inter-group relations. The form of assimilation resulting from blurring differs from that characteristic of cross-ing. In the latter, the conversion-like move across boundaries produces a radical disjuncture between people's past identities and their new identities. By contrast, blurring occurs when the mainstream's boundary is sufficiently porous to admit aspects of the minority group's culture. In other words, boun-dary blurring is a two-way, rather than a one-way pro-cess. The sort of assimilation made possible by boundary blurring can lead to the maintenance of a meaningful and substantive minority-group identity, something that can be more substantive than the thin-ner version of ethnic identity maintenance depicted in Gans's symbolic ethnicity and Waters's "ethnic options" thesis. A two-way process results in hyphen-ated or hybrid identities.

The Transnational Perspective

Transnationalism entered the lexicon of immigration studies in the 1990s, over a century after assimilation had begun to be used extensively. It was promoted by a number of principal advocates and embraced by many others, but it also confronted skeptics and crit-ics. The result is that the concept has undergone sub-stantial revision since its earliest formulation. Actually, transnational migration is but one way the term has been used in recent years. Thus, one can readily find publications referring to the transnation-alist capitalist class, transnational financial flows, transnational nongovernmental organizations, trans-national social movements, and transnational terrorist and criminal networks. The list could go on.

Those scholars who initially embraced the idea of transnational immigration did so because of a convic-tion that it was necessary to capture the distinctive and characteristic features of the new immigrant commun-ities that have developed in the advanced industrial nations. One of the realities of the contemporary world is that it is far easier for immigrants to maintain contact with their country of origin than was the case in earlier periods, due to improved communication and transportation technologies. Whereas a century ago, immigrants had to rely on letters to maintain con-tacts with friends and family left behind, today it is possible for many to be in contact on a routine basis due to the availability of the Internet, but in particular as a result of the telephone, especially since the advent of cheap phone cards. Likewise, improvements in travel technologies have made movement back and forth between place of origin and point of destination considerably easier. While immigrants in an earlier era had to rely on arduous journeys by steamship and train, today's immigrants make extensive use of air travel. Newcomers to the United States once arrived at Ellis Island by ship. Today, they land at JFK International Airport.

The net result, according to those who have studied transnational practices, is that a unique social field is often created that transcends political bounda-ries, a social space in which patterns of interaction arise that link the immigrants to those who stay behind. The result is that immigrants are more likely to preserve aspects of their previous ethnic or national identities than otherwise might have been the case, while at the same time those who have remained in the homeland are influenced by their émigré counter-parts who bring back with them new ideas and ways of living from their new country. The core group that makes such a field possible is the individuals who move back and forth between two localities with a certain regularity, living in effect with one foot in both places. These individuals are typically bilingual and have economic and/or political stakes in both the homeland and the destination country.

During the past two decades, a considerable body of research has been conducted on transnational immigration. On the basis of that work, a number of general conclusions can be drawn. First, contrary to the earliest characterizations of transnationalism, it is not a new phenomenon. Indeed, there is evidence that immigrants in the last great wave of immigration were prepared to move back and forth between sending and receiving counties. That being said, the technological changes that have occurred make transnationalism possible for greater numbers today than in the past. However, there is a need to avoid technological determinism, which presumes that the existence of the Internet, telephones, and jet airplanes means that large numbers of immigrants will attempt to maintain sustained and frequent contact with the homeland. As it turns out, the actual number of people who can be defined as transnational in this sense—the people who routinely live in two worlds—is relatively small. Barkan (2004) has described as "translocalism" the more attenuated relationship to the homeland that characterizes the majority of newcomers. While it is true that most immigrants are not transnationals, this does not necessarily mean that they do not have a larger impact both on the ethnic community in the United States and in the homeland community.

Within this context, what is the relationship between transnationalism and assimilation? The earliest formulations of transnationalism viewed the two as contrasting, antithetical modes of incorporation, with transnationalism being an alternative to assimilation. On the other hand, there have been those who have argued that transnationalism has actually been a far more limited phenomenon than many assumed was the case; and as such it did little not only to challenge, but also in any significant way to impact assimilation. Both of these positions have progressively given way to a view that sees the two not as mutually exclusive, but rather as interconnected. The call has been to overcome what is increasingly viewed as a false dichotomy.

The key, but generally unstated, point is that transnationalism is not to be conceived as a mode of incorporation akin to assimilation. Rather, as Alejandro Portes, one of the key proponents of transnationalism, puts it, "immigrant transnationalism is significant in that it can alter, in various ways, the process of integration to the host society of both first-generation immigrants and their offspring" (2001, 188). In other words, an individual's assimilation and transnational involvements can occur simultaneously; and since neither constitutes a uniform process as they play out in tandem, a number of different outcomes are

possible. It does need to be reemphasized here that assimilation and transnationalism ought not to be construed as competing alternatives, for while assimilation refers to a mode of incorporation into a receiving society, transnationalism alludes to a distinct dualism, an individual's or group's give-and-take relationship between the homeland and the settlement society in one or more arenas of their social life: familial, religious, economic, political, cultural, and so forth.

A final question about the relationship between assimilation and transnationalism needs to be addressed: is transnationalism a phenomenon limited to the first generation? Will the children and grandchildren of immigrants be as invested in transnationalism as their parents were? We can only speculate about what the future holds, but research that has recently begun on the second generation suggests that with generational succession, we can expect a decline in transnational practices. However, transnationalism can continue to be salient as long as new immigrants continue to arrive in the receiving society. The continuing interest of some groups in homeland politics, such as Jews as a paradigmatic example, and including such contemporary examples as Kurds, Taiwanese, Tibetans, Bosnians, and Macedonians, is an indication that transnationalism may prove to be durable.

Conclusion

Though there was much that the earliest, canonical formulation of assimilation got right, it also had various shortcomings. The three developments discussed herein—segmented or downward assimilation, boundaries and the mainstream, and transnationalism—ought to be seen as efforts aimed at overcoming some of those shortcomings, the first two being intended as efforts to revise from within the theoretical tradition, while the third has been conceived as offering a complementary approach from the outside. This survey of the historical development of assimilation theory from the late nineteenth to the early twenty-first centuries is intended to offer evidence that Nathan Glazer (1993, 123) was right when he wrote that "if properly understood, assimilation is still the most powerful force affecting the ethnic and racial elements of the United States."

Bibliography

Alba, Richard. 1990. *Ethnic Identity: The Transformation of White America.* New Haven, CT: Yale University Press.

Alba, Richard, and Victor Nee. 2003. *Remaking the American Mainstream: Assimilation and Contemporary Immigration.* Cambridge, MA: Harvard University Press.

Barkan, Elliott. 2004. "America in the Hand, Homeland in the Heart: Transnationalism and Translocal Immigrant Experiences in the American West." *Western Historical Quarterly* 35 (Autumn): 331–54.

Barkan, Elliott Robert. 1995. "Race, Religion, and Nationality in American Society: A Model of Ethnicity—from Contact to Assimilation."*Journal of American Ethnic History* 14, no. 2: 38–75.

Bodnar, John. 1985. *The Transplanted: A History of Immigration in Urban America.* Bloomington: Indiana University Press.

Gans, Herbert. 1992. "Second-Generation Decline: Scenarios for the Economic and Ethnic Futures of the Post-1965 American Immigrants."*Ethnic and Racial Studies* 15, no. 2: 173–92.

Gans, Herbert. 1999. *Making Sense of America: Sociological Analyses and Essays.* Lanham, MD: Rowman & Littlefield.

Glazer, Nathan. 1993. "Is Assimilation Dead?" *Annals of the American Academy of Political and Social Science* 530 (November): 122–36.

Glazer, Nathan, and Daniel P. Moynihan. 1963. *Beyond the Melting Pot.* Cambridge, MA: MIT Press and Harvard University Press.

Gordon, Milton. 1964. *Assimilation and American Life: The Role of Race, Religion, and National Origins.* New York: Oxford University Press.

Greeley, Andrew. 1974. *Ethnicity in the United States: A Preliminary Reconnaissance.* New York: John Wiley and Sons.

Handlin, Oscar. 1951. *The Uprooted.* Boston: Little, Brown and Company.

Kasinitz, Philip, John H. Mollenkopf, Mary Waters, and Jennifer Holdaway. 2008. *Inheriting the City: The Children of Immigrants Come of Age.* Cambridge, MA, and New York: Harvard University Press and Russell Sage Foundation.

Park, Robert E., and Ernest W. Burgess. (1921) 1969. *Introduction to the Science of Sociology.* Chicago: University of Chicago Press.

Pearlman, Joel. 2005. *Italians Then, Mexicans Now: Immigrant Origins and Second-Generation Progress, 1890–2000.* New York: Russell Sage Foundation.

Portes, Alejandro. 2001. "Introduction: The Debates and Significance of Immigrant Transnationalism." *Global Networks* 1, no. 3: 181–94.

Portes, Alejandro, and Rubén Rumbaut. 2001. *Legacies: The Story of the Immigrant Second Generation.* Berkeley: University of California Press.

Portes, Alejandro, and Min Zhou. 1993. "The New Second Generation: Segmented Assimilation and Its Variants." *Annals of the American Academy of Political and Social Science* 530 (November): 74–96.

Waldinger, Roger. 2007. "Did Manufacturing Matter? The Experience of Yesterday's Second Generation: A Reassessment." *International Migration Review* 41, no. 1: 3–39.

Warner, W. Lloyd, and Leo Srole. 1945. *The Social Systems of American Ethnic Groups.* New Haven, CT: Yale University Press.

Waters, Mary C. 1990. *Ethnic Options: Choosing Identities in America.* Berkeley: University of California Press.

Zolberg, Aristide R., and Long Litt Woon. 1999. "Why Islam is Like Spanish: Cultural Incorporation in Europe and the United States." *Politics and Society* 27, no. 1: 5–38.

Immigrant and Ethnic Experiences in Urban and Metropolitan America

Jason MacDonald

Immigration to the United States was once famously described as a movement from European farms to American cities. Indeed, for much of American history, the foreign-born and the native-born of foreign parentage displayed markedly greater tendencies than the old-stock native-born to reside in cities. Immigrants and their offspring usually comprised a disproportionately large share of the total urban population, making most American cities more ethnically diverse than the country as a whole. Moreover, some of the nation's earliest and most important cities were even founded by immigrants. Nieu Amsterdam (1625)—later renamed New York—and Philadelphia (1682) were established by Dutch and English colonists, respectively. Newcomers also played a major role in the spiraling urbanization initiated in New England by the founding of Boston in 1630.

While the characterization of urban America as a magnet for old-world—and not just European—immigrants clearly contains much truth, it would be inaccurate to suggest that cities were the preferred destination of all or even the majority of immigrants during most of American history. The emergence of urban America as the prime location of immigrant settlement and ethnic cosmopolitanism has been a gradual process. During the seventeenth and eighteenth centuries, as they headed for rural destinations, immigrants were more likely to pass through rather than settle in American coastal and inland cities. Although immigrants increasingly gravitated toward urban centers during the course of the nineteenth century, at the turn of the twentieth century, most immigrants and their offspring still resided in rural areas. It was not until the twentieth century that urban America finally became established as the nation's principal site of immigrant residence. The history of immigrant and ethnic experiences in urban and metropolitan America divides into three distinct periods: (1) the age of the native-born-dominated commercial city, which lasted from colonial times until the Civil War; (2) the age of the immigrant-dominated industrial city that emerged during the late nineteenth and early twentieth centuries; and (3) the age of the post-industrial metropolitan ethnic mosaic that began around the time of World War II. Each of these periods witnessed a transformation in urban America that brought about ever-expanding and, in comparison with rural America, increasingly unrivaled opportunities for economic advancement, social mobility, political power, and cultural expression.

The Commercial City and the Immigrant (c. 1625 to 1865)

From the founding of British North America to the eve of the American Civil War, the overwhelming majority of voluntary immigrants came from northern and western Europe. During the seventeenth century, with the exception of the Dutch and Swedish settlers, whose colonies were incorporated into Britain's American possessions by 1664, most immigrants were English and Protestant, but there were also Welsh, Scotch-Irish, Germans, French Huguenots, and Jews, as well as enslaved Africans. The eighteenth century witnessed large increases in the numbers of Protestant immigrants from Ulster and the German Palatine states, as well as in the proportion that African slaves made up of all newcomers. The geographic origins of immigrants changed little after the American Revolution, with over nine-tenths coming from the west and north of Europe during the decades preceding the Civil War. However, immigrants from Britain comprised less than one-seventh of all newcomers arriving between 1820 and 1860, while those from Germany and Ireland accounted for three-tenths and two-fifths, respectively. Moreover, the vast majority of immigrants from Ireland were now Catholic, as were a large share of those from Germany. Other significant sources of immigration at this time were Canada, France, Switzerland, Norway, China, and the Netherlands.

During the seventeenth century, Boston was the main port of entry for immigrants, but in the 1700s, it was increasingly rivaled and eventually supplanted by Philadelphia. However, both were soon overtaken by what became the quintessential immigrant gateway—New York City. By the early nineteenth century, Boston had regained some of its former prominence as an immigrant-entry port and by the 1840s, it surpassed Philadelphia, which gradually declined in importance as a port of admission; but neither could challenge the preeminent position now held by the port at the mouth of the Hudson River. Out of the more than 7 million immigrants admitted to the United States between 1830 and 1870, over 5 million, or 72 percent of the total, entered through New York City, compared with 452,000 (6 percent) through Boston, 236,000 (3 percent) through Philadelphia, and 267,000 (4 percent) through Baltimore, the other great port on the Atlantic seaboard. Following the Louisiana Purchase, the Gulf of Mexico port of New Orleans, with its 554,000 immigrant arrivals (8 percent of the national total), emerged as the country's second-largest entry point; After the Mexican-American War, San Francisco became its West Coast equivalent, accounting for 144,000 (2 percent) of all entrants.

Many of these new arrivals settled in urban areas. Compared to the native-born population, a higher proportion of the foreign-born resided in cities. In 1860, the nation's 44 leading cities contained less than one-eighth of the total population but more than one-third of the foreign-born. The cosmopolitan character of urban America was apparent early on in its

history. In the late seventeenth century, the English comprised one-fifth of Nieu Amsterdam's population, which also contained large numbers of Dutch, French, African, and Jewish inhabitants. Philadelphia contained sizable Welsh, Swiss, German, Irish, and Scotch-Irish populations. At about the same time, circa 1700, the English vastly outnumbered other European immigrants in colonial Boston and Charleston, but Africans made up one-sixth of the total population in the former and one-half in the latter. By the eve of the Civil War, the newer urban centers that had appeared in the Mississippi River Valley were rivaling the coastal cities as magnets for foreign-born migrants.

This development was facilitated by transportation and communication improvements, such as the building of the Erie Canal, which connected the Great Lakes to the Atlantic Ocean. Immigrants made up a noticeably higher proportion of the total population in Midwestern cities, such as St. Louis (60 percent) and Chicago (50 percent), than in some traditional destinations, notably Boston (36 percent), Philadelphia (29 percent), and Baltimore (25 percent). However, in 1860, the foreign-born population was still high in the two leading ports of entry, New York (48 percent) and New Orleans (38 percent), as well as in San Francisco (50 percent). New York City contained the nation's largest foreign-born population (383,000), followed by Philadelphia (169,000), Brooklyn (104,000), St. Louis (96,000), Cincinnati (73,000), New Orleans (64,000), Boston (63,000), Chicago (54,000), and Baltimore (52,000). Some immigrant groups were more likely than others to settle in urban places. Irish, German, and French newcomers, for example, were significantly more inclined than immigrants from Britain and Canada to settle in urban America. In 1860, the Irish were the largest and most urbanized immigrant group, 705,000 (43.8 percent) of whom resided in the nation's leading urban centers, followed by the 491,000 Germans (37.7 percent). In comparison, 28.3 percent (122,000) of English and 14.4 percent (35,000) of Canadian immigrants had settled in the main cities, whereas 36.7 percent (40,000) of French immigrants were in the cities.

Even though the Irish tended to be the most numerous foreign-born group in antebellum cities, including New York, Philadelphia, Boston, and New Orleans, the Germans outnumbered them in Midwestern cities located within the so-called German Triangle—the three points of which were Cincinnati, St. Louis, and Milwaukee—as well as in Chicago, Buffalo, and Baltimore. Settlement within cities also displayed some variation. Poorer immigrants tended to reside in locations close to the center of cities, or along the waterfront in ports—as was true of many of the Irish in Boston—or in outlying areas if the central city remained gentrified, such as in heavily German Milwaukee. Distinct ethnic enclaves even appeared in some cities, such as a New York City's Kleindeutschland (Little Germany) in the 1820s. Nonetheless, immigrants were generally distributed throughout the antebellum American city, and not just concentrated in one or a few neighborhoods. Ethnic residential patterns in antebellum Boston, measured with an index of dissimilarity—in which a value of 100 represents total segregation between two groups and a value of 0 represents no segregation—reveal that while segregation between the native and foreign-born populations was low, it was gradually rising. The degree of dissimilarity for native whites and Irish immigrants rose from 21 to 26 during the period 1850–1855, while native white-German immigrant segregation increased from 31 to 39. German and Irish immigrants were actually more segregated from each other than they were from native whites, the dissimilarity value for these groups rising from 36 to 45. But the highest levels of segregation were between African Americans and whites of any nativity, with values ranging from 51 to 62 in 1850. Black-white segregation had also increased by 1855, with the levels for Germans (73) and Irish (65) being higher than for native whites (51).

Immigrant neighborhoods in the commercial city were typically cramped and squalid, and the lower the immigrants were in the urban occupational hierarchy, the more cramped and squalid were the neighborhoods in which they lived. Irish neighborhoods were the most impoverished and their occupants particularly prone to the ravages of disease, such as the cholera epidemics that struck in Philadelphia, New York, and Boston in 1849. In all three cities, the mortality rate during the epidemics was much higher among the Irish, who accounted for more than two-fifths of the victims in New York City. Municipal social services were meager throughout the colonial and antebellum eras, but immigrants were disproportionately represented among the inmates of such institutions as did exist, such as almshouses, orphanages, prisons, and asylums. In 1855, two-thirds of the people in Philadelphia's Blockley Almshouse were Irish, a pattern replicated in Boston and in other antebellum cities. Although many Protestant charitable organizations appeared during the antebellum period and eventually performed a large share of the urban social work, these volunteers were frequently viewed with mistrust by immigrants, particularly Catholics, who resented the heavy dose of evangelizing that was usually served with urban relief.

Occupations and Urban Self-Employment

Immigrants entering the commercial city experienced a segmented incorporation into the American economy. Newcomers possessing money, skills, or education stepped onto the urban occupational ladder at a higher rung than those who were deficient or lacking in any or all of these attributes. Out of the two largest groups of foreign migrants to urban America during the antebellum period, Germans were more evenly distributed throughout the occupational structure than were the Irish. Germans figured prominently among the urban artisan class, in fields ranging from carpentry to brewing; on the other hand, the Irish were preponderantly in unskilled occupations, for example, stevedore and construction laborer. In antebellum Buffalo, 49 percent of German men were skilled or semiskilled workers, compared with only 17 percent of the city's Irish male population. At the same time, 68 percent of the Irish male immigrants were unskilled laborers, but only 42 percent of the German males were so identified. In Milwaukee, Philadelphia, and New York, Germans comprised between one-half and two-thirds of the skilled workforce in 1850, while, as noted, about two-thirds of Irish workers were unskilled in the cities of Boston, Milwaukee, St. Louis, and New Orleans.

Furthermore, married German women rarely worked outside the home, but Irish women frequently did, and they comprised three-fourths of all the domestic servants in New York City by the mid-1850s. Moreover, given that upward occupational mobility was possible for urban immigrants during the antebellum era, yet it was not typical, and it was definitely not as easy for immigrants to achieve as it was for native-born workers. In Newburyport, Massachusetts, 72 percent of immigrant men employed as unskilled laborers in 1850 were still engaged in the same type of work in 1860, compared with only 47 percent of native-born workmen. Significantly, only 8 percent of these immigrant laborers managed to work their way up into semiskilled occupations during this 10-year period, whereas 32 percent of native laborers accomplished the feat. However, the children of foreign-born workers fared better than their parents. Although 71 percent of the sons of immigrant laborers were engaged in unskilled work in 1850, only 8 percent were in 1860, with the proportion employed in semiskilled occupations rising from 21 percent to 88 percent. Nonetheless, almost one-fifth of the sons of native-born laborers were employed in skilled work and the same proportion in nonmanual occupations, while only 3 percent and 1 percent, respectively, of immigrant workmen's sons were so employed.

Although, as a rule, German immigrants tended to experience upward mobility more frequently than did Irish immigrants, the pattern of economic opportunity varied from city to city. In Boston, for instance, the Irish rarely achieved the status of independent entrepreneur, while in Philadelphia it was common for them to do so. During the 1850s, less than 1 percent of grocers in Boston were Irish, but more than one-fifth were in Philadelphia. That said, Germans really constituted the immigrant success story of the antebellum city, where by the 1850s they usually operated the majority of bakeries, butcher shops, confectionaries, and breweries.

Churches, Schools, and Politics

Immigrant social, cultural, and religious organizations flourished in the commercial city. Most ethnic groups established an organization for the support of newly arrived immigrants from their homeland. In New York City, such bodies as the German Society, Irish Emigrant Society, Saint George's Society, and Saint Andrew's Society, as well as offering newcomers help and advice on finding accommodation and employment, successfully lobbied for legislation to protect immigrants from being cheated and exploited upon their arrival at the port. No group was more active in setting up organizations than the Germans. Fraternal bodies, literary and artistic associations, mutual-aid societies, sports clubs, and newspapers were just a few of the institutions that multiplied in cities housing German immigrants. Philadelphia had over 50 German mutual-aid societies during the Jacksonian era. By 1850, there were on average two German-language daily newspapers published in most American major cities and as many as four in Cincinnati. The urban Irish developed similar social and cultural institutions, but they were neither as numerous nor as enduring as their German counterparts.

However, the Irish were able to match Germans in the realms of church building and participation in religious organizations. The number of Catholic churches in New York City rose from 2 to 32 between 1820 and 1865. Out of these 32 churches, 1 catered to French speakers, 8 to Germans, and 23 to mostly Irish parishioners. In 1838, John Hughes became the first Irish bishop of New York. Hughes became an archbishop in 1850 when the diocese was upgraded to an archdiocese by the pope, and Hughes' successor, an Irish American, like all subsequent holders of the post, became the first American cardinal in 1875. Objecting to the Protestant bias of the curriculum and proselytizing efforts of teachers in New York City's schools, Bishop Hughes successfully petitioned for the establishment of a public school system that was free of sectarian influences. And yet, his campaign to set up public funding of Catholic schools met with failure. By 1840, one-fifth of the city's schoolchildren were enrolled in the privately financed parochial school system developed by the Catholic Church. During the two decades prior to the Civil War, the Sisters of Mercy set up parochial schools in Pittsburgh, Philadelphia, Cincinnati, St. Louis, and San Francisco. As well as educational institutions, Irish Catholics established a whole host of charitable and social welfare agencies, including hospitals, such as Mullanphy in St. Louis (1829), Saint Vincent's in New York (1849), Saint Joseph's in Philadelphia (1849), Saint Mary's in Detroit (1854), Saint Joseph's in New Orleans (1858), and Carney in Boston (1863). The churches, schools, and hospitals established by immigrants not only provided essential social services but also helped strengthen ethnic ties. In New York City, German Catholics formed their own parishes in order to have services conducted in their own language, a concession to which the Irish-dominated hierarchy reluctantly consented.

The nation's liberal naturalization laws and active encouragement from political parties, especially the Democrats, for immigrants to naturalize and become eligible to vote, ensured that urban immigrants would play an important role in antebellum politics. In Buffalo during the 1840s, local courts commonly processed 200 applications for naturalization per week in the run-up to spring or fall elections, with virtually all of the applicants being Democrats. Voter participation varied by ethnic group, with the Irish being considerably more politically active than Germans. While about four-fifths of native-born voters regularly turned out on Election Day in Buffalo during the late 1840s and early 1850s, almost three-fourths of Irish voters did so, which was about the same as the average for the city as a whole. In contrast, less than two-thirds of Buffalo's German voters generally participated in elections during this period. Although class played some role, the two dominant determinants of political affiliation among urban immigrants were nativity and religion. Native-born Protestants as well as immigrants with shared or similar culture, such as the English, the Scotch-Irish, and German Protestants, supported the Whigs. Other immigrants and Catholics supported the Democrats. Irish Catholics were the most partisan group of voters. The Democrats lost only 2 out of 17 elections in Buffalo's Irish-Catholic First Ward during the period 1843–1853, but they lost six in the German Fourth Ward.

During the 1850s, nativity became almost as salient as religion in urban politics, due to the rise of the nativist Know-Nothing Party. In San Francisco, Catholic and Protestant Irish voters put aside their sectarian differences to unite against a local Know-Nothing movement; while in Pittsburgh, native-born voters abandoned the Whig Party after it had sought the support of local Catholic immigrants. The spoils system usually ensured that ethnic voting blocs were rewarded for their party loyalty, commonly in the form of municipal jobs. In 1855, two-fifths of New York City's policemen were immigrants, three-fourths of whom were Irish. In Buffalo, over 40 percent of the police were Irish in 1859, and Irish Democrats monopolized 45 other local government positions from which they derived $38,000 a year in salaries. Nonetheless, while the influence of immigrant elements was growing within the emerging American urban political machines, the reins of power were still held by native-born and old-stock politicians. In New York, Philadelphia, Buffalo, and Boston, immigrant candidates for office were a novelty, and prior to the 1850s, they were rarely elected to places on the boards of aldermen or city councils. In Boston and Philadelphia, Irish-Catholic voters were too consumed with resisting nativist attempts to dilute the immigrant vote through gerrymandering to even contemplate achieving dominance within the local Democratic Party, let alone the city as a whole.

The commercial city was characterized by much competition and conflict between ethnic and racial groups. Whether as instigators or victims, Irish immigrants were the group most commonly involved in manifestations of ethnic conflict during the antebellum era. They were the principal target of anti-immigrant nativist movements, as well as the main antagonists in antiblack racist movements. By contrast, German immigrants rarely became embroiled in ethnic or racial conflict during this era. Religion played a major part in antebellum ethnic tensions. In 1834, an outburst of nativist violence in Boston, directed at the Irish-Catholic population, resulted in the burning of an Ursuline convent. Ten years later, Philadelphia witnessed two major outbreaks of ethnic violence in the same year, the Kensington riots in May and the Southwark riots in July. The anti-Catholic riots that engulfed the Kensington neighborhood for three days resulted in the razing of two Catholic churches, the destruction of many immigrant homes, and 16 fatalities, while the Southwark riots left 12 people dead.

Protestant immigrants from Ulster instigated the riots, but two years of anti-Catholic tirades from the American Protestant Association, a local forerunner for the American "Know-Nothing" Party, ensured that plenty of native-born Protestants were sufficiently instilled with religious intolerance to participate in the violence. Economic competition was the main cause of the conflict between Irish immigrants and African Americans that periodically erupted in antebellum cities. Philadelphia witnessed such disturbances in 1832 and 1842, but the worst outbreak by far took place in New York City in July 1863, the infamous Draft Riots. During four days of rioting and mayhem in Manhattan, a predominantly Irish mob burned an orphanage for black children and lynched more than a dozen African Americans. More than 100 people were killed before order was finally restored by a force comprised of police, militia, and army units. Although the Conscription Act was the immediate cause of the disturbance—because it made the burden of military service fall more heavily upon those too poor to afford the purchase of an exemption from the draft—Irish rioters also used the occasion to vent long-harbored animosities toward black New Yorkers.

Immigrant Cities in the Industrial Age (c. 1865 to 1945)

Between the end of the Civil War and the beginning of World War I, urban America attracted an ever-mounting volume of immigrants, originating in an increasingly varied array of sending countries. Assuredly, immigrants continued to arrive in large numbers from the traditional sources of immigration in northern and western Europe, and the movement from Asia that started just before the Civil War gained pace after it, but southern and eastern Europe soon became the main sending region. After World War I, new immigration laws severely curtailed immigration from the Old World, allowing New World countries, particularly Canada and Mexico, to become the leading sources of foreign migration to American cities.

During the period of mass immigration, between 1870 and 1920, New York City retained its place as the preeminent port of admission for newcomers to the United States. A staggering 18.8 million immigrants (72 percent of the total) entered the country via New York during this period. In second place, Boston admitted the not-inconsiderable number of 1.6 million (6 percent), followed by Baltimore with 1.2 million (5 percent) and Philadelphia with 984,000 (4 percent). Southern and western ports declined in importance as disembarkation points for immigrants. San Francisco admitted 361,000 immigrants (1.4 percent), more in absolute numbers than during the antebellum period, but a lower proportion of the national total; while New Orleans admitted 143,000 (0.5 percent), barely more than one-fourth of the number it had before 1870.

During the period 1900–1919, more immigrants entered the United States through Galveston (67,000) than through New Orleans (55,209). Only Honolulu came close to rivaling the Atlantic seaboard ports during the first decade of the twentieth century, with over 93,000 admitted there between 1900 and 1909; but when restrictions on immigration from Asia were imposed (1904, 1907–1908, 1917), the number fell to about 42,000 for the period 1910–1919.

During the 1920s and 1930s, an increasing proportion of immigrants entered the United States by crossing the land borders with Canada and, particularly, Mexico (because many Canadians still entered by sea, through such ports as Boston and Seattle), turning cities like El Paso, Texas, into major entry points.

Immigrants arriving in the United States between the end of the Civil War and the end of World War I entered a country undergoing rapid urbanization. In 1870, just over one-fourth of the total population lived in urban areas; by 1920, more than half did. Immigrants contributed significantly to the United States' transition from a rural to an urban society. In 1920, three-fourths (75.5 percent) of the foreign-born white population resided in cities, compared with two-fifths (42.0 percent) of old-stock whites. As a rule, the larger the city was, the higher the proportion of immigrants in its population. White immigrants made up 12.5 percent of the population in cites of fewer than 25,000 inhabitants, but 28.4 percent in those over 500,000. Moreover, immigrants and their children comprised over one-third of the population in smaller cities and two-thirds in the emerging metropolises. Among the country's principal cities at the close of World War I, New York City had—at 76 percent— the highest percentage of foreign stock, that is immigrants and their children, in its population, followed by Boston (73 percent) and Chicago (72 percent). But Cleveland, Newark, Jersey City, Buffalo, Detroit, Minneapolis, San Francisco, and Rochester all had over 60 percent. Cities where those of foreign stock comprised more than one-fourth of the population included, in rank order, Philadelphia, Seattle, Pittsburgh, Portland, St. Louis, Los Angeles, Cincinnati, Denver, Baltimore, and Kansas City.

When immigration levels peaked shortly after the beginning of the twentieth century, immigrants from central, eastern, and southern Europe displayed a much greater propensity for urban residence than did their counterparts from the more traditional sources of immigration in northern and western Europe.

Although the majority of immigrants from such countries as England (76.3 percent), Germany (67.5 percent), and Sweden (63.1percent) resided in urban centers by 1920, the proportions were much higher for those from such places as Russia (88.6 percent), Poland (84.4 percent), Italy (84.4 percent), and Hungary (80.0 percent). Only the Irish achieved a level of urbanization (86.9 percent) comparable to that of the newer nationalities of immigrants, while less than half (47.2 percent) of all Norwegian newcomers lived in cities. New World immigrants also had diverse patterns of urbanization. Almost four-fifths (79.2 percent) of French-Canadian immigrants in the United States were urbanized, compared with under half (47.4 percent) of Mexicans.

The ethnic composition of American cities was radically altered by the changing origins of immigration and diverse levels of urbanization. Out of the nation's 20 largest cities in 1920, Germans had been

A street scene in New York's "Little Jerusalem" neighborhood, about 1910. (Library of Congress)

the largest foreign-born group in 15 of them in 1900 (including New York, Chicago, St. Louis, Baltimore, and San Francisco), with the Irish occupying the same position in three cities (Boston, Philadelphia, and Washington), Swedes in one (Minneapolis), and Canadians in one (Seattle). By 1920, Russians (mostly Jewish immigrants and their children) were the largest foreign-born group in five of these cities (New York, Philadelphia, Pittsburgh, Baltimore, and Washington), Poles in three (Buffalo, Cleveland, and Chicago), Italians in three (Newark, New Orleans, and San Francisco), Canadians in two (Seattle and, now, Detroit) and Mexicans in one (Los Angeles). While Swedes retained their preeminent position in Minneapolis, Germans now remained the largest foreign-born group in only four of the cities (Cincinnati, Milwaukee, and St. Louis, and Kansas City) and the Irish in one (Boston).

Ethnic residential patterns in urban America during the industrial age contrasted sharply with those of the earlier commercial city. The tendency for immigrants to reside in segregated neighborhoods became far more pronounced in the decades following the Civil War, although the pattern started to reverse itself after the turn of the twentieth century. Moreover, immigrants from central, eastern, and southern Europe experienced higher levels of residential segregation than did their counterparts from traditional sources of immigration, notably Germany, Ireland, and Britain. In 1880, the indexes of segregation from the native white population in Boston were much lower for immigrants from England (13), Ireland (15), and even Germany (31), than they were for those from Russia (54), Poland (62), and Italy (74). By 1930, the index of dissimilarity value in Boston for old-stock whites and immigrants from northern and western Europe was 24, compared with 60 for old-stock whites and foreigners from eastern and southern Europe. The pattern of ethnic residential segregation was broadly similar in Buffalo, Chicago, Cincinnati, Philadelphia, Pittsburgh, and St. Louis. During the industrial era, the immigrant ghetto became a standard feature in cities across the United States, from Little Italy in Manhattan to Chinatown in San Francisco, from Polish Downtown in Chicago to the Mexican West Side in San Antonio.

After an initial concentration in poor inner-city areas, most immigrants and their offspring dispersed to ethnic clusters located in more affluent outlying areas. A pattern of neighborhood succession emerged in which the newcomers of one ethnic group moved into the neighborhoods vacated by the members of longer established ones. Each mini-migration was a movement away from downtown poverty toward suburban prosperity. In the late nineteenth century, New York City's East European Jews were concentrated in the Lower East Side of Manhattan Island; but by the turn of the century, many had moved to the more desirable location of Harlem, and by World War II, they were increasingly abandoning Manhattan altogether and dispersing to the outlying boroughs. Just as the neighborhoods vacated by Germans were settled by East European Jews, those vacated by East European Jews were settled by African Americans, Puerto Ricans, and other newcomers to New York City.

While many immigrant neighborhoods had been crowded during the antebellum era, in the industrial city they were positively teeming with inhabitants. The development of the dumbbell tenement in New York from the late 1870s onward enabled more and more people to be crammed into less and less space. In 1890, Jacob Riis, the famous chronicler of slum conditions in Gilded Age New York, figured that a single square mile of slum housing contained 330,000 people, with more than 700 persons per acre in some parts. Tenements were ill lit and poorly ventilated, and they exposed their residents to high risks of both disease and fire due to faults in design. In cities across the United States, municipal leaders generally ignored the needs of foreign-born slum dwellers and even tolerated prostitution, gambling, and other criminal behavior in immigrant neighborhoods, with a view to confining such activities to a single geographic area of the city and protecting respectable districts.

The industrial city offered immigrants a variety of occupational opportunities, although they tended to enter the workforce at a younger age than native whites, as well as to be more heavily concentrated in lower-skilled and lower-paying jobs. In Pittsburgh, more than one-half of foreign-born white males were industrial workers in 1930, compared with under two-fifths of native-born white males. While foreign-born men were slightly underrepresented in trade, transportation, and public service jobs in the Steel City, only 7 percent worked in professional and clerical positions, compared with 21 percent of native white males. Immigrants' position in the industrial city's occupational hierarchy is best illustrated by examining the numbers employed in domestic service, generally viewed as being the least desirable field of employment due to its long hours and low pay. Less than one-tenth of Pittsburgh's foreign-born white males worked as domestic servants at the beginning of the Great Depression, compared with under one-twentieth of their native-born counterparts, but one-fourth of African Americans. The occupational distribution of the city's native-born white, foreign-born white, and African-American women was similar to that of the men, except that foreign-born women were much less likely to be engaged in paid employment—only 16 percent in 1930—than their native-born white (27 percent) or African-American (32 percent) counterparts. More than one-half of foreign-born women in the labor force worked as domestics in Pittsburgh, compared with less than one-fourth of native-born white women workers but nine-tenths of black female workers.

Whether it was a steel town like Pittsburgh or a textiles manufacturing center such as Lawrence, Massachusetts, immigrants in American cities during the industrial age occupied a position in the workforce slightly below that of native-born whites but usually significantly higher than that of African Americans. As in earlier periods, the more skills and capital an immigrant group brought with it to the American city, the more likely it was to succeed in the economic sphere. British and German immigrants, coming as they did from industrialized nations, brought expertise and skills that were highly valued in the American economy. Many Russian Jews possessed artisanal skills that enabled them to easily find a niche in the burgeoning garments industry in New York City. Italian immigrants in American cities tended to have fewer easily marketable skills than did German, British, or Jewish immigrants, but more industrial though not professional skills than those of their Slavic counterparts.

Upward occupational mobility was even less common for urban immigrants during the industrial era than it had been in the antebellum town or city. Some immigrant groups clearly did better than others in this respect, but all did better than urban blacks. In New York City, the quintessential city of opportunity during the industrial era, Italian immigrants followed the pattern set by the Irish in antebellum cities by finding employment in mostly unskilled, low-paid work, while Russian Jews emulated the German experience and mostly entered skilled occupations. Russian-Jewish immigrants enjoyed much greater upward occupational mobility than did their Italian counterparts. The proportion of Russian Jews employed in high white-collar jobs in New York rose from 5.2 percent to 15.1 percent between 1880 and 1905; while for Italians the figure barely changed at all, increasing from 2.0 percent to 2.3 percent. In 1905, two-fifths of the city's Italian immigrants workers were employed in unskilled occupations, compared with less than 2 percent of Russian Jews.

A foreign-born industrial worker rarely earned enough to support a family, so working children were essential to the economic well-being of the immigrant urban household. Immigrant wives rarely worked outside the home, while a majority of their unmarried daughters did. Moreover, the daughters of Italian, Jewish, and Slavic immigrants were far less likely to work as domestics than were their Irish or Scandinavian counterparts. Instead, unmarried women from southern and eastern Europe displayed a preference for working in urban sweatshops, factories, and canneries. Asian women, married and unmarried alike, had higher rates of participation in the urban labor force than their white counterparts. Their work patterns were also different from both the old and the new European immigrant groups. In 1870, one-half of the adult Chinese women living in San Francisco worked as prostitutes, an occupation that in New York City was less than common among Irish and East European Jewish immigrant women, and very rare among Germans and Italians. On the eve of World War II, a relatively high proportion (57 percent) of the working daughters of San Francisco's Japanese immigrants were employed in domestic service, while in Seattle an unusually large number of Japanese immigrants' wives, almost two-fifths of those in gainful employment, worked as managers or sales staff in retail businesses.

While occupational advancement varied from group to group, in general it was rare, mostly involved workers moving from unskilled up to semiskilled jobs rather than into skilled or professional employment, and was an essentially intergenerational phenomenon. In Steelton, Pennsylvania, in the early years of the twentieth century, the sons of German and Irish immigrants were equally or more likely to improve upon the occupational status of their fathers as were the sons of native-born whites. On the other hand, the sons of Slavic and Italian immigrants experienced markedly lower rates of intergenerational mobility than did both groups, although higher ones than local blacks. The patterns were similar for immigrant women. During the 1900s and 1910s, there was an intergenerational shift among Italian-American women in New York City away from blue-collar factory work and toward white-collar clerical jobs.

A plethora of immigrant institutions and organizations emerged designed to ease the newcomer's adaptation to life in the American industrial city. Mutual-aid societies, providing such services as insurance, sick benefits, and interest-free loans, were popular among immigrant groups. In New York City, thousands of such bodies, known as *landsmanshaftn*, were founded by Jewish immigrants from Eastern Europe between 1880 and 1920. About one-half of the two million Jewish immigrants entering New York during this period belonged to such a body.

The Catholic Church provided essential support to Polish, Italian, and other immigrants from central and southern Europe, as it had done to Irish and German newcomers in the antebellum era. Yet, its domination by Irish clergyman and opposition to the creation of parishes based on ethnicity gave rise to much animosity and sometimes led to wholesale desertions, as in the case of disgruntled Polish parishioners in numerous American cities who set up their own splinter church. Southern Italians were less reliant upon and more mistrustful of the church than were other Catholic immigrants, preferring instead to mediate with the unfamiliar milieu of urban America through a *padrone*, an individual who, for a fee,

helped immigrants find lodgings and employment. Regardless of the form they took, ethnic organizations and informal institutions generally eased immigrant incorporation into the economy and promoted adaptation to the new cultural environment, thereby promoting the process of assimilation. Those ethnic bodies that survived until the Great Depression mostly collapsed under the strain of the economic crisis and were replaced by New Deal agencies as the first recourse of ethnic urbanites in time of need.

The age of the industrial city coincided with that of the urban political boss, a leader whose power base invariably was inner-city immigrant and ethnic voters. In the heyday of machine politics, political parties depended upon ward bosses, who frequently belonged to the same ethnic group as the majority population in their electoral unit, to ensure that immigrants voted en masse for the official candidate. Although the political machines that dominated American cities during the industrial era bore many similarities to their antebellum predecessors, a major new feature of municipal politics after the Civil War was that immigrants and ethnics not only exerted influence as voters, but also rose to positions of power within the political party and city government alike. No group was more successful at turning disciplined voting into political power than the Irish. In early-twentieth-century San Francisco, for instance, 70 percent of Irish men were registered to vote, which equaled the native-born rate, compared with only 37 percent of other foreign-born men. Through their control of the local Democratic Party, Irish politicians established machines that dominated such cities as New York, San Francisco, Pittsburgh, and Chicago. In New York City, Tammany Hall, the Democratic machine that controlled the city from the 1870s to the 1930s, was led by a string of Irish and Irish-American bosses: "Honest John" Kelly, Richard Croker, Charles Murphy, and George Olvaney.

Two prominent cities that failed to produce all-powerful Irish-Democrat machines were Philadelphia, where a Yankee Republican machine ruled, and Boston, where Irish-Democrat factions continually battled among themselves for power. Nonetheless, Boston still managed to elect a string of Irish and Irish-American mayors from the mid-1880s onward, including John F. Fitzgerald, the grandfather of a future president of the United States, John F. Kennedy. The success of the machine rested on the loyalty of its constituents, and that loyalty was guaranteed by the provision of jobs and services. Between 1870 and 1900, the proportion of public employees in the nation's 14 largest cities that were of Irish parentage rose from 11 percent to 30 percent, whereas the overall size of the Irish-parentage workforce remained stable at 20 percent. At first, Irish politicians attempted to minimize the electoral power of the newly arriving Italian and Jewish immigrants. However, by the Progressive Era, the latter groups had themselves come to appreciate the potentialities of ethnic-bloc voting, and Irish politicians, to maintain their grip on power, were forced to distribute the spoils of victory beyond their own ethnic group.

Irish machines were essentially a conservative force in urban politics. They did not challenge the rectitude of the spoils system; they just competed with Yankee-dominated machines for control of it. Consequently, Irish machines sided against radical and anti-capitalist movements, such as the coalitions of left-wing immigrants, mostly Germans but also many Irish, who tried unsuccessfully to elect labor candidates as mayor in cities such as New York and Chicago during the Gilded Age. The Great Depression severely weakened the influence of the Irish-Democrat machines in numerous cities, enabling other groups to supplant the Irish in power. In New York City, for example, Fiorello La Guardia, a Republican Party reform candidate of mixed Italian and Jewish ancestry, used his support among Italian, Jewish, and Polish voters to win election as mayor and bring Tammany's dominance of municipal government to an end.

Ethnic conflict was prevalent in the industrial city. Tensions between white immigrant groups usually originated in competition for housing, jobs, and political power. This is the form that ethnic relations took in New York City between the Irish and the newer immigrant groups, such as East European Jews and Italians, who posed a challenge to Irish dominance of municipal government. Usually taking the form of an electoral contest or war of words, such tensions rarely erupted into the violence that characterized ethnic relations in the antebellum city or race relations in the industrial era. Sometimes, however, external events and old-world animosities did spark violent conflict between ethnic groups, as happened between Jews and both Germans and Italians in New York City during the 1930s. The rise of Italian fascism and German Nazism in Europe ignited ethnic tensions in urban America, because Jewish immigrants feared that German and Italian immigrants sympathized with the anti-Semitic policies adopted by the governments of their homelands.

Nativism had also reared its ugly head in urban America during the industrial era, most notably in the form of the anti-immigrant, anti-Catholic, and anti-Semitic Ku Klux Klan, which enrolled tens of thousands of members in many of the largest American cities during the 1920s. While no immigrant group experienced the same levels of violence leveled at urban African Americans during the industrial era—in the form of lynchings and race riots, the latter increasingly occurring in northern as well as southern cities—Asians, and particularly the Chinese, came close. During the late nineteenth century, Chinese neighborhoods in many western cities were overrun by rampaging white mobs, not infrequently led by, or mostly composed of, Irish immigrants. Major anti-Chinese disturbances occurred in Los Angeles (1871), San Francisco (1878), Denver (1880), and Rock Springs (1885); the latter left 25 Chinese dead and another 15 wounded, plus $150,000 worth of destruction to property. Mass expulsions of Asian immigrants were also a common occurrence in the urban West during the industrial era.

The Postindustrial Metropolitan Mosaic (c. 1945 to Present)

After World War II, and particularly from the late 1960s onward, immigrants to urban America came from an increasingly diverse range of sending regions. During the 1940s, Europeans made up more than half of the immigrants entering the United States; in 2008, they accounted for only 1 in 10. While the share of immigrants coming from the Americas increased steadily during this period, from 38 percent to 45 percent, the most marked increases were those for Africa

(1 percent to 9 percent) and, especially, Asia (4 percent to 34 percent). Overall, Europeans comprised 1 in 5 of the immigrants entering the United States between 1940 and 2008, while Africans made up 1 in 33, Asians nearly 1 in 3, and North and South Americans almost 1 in 2. By the beginning of the twenty-first century, Mexico, Cuba, the Dominican Republic, and the Philippines, India, and China, had replaced countries in southern and eastern Europe as the major sources of immigration, just as the latter had displaced Germany, Ireland, and Great Britain at the turn of the twentieth century.

The proportion of immigrants entering the United States via seaports declined further after 1940, with border cities, such as El Paso and San Diego, continuing to grow in importance as points of entry. However, during the late twentieth century, air travel emerged as the dominant form of immigrant transportation. Consequently, immigrants increasingly flew directly to their final destination in the United States. This development produced a far more even distribution of newcomers arriving through the main entry points, but it also facilitated the increasing geographic concentration of the foreign-born population. In 2008, more than half of all recent arrivals resided in just 10 cities. Although New York remained the most favored destination of immigrants, attracting 16.3 percent of the total, compared with earlier periods its share was not so glaringly different to that of its main competitors, which were now Los Angeles (8.7 percent) and Miami (7.9 percent). Other top destinations included Washington (3.9 percent), Chicago (3.6 percent), San Francisco (3.3 percent), Houston (2.8 percent), Dallas–Fort Worth (2.4 percent), Boston (2.2 percent), and Atlanta (2.0 percent). At the beginning of the twenty-first century, as in earlier periods, immigrants were more likely than the native-born population to live in cities. In 2000, while 80.9 percent of the total population and 79.3 percent of the native-born population resided in metropolitan areas, 94.9 percent of the foreign-born did.

Moreover, while the native-born were evenly distributed among cities of varying sizes, immigrants were less likely than the native-born to live in smaller cities and much more likely to live in large ones. Just over half (51.7 percent) of the native-born lived in cities with populations of over one million, compared to over three-fourths (78.2 percent) of immigrants. The cities with the largest immigrant populations were Los Angeles (4.7 million), New York (4.7 million), San Francisco (2.0 million), Miami (1.6 million) and Chicago (1.1 million). Although the proportion of the population that was foreign-born declined in most cities during the early and middle parts of the twentieth century, the last three decades of it witnessed a marked increase. In New York, the figure rose from 15.2 percent in 1970 to 22.8 percent in 2000; in Los Angeles from 11.3 percent to 29.6 percent; and in San Francisco from 11.2 percent to 28.3 percent. By 2000, immigrants also made up more than 1 in 10 of the population in Chicago, Washington, Boston, and Dallas; but in Philadelphia and Detroit, the foreign-born comprised the same share of the population as they had 30 years earlier, 5 percent and 7 percent, respectively.

As in earlier periods, some immigrant groups displayed a greater preference than others for urban residence. However, at the beginning of the twenty-first century the differences were negligible. In 2002, Mexicans and Filipinos were the least urbanized of the major immigrant groups, but the proportions of each living in metropolitan areas were still 91 percent and 92 percent, respectively. By this time, the question of which immigrants most preferred to live in cities was much less relevant than the one concerning which immigrants preferred which cities, because over 95 percent of immigrants settled in urban areas. Mexicans, Salvadorans, Filipinos, and Koreans displayed a preference for Los Angeles; Chinese, Dominican, and eastern European immigrants gravitated to New York, while Asian Indians preferred San Jose and Cubans settled overwhelmingly in Miami. As these preferences suggest, propinquity to place of origin has played a major role in determining settlement patterns, but so did the existence of established ethnic communities. The large Polish-American presence in the urban Midwest, for instance, acted as a strong magnet for a new wave of immigrants from Poland after the end of the Cold War.

These changes in immigration and settlement patterns radically altered the ethnic landscape of urban

America. Like before, immigrants in the postindustrial era tended to congregate in the inner cities. In 2000, foreign-born residents of metropolitan areas were significantly more likely than the native-born to live in the central city. Forty-five percent of the foreign-born lived in central cities, compared with just 27 percent of natives. Moreover, in cities across the United States, European immigrant groups were displaced from their positions as the largest foreign-born populations by newcomers from Latin America and Asia. By 2003, Mexicans were the largest immigrant group in Houston, where they comprised 38 percent of the foreign-born population, Los Angeles (37 percent), and Chicago (25 percent). The largest immigrant populations in New York were Dominicans (11 percent), Chinese (9 percent), Guyanese (7 percent), Jamaicans (5 percent, and Ecuadorians (5 percent). In Miami, Cubans made up a whopping 46 percent of the city's foreign-born, followed by Haitians (9 percent) and Nicaraguans (9 percent).

As with prior patterns, immigrant incorporation into the urban economy during the postindustrial era was segmented, with the better educated and more highly skilled generally entering into middle-class occupations, while those with less human and social capital were mostly confined to manual jobs that offered little hope of advancement. At the turn of the twenty-first century, more than two-thirds of Indian immigrants possessed college degrees, compared with fewer than 1 in 20 Mexican immigrants. The median household income of Indian immigrants, at $70,000 a year, was way above the national average and more than double that of Mexican immigrants; while the poverty rates for Mexicans, at 29 percent, was triple that of Indians. A large minority of Filipino, Korean, and Chinese immigrants also possessed college degrees that facilitated their entry into middle-class jobs, while the pattern of incorporation for the vast majority of Salvadoran, Dominican, and other Latin American immigrants was similar to that of Mexicans.

Intergenerational mobility among urban ethnic groups was complex in the industrial era, with the grandchildren of immigrants having lower poverty rates and higher home ownership rates than

immigrants and their children, but also being less likely to have college degrees than the first and second generations. Once again, patterns varied from group to group. In early-twenty-first century San Diego, 2 out of 5 Mexican-American youths failed to graduate from high school, compared with 1 in 20 Chinese Americans. The unemployment rates among young adults from both groups were 7 percent and 3 percent, respectively. Moreover, one-fifth of Mexican-American young men had been to prison.

Compared with earlier periods, ethnic conflict was generally not as common or virulent as in the postindustrial city, but ethnic tensions were ever present and occasionally erupted into violence. In the wake of the black civil rights movement and federal initiatives to desegregate schools and residential neighborhoods, white ethnics launched campaigns to resist integration. In Canarsie, a lower-middle-class district of Brooklyn inhabited mostly by the children and grandchildren of Italian and Jewish immigrants, the residents boycotted the public schools in 1972 in protest over the busing in of African-American pupils. In South Boston, it was mostly Irish Americans who spearheaded the sometimes violent resistance to busing.

In cities across the United States, white ethnics seemed as determined to maintain the racial composition of their neighborhoods as were diehard segregationists in the South. In cities experiencing a large influx of Latino immigrants, ethnic tensions took a different form. After Cuban immigration during the 1960s and 1970s had turned Miami into a predominantly Hispanic city, Dade County passed an Anti-Bilingual Ordinance, requiring all official business to be conducted solely in English, which was not overturned until 1993. In 1994, anti-Latino sentiment was behind the passage of California's Proposition 187, which denied undocumented immigrants access to public services. While Latinos voted overwhelmingly against the proposal, non-Latinos voted overwhelmingly for it. A blend of nativist and racist sentiments also surfaced in West Coast urban areas experiencing heavy influxes of Asian immigrants. During the 1980s, whites in Monterey Park, an affluent suburban municipality in Greater Los Angeles, launched an assault upon the economic, cultural, and political influence of prosperous Chinese immigrants whose numbers had increased rapidly in the previous two decades. Far more explosive, however, were relations between Korean immigrants and African Americans during the 1980s and 1990s in cities as distant from each other as New York, Chicago, and Los Angeles. In New York City, African Americans, complaining of mistreatment and exploitation, staged dozens of boycotts of Korean-owned stores during the 1980s. During the Los Angeles riots of 1992, Korean merchants organized armed vigilante groups to protect their stores, which had become had a prime target of rioters and looters in the predominantly black and Latino neighborhoods where the disturbances occurred.

Conclusion

While immigration to the United States did at some points in time resemble a movement from the farms of the Old World to the cities of the New World, it increasingly became a movement from cities in one part of the world to those in the United States, as well as one from part of the New World to another. Over the course of time, immigrants and their offspring witnessed great changes in the opportunities American cities offered for economic advancement, social mobility, political power, and cultural expression. During the age of the commercial city, lasting from colonial times to the Civil War, urban immigrants generally experienced less promising economic prospects than their rural counterparts and made only slow progress in attaining social mobility and political influence.

Moreover, displays of cultural distinctiveness regularly invited outbursts of intolerance and even violence from the native-born population. Between 1865 and 1945, the industrial city vastly expanded the occupational opportunities available to immigrants and ethnic minorities, as well as improving their prospects of social mobility. During this period, coalitions of immigrant and ethnic voters also emerged as the dominant force in municipal politics in most parts of the United States. Residential and occupational concentration facilitated the maintenance of ethnic ties and culture for most groups, but

immigrants and their children in industrial cities increasingly encountered organized and government-sanctioned attempts at forced Americanization. After World War II, immigrants and ethnic minorities residing in the nation's postindustrial metropolitan centers enjoyed unparalleled opportunities for economic advancement, social mobility, political power, and especially cultural expression.

However, the economic benefits of residing in the postindustrial city were experienced more unevenly than in the age of the industrial city, with immigrants from developed countries, or those from developing countries who possessed high levels of education, finding it much easier to enter into the urban middle class. Many immigrants and their children, particularly those from Latin America, failed to achieve any social mobility and became part of a permanent urban underclass. Political power, mirroring the residential patterns of the white ethnic population, rapidly shifted away from urban centers to the suburbs, leaving African Americans and the more impoverished elements of recently arrived immigrant groups to compete with each other for control of inner-city politics. Despite the homogenization of urban culture that resulted from the growth of mass marketing and the national media, immigrants in the postindustrial city enjoyed greater freedom to express their cultural distinctiveness than at any previous time in American history. Forced Americanization fell out of vogue after World War II. By the turn of the twenty-first century, multiculturalism had become the new watchword of most private and official agencies dealing with urban immigrants and ethnic minorities, with policy and funding actually being directed toward encouraging the development and survival rather than the elimination of ethnic cultures.

Bibliography
Bayor, Ronald H. 1988. *Neighbors in Conflict: The Irish, Germans, Jews, and Italians of New York City, 1929–1941.* 2nd ed. Urbana: University of Illinois, Press.
Bodnar, John. 1985. *The Transplanted: A History of Immigrants in Urban America.* Bloomington: Indiana University Press.

Chen, Yong. 2000. *Chinese San Francisco, 1850–1943: A Trans-Pacific Community.* Stanford, CA: Stanford University Press.

Conzen, Kathleen Neils. 1976. *Immigrant Milwaukee, 1836–1860: Accommodation and Community in a Frontier City.* Cambridge, MA: Harvard University Press.

García, María Cristina. 1996. *Havana USA: Cuban Exiles and Cuban Americans in South Florida, 1959–1994.* Berkeley: University of California Press.

Gerber, David A. 1989. *The Making of an American Pluralism: Buffalo, New York, 1825–60.* Urbana: University of Illinois Press.

Handlin, Oscar. 1941. *Boston's Immigrants, 1790–1865: A Study in Acculturation.* Cambridge, MA: Harvard University Press.

Kessner, Thomas. 1977. *The Golden Door: Italian and Jewish Immigrant Mobility in New York City, 1880–1915.* New York: Oxford University Press.

Lieberson, Stanley. 1963. *Ethnic Patterns in American Cities.* Glencoe, IL: Free Press.

Zunz, Olivier. 1982. *The Changing Face of Inequality: Urbanization, Industrial Development, and Immigrants in Detroit, 1880–1920.* Chicago: University of Chicago Press.

Immigration and Settlement Patterns

Samantha Friedman, Emily Rosenbaum, and Katherine L. Moloney

The United States has always been a nation of immigrants. The late nineteenth and early twentieth centuries were a time when the country witnessed significant levels of immigration. Between 1860 and 1920, the share of the American population that was born abroad hovered between 13 and 15 percent. With the passage of several pieces of restrictive immigration legislation in the early 1900s (until 1929), there was a significant period of decline in the influx of immigrants. Not until the mid-1960s, when the restrictive caps on immigration were removed, did immigration to the United States increase again. Since 1990, the levels of immigration have been exceeding those witnessed in the earlier period (For example, 1900–1909 admissions, 8.2 million; 1990–1999 admissions, 9.78 million; and 2000–2009 admissions, 10.3 million. Peak years: 1907, 1.28 million; 1990, 1.54 million; 1991, 1.83 million; and 2006, 1.27 million.) According to the U.S. Census Bureau, in 2008, the foreign-born population comprised 12.5 percent of the American population, up from 11.1 percent in 2000.

With immigration has come diversity. The earliest waves of immigration disproportionately came from northern and western Europe. However, from 1880 until 1920, immigrant origins changed. Immigration from southern and eastern Europe (as well as from China and Japan) increased, bringing much diversity to the United States in the way of language, religion, and culture. A more substantial shift in origins has been witnessed in recent years. Since the 1990s, the large majority of immigrants are coming from Latin America and Asia. In 2008, just over 53 percent of immigrants came from Latin America and 27.3 percent came from Asia. Immigrants from Europe comprised only 13.1 percent of the foreign-born population.

This chapter explores the settlement patterns of immigrants to the United States. Residential patterns are reflective of the way groups are incorporated into the American stratification system. Where people live is inextricably linked to their current and future economic and social well-being. As such, it is important to document immigrant settlement patterns in order to gauge immigrants' level of integration into American society and their position in the stratification system. This chapter focuses on several layers of settlement from both historical and contemporary perspectives. At a more macro level, immigrant settlement at the regional, state, and metropolitan levels is documented. While such settlement has typically clustered in particular areas within the United States, recently there has been a shift away from the more traditional gateways. Within metropolitan areas, have immigrants been clustering with co-ethnics, or have they been integrating into the urban landscape? Finally, the chapter zooms down to a more micro level, specifically to the neighborhoods in which immigrants reside. What are their neighborhoods like? Do they afford immigrants access to high-quality amenities, such as upscale shopping, good schools, access to transportation, and job opportunities? Do immigrants experience upward geographical mobility into such neighborhoods once they have been in the United States for a while?

Contemporary Theories on Immigrant Residential Attainment

Derived from general assimilation theory, spatial assimilation theory is one of the main models explaining variation in the residential patterns of immigrant households, especially relative to native-born households. Spatial assimilation theory, developed by Douglas Massey, draws on the basic tenets of general assimilation theory and seeks to specifically characterize the incorporation of immigrants into geographic space, focusing on how residential mobility is associated with social mobility more generally. In other words, the theory seeks to characterize social stratification as it is reflected in geographic space.

Spatial assimilation theory derives from the observation, rooted in the experiences of European immigrants around the turn of the twentieth century, that immigrants settle together among their co-ethnics in older, inner-city neighborhoods. New immigrants tend to be physically segregated from native-born households and live in low-quality, inexpensive housing located in deteriorating neighborhoods that serve as filters for successive waves of immigrants. It is thought that such ethnic neighborhoods develop out of processes that sustain migration streams—social networks of family, friends, and co-ethnics who share information about housing and job opportunities and provide assistance in transitioning to life in the host society. As such, these processes cause immigrants to be residentially segregated from native-born households.

In contrast, at work on the individual level are processes of social mobility and acculturation. As members of ethnic groups acquire advanced levels of education, higher-status occupations, greater levels of English proficiency, and more income, they seek to translate these gains into better residential circumstances. The neighborhoods in which they desire to live tend to be inhabited by fewer members of their co-ethnic groups and more by members of the majority group. As such, over time and across generations, immigrants are expected to become less segregated from majority group members than when they initially arrived in the United States.

The spatial assimilation model relies on the tenets of traditional residential mobility theory to conceptualize the process of spatial mobility. In general, the sorting of households across housing units and neighborhoods is a function of their residential needs and preferences and their economic ability to satisfy those needs and preferences. Demographic transitions through the life course, such as marriage and childbearing, constitute one of the main sets of factors that shape housing needs and preferences. The ability of a household to satisfy its needs and to realize its residential preferences, however, depends upon the resources it has available.

Households with higher levels of income and more access to wealth are likely to enjoy the most freedom in choosing where to live and are particularly likely to occupy the highest-quality housing and neighborhoods. Those with greater levels of education and high levels of English proficiency also have more choices about where to live and are better equipped to purchase the full range of amenities that may comprise high-quality housing (a unit in sound condition, in a safe neighborhood, and with sufficient space for the household). Those with lower levels of English proficiency, less income, and less education are arguably the most constrained in their options, particularly those receiving public assistance. Not only do these households lack the resources to purchase a home, but landlords are also generally more hesitant to rent to them because of concerns about behavior and the ability to pay rent, thereby increasing the chance that they live in low-quality housing and neighborhoods.

While the spatial assimilation model would predict an overall disadvantage to foreign-born households because of limitations in resources, it also predicts that these limitations will diminish over time and generation in the course of acculturation and social and economic mobility. Specifically the model asserts two kinds of outcomes. First, that housing and neighborhood conditions of later generations should be superior to those experienced by newly-arrived immigrants. Second, because economic-status differences are responsible for variation in housing and neighborhood quality, reductions in such differences should reduce if not eliminate differences in housing and neighborhood quality among immigrants, and between immigrants and native-born whites.

A large body of research suggests that the spatial assimilation model may not completely explain away differences in the housing and neighborhood quality that exist between foreign- and native-born households. In other words, disadvantages in housing and neighborhood location experienced by blacks, and to a lesser extent Hispanics, have been found to persist with controls for characteristics central to the spatial assimilation model, including income and education. This weakness has given rise to a second model—the place stratification model—that is better equipped to account for persistent inequalities by race and ethnicity.

The place stratification model highlights the role that structural factors play in causing there to be persistent racial and ethnic inequalities in the locational attainment of individuals in the metropolis. The model takes as a starting point the hierarchical ordering of places and social groups and maintains that the spatial hierarchy that exists in the residential patterns of whites and minorities reflects the inequality in their social positions in society. More advantaged groups, such as whites, use their power to create social and spatial distance from less advantaged groups, like blacks and Hispanics. Power is manifested in the form of discriminatory acts either by individuals or the institutions over which they have control. Such acts include the adverse treatment of minority home-seekers by realtors and landlords, opposition to minority in-movement by individuals and neighborhood associations, predatory lending practices, and the redlining of minority communities by financial institutions. Taken together, these actions have helped to create and maintain a dual housing market, which constrains minorities to live in neighborhoods that are more ethnically heterogeneous, less affluent, and of lower quality than whites. The model argues that even after taking into account individual-level characteristics related to acculturation, socioeconomic status, and life-cycle stage, significant disadvantages in residential outcomes will remain for minorities, relative to whites.

The fact that race, particularly black race, remains a powerful predictor of integration of immigrants has given rise to an alternative, general theory of immigrant integration—segmented assimilation theory (also discussed in "Integration and Assimilation: The Core Concept and Three Contemporary Developments" in Part 4). This theory, developed by Alejandro Portes, Ruben Rumbaut, and Min Zhou, maintains that contemporary immigrants enter a society that is not characterized by one culture, but instead by a variety of subcultures and opportunity structures that are largely shaped by race and ethnicity. As opposed to following the "straight-line" path of assimilation conceived of by Robert Park, Milton Gordon, and others, and the "new assimilation theory" as conceived by Richard Alba and Victor Nee, segmented assimilation theory suggests that contemporary immigrants and their descendants may follow various paths of integration into American society, including upward, downward, or lagged trajectories. The particular path immigrants take will be influenced by the segment of American society into which they are received and their race and ethnicity. More specifically, the persistence of forces that maintain racial and ethnic stratification in American society means that the integration of some immigrants may be characterized by a degree of downward mobility.

According to segmented assimilation theorists, one of the key determinants of assimilation outcomes for immigrants and particularly their children is where they settle. As will be discussed in more detail further on in the chapter, some immigrants settle in resource-rich, suburban neighborhoods and have easy access to the opportunity structure (e.g., good schools and prestigious schools). Others settle in inner-city neighborhoods, exposing their members to the "urban underclass" whose very existence and behaviors are the legacies of past discrimination and blocked opportunities. According to the theory, exposure to the underclass and to prejudice and discrimination, in general, has the potential to thwart the progress of immigrants and particularly their children. Through such exposure, the second generation or children of immigrants may develop an "adversarial stance" to middle-class culture, causing them to drop out of school or engage in deviant behavior and derailing them from a path of upward social mobility. Thus, implicit within segmented assimilation theory is the idea that structural constraints on the housing choices of immigrants of African and Hispanic ancestry may limit them to disadvantaged neighborhoods and could impede their chances for social and economic success.

No doubt there has been criticism of segmented assimilation theory. Some argue that the notion of an "urban underclass" detracts attention away from the many blacks and Latinos in impoverished neighborhoods who exhibit mainstream behaviors, such as high school graduation and productive employment in the labor market. Similarly, others point to the role that minority institutions and organizations have played in facilitating the positive integration of black and Latino immigrants from such neighborhoods into American society. However, most if not all of these scholars agree that some groups may be vulnerable to the chances of downward mobility.

How well the spatial assimilation, place stratification, and segmented assimilation models characterize contemporary immigrant settlement patterns is the issue to which we turn now. Until recently, most of the discussion of immigrant settlement patterns has been focused at the neighborhood level. With the movement of immigrants to new destinations, attention has been refocused back up to the metropolitan level. In the next section, we explore such settlement patterns and their implications for immigrant integration into neighborhoods and housing. Following that, we review the literature on current patterns of immigrant settlement and discuss the implications of such patterns for theories characterizing immigrant settlement.

Regional, State, and Metropolitan Trends in Immigrant Settlement

Immigrant settlement has hardly been uniform throughout the United States both in contemporary and historical periods of large-scale immigration. Instead, immigration has largely been simultaneously a regional and urban phenomenon, with immigrants concentrating in particular ports of entry or gateways. From a historical perspective, immigrants of particular origins concentrated in specific regions of the United States mainly based upon the proximity of their regions of origin. It is hardly surprising that European immigrants initially settled in cities and states in the Northeast, Asian immigrants on the West Coast, and Latin Americans in the Southwest.

During this time period, immigration was largely urban in nature. Stanley Lieberson characterized the settlement patterns of immigrants from South, Central, and Eastern (SCE) Europe and found that "essentially half of all urban residents in 1920 were either immigrants or the children of immigrants" (Lieberson

1980, 23). According to Lieberson, at the end of the nineteenth century and the beginning of the twentieth century, the largest numbers of European immigrants settled in New York City, with Italians, Russians, and Austrians comprising the largest proportions. (Note: Russians and Austrians are ethnic groups and do not necessarily link to country-of-origin groups; nevertheless, the labels are adequate for the purposes of discussing residential patterns because ethnicity matters more than country-of-origin.) Large numbers of Italians also settled in Boston, Chicago, Philadelphia, and San Francisco, while somewhat smaller numbers settled in Buffalo, Newark, Cleveland, and Pittsburgh. Although New York City was the primary destination for Russians, large numbers of Russian immigrants also settled in Philadelphia, Chicago, and Boston. New York City, Chicago, and Cleveland were the primary destinations for Austrians and Hungarians during this time period, while Greeks settled predominantly in Chicago and New York City, and Romanians primarily in New York City, with much smaller numbers residing in Philadelphia and Chicago. Regionally, SCE groups were much more concentrated in northeastern and Midwestern cities than western cities largely because employment opportunities in the industrial sector were concentrated in these areas.

Immigrants today are still settling in the traditional destination states of the Northeast (New York and New Jersey), the Midwest (Illinois), the West Coast (California), and along the Mexican border (Texas). Florida is also a state with large shares of immigrants. Data from the 2009 American Community Survey (ACS) reveal that over half of the foreign-born population (56 percent) lived in four of the six states—California, New York, Texas, and Florida. As far as the total American population is concerned, however, these four states were home to only 33 percent of the entire American population, revealing the concentration of the foreign-born population in these areas. Immigration continues to be an urban phenomenon, and perhaps even more so than at the turn of the twenty-first century. According to data from the 2009 ACS, 95 percent of the U.S. foreign-born population resided within metropolitan statistical areas. However, out of the foreign-born population living in such areas, just over 50 percent lived in suburbs, making the "urban" character of this settlement a bit different from the earlier period.

One of the biggest changes in the settlement of immigrants between historical and contemporary periods of large-scale immigration to the United States is that since the 1990s, increasingly larger proportions of immigrants have moved from or bypassed entirely the traditional gateway metropolitan areas within the four states identified above. Contemporary immigrants have been moving to "new destinations" or "new gateways." These areas have been found to be places in smaller metropolitan areas and rural areas that are largely in the Midwest and South. Hispanics make up the majority of immigrants to new destinations, but refugee groups, such as Kurds, Iranians, Somalians, Bosnians, and Sudanese, have also been the catalyst for the growth of these "new places." While the U.S. Office of Refugee Resettlement has actively created refugee communities in nontraditional areas, Hispanic immigrants, especially, have been pulled to new destinations, in part by recruiters from the poultry-processing, construction, agricultural, forestry, landscaping, carpet-making, and oil-refining sectors, away from the saturated labor markets of the Southwest and Northeast. Immigrants have also been motivated to leave or have felt "pushed" out of traditional areas by the perceived and actual economic decline and social problems of traditional gateway cities, and they have been motivated to move to new destinations or "pulled" by the perceived and actual lower levels of crime, greater educational opportunities, affordable housing, and the lack of scrutiny by the FBI, Homeland Security, and U.S. CIS (Customs and Immigration Service) agents working to combat the illegal immigration problems in many traditional destinations.

Given the regional and urban concentration of immigrant settlement today and historically, the next issue to which we turn is evaluating the extent to which immigrants have been living exclusively among their co-ethnics or instead among non-Hispanic whites or members of the "majority" group in American society. As discussed in the theory section above, gauging the extent to which contemporary and historical waves of immigrants are residentially segregated from majority-group members or isolated among their co-ethnics is important because it can be used as a barometer to gauge immigrant access to the larger American opportunity structure. Consistent with the tenets of the spatial assimilation model, do immigrant groups become less segregated from native-born, non-Hispanic whites as they spend more time in the United States? Or do race and ethnicity ultimately dictate residential segregation patterns, consistent with the place stratification models? Do the trajectories of segregation vary across generations such that some groups' exposure to white increases and other groups' exposure to whites actually *decreases*, consistent with the segmented assimilation model?

Lieberson's analysis of historical patterns of segregation reveals support primarily for hypotheses derived under the spatial assimilation. In 1910, white SCE immigrant groups were more residentially segregated (as measured by the isolation index) than blacks in such cities as Boston, Buffalo, Chicago, Cleveland, Detroit, Milwaukee, Newark, New York City, Philadelphia, and San Francisco. However, as early as 1920 and continuing beyond 1920, the segregation of SCE groups declined. Lieberson explains this decline in isolation as reflecting the fact that their segregation was primarily done on a voluntary basis.

When these SCE groups initially arrived in the United States, American culture and language were alien to them. Thus, to facilitate their integration into their new homeland, they chose to live among their co-ethnics. However, once they learned the language and culture, members of the SCE groups felt more comfortable dispersing from their co-ethnics, particularly the adult children of the initial migrants. In addition, because of restrictive immigration laws put into place in the 1920s, immigration from SCE countries came virtually to a standstill, weakening these groups' networks to their homelands and thereby speeding up their acculturation into American society. Consistent with the tenets of the spatial assimilation model, Lieberson found that the cities that remained segregated during this time period had larger proportions of immigrants who had been in the United States for less than 20 years.

During the same period, while SCE group isolation was declining, black isolation was increasing.

Lieberson attributes this increase initially to the beginnings of the Great Migration from the South to the North and also to the fact that the economy was changing in cities with blacks moving more into manufacturing jobs and leaving behind their employment as servants or sharecroppers for whites. The segregation of blacks in such areas increased dramatically during this period not only because of the demographic impetus of the Great Migration, but also because of institutionalized practices of discrimination that were built into the home mortgage industry in the 1930s and 1940s. The reasons for the increases in black segregation during this historical period are more consistent with the tenets of the place stratification than with the spatial assimilation model.

With this shift in the nature of the operation of the housing market and the fact that the majority of today's immigrants are racial and ethnic minorities, what is the nature of residential segregation among contemporary immigrants to the United States? Do they adhere to the patterns hypothesized under the spatial assimilation model, or are they more in line with the tenets of the place stratification model?

In examining the "evenness" of the overall foreign-born population with the native-born, non-Hispanic white population or the "index of dissimilarity," the patterns conform to that predicted under the spatial assimilation model. The analyses of 1990 and 2000 decennial census data reveal that between this period, the index of dissimilarity, or "d-score," rose modestly from .411 to .443, indicating that at least 41 percent of the foreign-born population would have had to move to achieve an even distribution with the native-born, non-Hispanic white population. (D-scores that fall below 30 are generally thought to be low; those between 30 and 60 are in the middle; and those over 60 are considered to be high.) Examining the trends disaggregated by the foreign-born population's year of entry reveals two important findings. First, more recent immigrant arrivals had greater levels of residential segregation than those who had been in the United States for a longer period, regardless of looking at the 1990 or 2000 census data. Second, in examining immigrants disaggregated by year-of-entry cohorts, segregation has declined between 1990 and 2000 for the 1980–1989 and 1970–1979

cohorts and increased slightly for those arriving before 1970. Taken together, the overall results indicate support for the spatial assimilation model.

When examining the metropolitan levels of residential segregation for nativity-status groups disaggregated by race and ethnicity, the results reveal patterns both consistent and inconsistent with the tenets of the spatial assimilation model. Foreign-born Hispanic segregation from native-born, non-Hispanic whites is .60, while that of foreign-born Asians from native-born, non-Hispanic whites is .48. The segregation of foreign-born whites from native-born whites is .271, which is considerably lower and falls in what is considered to be the "lowest" tier of segregation. Interestingly, foreign-born Hispanic segregation falls in the highest tier. As with the results for immigrants as a whole, Asian, Hispanic, and white recent immigrant arrivals tend to have higher levels of residential segregation from native-born, non-Hispanic whites than Asian, Hispanic, and particularly white immigrants who have been in the United States longer. Between 1990 and 2000, segregation declined modestly for most cohorts of foreign-born Hispanics; but for foreign-born Asians, the changes were not statistically significant. For foreign-born whites, the declines in segregation between 1990 and 2000 were most significant for the 1980–1989 cohort. Taken together, for the most part, these patterns adhere to the patterns expected under the spatial assimilation model.

The patterns for foreign-born blacks differ, however, from those of foreign-born Asians, Hispanics, and whites. The segregation of foreign-born blacks, overall, from native-born non-Hispanic whites is .747, which is much higher than the other racial and ethnic subgroups of immigrants. Thus, nearly 75 percent of foreign-born blacks would have to move to achieve an even distribution with native-born, non-Hispanic whites. Contrary to the pattern found for the other subgroups, as foreign-born blacks spend more time in the United States, they actually become *more* rather than *less* segregated from whites. These patterns are inconsistent with the expectations generated under the spatial assimilation model. The fact that the index of dissimilarity gauging foreign-born black/native-born white segregation is substantively much higher than that for foreign-born Asians, Hispanics, and whites indicates support for the tenets of the place stratification model. Moreover, the fact that residential segregation increases among foreign-born blacks as they have been in the United States longer suggests support for the patterns expected under the segmented assimilation model.

How these patterns of segregation look today remains to be seen. Unlike in previous decennial censuses, the 2010 census did not collect data on the nativity status of persons in households across the United States. The nativity-status question was on the "long-form" of the decennial census, which is no longer administered to the U.S. population every 10 years. Instead, data collected for the American Community Survey (ACS) on a yearly basis has replaced the data that had been collected every 10 years in the long-form survey of the decennial census questionnaire. The data at the census-tract level, which are required to tabulate indices of dissimilarity or d-scores, were released in December 2010 through the 2005–2009 five-year estimates of the ACS. Because of confidentiality concerns, the public use files of the ACS do not disaggregate census-tract level counts of the population by race, ethnicity, and nativity status. Therefore, in order for the work to be updated with more recent data, future research will have to obtain special access to the 2005–2009 census-tract level data.

Given these data limitations and the fact that the immigrants to the United States have increasingly settled in new destinations since 2000, researchers working in this area revisited 2000 census data and began examining residential segregation in new destinations and comparing them to segregation patterns in traditional destinations. Few studies have been done in this vein, but clearly this is the direction in which the latest research is moving. These studies reveal that the patterns of residential segregation vary depending upon the geographic level of analysis employed. When examined at the metropolitan-area level of analysis using census tract data, there appears to be overall less segregation of Hispanics and Asians in new destinations than in traditional gateways. Taking a closer look at the within-group differences, however, nativity status matters. Hispanic and Asian immigrants are more likely to be segregated from the white population in both new destinations and the

traditional gateways than their native-born counterparts are. When the new destination is defined at the place level of analysis rather than at the metropolitan level of analysis, rates of Hispanic-white segregation have been shown to be *higher* in the new destinations than in the traditional destinations. Qualitative research has also described the clustering of Hispanics in particular neighborhoods of new destinations, separated from the predominantly white areas.

What explains the higher levels of Hispanic-white residential segregation in new destinations defined at the place level of analysis? Part of this can be explained by the low incomes of Hispanics in these places, since the jobs that attract Hispanics to these places are typically low-wage jobs. However, income inequality has been shown to have a greater effect on segregation in traditional gateways than in new destinations. Because Hispanic-white segregation in new destinations has been shown to be associated with an increase in the Hispanic population and an increase in the black population, it is possible that the segregation of Hispanics from whites in these areas might be due to Hispanics moving into cities and suburbs with preexisting black-white segregation.

Much more research needs to examine the neighborhoods of immigrants who settle in new destinations and to compare them to those of immigrants settling in traditional gateways. It is crucial to study the patterns of segregation in new destinations because of the spatial separation that leads to separation in the economic, social, and political spheres of life. Living separately can raise fears, exacerbate discrimination, and intensify anti-immigration feelings and actions. The anti-immigrant legislation passed in Arizona in 2010 (but partially struck down by the Supreme Court in June 2012, leaving only the ability of the police to check immigration status of those arrested for lawbreaking) and Georgia and Alabama in 2011 no doubt reflects the new and rapid growth of immigrants in these states.

Immigrant Settlement in American Neighborhoods: Assimilation or Stratification?

While levels of segregation are high between recent immigrant arrivals and the native-born population, the literature focused at this aggregate level of analysis does not speak to the individual-level experiences of immigrants, nor does it explicitly assess immigrant residential attainment across immigrant cohorts or generations. Immigrants could be segregated because of their preferences to live with co-ethnics, because of discriminatory forces that constrain their residential opportunities, or due to a combination of both reasons, and the extent to which these explanations are valid could vary with their time in the United States. Although it is extremely difficult to assess which of these explanations is most supported, examining the neighborhood characteristics of individual immigrants and their households can shed light on the extent to which immigrants and native-born households live in "good" and "bad" neighborhood environments. Presumably everyone wants to maximize their opportunities to live in the best neighborhood environments. To the extent that they do not, and their individual resources are accounted for, such inequalities could reflect the operation of discriminatory mechanisms at work.

We focus on the residential characteristics of immigrant- and native-born households with the following questions in mind. What are the patterns of residential attainment of foreign-born households, relative to native-born households, historically and in contemporary periods? How do these patterns vary by immigrants' year of arrival, race and ethnicity, and by generation? Do the patterns adhere to those predicted by the spatial assimilation model, place stratification model, or segmented assimilation model?

Immigrant Residential Attainment in a Historical Context

In order to understand contemporary immigrant residential attainment, it is necessary to examine the settlement of immigrants historically. We focus here on the residential circumstances in New York City (hereafter referred to as "New York") in the late nineteenth and early twentieth centuries. New York was one of the major immigrant-receiving cities at that time. In 1920, nearly half of New Yorkers were immigrants or the children of immigrants, comprising the highest diversity in any American city at that time. An additional reason why New York provides a useful context in which to examine immigrant settlement patterns relates to the fact that housing policy reform got its start there.

Two large waves of immigration to New York occurred during the nineteenth century. The first started in the 1830s and lasted until the 1880s and was comprised largely of Irish and Germans. The second wave began in the 1880s and lasted until the first decades of the twentieth century. It was comprised of immigrants from eastern and southern Europe and was dominated by Italians and Russians.

With respect to the first wave of immigrants, the settlement patterns of the Irish and the Germans were quite different in nature, owing largely to economic differences and preexisting settlement patterns. The Irish were unskilled and quite impoverished. In 1855, "Irish immigrants represented approximately 87 percent of the city's unskilled laborers, and this occupational category was the largest one for Irish-born men" (Rosenbaum and Friedman 2007, 61). As a result of their poverty, the Irish tended to be concentrated in poor neighborhoods and poor-quality housing. A core group of the Irish community was located in the Five Points slum neighborhood of New York, which was notorious for its poverty and disease. As the number of Irish immigrants increased, their settlement spread eastward from Five Points into the Fourth Ward, located near the docks and shipyards that provided such immigrants with employment. And, although a core of Irish immigrants was confined to settlement in such poor areas, others were more spread out, living in areas in the Bronx, Queens, and Brooklyn.

Unlike the Irish coming to New York, the Germans had more skills, higher rates of literacy, and generally more money. Many German immigrants settled in the well-established ethnic community Kleindeutschland. Germans were a bit more concentrated in their settlement in this community than Irish were in the Five Points slum. However, there were Germans who lived in a dispersed manner throughout the city. In general, the neighborhood and housing conditions of these immigrants was better than those of their Irish counterparts, and because of Germans' higher socioeconomic status, they were able to integrate into American society a bit faster than the Irish.

For both groups, the variety in neighborhood locations translated into variation in housing conditions. The Irish who were "live-in" domestics likely had experienced the best housing conditions, as they lived in affluent housing in newer neighborhoods. In the newer portions of Kleindeutschland, the housing was also relatively decent. However, the poorest of newcomers who could not afford to pay much for housing, as in the case of many of the Irish, had few housing options and lived in tenements or slum housing.

As wealthier residents began relocating to newer wards in the uptown area of Manhattan, the houses that they left behind were divided up for use as boardinghouses or multiple-family dwellings. These units, which became known as tenements or barracks, consisted of housing that was small, dark, and contained poorly ventilated rooms. Other newcomers who could not even afford to live in tenements ended up in basements, attics, sheds, and stables. Because of the great waves of Irish and German immigration, the population living in basements and cellars expanded dramatically from 7,200 persons in 1843 to more than 29,000 by 1863.

To meet the housing demands of the growing poorer, immigrant populations, developers adapted their construction of row houses for the middle and upper classes to produce housing in the lower wards of Manhattan where these newer groups were locating. They constructed stripped-down versions of the row houses that they were producing for their more affluent clients. Due to the absence of windows in these tenements, the internal hallways and stairways were dark, and the five or six stories were joined together by narrow and deep stairways. The rooms in the apartments within these tenements were lined up in a row like train cars and became known as "railroad flats." Only the rooms in the front and rear of the tenements received light, but sometimes tenements in the back blocked the light in the rear apartments. Although the construction of these tenements reduced the size of the cellar-dwelling population, the new housing coupled with the large influx of immigrants produced high rates of neighborhood density. Between 1820 and 1850, the average block densities

in the seven wards below Canal Street increased from 157.5 to 272.5 persons.

The quality of construction of these tenements and the levels of crowding that existed within them and within the neighborhoods that they occupied led to a serious public health crisis around the early to mid-1800s. The danger of fire was a constant threat to residents in these areas, and contagious diseases spread rampantly in these communities. Indeed, in the late 1850s, the mortality rate in New York exceeded that in all other large American cities. The combinations of poverty, crowding, little available drinking water, and poor sanitary conditions facilitated the spread of diseases like tuberculosis and diarrhea. In these poorer areas, epidemic diseases, such as yellow fever, cholera, and typhoid/typhus, took their greatest toll. In 1856, roughly 1 in 23 persons died in the poorest ward, whereas 1 in 55 persons died in the more affluent wards.

City inspector and physician John Griscom was the first major public figure to link the city's poor public health conditions to high levels of population density and to the lack of ventilation in working-class homes. His report, *The Sanitary Conditions of the Laboring Population*, provided significant impetus for the housing reform movement in New York City and for the nation as a whole. In 1864, the Council of Hygiene carried out a detailed survey of the city's housing and sanitary problems. The report generated from the survey formed the basis of the state's first comprehensive housing law, the Tenement House Act of 1867. The act focused mainly on the structural aspects of housing, specifying proper room dimensions and ceiling heights, mandating provisions for ventilation and light, and requiring a minimum of one toilet for every 20 residents. The legislation helped to improve the housing stock in New York, but the forces of immigration and migration continued to place severe demands on the housing market in subsequent years.

Between 1880 and 1920, New York City experienced significant events that would change the city's character, both in its geography and population. The first event was the consolidation of the counties, New York, Kings, Queens, Bronx, and Richmond, into Greater New York City on January 1, 1898.

On a single day, New York would become the most extensive geographically and the most populous city in the United States. The second event that shaped the city's character was the shift in immigration from northern and western Europe to southern and eastern Europe. Irish and German immigrants continued to settle in New York, but the inflow of other immigrant groups from Italy, Russia, Poland, Austria-Hungary, and Romania became more prevalent. In particular, the influx of Italians and Jews would alter the city's ethnic composition and the geographic organization of its ethnic communities.

Not only did the ethnic character of New York's population change, but the race of the population changed as well. During this period, there was a significant in-migration of blacks from the South. The 1900 census counted 60,666 blacks in the city, but by 1920, there were an additional 90,000 blacks counted in the census. By the 1930 census, the black population numbered 327,706. In addition to native-born blacks migrating to New York from the South, the city also witnessed growth in its foreign-born black population. In the 1900 census, foreign-born blacks numbered 3,552. By the 1930 census, the foreign-born black population reached over 54,000, comprising the largest foreign-born black community in the nation. The final force that changed the character of the city's population was the significant in-migration of Puerto Ricans at the end of the Spanish-American War in 1898.

How were these changes to the character of New York City's population during this 40-year period reflected in the spatial distribution of groups throughout the city's neighborhoods? By and large, the evidence suggests the most support for the tenets of the spatial assimilation model. By the 1880s, a significant number of German immigrants and their descendants who had come to New York in the earlier part of the nineteenth century had entered the middle class. Improvements in their socioeconomic status resulted in their migration out of the ethnic community Kleindeutschland to neighborhoods further from the core, such as Yorkville, Central Harlem, Williamsburg (Brooklyn), and Astoria (Queens). Expansions in transportation lines created newer communities that facilitated the out-migration of the Germans. The

Irish, who were poorer than the Germans at the outset, took longer to achieve middle-class status, but like the Germans, they also moved to better housing and new communities on both the west and east sides of Manhattan and to areas in Brooklyn and Queens.

Italians and Jews of the "new" immigration moved to many of the areas vacated by the Germans and Irish, producing large-scale ethnic turnover in many of New York's congested tenement districts in the lower wards. Like the Irish and Germans before them, many of the Italians and Jews arrived with few economic resources and had to live in older neighborhoods with lower rents and that were within walking distance of their workplaces. Meanwhile, the size of the new immigration was quite large and produced significant levels of crowding in destination neighborhoods. By 1910, Jews constituted one-fourth of New York City's population. Meanwhile, the size of the population of foreign-born Italians in Manhattan and Brooklyn had doubled between 1880 and 1890.

Italian and Jewish immigration flows were quite different, and these differences were reflected in their initial residential attainment. Italians arriving in New York after 1880 were largely illiterate peasants and laborers originating from agricultural regions of southern Italy and Sicily. Of Italian immigrants arriving between 1880 and 1910, 80 percent were male, and 83 percent were between the ages of 14 and 44. In the early years of migration, the goal of these immigrants was to make enough money to return home and purchase land in Italy. Because of their lack of skills, Italians, like their Irish predecessors, took their place at the bottom of the occupational ladder. To a very large degree, their residential location was determined by their place of work; and because of their limited economic means, they settled in very poor-quality housing—tenements, many without running water or fire escapes, and few with toilets on all their floors.

By contrast, the Jewish migration was more of a family migration and far more likely to be permanent, and Jewish immigrants were also more likely than the Italians to be literate and to possess skills. In the early years of East European Jewish migration, Jews settled in and around Kleindeutschland and began replacing the upwardly mobile Germans leaving that area. The area gained greater fame as the Jewish Lower East Side than as Kleindeutschland. By 1892, fully 75 percent of the city's Jews lived in that area. The population density there was the worst in the whole city, but one study by the Immigrant Commission found that the unit quality of Jewish tenement apartments was better than that of the Italians.

Over time, and consistent with the tenets of the spatial assimilation model, both Italian and Jewish immigrants and their descendants achieved upward residential attainment. The rising socioeconomic status of many Jewish immigrants enabled them to afford better housing in less densely populated areas. As a result, Jews dispersed to areas in upper Manhattan, the Bronx, and Brooklyn. Italians were a bit slower in making economic gains, yet by World War I, many Italians and their descendants had achieved middle-class status and moved to areas like the Bronx, where there were better residential opportunities. For the immigrants left behind in the original settlement areas, there were slight improvements in their housing conditions with the passage of the Tenement House Act of 1901. The act required improvements to be made to existing tenements, including the provision of running water, a toilet, and a fire escape for each family. With respect to new construction, the law led to the building of more solid tenements and featured amenities such as light, air, and plumbing.

While the residential attainment of the Italians and Jews largely mirrored those of the Irish and Germans, the settlement patterns of black and Puerto Rican migrants to New York were different and more consistent with the place stratification model. Until about 1880, before the arrival of many southern black migrants, a primary black settlement existed in Greenwich Village. However, the fivefold growth in black population between 1900 and 1930 created a significant demand for housing, particularly cheap housing. Harlem became the area to which these migrants flocked. Interestingly, at the turn of the century, Harlem was predominantly white, serving as home to middle- and upper-class Jews and Germans as well as older immigrants from Britain and Ireland and native-born Americans. With the construction of the elevated train lines from 1878 to 1881, the area underwent a huge building boom. In anticipation of

the completion of the Lenox Avenue subway, speculators, who made good profits on increasingly valuable land, continued building luxury apartment buildings in the late 1890s and early 1900s along Seventh and Lenox Avenues up to 130th and 140th Streets. However, the construction happened too far in advance of the completion of the subway, and the housing stock was priced too high. As a result, the housing market in Harlem collapsed in 1904–1905, and numerous new apartments remained vacant.

The housing bust coincided with the tremendous growth in the city's black population. Greedy speculators played upon whites' antipathy toward blacks to hasten the transition of Harlem from an all-white to an all-black neighborhood. Although New York had never been a place where blacks were considered equal to whites, the significant growth of the black population caused the deterioration of whites' more permissive racial attitudes; the color line in the city grew more rigid, and in Harlem, landlords, realtors, and other housing-market actors opened their housing units to blacks to avoid financial ruin. Such tactics, which became known as blockbusting, caused many whites to flee because of the subsequent decline in housing values. With the opening of access to Harlem housing, many blacks moved from other areas that were much more crowded and significantly lower in quality. The supply of housing and the demand for better housing prompted the relatively quick transition of Harlem from white to black.

Although Harlem initially offered blacks the opportunity to live in high-quality accommodations, by 1920, the desirability of the neighborhood and housing stock diminished and Harlem was transformed into a slum. In large part, this had to do with the fact that this was one of the few areas in the city in which blacks were welcomed to live. Population density increased significantly. The fact that residents had to take in boarders to help pay the rent did not alleviate the population density in the area. In addition, much of the housing stock was built prior to the Tenement Housing Act of 1901. Therefore, the overpopulation taxed the already poor-quality housing in the area. Many structures were subdivided and transformed into boardinghouses, and landlords allowed their properties in the area to deteriorate. Sadly, unlike the case for the white immigrants to New York, black residential attainment deteriorated further with the establishment of discriminatory polices under the country's mortgage financing system (see below). Thus, the trajectory of black residential attainment was much less consistent with the tenets of the spatial assimilation model than was the case for the white immigrants.

Puerto Rican migrant settlement patterns in New York City may be characterized as falling in between those of black migrants and the experiences of white migrants. Initially, Puerto Ricans sought housing near potential job opportunities. Early settlements were found in East Harlem, the Lower East Side, and near the Brooklyn Navy Yard. Between 1920 and 1940, the Puerto Rican migrant population to the city increased eightfold, from about 7,000 to more than 60,000. The East Harlem community became the most significant Puerto Rican community in the city. Like their white and black immigrant counterparts, Puerto Ricans inherited some of the city's oldest and worst housing. What made their settlement more like that of blacks was the fact that over time, the spatial patterns of Puerto Ricans in the city were far more similar to those of blacks than whites. Puerto Rican segregation from whites would eventually reach levels as high as that of blacks. The fact that a sizable percentage of Puerto Ricans identified themselves as nonwhite no doubt created many of the same structural constraints with regard to access to housing opportunities, as was the case for blacks.

What further constrained both black and Puerto Rican housing choices historically and up through the present day were the housing programs instituted in the 1930s. Perhaps the most damaging program in this regard was the Home Owner's Loan Corporation (HOLC) created in 1933. HOLC introduced the long-term, self-amortizing mortgage featuring uniform payments throughout the lifetime of the loan. The most significant and notorious legacy of HOLC was its institutionalization of the practice of "redlining," which systematically denied capital and undervalued ethnically mixed, densely populated, and physically aging neighborhoods. Such discriminatory practices accelerated the decline of these neighborhoods and hastened their turnover to predominantly

black occupancy. The actions of subsequent programs—the Loan Guarantee Program of the Federal Housing Administration (FHA) and the Home Loan Guarantee Program of the Veterans Administration (VA)—helped solidify the creation of ghettos in New York City and beyond. Relying on the discriminatory appraisal system established by the HOLC, the majority of these loans went to suburban locations and significantly increased racial residential segregation between whites and blacks. Not until the passage of the Fair Housing Act in 1968 was the practice of redlining outlawed.

From a historical perspective, the patterns of the residential attainment of immigrants in New York City appear to fit well with that predicted by the tenets of the spatial assimilation model. However, at the same time, the increasing diversity of the flows of population to New York City as well as the institutional practices of racial and ethnic discrimination clearly gave rise to the saliency of hypotheses predicted under the place stratification model. While the focus of this section has been on New York City, the patterns uncovered and discussed here should not be thought of as unique to this city. Instead, because of its stature as a city of immigrants around the turn of the twentieth century, the experiences in New York City should be considered as normative of that era.

The question to which we now turn is the extent to which today's immigrants to the United States exhibit the patterns of residential attainment that existed at the turn of the century. Today's immigrants are far more racially and ethnically diverse than those at the turn of the twentieth century, largely immigrating from Latin America and Asia rather than almost exclusively from Europe. As noted above, the segregation of foreign-born Hispanics and blacks from native-born whites is relatively higher than that of foreign-born Asians and whites from native-born whites. While these scores do decline over time, they appear to decline at different rates for individuals of different races and ethnicities. However, what we do not know from these aggregate-level analyses is the extent to which the segregation of these groups translates into poor neighborhood quality or residential attainment. Perhaps immigrant groups are choosing to live with their co-ethnics and they live away from whites residing in high-quality residential locations. Or, perhaps immigrants are constrained in their housing choices and are segregated from whites, and compelled to reside in poorer-quality areas.

Immigrant Residential Attainment in the Contemporary Period

A large and growing literature focusing on the locational attainment process of individuals and households, in general, has demonstrated that members of different racial and ethnic groups experience varying levels of access to high-quality neighborhoods. Such more affluent neighborhoods offer greater connections to the opportunity structure in that they provide more access to jobs, better-quality schools, safer neighborhoods, and more resource-rich environments. These studies have contributed greatly to our knowledge concerning the extent and nature of racial and ethnic inequality by consistently demonstrating a general pattern of access to advantaged areas whereby whites enjoy the highest levels of access, followed by Asians, Hispanics, and finally blacks. These studies, however, have been limited in that they have not explicitly analyzed the foreign-born contingent of a given ethnic group separately from the native-born contingent of that group, nor have they examined characteristics beyond those available from the decennial census data (i.e., percentage of whites in the neighborhood and median household income).

In recent years, several studies have filled this gap in the literature and have explicitly focused on immigrant residential attainment. With these data, we attempt to make explicit several comparisons in order to consider how these findings relate to the spatial assimilation, place stratification, and segmented assimilation theories discussed at the outset of this chapter. First, we compare the general neighborhood outcomes of foreign-born and native-born households. Then we focus on such comparisons within and between racial and ethnic groups. Finally, our discussion turns to an analysis of the residential attainment of foreign-born and native-born households grouped by their generational status (i.e., first, 1.5, second, and third-plus generations).

When comparing foreign-born and native-born households, overall, the findings in the literature based upon national data generally reveal that foreign-born households live in worse-quality housing and neighborhoods than do native-born households, similar to their counterparts at the turn of the twentieth century. Foreign-born households have been shown to have lower rates of homeownership than do native-born households—as much as 15 percentage points lower, providing them less access to wealth. In addition, foreign-born households are significantly more likely to experience housing cost burdens than their native-born counterparts. In particular, foreign-born owners are more likely to pay more than 50 percent of their income toward housing than is the case for native-born owners.

Like immigrants in New York City in the late 1800s and early 1900s, today's foreign-born households are more than 10 times as likely as native-born households to experience household crowding at both standard (more than 1 person per room) and extreme (more than 1.5 persons per room) levels. Today's immigrants are also more likely than native-born households to live in severely inadequate housing. One can be sure, however, that such housing is not nearly as inadequate as the tenements that existed in New York City long ago. With the housing reforms passed at the turn of the twentieth century and later, significant regulations now exist in the construction of housing that prohibit the squalid conditions existing in our urban history.

With respect to their neighborhood characteristics, studies have revealed that foreign-born households, overall, are more likely than native-born households to live in neighborhoods located in the central city and that are less desirable with respect to physical quality and land use. For example, immigrant households are less likely than their native-born counterparts to report the presence of open spaces within a half a block of their housing units. At the same time, foreign-born households are more than twice as likely as native-born households to report the presence of buildings with bars on windows within a half a block of their housing units. Interestingly, despite the poorer physical quality of their neighborhoods, immigrants are significantly less likely than native-born households to live in neighborhoods with higher levels of social disorder. For example, foreign-born households are less likely than native-born households to find crime to be bothersome within their neighborhoods.

The fact that foreign-born households, overall, have relatively worse housing and neighborhood conditions than native-born households is attributable to several differences that exist between the two groups with respect to their socioeconomic and demographic characteristics. With respect to socioeconomic status, foreign-born households are generally more likely than native-born households to be headed by a person with less than a high school education and making a lower median income. Therefore, immigrants have fewer economic resources to buy better-quality housing and buy into better-quality neighborhoods.

The fact that just about one-third of present foreign-born households entered into the United States since 1990 is also likely to contribute to the immigrant disadvantage in housing and neighborhood conditions. With less time in the United States, immigrants have had less of a chance to acquire the socioeconomic resources they need to locate in better housing and neighborhoods. Foreign-born households also differ from native-born households in their household size, which likely contributes to the situation in which they are more crowded than their native-born counterparts. Immigrant households are significantly more likely than native-born households to be headed by a couple and to have children under age 18 and other adults beyond those who are part of the nuclear family. Taken together, the differences found between foreign- and native-born households, overall, are most consistent with the spatial assimilation model.

Do the general differences found in housing and neighborhood conditions between foreign- and native-born households exist overall within racial and ethnic groups? Except in the case of Asians, foreign-born households have been found to be significantly more likely than native-born households to experience negative housing conditions, mirroring the pattern for native- and foreign-born households overall. For example, on a national level, foreign-born whites, blacks, and Hispanics are significantly

less likely than their native-born counterparts to own their homes. Foreign-born owners within these racial/ethnic groups have been shown to be significantly more likely than their native-born counterparts to experience moderate and severe housing cost burdens. The findings regarding household crowding are also consistent with the findings for households across the board. Foreign-born white, black, and Hispanic households are more likely than native-born white, black, and Hispanic households, respectively, to have more than one person per room within their housing units.

The one housing condition in which the comparisons between foreign- and native-born households within racial/ethnic groups are not as consistent as those found for households, overall, is for housing quality. For whites and Asians, there is no significant nativity-status difference in housing quality. For blacks and Hispanics, foreign-born households are significantly *less* likely to live in moderately inadequate housing than native-born households, contrary to the pattern for the total sample. However, with respect to severely inadequate housing conditions, foreign-born black households are significantly more likely than native-born black households to live in such housing.

While for the most part nativity-status differences in housing conditions within racial and ethnic groups mirror the patterns in the total sample, it is instructive to examine the differences that exist between whites and foreign- and native-born minorities. For example, the access to homeownership is stratified just as much, if not more, by the race and ethnicity of households. Whites, irrespective of their nativity status, are the most likely to own their homes, and Asians are a close second. However, Hispanics and blacks are less likely than whites and Asians to own their homes. The lowest level of homeownership is among foreign-born blacks. A racial and ethnic hierarchy in housing conditions is also evident when considering housing quality and owners' housing costs. Whites and Asians, irrespective of nativity status, tend to live in units that are less likely to be moderately or severely inadequate than Hispanics and blacks. Native-born blacks and Hispanics are the most likely to live in *moderately* inadequate housing, while foreign-born blacks are the most likely to live in *severely* inadequate housing. White and Asian owners are also less likely than black and Hispanic owners to pay a larger share of their incomes toward their housing costs.

With respect to neighborhood conditions, there is more variability in nativity-status differences across racial and ethnic groups with respect to the general nativity-status difference for all households. Among whites and Hispanics, foreign-born households are significantly less likely than their native-born counterparts to report that open spaces are present within a half a block of their housing units and significantly more likely than native-born households to report that buildings with bars on windows are present within a half a block of their housing units. For Asians, these differences also exist, but are not statistically different. Moreover, foreign-born white and Asian households are statistically more likely than their native-born counterparts to live in central cities. There is virtually no difference in the residential location of foreign- and native-born Hispanic households.

While foreign-born households in these groups tend to live in neighborhoods of slightly poorer physical quality and with more undesirable land use than their native-born counterparts, the opposite is true with respect to neighborhood conditions indicative of social disorder, consistent with the findings for all households. For example, among whites and Asians, immigrant households are significantly less likely than native-born households to report that abandoned buildings are present within half a block of their housing units. For Hispanics, the same pattern exists, but the difference is not statistically significant. Among whites, foreign-born households are also significantly less likely than native-born households to report that crime is a problem within their neighborhoods. While the same pattern is evident among Hispanics and Asians, the nativity-status difference on this indicator is not statistically apparent.

Contrary to many of the patterns present in the whole sample, foreign-born blacks are significantly more likely than native-born blacks to live in neighborhoods with better physical conditions. For example, foreign-born blacks are about half as likely as native-born blacks to report the presence of trash or junk and factories within a half a block of their housing units, and that odors are bothersome in their neighborhoods. What is interesting is that this pattern exists even though immigrant black households are slightly more likely than native-born black households to live in central cities. With respect to neighborhood conditions more indicative of social disorder, black foreign-born households are significantly less likely than black native-born households to report the presence of abandoned buildings and that crime is bothersome in their neighborhoods.

Despite the fact that black foreign-born households tend to reside in better-quality neighborhoods than do their native-born counterparts, in general there exists a hierarchy in neighborhood conditions when considering comparisons across racial and ethnic groups. Blacks and Hispanics generally occupy lower positions in this hierarchy than whites and Asians, as was the case with the housing conditions. For example, black and Hispanic households are more likely than whites, Asians, and all households combined to live in neighborhoods within the central city, regardless of nativity status. Black and Hispanic households are more likely than whites, Asians, and all households combined to report the presence of buildings with bars on windows, abandoned buildings, and trash or junk, and that crime and odors are bothersome within their neighborhoods.

In part, the nativity-status differences that exist in housing and neighborhood conditions within racial and ethnic groups are attributable to the variation that exists between foreign- and native-born households in their socioeconomic and demographic characteristics. The worse-quality housing and neighborhoods experienced by foreign-born households among whites, Hispanics, and Asians is attributable to the fact that compared to their native-born counterparts, immigrant households within these groups have less education and income, have larger families, and have been in the United States for less time, consistent with hypotheses derived from the spatial assimilation model. However, the fact that foreign-born black households experience *better* neighborhood conditions than native-born black households is a pattern inconsistent with hypotheses derived under the spatial assimilation model. Likewise, the findings that, regardless of nativity status, black and Hispanic housing and neighborhood conditions are consistently of poorer quality than those of whites and Asians, even after accounting for the variation across groups in their socioeconomic and demographic characteristics, are consistent with hypotheses derived under the place stratification model. It is evident that structural barriers in the housing market are constraining the residential opportunities of minorities regardless of their nativity status.

Nonetheless, one of the main limitations with the existing research that explores foreign- and native-born residential attainment is that most of the data used by researchers (e.g., decennial census data) cannot identify the generational status of individuals. Such distinctions are relevant when considering the unexpected findings for foreign-born blacks relative to native-born blacks and the findings of no differences between native- and foreign-born households. Foreign-born households are comprised of householders who came as adults and as children (i.e., the first and 1.5 generations). Native-born households include the children of immigrants (second generation), the grandchildren of immigrants, and the great-grandchildren of immigrants (third-plus generation). If few differences exist between foreign- and native-born households, it could be because the foreign-born households are being compared to native-born households largely comprised of second-generation householders, who are not very far removed from the immigration process. In general, because of data limitations, little research has explored generational patterns in the residential attainment of households.

The recent research on this topic is limited to two studies, one examining New York and the other analyzing Los Angeles data. Both the Rosenbaum-Friedman and the Brown studies find the spatial assimilation model to be lacking in some respects in characterizing contemporary immigrant settlement patterns. In the Los Angeles study, there appears to be a pattern of delayed spatial assimilation among Mexicans, whereby generational improvements occur only between the third- and fourth-plus generations. Brown attributes the delay in spatial assimilation to the fact that adult children in the 1.5 and second generations bear extra expenses of caring for their relatives in the United States or abroad. Therefore, they have less money and time to improve their residential circumstances.

In the New York study, while generational improvements in housing and neighborhood conditions were evident for white and Hispanic households, these trends in improvements were almost entirely explained by economic differences. And yet, consistent with the tenets of the spatial assimilation model, the same was not true for blacks. On a majority of housing and neighborhood outcomes, the generational patterns for blacks exhibited a pronounced and consistent pattern of decline from the first and 1.5 generations to the second generation and then again to the third-plus generation. Even after controlling for differences in socioeconomic status, such generational declines persist, providing evidence to support the expectations generated under the segmented assimilation theory. It is likely that the frequency and intensity of discrimination vary across generations of blacks. As markers of ethnic origins dissipate (e.g., accents, ways of dress), descendants of black immigrants are more vulnerable to prejudice and discrimination than their immigrant parents or grandparents. As a result, becoming American does not result in upward mobility but instead results in a loss of status in the society.

Conclusion

In summary, the chapter here tells a compelling story about the salience of race and ethnicity in American society both historically and today. Residential attainment is inextricably linked to households' current and future social and economic well-being, and the fact that the structure of opportunity available in the United States has and continues to be shaped by race and ethnicity does not bode well for the future stratification of our society. The chapter makes clear that housing and neighborhood outcomes remain unevenly distributed across racial and ethnic groups. Blacks and, to a lesser degree, Hispanics disproportionately occupy the least desirable units located in neighborhoods with the fewest resources necessary for upward social and economic mobility in American society. What the research reviewed here has shown is that even if immigrants have sufficient socioeconomic resources at their disposal to facilitate improvement of their residential circumstances, the way that their resources are translated into such residential outcomes depends upon race and ethnicity.

The bottom line is that current debates among scholars and policy makers may be misguided. Many argue that current waves of immigrants are of lower quality than their counterparts from earlier times. The thought is that today's immigrants are unable to, or unwilling to, "make it" in American society. As seen from this chapter, such thinking may be irrelevant. Many immigrant groups do "make it" and are successful in their residential attainment. On the other hand, those that do not "make it" are not unsuccessful because of their lack of desire. Rather, as this chapter makes clear, structural barriers and not individual traits play a very influential role in shaping the trajectories that immigrants will take in their residential attainment. Therefore, policies that are restrictive against immigrants will not work. Instead, policy makers must identify ways to remove the barriers that prevent Americans of color from having full access to the residential opportunity structure. It is only through such efforts that the children and grandchildren of today's immigrants can truly have the means to become Americans.

Bibliography

Alba, Richard D., and Victor Nee. 2003. *Remaking the American Mainstream: Assimilation and Contemporary Immigration*. Cambridge, MA: Harvard University Press.

Alba, Richard D., and John Logan. 1993. "Minority Proximity to Whites in Suburbs: An Individual-Level Analysis of Segregation." *American Journal of Sociology* 98: 1388–1427.

Brown, Susan K. 2007. "Delayed Spatial Assimilation: Multigenerational Incorporation of the Mexican-Origin Population in Los Angeles." *City and Community* 6: 193–209.

Friedman, Samantha, and Emily Rosenbaum. 2003. "Housing and Neighborhood Conditions: How Do Immigrants Fare?" Unpublished report for the Fannie Mae Foundation.

Iceland, John. 2009. *Where We Live Now: Immigration and Race in the United States*. Berkeley: University of California Press.

Lieberson, Stanley. 1980. *A Piece of the Pie: Blacks and White Immigrants since 1980*. Berkeley: University of California Press.

Logan, John, and Harvey Molotch. 1987. *Urban Fortunes: The Political Economy of Place*. Berkeley: University of California Press.

Logan, John, Richard D. Alba, and Wenquan Zhang. 2002. "Immigrant Enclaves and Ethnic Communities in New York and Los Angeles." *American Sociological Review* 67, no. 2: 299–322.

Massey, Douglas S. 1985. "Ethnic Residential Segregation: A Theoretical Synthesis and Empirical Review." *Sociology and Social Research* 69: 315–50.

Massey, Douglas S., and Nancy A. Denton. 1993. *American Apartheid: Segregation and the Making of the Underclass*. Cambridge, MA: Harvard University Press.

Portes, Alejandro, and Ruben Rumbaut. 1996. *Immigrant America: A Portrait*. Berkeley: University of California Press.

Rosenbaum, Emily, and Samantha Friedman. 2007. *The Housing Divide: How Generations of Immigrants Fare in New York's Housing Market*. New York: New York University Press.

Zhou, Min. 1997. "Segmented Assimilation: Issues, Controversies, and Recent Research on the New Second Generation." *International Migration Review* 31: 975–1008.

Urbanization and Immigrants in America

Dominic A. Pacyga

Colonial and Postcolonial Urban Centers

Since the very beginning of European settlement in North America, cities have been intimately connected with immigration. Some 10,000 Englishmen arrived in Massachusetts through the port of Boston in the 1630s. The Atlantic seaports later most identified with immigration had long established themselves as beachheads for the European invasion of the continent. Boston, New York, Philadelphia, and Newport and later Baltimore all tied the new settlements to the flow of people across the Atlantic that eventually transformed the lands occupied originally by Native Americans. These cities, and others like them, would be havens for immigrants as the new republic rose after 1776.

Unsurprisingly, the English experience shaped the attitude of early Americans toward immigration, but this was soon overwhelmed by the realities of settling a continent and defeating and replacing an indigenous population that held on to its traditional lands. Warm bodies were needed, and immigration was encouraged even in Puritan Boston, with its hope of building a new Christian community based on Calvinistic principles. Skilled Polish glassmakers were imported into Jamestown in the early seventeenth century. Later, Germans threatened to outnumber their Quaker neighbors in Pennsylvania, entering through the busy port of Philadelphia, where many stayed to make their new lives. Dutch and Swedish settlers came under British rule as Britain expanded and secured its domination of the East Coast. After the French and Indian War (Seven Years' War), the English monarch saw his rule extend over French-Canadian Catholics. Diversity was to be a constant reality of life in the British colonies even as settlers from Britain itself continued to dominate them both culturally and economically.

Immigrants and prosperity seemed to go hand in hand as the nation formed. Even in such a seminal document as the Declaration of Independence, immigration was recognized as a factor in the growth of those societies sprouting along the Atlantic seaboard. Jefferson and his colleagues argued that King George III had "endeavored to prevent the population of these states; for that purpose obstructing the Laws of Naturalization of Foreigners; [and] refusing to pass others to encourage their migration hither." Many of the Founding Fathers saw immigration as a spur to further economic growth. Washington, in referring to recent Irish immigrants, declared in 1783 that America "is open to receive not only the opulent and respectable stranger but the oppressed of all Nations and Religions." James Madison declared in 1787 at the Constitutional Convention, "That part of America which has encouraged them [foreigners] most has advanced most rapidly in population, agriculture, and the arts." Despite the agrarian orientation of the new republic, this statement would in fact be a watchword for developing American cities, especially in the northern states of the new republic. In 1800, only 6 percent of all Americans, both native-born and foreign-born, lived in cities. That would rapidly change over the next 100 years.

While urbanization, industrialization, and immigration are distinct processes, they came together in the nineteenth century to transform the United States more completely than anyone might have imagined in the previous century. Immigration became a widespread phenomenon after 1820. During the century of mass immigration, over 40 million immigrants arrived in the United States, the vast majority from Europe. It was also during this era that the United States evolved into an industrial power and an urban nation. Cities grew at phenomenal rates largely as a result not only of migration from rural areas but also of immigration first from northern and western Europe, and then from southern and eastern Europe. Immigrants from Asia, Latin America, and Africa would also impact the development of the American city. Much of this was a response to an aggressive and rapidly industrializing capitalist economy. The new industries needed large numbers of both skilled and unskilled labor. Foreigners flooded into American cities, particularly among the eastern ports. From there they made their way across the nation, often settling in cities and towns undergoing industrial transformation.

The period between the 1830s and the 1850s saw the takeoff point for the American Industrial Revolution. The contribution of manufacturing to the economy nearly doubled between 1839 and 1859. The older urban areas witnessed much of this industrialization, first powered by water but then expanded with the use of steam. At this point, the northeastern and Mid-Atlantic states contained the largest urban population in the United States. These states in turn attracted the largest proportion of immigrants. In the United States, a dynamic market economy stimulated both rapid urbanization and immigration. Philadelphia, Boston, and Baltimore provided major ports of entry for immigrants. After 1825, with the rise of the port of New York, Castle Garden and then later Ellis Island became the symbolic—and principal—gateway for the migrations from Europe to the United States.

The original urban core along the seaboard benefited greatly from the growth of immigration after 1820. The population of New York increased substantially by 1830 to over 200,000 residents. Neighboring Brooklyn contained more than 15,000 inhabitants, while nearby Newark boasted over 10,000. Immigrants in general tended to settle in the most rapidly urbanizing areas. The seaports were part of established trade routes between the United States, England, and Western Europe. This trade frequently determined both the sources and destinations of

immigration. Immigrants repeatedly acted as ballast for ships returning to the American ports after bringing agricultural products to European ports. For example, Irish immigrants often arrived on sailing ships that had crossed the Atlantic with lumber for the British Isles. Germans likewise journeyed in large numbers to Baltimore on tobacco ships returning from Bremen and Hamburg. The trip by sailing ship could take anywhere from one to three months. As Britain attempted to reduce immigration to the United States by imposing high prices on passage to New York, the Irish often entered the country through Canada, taking advantage of relatively low passage to British North America.

At midcentury, a distinct urban industrial core emerged, stretching from New England through the Mid-Atlantic states. These cities attracted large numbers of immigrants in the nineteenth century. By 1850, Chicago, Milwaukee, and Detroit emerged on the Great Lakes as major manufacturing centers, and these too attracted large numbers of German immigrants. That year, Cincinnati held the title of the largest inland city with 115,000. St. Louis provided a home for more than 75,000 in 1850. Twenty years later, Chicago and St. Louis each had more than 250,000 people and ranked fourth and fifth among American cities. With more than 200,000, Cincinnati stood at eighth largest. Chicago, Detroit, and Cleveland had grown rapidly due to the expansion of transportation technologies, particularly canals and railroads, and to wartime (Civil War) manufacturing. In the West, San Francisco's rise as a city resulted in attracting large numbers of immigrants, especially the Irish and Germans. Competition between these two groups as well as with the Chinese resulted in various clashes. Anti-Chinese feeling proved especially strong and resulted in the emergence of the Workingmen's Party of California and the Workingmen's Party of San Francisco, along with an anti-Chinese riot in 1877, all of which eventually resulted in a ban on Chinese immigration.

The transportation revolution had made this interior growth possible. The opening of the Erie Canal in 1825 set off a flurry of canal building across the country, opening up the interior to settlement by native-born and immigrant alike. In turn, these massive public works projects attracted a large number of immigrants who then settled in the cities reached by the canals. Gangs of Irish and other immigrants worked on the Erie Canal, and many would settle in the urban centers that benefited from the new man-made waterway. Albany, Lockport, and Buffalo all saw their populations grow, as did other upstate New York cities such as Syracuse, Rochester, and Utica. Fifteen years later, the United States had over 3,000 miles of canals.

For example, the opening of the Erie Canal was important for Chicago by tying it to New York City via the Great Lakes. Chicago then built its own canal, the Illinois & Michigan Canal, which opened in 1848, extending eastern capital's reach further west and giving Chicago an advantage over St. Louis. In Ohio, canals joined the state together, allowing trade to go either north to the Great Lakes or south to the Ohio River and the Mississippi. Cincinnati and St. Louis had already benefited from the development of steamboats, causing them to rely on that mode of transportation even in the face of the development of the railroad, which eventually replaced the canal system as a major mover of goods and people across the country. In 1848, Chicago tied into the railroad system; three years later, it was connected to the East by rail, and by 1854, it stood as the center of the rapidly expanding system that would join the two coasts together in 1869. Immigrants proved crucial to the construction of these transportation routes, Europeans in the East and the Chinese in the West.

Now immigrants disembarking in New York City could easily reach the interior of the nation if they had the financial means and will to do so. The railroad also played an important part in the Northern victory during the Civil War, as did immigrants who sought their future in the United States. Recruiters met immigrant ships in New York and brought many new arrivals into the armed services of the North during the war.

Civil War Era

The first wave of Europeans established institutions throughout urban America. An abundance of churches appeared around which a sense of community developed. Not surprisingly, English immigrants often felt at home in American congregations, but they established separate ethnic organizations, such as the St. George Societies. Their fellow immigrants from the British Isles, the Scotch and the Welsh, in turn formed churches and also fraternal societies named after their patron saints St. Andrew and St. David. These institutions provided not only a feeling of camaraderie, but also political power in the new American urban settings. The Irish, in particular, settled primarily in cities and showed a penchant for political organization. While many could not at first afford to move beyond the Eastern seaports and so settled in large numbers in Boston, New York, Brooklyn, Baltimore, and Philadelphia, by the 1850s many had moved to the booming cities of the interior. Like their fellow immigrants from the British Isles, they showed a great ability to create institutions; unlike the immigrants from Britain, they felt the lash of prejudice.

The Irish-Catholic immigrant community quickly established a Roman Catholic parish model to be followed by others as they arrived in American cities. The parish provided both a place of worship and an organizational home for the creation of an urban power base. The first waves of Irish immigrants faced extreme discrimination both because of their ethnic origins and because of their Catholicism. Many had been pushed off their land in Ireland initially by the enclosure acts and then by the potato famine that ravaged that country in the 1840s. These impoverished Irish came to the United States with little education and only a meager understanding of traditional Catholic beliefs. Meanwhile, back in Ireland after the potato famine, a rejuvenated Catholic Church appeared, benefiting from what is often referred to as the Devotional Revolution, tying Irish nationality much more strongly to both Catholicism and middle-class values. The Irish, who would continue to come in large numbers to American cities throughout the nineteenth century, brought these new attitudes with them and constructed a powerful institutional church, which in turn would provide Irish Americans would a strong political and social base.

The Devotional Revolution in Ireland resulted in the founding of various dynamic religious orders that soon addressed the problem of immigration. Among these, one of the most important was the Sisters of Mercy, founded by Catherine McAuley in 1827, and, at the same time, Dublin Orders, such as the Sisters of Mercy, which followed immigrants to the United States and settled among their coreligionists in the industrial cities. Other Catholic orders also came to serve the growing Irish population, including both the Lasallian Christian Brothers, a French order, and the Irish Christian Brothers. These religious groups created a large institutional base for the ethnic community and provided a model for other ethnic groups to build upon. The Irish Catholic parish system was built largely by the communities that they served. Despite low pay and poor housing conditions, immigrants were able to raise large amounts of money and labor to build a web of churches that served their neighborhoods.

In turn, such orders as the Lasallian Christian Brothers and the Sisters of Mercy built institutions beyond the parish to benefit the immigrants. The Sisters of Mercy arrived in Chicago in 1843, opening their first school for girls in the city in 1846. It would later develop into St. Xavier University. The Irish order established Mercy Hospital in Chicago in 1852. The Christian Brothers served schools that taught boys first in parishes across New York City and Boston and then via a network of high schools and colleges across the country dedicated to the education of working-class boys. The Jesuit order likewise operated inner-city high schools as well as colleges and universities. The Jesuit institutions welcomed a more ethnically, and at times religiously, diverse group of students than did the locally based parochial schools, providing an institutional foundation for the large numbers of Irish and other Catholic immigrants.

The Irish institutional model presented an example for groups that would come after them. So, too, did the Irish political model. The Irish were familiar with the British political system, even if they rarely benefited from it. The leap to American politics was hardly a great one. In addition, most Irish spoke English and, in some states before the Civil War, could vote in local elections even as noncitizens as long as they were residents of the area for the prescribed time. This, along with a firm institutional base

in the Catholic Church, gave the Irish a tremendous political advantage in the American city. Another factor was the development of a strong sense of folk culture, which centered on family, kinship, church and community. This sense of community would prove crucial as the Irish faced life in the American city.

In the antebellum years, the Irish lived in crowded and neglected neighborhoods throughout urban America. The slums of Buffalo proved typical of these conditions. In 1851, Buffalo's *Courier* described the heavily Irish First and Eighth Wards where one saw "the spectacle of a most squalid poverty hardly credible in this land of plenty." Some 57 percent lived in lakeshore and canal corridor slums; the poorest of the Irish huddled in shacks no more than 12 feet to a side in neighborhoods known as "the Patch," "the Flats," "the Beach," "the Hook" and "Sandytown." These were constructed from waste boards discarded by local industries and warehouses. Some residents even lived in beached canal boats. Fires and storms often decimated these meager dwellings. On top of all this, the inhabitants owned few of these structures. In 1855, only 23 percent of Irish household heads owned homes, as compared to 56 percent of Americans and 54 percent of Germans! Of those Irish-owned structures, 90 percent were made of plank or wood frame.

Such conditions replicated themselves throughout urban America. The Irish tended to fill the ranks of unskilled labor and occupied a limited niche even within that category. In Chicago, many had come to work on the construction of the Illinois & Michigan Canal. They stayed behind to fill the ranks of laborers in the packinghouses and steel mills that soon opened adjacent to the waterway in suburban Bridgeport and later farther to the south in the town of Lake.

In the years before the outbreak of the Civil War, many cities saw clashes between immigrants and native-born Americans. Often these riots were based on religious as well as ethnic differences. Foremost in the case of the Irish, anti-Catholicism became an issue, but labor competition also played a role. Native-born weavers attacked Irish weavers and destroyed their looms and houses in Philadelphia's Kensington neighborhood in 1844. Anti-Catholic and anti-Irish riots occurred in Baltimore, St. Louis, and

Louisville during this period. Germans too felt the wrath of nativist sentiment, especially around the issue of temperance. The so-called German or Continental Sunday upset American Protestant sensibilities. After going to church, immigrant communities often celebrated their day off from work in saloons, picnic groves, beer halls, and gardens. Beer flowed freely, while bands played ethnic music and women and children attended what nativists saw as sinful violations of the Sabbath. Sunday blue laws restricting such entertainment resulted from the unreconstructed drinking habits of immigrant workers. In 1855 in Chicago, this resulted in the Lager Beer Riot, pitting the German community against the Know-Nothings who temporarily ran the city government and attempted to restrict German taverns by arresting various saloonkeepers. The riot resulted in one death and some 60 injuries; more importantly, it set the stage for both ethnic politics and further urban clashes in Chicago and across urban America.

Many of the Germans who left Europe after 1848 brought radical ideas with them and found freedom in the American city to express them openly. Cities with large German populations, such as Milwaukee, Cincinnati, Chicago, and Detroit, saw mass socialist and even anarchist movements in the nineteenth century. Indeed, socialists would continue to have a good deal of political power in Milwaukee well into the twentieth century. The 1877 railroad strikes across the country, particularly in cities including Pittsburgh, Chicago, and St. Louis, saw Germans emerging in the leadership of labor unions and radical political parties. Nine years later, the police rounded up German immigrants and closed immigrant radical newspapers in Chicago after the tragic Haymarket Affair.

Native-born Americans often feared that the immigrants would never be assimilated into American life. They worried about the impact of European radicalism and felt that the second wave of European immigrants from eastern and southern Europe seemed too different to assimilate into the dominant Protestant middle-class culture. Catholics, Orthodox Jews, and Orthodox Christians presented problems in the eyes of those who feared the new immigration. The earlier, largely Protestant, and often English-speaking immigration seemed more flexible, more assimilable. Despite these differences, the experiences of both groups of Europeans largely mimicked each other.

Post Civil War to 1920

The emergence of steam, of course, transformed more than the interior transportation system of the United States. It dramatically changed travel and communications across the Atlantic Ocean and within the interior of Europe itself. In the 1860s, British steamships cut the time it took to make the ocean voyage from Liverpool to New York City from one to three months to an astonishing 10 days to two weeks. Travel and communication between the continents improved quickly. As more technological changes came to sea travel, the trip became quicker, more reliable, and less dangerous as well as more comfortable. At the same time that the railroads and canals were opening the American West to more and more settlement, they were transforming European travel. Now people in areas of that continent who had found emigration difficult were able to respond to the migration impulse.

After 1880, northern and western European immigration began to decrease, and immigration from the "other" Europe—that is, eastern and southern Europe—increased as railroads reached Warsaw, Krakow, Kiev, Moscow, and southern Europe between the 1840s and 1860s. These parts of Europe found themselves more engaged in the capitalist market system. As capitalism emerged in these areas, it displaced old ways of doing things and traditional beliefs and customs. The new economic system also provided opportunities for millions of individuals to change their lives either within the homeland's economy or outside of it. Italians, Greeks, Poles, Jews, and others from east of the Elbe and south of the Alps soon flooded American cities and added to the ethnic diversity of the streets. Immigration increased as transportation became more efficient and as industrialism stoked the imagination of people on both sides of the Atlantic.

To the native-born, American cities seemed to lose their American character as immigrants and their children came to dominate them. After the Civil War, a continental pattern evolved with the northeastern manufacturing belt leading the nation in population, stretching from New England through the Mid-Atlantic states and including the Great Lakes states. Naturally, immigrants flocked to this industrial core. In 1870, almost 60 percent of the urban population of the United States lived within the New England and Mid-Atlantic states, making up more than 40 percent of the region's population. Immigrants and their American-born children made up two-thirds or more of these urban residents.

While large German and Irish communities appeared in all the ports, differences in final destinations showed various trends. The Irish often stayed on in the eastern ports that had the highest concentration of that group; while Germans had greater economic means and skills, which often allowed them to push into the nation's interior and settle in the quickly rising cities of the North Central region around the Great Lakes and the Ohio and Mississippi River systems. In 1880, Manhattan saw 198,595 Irish immigrants call it home. Brooklyn, just across the East River, now contained 83,378 Irish-born residents. In 1847, Boston, a city of about 115,000, had been swamped with 37,000 Irish immigrants. In 1880, 67,030 Irish immigrants called Boston's Suffolk County home. Over 74,000 resided there 10 years later. Numerically, the Germans almost matched the Irish in Manhattan in 1880, with 163,482 foreign-born Germans. In that same census year, nearly 60,000 Brooklynites were born in Germany. Interior cities, such as Chicago, St. Louis, Cincinnati, Detroit, and Milwaukee, housed large German populations.

After 1880, the source areas for immigrants began to shift and their numbers increased substantially. Fewer than one-third of all immigrants entering the country between 1820 and 1920 had arrived prior to 1880. Over the next 40 years (1880–1920), immigrants flooded into the country, as an average of six million entered each decade. From 1900 to 1909 alone, some eight million immigrants came to the United States. Southern and eastern Europeans predominated in this second wave of European immigration. Observers made much about the fact that these newer immigrants seemed to settle more intensely in

cities than their predecessors. In fact, even the wave of immigrants from northern and western Europe settled heavily in cities. In 1910, immigrants and their children made up nearly 80 percent of the populations of Chicago and New York. Irish immigrants came to dominate several smaller western cities, such as Butte and Anaconda, Montana. In Anaconda, over half of the population was foreign-born in 1907, with the Irish making up nearly 25 percent of the city's population.

By 1920, the census counted 75 percent of immigrants from the United Kingdom living in cities. Irish immigrants were urban at a rate of 86.9 percent, the highest percentage for the first wave. More than 67 percent of German immigrants also found themselves in cities, as did 54.6 percent of all Scandinavians. The high rates for Russians (88.6 percent), Poles (84.4 percent), Italians (84.4 percent), and Hungarians (80 percent) resulted from several factors, including the shrinking of the frontier by the 1890s. In some areas, land was simply more available to the earlier wave of newcomers.

Overall, the fact was that by 1900, it was the city, urban living, that had become the frontier. Also, the large number of East European Jews coming from Russia, Poland, Lithuania, and Austria-Hungary had a long tradition of living in urban centers. In either case, whether from a Welsh coal town, a Ukrainian farm, or a Polish shtetl, it was the industrial American city that attracted immigrants after 1880. In 1920, the United States contained a population of nearly 106 million people; of these, over 36 million of the white population was made up of foreign stock; that is, either foreign-born or with one or more foreign-born parent. In addition, some 186,000 Asians lived in the continental United States with another 160,000 Asians in the territory of Hawai'i. As the Norwegians said, urbanization meant Americanization. In 1920, a full three-quarters of immigrants lived in cities. This proved to be even more true for the largest cities, for immigrants had a kind of multiplier effect on both the population and economic levels of these cities.

The demand for low-paid, unskilled labor attracted immigrants to the burgeoning industrial cities. From Lynn, Lowell, and Providence through New York City, Newark, Hoboken and other East

Coast industrial centers; to the Midwest's Pittsburgh, Cleveland, Chicago, Gary, and Minneapolis–St. Paul; and on to many Western cities, notably Seattle, San Francisco, and Los Angeles, immigrants found themselves at the bottom of the industrial ladder, filling unskilled positions across the industrial spectrum. Like the Irish in Buffalo, they lived in crowded housing near the industrial plants that attracted them. Chicago's teeming West Side drew residents from around the globe. Irish, Germans, Czechs, Poles, Italians, Dutch, and East European Jews mixed on Halsted Street as they made their way in the new American urban world. What had once been a country retreat, Hull House, had by 1889 become the city's first and most famous social settlement house dedicated to serving the vast numbers of poor immigrants who inhabited the West Side.

A few miles to the south, the Back of the Yards neighborhood huddled up against the stockyards and packinghouses that served as magnets for immigrants. In less than two square miles, Catholics organized nine Catholic churches, while over 30 Catholic parishes surrounded the stockyards. Five of these churches were Polish, but all served various ethnic groups. These immigrant groups tended to gather together, but none totally dominated the neighborhood. Often immigrants lived in what might be called spatially integrated/socially segregated districts. While they might live together, they tended to socialize among themselves and attend separate institutions, whether it was the local ethnic parish, parochial school, tavern, grocery store, or funeral parlor.

To outsiders, these immigrant communities seemed disorganized. Observers saw bedlam on these streets of the American city. Community members, however, realized these neighborhoods were highly organized and institutionally developed. The initial reaction of immigrants was what might be called a "communal" response. New York's Jewish Lower East Side was home to many synagogues, stores, theaters, and other institutions. The Bialystoker Synagogue, Beth Hamedrash, the Eldridge Street Synagogue, Kehila Kedosha Ianina, and Angel Orensanz Center are among the more famous synagogues in the neighborhood. Yiddish theaters opened along the streets of the Lower East Side. At least 12

operated in the district centered on Second Avenue and known as the Jewish Broadway. In addition, Yiddish newspapers, such as the *Yiddish Daily Forward*, provided information and a point of view for the community. This institutional base was also eventually translated into considerable political power for immigrant communities.

Urban Machines: Political and Labor

Immigrants and the political machines, particularly Democratic ones, seemed intimately connected throughout urban America in the nineteenth and early twentieth centuries. The newcomers seemed as vital to these organizations as they did to the sweatshops, factories, packinghouses, and steel mills in which they worked. Immigrants were not simply sheepish followers of ethnic and political leaders. The machines provided an opportunity for immigrants and their American-born children to exert a sense of countervailing power against those who ruled the American city. Faced with the tremendous power of the large corporations that emerged, especially after the Civil War, immigrants found it difficult to exert any influence in the American city. The inward-looking communal response provided only a limited sense of security. Once those communal institutions, notably the churches, parochial or synagogue schools, taverns, local banks, and fraternal organizations, were established, it soon became evident that these urban communities had to band together to further protect themselves and gain prosperity. An urge to organize in both the political arena and on the shop floor generally meant reaching out to other groups and attempting to overcome the constant fragmentation of the urban working class that immigration and diversity of all kinds often engendered. Thus, an extra-communal response emerged that would include both political activism, often in the guise of political machines, and the labor movement.

Native white Americans often complained that the so-called big city political machines were fueled by the votes of immigrants and their children. New York City's legendary Tammany Hall organization, although founded by such prominent native-born whites as Aaron Burr as part of the Democratic-

Republican Party, was soon seen as an instrument for immigrants to gain control of the city. By the 1850s, Tammany Hall had garnered the support of immigrants who settled there, particularly the Irish. In 1854, the political club elected its first mayor. Over the years John Kelly, William Tweed, and Richard Croker played crucial roles in the development of the Tammany Hall organization, which finally went into decline only during the Great Depression of the 1930s. Political machines appeared throughout urban America, convincing many that democratic ideals had been lost to power-hungry professional politicians who had wrested control from the native-born elite in a number of cities, including New York, Philadelphia, Chicago, and San Francisco.

Immigrant communities often turned toward organized labor as another answer to protecting themselves in the capitalist city. First Wave immigrants who brought skills with them to the United States often brought labor union traditions. For example, skilled immigrant textile workers were not only familiar with production methods, but also knew how to deal with owners, managers, and workplace issues. They often had been prominent members of union organizations in their homelands. Some unions were even transplanted from Britain to the United States as more and more of their memberships migrated to American textile centers in New England. In Chicago, German unionists and radicals helped organize the labor movement. British coal miners organized Illinois coalfields and influenced Illinois' passage in 1872 of the first law in the United States to protect coalminers. The Irish iron molders in Troy, New York, even agitated for a "worker" city that would result in greater Irish and labor political control.

Not only did First Wave immigrants have such experiences, but many southern and East European immigrants also brought labor union and socialist organizing skills with them. In Providence, Rhode Island, East European Jews brought their experiences in the Socialist Bund to help organize workers. Italian immigrants, with experience in farmers unions in Italy, also came to Providence and helped organize labor. In Butte, Montana, in 1907, 500 Finnish miners were fired for being socialists. In Chicago, Polish immigrant workers actively supported the

Amalgamated Association of Iron and Steel Workers in the 1919 steel strike and helped to organize the packinghouses during the same era. While the American Federation of Labor (AFL) often agitated for immigrant restriction and discriminated against unskilled immigrant labor, even that union had to embrace immigrants in the steel, meatpacking, coal mining, and garment industries. In the 1930s, immigrants and their children, as well as African Americans, would prove vital to the revitalization of organized labor and the rise of the Congress of Industrial Organizations (CIO).

Urban West, Urban South

While the majority of immigrants in the nineteenth and early twentieth centuries settled in the Northeast and Great Lakes states, immigration also had a great impact on the West. Immigrants from Europe as well as from Asia and Latin America have consistently provided a large proportion of the population of Western cities. Although in 1900, less than 10 percent of the nation's immigrant population lived in the West, they made up 15.4 percent of the region's population. The urban West would see even greater concentrations. Once again immigration to the West resulted from a great need for cheap labor as white settlers rolled back the frontier. Labor was to be cheap, ample, and expendable. In 1880, the foreign-born made up more than 44 percent of the population of San Francisco County. At that time, immigrants from the British Isles predominated, with over 30,000 immigrants coming from Ireland alone. Here they clashed with over 21,000 Chinese, who had been attracted to California first by the Gold Rush and then by the building of the railroads tying the state to the East.

Thirty years of anti-Chinese agitation by the working class culminated in the passage of the Chinese Exclusion Act of 1882, which barred most Chinese immigration for 10 years (and was twice renewed). During that decade, 5,212 Italians joined San Francisco's diverse workforce, whereas the China-born population only grew by about 3,000, to just over 24,000—a consequence of the exclusion act and other discriminatory legislation and federal court decisions. Anti-Chinese riots in the mid-1880s also occurred in other West Coast cities, including Seattle and Tacoma. The Chinese had first arrived in Seattle in the 1860s. Twenty years later, many found themselves unemployed after the completion of the Northern Pacific Railroads line from Lake Superior to Tacoma. In 1883 the Chinese had helped dig Seattle's Montlake Cut to connect Lake Union's Portage Bay to Lake Washington's Union Bay. The Chinese tended to locate in what became known as Seattle's Chinese District, near today's Occidental Park. Anti-Chinese feelings rose in the mid-1880s due to an economic collapse and rising unemployment. Anti-Chinese mobs attacked the small community. Various labor groups agitated against the Chinese, including socialist leaders and the heads of the Knights of Labor.

The results of the 1882 exclusion act had a definite impact on the West Coast's Chinese-born population. By 1900, that community in San Francisco had fallen to 10,762. In Seattle's King County, which always contained only a small population of foreign-born Chinese, fewer than 400 lived in the area in that year. Los Angeles contained a population of nearly 3,000 Chinese in 1900. At the same time, Chinese communities were growing in the Great Lakes regions and the East, particularly in New York and Brooklyn. In contrast, the Chinese population of the West Coast would not see significant gains until after World War II, when the 1943 repeal of the acts excluding most Chinese immigrants was followed a few years later by special provisions in the War Brides' Act allowing for the admission of Asian spouses of American military personnel. Like African Americans, the Mexicans, Filipinos, and Asians in the West would be treated as racial minorities and would face discrimination and even violence.

The immigrant populations of the West continued to expand, including the Japanese community. In 1890, only 137 Japanese lived in the Seattle area, but 10 years later 3,338 called King County home. The San Francisco Japanese population rose by nearly 300 percent during the same decade to 1,852 residents. By 1890, San Francisco County's foreign-born population stood at just over 42 percent, with the Irish and Germans the largest groups; while the Seattle area

foreign-born population was nearly 28 percent of the total number of residents. Seattle's population proved extremely diverse in 1880, and Canadians, English, Germans, Swedes, and Norwegians provided the largest numbers of immigrants. As in eastern cities, these groups formed crucial communal institutions such as churches, ethnic fraternal associations, and neighborhood clubs, and of course also illegal criminal organizations.

Not surprisingly, Texas, California, and the Southwest saw a large influx of Mexicans across a largely artificial border created after the Mexican-American War (1846–1848). By 1920, over 33,000 Mexican immigrants had settled in the Los Angeles area out of a total population for Los Angeles County of 936,455. Both neighboring Orange and Ventura Counties also had growing Mexican populations. These were, however, still very rural counties. Nevertheless, much of the demographic growth in the West is attributable to cities, especially after 1920. Immigrants played vital roles in these western cities as they did in the East. Germans, Italians, Irish, Chinese, and German Jews were well settled in San Francisco. Norwegians and Canadians made up large percentages of Seattle's population at the time, with over 11,000 Norwegians and 18,000 Canadians in that city by 1930. Over the years, Norwegian immigrant numbers would decline precipitously, but the closeness of Canada and an open border would guarantee a long-lasting Canadian community in Seattle. Swedes and Canadians would have an important role in Tacoma, as did Germans, German Jews, Swedes, and Chinese in Portland and Italians in Denver. Chinese, Japanese, Italians, and Jews played large roles in Los Angeles.

Los Angeles saw its foreign-born population double in the 1920s. In a study of 15 specific groups examined in Western cities, in Los Angeles only the Chinese did not increase in number. The Jewish population of Los Angeles skyrocketed. It jumped to nearly 20,000 by the end of World War I and then more than doubled by 1923, surpassing San Francisco's Jewish community and becoming the largest Jewish settlement in the West. By 1927, 67,000 Jews called Los Angeles home. On the eve of World War II, some 130,000 Jews lived in the city, a population three times the size of San Francisco's Hebrew community.

In Houston, a 9 percent growth in the foreign-born population during the 1920s was spread across 11 groups. Only Denver saw a decline in its foreign-born population, with only a small increase among Mexicans. Between 1910 and 1930, faraway Honolulu grew rapidly, largely once again because of immigration. The city's population expanded by 164 percent in this period, and Asians made up 58 percent of the city's population on the eve of the Great Depression. Nearly 47,500 Japanese lived in the city, while the Filipino population grew from just 87 in 1910 to almost 4,800 during the same period. The Portuguese made up the largest European immigrant group in Honolulu, with 12,100 members.

In the era up to 1950, with the exception of New Orleans and to a lesser extent Charleston, southern cities attracted the fewest immigrants, which is not surprising given the nature of the South's economy both before and after the Civil War. In 1880, over 13,000 Germans called New Orleans home along with nearly 12,000 Irish and just over 1,800 Englishmen. That same year, just 1,600 Irishmen settled in Charleston, as did about the same number of Germans. Southern cities offered fewer opportunities for immigrants and had large African-American and white working-class populations to take up the low-paying jobs. Some English immigrants found their way to Birmingham, Alabama, to work, attracted by the emerging steel industry at the turn of the twentieth century. Immigration, however, would become a much larger factor in southern cities after 1960, with, for example, over one million immigrants in 2000 calling Miami City's Dade County home.

World War II and the Postwar Era: Reforms and Refugees

A series of laws restricting immigration were passed in the twentieth century with varying results. The years of large-scale European immigration ended in the mid-1920s. After that, with a few exceptions, such as the 1942 wartime Bracero agreement with Mexico that allowed labor to be imported into the United States (mostly) from Mexico. Indeed, with the enactment of the post–World War II Displaced Persons Acts in 1948 and 1950, the era of mass immigration

was seen as over. The 1948 act enabled many Europeans—who had seen their homelands overrun by Germany and its allies and later occupied by Soviet forces—to enter the United States. Among these were survivors of the Holocaust and those former residents of occupied nations who saw their populations moved to Germany to work in labor camps. Some also refused to return to their countries of origin for political reasons, particularly Polish soldiers who had fought in the West during the war and were opposed to the implementation of a Communist regime in Poland after 1945.

One result of the Displaced Persons Act was that the newcomers rejuvenated a number of older ethnic communities, providing them with new members and helping to anchor many inner-city immigrant neighborhoods across urban America, especially eastern European ones. Ethnic organizations often found new memberships as well. To reiterate, despite this and various other legislated exceptions during the 1950s, it seemed to most Americans as if the era of mass immigration was over.

In 1965, however, Congress passed new laws regulating immigration, and by the end of the twentieth century, the United States had clearly entered yet another massive immigration era. The full implication of the reforms would not at first be apparent, but by the mid-1970s, it was visible in major urban areas who the new immigrants would be. This time the major providers of immigrants would not be European countries, but Asian, Caribbean, and Latin American ones.

The United States has seen an incredible increase in the number of immigrants arriving from Latin America, particularly Mexico, and other Spanish-speaking countries in the Western Hemisphere. In turn, while the numbers have been somewhat smaller, the impact of Asians arriving in the country—their roots extending from India to the Philippines—has also been great, expanding or establishing many new settlements in urban areas. Much of the stability and growth of urban America in the past 30 years has been due to this new wave of immigrants. By 2009, 54 percent of the nation's 38 million foreign-born residents came from Latin America, 27 percent from Asia. These figures do not include the approximately

A Kurdish immigrant buys bread at a market in Nashville, Tennessee, 2005. There are an estimated 8,000 Kurds living in Nashville, which they call "Little Kurdistan." (AP Photo/John Russell)

12 million illegal immigrants who entered the United States. The period since 2000 has seen the largest overall numbers of immigrants enter the country than in any comparable period of time, with approximately 7.9 million legal and illegal immigrants entering the country in the first five years of that decade (along with those who overstayed their visas).

The destination of immigrants has also widened in this period. While major traditional immigrant cities, such as New York, Los Angeles, Chicago, and San Francisco continue to attract immigrants, newer centers in the South, Midwest, and West have experienced explosive growth, notably Cape Coral–Fort Myers, Nashville, and Indianapolis. Cape Coral witnessed a 122 percent growth in its immigrant population between 2000 and 2007. Nashville's foreign-born population increased by 74 percent during the same time period, while Indianapolis saw a 71 percent growth. Indianapolis's Mexican immigrant

community numbered only 210 in 1970, but 30 years later, 13,222 Mexicans called the Indiana city home. In 1980, merely 319 Africans lived in the Indiana capital, but 20 years later, that figure mushroomed to 2,799. Vietnamese immigrants numbered over 1,300 in 1980; by 2000 over 39,000 lived in Indianapolis. Orlando, Florida's immigrant population rose by 64 percent, and Raleigh, North Carolina, saw a 62 percent increase. In contrast, Asians accounted for the largest immigrant population in Columbia, South Carolina, providing up to 40 percent of the foreign-born. Nashville is home to the largest Kurdish population in the United States. It also has a growing Mexican community, which in 2000 included 10,523 of Davidson County's 39,523 immigrant residents. The South is witnessing immigration as it never has before. Immigrants, who made up 80 percent of the increase in recent years, have largely fueled Dallas–Fort Worth–Arlington's amazing population growth.

In 2000, nearly 300,000 Mexicans lived in Dallas County alone, with over 104,000 in neighboring Tarrant County, home to Fort Worth and Arlington.

As in the past, chain migration and early settlers have often determined the destination of immigrants entering the country. Since 1980, immigrant numbers have greatly expanded across the southwestern United States. In Phoenix, the nation's sixth-largest city, more than 70 percent of its immigrant population was Latino, including nearly 285,000 Mexicans across Maricopa County, together with nearly 4,000 Salvadorans and 2,000 Cubans. Moreover, immigrants made up roughly 41 percent of the city's whole population in 2008. Meanwhile, Los Angeles County, long a destination for immigrants, has seen its foreign-born population grow by more than 400 percent from 1970 to 2000, of which about one-third were Mexican (1,166,754). At the turn of the century, over 213,000 Salvadorans, 161,000 Filipinos, 114,000 Koreans, 87,000 Chinese, 76,000 Vietnamese, 58,000 Middle Easterners, 51,000 former Soviet or Russian immigrants, 43,000 Canadians, 40,000 Japanese, 39,000 English, 34,000 Cubans, 26,000 Germans, 24,000 Indians, and 13,000 Poles together comprised one of the country's most diverse populations.

Traditional havens for Cuban and other refugees, particularly Miami, of course still lead southern cities, although since the Cuban Revolution in 1959, Miami often sees itself as a Caribbean rather than a southern city. In 1960, Miami–Dade County provided a home for a largely Russian immigrant population of 15,341, along with just over 7,000 immigrants born in Poland. This largely Jewish population, many of whom were retirees and formerly lived in northern cities, provided the city's ethnic diversity. After Fidel Castro came to power, the Cuban population began to skyrocket to 207,139 in 1970 and 324,976 in 1980. In 2000, as the eastern European population dwindled, Cubans made up 45.8 percent of Miami-Dade's immigrant population of 1,147,646 people. Other Spanish-speaking immigrants joined the nearly 777,500 Cubans (2006–2008), including over 105,100 Nicaraguans, more than 36,000 Dominicans, almost 21,000 Mexicans, and about 11,000 Salvadorans. Less than 1 percent of Miami-Dade's population is Asian. The population is very diverse and with a definite Latin accent. The 2000 census recorded that 66.7 percent of Miami proper's residents listed Spanish as their first language, while English accounted for 25.45 percent. Nearly 75 percent of Miami's population spoke primarily languages other than English at home.

War and revolution have shaped much of the new wave of immigrants. In 1975, with the fall of Vietnam, Cambodia, and Laos to Communist forces, many refugees from Southeast Asia fled to the United States. The Hmong, an ethnic people that lived along the Vietnamese-Laotian border and had been allied with the South Vietnamese and American forces during the Vietnam War, were also among those who escaped to the United States (along with other destinations). Minneapolis–St. Paul has openly taken steps to attract immigrants from Southeast Asia, particularly the Hmong. While humanitarian reasons originally prompted this, the urban economy has greatly benefited from the immigrant arrivals, as they have proven to be a crucial part of the revitalization of the Twin Cities. In the 20 years after 1980, the Twin Cities saw their immigrant population grow by 196 percent. Vietnamese, Laotian, Hmong, Somali, and Latino immigrants made up the bulk of these newcomers. Today, over 60,000 Hmong live in Minnesota, and their language is the second-most spoken language in the Twin Cities public schools. In addition, the 2000 census counted about 10,000 Vietnamese-born residents living in Hennepin and Ramsey Counties, where the Twin Cities are located. Officials and organizations, especially the Lutheran Brotherhood and the Minneapolis Foundation, played a key role in bringing these immigrants to the Twin Cities.

The next group welcomed there was Somali refugees. These African immigrant families often arrived without men, many of whom had been killed in the Somali civil war. However, like the Hmong before them, they quickly became integral parts of the local economy. In 2000, over 26,000 Africans lived in Hennepin and Ramsey Counties. On the other hand, only 729 Swedish-born residents called the two counties home, whereas nearly 40,000 had lived there in 1910, a result of the changing composition of immigration. By the beginning of the current century, the

Twin Cities were also looking to attract refugees from the civil war in Bosnia. By the early twenty-first century, Minneapolis–St. Paul had become a diverse urban area with an energetic economy largely because it welcomed immigrants with open arms.

Cities that already have large immigrant populations usually attract more foreign-born. New York and Los Angeles both attracted over one million immigrants in the 1990s, while Miami drew roughly 485,000 newcomers. About 50,000 Polish immigrants made their way to Chicago in the 1990s, joining that city's already-large Polish community. Immigrants tend to follow paths already pioneered for them by earlier settlers. Thus, Hmong, Vietnamese, and Somali immigrants looked to their co-nationals' migration streams to the Twin Cities.

Twenty-first Century

The new immigrants have buttressed cities as their older populations have moved out. This is a historical trend as well as a contemporary one. In the nineteenth century, as native white elites and the middle class fled the industrial cities, they were first replaced by immigrants from northern and western Europe and then by those from southern and eastern Europe. Today, the descendants of those Europeans are leaving the central cities and in turn are being replaced by a new wave of immigrants. The Pittsburgh metropolitan area, which does not attract a large number of immigrants, lost some 60,000 residents between 2000 and 2006. On the other hand, New York and Los Angeles look to gain populations after the first decade of the century.

New York and its suburbs received one million immigrants from 2000 to 2006. It is estimated that without this influx the region would have lost nearly 600,000 people. A state report claimed that immigrants accounted for $215 billion, or nearly one-third of the state of New York's economic activity in 2008. Immigrants made up 34.6 percent of New York City's population and 43 percent of its workforce. Its immigrants hail from 148 different countries, although 52 percent are from just 10 countries. Dominicans make up the largest group, followed by Chinese, Jamaicans, Mexicans, Guyanese, Ecuadorans,

Haitians, Trinidadians and Tobagonians, Russians, and Koreans.

Between 2000 and 2008, the number of immigrant workers grew by 68 percent and their wages increased by nearly 39 percent in New York. Queens had the largest concentration of immigrant workers, with Brooklyn, not surprisingly, just behind with nearly half of all foreign-born workers. The immigrant contribution to the gross city product rose 61 percent. These gains all exceeded figures for the native-born workforce. Foreign-born residents owned 60 percent of the homes in the city. Immigrants made up 46 percent of the city's physicians and surgeons and 55 percent of its registered nurses. Twenty-seven percent of chief executives and 21 percent of elementary and middle schoolteachers were born outside the United States. Between 2000 and 2007, the 10 New York neighborhoods with the highest concentration of foreign-born residents had stronger economies than the rest of the city's neighborhoods, as the median household income of the city's immigrant population nearly doubled from 1990 to 2007, a rate higher than that of inflation.

From 2000 to 2006, Los Angeles's immigrants prevented a decline of roughly 200,000 residents. The immigrant population of the Los Angeles–Long Beach area rose from 2,895,066 in 1990 to 3,449,444 in 2000, out of a total population of 9,519,338. During the same years, the Boston area took in about 160,000 immigrants, also preventing a population loss. The recession in the years after 2008 may overturn some of these gains as immigrants felt compelled to return to their homelands. For example, Chicago's population is likely to decline as a result of a falling off of immigration, and this despite an increase in the 1990s. Chicago's Mexican population remains one of the largest in the United States. Nevertheless, the majority of Chicago Hispanics now live in the city's suburbs, which points to an interesting trend among the new urban immigrants; for, as with many other older industrial cities, manufacturing jobs have fled the city proper and have moved to the suburban locations. Consequently, the significant demographic trend across urban America over the last 30 years has been the movement of the population to the periphery. In many ways, this trend has made the old immigrant portals obsolete.

The new immigrants, whether highly qualified professionals or unskilled workers, began to be attracted to these new job locations beyond the city's boundaries. As employment decentralization quickened, the new immigrants found themselves in a more enviable spot as compared to the city's traditional poor. Chicago's inner-city African-American community was at a distinct geographic disadvantage when it came to employment. Stuck in the central city, they realized the source of new jobs was a long commute away. Add the realities of racism and poor public transportation to the distant suburbs, and it becomes obvious that Chicago's working-class blacks suffered from a geographic disadvantage. These traditional South and West Side African-American neighborhoods had once been close to major industrial employers such as meat packinghouses, steel mills, warehouses and small manufacturing plants.

Much of that is now gone. Mexicans and other Latinos were moving to industrial suburbs, especially Cicero, Berwyn, and Melrose Park; and even to outlying satellite cities, for example, Aurora and Joliet. Others were also moving to the suburbs. The vast majority of Japanese, Filipino, Indian, Pakistani and recent Polish immigrants have likewise relocated to more employment-rich suburbs. Many of these had arrived with professional skills and could easily make their way out of the city to at least the older suburbs. Concurrently, Chicago's southwest suburbs, just beyond the city proper, have been receiving large numbers of Palestinians and other Arabs.

Conclusion

While numerous groups have been migrating to suburbia—at times bypassing older immigrant neighborhoods, such traditional immigrant-ethnic enclaves have found themselves resettled by a mixture of urbanites bent on gentrification (as well as some newer populations). While this newer demographic movement takes place, it puts pressure on older inner-city neighborhoods generally identified as either black or immigrant. Taxes and rents go up, and neither poor blacks nor immigrants can afford to live in these communities. Or, in another scenario, outside of Los Angeles, new communities have taken root, especially in San Bernardino and Riverside Counties, with thousands of first- and second-generation families acquiring new, first-time "dream" homes only to be confronted with the worst recession since the 1930s Great Depression and a multitude of foreclosures.

Although suburban areas have certainly attracted many diverse newcomers, a 2008 study also revealed that, in terms of employment, in "14 of the 25 largest metropolitan areas, including Boston, New York, and San Francisco, more immigrants are employed in white-collar occupations than in lower-wage work like construction, manufacturing or cleaning" (Preston 2010, A1). In fact, in 2006–2008, metro areas long overlooked as indices of growth due to immigration—including Pittsburgh, Baltimore, Detroit, Cleveland, Cincinnati, and Philadelphia—have found that three-to four-fifths of the immigrants present were white-collar workers. Moreover, "immigrants played a central role in the cycle of the economic growth of cities" since 1990. A stunning example has been the Bosnian refugees during the two decades following 1990 who have concentrated chiefly in St. Louis, displaying a broad array of occupations and investing in an exceptional number of new businesses on formerly blighted streets. Many Chinese settling there have similarly impacted that city.

Over the expanse of American history, cities have proven to be both constant magnets and beneficiaries of the massive waves of immigration that have entered the United States. That is not to say that there have not been downsides. Immigrants have often faced prejudice, poor living and working conditions, and even violence. Immigrants have also been involved in various types of crime, although the extent to which this is true has often been exaggerated. In most cases, however, the economies of urban and suburban areas have grown in the past and have recovered from economic contractions and recessions. In the early years of the twenty-first century, it is clear that the nation's postindustrial economy will continue to pose challenges and setbacks for some urban centers and opportunities for others to grow. Undoubtedly, immigrants will continue to be an important factor in many metropolitan regions.

Bibliography

Barkan, Elliott Robert. 1996. *And Still They Come: Immigrants and American Society, 1920 to the 1990s*. Wheeling, IL: Harlan Davidson.

Barkan, Elliott Robert. 2007. *From All Points: America's Immigrant West, 1870s–1952*. Bloomington and Indianapolis: Indiana University Press.

Barkan, Elliott Robert. 1990. "New Origins, New Homeland, New Region: American Immigration and the Emergence of the Sunbelt, 1955–1985." In *Searching for the Sunbelt: Historical Perspectives on a Region*, edited by Raymond A. Mohl, 124–48. Knoxville: University of Tennessee Press.

Bodnar, John. 1985. *The Transplanted: A History of Immigrants in Urban America*. Bloomington: Indiana University Press.

Daniels, Roger. 2004. *Guarding the Golden Door*. New York: Hill and Wang.

DiNapoli, Thomas P., and Kenneth B. Bleiwas. 2010. *The Role of Immigrants in the New York City Economy*. Report 17-2010. Albany: Comptroller of the State of New York.

Diner, Hasia. 2002. *Lower East Side Memories: A Jewish Place in America*. Princeton, NJ: Princeton University Press.

Gerber, David. 1989. *The Making of an American Pluralism: Buffalo, New York, 1825–1860*. Urbana and Chicago: University of Illinois Press.

Greene, Richard P. 1997. "Chicago's New Immigrants, Indigenous Poor, and Edge Cities," *Annals of the American Academy of Political and Social Science*, Vol. 551, Globalization and the U.S. City (May): 178–90.

Immigration Explorer Map, *New York Times* website. http://www.nytimes.com/interactive/2009/03/10/us/20090310-immigration-explorer.html.

Kraut, Alan M. 2001. *The Huddled Masses: The Immigrant in American Society, 1880–1921*. 2nd ed. Arlington Heights, IL: Harlan Davidson.

Muller, Thomas. 1993. *Immigrants and the American City*. New York and London: New York University Press.

Pacyga, Dominic A. 2003. *Polish Immigrants and Industrial Chicago: Workers on the South Side, 1880–1922*. Chicago: University of Chicago Press,

Preston, Julia. 2010. "Immigrants in Work Force: Study Belies Image," *New York Times*, April 16: A1, A3.

Skerrett, Ellen, ed. 1997. *At the Crossroads: Old Saint Patrick's and the Chicago Irish* Chicago: Wild Onion Books.

Ward, David. 1971. *Cities and Immigrants: A Geography of Change in Nineteenth Century America*. New York, London, and Toronto: Oxford University Press.

Zachary, Gregg. 2010. "Immigrants as Urban Saviors: When Immigrants Revive a City and When They Don't: Lessons from the United States." *Intercultural City: Making the Most of Diversity*. http://www.interculturalcity.com/people.htm (accessed February 25, 2010).

Rural America and the Immigrant Experience

James M. Bergquist

For over 300 years, farming provided the livelihood of a majority of Americans, and for all of that time, immigrants played a role in forming the culture of rural America. During that period, many came from European countries where the amount of land was limited, and maintaining a family continuously on the land was difficult. The lure of land that was more freely available motivated many of these newcomers. They also came in hopes of maintaining in the United States some new creation of the rural life they had known in their mother countries. What developed in the United States was a unique North American rural culture, inspired by these goals but also formed by such factors as a different system of land tenure, environmental differences, varying soil and climatic conditions, a more mobile and free population, the influence of national and world markets, and agricultural products different from what they had known in Europe. Agricultural ways and rural life would become distinctly American, but their development would nevertheless show the mark of the immigrant, especially in the ethnic communities they founded.

The Colonial Period

In the 150 years before the American Revolution, the creation of a new agricultural system was carried out by many Europeans who migrated to the New World. In the English colonies, the majority came from the British Isles. However, there were also settlers from Germany, the Netherlands, Ireland, and Sweden who found their way to the agricultural areas. As would be the case in later times, their work was often defined by the opportunities presented by the market for cash crops. This would include new commodities not grown in Europe, most notably tobacco and Indian corn (maize). Additionally, they would adjust themselves generally to a new land system, with land granted in fee simple–conveying outright ownership with no feudal or other obligations, except to the government itself. With new possibilities presenting themselves for settlers to gain their own land, those who came as tenants or indentured servants could look forward to being on their own as the colony expanded. Only a few, given other choices, would be attracted to lands under conditions similar to feudal Europe, as for example in the large Dutch patroonships along the Hudson River.

In Massachusetts and other parts of New England, the countryside was organized in the seventeenth century on the basis of towns. Colonial governments granted charters to groups of settlers to establish towns in the unoccupied areas to the west. The towns were granted control of the land within their boundaries, and committees organized from the original settlers were given the power to allocate the lands to settlers. The purpose was in part to promote compact settlements and prevent a dispersal of population toward an unguarded frontier. The granting of land was by no means egalitarian, and those higher up in the social structure usually fared better when land was allocated. Those Europeans who envisioned some renewal of their customary village life, where farmers had houses clustered together in a village and went out to cultivate outlying fields, would by around 1750 find that pattern giving way to one in which the farmers lived on the outlying fields, often consolidating their dispersed holdings and maintaining livestock within view of their homes. The tight-knit character of the Puritan towns in the seventeenth century would also yield to a looser social structure as the Puritan control declined and the Great Awakening (the evangelistic movement of the 1740s) created greater diversity among and within the towns. New England, however, would remain the region with the fewest non-English immigrant settlers during the colonial period.

The region of the American colonies most favored by non-English immigrants was the middle colonies (New York, New Jersey, Pennsylvania, and Maryland). Pennsylvania in particular offered tillable land stretching back from the port of Philadelphia over 100 miles to the north and west. The land grants offered by the proprietor William Penn and his successors offered sizable farms to actual settlers, at prices that were not considered exorbitant. English and Welsh farmers settled closer to Philadelphia. Immigrants from the German states moved into an arc of territory surrounding Philadelphia at a distance of about 50 miles. Migrants from Ireland, mostly Protestants, settled further out in the backcountry. Southeastern Pennsylvania became the most productive agricultural area in the colonies, exporting crops, such as wheat and flax to other colonies, to Europe, and to the West Indies through the port of Philadelphia.

The Germans in the region became known (misleadingly) as the Pennsylvania Dutch, and the image often conjured up in the minds of outsiders was that of the pietistic sects such as Amish and Mennonites, who founded close-knit communities centering on common religious congregations and striving to maintain inherited traditions. The variety of German farmers was, however, much larger, and although their settlements were drawn largely from areas along the Rhine and the states of southwestern Germany, they were divided among Lutheran, Reformed, and Catholic religious affiliations as well as the pietistic sects. The fee-simple grants of land they took up were a sharp change from the declining feudal ties still surviving in parts of their German homeland. The German farmers became known for the stability of their communities and for the intensive farming practices they followed. These characteristics came particularly from the high value they put on ownership of land and using the land as a basis for family preservation.

The other pioneering rural immigrants of colonial days were the Scotch-Irish, who also entered through southeastern Pennsylvania. These were immigrants from Ireland who were descended from Scots who had migrated to Ireland during the seventeenth century. In religion, they were primarily Presbyterian Protestants; the number of Catholic Irish in colonial days was a minority of the immigrants coming from Ireland. The Scotch-Irish settled in the backcountry of Pennsylvania, beyond the German settlements and close to the frontier. Their settlements were vulnerable to hostilities from the Indians and French—a condition that made them a political group critical of pacifist Quaker policies. In contrast to the Germans, the Scotch-Irish became known for their greater mobility and their less intensive farming practices. Many on the frontier were subsistence farmers and lived partially by hunting. They often squatted on open land, and their attitude toward the land was more exploitive. Their restless nature caused them often to move on and become the vanguard of other frontiers to the west.

From Pennsylvania, the Scotch-Irish and their descendants moved into the mountain valleys of the colony and, during the late eighteenth century, migrated down the Cumberland Valley, into western Maryland and the Shenandoah Valley of western Virginia, then into western North Carolina. While there were also some German settlements in these same regions, the Scotch-Irish were poised to play an historic role as the prototypical American frontiersmen—eventually migrating over the Appalachians to Tennessee and Kentucky, then providing a significant proportion of the population in the Ohio Valley and the lower Midwest.

The tidewater areas of the southern colonies began a separate rural tradition of American large-scale plantation farming. The overseas markets demanded supplies of tobacco and rice; these were labor-intensive crops that demanded continued labor for much of the year. European immigrants were not inclined to undertake wage labor on such plantations, and the answer for the landlords came to be slavery, an institution to which the southern planters had turned overwhelmingly by the end of the seventeenth century. Thus, few immigrants were induced to come to the southern colonies, other than those British immigrants who came as indentured servants to be skilled craftsmen, teachers, or domestic servants. The possibility of land available in Pennsylvania and beyond was far more attractive than wage labor on the plantations of the South. The lack of involvement by immigrants would continue to be a distinguishing factor in the agricultural economy of the South as it expanded into the Cotton Belt after the American Revolution.

The Midwest and the Family Farm

The rural culture that developed in the early Midwestern states (then known as the Old Northwest) in the years after the American Revolution is often considered in the popular mind as the archetype of the American family farm. This developing system was based on independent farmers, holding lands in fee simple, producing crops to be sold in a market economy. As new transportation routes into the region developed in the nineteenth century, the new culture would become most attractive to immigrants, who would become an important part of the rural population of the region as the century developed. Thus economic and environmental circumstances contributed greatly to the formation of rural life, but the immigrants now migrating more freely into the region would have their own effect.

The original migration path into the region north and west of the Ohio River was from western Virginia and North Carolina, over the Appalachians and into Tennessee and Kentucky and then into southern Ohio and southern Indiana. The migrants who followed that path included many of Scotch-Irish descent, but these were now two or three generations removed from their Ulster origins. The western populations were still mostly Protestant, yet many changes in religious culture were brought about by the evangelical movement known as the Second Great Awakening, which originated in Kentucky in the first decade of the nineteenth century. There were also movements of Scotch-Irish and German descendants through Pennsylvania and the headwaters of the Ohio River.

The development of a rural life that went beyond mere subsistence agriculture had to await a number of critical developments. As long as the outlet from the Mississippi River into the Gulf of Mexico remained in foreign hands, exporting of cash crops from the region would be difficult. The Louisiana Purchase of 1804 transferred the mouth of the Mississippi from French to American hands, opening that trade route (and also acquiring a vast quantity of land that seemed to ensure the future of American agriculture). Before the War of 1812, the presence of Indians still defending their territorial claims in the Old Northwest also deterred settlement. By 1815, the end of the war with Britain, Indians were more easily removed and persuaded (sometimes under considerable pressure) to hand over their land claims to the United States. Also by that time, the development of the steamboat on western waters facilitated exports and the migration of settlers from the port of New Orleans up the Mississippi, Ohio, and Missouri Rivers. Over the next two decades after 1815, a remarkable settlement of newcomers would occur in Ohio, Indiana, and Illinois. The migration would include an increasing number of immigrants bent upon acquiring farms.

The great attraction for immigrants was, of course, the promise of American land—fertile land, at prices far lower than the limited lands of European countries. In Europe, those farmers who held land, either as owners or tenants, often found themselves unable to provide viable farms to multiple heirs. The persons with no hope of holding land were then faced with the choice of either migrating to the towns and industrial cities of Europe or setting off for the United States. Those who could sell land they already owned in Europe could think of migration, in the hopes that the money realized from the sale of their previous holdings might purchase a much larger tract of land in the United States–perhaps enough to provide for the next generation as well as themselves. Increasingly, as the nineteenth century went on, the regions of the west just being opened up became the goal for immigrant farmers. The goal of possessing land was closely tied to the desire for the stability and perpetuation of the family.

The key to satisfying that goal lay in the system of land disposal that had developed in the United States since the passage of a basic land ordinance in 1785, under the government of the Articles of Confederation. That land system would be applied to government lands owned within the Northwest

Territory—the lands north and west of the Ohio River. The system would subsequently be adopted in new territories that would be opened all the way across the West to the Pacific coast. The federal government had previously acquired sovereignty over the region from various states on the Atlantic coast. The territorial government would be formally organized under a separate ordinance in 1787. The federal government also obtained title to the unoccupied lands previously claimed by the individual states. This acquisition of millions of acres of land by the federal government was a fateful step that would affect the settlement of much of the United States for the next century.

The Ordinance of 1785 provided that the federal government first clear all the lands under its control of any claims to titles by Indian tribes, which were judged to hold them in common for all their members. The clearance of these lands by many tribes over time was sometimes the result of an Indian war, and often the result of fraud, bribery, or intimidation. After the Indians had been removed from the area in question, the land was surveyed and divided into one-square-mile "sections" of 640 acres each, and then subdivided into "quarter-sections" of 160 acres. Townships were created consisting of 36 sections; These surveyed towns were often used to define governmental units within the counties of the new territories or states. After the land was surveyed, it could then be put on sale by the federal land offices. Beginning in 1820, the price was set at $1.25 an acre, and would remain at that level for the next century. (The Homestead Act, offering free land to the settlers, would not be passed until 1862.) Settlers could buy smaller tracts of land, but as the century went on, the 160-acre farm became the standard for both foreign-born and "Yankee" settlers.

From its beginning, the policy allowed unnaturalized immigrants to buy the federal land. The system that developed formed the matrix for both immigrants and the native-born to establish communities in the expanding West. The land system would also create differences in the agricultural habits of immigrants from those they had practiced in European countries. Instead of close-knit villages from which immigrant farmers went out to open fields dispersed around the area, they now lived in the countryside on their own

plots of land, purchased from the checkerboard survey pattern set up by the federal government. The land was bought in fee simple, with, as noted, none of the remnants of feudal obligations they might have known in Europe. This dispersal of settlers throughout the countryside and away from towns caused sharp changes in community life from what they had known in Europe. For many of the immigrants, the basis of community life became the churches that spread across the countryside, serving as centers for preserving their identity and their native language. The immigrants thus had, at the same time, to adjust to an American system of agriculture while preserving their own unique traditions that they had brought with them.

The life of the immigrant would also be shaped by the development of the transportation system within the new regions. These new lines of transportation would open up access from the farms to national and international markets, which created a demand for certain crops of the region. As a general rule, with the inadequate roads and slow wagon transportation of the time, farmers needed to be within about 15 miles of transportation in order to export goods to a market. Lands at a distance from transportation had to await the arrival of newer modes before settlement could take place.

When waterways were still the principal routes for moving heavy goods, farmers seeking land settled along the Ohio River and its tributaries. Before the War of 1812, hostile Indians blocked access to the northern regions of the Midwest, and there was meager settlement there until after 1815. Beginning in the 1820s, canals being built in the region extended water transportation between major waterways. The Erie Canal in western New York, completed in 1825, made possible traffic from the East into the Great Lakes, giving access to the northern Midwest. During the 1820s and 1830s, canals were extended through the region, opening up to settlement sections of central Indiana, Ohio, and Illinois. By the 1840s, railroads were being built into the region, and new farming country was being opened up near railroad stations in places previously remote from transportation. The implications of these developments for immigrants seeking new land were to link them to a market economy. They could then specialize in certain crops demanded by the market, and thus move away from the earlier practices of self-sufficient agriculture they had followed when farms remained remote from any market.

The earlier population movement arriving from the south into the Ohio Valley had relatively few immigrants. Most were natives of the Appalachian regions of Kentucky, Tennessee, North Carolina, and western Virginia. Although some of these were descendants of Scotch-Irish immigrants, relatively few were foreign-born. As indicated above, after 1815 the port of New Orleans would become, by the 1830s, the second major port of entry for immigrants (New York City being foremost). The development of the new canals and railroads enabled immigrants to seek out tracts of land with easy access to the markets. Rapidly, they sent word to friends and relatives across the Atlantic, telling them of the new opportunities developing in the Midwest.

This could inspire "chain migration" of various kinds, where specific groups originating in Europe contributed to the settlement of particular American communities, frequently based upon specific towns in the Old World trying to recreate themselves in the New World. Indeed, they might be more broadly based on regional, provincial, or religious affiliations existing in the homeland. Some settlements were even organized by Catholic missionary societies in Europe. As settlements moved westward through the states of the Old Northwest, more native-born farmers migrated from the Mid-Atlantic states. By the 1820s and 1830s, Michigan and Wisconsin were being opened up, and migrants from New England and western New York were a strong element in those regions.

The Germans were by far the largest element among immigrants coming into the early rural Midwest. The majority of them came from the southern and western states of Germany (at a time when the many states there were not united) and migrated through the ports of New York and New Orleans, which had become by the 1830s the second-largest port of immigration. Most Germans, however, quickly bypassed the southern states and headed to the regions accessible to the Ohio, upper Mississippi, and Missouri Rivers. The Germans found homes both in cities and in rural areas. Cincinnati was the German center of the early Midwest, but other cities, such as St. Louis, Chicago, Milwaukee, and Indianapolis, would become urban centers for the growing rural populations around them.

The various Scandinavian groups would follow, becoming a distant second in immigrant rural populations. As the railroads began to spread across the upper Midwest and westward from Chicago, the new states of Wisconsin and Minnesota offered opportunities for land. The opening up of these regions by a boom in railroad building coincided with the peak period in the flow of pre–Civil War immigration. Norwegians, who had come to Illinois as early as the 1820s, found new opportunities in Wisconsin and Minnesota. The migration of Swedes would swell in the 1850s. Finns would find a new homeland in the Upper Peninsula of Michigan, and a new migration of Dutch would find their way to western Michigan.

Perfecting the Model of the Family Farm

The formation of tightly knit ethnic communities in the Midwest created a new immigrant culture, partly formed by economic and environmental factors, partly by the desire to maintain traditional ways of life. Immigrants were obliged in many ways to adapt to the new Midwestern environment. They came into a different land system, one that offered opportunities unknown in the Old World and assured them of the ability to pass land onto their heirs. They now raised products for an international market—such as Indian corn, the hogs produced with Indian corn, and, in the more northern parts of the region, wheat and other small grains. In concentrating on these, they moved away from the habits of self-sufficiency that characterized many places in the Old World. They had to accept a new role as businessmen, playing their chances in a world market, abandoning the old-fashioned system in which weaving, vegetable production, harvesting wood for fuel, and slaughtering animals for meat would give away to practices aimed at greater efficiency, putting the most effort into marketable commodities and less into household production. Toward the end of the nineteenth century, of course, their dependency on the vagaries of the market would create financial problems, as deflation caused agricultural prices to drop. But the market and environment would induce further changes, as when many in the northern Midwest turned from wheat and other small grains to dairy production.

These adaptations to a new agricultural system contributed to the assimilation of rural immigrants. But there were other ways in which they could resist assimilation and manage to preserve their cultural traditions. Their goals of acquiring land and preserving it within the family led to a stability in their farm life and in their communities. In the United States as in their mother countries, immigrants sought to develop their farms and pass them on to the next generation. They sometimes sought to acquire more land nearby in order to provide for all their sons, rather than the eldest. Only their churches and other associations helped to maintain stability, and also to provide protection for much of their inherited culture, particularly language. There is no question but that ethnic-language retention could be preserved longer in rural areas than in the city.

There were wide variations in the structures of the immigrant communities that developed in the nineteenth-century Midwest. In some cases, they consisted of settlements where farmers of similar ethnicity clustered together closely. In others, communities were more widely dispersed, using churches or ethnic associations as a means of communication or interaction. Scholars who have studied the rural communities have often remarked that in general, these communities were more stable than those created by native-born "Yankees," who often arrived in the earlier stages of settlement, exploited their land claims with less intensive farming, and then sold their lands and moved on to new lands being opened up further west. British immigrant farmers brought habits of more scientific and intensive farming with them, but these often gave way to the more exploitive customs of the native-born farmers; the British had less fear of assimilation, since they faced no language barrier and could easily fit into the society and institutions of the American-born.

This restless, speculative attitude toward the land was in sharp contrast to the practices of the immigrants who tended to hold on to the land or to convey it to family or friends over several generations. The contrasting behaviors of the two types led to tying together the immigrant network more tightly as the Yankees moved out and were replaced by others of immigrant stock. The promise of land for younger generations helped to keep them tied to the community and its family values, while the "Yankees" might succumb to the promise of other opportunities, such as those promised by the increasing lure of the city in the late nineteenth century.

Thus, even while their lives were changed drastically by the realities of American economic life and prevailing agricultural practices, rural immigrants nevertheless sought to preserve their identities, perpetuate their language, and preserve cultural inheritances brought from the old country. Their rural activities were especially centered on the immigrant churches. In some cases this might involve divisions within the communities; the rural Germans, for example, might be of Catholic, Lutheran, or Reformed affiliations. Often, however, specific clusters of immigrants tended to be of one religious persuasion. In time, as the communities developed in the late nineteenth century, other organizations, such as mutual-assistance societies or cooperatives, were formed.

The differences in behavior between native and foreign-born settlers led in many cases to an increasing concentration of the population in immigrant communities as native-born settlers moved on to other regions. Immigrant farms were clearly seen as a family enterprise, using the labor of the younger generation and providing them with land in the future. Usually the oldest son would be able to inherit the farm; sometimes it was transferred by an agreement in which the son would care for the aging parents on the farm. Other sons might be provided for by dividing a larger claim of land, or by purchasing land being vacated by others, often Yankee farmers moving west. Since the promise of an independent livelihood encouraged individuals to stay with the family, they stayed on the farm and provided the labor necessary for the intensive agricultural practices that prevailed.

Immigrant communities like these, then, were based on the family farm as both a cultural and an economic unit, which aimed at producing a profit based upon the labor and resources available within the family. The economic future of each individual was tied to the success of the family farm; it would produce more land for younger generations who awaited their own property, either by inheritance or by being acquired from family resources. Such family farms were not necessarily democratic units. The principal landowner, in charge of the farm, had to organize the labor needed, and then assign roles to various of the family members. If additional labor was needed, either full-time or seasonal, this was assigned to wage laborers. Hired hands on the immigrant farms were often new immigrants who had their own desires to acquire farms of their own, either as tenants or as owners.

Women and children were also enlisted in the family enterprise. Even younger children could herd cows or feed hogs. In contrast to old-world practices, however, American immigrant farmers milked the cows themselves and left women to the kitchens and gardens, although women "wives/mothers" might work in the fields at times of planting and harvesting, when additional seasonal labor was required. Still, one immigrant tradition that did not change was the inferior status of women. According to long-standing tradition, they remained committed to their proper domestic roles. As the German immigrants particularly expressed it, women's activities should properly be confined to "*Kirche, Küche und Kinder*"—church, kitchen, and children. Women might sometimes work in the fields, but that declined as farms became more mechanized. They devoted their activity to gardening and (often) the raising of poultry. Most important, of course, was the raising of offspring, who were the future of the family enterprise.

Meanwhile, other immigrant traditions brought from the mother country were cultivated, and often links to the old homeland were maintained. Churches were especially important to the maintenance of ethnic identity. Rural churches in the Midwest were often found in the countryside away from towns, but sometimes immigrant churches developed in the small towns and villages that sprang up around railroad stations. The immigrant churches were often the nucleus of other organizations, such as mutual-assistance

societies, musical organizations, and especially schools. All of these were fundamental to preserving the use of the immigrant language as the basis of ethnic solidarity. Thus immigrants developed schools in which most of the instruction was in the foreign language. In 1889, there were legislative efforts in Illinois and Wisconsin to require that the basic instruction in all schools must be in English. These efforts seemed a direct attack upon the immigrant culture, and they mobilized the immigrant vote in politics out of its usually divided state, creating an uproar in the party politics of the time. Immigrant voters managed to repeal the efforts. The only other issue that could unite them as much was that of liquor prohibition.

The immigrant culture, influenced by both environmental and traditional factors, played a role in the formation of the general agricultural life of the Midwest in the nineteenth century. While the integration of immigrant groups was slower in the rural context than in the urban environment, it nevertheless occurred as younger people tended to leave the immigrant community, and intermarriage between groups became more commonplace. As the rural population moved further west into Wisconsin, Minnesota, and Iowa, reaching the Missouri River in places by the eve of the Civil War, new communities based on the pattern of the family farm would be created. And in further frontiers, offspring of the Midwestern rural type would be found, in places like the Dakotas, the Willamette Valley of Oregon, and the panhandle of Texas. While eventually other factors would work to change rural immigrant life, the Midwestern family farm would remain the model in the American imagination.

Into the Plains and Plateaus

By the eve of the Civil War, the western edge of settlement moving out from the Midwest reached just beyond the Missouri River, into the eastern portions of Nebraska and Kansas. The immediate aftermath of the war saw renewed movement of settlers toward the middle of those territories (which became states during the 1860s). A crucial factor in the onward movement of settlement was the declining rainfall as settlers moved west on those prairies; below 20 inches of rainfall annually, the traditional farming methods of the Midwest were not possible. The semiarid region of what became known as the Great Plains stretched westward from the middle of Kansas, Nebraska, and later the Dakotas, toward the Rocky Mountains. That region required definite adjustments and new ways of farming.

Immigration to rural areas was renewed after the Civil War, and a new factor adding to the attraction of the open lands of the West was the 1862 passage of the Homestead Act. Southerners were no longer able to oppose it. The act offered 160 acres of land to actual settlers who would live on it for five years and bring it into cultivation. Immigrants could qualify to apply if they simply declared their intention to become citizens. This might seem attractive for immigrants who were bent upon establishing stable communities where they could bring friends and relatives together in a newly opened region. Yet many might

be deterred by the challenges offered in proving their claim on that 160 acres. Although the homestead land was "free," there were additional costs to be met, such as fencing, housing materials, and farming equipment. Being able to survive for five years could sometimes be difficult while dealing with problems of drought, pestilence, and uncertain markets. It was not surprising that some turned instead to other sources to establish their farms. Government land was still available at the price of $1.25 per acre, and title to the land could be achieved right away. Land was also available from the railroads building through the region; these were lands granted by the federal government to encourage the railroad companies to build into the sparsely settled region. Eager to develop more business along their rights-of-way, the railroads were willing to compete in the prices of desirable lands that were close to transportation. Another deterrent to homesteading was the fact that 160 acres in the Great Plains environment was often not

A family pose with their wagon in Loup Valley, Nebraska, on their way to their new homestead. (MPI/Getty Images)

sufficient to produce enough to maintain a family. Eventually, changes in the law would be passed to allow homesteading on larger tracts of land; but meanwhile, immigrants, particularly those who came with the price of a farm in hand, could purchase land in other ways.

Movement onto the Great Plains required changes and accommodations by the immigrant even greater than what had been necessary in the Midwest. Despite the seeming isolation of the environment, the economy of the region was entirely dependent on the capitalist, urban economic structure of the East, and on international markets as well. The railroads were the only outlet for the principal crops, primarily livestock and wheat. These products were sent forth from the "cattle towns" of the plains to the centralized packing houses of Chicago, Omaha, Kansas City, and other cities. Grain was sent to the large mills of Minneapolis and elsewhere. In return, the farmer was dependent on the railroads for bringing in most other necessities: foodstuffs, machinery, fuel, building materials, and clothing, among other things.

Many of the western states, eager to increase their population, actively promoted the opportunities for obtaining land. Colonization agencies representing state governments met new immigrants on the docks of port cities and sent agents into eastern Europe to attract settlers. The railroads also actively sought prospective settlers in Europe, sending out agents to offer settlement opportunities, sometimes granting lots in the new towns of the West for the use of immigrant churches and organizations that might function as community centers. Thus they promoted the attractions of a homogenous community that were particularly desired by many immigrants. These colonization efforts by states and by railroads strengthened chain migration, creating towns and surrounding areas densely populated by immigrants of a specific ethnicity or religion.

The settlement of the plains by both immigrants and "Yankees" was conditioned by the economic cycles of the times. In the late 1860s, the railroads began building westward toward the Pacific coast, and the first transcontinental railroad was completed in 1869, linking the Central and Union Pacific railroads. This opening to the Great Plains of Nebraska was soon followed by other railroads across Kansas and, by the 1880s, through the Dakotas. The developing railroad lines brought a flood of settlers into the region, until the Panic of 1873 introduced a period of depression that discouraged both immigration and settlement for the rest of the decade. In the early 1880s, immigration revived, and the next few years constituted one of the high points of immigration to the United States, when migration into the Dakotas was especially strong. In 1883, it was reported that the Northern Pacific Railroad, then being built westward through the Dakotas, had 124 agents at work in Europe recruiting both laborers to build the railroad and farmers to occupy the lands nearby. But another depression slowed migration toward the end of the decade. Then a new revival of migration occurred, which was unexpectedly cut off by the Panic of 1893, the most serious economic depression of the nineteenth century.

Not all the efforts to populate the Great Plains were successes, then, and immigrants as well as others sometimes had to retreat to locations further east, as drought, depression, or falling agricultural prices led them to give up and seek another environment, either rural or urban. Among the most gripping accounts of the hardships of the time was a novel written by an immigrant, Ole Rolvaag, born in a fishing village in Norway in 1876, who migrated to the United States in 1896 when his uncle in the Dakotas sent him a ticket to come to America. Rolvaag worked as a field hand in the Dakotas for several years before entering college. His most famous work, *Giants in the Earth*, portrays life on the northern plains in the 1870s as experienced by a struggling family of Norwegian pioneers. Among the dispiriting events they encountered were tremendous blizzards, grasshopper plagues, drought, and near starvation. Rolvaag's account and other similar ones reflect the withering away of the family farms as an immigrant ideal; rather than staying in hopes of acquiring land, the younger generation tended to look elsewhere, often in the cities, for the prospects of success. Rolvaag also emphasizes the distress of women on the plains, as they faced increasing loneliness and isolation.

Norwegians and other Scandinavians were among the most active European immigrants in the settling of the plains. Some migrated from previous homes in Minnesota or Wisconsin, while others came directly from Sweden or Norway, with fewer numbers coming from Denmark, Finland, or Iceland. In the late nineteenth century, young people in the Scandinavian countries faced some of the same conditions as those facing other Europeans earlier in the century: limited land available for those who wanted to continue a rural life, and limited opportunities in urban occupations. In the years after the Civil War, Sweden was struck by crop failures, particularly in the period 1867–1869. Some migrants in those years would seek land in the just-opened Dakota Territory. Some form of chain migration affected many of these, as they sought places where new communities were founded around an immigrant church. In Kansas, for instance, a group of Swedes from the province of Värmland arrived in 1869, having acquired in common a large tract of railroad land bought for them by a Swedish settlement company. Most were dissenters from the

established Swedish Lutheran Church and immediately founded their own pietist church as the center of the community. The distribution of the land attracted other Swedes, eventually creating a large Swedish farming region in the middle of Kansas, of which the town of Lindsborg became the Swedish "capital." Both Norwegians and Swedes were divided in allegiance, either to the established Lutheran church of their homeland or to a dissenting group. The high point of the Scandinavian settlements on the Great Plains would occur during the early 1880s, as railroads opened up more land near their routes.

Germany continued to provide the largest number of European immigrants headed for farmlands on the Great Plains. In the post–Civil War era, they were coming into Nebraska; the town of Grand Island, promoted by a German-born colonization agent, developed as the center of a large German-settled agricultural region in eastern Nebraska. It was located on the western end of the corn-belt environment and

A pioneer family stands outside their sod house in Nebraska, circa 1886. (Library of Congress)

occupied a desirable location on the new transcontinental railroad. Other plains states would welcome new migrations of Germans, especially in the peak years of the 1880s. The immigrants from Germany, after 1871 a united empire under the leadership of Prussia, came increasingly from the eastern sections. Agriculture there was often practiced on large estates, hiring wage laborers who had little chance to own land of their own. In the post–Civil War period the available transportation for Germans was provided by the two great steamship lines, Hamburg America and North German Lloyd. Their agents held out to Germans the attractions of a low fare to America and the promise of land in the West in communities of similar ethnicity. While some came to America bringing with them the proceeds of their previous landholdings, which enabled them to buy new land, others who had owned no land began their careers as farm laborers or tenants. As before, the Germans were divided in religion between Catholics, Reformed, and Lutheran, and churches of every type could be found as community centers in the railroad towns of the plains.

There were, however, Germans who came to the United States from regions outside the German Empire. The most numerous were those coming from the Russian Empire, especially from regions along the Volga River. Germans had migrated to Russia in the mid-eighteenth century, when Empress Catherine the Great had encouraged their settlement. In the late nineteenth century, crop failures and prejudicial Russian policies against them started a movement to emigrate among the Russian Germans. In the early 1870s, two railroads, the Atchison, Topeka and Santa Fe and the Kansas Pacific, began active recruitment of Russian Germans to settle on the more arid parts of the Great Plains in Kansas, and sent agents to Russia to promote the state. By the end of the decade, two centers of Russian German immigrants were developing, one of Germans from the Volga region, primarily Lutherans and Catholics, the other primarily Mennonites.

Their communities were unusually tight-knit, and the German language would be preserved in many of them until well into the twentieth century. Other German Russians would settle in western Nebraska and the Dakotas, and eventually some would start a secondary migration to the plains of eastern Washington. Many of them came from regions of Russia not unlike the Great Plains, and they continued many of their agricultural practices for farming in semiarid regions. While they maintained mixed-farming practices like their Yankee and immigrant neighbors, they put more emphasis on wheat raising. They have been credited particularly with the introduction of winter wheat, a hardy type that could sustain severe weather, into the Great Plains.

Other immigrants came from eastern Europe, and especially from the Austro-Hungarian Empire. Nebraska was particularly the destination for many Czechs, usually referred to in those days as Bohemians. Many were attracted to that state by Edward Rosewater, a Jew from Bohemia who edited a newspaper in Omaha and established a Czech-language newspaper primarily to advertise the availability of land in the state. Another factor was the land activities of the Burlington and Missouri Railroad, one of the most active railroads in promoting land sales in Europe. Nebraska held the largest number of Czechs among the western states, followed by Texas, Kansas, and the Dakotas. The Czechs who settled on the plains in many aspects of their culture resembled the Scandinavians and the Germans but differed from other immigrant groups in that, following traditions brought with them from Europe, they were in the majority free-thinkers of varying degrees of radicalism. The churches were a smaller element in their ethnic identity, and the creation of a network among Czechs was more accomplished through mutual assistance and fraternal organizations.

English-born immigrants, though fewer in number than the Scandinavians or the Germans, were also migrating to the Great Plains. The land boom of the 1870s occurred at the same time as an agricultural depression in England. Those fleeing the depression were often farm laborers or tenant farmers who were being pushed off the land. They were encouraged by British reformers, who recommended the American West, Australia, or western Canada as the future for the oppressed farmer. They also were encouraged by the steamship lines and the western railroads, the latter eager to dispose of its western lands. The Kansas

Pacific Railroad sold 70,000 acres of land in Kansas to the English capitalist George Grant, who proceeded to develop the area as American landed estates for English gentlemen around the town he named Victoria. Grant promoted cattle raising on the large tracts of land purchased by his followers, and while living in Victoria from 1873 to 1878, he introduced the first Aberdeen Angus cattle in the United States. Other English gentlemen, hoping to create new estates, tried their luck at cattle raising, most of them in Colorado. Most English settlers migrated in the simple desire to hold land of their own, and suffered success or failure in the same ratio as others who ventured out onto the plains at the time. The British immigrants here as elsewhere were not obsessed with the desire to preserve a separate culture or ethnicity, as they could easily merge into the general American society with no language barriers to deal with.

In general, the European migrants to the Great Plains tended to settle east of the semiarid area, at the western edge of the old Midwestern corn-belt culture. West of that, the primary agricultural products were either cattle from the open range, or wheat. Few European immigrants provided the labor for cattle ranching. But European immigrants were considerably involved in the wheat farming in the High Plains, using the hard Turkey Red wheat from Russia that adapted well to the semiarid region.

In the 1870s and 1880s, attempts were made to introduce irrigation methods to the High Plains, but most of these efforts were unsuccessful, due to the lack of sufficient water resources and the very deep water tables of the region. Immigrants, however, were playing a role in the more successful irrigation attempts in the Great Basin, begun in the 1840s when the Latter-day Saints arrived on the shores of the Great Salt Lake. The salty waters of the lake were unusable for agriculture, but the Mormons began to conduct water from the mountain streams debouching onto the level flatlands from the Wasatch range to the east. Distribution of these waters required something of a communal effort to apportion the water and distribute it through canals. This tended to cluster together settlements near the water resources, making for a compact development of the area, with the settlers living in villages rather than in isolated farmsteads, somewhat reminiscent of the early New England towns. This proved to be a particular attraction for the foreign-born immigrants, which the Mormons began to recruit from abroad. Converts to Mormonism in Europe often received support in their migration from the Perpetual Emigrating Fund Company and other church agencies. About a third of the Latter-day Saints who arrived in Utah between 1852 and 1887 were foreign-born. The European migrants to the Great Basin came in larger numbers from Britain, Norway, and Denmark, with others coming mostly from northern European countries.

In the high plateaus and mountains of the West, another group of immigrants provided the principal example of a wandering and nomadic rural life. These were the Basque sheep herders, who had been in the West since the California Gold Rush, but migrated to the region in greatest numbers between 1880 and 1920. Their homeland lay along the Pyrenees mountains between Spain and France; they had a separate language of their own and were independent of both French and Spanish cultures. The original Basque settlers in California came from South America; later, there was more migration directly from the European homeland. Many Latin American Basques had been shepherds in South America before migrating to California; they taught the skills to newcomers from Europe who had less acquaintance with it. The Basques took up sheep raising in California in the gold-rush days, but by 1900 had expanded into Nevada, Oregon, Idaho, Wyoming, and other states in the Rocky Mountains. The low rainfall and the quick depletion of grasslands meant that sheep had to be moved constantly as the seasons changed. The unoccupied public lands of the mountain regions offered abundant pasturage for raising sheep, but required a lonely life in which shepherds and their wagons were constantly moving and were away from organized society for months at a time.

The establishment of foreign-born immigrants on the Great Plains and the plateaus of the West was one part of the larger story of the closing of the American frontier (which the historian Frederick Jackson Turner famously dated in 1890). By that time, the attractions of agricultural land would be drawing fewer European immigrants from rural areas in the old country, and more would be drawn instead to the American cities and industrial areas. Immigrants migrating from Asia and Latin America would come to rural areas under different conditions, ones more likely to exploit rather than uplift the immigrants.

Immigrants and Large-Scale Agriculture

The typical large-scale agriculture of the early nineteenth century was, of course, the southern slave plantation, devoted to such labor-intensive crops as tobacco, cotton, and sugar. The aftermath of slave emancipation after the Civil War brought vast changes to this system; in many locations, the result was a sharecropping system of small farmers. Although some southern states started their own efforts to attract immigrant farmers, these had little result, as the immigrants naturally responded more to the offers of free or cheap land in the northern Great Plains. The only southern state with some success was Texas, where some new immigrant towns, mostly German, were established in the western part of the state, which was part of the Great Plains environment.

Meanwhile, on the Pacific coast, there developed a system of large-scale commercial agriculture, which eventually would employ various immigrants from Asia and Latin America. Their experience was far from that of the European immigrants on the family farm. The new immigrants constituted a labor force easily exploited, made up largely of transients, and in most cases overwhelmingly male and without families. Before the Mexican-American War and the annexation of the Southwest, commercial farming of produce had been practiced on the ranches of the *Californios*, Mexicans who held large grants of land, much of it acquired from the former Spanish missions. As in the missions, they employed mostly Indians in the fields. The principal produce of the California ranches was cattle, mostly marketed for their hides, which were exported both to the United States and to the Far East. Some Mexican grants of land were made to Americans and to immigrants from Europe, like the vast holdings of Martin Murphy, whose Irish family acquired over 90,000 acres along the California coast, and of John Sutter, the Swiss-born adventurer who established an agricultural and fur-trading empire on the northern frontier—and on whose property gold was first discovered in 1847.

The California Gold Rush brought gold-seekers from all parts of the world to the mines. Most went to the mining camps, but some saw the opportunity to supply the burgeoning mining towns and port cities with food. Thus large-scale farms producing foodstuffs and ranches producing cattle began to emerge in the Sacramento River Valley, and eventually in the San Joaquin Valley further south. In the beginning, these farms used labor of people hoping to go on to discover gold, or those who returned from the mining towns discouraged at their lack of success. This proved to be a very unstable source of agricultural labor. As the mining boom went into decline, the employers of agricultural labor turned to the Chinese.

The Chinese laborers who had come to work in the mines were in time pushed out of the desirable locations, and they eventually turned to other labor, including railroad construction. They also provided the first element of migratory workers in the large-scale agricultural enterprises that would dominate the California scene for the next century and a half. The Chinese satisfied the demand for cheap labor in a labor-intensive agricultural economy. Although they would accept wages considerably lower than was common for other American working-class jobs, this was still better compensation than would be received for similar work in China. The numbers of Chinese agricultural workers grew in the 1860s and 1870s. Then Congress passed the Chinese Exclusion Act (1882), forbidding the admittance of Chinese laborers to the United States. The numbers of Chinese in the U.S. population began to decline, as did Chinese workers in the fields of the West; but by 1900, Chinese still constituted about 40 percent of the field workers. They had helped to reclaim land in the swampy delta of the Sacramento River; some of them became tenants there, raising potatoes and beans; others worked in vineyards and fruit orchards in California's Central Valley.

Japanese workers began to be admitted to California as replacements for the declining Chinese laborers in the last two decades of the nineteenth century. Some came directly from Japan. Others who had been living as agricultural laborers in Hawai'i came to California after 1898, when the United States annexed Hawai'i. Since the Chinese had encountered hostility from white labor groups in working in industrial jobs, the Japanese shunned such work and turned to the agricultural fields. Japanese labor was recruited by Japanese contractors, and some Japanese bought lands and developed their own large farms. The most famous of these was George Shima, who came to the United States from Japan in 1889, worked for a while as an agricultural worker, then turned to contracting to supply Japanese laborers, and finally bought land in the Sacramento River delta, which he drained and turned to the production of potatoes. By 1913, he had 28,000 acres under cultivation, and was known as the "Potato King." California's Alien Land Law, passed that same year, tried to limit land ownership by aliens ineligible for citizenship, but was only moderately successful and evaded by many Asians. By 1925, about one-fourth of the Japanese in California were employed in agriculture, mostly in the Central Valley and the delta.

The increasing control of California land by Japanese led to nativist reactions and contributed to the informal "Gentlemen's Agreement" between the United States and Japan (1907), in which Japan agreed to limit the migration of Japanese laborers to the United States. Other ethnic groups began to replace the declining numbers of Japanese in the California fields. Filipinos were among the most prominent. After the United States took control of the Philippines at the turn of the twentieth century, Filipinos were designated nationals—with the right to enter and depart the United States. They began to migrate both to Hawai'i and to the West Coast. Like previous migrant workers, they were mostly male and worked in truck garden farms producing various vegetables and fruits. In the 1930s, immigration from the Philippines began to decline after the United States made promises of Philippine independence. There were other immigrant groups as well who entered the "factories in the fields," the large-scale commercial agricultural farms. These included Sikhs from South Asia and Armenians, who eventually came to dominate raisin production in the Central Valley of California.

But the story of migrant farm workers in the twentieth century came to be predominantly Mexicans—both Mexican Americans, citizens who were descended from those who had been incorporated into the United States after the Mexican-American War in 1848, and others who crossed the border later from the Republic of Mexico. Their experience differed from most of the other immigrant groups in that (as with French Canadians, for example) the homeland was always close by, and passage back and forth into the United States was fairly easy. It was convenient for agricultural employers to turn to them as replacements for other laborers when those sources declined. The number of Mexicans began increasing in the fields of California, Texas, and other areas near the border in the early 1900s. After the Mexican Revolution broke out in 1910, many fled to the United States and became the principal part of the largest population of migrant agricultural workers. Others who pursued seasonal agricultural employment migrated frequently across the borders and back again. After increasing in the 1920s, the numbers of Mexicans in the United States were reduced sharply in the years of the Great Depression. This was partly due to government policies based upon a supposed surplus of agricultural labor, and many who were Mexicans were repatriated forcibly during the 1930s.

For a while, migrants from the "Dust Bowl" on the Great Plains replaced immigrant workers. Policies were reversed again during World War II; since farm workers were very difficult to find, the Bracero Program was initiated to import Mexican laborers as temporary farm workers, but was later terminated after the war. Without introducing a complete history of Mexican immigration and its issues, it will suffice to say that the need for immigrant farm workers continued to be a bone of political contention through the rest of the twentieth century. While agricultural employers continued to desire the supply of cheap labor, others claimed immigrants undercut American labor standards and led to the increase of impoverished sectors of the population.

The increasing dominance of large-scale agriculture and its demand for migrant labor has created a picture of immigrant life far different from the rural communities of the nineteenth-century Midwest.

With the use of primarily male migrating labor, there was little room for family continuity or identity. The need for mobility of the workforce worked against any goal of ethnic stability. Low wages prevented any possibility of upward social mobility. While the needs of a capitalistic market economy have always shaped the life of immigrants in rural areas, the needs of large-scale agricultural production have dispensed with any relationship to immigrant cultures.

The Immigrant and Commercial Agriculture in the Twentieth Century

Through most of American history, two factors have formed the immigrant rural experience: the need to adapt to a capitalistic market economy, and the desire to retain ethnic identity and ethnic culture. Over the length of the twentieth century, the family farm became overtaken by "agribusiness," which encouraged the consolidation of farmland in the interest of greater efficiency. The trend was particularly strong during and after World War II, as mechanization was increased to meet the lack of farm labor and many of the younger generation left the farm for the military or jobs in industry. The old 160-acre family farm now became inefficient; farms were sold to create larger tracts, and the sellers moved to the towns or cities. By 1990, the average farm in the United States was 460 acres, and many claimed that was insufficient to support a family. While larger farms, even ones owned by corporations, might still be controlled by families, the process of consolidation eroded the tight-knit rural communities, including those established by immigrants.

The displacement of many from those communities speeded the process of assimilation that had been going on slowly for several generations. Language retention persisted longer in the rural communities, but after several generations, the number of those within the communities decreased, and fewer new immigrants arrived and were recruited by large agricultural enterprises—"factories in the fields," from Hawai'i to Texas and, in recent years, in many locations from Florida northward. What had begun with the Bracero programs was continued by combinations of official temporary workers, undocumented laborers, and increasingly diverse teams of workers from Central America and indigenous migrants from southern Mexico.

Country churches were often the last influences still protecting immigrant cultures, but many of those were consolidating or closing down. The more mobile immigrants leaving the farm were more likely to intermarry. Newer streams of migration, except for the migratory farm workers, were more likely to seek urban communities. The ideal of the rural immigrant community as a center of stability and cultural harmony was no more.

Bibliography

Alexander, June G. 2009. *Daily Life in Immigrant America, 1870–1920*. Rev. ed. Chicago: Ivan R. Dee.

Bailyn, Bernard, and Philip D. Morgan, eds. 1991. *Strangers within the Realm: Cultural Margins of the First British Empire*. Chapel Hill: University of North Carolina Press.

Barkan, Elliott Robert. 2007. *From All Points: America's Immigrant West, 1870s–1952*. Bloomington: Indiana University Press.

Bergquist, James M. 2009. *Daily Life in Immigrant America, 1820–1870*. Rev. ed. Chicago: Ivan R. Dee.

Billington, Ray A., and Martin Ridge. 1982. *Westward Expansion: A History of the American Frontier*. 5th ed. New York: Macmillan.

Cayton, Andrew R. L., and Peter S. Onuf. 1990. *The Midwest and the Nation: Rethinking the History of an American Region*. Bloomington: Indiana University Press.

Conzen, Kathleen M. 1990. *Making Their Own America: Assimilation Theory and the German Peasant Pioneer*. Washington, DC: German Historical Institute.

Ferleger, Lou, ed. 1990. *Agriculture and National Development: Views on the Nineteenth Century*. Ames: Iowa State University Press.

Gjerde, Jon. 1997. *The Minds of the West: Ethnocultural Evolution in the Rural Middle West, 1830–1917*. Chapel Hill: University of North Carolina Press.

Hahn, Steven, and Jonathan Prude, eds. 1985. *The Countryside in the Age of Capitalist Transformation: Essays in the Social History of Rural America.* Chapel Hill: University of North Carolina Press.

Kamphoefner, Walter D. 1987. *The Westfalians: From Germany to Missouri.* Princeton, NJ: Princeton University Press.

Luebke, Frederick C. 1997. "Ethnic Group Settlement on the Great Plains." *Western Historical Quarterly* 8: 405–30.

Luebke, Frederick C., ed. 1980. *Ethnicity on the Great Plains.* Lincoln: University of Nebraska Press.

McWilliams, Carey. 1939. *Factories in the Field: The Story of Migratory Farm Labor in California.* Boston: Little, Brown.

Miller, Sally M. 1995. "Changing Faces of the Central Valley: The Ethnic Presence." *California History* 74: 174–89.

Ostergren, Robert C. 1988. *A Community Transplanted: The Trans-Atlantic Experience of a Swedish Immigrant Settlement in the Upper Middle West, 1935–1915.* Madison: University of Wisconsin Press.

The Economic Impact of Immigration

Harriet Orcutt Duleep

With the movement away from the national-origin quota system in 1965, immigration to the United States increased substantially. Given differences in the relative economic opportunities between the United States and the countries whose immigration had been severely restricted prior to 1965, the source-country composition of American immigration shifted from one of largely European origin to being predominantly from Asian and Latin American countries that are less economically developed than the United States. This sea change in the quantity and character of American immigration—like the waves of immigrants that arrived in the nineteenth and twentieth centuries—has led to concerns about the impact of the new immigrants on the U.S. economy. These concerns are bolstered by statistics showing high poverty rates of immigrants relative to the native-born as reported in the "Income and Poverty" fact sheets of the MPI Data Hub (http://www.migrationpolicy.org/datahub).

This chapter reviews research on two key elements of the immigration–U.S. economy nexus. Part I below focuses on immigrant economic assimilation; Part II studies immigration's effect on the wages and employment of American natives. Linking Parts I and II are two leitmotifs: the hazards of embedded assumptions and of drawing policy conclusions from initial conditions. The chapter ends by tying a key result from Part I—the propensity of immigrants to invest in human capital—to the impacts of immigration on economic growth.

Part I: The Economic Assimilation of Immigrants

With the restrictive immigration policy of the 1920s and subsequent decline in the number of immigrants entering the United States, immigration lost its luster as an interesting research topic. Following the reopening of the U.S. admission gates in the 1960s, immigration reemerged as an exciting topic. A key question for scholars and policy analysts has been, how do immigrants fare in the U.S. labor market? Though a seemingly simple question, answering it requires discerning from available data the earnings growth of immigrants. Estimates of immigrant earnings growth reflect interplay between how researchers perceive changes in immigration over time, the methods they use to measure immigrant earning growth, and the assumptions behind those methods.

A Decline in Immigrant Entry Earnings

Following immigration's peak in the early twentieth century, a model of immigrant assimilation was spawned in the University of Chicago's Department of Sociology and closely associated with the works of Robert E. Park. This model portrayed immigrants' trajectories in the host country as a single process that applied to all immigrants, eventually leading to their cultural and economic assimilation.

In the 1970s, echoing Park's thesis but focusing on labor market outcomes, Barry Chiswick introduced the concept of skill transferability wherein migrants often lack skills specific to their destination country that would permit their home-country human capital to be fully valued—"transferred"—to the host-country labor market. According to that model, immigrants start with low earnings but acquire host-country-specific skills, such as fluency in English, to restore the market value of their homeland human capital. As English and other U.S.-specific skills or credentials are gained, the value of the immigrant's home-country human capital is restored: the aerospace engineer, who could not get a job in aerospace engineering, or even engineering, now lands a job in his field.

The model was most often tested using a single year of census data. Researchers measured earnings growth by comparing the earnings of recently arrived immigrants with the earnings of immigrants of similar age and education who had been in the United States longer. This method of analysis assumes that the earnings path of recently arrived immigrants follows the earnings path of earlier immigrants once differences in years of schooling and experience have been accounted for. The difference between recent entrants' earnings and that of longer-term residents with similar years of schooling and experience then provides an estimate of immigrant earnings growth. Cross-sectional research in the United States and elsewhere confirmed Chiswick's thesis: following an initial period of adjustment, immigrants have high earnings growth, their earnings generally approaching those of natives with similar years of schooling and experience after about 15 years.

In a 1980 work, however, Chiswick discussed the possibility of cross-sectional bias—changes across year-of-entry immigrant cohorts in unmeasured variables that affect earnings could create biased estimates of immigrant earnings growth in a single cross-section of data. In addition to articulating the problem of inferring longitudinal effects from cross-sectional data, Chiswick introduced analyses to measure cross-sectional bias.

Building on Chiswick's work, George Borjas used multiple censuses to examine immigrant earnings and found that the entry earnings of immigrants had declined even holding years of education and experience constant. Tracing the earnings of earlier cohorts across censuses revealed immigrant earnings growth to be quite modest, substantially lower than the cross-sectional prediction. Much of the cross-sectionally measured earnings growth stemmed from linking the lower entry earnings of more recent cohorts with the higher earnings of earlier cohorts. However, the entry earnings of the earlier cohorts greatly exceeded those of their successors.

Borjas's research launched a new model of immigrant earnings that continues to be standard methodology. This model permits the initial earnings of year-of-entry immigrant cohorts to change. Yet it assumes that earnings growth rates are constant across year-of-entry cohorts, once observable variables, such as age and education, are accounted for.

The finding that immigrant entry earnings had declined, even holding schooling and experience levels constant, along with the underlying assumption of constancy in earnings growth rates, spurred speculation that the labor-market "quality" of recent immigrants had declined. It challenged the traditional notion that immigrants are a select group of highly motivated individuals and raised the specter of recent immigration being a bane rather than a blessing for the U.S. economy. Borjas suggested that underlying the decline in immigrant entry earnings was a decline in the labor-market "quality" of immigrants, reinforced by the greater income inequality of the countries contributing to U.S. immigration. He reasoned that immigrants coming from such countries with greater income inequality than the United States will be of relatively low labor-market quality because persons of low labor-market ability would have the most to gain by migrating to a country with a more equal income distribution.

Borjas correctly showed that in a situation, as in the United States, where immigrant initial earnings were falling over time, estimating earnings growth from a single year of data by pairing the initial earnings of more recent immigrants with the earnings achieved by earlier immigrants after 10–15 years in the United States overstates the earnings growth of the earlier immigrants. It does not follow, however, that the earnings growth of the earlier immigrants predicts the earnings growth of more recent immigrants.

An Alternative Explanation for the Decline in Immigrant Entry Earnings: The Economic Development–Skills Transferability Hypothesis

An alternative hypothesis for the decline in the education- and age-adjusted entry earnings of immigrants is that it reflects a decline in the extent to which the country-of-origin skills of immigrants transfer to the

United States. The initial earnings of U.S. immigrants vary enormously depending on where they come from. Immigrants from the source regions that dominate recent U.S. immigration (Asia, Central America, and South America) initially earn about half or less than half what U.S. natives earn, whereas the entry earnings of western European immigrants resemble those of the U.S.-born. These differences persist even when controlling for age and education.

A key factor underlying the variation in immigrants' initial U.S. earnings is the source country's level of economic development. Those hailing from economically developing countries have low initial earnings relative to their U.S.-born counterparts. Plotting the median 1989 U.S. earnings of immigrant men who entered the United States in 1985–1990 against the 1987 per adult GDP of each source country reveals a positive relationship between immigrant entry earnings and level of economic development.

Post-1965 immigrants are more likely to come from countries that are less economically developed relative to the United States than was true of immigrants who came to the United States in the years following the 1929 National Origins Act. This decrease in the economic development of the countries contributing to U.S. immigration could have contributed to a decline in immigrant skill transferability —that is, a decline in the extent to which immigrants' home-country education and experience are valued in the U.S. labor market.

One would expect immigrants from less-developed countries to have lower skill transferability to the United States because the limited opportunities in less-developed countries make it worthwhile for them to migrate to the United States even when immigration entails substantial post-migration investments in new skills and credentials, such as learning English, undertaking a U.S. degree program, changing their field of work, or starting a business. Persons in economically developed countries, with opportunities similar to those in the United States, would typically only migrate if there were positions for them in the United States that immediately valued their source-country skills, and they did not have to invest in new human capital, whether it be learning English or undertaking additional training.

This opportunity selection explanation for variations in the skill transferability of immigrants accommodates otherwise inexplicable intergroup patterns: The English proficiency of Asian Indian immigrants far surpasses that of non-British European immigrants. Yet their initial earnings in the United States are low relative to those of European immigrants. Filipino immigrants are more proficient in English than their non-British European counterparts, yet have lower initial earnings. Conversely, the initial earnings of Japanese immigrant men are very high, despite their very low English proficiency. The entry earnings of Korean, Indian, Filipino, and Chinese immigrants are similar despite enormous variation in their English proficiency. The similarity in their entry earnings is not surprising, however, if intergroup differences in skill transferability stem from variations in immigrant selection based on inter-country differences in economic opportunity. The common link among these countries is a low level of economic opportunity vis-à-vis the United States.

Immigrant Skill Transferability and the Propensity to Invest in Human Capital

A decline in the initial earnings of immigrants caused by a decline in immigrant skill transferability should be accompanied by an increase in earnings growth. This prediction flows from a simple Immigrant Human Capital Investment (IHCI) model developed by Duleep and Regets that builds on Chiswick's assimilation model. In the original Chiswickian model, which introduced the idea of international skill transferability, immigrants initially earn less than natives because the skills they possess do not transfer completely to the U.S. labor market. Chiswick hypothesized that as English and other U.S.-specific skills or credentials are gained, the value of the immigrant's home-country human capital is restored.

The IHCI model highlights two aspects of immigrant skill transferability. First, immigrants whose home-country skills transfer poorly to the new labor market will, by virtue of their lower wages, have a lower opportunity cost of human-capital investment than natives or immigrants with high skill transferability. Second, home-country skills are useful for

A legal immigrant from Venezuela works from his desk at a suburban Atlanta bank operation, May 24, 2006. (AP Photo/Gene Blythe)

learning new skills even if those skills are not valued in the host-country labor market: Persons who have learned one set of skills have advantages in learning a new skill set.

With its emphasis on the low opportunity cost of human capital investment for immigrants lacking transferable skills—paired with the value of home-country human capital for learning new skills—a distinguishing feature of the IHCI model is its conclusion that the higher incentive to invest in human capital pertains not only to U.S.-specific human capital that restores the value of specific source-country human capital—the foreign-born aeronautical engineer who learns English so that he can pursue aeronautical engineering again—but to new human capital investment in general.

A native-born aerospace engineer well launched into his career, or an immigrant with highly transferable skills allowing him to immediately pursue a job in his field, would be reluctant to undertake computer training or an MBA. This would be true even if the training facilitated an ultimately better-paid line of work because of the lost wages that such training would incur. The low opportunity cost for a similarly educated immigrant who could not initially transfer his home-country human capital—paired with the value of this undervalued human capital in producing new human capital—might make pursuing further training an attractive option.

Another prediction from the model is that the difference in the propensity to invest between immigrants and natives will likely be greatest for the highly educated. In most human capital models, prior education has an ambiguous effect upon investment decisions: An increase in an individual's education increases both the opportunity cost of time spent in human capital investment and the productivity of that time. In the IHCI model, source-country human capital that is not valued in the destination-country labor market is useful for gaining new skills, and it does not increase the opportunity cost of time spent in human capital investment. Thus a potential benefit of immigrants—particularly highly educated immigrants—lacking immediately transferable skills is a high rate of human capital investment that is not tied to restoring specific home-country skills.

Consistent with the IHCI model's predictions, studies have found that recent immigrants have a higher propensity to invest in human capital and do so over a longer period than otherwise similar natives. Adult immigrants are more likely to be enrolled in school and at older ages than natives. A study of Canadian immigrants by David Green (1999) reports higher rates of occupational change and at older ages for immigrants than for natives.

A lower opportunity cost of human capital investment combined with the usefulness of undervalued human capital for creating new human capital creates a greater incentive for low-skill-transferability immigrants to invest in human capital than will be true of either high-skill-transferability immigrants or natives with similar levels of education and experience. Since greater human capital investment fuels greater earnings growth, the IHCI model predicts that immigrants will experience higher earnings growth than natives, and among immigrants, there will be an inverse relationship between entry earnings and earnings growth. Immigrants whose skills initially transfer poorly to the United States will have lower initial earnings but higher earnings growth than natives or than immigrants with similar levels of schooling and experience, yet more transferable skills.

The Importance of Being Permanent

The IHCI model's predictions are predicated on an important condition: Whether immigrants invest in American human capital will be affected by whether they intend to stay in the United States. Starting a business, pursuing jobs with on-the-job training, and learning English take time and money and generally result in lower earnings at first. Immigrants would embark on these pursuits only if the benefits from making them could be reaped in the future. Of course, individuals who initially plan on returning to their home country may end up making the United States their permanent home. And, the very act of investing —particularly when skills learned in the host country do not easily transfer back to the home country— encourages permanence in the host country. Nevertheless, initial intentions are likely reflected in the investment behavior, hence earnings profiles, of immigrants. Consistent with this expectation, we find that among all immigrants, the highest earnings growth occurs for those whose first U.S. earnings coincide with an expressed intent to stay permanently in the United States.

As long as immigrants are permanently attached to the United States, earnings growth appears to occur even for undocumented (illegal) immigrants with minimal levels of schooling. The importance of permanence is vividly illustrated by comparing two groups of poorly educated, primarily undocumented, immigrants.

Traditional sources of information on immigrants, such as the census, shed little light on the experiences of the undocumented. To illuminate their experiences, Douglas Massey launched a novel information-gathering strategy, the Mexican Migration Project (MMP), in which data on migrants are gathered in those communities in Mexico that are prime sources of undocumented immigration to the United States, and in the communities in the United States that are prime receiving communities for undocumented immigrants. Analysis of the MMP data shows extensive transiting back and forth of the Mexican border, hence low levels of permanence for Mexican illegal immigrants and little or no earnings growth.

Liang applied Massey's strategy to learning about illegal immigrants in the United States from China and created the China International Project. Taking advantage of the newly available data from the China International Project, Miao Chunyu traces the work trajectories of immigrants from China's Fujian province, the source of the largest wave of Chinese emigration in the 1990s. Like their Mexican counterparts, most of these immigrants are illegal and poorly educated: 41.4 percent possess only elementary-school education or less, 37.9 percent only junior high school. Yet, in stark contrast to the Mexican undocumented immigrants, the Fujianese immigrants plan to stay permanently in the United States; few return to China. As a result of being part of a permanent community in the United States, Fujianese immigrants often work for co-ethnics. Chunyu (2011, 10, 12) finds that these immigrants experience substantial earnings growth: " U.S. experience, both in residence and in the labor market, tends to produce a substantial and positive impact on their earnings ... Such effect is twofold—one is the living experience as measured by the total length of residence in the U.S. and the other is the labor market experience as measured by the total number of jobs had by an immigrant."

There are also intergenerational implications of permanence. Historically, groups that were permanently attached to the United States showed greater intergenerational progress in educational attainment than groups who were less permanent. A likely reason for this is that educational expectations are tied to the place to which one is attached. If a significant part of the community is tangentially attached to the United States, as would be the case in communities where a large percentage are going back and forth, then expectations for their children's education will be influenced by the "home" country.

Differences in level of permanence may explain the lower intergenerational progress in education for the cohorts of Mexican Americans who entered the United States in 1880–1920 compared with cohorts of southern and eastern European immigrants entering the United States during the same time period. Southern European immigrants included persons of Italian and Greek origin; East European immigrants included the Czech, Slovak, Polish, Russian, Ukrainian, Romanian, Hungarian, Serbian/Croatian, and Estonians, Latvians, and Lithuanians. These immigrants arrived in the United States with very little formal education. This situation, however, was to change quickly. Over a course of a single generation, the mean years of schooling by persons of southern European origin increased by five years. For East Europeans, the corresponding increase was almost four years. In stark contrast with the same time-period cohorts of Mexican Americans, persons of East and southern European origin went from an education deficit relative to the native-born to one of relative advantage.

If one uses the male/female ratio as an indication of permanence, with a more equal gender distribution denoting more permanent communities, then the early immigrants from China and Japan who came in the nineteenth and early twentieth centuries are another case in point. Early Chinese immigration reached a peak in the 1870s; Japanese immigration in the 1900s was as large as the Chinese migration of the 1870s. Although both groups were dominated by unskilled laborers, the Japanese, who exhibited a much more equal gender distribution than the Chinese, showed much higher intergenerational growth in schooling levels than did the early Chinese Americans.

An Inverse Relationship between Entry Earnings and Earnings Growth

With immigrants who are permanently attached to the United States, the IHIC model predicts that an increase in earnings growth will accompany declines in immigrant entry earnings caused by declines in immigrant skill transferability. Ample empirical evidence supports this prediction.

Without imposing any restrictions on entry earnings or earnings growth, following year-of-entry cohorts of immigrants defined by country of origin, age, and education across the 1960 through 1980 decennial censuses and across the 1970 through 1990 censuses reveals that as immigrants' entry earnings decreased, their earnings growth increased. Despite a 23 percent drop in immigrants' initial earnings relative to the native-born between the 1965–1970 and the 1975–1980 immigrant entry cohorts, there is very little difference in the relative earnings of each cohort after 10–14 years of U.S. residence. This is because the more recent cohort, with lower relative entry earnings, had a much higher earnings growth rate. The effect is even more dramatic when separating into age and education groups. In each case, the cohort with lower relative entry earnings surpasses the initially higher-earning immigrant cohort.

Dividing countries of origin by level of economic development reveals that immigrants from less economically developed regions of the world have lower entry earnings but higher earnings growth than immigrants of similar age and education from economically developed countries. This is true at all levels of education, but particularly true of the highly educated, in keeping with the IHCI model's predictions.

To circumvent potential problems with following cohorts across censuses, Duleep and Dowhan used longitudinal administrative record data to follow the annual earnings of working-age foreign- and native-born individuals, from numerous year-of-immigration cohorts. Their results show that the initial earnings of immigrant men fell over time in relation to native-born men. Foreign-born men who immigrated in 1960–1964 earned on a par with U.S. natives, those who immigrated in 1965–1969 earned 17 percent less than their U.S.-born statistical twins, and those who immigrated after 1969 earned 28–46 percent below the earnings of comparable natives. The data on women tell a similar story.

Yet, for both men and women immigrants, as their entry earnings (relative to U.S. natives) fell, their relative earnings growth increased. The earnings growth rates of the early cohorts of immigrant men and women closely resemble those of the U.S.-born. Then, starting with the 1970–1974 cohort, their earnings growth rates exceed those of the U.S.-born. Moreover, whether following cohorts or individuals, a dramatic increase in earnings growth occurs, even with no control for over-time changes in the educational composition of immigrants relative to U.S. natives. As entry earnings have decreased, earnings growth has increased to such an extent that when one looks at immigrants after they have been in the United States for 15 to 20 years, immigrant earnings do not look like they have declined at all, and in some instances, have increased.

Reconsidering Studies of Immigrant Quality

The decline in immigrant entry earnings has been interpreted as a decline in the labor-market quality of immigrants. Yet, the increase in earnings growth, which has accompanied the decline in entry earnings, is incompatible with declining immigrant quality.

What, then, are the flaws in studies that have led analysts to believe that recent immigrants are of lower labor market quality than earlier immigrants?

Tests of immigrant selectivity have often been done using region-of-origin variables. Source-region variables offer the tantalizing prospect of achieving a more holistic understanding of immigration. Nevertheless, deceptions that we have found something when we have not stem from two sources. The limited number of effective observations (since all sample individuals from a given country are assigned the same average value) makes it difficult to test competing hypotheses. Moreover, average values of country-of-origin characteristics may provide grossly inaccurate information about the immigrants whose behavior we seek to explain.

A potential specification error of the empirical test of Borjas's income distribution–immigrant ability thesis is that the relevant distribution for a potential emigrant, in an analysis that focuses on immigrant earnings controlling for education, is the earnings distribution associated with that person's level of education, not the income distribution of the entire country. This would not be a problem if there were a high correlation between the overall income distribution of a country and the income distribution that individuals with specific levels of education face. Yet, the overall earnings distributions of countries may have little relationship to the earnings distributions that individuals with specific levels of education face.

Moreover, "Because educational supply constraints are more likely to bind in rural areas [of developing countries] . . . levels of education attainment in rural areas will be lower. If this is the case, interpreting education differences across the population of migrants from developing countries as reflective of broader quality differentials clearly is problematic, since high-ability individuals from educationally supply-constrained rural areas may have low levels of education attainment. . . . If . . . educational attainment is supply constrained, completed years of education is flawed as a measure both of the entry-level stock of human capital and the possible trajectory of human capital over time" (Jensen et al. 2006, 2–3, 23).

Former Seo employees searching for work in New York's garment district. The sisters lost their jobs when the Seo factory where they worked, closed after it was found to violate state and federal labor laws. (AP Photo/Kathy Willens)

Parenthetically, concerns about declining immigrant quality, as evidenced by a decline in immigrant entry earnings, have been cultivated by a rather unusual comparison. The 1929 National Origins Act, following a series of restrictive laws (particularly the Immigration Acts of 1921 and 1924), imposed the country's first permanent immigration limit and established a national-origin quota system that governed U.S. immigrant admissions for decades. The small annual quotas prescribed for most nationalities reflected the stock of immigrants who were living in the United States in 1920, favoring migrants from northern and western Europe while sharply reducing the size of the total immigrant inflow. The Great Depression and World War II further contributed to a 40-year hiatus in U.S. immigration. The finding of declining entry earnings is based on a comparison of recent immigrants with immigrants who entered the United States during and immediately following this very restrictive period of American immigration history.

The European immigrants in the 1930s through 1960s who dominated U.S. immigration during this restrictive immigration period had earnings profiles exactly fitting the predictions of the IHCI model. They would not have come to the United States if they had to invest in new skills. As predicted by the IHCI model, their entry earnings were similar to those of natives of similar education and experience, and their earnings growth were also similar to that of U.S. natives and substantially below the earnings growth of the immigrants who followed in 1970 and beyond.

Immigrant Economic Assimilation— Main Points

In summary, the earnings profiles of immigrants from economically developed countries/regions, such as Japan, Canada, or western Europe resemble those of American natives who are of the same age and education. In contrast, the earnings of immigrants from developing nations, given that they are permanently attached to the United States, tend to start well below those of U.S. natives with comparable years of schooling and experience, but rise more rapidly.

Comparing the earnings profiles of immigrants of similar age, gender, and years of schooling, over time and across groups, a strong inverse relationship emerges between the initial earnings of immigrants and their subsequent U.S. earnings growth. In other words, the lower the initial earnings are, the higher the earnings growth. During the unusual period of highly restricted immigration, immigrants had earnings profiles resembling U.S. natives of similar age and schooling. With the opening of U.S. immigration in 1965, immigration from countries economically less developed than the United States increased. As this occurred, the entry earnings of immigrants fell, but their earnings growth increased, a phenomenon reflecting higher rates of investment in human capital.

A strong inverse relationship between entry earnings and earnings growth yields a much more optimistic picture of the prospects of recent immigrants. It suggests that the unexplained decline in immigrant entry earnings reflects changes in skills transferability (as opposed to a decline in immigrant innate ability or motivation) and that recent immigrants starting at low adjusted entry earnings have high rates of human capital investment. The increase in earnings growth is such that at the 15-year mark, the most recent immigrants earn at the same level as their predecessors who started their U.S. earnings trajectory at a higher point.

A widely shared perspective is that desirable immigrants are those who immediately fit into the host country's labor market and earn on a par with natives. Immigrants who come to the United States and intend to stay because of the greater opportunities it offers relative to their home countries will always initially lack transferable skills and earn less than

U.S. natives. Yet, as the end of Part II highlights, because human capital that is not valued in the U.S. labor market is useful for learning new skills, these immigrants provide the United States with an undervalued, highly malleable resource that promotes a vibrant economy in the long run.

Part II: The Effect of Immigration on the Wages and Employment of U.S. Natives

In addition to how well immigrants fare in the U.S. economy, a key policy concern is their impact on the wages and employment of persons born in the United States, particularly those with low levels of schooling. Although a long-standing concern, some would argue that its importance has risen in recent years with dramatic changes in the U.S. wage structure. Nevertheless, today's scholars are no closer to a consensus as to whether immigrants hurt, help, or have no significant effect on native-born employment and wages than they were nearly a century ago. Clouding a definitive consensus are unresolved issues in the following areas: (1) the measurement of immigration, (2) disentangling the effect of immigration on natives' economic status from the effect of economic conditions on immigration, (3) the concentration of immigrants in a few states, (4) the migration of natives in response to immigration, (5) estimating an immigration effect at a nationwide level, and (6) reconciling statistical evidence with anecdotal evidence and theoretical expectations.

The Measurement of Immigration

Most studies of the impact of immigration on native-born employment and wages measure immigration's effect by comparing natives' wages and employment in localities or time periods with varying levels of immigration. The following principle guides such efforts: If we succeed in controlling for other variables that may affect native-born economic status, then the estimated relationship between the presence of immigrants and native-born economic status across areas or time periods will reflect the effect of immigration on natives' economic status. However, the estimated effect will also depend on how the extent of immigration is measured and defined.

(1) The number of immigrants. Simply counting the number of immigrants in a particular area or time period is a problem that afflicts all studies relating immigration to natives' economic status. Although the Immigration and Naturalization Service (now part of the Department of Homeland Security) maintains annual records of legal immigration, illegal immigration by its very nature is difficult to quantify. This would not be a problem if immigrants, regardless of their legal status, were accurately counted in survey data, such as the decennial census, the American Community Survey, and the Current Population Survey. However, some scholars in this volume suggest that the census may miss one-third to one-half of the total number of illegal immigrants.

The inability to measure immigration accurately introduces a source of measurement error (of unknown proportion) in all analyses relating immigration to natives' wages and employment. Since measurement error obscures the underlying relationship we seek to estimate, its presence makes it less likely that we will be able to detect an immigration effect on natives' wages and employment. As illegal immigrants tend to have lower levels of education than legal immigrants, the discrepancy between the actual number of immigrants in a particular area and the measured number of immigrants is likely greatest for the poorly educated. Measurement error may be particularly troublesome for analyses focused on the effect of immigration on poorly educated natives.

(2) The human capital endowments of immigrants. Economic theory suggests that immigration may have a variety of effects on natives' economic status—including raising the demand for native-born labor—depending on the extent to which immigrants are substitutes or complements for native-born labor. The greater the extent to which immigrant workers are substitutes for native-born workers, the greater the potential for a negative effect on natives' wages and employment. The extent to which immigrants and natives are complements or substitutes would depend on their human-capital endowments and in particular their level of education.

In comparing native-born economic status in areas with high and low immigration, several studies separately analyze the effect of immigrants on native-born workers of various education levels. However, these studies do not typically separate immigrants by their level of education. Cross-area analyses generally examine the economic impact of increases in the percentage of all immigrants on low-skilled natives, or the percentage of immigrants with low predicted earnings, as an indicator of the skill level of immigrants. The latter measure is a poor indicator of skill, since it groups together poorly educated immigrants (those in the low skilled levels who have low initial earnings but high earnings growth) with highly educated immigrants.

A rationale for using as the independent variable all immigrants, as opposed to immigrants of a given educational level, is that recently arrived immigrants often go through a period of adjustment in which their occupational status is diminished from their country-of-origin status. Indeed, college-educated immigrants may start their U.S. careers by doing dishes in a restaurant. Thus, all immigrants, regardless of their educational level, may compete with low-skilled natives. However, the effect on natives' employment and wages of an additional person washing dishes for six months differs from the effect of an additional person who works for years as a dishwasher.

Even if substitution or complementary relationships between immigrant and native workers of various education levels are impervious to time period and region, we would still expect a diversity of results from cross-area (and over-time) analyses depending on the particular schooling-level mix of immigrants going to different areas that varied in their level or rate of immigration. In our efforts to measure immigration effects on natives' wages and employment, dividing immigrants by education level would be one step toward unraveling differences among studies and would also provide information on a key policy question: Is the immigration of poorly educated immigrants detrimental to the economic status of poorly educated natives?

(3) Other characteristics. The admission criteria through which immigrants enter the United States and whether they enter legally could also affect the

types of jobs immigrants pursue and the extent to which they are substitutes or complements for U.S. natives. By having a lower level of readily transferable skills to the United States, family-based immigrants may compete less with natives than immigrants admitted on the basis of occupational skills. A lack of readily transferable skills to the United States may foster the development of employment opportunities for immigrants that are distinct from the employment opportunities of natives.

Lindsay Lowell (1996, 362) concludes: "Skill-based immigrants, in part because their admission depends on formal links to U.S. employers ... may enter directly into job competition with U.S. workers. ... Conversely, the nature of the jobs that are initially filled by family-based immigrants, precisely because they are not as tightly linked to the primary labor market, may mean that family-based immigrants compete less with U.S. workers."

A 1992 study sheds empirical light on this issue by using census data matched to immigrant admissions data. Dividing by admission status, immigrants admitted on the basis of occupational skills (employment-related immigrants) are found to have a small but statistically significant negative effect on the employment opportunities of native-born white males. In contrast, family-preference immigrants have a statistically significant positive effect on the earnings and employment of U.S.-born whites and on the earnings of U.S.-born blacks. Foreign-born naturalized citizens have a negative effect on native male workers. Elaine Sorensen (1996, 256) notes, "[This] finding is not surprising if immigration is viewed as a process whereby immigrants become increasingly more competitive with native-born workers as they adjust to the U.S. labor market."

(4) Immigrant emigration and immigrant/native labor market competition. To what extent immigrants choose to stay in the United States and for how long will affect their impact on natives' wages and employment. There is, as previously mentioned, a duration effect: the effect on natives of an immigrant employed in a particular type of work will vary depending on whether the employment is for a few years or for a working life.

The amount of time immigrants expect to stay in the United States may affect the type of jobs they pursue by affecting social attitudes toward employment. Based on studies of guest workers in Europe, undocumented workers in the United States from Mexico and the Caribbean, and the migration of southern and East European peasants to the United States in the late nineteenth and early twentieth centuries, Michael Piore (1979, 17) argues that it is the temporary nature of some immigration that permits those immigrants to take jobs that would otherwise be considered undesirable.

The extent that across-area or over-time immigrant populations vary in their permanence is another source of variation in the results of studies measuring the effects of immigration on the wages and employment of natives. Supplementing current studies measuring the effect of all immigration with approaches that disaggregate by "type" of immigrant would help explain discrepancies among the results of empirical studies and provide useful information for discussions concerning U.S. immigrant admission policy.

Disentangling the Effect of Immigration on Natives' Economic Status from the Effect of Economic Conditions on Immigration

Regardless of how immigration is measured, a serious difficulty with cross-area analyses is that immigrants may move to areas with better-than-average wages and employment opportunities, thereby obfuscating any potential adverse immigration effect on natives' economic status. If areas of high immigration are areas of high wages and good employment opportunities for natives, does this mean that immigration positively affects natives' economic status, or does it merely reflect immigrants moving to high-wage and good-employment areas? The wages of natives in high-immigration areas may be lower than they would have been in the absence of immigration. The same problem afflicts over-time studies; historical analyses consistently show an inverse relationship between immigration and the host country's unemployment rate.

To isolate the effect of immigration on natives' economic status, analysts can relate changes in native-born economic status to changes in immigration. If, however, changes in native-born employment and wages affect changes in immigration (immigrants are more likely to move to areas where wages are rising and less likely to move to areas where wages are declining), then immigration's effect on native's wages and employment will still be obscured.

Another approach is to use instrumental variables (proxy variables that are correlated with immigrant inflows but uncorrelated with changes in economic conditions that may affect immigrant inflows). A problem with this approach is the imprecision inherent in using a proxy for the variable whose effect we wish to estimate. If the instrumental variable and the original variable are not highly correlated, then the estimated effect will be imprecise.

Researchers have been moderately successful in instrumenting changes in the fraction of immigrants. We would, however, like to learn the effect of changes in the fraction of less-educated immigrants, as opposed to changes in the fraction of all immigrants. Efforts to do this have been less successful. One analysis uses the fraction of less-skilled immigrants in an earlier period as an instrument for the change in the fraction of less-skilled immigrants by Standard Metropolitan Statistical Area (SMSA). (The Census Bureau defines urban centers by breadth and population size, with SMSA representing one of the largest and wherein economic links bind regions into larger entities.) Yet the correlation between these two variables is very low. The result are imprecise estimates that preclude any conclusion as to whether the potentially important estimated effect of "less skilled" immigration on the wages of less-skilled natives reflects a real effect or simply random variation. Clearly, alternative approaches are needed to isolate the effect of immigration on natives' employment and wages from the effect of economic conditions on immigration.

Alternatives to Instrumental Variable Estimation

To isolate an immigration effect from the correlation of immigration and economic conditions, scholars may analyze areas and time periods that experience an abrupt influx of immigrants due to factors that are unrelated to the host region's employment conditions.

These are called natural experiments because they mimic an experimental design but in a natural setting. For instance, scholars have examined the unemployment and wages of low-skilled blacks and other non-Cuban groups in Miami before and after the Mariel boatlift (composed primarily of Cubans with low levels of schooling), and found no effect. Other potential "natural experiments" include the influx of refugees after World War II and the influx of Indochinese refugees beginning in 1975. Nevertheless, this approach is limited by a paucity of appropriate natural experiments and by the special circumstances that accompany them.

The need for using instrumental variable estimation arises from the belief that there is a simultaneous relationship between changes in native-born wages (or employment) and changes in the fraction of immigrants in a specific area. Simultaneous means occurring in the same time period. We want to measure the effect of changes in immigration on native-born wages and employment, but our estimates will also reflect the effect of changes in native-born economic status on immigration.

But is the relationship truly simultaneous? It seems more likely that an inflow of immigrants into an area would affect native-born wages with a lag. There would be a delay between the entry of immigrants into an area and their labor-market search. There would also be a delay between immigrant arrivals in an area, the realization by employers of the increased labor supply, and the decision by employers to lower wages. (Simultaneity may arise because the data we use are not sufficiently subdivided in time to permit us to observe immigrant inflows and their subsequent effect. This is an argument for using annual data, instead of decennial census data, in across-area studies of the effect of changes in immigration on changes in native-born wages and employment.)

It seems reasonable to hypothesize that changes in an area's immigration would affect changes in native-born wages with a lag of one year. We would then want to estimate, for instance, the effect of a change from 2001 to 2002 in the fraction of immigrants in area i on the change from 2002 to 2003 in native-born wages in area i.

This type of model circumvents the simultaneous relationship, since although changes in immigration may affect changes one year later in native-born economic status, the reverse cannot occur. It would still be true that variables that affect both the change in immigration in year *t* and the change in native-born wages in year *t*+1 will bias the estimated effect of immigration on native-born wages. Nevertheless, by distancing our dependent and explanatory variables in time, we have moved from a potentially intractable simultaneous relationship to an omitted-variables problem. If there are variables that affect both the change in immigration in year *t* and the change in native-born wages in year *t*+1, then the solution is to include these variables in the estimation. For instance, including information on the trend in wages for the area would help safeguard against this type of omitted variable bias.

The Concentration of Immigrants in a Few States

Historically, immigrants have clustered in just six states (California, New York, New Jersey, Illinois, Texas, and Florida) with the largest percentage in California, followed by New York. Within those states, immigrants are concentrated in the largest cities or SMSAs. Since 1990, a major shift has occurred, and the new major destinations include Georgia, North Carolina, South Carolina, Alabama, Massachusetts, Virginia, and Maryland. Within those states, foreign workers cluster in specific industries. Note the impact of Latinos in industries such as carpet making in Georgia and the meat and chicken processing plants of Alabama and North Carolina.

Scholars need to consider the impact of this clustering on their analyses. Using pre-1990 data, one-time cross-state estimates of the effect of immigration on native-born employment and wages (or the effect of changes in immigration) will be sensitive to economic circumstances (or changes in economic circumstances) in any of the six states with heavy immigration. A downturn or upturn in California's economy (not captured by the explanatory variables in the regression) would likely be captured by the immigration variable and be reflected in estimates of the effect of immigration on native-born economic status. One-time cross-state analyses of data since 1990 will be sensitive to the clustering that has occurred since 1990.

Analyzing SMSAs instead of states may give the impression of more data. However, the effective gain in information with which to separate the effect of immigration from the effect of other variables may be minimal, since large cities within a state are likely subject to similar economic circumstances and changes in those circumstances. The limited number of effective observations may explain why analysts estimating the effect of immigration on natives have found very different results using similar methodologies but estimating in two different time periods. Given the concentration of immigrants in a few states, the problem of isolating the effect of immigration on native-born economic status from the effect of perturbations in these states' economies can be overcome only by using time-series information in combination with cross-sectional information.

The Migration Response

Analysts may find no effect or only a small effect of immigration on native-born wages and employment in cross-area comparisons if natives migrate in response to immigrant inflows. According to this scenario, immigrants reduce the wages and employment opportunities of natives and, in response, the native-born leave. No wage or employment effect is observed, since the supply of native-born labor in high-immigration areas has decreased with the out-migration of natives from these areas.

Scholars have found that low-educated natives have been moving out of areas with large increases in immigrants, and high-educated natives have been moving into these areas. The differential response has been interpreted as evidence that immigrants, and in particular recently arrived immigrants, are substitutes for low-educated natives and complements for high-educated natives. According to this interpretation, the migration response of natives provides evidence of a negative wage and employment effect of immigrants on low-educated natives and a positive wage and employment effect on high-educated natives. There are, however, alternative explanations. If immigrants make location decisions based on different criteria from those of low-educated natives, then you could still find a negative relationship between rates of immigration and native out-migration, even if immigrants have no economic effect on low-educated natives.

The destinations immigrants choose have tended to be large cities in coastal states, such as California and New York. Immigrants are attracted to these areas because of immigrant communities; employment opportunities and other forms of social and material support run through well-established networks. Immigrant inflows positively correlate with the immigrant fraction of an area's population. *Highly educated natives may move to the same areas that immigrants favor because of employment opportunities* (which may or may not reflect a complementary relationship with immigrant labor), *and because these areas are cultural centers, ethnically diverse, and have other attributes that attract highly educated individuals.*

Concomitantly, these cities share the problems of all big cities—crime, poor public schools, drug marketing—that grew over time at the same time that immigration grew. The highly educated insulate themselves from these problems by sending their kids to private schools and living in safe areas. Yet low-educated natives may leave these areas, not because they have experienced adverse immigration effects, but because of the urban problems from which they cannot insulate themselves.

In thinking about the tendency for low-educated natives to move out of areas of high immigration, three potential explanations come to mind. One is that low-educated natives migrate in response to economic conditions caused by an influx of immigrants. Another is that low-educated natives move out of high-immigration areas because they dislike immigrants or because they believe immigration will harm their economic opportunities. Finally, the correlation may be caused by factors other than immigration as in the scenario depicted above.

Of primary policy concern would be if low-educated natives are moving in response to an adverse effect of immigrants on their employment and wages. This would suggest that even if we do not find a detrimental immigration effect in the cross-area wage and employment analyses, it may still be the case that the wages and employment of natives are being hurt by immigration. If, on the other hand, natives are moving because of an aversion to immigrants, or because of the perception that immigrants decrease economic opportunities, not because of any economic harm, then this would be cause for concern from a social harmony perspective; although it is not clear what type of immigration policy response, if any, is warranted. If the native-born migration is not due to immigration at all but is caused by other non-immigration factors, then it would seem that no immigration policy response is merited, although we would still want to explore the sensitivity of our estimates of the effect of immigration on native-born wages and employment to native-born migration patterns.

How can we distinguish between these three hypotheses? A stronger test of whether native-born migration and immigration are causally related is to relate changes in the size of immigrant inflows to particular areas to changes in the out-migration of low-educated natives from these areas. Here we do not have a problem of simultaneity since we are assuming that the inflow of immigrants into an area affects the migration of natives but not vice versa. (If it were believed that changes in the inflow of immigrants affected native-born migration with a lag, then the model could be altered to reflect that.)

As before, the fact that immigrants are concentrated in a few states (and the cities within those states where they reside likely share many attributes) presents an estimation problem. The estimated "effect" of immigrant inflows on native-born migration may be sensitive to nonimmigrant changes (in any of the immigration states) that affect the out-migration of natives from the big cities in those states but that are not controlled for in the estimation model. Estimating the above relationship over several time periods may help in this regard.

A second strategy for determining whether immigration causally affects the migration patterns of low-educated natives is to make predictions that are compatible with the hypothesis that low-educated natives are migrating in response to immigration and see if the predictions hold true. For instance, if we believe that the out-migration of low-educated natives is in response to an immigration-induced decline in their economic opportunities, then we would expect that increases in low-educated immigrants would have a greater effect on the out-migration of low-educated natives than would increases in high-educated immigrants. However, the correlation between inflows of low-educated immigrants and the out-migration of low-educated natives across SMSAs is no more negative than the correlation between inflows of highly educated immigrants and the out-migration of low-educated natives.

We would also predict the greatest migration effect for the most economically vulnerable. We would therefore expect a stronger migration response to immigration for native-born blacks than for native-born whites. Yet, some scholars have found these estimated migration effects to be weakest (or even positive) for blacks.

If our hypothesis is that low-educated natives move out of areas with high immigrant inflows because of an aversion for immigrants, then we would expect that the relative magnitude of immigrants in specific areas would be important. The relevant variable in this case would be the percentage of immigrants in the state, not the percentage of recent immigrants. However, separate the effect on native-born migration of recent immigrant arrivals from previous immigrant arrivals and one finds that native-born migration is negatively related to the inflow of recent immigrants into states, but positively associated with the percentage of immigrants.

A third approach for determining whether the migration patterns of low-skilled natives are causally related to immigration would be to obtain more information on the causal links in each proposed model. If our hypothesis is that immigrants move in, depress economic opportunities, and natives move out, we should be able to observe changes in immigration affecting changes in unemployment and/or wages using annual data. If the responses are so quick as to elude annual data, which seems unlikely, then other research strategies need to be pursued to get actual information on the relevant causal links. For instance, it might be possible to survey natives who have moved and determine the causes of their move and their current employment situation. This information

could then be related to detailed information on the jobs immigrants fill.

Determining whether immigration causes native displacement is crucial. "There is a long-standing debate . . . about the effect of immigration on native internal migration decisions. If immigrants displace natives, then native workers suffer a direct cost of immigration in the form of decreased employment opportunity. Moreover, displacement would also imply that cross-region analyses of wage effects systematically underestimate the consequences of immigration" (Peri and Sparber 2011, 82).

Hampering consensus on this and other immigration issues has been the estimation of models with built-in assumptions that yield biased results. To guard against such misinformation, analysts should routinely test for embedded and seemingly innocuous assumptions by estimating their models on data generated so that the explanatory and outcome variables are uncorrelated. When this technique is applied to the issue of immigrant displacement of natives, Peri and Sparber find that a leading model predicts displacement even when estimated on data constructed so that the migration decisions of immigrants and natives are uncorrelated. "This is likely due to an inherent and mechanical bias created by including a measure of native employment in the denominator of the explanatory variable and in the numerator of the dependent variable" (Peri and Sparber 2011, 90).

Estimating the Effect of Immigrants on Native Economic Status at a Nationwide Level

The possibility that natives may migrate in response to immigration and the issue of endogenous immigration location choice has led several researchers to reject the use of cross-area variation in immigrant concentrations to estimate the impact of immigration on native labor market outcomes. Instead, these researchers estimate the effect of immigrants on natives' earnings at a whole-economy level. A whole-economy approach captures the potential effects on natives' earnings of migration responses within the nation. Another positive trait is an emphasis on measuring the effect of increases in poorly educated immigrants on the earnings of poorly educated natives. These studies find a large negative effect of immigration on the wages of natives with low levels of schooling. Given the policy implications of this result, it is important to examine the three steps that comprise the national economy approach.

The first step calculates the effect of immigration on the supply of low-educated labor. The second step estimates the effect of increases in the supply of low-educated labor on the earnings of low-educated workers, using aggregate time-series data. The third step involves multiplying the first and second steps. The product provides an estimated effect of poorly educated immigration on the earnings of poorly educated natives.

The Achilles' heel of this approach is the underlying assumption in the second step that an increase in the supply of low-educated workers, primarily composed of natives, has the same effect on natives' earnings as an increase in the supply of low-educated immigrants. Poorly educated immigrants and poorly educated natives are assumed to be perfect substitutes. If this assumption is incorrect—as suggested by case-study evidence discussed in the section "Theoretical Expectations" below—then the estimated effect of immigration on natives' earnings will also be incorrect.

A better strategy would be to estimate the effect of changes in immigration on changes in natives' earnings, controlling for the size of the labor force and changes in the size of the labor force as well as other factors that could potentially affect natives' earnings. This approach directly estimates the effect of immigration on natives' earnings, obviating the need to assume that immigrants and natives have similar effects on natives' earnings, while taking into account potential offsets in the total labor supply. Such a model could be estimated disaggregating all relevant variables by the education level of immigrants and natives.

Reconciling Statistical Evidence with Anecdotal Evidence and Theoretical Expectations

Anecdotal and theoretical considerations suggest that an influx of unskilled immigrant labor will adversely affect unskilled native labor. Most people have observed incidents in which jobs that were once held by natives, such as a building's cleaning crew, are now held by immigrants. Economic theory suggests that the greater the extent to which immigrant workers are substitutes for native workers, the greater the potential for wages to fall and/or for native workers to be displaced. It logically follows that an increase in unskilled immigrant labor will detrimentally affect unskilled native-born labor. If statistical studies ultimately fail to find a negative employment or wage effect of unskilled immigrant labor on unskilled native labor, how can we reconcile this finding with our personal observations and theoretical expectations?

Anecdotal Evidence

One problem with reconciling anecdotal evidence of native job displacement with statistical estimates stems from a tendency of researchers to conclude that an estimated negative relationship between percentage of immigrant and native-born wages and employment means that immigrants and natives are substitutes, and a positive relationship indicates that they are complements. In fact, there is no direct evidence in these studies on the nature of the relationship in production between immigrants and natives.

A positive or negative estimated wage or employment effect of immigration only suggests that there is on balance a positive or negative effect of immigration on native-born employment and wages. A positive or null relationship between immigration and native-born wages and employment in statistical studies is not inconsistent with specific cases of displacement and immigration-induced wage declines.

Furthermore, a turnover from native to immigrant labor does not necessarily constitute evidence of displacement. Where jobs that were traditionally filled by natives become dominated by immigrants, case-study evidence is needed on how this occurred and what happened to the native workers who were formerly employed in these jobs. Although it may be impractical to follow numerous firms in order to observe the process by which immigrants come to dominate certain jobs once filled by natives, it would be possible to study work locations that are currently dominated by immigrant labor and to find out what happened to the previous employees, the processes that led to the replacement of immigrants for natives, and the processes that perpetuate the employment of immigrants in those positions. Evidence on whether natives want these jobs could be gleaned from the composition of applicants for these jobs when they are advertised.

Roger Waldinger, in his 1996 study of "Black/Immigrant Competition," provides case-study evidence that immigrant networks work to displace blacks from job opportunities in hotels and restaurants in Los Angeles. Yet, displacement requires that employers prefer immigrants to U.S. natives, and that U.S. natives want the jobs employers have to offer. That African Americans want these jobs is not clear from Waldinger's evidence. In his interviews, employers state that because blacks want better jobs with career potential, few apply for low-level jobs. In contrast, Hispanic immigrants clearly want the jobs, as evidenced by employer accounts of their sometimes long commutes to work. These findings are consistent with Piore's observation that jobs that are acceptable to first-generation Americans are often unacceptable to their descendants, who harbor higher expectations. On the other hand, the fact that African Americans are less likely to apply for these jobs may reflect a rational response to a likely rejection. Waldinger's interviews do suggest that employers favor immigrants, at least for certain types of jobs.

Given that blacks may respond to discrimination by not applying for jobs, definitive evidence of employer discrimination requires an experimental approach, in which discrimination is measured by the responses of employers to actors portraying Hispanic immigrant and native-born black job seekers. Such an approach, which provides information uncontaminated by minority responses to discrimination, has typically been used to measure discrimination against black and Hispanic men versus non-Hispanic white men. Waldinger's findings make a convincing case for using the experimental approach to measure possible employer discrimination among native-born minority and immigrant groups.

The interviews in Waldinger's study also suggest that employee discrimination as well as an employer preference for one group over another may lead to single-group hiring. To avoid interethnic tension at the workplace, employers may simply let immigrant networks find new employees; eligible blacks may never learn of the job openings. Even in the absence of intergroup tensions, Waldinger describes several advantages for the employer of network hiring that would encourage single-group hiring. In such a scenario, immigrant groups with well-developed networks are at a distinct advantage.

The preceding observations suggest that statistical evidence of no adverse effect of immigration on natives' wages and employment, or even a positive effect, may go hand in hand with definitive evidence of displacement in particular instances. Case-study evidence, such as Waldinger's study, can help illuminate the dynamics underlying the concentration of particular groups in particular jobs.

Theoretical Expectations

The theoretical expectation that an increase in unskilled immigrant labor must harm the employment and wages of native unskilled labor comes from a tendency to think only in terms of two types of labor—skilled and unskilled—in discussions and models concerning the effect of immigrant labor on native-born labor. There are, however, many gradations within the unskilled category. And, even within the same observationally equivalent job categories, there are a variety of attributes that make people substitutes or complements.

In detailed analyses of the impact of immigrants on the California labor market, Muller and Espenshade (1985, 101–2) conclude: "[T]he influx of Mexicans to Los Angeles and southern California during the 1970s did not increase the aggregate level of unemployment among non-Hispanic California residents, including blacks. . . . The reason for this, at least in southern California, is that there appears to be relatively little direct competition between Mexican immigrants and native blacks for the same jobs. . . . [T]he differences in education and occupation between Mexican immigrants and blacks in Los Angeles suggest that these workers are labor market complements rather than substitutes."

Even within specific unskilled occupations within specific industries, immigrants and American natives are differentiated by the nature of their work. Carmenza Gallo and Thomas Bailey (1996, 206–7) observe: "[W]hile immigrants were concentrated in the low-skilled positions of the full-service restaurant and in the immigrant restaurant sectors, low-skilled natives were concentrated in the more formally organized fast-food and chain-restaurant sectors. While immigrants populated the small food retail shops, low-skilled natives are concentrated in large supermarkets, and while immigrants are concentrated in the non-unionized renovation sector in the construction industry, native minorities are in the unionized and more established construction firms. To a significant extent the role of networks in job and in informal specific skill acquisition differentiates low-skilled immigrants from low-skilled native workers in the secondary labor market." This insight from case-study analyses of the nature of work that immigrants and natives pursue and the processes by which they become employed may help elucidate why, in several nationwide statistical studies, immigration does not appear to have much of an effect on native-born employment.

Beyond the relationship between native and immigrant labor in the production process, immigration may affect the demand for products produced by natives through several routes. Immigrants spend money and buy native-produced products. The incomes of natives will also be affected by the extent to which the products produced by immigrant and native labor are substitutes or complements. If the presence of immigrants makes one product cheaper, the demand for complementary products will increase.

There is also an interplay between immigrant/native relationships in production and consumption effects. The availability of immigrants to care for kids and clean homes allows middle-class women to work and spend money on goods and services that may be produced by low-educated U.S.-born labor. These types of relationships could have potentially important effects on whether and how immigrant inflows affect the wages and employment of native labor.

Employer Responses to Population Changes

Finally, employers may respond to labor force changes brought about by immigration in ways that minimize or even improve the employment and wage picture of U.S. natives. A particular concern is that immigrants may take the jobs that would otherwise go to poorly educated natives. Yet, businesses may develop or persist in response to the availability of certain types of labor that particular immigrant groups provide. With a growth in low-skilled labor, businesses that may have otherwise left the United States may decide to stay, or opt to produce their products with more labor and less capital. Maria Enchautegui and Ethan Lewis find evidence of a positive effect of immigration on low-skilled employment opportunities.

Economic growth is critical to the jobs and wages of U.S. natives. A voluminous literature points to innovation being the key ingredient of economic growth. As discussed in Part I, immigrants' human capital acquired in their home countries may not immediately and fully transfer to the United States. Yet, this human capital is useful for learning new skills. Immigrants are able to learn new skills and methods at a lower opportunity cost than observationally equivalent natives. According to this theoretical perspective, the presence of immigrants in the United States, particularly the highly educated from economically developing countries, fosters and encourages innovation, entrepreneurship, and business development by native Americans. Indeed, "variation in concentrations of highly educated immigrants across time and space positively correlates with business development by U.S. natives and job creation" (Duleep and Jaeger 2011, 31).

Sharpening Our Ability to Measure Immigration's Effect on Natives' Employment and Wages—Main Points

In conclusion, the jury is still out on whether immigrants, on balance, harm, help, or have no effect on the wages and employment opportunities of U.S. natives. Part II of this chapter highlights interrelated problems that contribute to the variety of estimated results. These include combining various types of immigrants with potentially different effects on natives' earnings into one explanatory variable, overcoming simultaneity issues (immigration affects natives' economic conditions, but economic conditions affect immigration) via the use of instrumental variables, and the historical concentration of immigrants in the big cities of a limited number of states.

To sharpen our ability to measure immigration's effect on native's employment and wages, particularly for natives with low schooling levels, a number of approaches could be pursued, ideally in combination. These include disaggregating the explanatory variable into immigrant inflows by level of immigrant education, considering whether the relationship we seek to unravel is truly simultaneous or whether we could instead relate changes in immigration in one year to changes in natives' economic status the following year; thereby moving the estimation challenge from an intractable simultaneity problem to an omitted-variables problem, controlling for population changes in the estimation rather than assuming that immigrants and natives have similar effects on natives' earnings, using cross-sectional data over numerous time periods, and exploiting natural experiments—situations with sudden and unanticipated influxes of immigrants that are unrelated to the economic conditions of the host region.

Finally, progress in immigration research has been slowed by the estimation of models with built-in assumptions that yield biased results. To guard against such misinformation, analysts should routinely test for embedded assumptions by estimating their models on data generated so that the explanatory and outcome variables are uncorrelated. If, however, it is conclusively determined that immigrants have no effect or even a positive effect on natives' employment and wages, the reason may lie in the high propensity of immigrants to invest in human capital and employer responses to that.

Bibliography

Bohn, Sarah, and Seth Sanders. 2007. "Refining the Estimation of Immigrations' Labor Market Effects." Duke University working paper.

Card, David. 1990. "The Impact of the Mariel Boatlift on the Miami Labor Market." *Industrial and Labor Relations Review* 43 (January): 245–57.

Chiswick, Barry. 1980. *An Analysis of the Economic Progress and Impact of Immigrants.* Employment and Training Administration, U.S. Department of Labor. National Technical Information Service, (August), PB80-200454.

Chiswick, Barry R. 1978. "The Effect of Americanization on the Earnings of Foreign-Born Men." *Journal of Political Economy* 86, no. 5: 897–921.

Chunyu, Miao David. 2011. "Earnings Growth Patterns of Chinese Labor Immigrants in the United States." Paper draft prepared for the Annual Meeting of the Population Association of America, Washington, DC. http://paa2011.princeton.edu/download.aspx?submissionId=110457.

Duleep, Harriet, and Daniel J. Dowhan. 2002. "Insights from Longitudinal Data on the Earnings Growth of U.S. Foreign-Born Men." *Demography* 39, no. 3: 485–506.

Duleep, Harriet, and David Jaeger. 2011. "The Effect of Immigration on U.S. Natives' Innovation and Entrepreneurship: Theoretical Foundations and Preliminary Results." Working Paper, Department of Economics, College of William and Mary.

Duleep, Harriet, and Mark Regets. 1999. "Immigrants and Human Capital Investment." *American Economic Review* 89: 186–91.

Duleep, Harriet, and Mark Regets. 2002. "The Elusive Concept of Immigrant Quality: Evidence from 1970–1990." Discussion Paper No. 631, IZA.

Enchautegui, Maria E. 1995. "Immigrants and the Low-Skilled Market." Discussion Paper. Washington, DC: Urban Institute.

Filer, Randall K. 1992. "The Effect of Immigrant Arrivals on Migratory Patterns of Native Workers." In *Immigration and the Work Force*, edited by George Borjas and Richard Freeman, 245–70. Chicago: University of Chicago Press.

Gallo, Carmenza, and Thomas R. Bailey. 1996. "Social Networks and Skills-based Immigration Policy." In *Immigrants and Immigration Policy: Individual Skills, Family Ties, and Group Identities*, edited by Harriet Duleep and Phanindra Wunnava, 203–18. Greenwich, CT: JAI Press.

Green, David. 1999. "Immigrant Occupational Attainment: Assimilation and Mobility Over Time." *Journal of Labor Economics* 17, no. 1: 49–79.

Jensen, Eric, Sarah Gale, and Paul Charpentier. 2006. "On Migrant Selectivity." Working Paper #32, College of William and Mary, Department of Economics, July.

Lewis, Ethan. 2011. "Immigration, Skill Mix and Capital-Skill Complementarity." *Quarterly Journal of Economics* 126, no. 2.

Lowell, Lindsay. 1996. "Skilled and Family-Based Immigration: Principles and Labor Markets." In *Immigrants and Immigration Policy: Individual Skills, Family Ties, and Group Identities*, edited by Harriet Duleep and Phanindra Wunnava, 353–71. Greenwich, CT: JAI Press.

Muller, Thomas, and Thomas Espenshade. 1985. *The Fourth Wave: California's Newest Immigrants.* Washington, DC: Urban Institute Press.

Peri, Giovanni, and Chad Sparber. 2011. "Assessing Inherent Model Bias: An Application to Native Displacement in Response to Immigration." *Journal of Urban Economics*, Elsevier, 69, no. 1: 82–91.

Piore, Michael. 1979. *Birds of Passage: Migrant Labor and Industrial Societies.* New York: Cambridge University Press.

Sorensen, Elaine. 1996. "Measuring the Employment Effects of Immigrants with Different Legal Statuses on Native Workers." In *Immigrants and Immigration Policy: Individual Skills, Family Ties, and Group Identities*, edited by Harriet Duleep and Phanindra Wunnava, 245–64. Greenwich, CT: JAI Press.

Waldinger, Roger. 1996. "Who Makes the Beds? Who Washes the Dishes? Black/Immigrant Competition Reassessed." In *Immigrants and Immigration Policy: Individual Skills, Family Ties, and Group Identities*, edited by Harriet Duleep and Phanindra Wunnava, 265–88. Greenwich, CT: JAI Press.

White, Michael J., and Zai Liang. 1998. "The Effect of Immigration on the Internal Migration of the Native-Born Population, 1981–1990." *Population Research and Policy Review* 17, no. 2: 141–66.

Labor Issues and Immigration

Robert Mikkelsen

Issues of immigration and ethnicity have bedeviled the labor movement since its beginnings in the United States. On the one hand, there is the obvious fact that without immigrants and their offspring, no labor movement could have been developed. During the years of the United States' most intensive industrialization, immigrants provided much of its leadership and membership. Indeed, it can be argued that immigration created the American working class. On the other hand, the constant and increasing stream of immigration prior to the 1920s placed the American labor movement in a dilemma: Should it try to organize all of the newly developing working class—both skilled and unskilled—in all its bewildering ethnic variety and conflicting interests? Or should it concentrate on organizing only that portion that had skills, focusing efforts within the workplace? The former would require some form of broad, industrial unionization encompassing the majority of the immigrants. The latter would mean organization on the basis of trade or craft unions, excluding the majority of immigrants, who were unskilled workers.

Related to and further complicating this dilemma were the issues raised by the differences between temporary immigrants and permanent immigrants. How were the two groups to be distinguished from one another? This was a necessary distinction to make because it was believed that immigrants with no intention of staying in the United States were not motivated to join the labor movement. Whatever their original intention, from the onset of mass migration to the present day, an estimated 30 percent of immigrants to the United States have decided either to return to their home countries or move elsewhere.

Yet at any given moment, the ethnic communities created by immigrants and their offspring have necessarily included both permanent and temporary workers. It would be hard put to separate the two, since intentions change and the heart may wander. In addition, ethnicity itself can often function as a basis for union solidarity, acting as a channel moving the temporary worker into permanent status and possible union membership. Several important unions were buttressed by such ethnic solidarity. For example, in the late nineteenth century, the United Brewery Workers, centered in Milwaukee, Wisconsin, was overwhelmingly German American in membership. In the middle of the twentieth century, the United Farm Workers were primarily Mexican American. In this sense, ethnicity fueled by immigration could function as a conduit to unionization. On the negative side, of course, barriers created by differences of culture and language could serve to exclude new potential union members outside the union's ethnic group, isolating it within an immigrant ghetto. In sum, ethnicity could be a source of strength or of division, a quality it has retained to the present day.

A subgroup of such temporary immigrants has included sojourners or "birds of passage." Between the years of 1880 and 1920, they became increasingly prevalent as transportation became more efficient, allowing them to move back and forth across the Atlantic according to seasonal work opportunities. Their increase was closely connected to the enormous waves of immigration coming from southern and eastern Europe during these years. With the imposition of immigration restrictions in the 1920s, the major source of sojourners became Latin America, particularly Mexico, a trend that has continued to the present day, when many sojourners are undocumented immigrants entering the country illegally.

Sojourners have generally been young, unskilled, and easy targets for exploitation, accepting low wages and poor working conditions out of ignorance, need, and the assurance that their situation was temporary. For most of organized labor's existence, such temporary immigrant workers have been seen as exerting a downward pressure on wages, job security, and working conditions. They were felt to have no interest in the labor movement and were, indeed, often used as strikebreakers. Antipathy between unorganized, temporary immigrants and unionized workers has occasionally been profound. This has been equally true of the labor movement's relationship to "contract" or "guest" workers, a variety of sojourners distinguished by being actively recruited in their homelands to come to the United States under contract for a stipulated period of time.

This chapter will trace the changing attitude of organized labor toward such permanent and temporary workers from the late nineteenth century until the present day. In doing so, it will examine the impact of immigration on forms of labor organization. It will look at various attempts by organized labor to control the flow of both permanent and temporary immigration through the years. And it will examine the changes in attitude and organizational strategy that permanent and temporary immigrants have caused in the labor movement, both during the 1930s and during the latter half of the twentieth century, when organized labor was once again faced with the challenge of mass immigration. As we shall see, dealing with these challenges has led to a sea change in organized labor's relationship to both permanent and temporary immigrants. Throughout these developments, the central question for the labor movement has remained the same: Who among the diverse elements of the American working class ought to be included within the union fold, and how are they to be organized?

Unions and Immigrants before Immigration Restrictions

Potential divisions within the labor movement between skilled and unskilled workers, natives and immigrants, or because of differing ethnic backgrounds were exacerbated by the extremely difficult conditions organized labor faced at the outset with regard to the governmental authorities working together with employers. From the beginning, unions risked being viewed as criminal conspiracies. The courts, the police, and, in the case of strikes or other direct confrontations, state militia or federal troops could be and were mobilized against them. A severe blow was dealt the movement in 1908 when the Supreme Court ruled on the basis of the Sherman Antitrust Act that a union engaged in a boycott against its employer was guilty of unlawful combinations to restrain trade. It issued an injunction and made the union in question liable for the payment of triple damages. It would not be until the 1930s that unions would gain full legal legitimacy within the institutional framework of American government.

Despite such opposition, attempts were made from the outset to organize immigrant workers on a broad basis, encompassing as much of the working class as possible. This was true of the short-lived National Labor Union (1866–1872) and, most notably, of the Knights of Labor, first established in Philadelphia in 1869. The Knights' policy was to include both skilled and unskilled workers, regardless of race or gender or national origin. When Terrence V. Powderly took over leadership in 1878, the Knights entered into a period of explosive growth, expanding from 9,000 members in 1879 to a peak of 729,000 members in 1886. Its liberal membership policy and rapid expansion created a widespread, but poorly disciplined and heterogeneous organization. Its primary wish was to improve the conditions of the working class though political action that would lead to government legislation favoring labor. As such, it opposed the use of strikes and other forms of direct militant confrontation with employers to settle labor disputes, favoring arbitration. It is therefore ironic but illustrative that it was unauthorized strikes within its ranks that fueled the Knights' growth. Equally, it was a disastrously unsuccessful strike in the Southwest that later took the bottom out of the movement, reducing it to fewer than 75,000 members by 1893.

Although some national trade unions were affiliated with the Knights, most viewed its rapid rise and fall from a distance. The Knights' debacle served to reaffirm the trade unionist view that the only certain basis for worker solidarity was through the common interest generated by a common workplace, a workplace defined by skill and craft. Newly arrived and unskilled immigrants could not be expected to generate such solidarity. This became the bedrock for the organization of the American Federation of Labor (AFL), a federation of national craft and trade unions that emerged in 1886 as the dominant and enduring center of the labor movement. The AFL concentrated on improving wages and working conditions within the workplace and eschewed ideological political objectives. The emergence of this brand of "pure-and-simple" trade unionism as the dominant form of labor organization was intertwined with the AFL's position with regard to immigration and ethnicity. AFL trade unionism focused on improving the wages and working conditions of its members at the exclusion of unskilled workers, which meant the exclusion of most immigrants and the greater part of the working class. It was willing to use the strike as a weapon in its direct confrontations with employers. For this to be successful, however, it had to control access to its skilled pool of labor. Unrestricted immigration potentially threatened this control. This was an important reason why the AFL opposed unrestricted immigration from the start.

Despite differences in organizational strategy, on one issue, the Knights of Labor and the trade unions were in complete agreement—opposition to temporary immigrants in the form of contract laborers. Like all temporary immigrants, they were believed to exert downward pressure on wages, job security and working conditions—all of which undermined the bargaining position of unions. In the 1880s, both the Knights of Labor and the craft unions of the day opposed imported Chinese "coolie" labor on the West Coast. "The Knights believed that it was impossible for unskilled American workers to compete with unskilled coolie workers who were contractually obligated for seven years or more to the Chinese employers who bought them to the United States" (Briggs 2001, 39). In 1882, the labor movement was a key player in the passage of the Chinese Exclusion Act, virtually ending most immigration from China for

more than 80 years. This was the first significant piece of legislation by Congress to restrict immigration to the United States. In 1885, this victory was extended to include organized labor's opposition to contract labor from Europe as well. The Knights successfully worked for the passage of the Alien Contract Law, which titularly banned all foreign recruitment of workers by American companies (commonly referred to as the Foran Act). However, like many similar laws that were to follow throughout the twentieth century, it proved ineffective in practice, lacking effective penalties or means of enforcement.

The AFL, Ethnicity, and Unskilled Immigrant Workers

Part of the logic of the AFL's brand of pure-and-simple trade unionism was the idea that making skill the sole basis of for membership and solidarity could circumvent the potential splits that different ethnic heritages might bring to the workplace. In fact, however, the organizational structure of the AFL often both reflected and reinforced existing ethnic divisions within the growing working class because differences of skill often closely paralleled differences of background. During the period of intense industrialization and immigration between 1880 and 1920, many of the unskilled immigrants came from southern and eastern Europe. They encountered ethnic communities from northern and western Europe that had already been established during the first wave of mass immigration between 1820 and 1880. It was members of these groups that had founded both the Knights of Labor and the AFL (see Table 1).

From the outset, the immigrants of this first wave and their children had made up a disproportionate number of those active in union movements in the United States. Many of the early craft and trade unions were formed by workmen who brought their union experience as well as their skills with them across the Atlantic. In this way, the experience of many early trade unions in England and Germany was transferred to American environs. Some English unions, such as the Amalgamated Society of Engineers, even set up American branches. Similarly, the

Table 1. Immigration to the United States, by Decade. Persons Obtaining Legal Permanent Resident Status: Fiscal Years 1820 to 2010

Decade	Number
1821–1830	143,439
1831–1840	599,125
1841–1850	1,713,251
1851–1860	2,598,214
1861–1870	2,314,824
1871–1880	2,812,191
1881–1890	5,246,613
1891–1900	3,687,564
1901–1910	8,795,386
1911–1920	5,735,811
1921–1930	4,107,209
1931–1940	524,431
1941–1950	1,035,039
1951–1960	2,515,479
1961–1970	3,321,677
1971–1980	4,399,172
1981–1990	7,255,956
1991–2000	9,080,528
2001–2010	10,501,053

Source: U.S. Department of Homeland Security.

leadership of early American unions held a disproportionate number of immigrants from northern and western Europe. Of 77 American labor figures who were prominent between 1860 and 1875, 45, or 58 percent, had been born in Europe—13 in England, 11 in Ireland, 9 in Germany, 5 each in Scotland and Wales, and 2 in France. Eleven of 25 of the leaders in the Knights of Labor in 1886 were northern and western European immigrants and, then, responding to strains in the labor movement, in February 1885 Congress banned the importation of contract laborers (Foran Act).

Samuel Gompers, president of the AFL from 1886 until his death in 1924 (with a brief break in 1894) typifies this first wave. Born in London in 1850, he immigrated with his Jewish Dutch family to the United States in 1863, where he gained citizenship in 1873. He was active in the Knights of Labor through the National Cigarmaker's Union he helped establish. He watched their unsuccessful attempt to establish a broad-based union movement including unskilled labor and went on to found and lead the AFL. Like the craft and trade unions he led, Gompers took a dim view of the new immigrants flooding the

nation from southern and eastern Europe after 1880. He helped create and strongly supported the anti-immigration policy of the AFL for many years.

In addition to economic reasons, there was an element of racist and ethnocentric justification for the AFL's policy. For example, in a resolution approved in 1904 by the AFL to explain its support of the Chinese Exclusion Act of 1882, the reasons given focused explicitly on racial issues, contending that "the racial incompatibility, as between the peoples of the Orient and the United States, presents a problem of race preservation which it our imperative duty to solve in our own favor, and which can only be thus solved by a policy of Exclusion" (AFL 1904, 172). Later, similar attitudes were expressed when opposing immigration from southern and eastern Europe. The AFL supported the restrictionist views of the Dillingham Commission, a congressional commission on immigration appointed in 1907. In addition to agreeing with the commission's suggestion urging the adoption of limits on the entry of unskilled immigrants, the AFL shared the commission's view that these new immigrants were by nature far less intelligent than the old immigrants, and therefore detrimental to both the nation and the union movement.

Attitudes such as these led workers in older trade unions with roots in established ethnic groups, such as the German Americans, to look askance at their newly arrived, unskilled, and unorganized comrades, such as the Polish Americans. Little effort was made by the AFL trade unions to organize such workers. In fact, "many of the AFL unions used various measures to block immigrant workers from joining craft unions. For example, making preconditions for membership that included such criteria as U.S. citizenship or declaration of intention to become a citizen, particularly high initiation fees for immigrants, approval of the national unions' officers and special evidence of competency" (Haus 2002, 52). In practice, a kind of ethnic hierarchy of unions grew up within the organization, with the older ethnic groups from northern and western Europe occupying the upper tier of craft unions and viewing with skepticism lower-tier unions with membership including eastern and southern European immigrants and their children.

The Industrial Organization of Immigrants

This is not to say that there was no such organization of newly arrived immigrants within the AFL or the labor movement. Within the AFL, the United Brewery Workers (UBW) has been mentioned as an example of ethnic and union solidarity supplementing one another—in this case, through the German-American community. The UBW organized both skilled and unskilled workers. However, the greatest exception within the AFL prior to the 1930s was the United Mine Workers (UMW), which was founded in 1890 and joined the AFL shortly afterward. The UMW was an industrial union. It had an inclusive approach and seriously sought to organize the entire workforce. This was a consequence of the kind of unskilled work that the vast majority of workers had within the mining industry. It was a pragmatic response to raise wages and improve working conditions. A large proportion of mine workers were immigrants from southern and eastern Europe. According to the 1920 census, 52.7 percent of mine workers were foreign-born. Of these, 18 percent were from Poland, 10.5 percent from Russia, and 6.5 percent from Italy.

Coal operators had begun to recruit immigrants from Italy and eastern Europe in the 1870s, leading to violent confrontations with established mine workers. In response to such interethnic hostility, the UMW took practical measures to unionize immigrants. It used organizers who spoke the languages of the immigrants, printed parts of the union newspaper in foreign languages, and forged links among the leaders of the ethnic communities, including religious leaders. These pioneering efforts paid off. In 1892, the UMW had fewer than 20,000 members. By 1908, that number had risen to 263,000. After World War I, it exceeded half a million members, making it by far the largest union in the AFL.

Another AFL union that practiced industrial unionization was the International Ladies' Garment Workers' Union (ILGWU). The ILGWU was granted its AFL charter in 1900 in New York City and gained most of its membership among young Jewish- and Italian-American immigrant women during a series of prolonged spontaneous strikes against sweatshop

A Russian-Jewish immigrant trims rayon underwear in a factory in New York City, 1938. The woman was a member of the International Ladies' Garment Workers' Union (ILGWU) Local 62. (Hansel Mieth/Time Life Pictures/Getty Images)

and industrial exploitation in 1909 and 1910. The ILGWU exemplifies how ethnic and—in this case—gender solidarity could in certain circumstances underpin industrial unionism. Interestingly, when voting for the first of the spontaneous strikes, women at the meeting took a traditional Yiddish oath: "If I turn traitor to the cause I now pledge, may this hand wither from the arm I now raise" (Newsinger 2008).

Yet the eastern European Jewish origins of these women did not prevent them from joining hands with their Italian-American sisters. The success of the ILGWU confounded more conservative trade unionists who did not believe that either women or immigrants could be organized. Like the UMW, the ILGWU also pioneered new techniques of organization and negotiation on an industry-wide basis, notably with the "Protocol of Peace" of 1910, an agreement by which the union won recognition and benefits while promising to settle grievances through arbitration rather than strikes during the term of the agreement—a landmark contract. By 1920, its membership had reached 100,000.

Outside of the AFL, there were additional attempts to organize immigrants within industrial unions. One of the earliest is the Western Federation of Miners (WFM). Founded in 1893, it was an independent union with a justified reputation for militancy that operated in the western United States and British Columbia. It briefly affiliated with the AFL in 1896–1897, but it was disappointed by that organization's lack of support and judged the AFL under Gompers to not be sufficiently interested in actively fighting for workers' rights.

By 1903, the WFM had 27,000 members in almost all the western states. Like the United Mine Workers of the AFL, the WFM welcomed all miners into its fold, irrespective of skill, ethnic background, time of arrival, or citizenship. Unlike the UMW, however, the WFM turned increasingly more radical and socialist as it battled corporations and state governments in the West in a series of bitter and bloody strikes. In 1898, it changed its name to Western Labor Union and, in 1902, once again to the American Labor Union. By 1905, it had suffered serious losses at the hands of state militias and sought allies. This led it to help found perhaps the most famous of the industrial unions before the 1930s, the Industrial Workers of the World (IWW).

The IWW believed in "one big union" for all—including all immigrants. It was the radical antithesis of the limited and cautious trade unionism of the AFL. The IWW favored direct economic action (e.g., sit-down strikes, chain picketing, and sabotage on the job) as opposed to political reforms. Its ultimate aim was a form of syndicalist control and ownership of the means of production. Though never very successful in its organizing efforts—it had perhaps 20,000 members in its peak years—it served to set the spotlight on the appalling conditions under which the unskilled workers lived at that time, left outside the union fold by the AFL. This was most evident in the successful strike it led in the textile industry in Lawrence, Massachusetts, in 1912.

Reflecting the working class of the day, the mills and the community of Lawrence were divided along ethnic lines. Skilled jobs were held by native-born workers of English, Irish, and German descent, many of them members of the AFL-affiliated United Textile Workers (which, incidentally, briefly tried to break the strike). Most unskilled jobs were held by young immigrant women of French-Canadian, Italian, Slavic, Hungarian, Portuguese, and Syrian background. It was these women who formed the backbone of the strike. They helped the IWW leaders to develop strategies to avoid ethnic splits among the workers, forming a strike committee made up of two representatives from each ethnic group in the mills and arranging meetings to be translated into 25 different languages. Even more than the UMW or the ILGWU, the success of the Lawrence strike demonstrated that neither gender nor ethnic background nor time of arrival was necessarily a barrier to the organization of unskilled, immigrant workers.

Although these and other efforts of industrial unionization among unskilled immigrants met with some limited success before World War I, they were the exception, not the rule. In general, immigrants, and particularly temporary immigrants, were viewed with skepticism by the majority of the labor movement as represented by the AFL. It was not until the interwar years and the coming of the Great Depression that industrial unionism made its breakthrough among unskilled immigrant workers. Two events precipitated that breakthrough: the imposition of immigration restrictions in the 1920s, and the coming of the New Deal under Franklin D. Roosevelt.

Organized Labor and Immigration Restrictions

Opposition to unrestricted immigration had been a popular policy in the labor movement since the days of the National Labor Union and the Knights of Labor. The aim of this policy was straightforward—to reduce the labor supply and thus improve the labor movements bargaining position vis-à-vis employers.

Regarding the AFL, as noted above, there was from the beginning a strain of racist and ethno-centric prejudice connected with this policy. These views placed the AFL in an unlikely alliance with the most conservative elements of the American nativist movement, including racist ideologues like Madison Grant and leading conservative Republicans like Senator Henry Cabot Lodge. Prior to World War I, the AFL supported the same positions as the most important anti-immigrant organization of the day, the Immigration Restriction League. This included promoting the imposition of a literacy test, a solvency test, and an increased head tax on incoming immigrants in order to reduce their flow, particularly from southern and eastern Europe. The attitudes underlying this support within the AFL come out clearly in Gompers's report to the AFL convention in 1902 supporting a literacy test: "This regulation will exclude hardly any of the natives of Great Britain, Ireland, Germany, France, or Scandinavia. It will exclude only a small proportion of our immigrants from North Italy. It will shut out a considerable number of South Italians and of Slavs and others equally or more undesirable and injurious. . . . It is good . . . to diminish the number of that class (of immigrants) which by reason of its lack of intelligence, is slowest to appreciate the value of organization" (AFL 1902, 21).

After World War I, the AFL went considerably farther in its opposition, calling for an end to *all* immigration to the United States for a number of years in order to avoid unemployment in a period of economic readjustment. Thus, it found itself in the 1920s in the unlikely position of viewing as insufficient the first permanent, as well as the most severe, restrictions ever imposed on immigration in the history the United States. However, since many of the aims for which it had been working were fulfilled by these restrictions, it supported their passage in Congress wholeheartedly.

The National Origins Act of 1924 established a cap of 165,000 on the overall number of immigrants allowed in, excluded Asian immigration, and set up a system of national quotas that limited the number of immigrants who could be admitted from any country to 2 percent of the number of people from that country who were already living in the United States in 1890—a time *before* the southern and eastern European immigrants had arrived in number. It had the results intended by its advocates. Immigration from southern and eastern Europe plummeted, while immigrants from Great Britain, Ireland, Germany, and other northern and western European nations were given the lion's share of places available within the cap stipulated. With minor adjustments, this quota system remained in place until the Immigration and Nationality Act of 1965.

The passage of immigration restrictions fulfilled many of the immigration policy goals that the AFL and organized labor had pursued for decades. The total number of immigrants was significantly reduced (see Table 1). The flow of cheap and potentially temporary immigrant unskilled labor from eastern and southern Europe was staunched. The bargaining position of the trade union movement was correspondingly improved, it was hoped. The AFL maintained its support of these restrictions for 30 years. However, this quota system held one abiding disappointment for the AFL: it did not include the Western Hemisphere. The same concerns about having organized labor's bargaining position undermined that had been expressed about the impact of unskilled immigrants from Europe were now transferred to the permanent and temporary immigrants arriving from Latin America, the Caribbean, and, to a lesser degree, Canada.

The AFL was particularly concerned about immigration from Mexico. Its extensive common border with the United States made both permanent and temporary immigration simple. In addition, hundreds of thousands of Mexicans annually moved back and forth across the border following seasonal agricultural work. The AFL leadership repeatedly and unsuccessfully called for Mexico to be included in the quota system that applied to European countries during the following decades. As the twentieth century progressed, the issue of Mexican and Hispanic/Latino immigration became increasingly intertwined with that of guest worker programs and undocumented, illegal immigrants—both of which were traditionally looked upon as detrimental to the interests of organized labor. This is an issue to which we will return below.

Unions and Immigrants after Immigration Restrictions: Industrial Unionism

In the opinion of many historians, the end of unrestricted immigration improved the position of the labor movement by removing the pressure of a constant stream of cheap labor undermining its bargaining position. It therefore helped set the stage for increased organization of unskilled workers—primarily immigrants and their offspring—into industrial unions. An equally important factor was the passage of the National Labor Relations Act—or Wagner Act—of 1935 during the New Deal. Previous to the Wagner Act, organized labor in the United States had traditionally faced the opposition of the federal and state governments, including the use of court injunctions, antitrust laws, and, at its most extreme, federal troops and state militia to break strikes and other forms of union activity. The Wagner Act reversed that. It guaranteed the right of employees to organize, form unions, and bargain collectively with their employers. Under the Wagner Act, workers could freely choose whether or not to belong to a union. It also created a new National Labor Relations Board to arbitrate deadlocked disputes, guarantee democratic union elections, and punish unfair labor practices by employers.

The improved conditions for the labor movement in the 1930s led unions within the AFL to challenge "pure-and-simple" trade unionism with its focus on the organization of skilled workers into trade unions. The unions that spearheaded this challenge were the same ones that had pioneered the organization of unskilled immigrant workers within the AFL in previous decades, including the United Mine Workers, the International Ladies' Garment Workers' Union, and the Mine, Mill and Smelter Workers Union (MMSWU, successor to the Western Federation of Miners). A "Committee for Industrial Organizations" (CIO) was established within the AFL in 1935 under the leadership of UMW president John L. Lewis and in the teeth of the opposition of the AFL leadership. CIO activities eventually led the AFL to exclude the 10 unions making it up in 1937. This, in turn, led to the transformation of the committee into the entirely independent labor federation, the Congress of Industrial Organizations (CIO) in 1938, with Lewis as president.

It would be hard to overestimate the impact the coming of the CIO and industrial unionism had on the relation of organized labor to immigrants, as well as to African Americans and women. The CIO made it clear from the start that it intended to be an inclusive union movement that would gain its strength in the labor market by organizing all potential workers in an industry, rather than select skilled workers at the exclusion of the unskilled majority. One of its stated goals was "to bring about the effective organization of the working men and women of America without regard to race, color, creed or nationality" (Chen and Wong 1998, 216). Many of the industries within which it organized were manned by precisely those groups of immigrants that had arrived in such numbers before immigration restrictions were imposed—i.e., the southern and eastern Europeans. An example of this is the United Auto Workers union (UAW). It was established in 1935 and developed extensive outreach programs to the many ethnic communities to which its membership belonged. It made good use of the methods developed by the UMW and other ethnically diverse unions prior to the Wagner Act and added to them a spirit of militancy in its use of tactics pioneered by the IWW, like the sit-down strike and mass picketing. By the end of 1937, the UAW was recognized by General Motors and had almost 500,000 members, a vast number of them first-and second-generation eastern and southern Europeans, as well as African Americans and women.

The founding of the CIO led to explosive growth for the union movement. The AFL replied to the CIO's challenge by modifying its organizing strategy to include forms of industrial unionization. The resulting intense competition between the two federations helped promote the most impressive upsurge of union membership in the history of the country. From about 3.5 million, or 11.6 percent of the labor force, in 1935, organized labor grew to encompass 8.7 million, or almost 27 percent of the workforce, in 1940. Under the impact of World War II, the movement grew to more than 14 million,

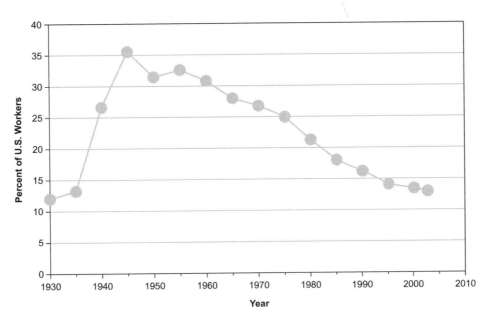

Figure 1. Union Membership.

or a fully a third of the workforce, a position it maintained into the 1950s (see Figure 1).

This was the birth of the modern labor movement, a movement made up of both trade and industrial unions that included within its fold large portions of the unskilled as well as skilled workers, of first- and second-generation Americans, of women as well as men, of African Americans as well as whites. Their inclusion within organized labor presaged a major shift in the policy of organized labor toward immigration in general.

Labor's Changing Immigration Policy and New Immigration Legislation

Despite its change in organizing strategy to include forms of industrial unionism and unskilled immigrant workers in the 1930s, the AFL did not change its position regarding the system of immigration restrictions. It continued to support the quotas favoring northern and western European immigrants over southern and eastern European immigrants, though it came to advocate revisions in the system after World War II. In contrast, the CIO opposed immigration quotas, reflecting its generally more inclusive, liberal position regarding ethnic identity and race. As

one representative put it, "Our unions are open to all, and all are accorded equal treatment, equal rights, and equal opportunity" (CIO 1955). On the pragmatic level, too, many in the CIO's membership favored more open immigration in order to be able to reunite with family members who had not entered the United States before the 1924 national origins restrictions were imposed. When negotiations for the reunification of the AFL and CIO began in 1955, this was one of the major differences to be ironed out between them.

Initially, the two decided on an ambiguous statement on the issue, one that gave the new AFL-CIO little guidance. Gradually over the coming decade, however, the more liberal views of the CIO took hold. This reflected the impact of the large numbers members of eastern and southern European ethnic heritage who had joined the labor movement through the industrial unions and their increasing levels of skills. And it reflected the times as well. During these years, people who held liberal values gained greater strength inside the labor movement. This normative liberalization was further strengthened through the activities of the civil rights movement, which broke the back of the racist ideology that had underlain the justification for the quota system adopted in

1924. Between 1955 and 1965, the reunited AFL-CIO gradually adopted the CIO's position on immigration.

In direct contrast to the alliance that the AFL had established in the early years of the twentieth century, with conservative forces working for immigration restriction, in the latter half of the century, the AFL-CIO joined liberal forces on policy toward legal immigration. It resisted restrictionist proposals to reduce legal permanent immigration and advocated family reunion as the main criteria for legal immigration, reflecting the liberal view that people with family ties to a member of U.S. society have moral claims to enter.

This is the background for organized labor's support of new immigration legislation adopted in 1965. The Immigration and Nationality Act of 1965 eliminated the national origin quotas that had been in place since 1924. An annual limit of 170,000 legal immigrants was set for the Eastern Hemisphere, ending the exclusion of Asians. No more than 20,000 were to come from any one nation. And for the first time, a yearly limit of 120,000 was set for the Western Hemisphere, with visas available on a first-come, first-served basis. The number of family reunification visas, however, was potentially unlimited. This would turn out to be a key provision of the bill. During the congressional debate on the measure, it was stressed that the intention was to redress the injustices of the past and create a balanced immigration policy free from racist overtones. It was not to set the stage for a new wave of mass immigration. In the words of Senator Edward Kennedy, a strong supporter of the bill, "The bill will not flood our cities with immigrants. It will not upset the ethnic mix of our society. It will not relax the standards of admission. It will not cause American workers to lose their jobs" (U.S. Senate 1965, 1–3).

In fact, the new legislation did bring about a new wave of mass immigration. Between 1971 and 2010, some 31 million new Americans reached the country's shores, the great majority heading for the cities (see Table 1). It also changed the ethnic mix of American society, shifting the origins of the great majority of immigrants from Europe to Asia and Latin America, particularly Mexico, which became the single largest sender country during the latter half of the century. Older, established ethnic groups from Europe, such as the German Americans, Irish Americans, Polish Americans, and Italian Americans, suddenly found themselves within the same broad category of European Americans when compared with the increasing numbers of new arrivals from China, Vietnam, India, Korea, and the Philippines as well as from Latin American and Caribbean countries such as the Dominican Republic, Colombia, Haiti, and El Salvador. The new immigrants brought with them new challenges to relations within the American labor movement.

The new legislation also relaxed the terms of admission to the United States. By 1996, the cap on annual admission had been raised to slightly less than 900,000. During the first decade of the twenty-first century, an average of slightly more than 1,000,000 legal immigrants have arrived per year (or were present and adjusted/admitted as Lawful Permanent Residents). Despite the return of mass immigration, organized labor did not change its basic policy, accepting the system of legal permanent immigration established after 1965, even though it suffered a steep decline in membership through these same years.

Unions and Immigrants after 1965

The change in the AFL-CIO's immigration policy also marked a change in focus regarding the debate on the impact of permanent and temporary immigration within organized labor. Gone were the days of restrictionism, but the debate about temporary immigrant workers—either as undocumented illegal workers or document guest workers—if anything grew more intense. Most unions within the AFL-CIO continued to see them as a threat to organized labor's bargaining position and wage standards. Some, however, came to see them as an unavoidable part of the workforce that needed to be included within organized labor in one form or another. This was a continuation of the ongoing debate about who was a suitable candidate for inclusion within the union fold. The grounds had now shifted from debating the issue of the recruitment of skilled workers versus unskilled workers to debating the recruitment of permanent legal immigrants versus temporary illegal immigrants or contract workers. Ethnicity continued to play an important role in these debates.

The influx of Mexican immigrants as contract workers and illegal immigrants in the latter half of the twentieth century became central to this debate. Mexicans had a long history of immigration, both permanent and temporary. Between 1900 and 1930, some 639,000 Mexicans had come, either drawn by the growth of the agricultural sector in the American Southwest, pushed out by the Mexican Revolution in 1910, or recruited to fill labor shortages during World War I and the boom years of the 1920s afterward. With the coming of the Great Depression, tens of thousands had been repatriated, often brutally and sometimes without regard to citizenship status. By 1940, their numbers had been almost halved, to 377,000.

The AFL had supported this policy wholeheartedly, calling for tougher border controls. When a similar labor shortage occurred during World War II, the Mexican government intervened to make certain its citizens would not suffer a similar fate if they took work in the United States. The result was the Mexican Farm Labor Program, informally known as the Bracero Program, a system of contract labor that guaranteed guest workers their wages and legal status and that ran intermittently from 1942 to 1964. During its existence, it sponsored more than 4.5 million border crossings by Mexican guest workers.

The AFL, and later the AFL-CIO, opposed it. Seen from the perspective of organized labor, the Bracero Program had clear negative consequences. First, it undermined repeated efforts to organize Mexican workers by provided cheap labor that undermined their bargaining position and could be used as strikebreakers. It was not, for example, until the Bracero Program was ended that the United Farm Workers (UFW) under the leadership of Cesar Chavez were able to gain ground in California and the nation. Secondly, it put in place a foundation for illegal immigration by forging networks of information about jobs in the United States. During a lull in the program, the arrest of undocumented immigrants jumped from half a million in 1951 to over 865,000 in 1952. The following year, over a million were apprehended during Operation Wetback, a government campaign

Table 2. Unauthorized Immigrant Population: 2000–2010

2000	8,500,000
2001–2004	*
2005	10,500,000
2006	11,300,000
2007	11,800,000
2008	11,600,000
2009	10,800,000
2010	10,800,000

*DHS estimates not produced for 2001–2004.
Source: U.S. Department of Homeland Security (DHS).

to round up illegal immigrants. The channels of migration between Mexico and the United States established during the Bracero Program would continue to exist long after its end, helping to set the stage for an illegal immigration that would come to number more than eight million by the end of the century, more than half being of Mexican origin (see Table 2).

When supporting the new immigration legislation of 1965, the AFL-CIO had pointedly urged the beefing up of border guards with just such illegal immigration in mind. Ten years later, this same attitude was reflected in an AFL-CIO resolution approved in 1975, which stated that "[The temporary immigrant workers'] presence takes jobs from American citizens and legal aliens and undermines the movement toward fair wages and working conditions" (AFL-CIO 1975, 27). Organized labor continued to feel threatened by illegal immigration until the end of the century.

Union Decline in a Globalized Economy

A significant reason for continued hostility toward illegal immigration was the pressure brought to bear by the general decline of the union movement during the last half of the twentieth century. From a high point of almost 35 percent of the workforce in the 1950s, unions organized less than 13 percent by the end of the century (see Figure 1). Numerous explanations have been given for this decline. Some have ascribed it directly to the new wave of mass immigration, creating a cheap labor pool and undermining labor's ability to organize and maintain unions.

One economist argued that "the hard reality of the lessons of labor history is that the more generous the immigration policy, the worse it is for all workers in their efforts to raise wages, to improve working conditions, and to secure employment opportunities" (Briggs 2001, 79). Others have emphasized the increasing globalization of the American economy and the restructuring that has accompanied it. The last half of the twentieth century witnessed the reduction of heavy industry in the Northeast, a stronghold of industrial unionism, reducing the "Steel Belt" to the "Rust Belt." Entire industrial concerns moved to the new "Sunbelt" of the south, shedding their union obligations along the way. Other industries went a step further, outsourcing their production abroad at the cost of union jobs. Simultaneously, American industries found themselves being challenged by cheaper imported goods, putting further pressure on them to cut costs and improve efficiency, often at the expense of previously agreed-upon union contracts.

At the same time that the industrial sector of the economy was shrinking, the service sector was growing. The United States had entered the era of the "postindustrial" economy. A significant part of this came to be known as the "informal" economy. The informal economy refers to enterprises that produce and sell goods and services outside of the governmental regulatory systems set up to maintain the minimum wage, taxation, health and safety standards, and other legal requirements for workplaces. The main motivation for being an employer in the informal economy was tax evasion, allowing greater profits. Much of the informal economy came to be found within the service sector. However, the American industrial sector also became involved in the informal economy in order to compete with low-wage labor in underdeveloped countries.

It was not the first time that such informal, mainly small enterprises had a significant impact on the American economy. In the previous period of mass immigration in the early twentieth century, many newly arrived immigrants—both permanent and temporary—had found employment in urban "sweatshops" operating on the fringes of the official economy (for example, the Jewish- and Italian-American women who had founded the ILGWU a century before). At the end of the twentieth century, however, a new factor was added. The growth of the informal economy went hand in hand with the development of a more flexible and decentralized system of industrial production in which private-sector enterprises subcontracted routine portions of their production to smaller, independent units, which then shipped products to central locations for "just-in-time" assembly. Many of these were, in turn, manned by immigrants who had been recruited by labor subcontractors. A labor subcontractor provided a specific number of workers for a certain period of time to undertake a defined task at a fixed rate of pay per worker, keeping some portion of the workers' wages. By using a subcontractor, an enterprise could avoid being held liable for the immigrant workers, since they were technically not its employees. The unstable, dispersed, and decentralized workplaces that resulted from this system further undermined the labor movement, eliminating high-paying union jobs and making new unionization drives extremely difficult.

Most of the new immigrant workers arriving in the United States were employed in businesses that lay outside the union fold. Many were employed in the informal economy. This was particularly true of the illegal temporary immigrant workers. They were subject to poor working conditions, low wages, exploitation, and—unlike sweatshop workers a century before—had no recourse to either the authorities or the unions to improve their conditions. That was why the labor movement was especially concerned with their impact on wages and job security. Potentially, they seemed to undermine both the older established organized workers and the new unorganized legal immigrant workers who might become future union members. On the other hand, as during earlier waves of mass immigration, it was not a simple matter to separate the interests of the legal permanent immigrant workers from the illegal temporary immigrant workers in the new ethnic communities springing up across the United States. For this reason, organized labor policies toward illegal immigration went through a series of changes during the last half of the twentieth century.

Employer Sanctions and INS Raids

In order to stem the flow of illegal immigration, organized labor had traditionally supported the imposition of employer sanctions; that is, the levying of fines and penalties on employers knowingly hiring undocumented illegal workers. For this reason, the AFL-CIO called for an effective, government-controlled system for the certification of workers by employers and supported Immigration and Naturalization Service (INS) raids to find and punish employers of illegal immigrants.

A tough stand on employer sanctions was one of the conditions set for the AFL-CIO's support for the 1986 Immigration Reform and Control Act. That act granted amnesty to selected illegal immigrants who had entered the United States before January 1, 1982, and had resided there continuously. The AFL-CIO put aside its skepticism to such an amnesty because the act also imposed a system that made it illegal for employers to knowingly hire or recruit illegal immigrants (immigrants who do not possess lawful work authorization) and required employers to attest to their employees' immigration status. It was hoped that this would end the tide of illegal immigration, bring those in the country into the official economy, provide them with rights and perhaps make them available for unionization.

By the 1990s, however, the AFL-CIO's policy with regard to employer sanctions began to change for a number of reasons. First, it gradually became clear the 1986 program was not effective. Illegal immigration had not been curtailed. False papers, spotty enforcement, and above all continuing demand for cheap, illegal immigrant labor undermined its effectiveness. Secondly, it became clear that employers were making use of the laws to thwart union organization. They could threaten to call in the Immigration and Naturalization Service (INS) to intimidate illegal workers trying to organize. Since a thriving business in the production of forged worker-certification documents had grown up, employers could believably claim ignorance of such illegal employees until they found it convenient to turn them in. Finally, and perhaps most importantly, organized labor became increasingly aware that these new immigrant workers—both legal and illegal—were a potential recruiting ground for the movement. Because many were badly exploited, they were ripe for unionization.

This was a potentially important source of membership during an era in which organized labor continued to lose ground. Understandably, it was unions involved in the service industries of the postindustrial economy that pioneered organization drives to reach illegal as well as legal immigrant workers. For example, the International Ladies' Garment Workers' Union (ILGWU) and Textile Workers Union (later UNITE) in New York took the lead in organizing a majority of New York City's Chinatown garment workers, netting an estimated 90 percent of both legal and undocumented workers. The Service Employees International Union (SEIU) and the Hotel Employees and Restaurant Employees International Union (HERE) actively pushed for change in the AFL-CIO policy. When SEIU's former president, John Sweeney, became president of the AFL-CIO in 1995, the percentage of the federation budget devoted to organizing was raised from about 5 percent to 30 percent, reflecting this influence.

By the turn of the century, the AFL-CIO had reversed its policy regarding employer sanctions and had come to oppose them. The Executive Council announced the shift in February 2000, calling for a repeal of the system of employment eligibility verification as a tool of workplace immigration enforcement. It also called for a new amnesty program for illegal immigrant workers. It promoted its new initiative with the slogan "Recognizing Our Common Bonds," an oblique reference to the unity to be developed between immigrants and native-born workers. Three years later, the AFL-CIO and its affiliates launched the Immigrant Workers Freedom Ride campaign. Modeled on the consciousness raising Freedom Rides of the civil rights era, this campaign promoted the rights of immigrants to organize and amnesty for undocumented immigrants. The coast-to-coast sustained demonstration attracted support for organized labor among both legal and illegal immigrants. It was clear that organized labor had now recognized that recruiting members from within these groups was important to its future.

A group from Miami, Florida, chant in support of immigrants' rights after arriving in Washington, D.C. October 2003. The group was part of the Immigrant Workers Freedom Ride, modeled after the original civil rights freedom rides of the 1960s. (AP Photo/Pablo Martinez Monsivais)

New Strategies

Increasingly, new organizing strategies were employed to reach legal and illegal immigrants. One strategy was to target industries outside of a union's traditional jurisdiction. This provided exploited immigrant workers with the expertise and resources of an established union while increasing union membership. For example, in the mid-1990s, the International Association of Machinists (IAM) in New York held a successful campaign to organize the city's limousine drivers, most of them South Asians. Employers preferred to view drivers as independent contractors and refused to deal with the unions. However, by making use of its expertise regarding the National Labor Relations Board and legal action, the IAM forced one of the major companies to negotiate a contract, providing its new members with significantly improved wages and working conditions.

Another strategy was to pursue and organize immigrant groups that had gradually taken over the jobs of established union workers within an industry. The organization of immigrant asbestos-removal workers from eastern Europe and Latin America by the Laborers International Union of North America (LIUNA) in New York is such a case. By the late 1990s, Local 78 had all but disappeared because its old-line Italian-American leadership, derived from the earlier wave of immigrant groups, had failed to reach out to immigrants of the new wave. The union successfully rebuilt its membership base by using many of the same tactics as multiethnic unions formed a century earlier. It organized new workers—many of whom were undocumented—by directly reaching out to their ethnic communities and recruiting respected members of those communities as union organizers.

A third approach was to use ethnic group solidarity within an existing union to extend that union's activities to new workplaces in which members of the ethnic group (or groups) in question had become active. For example, one local of the Union of Needletrades, Industrial, and Textile Employees (UNITE) in New York began organizing Mexican and Dominican workers employed in produce markets because the union's existing membership gave them excellent contacts within those ethnic communities. In the summer of 2004, UNITE and HERE merged to form UNITE HERE—a more powerful union with greater resources to pursue its organizing efforts among immigrants.

More broadly, ethnic groups within the labor movement formed their own interest organizations. The Asian Pacific American Labor Alliance (APALA) of the AFL-CIO is an example of this. Formed in 1992 by 500 labor activists from around the county, one of the stated goals of the APALA was to promote training, empowerment, and leadership of Asian-Pacific Americans within the labor movement. It further set out to defend and advocate for the civil and human rights of Asian-Pacific Americans, immigrants, and people of color and to develop ties within international labor organizations, especially in Asia and the Pacific. As with many of the new labor organizations, the APALA had an agenda that sought to reach out to allies beyond the union movement. Asian-Pacific Americans have a long history of labor organization, stretching back to the 1903 Oxnard strike in California, during which the first union among rural workers in the state was established, the Japanese-Mexican Labor Association (JMLA). Similarly, it was the combined efforts of the Filipino and Japanese sugar plantation workers that created the Hawaii Labors' Association (HLA) in 1919.

In addition to the efforts of established labor unions to reach immigrants, immigrant groups have organized among themselves to defend their interests. The campaign to establish the Immigrant Workers' Union (IWU) in 2001 in Los Angeles's Koreatown exemplifies this. Consisting of both Korean and Latino workers, the IWU hoped to utilize

collective bargaining to improve workers conditions at Assi Super, one of the community's largest supermarkets. The collaboration between the two groups was hailed by many unionists as the future of labor organizing. In 2006, the Immigrant Workers' Union (*Union de Tradajabores Inmigrantes*) was established in Madison, Wisconsin, defining itself not as a union, but as an immigrant rights organization that necessarily encompassed both legal and illegal immigrants.

The National Day Laborer Organizing Network (NDLON) is another, broader example. It was established in 2001 in California as an alliance of 12 community-based organization and worker centers for day laborers. Its program was to protect their civil liberties and workers' rights, create work centers for day laborers, promote their education and organization, and work for a legalization program for undocumented workers. By 2007, it had grown into a nationwide organization. Although not a union, at its conference that year, it affirmed its growing relationship to both the AFL-CIO and to the newly established Change to Win Federation member LIUNA (for Change to Win; see below). Such organizations sought the help of organized labor, but also lined up allies among civil rights groups, college students, ethnic group leaders, and members of the clergy. The object was to draw the larger community into the struggle for union recognition and improved working conditions for immigrants.

The massive nationwide demonstrations in 2006 against proposed federal legislation (H.R. 4437) to raise penalties for illegal immigration and classify unauthorized immigrants as felons may be viewed as an expression of this strategy of drawing the larger community into the struggles of illegal immigrants. Millions across the nation took part in the protests. The Mexican-American ethnic community turned out in force, encompassing both permanent and temporary workers, legal and illegal immigrants. Organized labor endorsed the protests. The AFL-CIO's executive vice president, Linda Chavez-Thompson, said: "We believe that there is absolutely no good reason why any immigrant who comes to this country prepared to work, to pay taxes, and to abide by our laws and rules should be relegated to this repressive, second-class guest worker status" (AFL-CIO 2006, website).

The strategies outlined here are not exhaustive, nor are they without precedent. They all draw in one way or another upon the earlier efforts of such pre–World War I unions as the UMW and the ILGWU and later CIO unions like the UAW and the MMSWU. The techniques of recruiting immigrants and promoting interethnic solidarity that had been developed during and directly after the previous era of mass immigration were applied to the new wave emerging after the changes in immigration policy in 1965. However, just as during the previous era, these activities were not pursued without meeting significant resistance within the union movement.

Ethnicity, Immigrants and the Change to Win Federation

Although a growing number of unions reached out to unorganized and undocumented immigrants during the last decades of the twentieth century, most unions in the AFL-CIO did not. Ethnicity once again emerged as both a barrier and resource in these new organizing efforts. On the one hand, established unions founded in the older, industrial sectors of the economy were often dominated by hierarchies recruited from the established ethnic communities with roots in the period of immigration before the Great Depression. Many among these groups, especially many second-generation men and women, had long ago acclimated to the language and customs of the United States and felt they had little in common with the new immigrants reaching American shores, whom they viewed with skepticism. Not only did these new arrivals have different languages and customs than the established communities, they also entered the workforce in a different sector of the economy from that of the older unions. As in the case of the asbestos-removal workers in New York noted above, this reinforced a reluctance among older unions to reach out to the new immigrants—particularly the illegal immigrants—to shore up falling membership. In this sense, ethnicity was a dividing factor.

On the other hand, within the new immigrants' established ethnic communities such as the Chinese Americans organized in UNITE in New York or the Mexican Americans organized in the UFW in California, ethnicity reinforced worker solidarity both among and between legal and illegal immigrants. This was clearly expressed when HERE invited the Mexican foreign minister to address the union's convention held in Los Angeles, and gave him a standing ovation when he called for illegal Mexican immigrants to be given legal status to prevent their exploitation.

Despite the organizing efforts mentioned above, union membership as a whole continued to fall throughout the 1990s. This led a group of unions within the AFL-CIO to grow increasingly impatient with what they viewed as inadequate efforts by the leadership to promote recruitment, particularly among immigrants. They created a new alliance within the organization in 2003 (mirroring the creation of the Committee of Industrial Unions within the AFL 70 years before). Known at first as the New Unity Partnership (NUP), it was made up of five unions working for greater organizing efforts within the AFL-CIO. These were the SEIU, LIUNA, UNITE and HERE (still separate at this point), and the United Brotherhood of Carpenters (UBC). In 2004, NUP was renamed the Change to Win coalition and was joined by the United Food and Commercial Workers (UFCW) and the International Brotherhood of Teamsters (IBT).

These coalition members were by and large service-sector unions with extensive experience recruiting immigrants and representing large numbers of women, immigrants, and people of color. They stood in contrast to the more conservative manufacturing unions, which had formed the basis of labor's strength for many years. After two years of disagreements and internal conflict, in 2005, a definitive break was made between the AFL-CIO and the Change to Win coalition. Like the earlier CIO, the Change to Win coalition established itself as a new labor federation, the Change to Win Federation (CtW), holding its first convention in September of that year. It was then joined by the United Farm Workers (UFW), making a total of seven member unions (UNITE and HERE had merged by that time). Chief among the priorities of CtW was the recruitment of new members through cooperation between the federation's affiliates.

Despite this break between the AFL-CIO and CtW, differences of policy between the two major federations with regard to legal and illegal immigrants were not great. Both supported providing a path to legalization for undocumented workers. Both defended immigrants' rights with regard to wages and working conditions, irrespective of legal status. Both wished to hold employers responsible for exploitation. Both opposed raids on workplaces by the Department of Homeland Security, successor to the Immigration and Naturalization Service. The difference between them was one of emphasis, with the CtW showing a much greater level of activity in recruiting legal and illegal immigrants as new union members.

Guest Worker Programs

The change of attitude toward legal and illegal immigrants that the AFL-CIO underwent during the last half of the twentieth century did not alter that organization's views on guest worker programs. As noted at the beginning of this article, the opposition to such programs has had deep roots in the labor movement, stretching all the way back to the Knights of Labor and its opposition to Chinese "coolie" labor. Contract labor has been viewed as detrimental to the interest of organized labor, undermining the bargaining position and wages of union workers. One group in particular has been the focus of such fears in the twentieth century: Mexican guest workers and the illegal immigrants who followed the network of job opportunities they established. The AFL-CIO had accepted only with reluctance the continuation of the World War II Mexican Farm Labor Program in the 1950s and had been among those who lobbied to have it shut down in 1964.

Nor was the AFL-CIO happy about the H-2 provision for temporary workers first authorized by the Immigration and Nationality Act of 1952 and allowed to continue after the end of the Bracero Program. The H-2 program allowed employers to hire workers from abroad on a yearly basis, provided they could show that no American workers were available for the jobs. Intended to meet the need for seasonal agriculture

workers in the Southwest, the H-2 program has had no limit on the number of applicants allowed in per year. In practice, however, the number was no more than about 40,000 per year by the early twenty-first century, not enough to make a significant impact on the working conditions for organized labor. However, in 1986, the H-2 program was expanded to include three categories: H-2A for seasonal agricultural workers; H-2B for seasonal nonagricultural workers; and H-1B, a new category, for high-skilled workers. Although no cap was put on the H-2 categories, the Immigration Act of 1990 set a ceiling of 65,000 per year on H-1B applicants. This was steadily increased, reaching 195,000 by 2000.

Including new and returning contract workers, the total number of temporary workers under these combined programs by 2008 was about 692,000 (including family members), prompting the AFL-CIO to complain that, "increasingly, employers have been permitted to use guest worker programs to suppress wages and other standards in entire industries, including construction (through the H2B program) and the professional and high technology sector (through the H1B program)" (AFL-CIO 2008).

Though a large number, 692,000 was dwarfed by the number of undocumented immigrant workers in the country by that time, an estimated 11.6 million. More than half of these were from Mexico (see Table 2). The difference between the two marked the difference between the ideal of regulating temporary immigrant workers and the reality of the labor market, particularly in the southwestern United States—though by 2008, the use of temporary contract workers had spread throughout the South and into the Midwest. It was this difference between intention and reality that led pressure to build in the late twentieth and early twenty-first centuries to establish a new guest worker program. It was argued that such a program would help repair a broken system by removing the need of temporary immigrants to enter the country illegally, relieve the pressure on American borders, bring temporary immigrants into the formal economy, and meet the clear needs of the business community.

The AFL-CIO's Executive Council was having none of it. It clearly stated its opposition to such programs in a statement issued in 2001: "The upshot of every guest worker program in the United States to-date has been to further depress wages for all workers, foreign and U.S. born, to cause greater exploitation, and to reduce overall employment opportunities" (Kelber 2001). The AFL-CIO lobbied to tighten rather than loosen the criteria for admission of temporary nonimmigrant workers. In 2005, when the Republican administration of George W. Bush floated the idea of a guest worker program in connection with an immigration reform bill jointly put forward by Senator John McCain (Republican) and Senator Edward Kennedy (Democrat), the leadership of the AFL-CIO promptly attacked it, warning that "a guest worker program of unlimited scale would depress wages and working conditions while creating a permanent underclass of foreign workers" (Swarms 2006).

At this point, however, disagreement on the issue surfaced within the labor movement, reflecting the deeper division of organized labor into two federations. The SEIU and other unions within the CtW coalition (soon to be federation), supported the idea of a new guest worker program, arguing that this view recognized the realities of the marketplace and the economy. What they wished was a guest worker program that would give immigrant workers the right to unionize and eventually petition for citizenship. This brought the CtW into an unusual alliance with the business interest of the U.S. Chamber of Commerce. The AFL-CIO's reply in 2007 was sharp: "The bells and whistles they are currently adding to the temporary workers programs are bound to fail, they have been proven to fail" (Williams 2007).

The impasse continued until the end of the Bush administration in 2008, reflecting a more widespread inability of the interested parties to agree on general immigration reform. It was not until the incoming Democratic administration of Barack Obama in 2009 that the rift appeared to be healed. Heeding the new administration's calls for a general immigration reform, the AFL-CIO and CtW sat down together and worked out a common set of policies, which they presented in April of that year. Among these were support for the legalization of undocumented immigrants and opposition to a guest worker program. Rather than a guest worker program, the AFL-CIO

and CtW proposed dealing with the issue of both legal and undocumented immigrants through the creation of a national commission to manage future immigration. The commission would determine how many permanent and temporary foreign workers would be admitted each year based on demand in American labor markets. This would make a specific guest worker program unnecessary. As of this writing, it remains uncertain how this proposal will be integrated into possible new immigration legislation. What was clear was that the AFL-CIO and CtW were once again working together on policy issues regarding both legal and illegal immigrants. Whether this presaged an eventual reunification of the two federations remained to be seen. Talks to that end began between the two organizations in April 2009.

Conclusion

From the late nineteenth century to the present day, the labor movement in the United States has moved a long way from its initial positions regarding permanent and temporary immigrants. From within a conservative and nativist opposition to all immigration and from outside of northern and western Europe in the years before permanent immigration restrictions were imposed in 1924, by the latter half of the twentieth century the labor movement, it came by support substantial yearly immigration from countries around the world on humanitarian as well as economic grounds. From fearing newly arrived unskilled immigrant labor as a threat undermining the solidarity and bargaining position of trade unions, by the 1930s, it came to view these same immigrants and their children as the basis for widespread and successful industrial unions within the labor movement. From viewing temporary and illegal immigrants as threats to wages, working conditions, and the establishment of unions, by the early twenty-first century, it came to view both groups as potential union recruits. In that connection, it moved from calling for the active enforcement of a system of employer sanctions, including raids on workplaces, to working for the repeal of such systems as hostile to the interests of organized labor.

These changes came as pragmatic answers to new conditions. In the latter half of the twentieth century, change was driven by the restructuring of the American postindustrial economy in an increasingly globalized world. As the manufacturing base shrunk, the service sector grew. The subcontracting of production and labor flourished, encouraging the growth of an informal economy outside the bounds of governmental or institutional control. In facing these difficult challenges posed by this economic environment, it remains to be seen if increased organizing efforts by the AFL-CIO and CtW among legal, illegal, and temporary immigrants will be able to help reverse the decline in union membership that the labor movement has suffered over the past 50 years. For those who wish to see such a reversal, a possibly optimistic sign is the increase of 480,000 new union members registered in 2008, raising the percentage of the workforce in unions from 12.1 percent in 2007 to 12.7 percent in 2008. This was the largest increase in 25 years. It remains to be seen if this growth can be sustained in times of economic recession.

Bibliography

AFL. 1902. *Report of the Proceedings of the Twenty-second Annual Convention.*

AFL. 1904. *Report of the Proceedings of the Twenty-fourth Annual Convention.*

AFL-CIO. 1975. *Policy Resolutions adopted October 1975 by the Eleventh Constitutional Convention*

AFL-CIO. 2006. *Press Releases, Speeches and Testimony,* "Remarks by AFL-CIO Executive Vice President Linda Chavez-Thompson at Immigration Press Briefing February 28, 2006." http://www.aflcio.org/mediacenter/prsptm/sp02282006.cfm (accessed June 15, 2009).

CIO. 1955. Statement of Victor G. Reuther on behalf of the CIO, before the Senate Judiciary Committee on Immigration and Naturalization, November 21.

Barkan, Elliott Robert. 1996. *And Still They Come: Immigrants and American Society, 1920 to the 1990s.* Wheeling, IL: Harlan Davidson.

Barkan, Elliott Robert. 2007. *From All Points: America's Immigrant West, 1870s–1952.* Bloomington, IN: Indiana University Press.

Briggs, Vernon M., Jr. 2001. *Immigration and American Unions.* Ithaca, NY: Cornell University Press.

Chen, May, and Kent Wong. 1998. "The Challenge of Diversity and Inclusion in the AFL-CIO." In G. Mantsios, ed., *A New Labor Movement for the New Century.* New York: Garland Publishing.

Climent, James, ed. 2001. "Unions and Union Organizing," *Encyclopedia of American Immigration,* vol. 2, 686–92. Armonk, NY: Sharpe Reference.

Fink, Leon. 1983. *Workingmen's Democracy: The Knights of Labor and American Politics.* Chicago: University of Illinois Press.

Foner, Philip S. 1955. *History of the Labor Movement in the United States.* Vol. 2, *From the Founding of the American Federation of Labor to the Emergence of American Imperialism.* New York: International Publishers.

Haus, Leah A. 2002. *Unions, Immigration, and Internationalization: New Challenges in the United States and France.* New York: Palgrave Macmillan.

Higham, John. 1981. *Strangers in the Land.* Rev. ed. Westport, CT: Greenwood Press.

Katsintz, Philip, John H. Mollenkopf, Mary C. Waters, and Jennifer Holdaway. 2008. *Inheriting the City: The Children of Immigrants Come of Age.* Cambridge, MA: Harvard University Press.

Kelber, Harry. 2001 "Inside the AFL-CIO; Legal Rights for all Immigrant Workers Is Organized Labor's Rallying Cry." *The Labor Educator,* August 28. http://www.laboreducator.org/inside23.htm (*accessed March 8, 2012*)

Milkman, Ruth, ed. 2000. *Organizing Immigrants, The Challenges for Unions in Contemporary California.* Ithaca, NY: Cornell University Press.

Mort, Jo-ann. 1998. *Not Your Father's Union Movement, Inside the AFL-CIO.* New York: Verso–New Left Books.

Ness, Immanuel. 2005. *Immigrants, Unions, and the New U.S. Labor Market.* Philadelphia: Temple University Press.

Newsinger, John. 2008. "The Uprising of The 30,000." *Socialist Review,* July–August. http://www.socialistreview.org.uk/article.php?articlenumber=10470 (accessed March 8, 2012).

Ngai, Mai M. 2004. *Impossible Subjects: Illegal Aliens and the Making of Modern America.* Princeton, NJ: Princeton University Press.

Parmet, Robert D. 1981. *Labor and Immigration in Industrial America.* Boston: Twayne Publishers.

Piore, Michael J. 1979. *Birds of Passage: Migrant Labor and Industrial Societies.* New York: Cambridge University Press.

Swarms, Rachel L. 2006. "Senator Introduces Bill Creating Guest Worker Program." *New York Times*, February 26. http://www.nytimes.com/2006/02/25/politics/25immig.html?_r=1&scp=1&sq=Rachel%20L.%20Swarns,%20Senator%20Drafts%20Foreign%20Labor%20Bill&st=cse (accessed March 8, 2012).

"Turn around America." 2008. *AFL-CIO Recommendations for the Obama Administration, Immigration, Introduction*, December. http://otrans.3cdn.net/fecfa5fa7b5bb9c58f_jim6btb7a.pdf (accessed March 8, 2012).

U.S. Senate. 1965. Subcommittee on Immigration and Naturalization of the Committee on the Judiciary, Washington, DC, February 10.

Waldinger, Robert D. 1996. *Still the Promised City: African Americans and New Immigrants in Post-industrial New York.* Cambridge, MA: Harvard University Press.

Williams, Krissah. 2007. "Unions Split on Immigrant Workers." *Washington Post*, January 27. http://www.washingtonpost.com/wp-dyn/content/article/2007/01/26/AR2007012601635.html (accessed March 8, 2012).

Wyman, Mark. 1993. *Round Trip to America.* Ithaca, NY: Cornell University Press.

Religion and American Ethnicity

Brett Jonathan Esaki

For many, religion has had a powerful role in determining life choices and making sense of the world, and hence it has greatly influenced the choices and experiences of American immigration. As a result, religion has been an essential characteristic of the complexity of American life.

Religion is often understood as the connection of humans to nonhuman powers. However, even this general definition does not encompass all religions. First, beliefs and practices that are considered religious in one context may have a different place in other peoples' societies and worldviews. This has legal ramifications, because new immigrants may find that their religious practices are considered illegal. Another common understanding of religion relates to the Latin *religare*, which means "to bind." This understanding implies that religious people bind together to pursue physical, mental, and spiritual endeavors. That is, they build a common culture and support one another. From this understanding we can see how religions can serve as emotional homes and centers for community resources and in this way can help new immigrants feel secure and adapt more smoothly to their new environment.

In addition to legal and sociological ramifications for immigrants, the conception of religion affects one's interpretation of the events of immigration. The experience of the connection to nonhuman powers can be powerful and can influence one to emigrate, can assist and complicate immigration, and can legitimate one's desires to immigrate. Religion can provide a relationship to gods, to a sacred cosmos, and to a sacred narrative, it can shape the categories with which the world is interpreted, and it can influence the sense of what is right and good. In these ways, religion profoundly affects the experience of immigration.

In order to illustrate the importance of religion in immigration, this chapter will focus on: religions' conceptions of the *sacred*; senses of *cosmic geography* and one's place within it; *rituals* that define a sense of sacred space and community; religion's role in the social construction of *race* and *racism*; and *laws* that protect and limit the practice of religion. These foci will be illustrated using case studies that are representative of larger trends of American religion and immigration. The trends and case studies are separated into three time periods: Early America to 1870, 1870 to 1940, and 1940 to the present.

With these foci, several themes of religion and immigration emerge across time periods. American religion has always been *diverse* and *complex*, though the diversity and complexity has varied by region and time. The variety of religions periodically leads to tensions over culture, beliefs, rights, and belonging. These tensions can initiate change, such as the development of new religious and social groups, can reinforce the already formed religious and social boundaries, and can spark interreligious violence.

Religion has also been central to many groups' senses of *welcome* and *alienation*. Religious organizations often take it upon themselves to aid or hinder the processes of immigration. For example, Catholic churches have provided a sense of home to Catholic immigrants and refugees of many ethnicities and national origins, yet some individual parishes have also purposefully marginalized Catholics of other ethnicities. In some instances, people experienced a sense of alienation or separation as part of their religious identity, such as the Puritans, who saw their immigration as an opportunity to establish a separate, exemplary society—a "City upon the Hill"—and some Jews who retained a sense of religious exile.

Sometimes the process of welcoming came along with the process of "othering"—or perceiving some groups as religious outsiders, foreign, and strange. For example, some Asian gurus were invited to teach their religions, while other Asians were excluded from citizenship in part because of the belief that their religions were dangerous.

Another theme is the *dissonance* between religious and political ideals and the practice of the ideals. Two significant cases of this dissonance are the treatment of Native Americans and African Americans. European immigrants wanted Native Americans to become more European and Christian, yet Native Americans were often forced to adopt this culture. During the early decades of the colonial period, some were forced to migrate from their native lands to "praying towns" and eventually to reservations. European immigrants strove to create a country independent of Europe and with religious freedom, yet they did so while forcing Africans to "immigrate" ("involuntary migration") as slaves and denying them independence, citizenship, and religious freedom. After the Civil War, the process of religiously uniting the country included granting citizenship to African Americans, yet they continued to face severe racism and government-backed marginalization. This led many African Americans to the desire to physically emigrate outside of the United States, and to spiritually migrate to Africa and Asia by founding religions and sovereign black nations with spiritual roots in Africa and Asia.

Put together, the foci and themes elucidate how a core of American life has been the adaptation to a vast and dynamic array of religions and immigrant ethnic groups. This adaptation includes developing a spectrum of relationships to other religions and ethnicities—from peaceful to violent, isolationist to integrationist, and exclusivist to pluralist.

Early America to 1870

Native Americans

The land of the present-day United States was originally occupied by many hundreds of indigenous tribes. Some, who came from Asia more than 10,000 years ago, could be considered the first immigrants to America. Indigenous tribes had different language bases, systems of organization and government, economies, relationships to land, and religions. Given this diversity, few generalizations can be made, but one stands out for religion and immigration. Native Americans did not divide land and time into squares, lines, and other even measurements. Rather, land was identified by spiritual events and intergenerational familiarity with the land's physical features, plants, and animals, and the other people who used it. Time was determined by rhythms of the natural world, the times for sacred stories and songs, and the moods and activities of spirits. Together, senses of land and time shaped their homes, celebrations, medicines, and competition and cooperation with other tribes.

Upon encountering Spanish imperialists of the present-day Southwest in the seventeenth century, Native Americans were confronted with the linear space and time of Catholic Christians. This was also the case in the Northeast, where Native Americans encountered the English Puritans. Both of these Christian groups held that their travels to the New World were part of a divine journey; for the Spanish, it was in search of Eden, gold, and trade markets, and for the Puritans, it was in search of Canaan, or a place to build their religious kingdom on earth. Both viewed the Native-American religions as savage and demonic and tried to convert Native Americans to Christianity as part of their divine missions. Moreover, the Europeans brought diseases, war technology, linear agriculture, and animals to the New World that together weakened and killed many Native Americans and contoured the landscape into lines and squares.

The intentional reconfiguration of New World space and time also affected Native-American migration. Some were prevented from seasonal migration by housing and transportation developments and by the decimation of animals and plants at migration destinations. After the American Revolution, this reconfiguration and denial of sovereignty was formalized in a system of "domestic dependent nations" in which land was allotted to Native-American tribes, but European-American settlement and U.S. law superseded any Native-American property claims. In the mid-to-late nineteenth century, this reconfiguration was further enforced by the reservation system. Many of the reservations were outside of traditional lands, and tribes were displaced and then forced onto the foreign lands. The physical displacement included a cosmic displacement that disrupted cultures' relationships to time, place, community, rivalry, and medicine.

Tribes formerly unknown to each other were often put into the same or bordering reservations. This led to conflicts of cultures but also provided the ground for empathy because all had undergone related experiences of colonialism. This empathy, combined with the forced intercultural contact, provided the grounds for pan-tribal religious practices. For example, periodically prophets appeared, providing leadership and spiritual guidance, such as the Shawnee Prophet (Tenskatawa) and later Wovoka. In the 1880s, dancing rituals, such as the Sun Dance among the Plains Indians, took on new significance in the context of oppression. In 1883, the government banned the Lakota's Sun Dance, and in 1889, it carried out a program to systematically eradicate Lakota culture and replace it with English and Christianity. Soon a pan-tribal ritual adapted by the Lakota (inspired by Wovoka) and called the Ghost Dance spread, and this ritual was for protection and to restore the spiritual order that was lost after European contact.

The American government feared that this ritual was a precursor to antigovernment attacks, so it banned such gatherings and arrested tribal leaders. In 1890, the government suppression resulted in the massacre at Wounded Knee. The power of the Ghost Dance came to symbolize resistance to government suppression, since the Lakota continued to use the ritual to defy military interventions. In the twentieth century, similar to the spread of the Ghost Dance, rituals using peyote spread through neighboring reservations by utilizing many tribes' systems of religious professionals and enclosed rituals, such as sweat lodges. These pan-tribal religious practices (the Native American Church) can therefore be seen as the results of forcing Native Americans to relocate and as reactions to the enforcement of the European-Christian cosmos.

European-American Identity

For European settlers, Native-American resistance added to the image of Native Americans. Native Americans were a physical threat and demonstrated political and technological knowledge, so they seemed to fit the European concept of the noble savage. The land of the New World was also depicted by Europeans as a female noble savage, a naked woman who submitted to European rule and ideas. The image of the noble savage inspired missionaries to come to the New World to "save" Native Americans by converting them and making them adopt a European language, dress, and behavior. Missionaries desired to be pioneers of religion—that is, to raise new Christians in supposedly pristine lands and upon untouched minds. In time, the noble-savage symbolism became attached to European settlers in the colonies. As the Revolutionary War approached, Europeans depicted colonists as ignorant and unruly noble savages. In response, colonists adopted the masculine aspects of this image as a representation of American difference from Europeans. Americans saw themselves as more fiercely independent and ruggedly masculine, and the male noble savage's freedom and physicality matched this well. This partly explains the stereotypical Indian dress used by colonists as disguises and their pseudo-Indian shouts during the Boston Tea Party.

The religiously diverse European settlers had different relations to the developing American identity. In the seventeenth century, English Puritans, Anglicans, and Quakers, and in the eighteenth century, English Presbyterians, Baptists, and Methodists, came to the colonies under a dual mandate to expand the English empire and to convert Native Americans. French Catholics, especially Jesuits, explored present-day Canada and went southward to compete with Spanish Catholics who had explored Latin America and spread north to the present-day United States. With so many settlers holding contrary national mandates, Europeans competed for land and governments that would support their national and religious lifestyles. Often people of the same religion and nationality would settle in the same colony, and each colony came to feature different national and religious groups, such as Alabama's and Louisiana's French Catholics, Florida's Spanish Catholics, Virginia's Anglicans and other English Protestants, and Pennsylvania's Quakers. This diversity led to a question of the relationship between religions, European nations, and colonial governments.

Examples of the combination of religious purpose, immigration, and government can be seen in the New England colonies. In 1630, the Puritans began most of the New England colonies, fleeing England's rigid regulation of non-Anglican religions. But, a decade earlier, the Pilgrims had left Holland's liberalism before coming to the New World and founding Plymouth. In America, both groups could be free to practice their version of Calvinism and to create a society that would be free of distractions from the faith. They would no longer be religious exiles, rather exemplary models of divine rightness. This blend of religious separatism, rigid morals, educational rigor, and single-minded work ethic led to the creation of such schools as Harvard and Yale, to the establishment of governments relatively unregulated by European nations, and to laws and policies designed to control or to exclude those of other faiths even where they were of the same nationality.

Freedom of Religion

The colonies' conflicting views of religious belief and the intertwining of political power with religious power helped shape the framing of the First Amendment to the U.S. Constitution. After the Revolutionary War, the newly formed states had differing relationships to religious organizations. Some with strong Anglican organizations maintained firm ties to the Church of England and authorized taxes to support the Anglican organizations or Christianity more broadly. Even in religiously diverse Pennsylvania, public officials were required to take an oath swearing belief in Christianity in order to hold office.

Virginia had a strong Anglican establishment, but there was also a strong Baptist and Methodist presence, and its constitution guaranteed the "free exercise of religion." In the late eighteenth century, this combination of religious influences led to a vociferous political debate in Virginia's legislature over the freedom of religion and multiple establishments. In 1785, James Madison wrote a strong message in this debate entitled, "Memorial and Remonstrance against Religious Assessments." He argued that religion is common to all mankind and is an unalienable right. By focusing on religion instead of church, Madison conceptualized a connection of humans to a divine creator that was not defined by a particular religious organization. This conceptualization of religion was echoed in the First Amendment, ratified in 1791, that states, "Congress shall make no law respecting an establishment of religion, or prohibiting the free exercise thereof."

With the words "an establishment" and "religion," the government could not tax on behalf of churches or create laws that regulated belief, as had been attempted in early colonial constitutions. This was a kind of separation of church and state that was cleverly not directed at any particular church or set of beliefs. It prevents government from formal, legal involvement with an establishment of religion but does not prevent government officials from involvement in and support of religious organizations. This seeming contradiction makes the Constitution a secular document while allowing individual government officials to be thoroughly non-secular. The mix of secular and non-secular explains in part the American mixture of religiously devoted government leaders and secular, pluralistic laws.

African-American Religion and Slavery

While the Constitution was crafted to include the free exercise of religion, the government was also actively denying this "unalienable right" to African slaves. Beginning in the early seventeenth century, slaves were brought by colonists and sold in the colonies. Unlike many Europeans who came to the colonies in debt bondage, African slaves had no agreement to be released from slavery, and very few were manumitted. The large-scale transport, sale, and separation of families were legitimated by several Christian ideas. Slave owners cited the biblical story of Ham, who was cursed to have his descendants be slaves, and it was believed that his descendants populated Africa after the biblical flood. Others read biblical passages addressing slavery as evidence that it was normal to have severely asymmetrical power relations of masters and slaves and to punish "disobedient" slaves. In the decades running up to the Civil War, some Southerners took up what they considered to be the moderate position on why slavery should be legal, namely, they would have slaves in order to teach them Christianity, not purely to exploit them. Some northern missionaries took it upon themselves to convert slaves and would travel to the South to live amongst them like other missionaries would live with Native Americans or other so-called heathens.

None of these paternalistic Christian movements would outweigh the fear of slaves assembling for any purpose. Slave revolts occurred infrequently, though slave owners were afraid of them. Fears increased after 1831, when news spread of the slave revolt led by Nat Turner. Turner's revolt alarmed slave owners because Turner and other rebels killed his master's family in order to free all of the plantation's slaves, instead of protesting conditions or enabling a few slaves to escape. In addition, Turner felt called to lead the revolt by inspiration from biblical passages and Christian prophetic visions. From these and other revolts, slave owners feared that rebellions could be organized and fomented during any kind of assembly, including Christian prayer and Bible classes that could help slaves develop their own interpretations of biblical passages. Moreover, the government upheld laws that would not allow slaves to testify in court and suppressed their literacy. Meanwhile, free African Americans—in spite of considerable oppression—assembled and worked together to build African-American Christian churches and denominations.

Even under the official lack of freedom of religion, African slaves practiced diverse religions. At least one-tenth of slaves were Muslim, and some maintained their daily prayers and use of Arabic. Others practiced religions indigenous to Africa and recreated their medicines, protections, and divinations as best they could, given the plants and animals in America. Some were already Christian in Africa; still others converted under African-American Christian preachers; and, many passed along Christian stories and mythology. Many hybridized their religions.

Some transformed non-Christian religions to appear Christian in order to make the traditions seem as non-threatening as possible. Alternatively, many practitioners of indigenous religions, who were often called "conjurers," explained the power of indigenous traditions by situating it in Christian cosmology or in contrast to the power of Christianity. Slaves' religions were found throughout the colonies and later throughout the states, and varied under the influence of charismatic leaders, countries of origin, and the benefits and penalties of particular religious practices in particular regions and plantations.

Those escaping slavery found strength in the different religions, and the religions also empowered their migration north, west, or out of the country. In the fight to survive, to escape, and to abolish the institution of slavery, religion was an important battleground. For one, African Americans, both enslaved and free, used religion to argue that they were equal to Europeans on a spiritual, intellectual, and moral level. Sacred cosmology also empowered slaves to escape. In the writings of free blacks and escaped slaves, Christian cosmology flattered northern abolitionists, because the North was linked to Christian freedom while the South was considered immoral. The escape from the South was often presented like the Exodus, which in brief is a biblical story about how the people of God were enslaved by a despot and how God aided their escape. Writers also depicted the North Star as a divine providential symbol of the holy land, which inferred that the North was this holy land.

A good example of the use of religion as rhetorical and spiritual legitimation of abolition is the autobiography of Sojourner Truth. This slave narrative was sold during Truth's speaking engagements to support the abolitionist movement and detailed her life in slavery, the escape from slavery, and life after slavery. In her narrative, Truth presented herself as a model of Christian character. She embraced the value of speaking the truth and keeping true to her word so faithfully that she refused to lie in order to feed her starving children. This allegiance to truth served several functions. The reader would trust the truth of her autobiography, and readers could feel that she was a Christian even though she was not part of a Christian congregation while she was a slave. In addition, total obedience to a divine law higher than the humanly created laws of slavery would make her spiritually correct even though she was legally considered a criminal as an escaped slave. The intricate negotiations of legal correctness and moral uprightness are examples of the intellectual and religious obstacles that African Americans encountered as they migrated to freedom. In such ways, African Americans adopted and adapted Christian cosmology to empower their spiritual and political gains in American citizenship.

What we find in this time period are contending interpretations of American cosmology. Native Americans fought to prevent their cosmology from becoming linear and disconnected from the land; European Christians sought to make their sense of Manifest Destiny into reality; and African slaves struggled to redirect European senses of Manifest Destiny toward an Exodus to freedom.

1870–1940

American Civil Religion

After the Civil War, the United States needed to come together symbolically as well as politically. Though this unity has never been complete, the northern victors offered a spiritual vision of the country that can be called the American civil religion. In his second inaugural address, Abraham Lincoln proposed that the death toll and financial expense of the Civil War was divine atonement for the violence and economic exploitation of slavery. In addition, in his Gettysburg Address, Lincoln explained that the death of northern and southern soldiers was part of the process of the nation's rebirth as a free, fully democratic country that would not perish. In these ways, Lincoln's vision did not blame either North or South for the war, and its resolution would free all from the sins of slavery and brotherly hate.

Forming an American civil religion also involved creating new rituals that would unite the country, such as Lincoln's setting the date of the Thanksgiving holiday. Just as President George Washington declared a day of thanksgiving, so in the middle of the Civil War Lincoln set the national holiday to appreciate divine blessings and to submit to divine punishment. In addition to shared rituals and a spiritual narrative for the country, civil religion included accepting one national flag, and later the national anthem and pledge of allegiance—rituals, symbols, and creed that newcomers could share as part of their Americanization. And yet, American civil religion did not fully unite the country, and other religious visions of the country competed with this civil religion. In addition, new immigrants from northern, southern, and eastern Europe, Mexico, and Asia were also confronted with this image of American religious unity, and many struggled to fit its image in order to appear more American.

Judaism and Catholicism

Jews and Catholics were present in the United States before the Civil War, but after the war, they became more numerous and internally diverse from the immigration of southern and eastern Europeans.

In the decades after the Civil War, Jews escaping persecution immigrated to the United States. European Jews were members of the Jewish Diaspora, and in the late nineteenth century, many uprooted again because of their religious background. Many from eastern Europe saw immigration to the United States as an opportunity to practice traditional Judaism, much like the first Puritan immigrants hoped for their practice of Calvinism. This practice of Orthodox Judaism contrasted with German-American Judaism, which had been reforming its practices and beliefs to be less insulated from nearby Christians and to be open to modernization. In these ways, new immigration brought about religious and ethnic tensions in Jewish communities and influenced the formation of three main streams of American Judaism. Reform Judaism had an ethic of universalism that was open to coalitions with moderate Christians. Orthodox Judaism retained traditional Jewish laws and embodied the separatist and sojourning spirit of early religious exiles in America. At the turn of the twentieth century, Conservative Judaism arose, taking a middle ground between Reform and Orthodox Judaism. Conservative Judaism embraced some gradual reforms yet conserved many of the rituals and Kosher laws that Reform Jews had stopped following.

Catholicism also experienced a shift in ethnic makeup, and this led to internal conflicts within individual churches. American Catholics were initially Spanish, French, English, German, and Irish, with pockets of Caribbean Catholics in the southern colonies. In the late eighteenth century, large numbers of Irish Catholics immigrated. Then, in the 1830s and during the Irish potato famine of the 1840s and 1850s, Irish increased their immigration. In the decades following the Civil War, Polish, Italian, Portuguese, Austrian, Russian, and other Baltic Catholics came to the United States. These waves of Catholic immigration led to internal conflicts over leadership, language, cultural mores (such as concerning alcohol consumption), and deciding which calendar to observe. The conflicts were particularly acute because the Roman Catholic Church relied heavily on the parish system, where membership was based on location. This meant that new immigrants often found themselves under priests of a different culture and language. In addition, with the large Irish immigration, German Catholics often saw their bishops and priests change from Germans who spoke German to Irish who spoke English.

The crisis of leadership had further ethnic dimensions because priests aided Irish immigration, and Irish more frequently sought ordination than did Germans, and much more often than Italians who were already anticlerical before immigration. Influenced by these conflicts of leadership and language, German, Polish, and French-Canadian Catholics often altered the parish system by developing national parishes. National parishes still served local communities, but the dominant ethnic group in the parish tried to keep control of its hierarchy, language, and cultural traditions.

The ethnic tensions from immigration were also felt in the development of Catholic schools. In the mid-nineteenth century, primary education became a focus for improving the nation, and Protestants organized public-school curricula and activities. With Protestant prayers, hymns, and readings from the King James translation of the Bible, many Catholics did not feel comfortable in public schools. Other people were similarly uncomfortable with Protestant practices in schools. For example, Catholics, Jews, and some Protestants, as well as some secular persons in Ohio, worked to ban Bible readings and hymns in public schools. In 1869, the Cincinnati Board of Education agreed. The Irish did not object as strongly as some other groups to the public education because English was the language of public schools. Other ethnicities that primarily spoke non-English languages were both concerned by Protestant curricula and disadvantaged by the language of public education, and so they were further motivated to create alternative primary schools.

Given the tensions of language and religion, Catholics created their system of parochial schools. By the late nineteenth century, the American Catholic hierarchy had the goal of having one parochial school per parish, and Catholic nuns staffed the schools with free labor. These efforts for Catholic schools with non-English curricula were at times hindered and at other times assisted by the government. Generally, in the nineteenth century, state governments allowed non-English-language instruction. In the last two decades of the nineteenth century, anti-Catholic and anti-immigrant fervor increased and led to several proposals for laws that required English tests for immigration and citizenship. This conflict could be seen in the 1923 U.S. Supreme Court decision of *Meyer v. Nebraska*, which declared unconstitutional Nebraska's 1919 Siman Act that banned foreign-language instruction in any school, including Catholic schools. Hence, these struggles over religious and linguistic education can be traced to conflicts of religion, ethnicity, and immigration.

The West and Its Religions

New Catholic immigration frequently impacted the Midwestern and western states. European immigrants traveled west in search of land that they could own, which was out of reach for a majority of Europeans. They were also in search of work as laborers in mines, railroads, agriculture, and other small businesses. Some took advantage of these opportunities to build ethnic communities, complete with an ethnic branch of religion, non-English language, and an ethnic-specific educational system. These communities were not necessarily accepted by other ethnicities in the area, and conflicts arose over culture, morality, and jobs.

Some saw the newly acquired Midwestern and western states as opportunities to start societies that were not marred by a history of slavery and other divisive issues of race. This purity of intention, however, would be confronted with the reality of non-Europeans with different religious intentions. Expansion west met with stiff opposition from Native Americans, who did not wish to see their religions disrupted and lands taken over and divided by European-American settlements. Mexicans in these states were declared American citizens after the Mexican-American War of 1846–1848. However, citizenship did not give them authority over local parishes, and Mexican and European Catholics battled over the nationality of ecclesiastical authority. Tensions also existed over Catholic practices influenced by Mexican traditions, such as the veneration of the Virgin of Guadalupe.

The first Asian-Pacific Americans who settled were Filipinos in the eighteenth century in present-day Louisiana. They came as sailors aboard Spanish trading ships, since the Philippines were a Spanish colony. The first large-scale immigration of Asians consisted of Chinese miners and laborers to present-day California in the mid-nineteenth century. Though China had a vast array of religions, including Taoism, Confucianism, Buddhism, and indigenous religions, immigrants focused on the gods that were most beneficial to life in the United States. For example, many paid tribute to Mazu, a goddess associated with the sea and compassion to children, in order for her to protect their journeys, to thank her for safe travels overseas to the United States, and to protect their families in China. Chinese immigrants started New Year's festivals with firecrackers and lion dances as early as the 1850s, which scare away bad spirits and invite spirits of good fortune into the newly settled communities. For many, burial became an important consideration because Taoism and Confucianism teach that the body's spirits must be near relatives in order to have a peaceful afterlife. Many were temporarily buried in the United States and then transported to China for final burial.

After the Chinese Exclusion Act of 1882, Japanese and Mexican laborers were hired to replace the excluded Chinese. The Gentlemen's Agreement of 1907 severely limited Japanese laborers. With a declining number of Japanese laborers, Korean, Filipino, and South Asian (mostly Punjabi) laborers were brought in to replace them. In total, this immigration from Asian nations included Christians who were Catholic, Methodist, Presbyterian, and Congregationalist, Hindus, Sikhs, Muslims, Buddhists who were Pure Land and Zen, and various indigenous religions. Mexican Americans and Mexican immigrant laborers, who brought Mexican Catholicism and indigenous traditions, also added to the West's diversity. In addition, Jewish communities, which were often begun by merchants, were growing in such states as Montana, Arizona, Washington, Oregon, and California.

Nativism and the Development of Whiteness

The West thus had a tremendous mix of ethnic and religious identities and practices, but this mixture tainted the purity of the West in the view of many European Americans. As stated earlier, many European Americans hoped to set up societies in the West that were free of problems with race. European-American migrants discovered that the West did not only include African Americans and Native Americans as did the East, but also Mexican Americans and Asian Americans. Moreover, many competed for the same positions in mines, railroads, lumber mills, agriculture, and urban professions. These economic competitions, often heightened in industrializing cities, helped develop conceptions of whiteness that encompassed northern and western Europeans and some that included southern and eastern Europeans.

Fears of Catholicism had many dimensions and aided the development of a Protestant whiteness. American Protestants often believed that Catholics were mental slaves to religious traditions and rituals, and also to the political whims of the pope. Protestants focused on the Catholic practices of same-sex cloisters and celibacy, believing that these practices stemmed from an excessive slavishness to religion and that they limited women's freedom. These perspectives were illustrated in popular fiction, such as the scandalous novels of Maria Monk that depicted cloistered nuns subject to physical and sexual torture by male priests. Some of these ideas can be traced to a fundamental difference between Protestants and Catholics—Catholics emphasizing the spiritual value of tradition, and Protestants emphasizing individual interpretation of the Bible. In the United States, the separation of church and state was initially directed toward the Anglican Church, but Protestant nativists also the saw this as a rejection of Roman Catholic influence. This anti-Catholic nativism erupted in several mob attacks on Catholic churches and monasteries in the 1830s and 1840s, such as the burning of an Ursuline convent in Charlestown, Massachusetts, in 1834.

Anti-Catholic nativism especially related to the nineteenth-century increase in immigration, urbanization, and migration west. In cities, one could see competitions between ethnic groups and religious groups over space, jobs, marriage and sexual partners, and morality. Many religious and social reformers believed that these competitions were attributed to five depravities: unassimilability, enslavement of women, drug use, organized crime, and poverty. In the eastern states, people accused eastern and southern Europeans of these depravities and sometimes believed that the depravities were connected to their religions, particularly Catholicism and Judaism. In the West, a similar process involved European Americans distancing themselves from Mexican Catholics. European Catholics used their involvement in the Mexican-American War to prove their American-ness and distance from the anti-Catholic image. Later, they further distanced themselves from the anti-Catholic image by ascribing it to Mexicans. Note that these ethnicities were legally considered white because of their European backgrounds (a Spanish background for Mexicans), but this process of "othering" rendered them strange, foreign, and lower kinds of white people, or "suspect whites," in popular opinion.

European Americans also feared Asians on religious grounds, and this aided the development of whiteness. Images of the Orient often depicted single, wealthy, Asian men in complete domination—physical, mental, political, economic, and spiritual—of harems of women. This image encapsulated Muslims, Middle Easterners, and other Asians. Naval literature and popular fiction, such as the Fu Manchu novels in England, attributed this image to the Chinese and Japanese. Mormons, with their early practices of polygamy, were also othered with this image of capturing and enrapturing young women. In many depictions of the race of Orientals or Mongols, it was claimed that spiritual authority was synonymous with political authority and that the great art and technology of the East were due to the slavish devotion to a divine political authority. This meant that common "Orientals" were indistinguishable slaves, and the leaders were slave drivers under the delusion of being a god on earth. In the western states, these images were superimposed on Asian ethnic enclaves, similar to the way Catholics in the East were depicted as immoral and foreign. Nativists and Protestant reformers took particular interest in Chinese prostitutes and Japanese and Korean picture brides, prejudicially charging that these institutions were intrinsic to Asian proclivities for lavishness, possession of women, disease, and organized crime.

In response to these issues of new immigrants, industrialization, and urbanization, social and religious reforms rarely took into account racist exclusionary policies, economic marginalization, and white exploitation of minority women. Many believed that the supposed ethnic and religious depravities were not removable from the group as a whole, so most reforms focused on individuals, such as Protestant Christianity's focus on "saving" one person at a time through conversion. Concordantly, in the widely accepted racial theories of the time, humanity was comprised of three or more distinct races that had sets of physical and mental potentials. One influential book of scientific racism was *The Passing of the Great Race* by Madison Grant (1916). This work influenced the authors of the American immigration acts of the early twentieth century and was subsequently used by Adolf Hitler to justify mass euthanasia. It included intense anti-Semitism and argued using scientific racism that Caucasoids (Europeans) consisted of three races, the best of which was the Nordic race that was tall, white-skinned, rugged, and governed by calculations and intellect. Grant argued that lower orders of Caucasoids and all the other races had poor hygiene and morality, so if left unchecked, they would eventually outnumber the Nordic race.

Scientific theories coincided with economic tensions, religious competition, religious and social reform movements, and racial prejudice. With this scientifically and religiously supported logic, nativist groups, such as the Ku Klux Klan, felt secure in their advocacy of the exclusion and/or extermination of Jews, Catholics, Asians, Mexicans, and Africans in the name of moral uprightness and American democracy. The confluence of ideas also influenced immigration legislation between the 1880s and the 1920s that limited or excluded the immigration of eastern Europeans, southern Europeans, and Asians.

World's Parliament of Religions

Even many white moderates made these connections, such as many of the organizers and participants of the Columbian Exposition of 1893, which included the World's Parliament of Religions. The Columbian Exposition was meant to celebrate the 400th anniversary of Columbus's voyage to the New World. It was supposed to represent the height of American civilization and its influence on the rest of the world. The World's Parliament of Religions was similarly supposed to prove the superiority of American religions, specifically American white, Protestant Christianity. In order to demonstrate the spiritual and intellectual superiority over all the world's religions, delegates from Asian countries were invited to speak about their religions.

While the trajectory of the exposition and the sheer number of white Protestant delegates made the case for American exceptionalism, in some ways the biggest winners were the Asian delegates. The Asian delegates were widely and excitedly covered by newspapers, and the delegates presented clear arguments, often in articulate English, of the scientific superiority, racial purity, practical benefits, and democratic values of Asian religions. In addition, several Asian delegates became founders of Asian religious movements in the United States that converted many non-Asian Americans. The founding of religious organizations and the well-formed arguments about Asian religions spread knowledge and acceptance of Asian religions in the United States. This coincided with a larger trend of white Americans who rejected

Christianity and sought alternatives, such as metaphysical religions. In the decades following World War II, this foundation would in many ways encourage the limited acceptance of Asian religions and Asian peoples.

1940–Present

African-American Migration and Immigration

The freeing of slaves in the Civil War and granting of citizenship in 1868 to African Americans via the Fourteenth Amendment to the Constitution brought about an important transition in American history. While the government did not support this political gain with economic and social aid, it enabled tremendous gains for former slaves in terms of religious freedom and the right to migrate and immigrate. African-American churches already existed across the country at the time of the Civil War, with a predominance of Baptist and Methodist organizations. Like ethnic enclaves for many minorities, the racism outside of African-American communities shaped religious organizations into becoming centers of education, economic opportunity, leadership roles, and political mobilization. Religious organizations, both formal and informal, also helped facilitate African-American migration northward and westward because these religious networks connected them to African-American resources in the North and West.

Overlapping these great African-American migrations was the immigration from Caribbean nations that began with Haitians at the end of the eighteenth century and sped up in the 1930s. At the turn of the nineteenth century, African slaves overthrew the French colonial government in Haiti. Many Haitians saw this overthrow as affirming the power of Afro-Creole religions. Many also considered their French Catholicism as a marker of spiritual pride and cultural uniqueness. Other Haitians came as slaves of French colonists who escaped before Haiti's revolution, though the slaves were not considered free and the United States did not recognize the new Haitian government until after the American Civil War. Nonetheless, Haitians who fled, or were taken, to the mainland brought with them a distinctive

African-American Catholic presence to Louisiana and elsewhere.

While African Americans mostly followed mainline Christian religions, freedom, urbanization, migration, and immigration spurred the growth of smaller Christian religions and other religions, such as Judaism, Islam, and metaphysical religions. Some converted to Judaism, and other African-American Jews traced their lineage to African and European Jews. The movement behind Marcus Garvey (UNIA—Universal Negro Improvement Association) illustrated how African Americans have changed their interpretation of religious cosmologies. He formed a vision of pan-Africanism in which the African diaspora would unite and form an independent government, and then would return to Africa as a free people. In this way, many African Americans changed their interpretation of their Exodus from going out of the South to the North to going out of America to Africa.

Some who did not seek a physical emigration performed a spiritual emigration by believing that their spiritual homes were in Africa and Asia. Some religious movements found strength in the ancient civilization of Egypt, epitomized by the intellectual and spiritual power of the pyramids and Egyptian mythology. Some of these movements were related to the founding and spread of the Nation of Islam, which is an African-American sect of Islam that advocates for the sovereignty of an independent black nation. Like some African-American movements in the early twentieth century, the Nation of Islam posited that Islam was the original religion of black people, whereas Christianity was the religion of Europeans and was imposed on Africans through slavery. In addition, the religion spread in large part from the efforts of preacher Malcolm X, whose father was a follower of Garvey. In these ways, African Americans have interpreted their multifaceted history of slavery and subsequent racial oppression and migration using different conceptions of the Exodus story and of divine peoplehood.

Asian Americans and Citizenship

Asian Americans also went through a significant transition from the late nineteenth and early twentieth centuries to contemporary America. The American government created exclusionary laws that centered on classifying Asian Americans as "aliens ineligible for citizenship," which prevented them from owning certain kinds of property and from running certain businesses. To combat the status, Asian Americans used religious arguments. For example, in the 1922 Supreme Court case *Ozawa v. United States*, Ozawa presented his Christianity as proof of his Americanness. In the 1923 case *U.S. v. Bhagat Singh Thind*, Thind contended that he was a high-caste Hindu, and therefore was Caucasian. Similarly, some Buddhists argued that Buddhism was the whitest religion because of its rationality and its Aryan roots.

These arguments did not convince the courts or popular opinion. In fact, as Japan grew in military power and as Japanese Americans became successful in agriculture, the American public became more convinced that people of Japanese descent were an imminent threat. The popular image of Japanese Americans followed older anti-Asian imagery and it emphasized the blind allegiance to a political and religious leader who was considered a god on earth, in this case the Japanese emperor. After Japan's bombing of Pearl Harbor launched World War II in the Pacific theater, the majority of the public and military believed that a significant number of Japanese Americans had sabotaged the United States and planned further attacks. They believed that certain religious affiliations made Japanese Americans more susceptible to blind allegiance to Japan's politico-religious authority. There was also the assumption that Japanese culture was inextricable from State Shintoism. For these reasons, leadership roles in Japanese culture classes, such as *haiku* clubs, made one more suspect and more likely to be imprisoned without trial.

In addition to these arrests, public outcry was so persistent and elected leaders and journalists so bent on catering to public fears that they pushed the government to put all Japanese Americans living in western zones into assembly centers and then internment camps. The centers and camps began with President Franklin D. Roosevelt's Executive Order 9066 in 1942 that authorized the creation of military zones from which people could be excluded as a result of "military necessity." In practice, the order authorized the exclusion of enemy aliens and all persons of Japanese descent—citizens and aliens. Internment was both a mass displacement of Americans and a massive loss of property, since Japanese Americans were unable to make payments for homes, farms, and businesses. This echoed the earlier mass displacement and loss of land by Native Americans, for many of the internment camps were built on Native American lands and because the camp administrators were frequently borrowed from the Bureau of Indian Affairs.

While Japanese Americans had their citizenship practically invalidated, other Asian Americans were gaining access to citizenship by joining the opposition against Japan. Chinese Americans, Korean Americans, and Filipino Americans all had transnational interests in the defeat of Japan, since Japan had invaded each of the related Asian nations. In fact, Korean Americans had long been organizing against the Japanese using Protestant churches as bases for political mobilization. In fact, Koreans have been exceptional in terms of the intense use of churches to reinforce cultural traditions and community bonds. Consequently, there is a very high percentage of regular church attendance among Koreans, with churches playing strong mobilizing community roles and serving as vehicles for persistent transnationalism with the homeland and with dispersed Korean communities. Partly to thank veterans for their passionate service and public speeches in opposition of Japan, immigrants from these and other Asian nations gradually became eligible for citizenship, starting with Asian veterans from World War I (June 1935) and Chinese, whose exclusion and ineligibility for citizenship were repealed in December 1943. Filipinos and Asian Indians became eligible in July 1946. The remaining Asian populations became eligible with the inclusion of a key reform prohibiting the use of race as a factor barring citizenship, which was included in the Immigration and Nationality Act of 1952.

Ending Policies that Used Race as a Category

After World War II, the political and religious threat of Communism came to the forefront of American concerns. With the ideology that sluggish democracy, greedy capitalism, and complicit religion created great inequalities of wealth, Communist countries depicted the United States and other Western countries as led by overfed racists. To make their point, they cited the history of paternalistic missionization and colonialism and the United States' legal segregation and tacit permission of lynching. This was not only a representational threat but an existential and religious threat for many Americans. The development of nuclear weapons and other scientific advancements threatened both American exceptionalism and the physical existence of the United States. During the onset of Communist control in Eastern Europe and then China, Communists' charges of American racism challenged American civil religion, which then included the nation's purging of slavery through Civil War deaths and included freeing Jews from Europe's World War II concentration camps. Moreover, Communist governments frequently and violently opposed organized religions, so that for many Americans, opposing Communism meant defending the worldwide existence of religion. This sense of mission was acute for Christians, who believed that their mission was to spread Christianity to the world.

The religious and political fight against Communism, having accelerated during the 1950s, continued during the time of the civil rights movement of the 1960s. Jobs from World War II's industrial demands and the unity of African-American church communities under racism provided the spiritual, educational, and economic foundations for African Americans' struggle for civil rights. Though many church communities decried the young Martin Luther King Jr.'s organized efforts to end segregation, he continually framed the political transformation in Protestant terms to maximize African-American mobilization and to gain sympathy from non-African Americans. It is also important to note that he modeled his practice and principles of nonviolence from the anticolonial mobilizations of Mahatma Gandhi. In this sense, King's vision was primarily African-American Protestant, but was also connected to anticolonial movements across Asia, movements that also inspired Malcolm X's later vision of world citizenship.

In the succeeding decades, the fight against Communism helped the American public to realize the importance of incorporating parts of King's vision into the larger American civil religion, namely the vision that people of all races should have equal rights. In addition, the victory over Germany was often shown as the elimination of racist eugenics, death camps, and other pogroms that systematically killed, experimented on, and marginalized people of certain ethnicities, nonwhite races, religions, disabilities, and nonnormative sexualities. Consequently, the scientific racism that had been used to support immigration acts in the early twentieth century was losing popular and scientific support. American reforms took shape in civil rights laws, the ending of segregation, and in the Immigration Act of 1965, which abolished race-based policies in favor of hemispheric and national quotas. In the decades to follow, the battle with Communism included creating refugee policies that especially assisted the admission of those who helped American wars against Communist countries and movements.

These changes to immigration policy have broadened the spectrum of immigrants, leading to more religious diversity. Skill and technology preferences in the policies have enabled more Asians with high social and economic capital to immigrate. There are also preferences for family reunification, which have enabled spouses and other nuclear family members to immigrate. Compared to earlier Asian immigration, post-1965 Asian immigrants had more access to higher paying jobs and more often had families in the United States. This has changed the foci of many Asian American religions. For example, some Taiwanese churches and temples help immigrants negotiate life in the United States and now focus on facilitating transnational networks, international politics, transnational identities, and educating the youth in Taiwanese language and culture. Some South Asian temples are built to house multiple gods and even multiple South Asian religions, an ecumenical practice not found in South Asia.

Refugees from Asia, the Middle East, Africa, Latin America, and the Caribbean also bring tremendous religious diversity. Those refugees who are Catholic, such as many Vietnamese, add to the already-multiethnic American Catholic church. Sometimes this can bring together those who speak the same language, though, like the earlier history of Catholicism in the United States, the diversity can lead to disputes over language, cultural mores, rituals, and leadership. Refugees and other immigrants have also increased the diversity of Pentecostal Christians, since many have come from Latin America, Asia, and Africa.

Middle East and North Africa

In recent decades, like the increase of immigrants and refugees from Asia, there has also been an increase in immigrants and refugees from the Middle East. Immigrants from the Middle East have been arriving since the late nineteenth century. At the beginning decades of the twentieth century, immigrants from the Levant (eastern shore of the Mediterranean Sea) were Muslim, Catholic, Eastern Orthodox, and other religions. After World War II, the United States took on the security of oil fields in the Middle East and North Africa, and the United States encouraged students from these countries to study in American schools in order to develop American allies. Like South Asian immigrants, those who arrived after 1965 were relatively well educated. Similar to Southeast Asian immigration, many immigrants and refugees left their countries due to war, political upheavals, and economic changes. Those who fled societal transformation comprised a variety of regional, ethnic, and religious groups who did not find a place in the new structure of their former countries. For example, many Palestinian Sunni Muslims escaped political and economic hardships after the 1967 Arab-Israeli War, and many Shia Muslims from Iraq were refugees after the Gulf War.

Immigrants from the Middle East and North Africa have been subjected to racism since their arrival, and this intensified with fears of terrorism. The diffuse fear of Muslims, Arabs, and Bedouins has a long history in American popular culture, and the fear often centers on the capture and abuse of women. After the 1967 Arab-Israeli War and terrorist attacks, such as the Munich Massacre of 1972, fears were increasingly aimed toward Islam. The fear of

Muslim women attend evening prayers during an open house at the Abubakar As-Saddique Islamic Center in Minneapolis. The center is the largest mosque in Minnesota. (AP Photo/Craig Lassig)

Islam can be traced to historic hostilities between Christians and Muslims. In general, both are exclusivist monotheisms, but Islam originated hundreds of years after Christianity, so it appeared to contest Christianity's claims of universality and eternal truth. Christian and Muslim empires also historically waged wars against each other, such as the Crusades in the High Middle Ages (1000–1300 AD).

The historic theological and violent battles served as a foundation of antagonism for the more recent fears. However, the religious antagonism in the forms of hateful attacks and social marginalization has frequently been directed at non-Muslims, because some attackers have followed the old assumption that Muslims are Arab and Arab-ness is marked by beards, brown skin, and hair coverings such as turbans and

veils. Consequently, South Asian Sikhs, Syrian Christians, and nonreligious Americans with some of these features have been conflated with Muslims. Besides being prejudiced, these attacks are further unjust given that many mosques in the United States have brought together multiple nationalities of Muslims, and some mosques have served as bases for interreligious and intercultural dialogues. This anti-Muslim racism that includes images of indistinguishable people and dangerous foreigners is another way that Asians, Middle Easterners, and North Africans have had similar racial and religious experiences in the United States.

Iranian Americans have experienced many of the aspects of the immigration of Middle Easterners and North Africans. In Iran, most of the population is ethnically Persian, and the vast majority is Shia Muslim. Like many immigrants from North Africa, the Middle East, and South Asia, there is a larger percentage of minority groups and religions among immigrants than are present in the home country. For example, besides Iranian Shiites, there were Zoroastrians, Jews, Christians, and Baha'is who moved to such cities as Los Angeles, Washington, D.C., and Atlanta. In the 1950s through most of the 1970s, Iran was increasingly dominated by secular trends, and many Iranian students came to the United States in these decades to study. Today, Iranian Americans remain one of the most highly educated ethnic groups. After the Iranian Revolution of 1979, many secular refugees escaped the new regime's hierarchy and lack of political freedom, and others came as refugees from religious oppression. Despite the reasons for choosing to immigrate and the number of generations in the United States, American perception of Iran has increasingly turned negative. As the anti-Muslim racism increased, so has the anti-Iranian rhetoric and fears. This was spurred on by the Iran hostage crisis beginning in 1979, and the increasing anti-Western, Islamic nationalist rhetoric of Ayatollah Khomeini.

Thus, many Iranian Americans have experienced painful misidentifications in the United States. Though largely ethnically Persian, they are grouped "racially" with Arabs. Though of many faiths, and though many are secular, they are also often grouped with Muslims. Though numerous Iranians have fled religious and political oppression and intolerance, they are often grouped with repressive regimes. From these experiences and other common issues of identity, Iranian Americans have come together across religions, such as for Persian cultural activities. In similar ways, in the post-1965 era, immigrants from South Asia, the Middle East, and North Africa have bound across ethnic and religious groups because racism has been applied across these lines; many are refugees with similar issues, and many share a high degree of education and social capital.

The new, wealthier immigrants in the post-1965 era, who have access to increased capital, education, and transnational mobility, also change the face of mission work. For example, Asian-American Protestants may feel better skilled, culturally sensitive, and racially acceptable than white Americans to missionize across Asia, Eastern Europe, and the Middle East. Meanwhile, transnational ties also help foreigners missionize and teach their religions in the United States, such as Korean-Christian missionaries striving to reconnect the United States to its presumed Christian roots and morality.

Asian Religions Among Non-Asians

Buddhism also transformed in the United States. Some western scholars in the eighteenth and nineteenth centuries were interested in Asian religions because they believed that Europeans and lighter-skinned Asians shared common ancestors and culture. Some who translated Buddhist scriptures claimed that Siddhartha Gautama (the Buddha) was white and his religion was the whitest. They saw Buddhist languages as sharing the same root as European languages and interpreted the statements of the Buddha as scientific and rational, which they believed were qualities of whiteness.

From the late nineteenth century through most of the twentieth century some non-Asian Americans who were interested in Asian religions consulted with Asian-American congregations, and others sponsored Asian priests to immigrate to teach Asian religions. This interest of non-Asian Americans expanded after World War II with the relaxation of immigration policies and popular cultural interest in Asia. For example, Nichiren Buddhism took root in the United States from marriages of servicepeople overseas to Asian spouses who were Nichiren Buddhist, and it gained new converts from countercultural interest and the active missionization of the United States. Today, Nichiren Buddhism is the most racially and ethnically diverse form of Buddhism in the United States, with such famous adherents as African-American musicians Tina Turner and Herbie Hancock.

The spread of Tibetan Buddhism in the United States relates to much of the history of Asian immigration and American interest in Asian religions. For historical and ideological reasons, China believes that the Kingdom of Tibet is part of China and has carried out this perspective by disassembling the religious authority and government of Tibet. Refugees from the brutal restructuring of Tibet have fled to many countries, and there are several refugee Tibetan communities across the United States. In exile and without military strength, the Dalai Lama uses several tactics to garner support in order to regain his country's sovereignty. He touts the value and essentiality of democracy, which is aligned with the image of American exceptionalism, post-King civil religion, and the American battle against Communism. He also encourages Tibetan Buddhists to work with Western scientists, doctors, and scholars to prove the necessity of preserving the wisdom of Tibetan Buddhism. This is in line with the history of Western scholars and Asian religious spokespeople who illustrated the scientific rationality of Asian religions. Also, the western support of the Dalai Lama's speaking tours is in line with the history of non-Asian Americans sponsoring the immigration of Asian priests.

Conclusion

This example of Tibetan Buddhism illustrates how the spread of Asian religions among non-Asian Americans has complex political and religious causes, though Asian religions are just one set of religions that have spread in the United States in the quickly expanding variety of religions in the current time period. The expanding variety has been facilitated by reforms in our immigration laws, yet the openness in policy has not been matched by an increase in religious tolerance. Instead, religious reactions to the changes in diversity have generally followed older patterns. For example, openness to Tibetan Buddhists followed the earlier process that Japanese Americans experienced of welcoming Asian Buddhists while depicting Asians as strange and dangerous. In the case of Muslims and those presumed to be Muslim, the twentieth-century rejection and hate crimes followed the earlier pattern of the rejection and hate crimes against Catholics in the nineteenth century.

In part, these patterns persist because there is still a struggle over the religious identity of the United States. Some have viewed the United States as a nation that will continually support their religion, some as a nation that will tolerate their religion, and

some as a nation that may never accept their religion. As a result, the United States remains a nation of a great variety of religious people and religious tensions. Whether it will become a nation that supports, tolerates, or rejects this diversity of religions remains an open question for the American people.

Bibliography

Alba, Richard, Albert J. Raboteau, and Josh DeWind, eds. 2009. *Immigration and Religion in America: Comparative and Historical Perspectives.* New York: New York University Press.

Barkan, Elliott Robert, ed. 1999. *A Nation of Peoples: A Sourcebook on America's Multicultural Heritage.* Westport, CT: Greenwood Press.

Bellah, Robert N. 2005. "Civil Religion in America." *Daedalus* (Fall): 40–55.

Butler, Jon. 1990. *Awash in a Sea of Faith: Christianizing the American People.* Cambridge, MA: Harvard University Press.

Deloria, Phillip J. 1998. *Playing Indian.* New Haven, CT: Yale University Press.

Dolan, Jay P. 1985. *The American Catholic Experience: A History from Colonial Times to the Present.* Garden City, NY: Image Books.

Gaustad, Edwin, and Leigh Schmidt. 2002. *The Religious History of America: The Heart of the American Story from Colonial Times to Today.* Rev. ed. New York: Harper San Francisco.

Iwamura, Jane, and Paul Spickard, eds. 2003. *Revealing the Sacred in Asian and Pacific America.* London: Routledge.

Joshi, Khyati Y. 2006. *New Roots in America's Sacred Ground: Religion, Race, and Ethnicity in Indian America.* New Brunswick, NJ: Rutgers University Press.

Lopez, Donald S., Jr. 2008. *Buddhism and Science: A Guide for the Perplexed.* Chicago: University of Chicago Press.

Martin, Joel W. 1999. *The Land Looks after Us: A History of Native American Religion.* New York: Oxford University Press.

McDannell, Colleen, ed. 2001. *Religions of the United States in Practice*, vol. 1. Princeton, NJ: Princeton University Press.

Miller, Randall M., Harry S. Stout, and Charles Reagan Wilson, eds. 1998. *Religion and the American Civil War.* New York: Oxford University Press.

Moore, R. Laurence. 1986. *Religious Outsiders and the Making of Americans.* New York: Oxford University Press.

Prentiss, Craig, ed. 2003. *Religion and the Creation of Race and Ethnicity: An Introduction.* New York: New York University Press.

Raboteau, Albert J. 1978. *Slave Religion: The "Invisible Institution" in the Antebellum South.* New York: Oxford University Press.

Seager, Richard Hughes. 1995. *The World's Parliament of Religions: The East/West Encounter, Chicago, 1893.* Bloomington: Indiana University Press.

Turner, Richard Brent. 2003. *Islam in the African-American Experience.* 2nd ed. Bloomington: Indiana University Press.

Waters, Mary C., and Reed Ueda, eds. 2007. *The New Americans: A Guide to Immigration since 1965.* Cambridge, MA: Harvard University Press.

Education and the Second-Generation Experience

Vivian Louie

The immigrant experience and education is important for at least two reasons: immigrants have long been central to the development of American schools, and their schooling plays a key role in intergenerational mobility (between different generations of a family) and assimilation.

This chapter looks at the schooling of second-generation individuals, or the U.S.-born children of immigrants and foreign-born children arriving by the age of 12, old enough to have been schooled and socialized in the United States. The focus here will be principally on second-generation students in public and Catholic parochial schools during two periods of large-scale immigration. Two benchmarks illustrate the comparable impact of immigration on children during these two periods. In 1910, 28 percent of children in the United States came from immigrant families, and in 2005, that figure was 23 percent. In the first period, the arrivals of immigrants largely from southern, eastern, and central Europe during the mid-nineteenth to early twentieth centuries coincided with the rise of the common school, the precursor to the American public school, and the Catholic school system as a possible alternative.

This period was also marked by a gradual increase in the number of years of schooling completed by Americans. The different experiences of comparatively smaller numbers of Mexicans in the Southwest, who faced greater institutional barriers, will also be considered. In the second post-1960s period, the arrivals of immigrants disproportionately from Latin America, the Caribbean, and Asia have coincided with the maturation and challenges facing both the American public and Catholic school systems and the rising importance of postsecondary education. This chapter will conclude with some thoughts on future considerations for this important population.

Mid-Nineteenth Century to Early Twentieth Century and a Different Kind of Schooling for the Many

To understand immigration and schooling during this period, one needs to understand the impact of industrialization. In the early 1800s to 1850, the American economy completed a shift from artisanship to factories, and from 1865 to 1920, a shift to large-scale industries made possible by technological and transportation advances, such as countrywide networks of railroads and the telegraph. By 1900, the nation was the largest industrial economy in the world. Labor recruiters went abroad to encourage the immigration of newcomers to accommodate the nation's labor-market needs. Between 1880 and 1924, more than 23 million immigrants arrived in the United States, with foreign-born individuals reaching nearly 15 percent of the overall population in 1910. They came largely from peasant, semiliterate backgrounds; they had few skills; and their homelands were likely to be in central, eastern, and southern Europe, or in the Caribbean, China, or Japan. Most were thus quite different from the typical immigrant to the United States prior to the 1880s, who, in many cases, arrived with more education, more money, and more skills. Proportionally, more of the new immigrants were also culturally quite different from native white and black Americans, as many of them practiced different religions (in particular, Catholicism or Judaism rather than the Protestant faith) and spoke languages other than English. While European immigrants and their descendants were legally accepted as white in the United States, their social acceptance as such was contested and took longer to achieve. The visibility of immigrants and their children, clustered as they were in ethnic neighborhoods in cities, whose growth was fueled by industrialization, such as New York City, Chicago, and Boston, along with smaller cities like Cleveland and Providence, further marking them as potential cultural and linguistic threats to American ways of life.

Industrialization also resulted in educational reforms that started prior to and then intersected with the needs occasioned by large-scale immigration. Reformers understand that industrialization would require a workforce skilled beyond the three Rs, i.e., reading, (w)riting, and (a)rithmetic. Education was also seen as a way to cope with the larger social problems emerging from industrialization, such as child labor, class tensions, labor conflicts, and crime. By the end of the nineteenth century, the common school, or free public education at the grade school level, available for all children and emphasizing reasoning and observation, replaced what had been highly localized educational systems available mainly to the wealthy. By 1918, all states had passed laws requiring children, both girls and boys, to attend at least elementary school. Secondary education became more common around the early part of the twentieth century, with the rise in public financing and compulsory attendance laws. Certainly, by the time the doors to large-scale immigration closed in 1924, the public school was thought to serve as both a possible channel of social mobility and a potential agent for social uplift through the development of citizenship.

As more children of immigrants started to enter the common schools, it also became clear that schooling could help to Americanize them. While some native white Americans viewed the first generation (newcomers arriving as adults) as perhaps incapable of becoming American, due to language, religious and other cultural issues, the second-generation child was viewed as a more promising possibility for Americanization. States and localities adopted

varying measures to promote English-language acquisition. By 1923, 35 states mandated that only English serve as the language of instruction in public schools. From the late 1880s to 1915, the study of foreign languages, which could serve as a way to introduce immigrant students' home languages into the curriculum, was often eliminated by local school boards. Studying a foreign language typically became a secondary school activity.

Interestingly, even secondary school foreign-language classes offered in cities with substantial immigrant populations did not necessarily get high enrollments of in-group members, e.g., children of Czech descent studying Czech. The schools may have taught a different or more formal version of the homeland language than immigrant students were used to in their homes. Public schools also adopted other practices intended to Americanize the children of immigrants, including the recitation of the pledge of allegiance and new textbooks emphasizing Americanism. Students read the King James Version of the Bible (generally used by non-Catholics) and recited the Protestant version of the Lord's Prayer.

However, after nativist movements led to the 1924 restriction of large-scale immigration from southern, eastern, and central Europe (the door to immigration from Asia had for the most part already been closed) and other kinds of popular ethnic fears, some educators countered with cross-cultural learning, notably intercultural education; during the 1920s and 1930s, these educational experiments emphasized the children's and youth's family histories and ethnic cultures.

How did the immigrant families themselves respond to such schooling experiences for their children? Certainly, there was an economic response. Immigrant families, on average, struggled economically enough that it often did not make sense financially to allow a child to attend school rather than work in the paid labor force and contribute to the family. In 1910, fewer than "10 percent of Italians, Polish, and Slovak children were attending beyond the sixth grade in Chicago and Cleveland. Jews admittedly were doing better, although two-thirds of all students regardless of their backgrounds were not in school at the time" (Bodnar 1985, 193). Before the 1930s,

Children of immigrants play on the roof of the Washington School in Boston, Massachusetts, 1909. (Library of Congress)

immigrant children in American cities, across national origins, overwhelmingly could be found in the labor force rather than schooling. This was in decided contrast to the nation's overall growing enrollment in and graduation from high school; in the 1930s, the high school enrollment rate was 73.1 percent among youth aged 14 to 17, and the graduation rate was 29 percent for 17-year-olds.

Catholic Schools

Some of the immigrant families had a cultural response to the Americanizing tendencies of public schools—they chose to enroll their children in Catholic parochial schools. Just as the development of the public school system had to do with the need to Americanize the children of immigrants and prepare them (and other children of native-born

parentage) for the industrial economy, the rise of the Catholic school system had to do with shielding immigrant children from the "alien" cultures advanced in public schools. Although Catholics made up 1 percent of the American population as early as 1790, it was really their increasing presence with immigration—by 1900, they were 16 percent of the American population—that led to the rise and maturation of the Catholic school system.

The expansion of Catholic schools, circa 1870–1910, depended on several factors: The recruitment of women from European nations as a low-cost labor force to run the schools (as newcomers themselves, these women were also reassuring to immigrant parents that their children would be taught home-country practices); the church's support of non-English languages in the schools, with some instruction in those languages, and along national lines; and the parents' perception of alienation from American religious norms and contentious relations with their children's public school systems. As a result, Catholic schools organized often along national origins and, eventually, parallel school systems. It is worth noting that social class background was an important factor in determining who was able to afford a Catholic school education. Overall, about three out of five Catholic children enrolled in Catholic schools.

While the goal of Catholic schools was to acculturate and assimilate children in ways tailored to a particular ethnic group, such as the Germans or the Irish, the schools were typically modeled in practice after public school norms. The tensions between public and Catholic schools notwithstanding, Catholic school leaders faced similar kinds of market and labor pressures and adopted like-minded responses. Authority became centralized, via school boards and superintendents, and the curriculum and textbooks in Catholic schools also became standardized. Over time, Catholic schools moved away from some of their original mission of national origins and linguistic and ethnic preservation to a new orientation of the parochial schools as places where students could identify ethnically but learn in English. By the 1950s, Catholic schools had become similar to public schools in the ways they were run and the characteristics of their teaching staff. The 1950s were significant for another reason: With the opening up of the opportunity structure to the third- and later-generation descendants of once-vilified European and Asian immigrants, Catholics joined the nation's movement from the cities to the suburbs. While Catholic schools remained a part of their educational landscape, these descendants also began to feel just as comfortable enrolling their children in suburban public schools. This shift signaled the assimilation of the descendants of European immigrants (and, to a lesser degree, of Asian Americans, too).

Despite the commonalities in their experiences, European immigrants and their descendants did not have monolithic trajectories. Jewish immigrants arriving after the 1880s, while being laborers, also had a middle-class orientation, high rates of literacy, and occupational skills well suited to industrial labor. As a result, they had a faster social mobility story.

Among white Catholics, the descendants of Irish immigrants typically did better in levels of schooling, incomes, and occupational status. It took Americans of Italian descent, longer, for instance, into the 1960s, to climb the educational and mobility ladders. By 1986, however, it was clear that Americans of southern, central, and eastern European descent were indistinguishable from whites of other European ancestries in educational level and earnings.

Mexicans in the Southwest: A Different Story

The story of Mexican Americans in the Southwest has to do with a different kind of settlement through strife and conquest, particularly as a result of the nation's westward expansion. Much of the Southwest was formerly the territory of Mexico, including Texas, which was annexed to the United States in 1845. In the aftermath of the Mexican-American War (1846–1848), the United States also acquired California and New Mexico and areas that would become incorporated as Arizona, Nevada, and Utah. The Mexicans living in these areas largely decided to remain in what was now the United States and become U.S. citizens. The Southwest Mexican-American population, which was comprised of 100,000 persons in 1910, increased, albeit with relatively small migrations (as compared to the European flows) in the aftermath of the Mexican Revolution of 1910 and later, in response to American labor shortages during World War I. It was during the labor shortage of World War II that the United States entered into an agreement with Mexico, known as the Bracero Program, to recruit Mexican laborers for agricultural jobs in the Southwest. [Editor's Note: There was a limited version of the Bracero Program initiated during World War I and continuing until 1921 known as the 9th Proviso.] By the time the principal program ended in 1964, more than 4.4 million Mexican citizens had participated in the guest worker program, and many were subject to working conditions that did not live up to agreed-upon benefits, including the same pay as that of American workers.

The experiences of Mexican Americans in the Southwest were similar to those of the Europeans in the North with regard to the Americanizing tendencies of public schools and the role of Catholic schools in response to those tendencies. Catholic schools, which predated the incorporation of the Southwest by the United States in 1848, thereafter became a more substantial presence. In part, this was due to Catholic officials' wish to maintain the religion in the wake of American incorporation. The schools also allowed the use of Spanish as the language of instruction and encouraged expressions of Mexican identity in other ways. Although public schools had an initial period of accommodation to Mexican Americans' Catholic faith, the Spanish language and Mexican cultural heritage, they were gradually transformed into English-only institutions with little mention of Catholicism and Mexican history. In short, these public schools adopted similar strategies as did their counterparts in the North.

However, there were also key differences. The children of Mexican-immigrant parents tended to have fewer years of schooling than second-generation European Americans (e.g., Italians and Poles). This was due to institutional reasons having to do with geography and race-based discrimination. Secondary schooling became more widespread earlier in the urban North (where European immigrants had tended to settle). And Mexican Americans in the Southwest also experienced far greater discrimination within schools, as compared to their European counterparts. The role of discrimination is crucial to the story of Mexican Americans, especially in the Southwest.

Analyses of a unique data set spanning four generations of Mexican Americans, with the original participants living in Los Angeles and San Antonio in 1965–1966, show that, while Mexican Americans made progress, they continued to trail native white Americans in educational and economic achievement. The schooling of Mexican Americans is similar to that of black Americans, namely, as a racialized minority group subject to strong institutional barriers and inferior schooling. From a young age, Mexican Americans disproportionately attend poorly financed public schools with less experienced teachers having low expectations of them. Even when they presently attend integrated schools, they continue to be tracked into less demanding courses.

The Contemporary Picture: Post-1960s to the Present

The Immigration Act of 1965, which partially owed its passage to the civil rights movement, reopened large-scale immigration to the United States. By 2009, about 38.1 million persons in the United States were foreign-born, or about 13 percent of the total population. There are several points of note about the newcomers and their children. First, post-1960s immigrants have brought unparalleled national origins and linguistic diversity to the United States and have been incorporated into each of the major racial and ethnic categories, Hispanic, Asian, black, and white, although they have been disproportionately from Latin America, the Caribbean, and Asia. In 2010, some 30 percent of foreign-born persons were from Mexico, nearly a quarter from the Caribbean, Central America, and South America, and another quarter from South Asia and East Asia.

Second, there is great class diversity in the immigrant flows. While earlier generations of immigrants tended to be low-skilled, the post-1960s newcomers have been bifurcated into those with high skills and many years of formal schooling and their counterparts, who have low skills and low educational attainment. Third, documentation status has emerged as a key characteristic. Although the Immigration Act of 1965 was intended to lift discriminatory quotas, it also imposed ceilings for the first time on immigration from Mexico and the Western Hemisphere. While pre-1965 migration from Mexico was largely documented, the proportions had shifted by the late 1980s, such that about three out of five Mexican migrants were undocumented. In 2009, it was estimated that the number of undocumented immigrants in the United States had slipped from 11.8 million in 2007 to close to 10.8 million in early 2009.

The newcomers and their children have encountered a vastly transformed public school system and labor-market stakes attached to schooling. Thanks to the civil rights movement, equity has come to be the expectation. In place of past explicitly assimilationist tendencies that characterized the cultures of native minority and immigrant families as inadequate, there is presently an emphasis on multiculturalism, or value placed on diversity, in contemporary schooling. Yet, significant achievement gaps remain. While high school completion is more the norm, there is variation by race and ethnicity; only 7.5 percent of non-Hispanic whites in 2002 dropped out of high school, as compared to 13.4 percent of blacks and 30.1 percent of Hispanics. Southeast Asians also have relatively high dropout rates. Given the shift of the American economy from a manufacturing to a service-based one, postsecondary education—whether a two- or a four-year degree or a vocational certificate—has become more important to higher earnings and a middle-class lifestyle. Even some postsecondary schooling, regardless of whether a degree is earned, proves materially helpful.

Public Schools: A System Facing Challenges

Given the changed labor market environment, the schooling of the children of immigrants is arguably even more important in this era. However, the public K–12 educational system has been struggling with several challenges. On the one hand, notable legislative acts, such as the landmark Elementary and Secondary Education Act (ESEA), the first and largest federally funded K–12 education legislation of the 1960s, have addressed issues of equity. ESEA was designed to reduce the gaps in schooling experiences between low-income students and their more well-to-do counterparts, and between whites and blacks.

Title I of ESEA, for instance, devoted extra funding to focus on the educational needs of children from low-income families and improvements in the schooling they received. On the other hand, while de jure segregation is no longer permitted, de facto segregation during this period along the lines of skin color, poverty, and language has brought persistent inequities in the distribution of school resources, and relatedly, school quality. From the academic years 1993–1994 to 2005–2006, minority majority schools, defined as those in which fewer than 5 percent of the students are white, rose dramatically. The result is that blacks and Latinos are more likely to attend public schools in which students have a greater probability of coming from low-income homes and yet have fewer institutional resources, including highly

qualified teachers and lower teacher-turnover rates. Such schools typically have lower academic expectations for students, less rigorous courses, and higher levels of dropping out and violence. Overall achievement gaps between blacks and whites, and Hispanics and whites in public school, continue to persist, although minority students' scores in mathematics and reading tests have risen over time.

Language

While public schools do not identify students by immigrant status, and national surveys typically do not collect systemic demographic data on immigrant children, there are a few issues clearly distinct to this population. One is English-language acquisition. While there is wide agreement on its importance, there is debate about how to achieve English-language proficiency among the children of immigrants (both foreign- and U.S.-born). One of several pedagogical strategies, structured immersion, or what is typically known as bilingual education in the United States, provides English instruction in a self-contained classroom. The teacher usually knows how to speak the students' native language, and the students learn the second language and subject matter content simultaneously. Bilingual education has been criticized as an infeasible instructional strategy. Such sentiments fueled the passage of Proposition 227 in California (1998), followed by the Question 2 ballot measure in Massachusetts (2002) along with other measures around the nation limiting the time children can spend in bilingual education. However, research suggests that much of the effectiveness of language programs depends on how they are implemented; e.g., they can be a strong form of academic support for students or set them apart as less likely to achieve.

An exception to the limited information we have available on immigrant children in schools are data on English-language learners (ELLs) as mandated by No Child Left Behind (2001), the federal educational statute. Two patterns seem to be cause for concern. Assessment tests of ELLs, who comprise more than 10 percent of the students in our nation's public schools and their public dissemination, both mandated by NCLB, reveal patterns of school-based

A classroom at the J.F. Oyster Bilingual Elementary School in Washington, D.C., 2002. (AP/Wide World Photos)

linguistic isolation in several states with high numbers of immigrants. ELLs in Arizona, California, Florida, New York, and Texas largely attend schools in which ELLs are the majority or a substantial minority. These schools tend to be larger, have higher proportions of students qualifying for free or reduced school lunch, and are more likely to be Title I schools. Such enrollment patterns appear to be linked to the achievement gap between ELLs and white students. A portion of the in-state math achievement gaps between ELLs and white students, for instance, was due to the fact that they tended not to be found at the same public schools.

Given the variation among states in the tests they use and the threshold to show proficiency, it is not possible to compare the gap between ELLs and whites across states. A second pattern is inconsistency in how language policies for ELLs in public schools are applied. The same student may be identified as ELL

and placed in English-as-a-second-language classes in one state but not in another. Further cause for concern is that the process of identifying an ELL is correlated highly with nonlanguage factors, including poverty. School districts with high numbers of ELL students also seem to be using different tests to judge whether the students have acquired successful levels of subject knowledge and English-language proficiency, now mandated by NCLB.

Documentation Status

Another issue specific to the immigrant population is documentation status. Under the Supreme Court decision *Plyler v. Doe* (1982), public K–12 schools are required to educate children, regardless of documentation status. However, documentation status can have indirect consequences on students' academic performance. Given that undocumented parents of

U.S.-born (and thus, citizen) young children are less likely to access institutional resources, including those to which the children are legally entitled and could benefit from developmentally, their children have lower cognitive skills. Undocumented adolescents can be understandably reluctant to share their legal status with school officials. Without this information, however, school officials may not be able to appropriately guide students toward completion of high school and the transition to college and the labor market. Finally, there are few financial aid provisions for higher education, with undocumented students not eligible for federal financial aid and qualifying for in-state tuition in only some states. Without financial aid, even academically qualified students are not able to attend college due to its prohibitively high cost.

Catholic Schools: New Constituencies

Similar to public schools, the situation for urban Catholic schools has also been transformed since the 1960s. This period has brought fiscal challenges to urban Catholic schools as a result of the lowered availability of relatively inexpensive teachers, a rise in the costs to maintain the buildings, and a dip in enrollment with the move of white Catholic families to the suburbs. Rather than close the schools, Catholic school officials have served the newcomers moving into urban centers, e.g., native and immigrant minorities. The result is that teaching staffs are no longer the same ethnic or racial group or, sometimes, the same religious background as their students. In the early 1990s, it was estimated that students of color comprised more than a fifth of Catholic school students, and only 20 percent of Catholic children attended Catholic grade schools. Nonetheless, Catholic schools have been praised as places where urban, low-income, immigrant, and native minority students thrive. What has been less clear are the factors driving this effect. The higher academic achievement might be due to self-selectivity; for example, the minority families who enroll their children in Catholic school are more economically advantaged and have higher educational aspirations for their children. Attention has also been paid to Catholic

schools' mean socioeconomic status of students, mean academic ability, and racial and ethnic composition. More academically oriented curriculums, higher teacher expectations accompanied by strong disciplinary standards, smaller class sizes, and a climate of care within Catholic schools have also been found to affect achievement for minority students.

We know relatively little about how second-generation students are engaging with and faring in Catholic schools, especially as compared to native white, Latino, and black Americans. However, Vivian Louie and Jennifer Holdaway's recent comparative analysis based in New York City reveals that for native-born whites and Puerto Ricans, religion, or at least a cultural sense of being Catholic, remained an important reason for attending Catholic school, as it was for students of European descent from the first period of immigration. Religion is not a driving force for the families of the second-generation individuals. Instead, like many native blacks and Latinos, these families choose Catholic schools because they wanted a refuge from poorly performing public schools.

However, there is variation in the extent to which families choose Catholic schools, in part due to how little or how much the families knew about the public education system in New York City. Some groups, particularly Dominicans, lack knowledge about better schools within the public system and see Catholic schools as the only exit strategy. Some poor families struggle to pay high fees even when their children have access to specialized or magnet high schools. In contrast, Chinese working-class families are able to access information from middle-class relatives and friends about which neighborhoods have better public schools. They are the least likely to use Catholic schools. There was also variation in use of the Catholic school system due to cost. Native-born whites are the only group for whom socioeconomic factors do not matter in influencing who can go to Catholic school and whether students can persist until graduation. Other families often could not afford to keep their children enrolled by high school, when costs rise sharply. Overall, there was a benefit in educational attainment for nearly all groups attending parochial school as well as a positive impact in terms of avoiding certain problems, such as early pregnancy for girls and trouble with police for boys.

Between-Group Differences

Just as the educational trajectories of earlier waves of immigrants to the United States were not the same, this is also the case for the post-1965 second generations. How the children of immigrants are faring educationally, the extent to which they have done better than their parents, and why there is variation in these outcomes have been much cause for scholarly debate. Most second-generation individuals still have better educational outcomes than their parents, which is understandable because their parents' outcomes are so low compared with those of native-born minority groups. Consistent with segmented assimilation theory, researchers have found that the highly educated among the second generation typically have parents with high socioeconomic status and/or are embedded in co-ethnic communities where social capital, or information about education, transmitted through one's connections, flows across class lines—for example, from the middle to the working classes.

The picture is not entirely rosy. There are also three distinct pathways for second-generation individuals, who come from low-income families, grew up in low-income, native minority areas, and went to struggling public schools. The majority do not do well in school and are found in low-skilled jobs, staying in the working-class position of their parents. A minority drop out of school and get into trouble, whether through teenage pregnancy or crime; an even smaller minority manage to overcome these substantial disadvantages and become highly educated.

What are the processes underlying these different trajectories? In reality, our use of broad racial and pan-ethnic categories collapsing differences along national origins and ethnicity makes it difficult to more precisely figure out these trajectories. Therefore, while Asian Americans in the aggregate are outperforming students of other backgrounds, there are also key differences according to generational status, national origins, ethnicity, and social class. As noted earlier, Southeast Asians, on average, have lower levels of educational attainment. Likewise, the term

Latino includes individuals from different generational statuses, nations, skin colors, and social class origins. For instance, there is particular cause to be concerned about the slower rate of progress among some Mexican Americans and whether this will persist into the third generation, which has been largely the case for Mexican Americans over the twentieth century.

Linguistic assimilation, for instance, occurs by the second generation for the most part and for Mexicans by the third generation. Even later generations of Mexican Americans continue to have less schooling than black and white Americans. *Additionally, because they are members of a group that continues to see large-scale immigration, Mexicans tend to be seen by Americans as foreigners rather than an ethnic group en route to assimilation.*

While popular explanations have tended to emphasize the cultural values of successful groups as key to their academic performance, studies have shown that there are other compelling reasons. The success of economically disadvantaged second-generation individuals, of varying national origins, can be attributed to the mentoring by a nonfamily adult to help them negotiate the schools they attend and the high quality of their schools, in addition to family discipline of children. However, immigrant youth, especially from such backgrounds, seldom get the kinds of mentoring that they need and access to high quality public schools.

Conclusion

Immigration and education continues to be a central concern of the United States. With their growing numbers, the outcomes of the children of immigrants stand to figure greatly in the United States' economic, social, and cultural future. There are several points to keep in mind as we move toward that future. First, the population of undocumented immigrants and their children (whether documented or not) deserves our attention. The current climate in several states, notably Arizona, Alabama, Utah, and Georgia, has grown decidedly inhospitable to immigrants, especially those who are here illegally, with charges that laws recently passed in those states invites racial profiling by authorities. Legislation passed in Alabama in

June 2011 asks public schools to check on the documentation status of students, for data-gathering purposes, which some have argued could lead some immigrant families not to send their children to school for fear of the potential consequences, namely deportation.

What kinds of financial aid opportunities should be available to undocumented youth, who are academically qualified for higher education, is another important question. Second, while we should continue to pay attention to the distinctive needs of the children of immigrants, as discussed earlier in this chapter, we also need to recognize that not all policies to improve educational opportunities have to target particular groups of children. It has been much the case that the children of immigrants from working-class and poor families have faced similar kinds of challenges that their native, minority counterparts have. These include growing up in under-resourced neighborhoods and attending inadequate schools. Many of the policies that have helped native minorities, such as programmatic interventions, have also promoted better outcomes among the children of immigrants. We need to do a better job of paying attention to *both* the shared and specific needs of students. [EDITOR'S NOTE: A major case in 1946 challenged segregation of Mexican school children. See Mendez vs Westminster School District in chapter on Latino politics.]

Bibliography

American Community Survey (ACS). 2008. September 28.

Associated Press (AP). 2011 (June 10). "Alabama Illegal Immigration Law Tougher than Arizona's."

Banks, James A. 1994. *An Introduction to Multicultural Education.* Boston: Pearson, Allyn & Bacon.

Bodnar, John. 1985. *The Transplanted: A History of Immigrants in Urban America.* Bloomington: Indiana University Press.

Cattaro, G. M. 2002. "Catholic Schools: Enduring Presence in Urban America." *Education and Urban Society* 35, no. 1: 100–110.

Clewell, Beatriz Chu, with Clemencia Cosentino de Cohen and Julie Murray. 2007. *Promise or Peril? NCLB and the Education of ELL Students.* Washington DC: Program for Evaluation and Equity Research, Urban Institute.

Coleman, J. S. 1981. "Quality and Equality in American Education: Public and Catholic Schools." *Phi Delta Kappan* 62: 159–64.

Dinnerstein, Leonard, and David M. Reimers. 1999. *Ethnic Americans: A History of Immigration.* New York: Columbia University Press.

Foner, Nancy. 2006. "The Challenge and Promise of Past-Present Comparisons." *Journal of American Ethnic History* 25: 142–52.

Foster, M. 1996. "Introduction." In *Growing Up African American in Catholic Schools*, edited by J. J. Irvine and M. Foster, 1–10. New York: Teacher's College Press.

Fry, Rick. 2007 (August 30). "The Changing Racial and Ethnic Composition of U.S. Public Schools." Washington, DC: Pew Hispanic Center. http://pewhispanic.org/files/reports/79.pdf (accessed March 12, 2012).

Gonzales, Roberto G. 2010. "On the Wrong Side of the Tracks: Understanding the Effects of School Structure and Social Capital in the Educational Pursuits of Undocumented Immigrant Students." *Peabody Journal of Education* 85, no. 4: 469–85.

Graham, Patricia. 2005. *Schooling America: How the Public Schools Meet the Nation's Changing Needs.* Oxford and New York: Oxford University Press.

Gutierez, K. 2002. "Beyond Essentialism: The Complexity of Language in Teaching Mathematics to Latina/o Students." *American Educational Research Journal* 39, no. 4: 1047–88.

Hing, Bill Ong. 2004. *Defining American through Immigration Policy.* Philadelphia: Temple University Press.

Jiménez, Tomás. 2010. *Replenished Ethnicity: Mexican Americans, Immigration, and Identity.* Berkeley: University of California Press.

Kasinitz, Philip, John H. Mollenkopf, Mary C. Waters, and Jennifer Holdaway. 2008. *Inheriting the City: The Children of Immigrants Come of Age.* Cambridge, MA: Harvard University Press.

Lazerson, M. 1977. Understanding American Catholic Educational History. *History of Education Quarterly* 17, no. 3: 297–317.

Louie, Vivian. 2005. "Immigrant Student Populations and the Pipeline to College: Current Considerations and Future Lines of Inquiry." *Review of Research in Education* 29: 69–105.

Louie, Vivian. 2012. *Keeping the Immigrant Bargain: The Costs and Rewards of Success in America.* New York: Russell Sage Foundation.

Louie, Vivian, and Jennifer Holdaway. 2009. "Catholic Schools and Immigrant Students: A New Generation." *Teachers College Record* 111, no. 3: 783–816.

Massey, Douglas, and Magaly Sanchez R. 2010. *Brokered Boundaries: Creating Immigrant Identity in Anti-Immigrant Times.* New York: Russell Sage Foundation.

McCabe, Kristen, and Doris Meissner. 2010 (January). "Immigration and the United States: Recession Affects Flows, Prospects for Reform." Migration Policy Institute. http://www.migrationinformation.org/usfocus/display.cfm?ID=766 (accessed October 22, 2011).

McGreevy, J. T. 1996. *Parish Boundaries: The Catholic Encounter with Race in the Twentieth Century Urban North.* Chicago: University of Chicago Press.

Passel, Jeffrey S., and D'Vera Cohn 2009. "A Portrait of Unauthorized Immigrants in the United States." Pew Hispanic Center. http://pewhispanic.org/files/reports/107.pdf (accessed March 12, 2012).

Perez, William. 2009. *We ARE Americans: Untold Stories of Undocumented Students in Pursuit of the American Dream.* Sterling, VA: Stylus Publishing.

Perlmann, Joel. 2002. "Polish and Italian Schooling Then, Mexican Schooling Now? U.S. Ethnic School Attainments across the Generations of the 20th Century." Working paper #350. Bard College, Levy Institute.

Pew Hispanic Center. Tabulations of 2000 Census (5% IPUMS) and 2009 American Community Survey (1% IPUMS).

Portes, Alejandro, and Patricia Fernandez-Kelly. 2008. "No Margin for Error: Educational and Occupational Achievement among Disadvantaged Children of Immigrants." *Annals* (AAPSS) 620: 12–36.

Portes, Alejandro, and Ruben Rumbaut. 2001. *Legacies.* Berkeley and Los Angeles: University of California Press; and New York: Russell Sage Foundation.

Ragan, Alex, and Nonie K. Lesaux. 2006. "Federal, State, and District Level English Language Learner Program Entry and Exit Requirements: Effects on the Education of Language Minority Learners." *Education Policy Analysis Archives* 14, no. 20: 1–32.

Reisner, E. H. 1930. *The Revolution of the Common School.* New York: Macmillan.

San Miguel, Guadalupe, Jr., and Richard R. Valencia. 1998. "From the Treaty of Guadalupe Hidalgo to Hopwood: The Educational Plight and Struggle of Mexican Americans in the Southwest." *Harvard Educational Review* 68, no. 3: 358–412.

Social Science Research Council. 2005. *Questions that Matter. Setting the Research Agenda on Access and Success in Higher Education.* http://www.ssrc.org/publications/view/18EC38AD-6357-DE11-BD80-001CC477EC70 (accessed October 22, 2011).

Steinberg, Stephen. 1982. *The Ethnic Myth: Race, Ethnicity and Class in America.* New York: Atheneum.

Stepick, Alex, and Carol Dutton Stepick. 2010. "The Complexities and Confusions of Segmented Assimilation." *Ethnic and Racial Studies* 33, no. 7: 1149–67.

Suárez-Orozco, Carola, Marcelo Suárez-Orozco, and Irina Todorova. 2008. *Learning a New Land.* Cambridge, MA: Harvard University Press.

Telles, Edward E., and Vilma Ortiz. 2008. Generations of Exclusion: Mexican Americans, Assimilation and Race. 2008. New York: Russell Sage Foundation Press.

Tyack, David B. 1974. *The One Best System: A History of American Urban Education.* Cambridge, MA: Harvard University Press.

York, D. E. 1996. "The Academic Achievement of African Americans in Catholic Schools: A Review of the Literature." In *Growing Up African American in Catholic Schools*, edited by J. J. Irvine and M. Foster, 11–46. New York: Teacher's College Press.

Yoshikawa, Hirokazu. 2011. *Immigrants Raising Citizens: Undocumented Parents and Their Children.* New York: Russell Sage Foundation.

Zimmerman, Jonathan. 2002. "Ethnics against Ethnicity: European Immigrants and Foreign-Language Instruction, 1890–1940." *Journal of American History* 88, no. 4: 1383–404.

Gender Issues and Immigration

Caroline B. Brettell

Engendering the Study of Immigration

Beginning in the 1970s, scholars across a range of disciplines, inspired by feminist analytical frameworks, began to develop a gendered approach to the study of international migration based on the principle that men and women experience migration differently. Prior to this time women were largely invisible in studies of migration, although in the late nineteenth century, the geographical statistician E. G. Ravenstein had already noted that women participate more heavily in short-distance moves while men are involved in longer-distance moves.

Gender is a social construct and refers to the ideals and expectations regarding men and women, or masculinity and femininity, and how these vary across both time and space. As thinking has developed, more attention has been paid to the intersections among gender, race, and class as these define and influence the unequal distribution of power. Research on gendered processes of migration has followed these developments, moving from an early emphasis on correcting the omission of women as subjects (often referred to as the "women only" and "just add women and stir" phases) to an approach that considers how gender structures the migration process and the immigrant experience for both men and women. Gender must be considered in both sending and receiving contexts, not only in relation to families, but also in relation to labor markets, immigration and citizenship policies, and the range of institutions with which migrants interact in places of origin and places of destination. An understanding of gender relations is vital to a full explanation of both the causes and the consequences of migration.

This chapter, which addresses the significance of gender to understanding migrations to the United States between the middle of the nineteenth century and the present, explores the demographics of migration streams and how these have in turn been shaped by gendered immigration and naturalization policies as well as a gendered labor force. It also explores the gendered aspects of immigrant institutions and gendered participation in "American" institutions. By using specific case examples, attention will be drawn to how gender interacts with national origins and social class. It should be emphasized at the outset that there is no generalized or uniform experience for male and female immigrants, although there are some shared experiences. Further, even within particular national groups, experiences of migration can and do vary by such factors as age, marital status, education, occupation, and place of settlement.

The Demography of Gendered Migration to the United States, 1850 to the Present

In the spring of 1888 a sixteen-year-old Irish girl named Mary Ann Donovan boarded a ship for Boston. Her parents had recently died and Mary Ann and her brother John were the only members of her family left in Ireland. Mary Ann's older sister Ellen was already in America and had sent money for her sister to join her. John planned to sell the family farm and then follow his sister to America. (Nolan 1989, 1)

In the middle of the nineteenth century, just over 40 percent of immigrants to the United States were female, while for the rest of the century, the proportion dropped to approximately 38 percent and to 30 percent in the first decade of the twentieth century.

After 1930, a period when immigration to the United States was restricted as a result of the National Origins Quota Act of 1924, the proportion of female migrants began to rise, and by the 1940s, women comprised 61 percent of all immigrants to the United States. Between 1950 and 1980, women were approximately 53.5 percent of all immigrants to the United States, and by 2000, the proportion had risen to 55 percent. According to combined 2005–2007 American Community Survey data, the female foreign-born were 49.7 percent of the total foreign-born population in the United States, and in 2008, according to the Office of Immigration Statistics, women were granted 54 percent of all the green cards issued in that year and accounted for 56 percent of all naturalizations.

Today, scholars write about the feminization of migration globally. In the United States, the higher proportion of women immigrants throughout the latter twentieth century can be explained both by an immigration policy rooted in family reunification and by a labor market, discussed further below, that provides specific opportunities for women. Further, throughout the course of U.S. immigration history, we can identify an association between gendered mobility patterns, economic and political conditions in the homeland, marital status, and the way in which reproductive and productive roles are culturally assigned.

In the nineteenth century, as today, the sex ratio of immigration has varied by national origins. For example, the absence of opportunities in their home country (including being excluded from the inheritance of land and often, by extension, the marriage market) resulted in high rates of outmigration for single Irish women, who went to England or the United States. Between 1885 and 1920, close to 700,000 young, mostly unmarried Irish women, like Mary Ann Donovan, emigrated from Ireland, taking their future into their own hands. Jewish immigrants, by contrast, were more likely to come to the United States in family units. During the first decade of the twentieth century, women comprised 43 percent of all Jewish immigrants. Pushed out of eastern Europe and Russia by pogroms and other forms of discrimination and persecution, they viewed their migration as permanent. By contrast, the Italian migration stream to the United States in the late nineteenth century was disproportionately male—between 1880 and 1910, approximately 80 percent of Italians entering the United States were men. In the period between 1911 and 1920, the proportion of Italian women rose to 31 percent. Italians were economic migrants who often expected to return to their homeland and hence initially left their families behind. Their migration represented a traditional pattern that was rooted in the separation of productive roles from reproductive roles, the first assigned to men and the second to women. Men migrated while women remained behind. The lives of rural Sicilian women were altered in the absence of men: their economic and social roles changed, the meaning of mothering changed, and their status in Italian civil society was repositioned. When Italian women came to the United States, it was generally as followers and dependents (wives and daughters) rather than as independent single women, and only after their husbands/fathers had abandoned the idea of returning to the homeland following a period of time working and earning money abroad.

In the late twentieth century, a demographic parallel to the nineteenth-century Jewish and Italian flows can be found in a comparison between Mexicans and Asian Indians. This comparison further illustrates how immigration policies in the twentieth century, also rooted in gendered assumptions and biases, have affected particular migration streams. At the end of the twentieth century, the sex ratio among the Mexican foreign-born was 118 males/100 females. However, while in 1985, women comprised only 41 percent of Mexican immigrants, only 15 years later, they were 60 percent. The Immigration Reform and Control Act of 1986, which allowed many unauthorized Mexican men in the United States to legalize their status and then bring their families to join them, had an important impact on the gendered dimensions of this flow from south of the U.S. border. In the same period between 1985 and 2000, the proportion of women among Asian Indian immigrants has remained at 50 percent, suggesting that this is a legal migration stream of families. Among Asian Indians, men have often entered on student visas or H-1B skilled worker visas, perhaps accompanied by dependent family members or later calling families to join them. Alternatively,

Filipino nurses are ubiquitous in the American medical scene. They demonstrate both the labor export aspect of the Philippine economy and the brain drain it has experienced for decades. (Dan Habib/The Concord Monitor/Corbis)

these men, particularly if they are single, may first acquire legal residence and then return to India to marry and subsequently return with their new wife. Only recently have young unmarried Indian women migrated on their own to the United States to study. Just a few decades ago, this would have been considered inappropriate, but gender ideologies are slowly changing in the Indian subcontinent.

More contemporary parallels to the heavily female migration stream of the Irish during the latter nineteenth century can be found in the flows of Filipinos and West Indians. While labor opportunities can explain the demographic nature of these flows, homeland culture and society must also be considered. In the Philippines, daughters are expected to contribute to the household economy; sending single daughters overseas, including to the United States to take employment as nurses or domestics, is therefore quite common. In many parts of the West Indies,

female-headed households are not unusual, and women are major breadwinners. These responsibilities at home and the opportunities abroad influence their decisions to migrate, including the decision to leave their children behind in the care of extended female family members. In the United States, Caribbean immigrant women outnumber Caribbean men with a sex ratio of 100 females to 85 males. By contrast, among African migrants to the United States, the majority of whom have entered since 1990, there are more men than women. However, while African economic migration streams, from countries such as Nigeria, Mauritania, and Senegal, tend to have higher percentages of men, African refugee streams, from countries like Liberia, tend to include more or equal numbers of women.

Indeed, for the more contemporary period of U.S. immigration, it is very important to consider refugees, many of whom are women and children. The UN

High Commissioner for refugees has estimated that there are approximately 21 million refugees (that is, people fleeing conflict and persecution) globally, with the highest numbers in Asia and Africa. Since 1980, when the U.S. Refugee Act was passed, the United States has admitted close to 2.7 million refugees. In 2008, when the annual ceiling for refugee admissions was raised from 70,000 to 80,000, 60,108 refugees were admitted to the United States; 48.5 percent of these were females. Since 1980, refugees have come to the United States from places where the United States has had geopolitical interests—Vietnam, Laos, Cambodia, Russia, Cuba, Afghanistan, Iran—and African trouble spots, including Ethiopia, Liberia, and Somalia. In 2008, two-thirds of refugees were from Burma, Iraq, and Bhutan. In other words, the source countries for refugees are often different from those for economic migrants.

Gendered Immigration and Citizenship Policies

In 1889 Chin Suey Kim was born in the United States to Chinese parents. Her mother eventually returned to China with her five children. In China her mother married her off to a Chinese herb doctor. By this marriage to a foreigner, Chin Suey Kim lost her U.S. birthright citizenship. Her brothers, who returned to the United States with their father maintained their U.S. citizenship. (Barkan 2007, 41)

Immigration and citizenship policies in the United States are rooted in assumptions about gender and have shaped migration flows. In the early 1900s, there were regulations restricting the entry of Asian women "to ensure greater profitability from immigrants' labor and to decrease the costs of reproduction—the expenses of housing, feeding, clothing, and educating the workers' dependents" (Espiritu 2003, 63). Temporary worker programs, such as the Bracero Program of the mid-twentieth century in the United States, exclusively or initially targeted male workers. Although both women and men were able to use the "War Brides Act of 1948" to bring spouses to the

United States, it was primarily men who used it, since it applied only to individuals who had served in the U.S. armed services.

Thus, if not explicitly a gendered immigration law, it was so implicitly. More broadly speaking, prior to the McCarran-Walter Act of 1952, which made immigration law gender-neutral, women could not sponsor an alien spouse's migration outside the nationality quotas that were in place. Even after the Immigration Act of 1965, the emphasis on family reunification in U.S. immigration policy to some extent continued to structure women and children as dependent rather than independent immigrants. U.S. H-4 visas that are attached to H-1B (skilled worker) visas are more commonly allocated to wives who enter as dependents and hence may not work. In summary, the impact of immigration policy on gendered flows is stark. In 1940, for example, there were six times as many Chinese men than Chinese women in New York City. Since the mid-1970s, the immigration of Chinese women has outnumbered Chinese men, and in 1980, a full 85 percent of all Chinese immigration to the United States was the result of family reunification. In 2008, for immigrants in general, 59 percent of the men who obtained legal permanent residence in that year were admitted to the United States under family-sponsored preferences or as immediate relatives of U.S. citizens, compared with 69 percent of the women.

Alternatively, other policies focus on the recruitment of skilled workers and may specifically target women. This is how many single or married Filipino, West Indian, and South Asian women have entered the United States, often with a green card in hand that makes it possible for them to bring their immediate family with them. In 2008, 17 percent of men who obtained green cards and 13 percent of women had been admitted to the United States under employment-based preferences. But an estimated 12 million unauthorized immigrants were also residing in the United States in 2008. Indeed, many U.S. immigrant families are of mixed legal status: perhaps a husband who is legal, a wife and some children who are undocumented, and other children who were born in the United States and hence are U.S. citizens. This mixed-status environment has important implications not only for the children of immigrants, an estimated four million of whom live in such families in the United States as of 2008; but also for immigrant women who may, for example, be victims of domestic violence but are fearful of reporting it because of their undocumented status.

Since the nineteenth century, laws of entry have shaped immigration flows in various ways. Laws of citizenship, as Chin Suey Kim's story above suggests, have also been highly gendered. At the turn of the twentieth century, immigrant women were considered derivative citizens. "Beginning in 1855, any alien woman who wed an American citizen became a citizen by virtue of her marriage, and until the 1920s and 1930s a woman's citizenship status was derivative, through her father as a child and through her husband as a married woman. The law remained mute on the status of American women who married alien men until 1907. That year, Congress legislated that any American woman who married an alien would herself become an alien" (Gardner 2005, 14). The Cable Act of 1922, passed two years after women in the United States finally won the right to vote, began to erode the idea of derivative citizenship by making female citizenship independent of marital status. After the Cable Act, the rate of annual naturalizations for female applicants increased and quickly equaled that of male applicants. By 2008, 56 percent of all people naturalizing in the United States were women; 67 percent of those naturalizing were married.

In particular, derivative citizenship affected Asian women whose racial categorization was equally important in limiting their access to the right to belong. Many of these restrictions on citizenship and rights of entry, applied to Asians in particular, were lifted during or after World War II. However, some scholars have suggested that while race and gender have been "eliminated from the body of immigration and naturalization law, each lingered within the shadow of the law, shading how respectability, domesticity, economic viability, and moral character were visualized at the border" (Gardner 2005, 254).

One more contemporary dimension of gendered immigration law can be found in debates about whether homeland cases of domestic violence or female genital mutilation (FGM)—that is, the excision of some or all of the genitalia of a young girl—constitute grounds for political asylum in the United States. So far, such cases have been difficult for attorneys to argue, since the courts have largely viewed them as forms of harm inflicted in the personal realm, or emerging from a social and cultural rather than a political context. Practices such as FGM have themselves raised often contentious debates about how sensitivity for cultural differences is to be balanced with basic ideas about human rights. In the late 1990s, Congresswoman Pat Schroeder was instrumental in passing a law banning FGM, which, as legal analyst Doriane Coleman (1998) points out, made it difficult for an intelligent compromise, such as one between a Seattle hospital and the Somali refugee community, to be put into place. [Editor's Note: Mexican birthrates declined dramatically by mid-2000s.]

Finally, in the twentieth century, we should consider the gendered dimensions of anti-immigrant attitudes that circulate around very vocal cries for immigration reform. As anthropologist Leo Chavez (2008) has argued, some of this is rooted in a fear of rampant and uncontrolled Latina fertility that will supposedly flood the "true" American WASP population, and of "anchor babies" who legitimize the presence in the United States of "hoards" of undocumented immigrants, male and female. Chavez suggests that the invasion and reconquest themes that are present in major anti-immigration texts of the early twenty-first century by such authors as Samuel Huntington are frequently associated with the reproductive capacities of Latina women. However, he is careful to observe that present-day gender stereotypes regarding Latina fertility (which, as he shows, actually declines among Latinas in the United States) are broadly comparable to those held by turn-of-the-twentieth-century authorities who eyed immigrant women carefully, assessing their virtue and the risk of their becoming public charges or prostitutes.

The Gendered Immigrant Labor Market

Donna Nguyen was born in Vietnam in 1973. Her father, an army nurse, entered the United States in 1981. Donna and her mother joined him in 1991. Donna attended beauty school in San Jose,

California, and once she had received her nail technician license she began work in a nail salon owned by her aunt. Donna later moved to Dallas, Texas, where she easily found work in another nail salon as an independent operator. Donna works to provide good service to her clients because word of mouth is the way her business grows. (Brettell 2007, 92)

Between 1850 and the present, the U.S. economy has moved from a predominantly agricultural to an industrial economy, and then to a service economy. The participation of men and women in the labor force has also changed. In 1900, women made up only 18 percent of the total labor force. By midcentury, this figure had risen to 29 percent, and by 2000, women comprised 47 percent of the total U.S. labor force. The labor force participation rate for women (that is, the number of women in the labor force divided by the total number of women in the population over 16 and eligible to work) in 1900 was 19 percent compared with 80 percent for men; a century later the labor force participation rate for women was 60 percent while that of men was 75 percent. By 2007, women's labor force participation had dropped slightly to 59 percent. Immigrant women of the so-called "third wave of immigration" (that is, those who entered the United States between 1880 and 1924) were generally more economically active than native-born women. In 1900, 21 percent of single white women participated in the labor force compared with 34 percent of single women with parents born abroad and 61 percent of those who were themselves foreign-born.

As women in the United States, in general, have sought waged employment outside the home, this difference has receded. In 2008, according to American Community Survey data, the labor force participation rate for foreign-born men was 81 percent (among native-born men it was 71 percent). By contrast, 55 percent of foreign-born women were in the labor force compared with 60 percent of native-born women. However, foreign-born mothers with children under age 18 had a lower labor force participation rate (61 percent) than did native-born mothers (74 percent), and among those foreign-born mothers with

children under age 3, the labor force participation rate was 45 percent compared with a rate of 65 percent for native-born women with very young children. Native-born and foreign-born men with children under 18 both participated in the labor force at a rate of 94 percent. The highest levels of foreign-born female employment were among Filipina and West Indian women, while Pakistani, Bangladeshi, and Mexican women were among the lowest. During the last decade of the twentieth century, among Arab populations in Detroit, fewer than 20 percent of Yemeni women were in the labor force, and only 33 percent of Iraqi and Palestinian-Jordanian women were employed. Lebanese and Syrian women participated in the labor force at much higher rates. It is both interesting and significant that the groups with low female labor force participation rates include Muslims and women who face issues of unauthorized status (i.e., Mexicans). Law and gender ideologies are both powerful influences on the lives of immigrant women.

In the United States, male and female immigrants have often filled different occupational niches, reflecting how gender ideologies (those of both the sending and the host societies) can define what is considered acceptable work for men and women. But sometimes these are tempered by economic and social circumstances, and in certain industries immigrant men and women worked alongside one another, as in the canneries of the American West or some of the garment factories and chicken-processing factories in the Northeast or American South. In the nineteenth century, immigrant men (Poles and Slovaks, for example) provided the labor for the steel mills of Pittsburgh and the slaughterhouses of Chicago. Across the country, they worked in agriculture and construction, and in the American West, they worked in such industries as logging, milling, and mining and, of course, helped to build the railroads.

In the late twentieth and twenty-first centuries, occupational niches for immigrant men have varied by national origin, by urban labor market, and by education and social class. Mexican men, in many cities across the United States, are largely employed in blue-collar jobs in construction, ground maintenance, manufacturing, and food service. In smaller towns, they can be found, together with Mexican women, in processing plants, and of course in California, they participate extensively in agriculture. In Chicago, a major receiving city for Polish immigrants in the nineteenth century as well as today, Polish men are employed in construction, while Polish women are either in skilled health care fields, or in light manufacturing, or in domestic service working for cleaning service enterprises, or as private domestics. By contrast with these largely blue-collar national origin groups, Asian Indians are primarily white-collar workers employed in the health care sector or the computer and technology sector. But, as discussed further below, there are also Indian men who are involved in the retail sector, as self-employed small business owners.

In the nineteenth and early twentieth centuries, single women found work in domestic service and in garment factories. Men also found employment in garment factories, but very often gender hierarchies influenced their assignment to skilled jobs, leaving women to work as operatives and machine tenders. As mentioned above, Irish women, pushed out of their homeland by poverty and the absence of opportunities, including the opportunities for marriage and employment, looked across the Atlantic for opportunities. A female migratory chain came increasingly to characterize this flow, and in the United States, Irish women came to dominate the domestic servant sector. As single women, they were free to take up positions as live-in maids, make decent money, and even send remittances home to support family members who were left behind or to help them emigrate. Working in middle- and upper-class homes not only was safer than factory work, but it also exposed these young Irish women to American culture and hence facilitated the process of "Americanization." Further, domestic service was often immune to economic depressions that impacted male immigrant employment sectors more seriously. Even today, domestic service accords an access to American life that should not be underestimated.

At the turn of the twentieth century, the garment industries of the East and West Coasts mostly employed single immigrant women. For example, in San Francisco in the early 1990s, there were more than 25,000 workers in the garment industry,

90 percent of whom were women. Of these women, 80 percent were Chinese. A similar concentration of Chinese immigrant women could be found in New York City, where approximately 60 percent were employed in small garment sweatshops in Chinatown. The high labor force participation of Chinese women in New York is accounted for by job availability within the ethnic economy. Despite low-wage menial jobs and poor working conditions, including long hours, women viewed this work as essential to the survival of their families. This is equally true of Latinas who have also entered this sector of the New York and Los Angeles economies.

Married immigrant women who had been employed in the homeland in small enterprises or in agriculture were relegated to the domestic sphere upon arrival in the United States. In New York City in 1905, in only 1 percent of Jewish households were wives working for wages outside the home; the comparable figure for Italian households was 6 percent. However, as the photographs of Jacob Riis so powerfully illustrate, Italian and Jewish wives (with their children) made money working at home as piece workers for a decentralized garment industry. Their economic contributions were essential to supplement the low earning capacity of their husbands. Women also took in boarders or helped their husbands in the small shops that proliferated in the Lower East Side of New York City and other urban immigrant neighborhoods in such cities as Chicago, San Francisco, and Philadelphia.

Domestic service and the garment industry continue in the present to be important sectors of the gendered immigrant workplace. More broadly, women in the late twentieth and early twenty-first centuries have moved in response to an international division of labor that offers them positions on the global assembly line in what is broadly referred to as "care work" (child and elder care, the health professions) and as sex workers. Immigrant women who are employed in domestic service and the garment industry often face very long working hours, low wages, and few benefits. For some of them, illegal status makes them particularly vulnerable, but at the same time, undocumented female migrants can often work more easily in the domestic sector precisely because it is private.

A distinctive feature of more recent migration streams by comparison with those of the past is the participation of skilled professionals. Professional women often migrate alone and eventually return, or they are the ones who pave the way for the migration of the entire family. Filipino, South Asian, Caribbean, and other individuals involved in this migrant medical labor force challenge the image of women as tied migrants. Further, immigrant women with skills who are responding to global labor-market shortages are often better able than those without skills to minimize the impact of traditional gender hierarchies. But such work also comes with challenges of licensing and with racialized working contexts that constrain opportunities for rising to managerial positions.

Like Donna Nguyen, many immigrant women and men in the United States have entered the realm of the self-employed sustaining the small-business sector of the U.S. economy for more than a century. The role of immigrant women in family business has a deep history. Immigrant women of various nationalities who came to the United States in the nineteenth and early twentieth centuries opened boardinghouses, hat and dressmaking shops, restaurants, and grocery stores. The same is true today, although added to these kinds of enterprises are those such as nail and beauty salons, motels, and real estate and insurance agencies. One study found that 38 percent of the Korean women in the labor force in New York were working with their husbands in the same business; 12 percent ran their own businesses independent of their husbands; and 36 percent were employed in co-ethnic business. At the time there were 1,500 Korean-owned nail salons in New York City. "Some Korean men just drive their wives to and from the nail shop and help them open and close it while they either babysit or play golf during the daytime" (Min 1998, 40).

Much of the research on immigrant entrepreneurs explores the impact of self-employment on gender roles, and several authors conclude that immigrant women in family businesses are often highly exploited. Alternatively, others find that self-employment has empowered women. Still others describe the blurring of boundaries between home and work, as well as the shared gender roles that are part of employment in this particular sector of the immigrant labor market. All this research underscores the significance of the intersections between work life and family life to the immigrant experience.

Immigrant Families: Gender Roles, Transnational Motherhood, and Domestic Conflicts

Gladys, a Salvadoran immigrant living in California, left four of her five children in El Salvador. Although she was sad not to be able to watch these children grow up, she felt as if she had protected them from the hardships of living in the United States. Gladys and her youngest daughter reside with her employer who initially quarantined the child to protect her own children. "I had to battle, really struggle ... just to get enough food for her." (Hondagneu-Sotelo and Avila 2007, 405)

A number of scholars have argued that gendered migration redefines family relationships and gender roles. Immigrant women, through their participation in the labor force, make important economic contributions to the household, and this in turn may give them a greater sense of power and autonomy within the family. Alternatively, other scholars have noted that the kinds of jobs that immigrant women do are poorly paid and lack benefits and hence yield little in the way of equality and independence. In many immigrant families, women bear a larger burden of responsibility for the care of their children and their household and therefore must juggle with the multiple roles of waged worker, wife, and mother.

For many immigrant women of the past, especially those who entered as wives and mothers, immigration was disempowering. Uprooted from their village communities and from extensive kinship networks that these afforded, these women found themselves living in small tenement apartments and often unable or forbidden to leave their households or the few local streets in their neighborhoods. They were confronted with American social reformers who contributed to the process of "institutionalizing social inequality between women, especially by nationality/race/ethnicity and class and between women and men in households and families" (Friedman-Kasaba 1996, 186). And yet, as one historian points out, immigrant children in turn-of-the-twentieth-century families viewed their mothers as powerful. "Children described immigrant mothers as collectors of wages, as organizers of expenditures and everyday life, as engagers of their help in domestic chores and industrial production, as dispensers of discipline and punishment, and as women who rewarded children with food, affection, small gifts and personal services. Immigrant mothers spent little 'quality time' with their children, yet fostered emotionally close ties to them" (Gabaccia 1994, 68). To a large extent issues, of public face and domestic realities were at play. Thus, writing about Chinese families in San Francisco in the late nineteenth and early twentieth centuries, a major Chinese-American scholar argues that immigrant women offered a submissive image in public but ruled at home. "As homemakers, wage earners, and culture bearers, [Chinese women were] indispensable partners of their husbands" (Yung 1995, 77). Most of these women, upon coming to the United States, were liberated from the traditional joint families of China, where they were dominated by their parents-in-law.

Late-twentieth-century scholarship on immigrant families is replete with analyses of the impact of women's waged labor and earning power on traditional gender ideologies, including ideas about patriarchy that are characteristic of many immigrant cultures today as they were in the past. Within Korean immigrant families, "wives . . . no longer take for granted husbands' dominance at home and relief from family work. Many wives become less obedient to their husbands by expressing their opinions or speaking out against them, consequently resulting in marital conflicts. With an awareness of their contribution to the family economy, wives also believe that they deserve their husbands' help with family work. Most wives also believe that their great efforts toward family survival legitimize their own decreased effort in homemaking. Therefore, they do not practice the superwoman ideal and feel no guilt about this" (Lim 1997, 48). However, these challenges to gender inequality do not subvert the marital hierarchy that is bolstered by a Confucian patriarchal ideology.

Instead, Korean women often apply a "politics of appeal" (Lim 1997, 49) to get their husbands to participate in family work as they participate in breadwinning. Similar patterns have been observed among Vietnamese immigrant families. While women's power within the family has increased as a result of their economic contributions, they do not challenge male authority overtly, but rather may work through more subtle community mechanisms to mediate conflicts and tensions that might emerge in the domestic sphere. Vietnamese continue to support the idea of patriarchy because it also helps to sustain their authority vis-à-vis their children and ensures their future economic security. Further, in these and other cases, women often adhere to traditional gender roles in order to present a unified and harmonious front vis-à-vis the outside world and to hold on to the middle-class ideal to which they aspire.

In many immigrant families of the late twentieth and twenty-first centuries, it is the men who see their status undermined and who experience downward mobility. This is particularly true of men of color in the U.S. context who are doubly disadvantaged, particularly in the public sphere. Among South Indian Christian families in the United States, women who work as nurses experience increasing social status and economic power, while their husbands experience a loss in status after joining their wives in the United States and often assuming more domestic responsibilities. To regain this status, men involve themselves in the activities of their church, even pushing women out of activities that they were used to doing in the religious sphere of Kerala. Some research on African refugee communities in North America also identifies differences between men and women with regard to status mobility. Men are confronted with a decline in social status that they find hard to cope with; while women, who not only experienced lower status in their home country but also particular traumas of being a refugee (including the threat or actuality of rape) view their host country as a place of security, possibility, and hope. A study of Afghan refugee women in northern California further identified generational differences—the elderly felt they had lost respect and were socially isolated; the middle generation were stressed by the multiple challenges of being

A Korean American store owner makes a sale at the store she owns in South Central Los Angeles in 2002. (AP Photo/Damian Dovarganes)

a housewife, an employee, and a household mediator (between husband and children); and young single women were confronted by cultural conflicts and the inability to find appropriate husbands (Lipson and Miller 1994).

For immigrant women, gender roles involve not only employment, but also motherhood. In the past, married women rarely came to the United States without their children, but this has become more common in the late twentieth and early twenty-first centuries. It has resulted in extensive discussion of what has been labeled transnational motherhood—that is, the "circuits of affection, caring, and financial support that transcend national borders" (Hondagneu-Sotelo and Avila 2007, 390). Transnational mothers, like Gladys described above, leave their children behind so that they can work as live-in nannies in the United States. Gladys and the transnational Latina mothers described by sociologists differentiate what they think

of as motherhood from things like the abandonment of or estrangement from children. They convince themselves that although they may be physically absent, they are not emotionally absent, and that their children are better off in their home communities than they would be in the United States. These women redefine motherhood to include the breadwinning role and expand their caregiving responsibilities to include the money they earn in the United States. Finally, to satisfy their own emotional needs, they transfer the nurturing aspects of mothering to the children of their employees.

Another late-twentieth-century immigrant family form, facilitated by the more rapid forms of communication and transportation today compared with the past, is the astronaut family characteristic among Chinese and Koreans in the United States. In these families, the husband returns to the homeland to work, while his wife remains in the United States so that the children can take advantage of educational opportunities. Husbands and wives maintain contact in transnational space through fax, telephone, e-mail, and travel. Clearly, this is facilitated by the class position of these families and is not necessarily possible for Latino families, who may find it cheaper to raise their children in the sending society and hence sustain the more traditional pattern of husbands going abroad to work by themselves.

Within immigrant families there is both cooperation and conflict. Some of the most intense conflict—across a range of immigrant groups from the Chinese in San Francisco in the 1920s, to the Italians and Greeks in New York in the 1930s, to Mexicans in the American Southwest in the 1950s and 1960s, to Arabs and South Asians today—occurs across generations and involves parental attempts to control dating and other activities commonly associated with American teen culture. Daughters generally face more intense restrictions and surveillance than do sons. For example, in the early 1900s, settlement house workers observed that Italian daughters "intended to be American girls" but were "sometimes beaten if they go out at night." Like their mothers, daughters were and are expected to uphold the values of traditional culture, including those associated with sexual mores and marriage patterns. Women's bodies are controlled in order to assert cultural identity and a sense of moral superiority vis-à-vis American culture and society and Americans.

Occasionally, the gendered patterns of parenting that circulate around the control of women's bodies erupt into serious forms of domestic violence. While scholars have argued that the incidence of domestic violence in immigrant families is not necessarily higher than that in the native-born population, isolation, limited English-language proficiency, and immigration status can make immigrant women particularly vulnerable. However, one form of domestic violence closely associated with immigrant cultural mores is that of so-called "crimes of honor" that are rooted in moral codes that define gender relations and appropriate gendered behavior.

For example, in 2008 in the United States, an Egyptian cab driver residing in a suburb outside the city of Dallas, Texas, killed his two teenage daughters

because they were meeting with non-Muslim boyfriends; a Pakistani pizza shop owner in the city of Atlanta, Georgia, killed his daughter when she admitted that she was seeking a divorce from her much-older husband, a marriage that had been arranged—he claimed this would dishonor his family; and in Chicago, Illinois, a South Asian man killed his pregnant daughter, son-in-law, and three-year-old grandson because he disapproved of his daughter's marriage to a lower-caste man. Those who have attempted to explain these crimes suggest that they relate not only to the role of immigrant women as bearers of group identity and preservers of culture, but also to the downward mobility and a loss of self-esteem experienced by immigrant men. These men turn inward, exerting patriarchal control over wives and daughters as a way to regain lost pride and protect their honor. *Powerlessness in the public sphere generates a desire to exercise more power in the domestic sphere.*

Gendered Migrant Participation in the Public Sphere: Schools, Religious Assemblies, and Ethnic Organizations

Maria Abastilla Beltran was born in the Philippines in 1903. She graduated from a nursing program and then emigrated to the United States to complete a public health nursing degree. After living in Philadelphia, Cleveland, and Chicago, she moved, in 1929, to Seattle where she married and became involved in the founding of a Filipino Women's Club. (Barkan 2007, 226)

Scholars generally agree that only when women arrive do communities and community institutions begin to develop within immigrant populations. Thus, how groups adjust socially and culturally as well as how they begin to become civically engaged are also gendered processes. The important roles of Italian, Polish, and Jewish women in their neighborhoods have described, including their activities in the public sphere to protest high prices and rent increases. Over time, "women's collective action, like men's, increasingly originated in the workplace, not in the neighborhood. And it was more and more apt to be based on voluntary association rather than informal neighborly solidarity or the kin network" (Gabaccia 1994, 80). In Lawrence, Massachusetts, for example, women working for wages, together with housewives, initiated the "Bread and Roses" a textile strike in 1912; while in Boston, the West End Mother's club launched protests to lobby for price-control laws.

Men and women each had their own voluntary organizations. Many men's organizations, including most mutual-aid societies, deliberately excluded women, or relegated them to auxiliaries. As one historian points out, "men argued that they joined the societies as a necessary part of their role as primary breadwinners for their families. It was through the societies, they claimed, that they provided their families with insurance against their loss of livelihood. Accordingly, the benefit structures of most orders and societies . . . reflected the needs and rhythms of men's work lives and assumed traditional patriarchal family relationships" (Soyer 2006, 534). Women, who often had to adapt organizational activities to their domestic responsibilities, founded their own networks of association, both formal and informal, depending on their class status. However, for both immigrant men and women, these organizations and activities facilitated the expansion of social networks, the development of civic and political skills, and benefits of economic support when needed.

Among the more important organizations were religious institutions, which quickly became centers of immigrant community life. Depending on the faith, immigrant men and women engage differently with these organizations, although immigrant religious congregations have often been described as bastions of male dominance. Among South Asian Christians in the United States in the late twentieth century, the church has become a male gendered space where they can exercise leadership responsibilities denied to them in the broader working world. Among Yemeni immigrants in Michigan, women are excluded from the mosque. In some Vietnamese Buddhist temples, women are more involved in voluntary activities, but mostly behind the scenes and not in leadership roles. In some Hindu temples, there is a similar frontstage/backstage or upstairs/downstairs divide, with men involved in ritual and priestly functions upstairs or

publicly, and women working in the kitchen downstairs or behind the scenes. These divisions, however, have to be put in context.

For example, regarding a Hindu temple in the Washington, D.C., area during the 1990s, an observer noted that, "For American feminists women in the kitchen marks gender segregation and subordination, but . . . South Asian women work in the temple kitchens, a task that in India is reserved for Brahmin men, whose ritual purity was a prerequisite for handling the holy food which was always served first to god." When women now make these sanctified meals, they are actually taking on a priestly role, with their domestic task expanding into temple service. Women find their status "enhanced by their greater role but also diminished because that role is no longer on an equal level (literally) with the other ritual functions of the temple" (Waghorne 1999, 124).

Historians have noted the important role of schools in producing an Americanized, disciplined, and literate labor force as well as the significant impact of immigrants on the growth of schooling in the United States. Immigrant sons and daughters engaged schools and other educational institutions in distinct ways. Concerning Italian and Jewish immigrant families in early-twentieth-century New York, it was observed that while women in the former group had minimal engagement with the public sphere, Jewish women became more involved in the cultural and educational dimensions of life in New York City. Jewish girls also participated in political activities and union organizing.

While Italian parents took their children out of school as soon as they could in order to put them to work for the family, Jewish families pursued education, particularly for sons but also for daughters, for whom at least some education was valued. Twice the percentage of Jewish men had completed high school than had the Italian men. Moreover, among the second-generation Jews, almost three times the proportion had completed high school than was the case with Italians. Although the educational accomplishment of foreign-born women of both groups was consistently less than that of men, among both the first- and second-generation Jewish women, more than two times the percentage had completed high school than was true for Italian women. Today, Asian populations and Latinos offer a similar contrast. Among Asian families, education is highly valued and viewed as the avenue to social and economic mobility for immigrant offspring. Latino children are more likely to be pulled out of school to work and hence show lower levels of school engagement. But even within Asian communities, there are gendered differences in the educational opportunities extended to children. While South Asian sons are often encouraged to attend competitive, upper-tier universities away from home, daughters are frequently steered to more local colleges and universities.

Conclusion: Gender and Transnational Space

Several scholars of recent immigrations have suggested that men experience a loss of status as a result of their immigration by comparison with women. They lose control of activities in the public sphere and possibly also of patriarchal domination. This orients them in many cases more strongly toward their home communities where they can maintain status, particularly, for example, if they are involved in hometown associations. It has been argued that Mexican men who engage in transnational citizenship have stronger ties to Mexico than do Mexican women who are more involved in social citizenship in the United States. Women, in relation to concerns about family health, their children's education, or domestic violence, become involved with host society state institutions, while men interact with the state "as a force of moral and legal regulation" (Goldring 2001, 508). Equally important are the constraints on the use of public space for Mexican men, who in their home villages could hang out on the village square. Mexican women recognize that if they returned to Mexico, they would not only face demanding household chores once again, but they would also have to submit to a patriarchal authority that has been weakened in the immigrant context. Thus, the reasons for engaging in transnational social space can differ for immigrant men and women.

These gendered differences in transnational attachments, and by extension to how immigrant men and women view the permanence of their migration, are common across a range of immigrant populations. For example, research has shown that while Dominican men view their migration as temporary and are eager to return to their home country where they would regain some of the traditional privileges of gender accorded to them, Dominican women want to avoid returning because they think that this would mean a loss of the freedoms they have acquired in the United States as well as of their ability to be involved in wage earning. Thus, while men save for return, women buy durable goods to outfit their homes and root the family in the United States.

Sociologist Pierrette Hondagneu-Sotelo, in a study of Mexican families in California, adopts a different approach by focusing on key activities of women that foster settlement and integration: creating patterns of permanent, year-round employment, provisioning resources for the maintenance and reproduction of the family on a daily basis, and building community life. However, she warns that this process of anchoring "does not proceed in any unilinear or predictable fashion" and "that neither settlement nor gender can be reduced to absolutes" (1995, 25, 41). She equally found cases of women who resisted the efforts of their husbands to send them back to Mexico as she found cases of men equally engaged in the kinds of activities that fostered more permanent settlement. Other scholars have emphasized the need for careful analyses of the home/host binary that avoids automatically equating the sending society with gender oppression and the host society with greater freedom.

Whether considering the migrations of the late nineteenth century or those of the late twentieth and early twenty-first centuries, the movement of families results in complex changes in gender roles and gender relations that are the result of political, economic, and social forces in both the societies of origin and the societies of destination. Further, the migrant experiences of men and women are also shaped by socially constructed ideas about masculinity and femininity that they bring with them or that they encounter in a new place of settlement. These ideas have of course changed over time, and they vary from one migrant population to the next. Any consideration of the relationship between gender and migration must be sensitive to both historical and cultural contexts.

Bibliography

Barkan, Elliott Robert. 2007. *From All Points: America's Immigrant West, 1870s–1952.* Bloomington: Indiana University Press.

Brettell, Caroline B. 2007. "Immigrant Women in Small Business: Biographies of Becoming Entrepreneurs." In *Handbook of Research on Ethnic Minority Entrepreneurship: A Co-Evolutionary View on Resource Management,* edited by L-P. Dana, 83–98. Cheltenham, UK: Edward Elgar.

Cameron, Ardis. 1993. *Radicals of the Worst Sort: Laboring Women in Lawrence, Massachusetts, 1860–1912.* Chicago: University of Chicago Press.

Chavez, Leo R. 2008. *The Latino Threat: Constructing Immigrants, Citizens, and the Nation.* Stanford, CA: Stanford University Press.

Cohen, Miriam. 1992. *Workshop to Office: Two Generations of Italian Women in New York City, 1900–1950.* Ithaca, NY: Cornell University Press.

Coleman, Doriane L. 1998. "The Seattle Compromise: Multicultural Sensitivity and Americanization." *Duke Law Journal* 47, no. 4: 717–83.

Connolly, James J. 1998. *The Triumph of Ethnic Progressivism: Urban Political Culture in Boston, 1900–1925.* Cambridge, MA: Harvard University Press.

Espiritu, Yen L. 2001. " 'We Don't Sleep Around Like White Girls Do': Family, Culture and Gender in Filipina American Lives." *Signs: Journal of Women in Culture and Society* 26, no. 2: 415–40.

Espiritu, Yen L. 2003. *Home Bound: Filipino American Lives across Cultures, Communities, and Countries.* Berkeley: University of California Press.

Friedman-Kasaba, Kathie. 1996. *Memories of Migration: Gender, Ethnicity, and Work in the Lives of Jewish and Italian Women in New York, 1870–1924.* Albany: State University of New York Press.

Gabaccia, Donna. 1994. *From the Other Side: Women, Gender, and Immigrant Life in the U.S., 1820–1990.* Bloomington: Indiana University Press.

Gardner, Martha. 2005. *The Qualities of a Citizen: Women, Immigration and Citizenship, 1870–1965.* Princeton, NJ: Princeton University Press.

George, Sheba M. 2005. *When Women Come First: Gender and Class in Transnational Migration.* Berkeley: University of California Press.

Goldring, Luin. 2001. "The Gender and Geography of Citizenship in Mexico-U.S. Transnational Spaces." *Identities* 7, no. 4: 501–37.

Grasmuck, Sherri, and Patricia R. Pessar. 1991. *Between Two Islands: Dominican International Migration.* Berkeley: University of California Press.

Hondagneu-Sotelo, Pierrette. 1995. "Beyond 'The Longer They Stay' (and Say They Will Stay): Women and Mexican Immigrant Settlement." *Qualitative Sociology* 18, no. 1: 21–43.

Hondagneu-Sotelo, Pierrette, and Ernestine Avila. 2007. " 'I'm Here, but I'm There': The Meanings of Latina Transnational Motherhood." In *Women and Migration in the U.S.-Mexico Borderlands: A Reader,* edited by D.A. Segura and P. Zavella, 388–412. Durham, NC: Duke University Press.

Lim, In-Sook. 1997. "Korean Immigrant Women's Challenge to Gender Inequality at Home: The Interplay of Economic Resources, Gender, and Family." *Gender and Society* 11, no. 1: 31–51.

Lipson, Juliene G., and Suellen Miller. 1994. "Changing Roles of Afghan Refugee Women in the United States." *Health Care Women International* 15, no. 3: 171–80.

Menjivar, Cecilia, and Olivia Salcido. 2002. "Immigrant Women and Domestic Violence: Common Experiences in Different Countries." *Gender and Society* 16, no. 6: 898–920.

Min, Pyong G. 1998. *Changes and Conflicts: Korean Immigrant Families in New York.* Boston: Allyn and Bacon.

Nolan, Janet A. 1989. *Ourselves Alone: Women's Emigration from Ireland, 1885–1920.* Lexington: University of Kentucky Press.

Reeder, Linda. 2003. *Widows in White: Migration and the Transformation of Rural Italian Women, Sicily, 1880–1920.* Toronto: University of Toronto Press.

Soyer, Daniel. 2006. "Mutual Aid Societies and Fraternal Orders." In *A Companion to American Immigration*, edited by R. Ueda, 528–46. Oxford: Blackwell Publishing Company.

Waghorne, Joanne P. 1999. "The Hindu Gods in a Split-Level World: The Sri Siva Vishnu Temple in Suburban Washington, D.C." In *Gods of the City*, edited by R. A. Orsi, 103–30. Bloomington: Indiana Univeristy Press.

Yung, Judy 1995. *Unbound Feet: A Social History of Chinese Women in San Francisco*. Berkeley: University of California Press.

Zhou, Min. 1992. *Chinatown: The Socioeconomic Potential of an Urban Enclave*. Philadelphia: Temple University Press.

Race Mixing and Intermarriage in the United States

Christine M. Su

On January 20, 2009, Barack H. Obama was inaugurated as the 44th president of the United States. When he was sworn in as commander in chief in front of the U.S. Capitol in Washington, D.C., millions hailed the event as a watershed in American history—the defining moment in which an African American became the leader of the country for the first time. Yet Obama's story is not only that of an African American. Rather, it is what *New York Times* journalist Jodi Kantor calls "a more complex narrative, about immigration, social mobility and the desegregation of one of the last divided institutions in American life: the family" (Kantor 2009, A1).

President Obama's story is one of national and racial boundary-crossing and intermarriage: he is the son of a black Kenyan father and a white American mother; the brother of a white and Indonesian half-sister; the brother-in-law of a Chinese Canadian; and the husband of a woman descended from both black American slaves and white American slave owners. While racial and ethnic mixing is not a new phenomenon, Obama's omnipresence in the public eye since his presidential campaign has helped to move discussions about intermarriage, blended families, and multiraciality out of the realm of academia and into everyday discussions, from theoretical tête-à-tête at scholarly conferences to dinner-table conversations.

Certainly, President Obama is not alone: according to the 2000 U.S. census, 2.4 percent (6,826,228) of the total adult population of the United States (281,421,906) identified as being of two or more races. Ethnohistorian Paul Spickard has commented that "the history of the world is a story of peoples on the move: invading, conquering, migrating, trading,"

and that, as a result of such movement, "ultimately they shared their personal lives as well, mixing socially and, eventually, maritally" (Spickard 1989, 4). This is certainly true in the United States, where most of the inhabitants are or were descended from immigrants (whether voluntary or involuntary, indigenous Native Americans notwithstanding). And interethnic and interracial mixing here are as old—indeed, older—than the nation-state itself. If interracial mixing and intermarriage are age-old occurrences, why, then, have they been the source of such contention?

The answer lies in that the history of the United States is not only a history of migration and mixing, but also a history of inequality. The mind-sets and motivations of those who set out to explore and "discover" new worlds influenced how they interacted with those they encountered along the way; and while the dynamics of particular individual and group interactions varied, by and large relations—interracial relations—in the United States have been characterized by inequality. While most scholars concur that race is more a social than a biological construct, the notion of race and the supposed attributes of a given race have, nonetheless, been used to justify power and privilege, discrimination and intolerance. Thus, "at a personal level, race is very much in the eye of the beholder; [but] at a political level, race is in the service of economic and social privilege" (Root 1992, 4).

This chapter briefly chronicles the history of interracial mixing and intermarriage in the United States. It proceeds chronologically and somewhat parallels what historians have outlined as the major "waves" of immigration, since these tended to bring large numbers of persons of different races into contact with each other. Each section is organized as follows: (1) each begins by outlining the *opportunity structures*—the conditions (geographic, economic, social, etc.) that allowed individuals of different races to meet and mix; (2) each then focuses on a discussion of the *interpretations* of such interracial unions by the larger groups of which the individuals were a part; and (3) culminating in a summary of the legal, economic, sociopolitical, and cultural *consequences* of these interpretations.

Setting the Context

In its broadest definition, *intermarriage* could refer to marriage between members of any two groups considered to be different, whether by themselves or others. For example, marriage between a white American man of Dutch heritage and a white American woman of French heritage could be considered an intermarriage, given the historical and cultural differences between the two. It could also refer to a marriage between two persons of the same race who are members of different religious groups, such as a black Muslim man marrying a black Baptist woman, or a white Jewish woman marrying a white Catholic man. And in some areas of the world, one's religious faith is indeed the most significant determinant of whether individuals are members of the same group. In the United States, however, race has most often been the dividing line between individuals and among peoples. As mentioned above, race is not easily defined.

However, because intermarriage in the United States is as much a discussion about who cannot or should not marry as who does, it is necessary to outline how Americans have delineated boundaries between groups. David Hollinger describes an "ethno-racial pentagon," a five-group demographic structure comprised of African-American, Asian-American, European-American, Hispanic/Latino-American, and Indigenous/Native-American groupings (Hollinger 2000, 8). While these categorizations are neither organic nor necessarily accurate (as Hollinger himself remarks), historically Americans have tended to classify each other according to these groups, and

interactions between one category and another have been considered interethnic or interracial. Consequently, the terms *interracial* and *intermarriage* for most of this chapter refer to any intimate or connubial crossing between individuals from one of the five ethno-racial categories to one or more of the others.

Early Encounters: Indigenous/Native Americans and Anglo-Europeans

Opportunity Structures

The first recorded interracial marriage in North American history took place in 1614 between Englishman John Rolfe and Pocahontas, an Algonquin Indian woman living in what is now the tidewater region of Virginia. However, Anglo-European social and sexual interaction with the indigenous peoples of what would become known as the Americas began with explorers' earliest arrivals.

Beginning in the fifteenth century, European nations in search of routes to India and the Far East landed in the "New World." There, they encountered numerous indigenous societies as diverse as the land itself, thriving as hunters, agriculturalists, fishers, farmers, and shepherds. Spain was the first imperial power, setting up colonies in the Caribbean and southern areas of North America. Voyagers from Great Britain settled along the Mid-Atlantic Coast. France explored and created an intensive fur and fish trade in the north and northeast. Because they arrived at different times in different areas of the country, the explorers met members of quite varied tribes. Each had its own name for its people and its own customs. The travelers' primary motives for their journeys were economic, but their interactions with the natives soon became more social, particularly given the indigenous peoples' hospitality and knowledge of the terrain.

The fifteenth-century Italian explorer Christopher Columbus, for example, who mistakenly called the indigenous peoples he encountered "los Indios," wrote in his journals about the native peoples' kindness and generosity: "So many came that they covered the land, giving a thousand thanks ... and they brought us all that they had in the world ... and all so bigheartedly and so happily that it was a wonder" (quoted in Nagel 2003, 64). Similarly, the Frenchman

A romanticized nineteenth-century depiction of Native American Pocahontas' wedding to colonist John Rolfe in 1614. (Library of Congress)

Jacques Cartier, who journeyed along the St. Lawrence River in the sixteenth century, described the native peoples as extraordinarily welcoming and lauded their knowledge of such things as the medicinal uses of plants and herbs.

They also reported social and sexual contact with the indigenous populations, which became evident in both informal unions and formal marriages, and the births of Native American–European children. Notably, despite their willingness to engage in such contact, many of the explorers attributed this mixing to the supposed licentiousness of the native peoples. Columbus's fellow Italian, Amerigo Vespucci, for whom the "New World" would eventually be named, commented at length in his reports on the nudity and seeming promiscuity of native women. Cartier in his writings chided the indigenous peoples for their paganism and lewd and

licentiousness behavior. The explorers' accounts admit that their male crewmembers were sexually attracted to the native women, although most accounts suggest that it was only the natives who were excessively lustful, and that their crewmembers "simply indulged native women's desires" (Nagel 2003, 66). Interestingly, a number of the sixteenth- and seventeenth-century Franciscan friars (who took vows of celibacy) settled in what is modern-day New Mexico fathered dozens of mixed-race children with the indigenous Pueblo women. There were also accounts of relationships between white women and Native American men.

Interpretations of Interracial Unions

For the most part, because mixing with indigenous individuals and groups, at least initially, supported the newcomers' goals of obtaining access to

America's natural resources and land for settlement, such unions were generally accepted. In 1514, for example, a Spanish law was passed explicitly permitting intermarriage of Spanish colonists with Native Americans. The fur trade in the northern United States and Canada led to extensive contacts between Europeans (primarily French but also British, Dutch, and Russian) and Native Americans, and the former relied heavily upon the latter as guides to assist them as they navigated the often inhospitable frontier. Therefore, it is not surprising that the French never banned such intermarriage. The offspring of white-native unions were generally accepted into tribal communities, which facilitated seventeenth- and eighteenth-century economic and political alliances. In some instances, intermarried whites and their offspring became tribal leaders.

There were even efforts to promote white-native intermarriage in the English colonies: in 1784, for example, Patrick Henry presented a bill to the Virginia legislature suggesting that "every white man who married an Indian woman should be paid ten pounds, and five for each child born of such a marriage; and that if any white woman married an Indian she should be entitled to ten pounds with which the county court should buy livestock" (quoted in Cruz and Berson 2001, 1). Henry's bill did not pass, but its introduction and the examples above provide evidence that intermarriage with Native Americans was not wholly forbidden, at least during the early colonial and revolutionary periods.

This is not to say, however, that relations between newcomers and natives were considered equal. On the contrary, many newcomers brought with them beliefs in the sophistication and superiority of their own cultures specifically—and the white, Christian race in general. Some historians assert that initial opposition to white-native couplings had little to do with "race" or skin color but, rather, with the natives' seeming paganism, which in the colonists' view made them uncivilized. The explorers' writings reflect these beliefs, for their accounts express both fascination and repulsion, describing them alternately as peaceful and vengeful, intelligent and primitive and, particularly in the case of native women, both childlike and licentious. The British captain Jonathan Carver wrote

of this perceived duality in 1767, noting that "the character of the Indians, like that of other uncivilized nations, is composed of a mixture of ferocity and gentleness. They are at once guided by passions and appetites, which they hold in common with the fiercest beasts that inhabit their woods, and are possessed of virtues which do honour to human nature" (Carver 1788, 334).

White male–Native American female relations in particular were for the most part tolerated if not encouraged, although the parity of these relationships is questionable. Consider the story of Sacagawea, a Shoshone woman who served as an interpreter for the Lewis and Clark expeditions in 1804 and whose legacy has been romanticized and immortalized on an American dollar coin. Of Sacagawea, the U.S. Mint of the Treasury comments: "She provided crucial knowledge of the topography of some of the most rugged country of North America and taught the explorers how to find edible roots and plants previously unknown to European-Americans. With her infant son bound to her back, she singlehandedly rescued Captain Clark's journals from the Missouri whitewater when their boat capsized. If she had not, much of the record of the first year of the expedition would have been lost to history" (U.S. Mint 2010). The heroine Sacagawea is described as the "wife" of the 18th-century French trader Toussaint Charbonneau; what is often sidestepped in history books is that Sacagawea was captured, sold into slavery, and then purchased by Charbonneau.

As it became clearer that the colonists of various national origins planned not only to stay in America but also to compete with each other and the natives for land ownership and governance, interpretations of white-native relations and intermarriage began to change. The British, Dutch, French, and Spanish struggled for control and sought various tribes as allies. Many were now seen as adversaries, and reports about the "sexually savage, brave new World" spread throughout Europe and "combined with those of later colonial and American chroniclers to form a general portrait of 'Indian life' as morally and culturally inferior to European and American societies" (Nagel 2003, 67).

Consequences

These changes in attitudes toward Native Americans and, by extension, white-native intermarriage had legal, economic, sociopolitical, and cultural consequences: the racialization of Native Americans; the forced removal and subsequent assimilation attempts; anti-interracial (sometimes called antimiscegenation) laws; and the development of blood quantum as the basis for Native American identification.

White Americans began to see Native Americans as racially as well as socially and culturally different. By the 1820s, "a notion had emerged that there was an essential biological difference between Indians and whites," and thus intermarriage "made many whites recoil in disgust and dismay" (Jacobs 2002, 33). Written accounts began to comment more on skin color, calling the native peoples "redskins," highlighting supposed racial differences between Native Americans and whites. Settlers came to feel it was their duty to protect white women from the alleged savagery of native males. They also felt that it was insulting (and perhaps emasculating) for white women to couple with native men. "A white woman who preferred a 'savage' over one of her own 'blood' upset the supposedly natural racial order, [and] that undermined the image whereby the 'civilized' white conqueror maintained superiority over the 'savage red-skinned' Indian" (Jacobs 2002, 33–34).

It was during this time that captivity narratives—stories in which whites, and in particular white women, were captured by native men—became popular reading. The typical captivity narrative involved an innocent, naive white female colonist kidnapped by a lustful male native, who usually ravished or otherwise assaulted her. As they solidified in the minds of the colonists, these portrayals of Native Americans became justifications for both attacks on various tribes and for laws and policies for forced removal of natives from areas chosen for expansion and settlement.

As the nineteenth century advanced, white Americans voraciously expropriated and exploited the resources of the various tribes in their rage for progress, an expropriation that was soon sanctioned by the U.S. government. In 1830, Congress passed the Indian Removal Act, which called for the forced migration of many of the southern and eastern tribes (in areas now known as Florida, Alabama, and Mississippi, for example), to lands west of the Mississippi River. These migrations were initiated in earnest by the late 1830s and included the infamous "Trail of Tears" of the Cherokee, Chickasaw, Choctaw, Creek, and Seminole tribes of the Southeast, during which thousands died of disease, starvation, and exposure. Unfortunately, settlers frequently were able to compel Native Americans to continue to move to new lands by seizing or driving away food sources (such as the buffalo, vital to the lives of the Plains tribes); at the time of European invasion and settlement, the number of Native Americans is estimated to have been between 1 million and 10 million. By 1800, due to disease, malnutrition, and extermination, that figure was about 600,000; and by 1850, it had shrunk to 250,000.

Following the American Civil War (1861–1865), a movement of white "reformers" emerged with the objective of righting the wrongs that had been inflicted upon Native Americans. They felt Native Americans could be "civilized" through assimilation efforts, including intermarriage. In the past, "mixed-bloods" had been able to act as cultural brokers between Anglo-European and tribal entities, and some believed that they had been able to do so because they had white blood: "the mixed offspring of Indian-white marriages were applauded by some reformers as superior to 'full-blooded' Indians (if not an improvement of 'pure' whites)" (Nagel 2003, 77). Mixed-bloods, it was felt, could also serve white social, economic and political interests, for example, brokering land deals, particularly after the Dawes Act of 1887 compelled individuals in designated tribes to accept allotted single parcels of land—for which most were unprepared.

Even before social and legal sanctions against interracial unions and intermarriage with Native Americans had surfaced, many Native Americans had begun to intermix not only with whites, but also with African slaves (as discussed below; some estimates claim that between 30 and 70 percent of the present African-American population has some Native-American ancestry). Mixed Native American–African–Anglo-European Americans, sometimes called *triracial isolates* by historians and social scientists, were particularly disturbing to whites. In due course, 14 states passed laws prohibiting white-Native intermarriage.

A final, enduring consequence of the interpretations of white–Native American mixing was the adoption of blood quantum as a basis for determining Native-American identity. Blood quantum is the degree of Native-American ancestry one has, expressed in fractions, such as one-half or one-fourth. Because there was substantial mixing beginning in colonial America, such references to blood quantum were used as early as the seventeenth century. Expressions, including quadroon (one-quarter African or "black" blood) or octoroon (one-eighth black blood), were used to determine whether one was free or slave, and defined his or her social status. For Native Americans, blood quantum became crucial in how the U.S. government administered its Indian-related policies.

The Indian Reorganization Act in 1934 turned management of land parcels over to tribes and made the latter largely self-governing. However, according to policies enacted by the Bureau of Indian Affairs, tribal membership was based upon having a particular percentage of Native-American blood. If not recognized as an enrolled tribal member, one could be deemed ineligible for federal resources and services; this means of determining tribal membership and benefit eligibility remains in effect today. While blood quantum was an externally imposed concept, it has been internalized by many Native Americans as a gauge of indigenous identity, rejected by many others, and remains the source of much dispute.

Involuntary Immigrants: African Slaves

Opportunity Structures

By the time that Columbus left Spain in search of India in 1492, Europeans had been enslaving Africans for nearly a century. Whereas European and British immigrants had little prior knowledge of indigenous American populations, their attitudes toward and treatment of Africans were well ingrained. When they came to the "New World," they brought their feelings of superiority over Africans with them; early on, this belief in superiority was associated with skin color, with race. They associated Africans, and blackness, with savagery, primitivism, and sexual insatiability.

The first Africans in what became the United States arrived in Virginia in 1619. Theirs was forced immigration. They were taken from different tribes and cultures, mostly from western Africa. Initially, the legal status of Africans in the colonies was not clearly defined, as some were indentured servants with anticipated rights to freedom after fulfilling contractual obligations. "[D]emography, social structure, and [w]hite people's images of Africans combined to produce a relatively high degree of interracial mating in the early colonial decades," at least some of which was consensual (Spickard 1989, 236). Some early white-black marriages have been documented, although informal unions were much more common. Indeed, a number of historians, most notably Winthrop Jordan, point out that there was proportionately more interracial mating in the colonial era than at any other time in American history (Spickard 1989, 237).

But the increasing need for labor, coupled with Anglo-European attitudes about blackness, soon led colonists to seek out permanent slaves. Beginning in the 1660s, the colonies ratified laws regulating slavery. The laws also asserted that slaves were property and thus could be bought, sold, given away, or done away with. Gradually, "consistent assertions of African savagery rendered them barely human in the European racial cosmology, and thus in possession of none of the rights reserved for civilized Christians" (Nagel 2003, 96).

The shift from servant to slave solidified negative attitudes—at least, publicly—toward interracial unions. Within a rather short period of time, black-white relationships were prohibited by law in most of the colonies, and transgressions carried severe penalties. By 1750, all of the southern colonies as well as Massachusetts and Pennsylvania had made interracial marriages illegal, and most made cohabitation illegal as well. Yet slaves were subject to the whims of their white masters, and these included the masters' sexual desires.

Beliefs about Africans' supposed hypersexuality had made their way into European thinking long before they landed in the New World, and thus, it is not surprising sexual contact with the Africans they brought with them was attributed to this. As with Native American women, perhaps white men were accommodating African women by having sexual relations with them. Slave owners and traders appealed to potential buyers by portraying African women as highly lascivious, and these characterizations provided masters with a "rationale" for the continued sexual violations of slave women.

At least 12 million Africans were shipped from Africa across the Atlantic Ocean—the notorious "Middle Passage"—primarily to colonies in North America, South America, and the West Indies. Of note is that while importation of slaves was outlawed by the United States in 1808, the reproduction of slaves was not. In addition to the prosperous domestic slave trade, "for the next fifty-seven years until slavery was ended in 1865 with the passage of the 13th Amendment to the U.S. Constitution, a slave owner's holdings could only be increased by 'breeding' slaves" (Nagel 2003, 106). Not surprisingly, the numbers of mixed race offspring multiplied exponentially in the antebellum years.

Interpretations of Interracial Unions

As with white-Native mixing, white male–black female mixing was initially tolerated or ignored by the larger (white) society, even though much of the sexual contact was unwelcomed by and abusive to the women involved. The existence of mixed-race children from these unions was to provide an increasing inventory of slaves; however, initially this was problematic because customary colonial law provided that the status (free or slave) of a child was determined by his or her father. Slave laws or "codes" reversed this: according to the codes, the children of slave women were slaves for life, their (free) white fathers notwithstanding. There were parallel codes that made the mixed-race children of white women and black slave men slaves as well. These children, known at the time by such varying terms as *mulatto*, could bring a higher price at the slave market, particularly if lighter-skinned. Some multiracial individuals, especially young females, were sold specifically to

serve as concubines. Known colloquially as "fancy girls," they were "auctioned off at 'quadroon balls' held regularly in New Orleans and Charleston," for example (Russell, Wilson, and Hall 1992, 18).

Some slave owners believed mixed-race slaves were more intelligent and capable than "pure" Africans. This had positive (given the overall circumstances) effects, as they were often given tasks requiring greater responsibility and/or skills, and indoor or less physically grueling assignments; it also had horrific ramifications, as the masters often subjected mixed female slaves they found particularly beautiful to their sexual advances. Additionally, resentful of their husbands' attraction to black and mixed females, some white female mistresses retaliated against them and their children with excessive punishment (particularly if they bore physical resemblance to the husbands).

Notably, it was much less acceptable for white women to mix and mate with black men, and, consequently, the interracial children of those unions occupied different yet still precarious places in the social order. "[W]hite women's mulatto children disrupted the patriarchy," as "mulattoes in the slave quarters were an economic asset, in the form of slave property, but a racially mixed child in the 'big house' created havoc and shame" (Russell, Wilson, and Hall 1992, 22). White women were chastised and disciplined for interracial unions, but often the responsibility for their transgressions was laid upon black men: If there were mixed-race children of white women and black men, it was assume that they must have been conceived through forced sexual contact. Hyperbolic accounts of black men's sexual prowess and insatiability circulated throughout the colonies and emasculated and threatened white males' control over "their" women. "[T]he conjunction of a supposedly violent Black nature and an alleged lust for White women was easily translated into a White preoccupation with rape" (Spickard 1989, 254). Consequently, black men who were sexually involved with white women were whipped, castrated, or murdered for defiling "the sanctity of white womanhood" (Russell, Wilson, and Hall 1992, 22–23). Amongst slaves themselves, multiracial children could be viewed with envy, resentment, or pity—or all three.

In some areas of the country, moreover, there were multiracial people who were not slaves but free-persons who occupied a middle tier between slaves and whites. In Charleston, South Carolina, and New Orleans, for example, multiracial persons formed their own communities, churches, clubs, and so forth. Multiracial individuals, who often had some schooling or training, "filled interstitial economic roles, particularly in the artisan, manual, and skilled trades, for which there were insufficient numbers of Whites" (Daniel 1992, 103). On one hand, members of this "mulatto elite" were sometimes accused of thinking themselves smarter, more attractive, or more astute than "pure" or darker-skinned blacks; on the other hand, while often not enslaved, they were treated as second-class citizens by whites. Theirs was an unstable existence that would become even more so after the Civil War.

The varied interpretations of mixed-race individuals were reflected in the contemporary literature. In the nineteenth century, stories and novels emerged with light-skinned black heroines, tormented by their racial duality, nearly all of whom came to tragic ends (such characters became known as the "tragic mulatta"). Some suggest that these stories can be interpreted in different ways: one interpretation holds that stories with multiracial characters served to "acknowledge the unsavory history of plantation rape; but the mulatta heroines had to die tragically, lest the stories appear to sanction miscegenation"; a second interpretation contends that "the mulatta represented the vanguard of a fully integrated society, and stories about her tragic downfall might have helped soothe White anxieties about unchecked mixing of the races" (Russell, Wilson, and Hall 1992, 136).

Many Americans struggled with the fact that slavery was incongruent with the ideals upon which the United States was founded. It was argued that the "[r]evered pillars of American political creed and social life, such as the principles of liberty, equality, and the pursuit of happiness, were rendered counterfeit and cynical in the face of slavery's unending misery, forced labor, and lifelong intergenerational servitude" (Nagel 2003, 99). This is not to say that white Americans considered or even wanted to consider blacks social equals (indeed, Abraham Lincoln's

detractors charged him in the 1864 presidential campaign with promoting the "mongrelization" of the races). However, they did admit that slavery was unacceptable in a country built on freedom and independence, and took steps to eradicate it. With the ratification of the Thirteenth Amendment to the U.S. Constitution in 1865, slavery was abolished.

Consequences

The legal and political changes anticipated for African Americans (whether "pure" or "mixed") in the aftermath of the Civil War and Reconstruction did not affect corresponding social changes, particularly with regard to intermarriage. In fact, they arguably strengthened social disparagement of, and sanctions against, interracial relations and unions, and multiracial people. This section discusses the following consequences: the development of the "one-drop" rule, the resurgence and strengthening of anti-interracial union (antimiscegenation) laws, and the emergence of what has been called "racialist pseudoscience" (Spickard 2010, 10).

After several generations of interracial mixing, it became clearer that phenotypical markers (e.g., skin color) were not sufficient to indisputably determine one's race. Complicating the issue were the existence of white–black–Native Americans, particularly in the Southeast, who, for example, might identify as white based upon physical appearance, Native American based upon blood quantum, or black based upon family history. This distressed whites, because "whiteness" and "blackness" were diametrical opposites: civilized and savage, moral and immoral, superior and inferior. Questions loomed: could a black person's blood become diluted enough such that the person "became" white? If an individual developed the skills necessary to function in a white world, could she or he live as a white person? The fear of contamination of whiteness and of the possible loss of white privilege led to what is known as the rule of hypodescent, or the "one-drop" rule: the conviction that if an individual had "one drop" of black blood from an African ancestor, no matter how distant, that individual was black. At the turn of the twentieth century, the African-American educator Booker T. Washington remarked:

"It is a fact that, if a person is known to have one percent of African blood in his veins, he ceases to be a white man. The ninety-nine percent of Caucasian blood does not weigh by the side of the one percent of African blood. The white blood counts for nothing. The person is a Negro every time" (Cruz and Berson 2001). The intermediate "mulatto elites" in most places suddenly became black. Or white.

The economy of the American South had been severely weakened during the Civil War and Reconstruction, leaving little business or employment opportunities for anyone, particularly blacks, whose new federal freedoms and constitutional guarantees were often thwarted at state and local levels. Former slaves unwittingly found themselves in competition with whites for food, shelter, and other resources. Resentment and rage manifested themselves in violence, particularly in the southern states, and while the Fourteenth Amendment guaranteed blacks equal protection under the law, much of the violence went unpunished. Furthermore, while slavery was no longer lawful, many southern states tried to reinstitute control over blacks through a series of policies and codes. They established curfews, for example, requiring that blacks have written permits to walk outside in the evenings or risk fines or imprisonment. Legislatures drafted measured that would limit African Americans' access to public facilities, such as street cars, waiting rooms, water fountains, and public restrooms.

While the Fifteenth Amendment was a move toward guaranteeing African Americans the right to vote (by prohibiting the use of prior enslavement and race as barriers to their right to vote), states established requirements for voting that essentially eliminated black participation, such as poll taxes, literacy tests, and proof of property ownership. Moreover, even the federal government's commitment to equality for blacks eroded, as exemplified by the Supreme Court's decision in the *Plessy v. Ferguson* case in 1896. In *Plessy*, the court upheld that segregated facilities—"separate but equal"—were not unconstitutional. Because of the one-drop rule, multiracial individuals who were categorized as black (with such categorization dependent upon the judgment of the person or responsible organization) were subject to the black codes and other injustices.

This fervent eagerness to keep blacks and whites apart, of course, extended to intimate interracial relations. The antimiscegenation laws in the Reconstruction years and beyond were distinct from those of the colonial and early antebellum period, however. While the structures (laws) banning interracial marriage were established beginning in the 1660s, racial mixing was seen to be more or less inevitable, although frowned upon, either because, it was said, white men could not help themselves (recall the licentiousness of African women), or because white women fell prey to the savagery of African men. The bans on intermarriage during this period were established so that black-white *marriage* was not legitimate. Interracial marriage "reflected an assumption that the two parties were social equals; this the slave regime could not tolerate." Hence extramarital affairs and concubinage with black women were tolerated by the dominant society, and while "the official ideology [was] that interracial sex was bad, most White men received only mild public censure for crossing the color line" (Spickard 1989, 245). (Besides, the offspring of such unions supplied additional slaves.)

In the years after the Civil War, however, it became increasingly important to whites that the "color line" not be crossed. Blacks were now legally free but by no means socially equal. By 1875, there were almost as many antimiscegenation laws in force in northern states (Maine, Delaware, Illinois, Indiana, Michigan, and Ohio) as in southern ones—and most western states, including California, had such laws as well. State and federal courts consistently upheld challenges to antimiscegenation laws, often with the added defense twist that interracial sexual relations were "unnatural," and produced "unnatural" offspring. In 1869, for example, a judge in Georgia prevented the marriage of a white man and a black woman, stating that "the amalgamation of the races is not only unnatural but is always productive of deplorable results. Our daily observations show us that the offspring of these unnatural connections are generally sick and effeminate" (*Scott v. State*, 39 Ga. 321 [1869]). Interracial procreation, they asserted, would result in children biologically and intellectually inferior to both parents.

In the late nineteenth and early twentieth centuries, influenced by Darwin's theory of evolution, a "racial science" movement emerged in the United States. White Americans became obsessed with protecting their racial integrity by showing that blacks and other nonwhites were, as proven scientifically, biologically and intellectually inferior. In 1916, for example, a physician and eugenicist named Madison Grant published a volume called *The Passing of the Great Race*, which postulated that humankind could be seen in terms of a hierarchy of different species, in which whites were at the top and blacks at the bottom. According to Grant, interbreeding of species was not only unnatural but would contribute to the degradation and possible extinction of those highest in the hierarchy (Spickard 1989, 284).

An American doctor and anthropologist, Samuel George Morton, attempted to classify human skulls he had collected from around the world to prove that whites were more intelligent than blacks. Morton believed that the larger the interior capacity of the skull, the larger the brain that had been inside it, and the higher the intelligence of the person to whom the brain belonged. Conversely, the smaller the skull, the smaller the brain and the lower the intelligence. Not surprisingly, Morton concluded that whites had larger skulls than other races and thus were more intelligent. The conclusions of Morton, Grant, and other eugenicists affected interracial-relations policies not only for African Americans but also for Native Americans and other "non-white" peoples.

In 1912, Virginia created the Bureau of Vital Statistics to register all births, deaths, and marriages within the state. The head of the bureau was Dr. Walter Plecker, a staunch supporter of eugenics and opponent of interracial marriage. As bureau director, Plecker required that all birth records have a racial description: either white or "colored," with corresponding blood percentages for the latter. These records would be used to determine whether requests for marriage licenses could be granted. Plecker ordered clerks in the bureau to refuse marriage licenses to anyone with any trace of nonwhite blood attempting to marry a white person. Plecker continued his crusade against interracial unions throughout his more than 30-year tenure at the bureau: in 1943, for

example, he issued a letter to bureau clerks identifying surnames he believed belonged to mixed-race families he suspected of trying to "pass" as white. Clerks were to make sure that anyone applying for a license to marry a white person was questioned and his or her birth certificate checked.

The beliefs and attitudes of Morton, Grant, and Plecker are indicative of American society's racialist, "one-drop" thinking of the time. While many of the theories were shown to be false, they nonetheless soon lent themselves to application to additional members of the growing population of the United States, many of whom were new arrivals from around the globe.

Others from Distant Shores: Immigrants from Asia

Opportunity Structures

At the same time that racialist, pseudoscientific thinking was escalating, the United States also experienced a surge in immigration. Whereas immigration has always underpinned American history, early immigration (the involuntary immigration of Africans notwithstanding) was primarily from northern and western Europe, especially Great Britain, France, and Germany. By the end of the nineteenth century, however, the United States was being flooded with immigrants from southern and eastern Europe: Russia, Italy, Austria-Hungary, and Poland, for example. These immigrants are sometimes called "second-wave" (1880–1920) immigrants. Many of them were Catholic or Jewish or Greek Orthodox, arriving in a largely Protestant America. Many also tended to have darker complexions than northern and western Europeans, and there was a growing paranoia that these new immigrants, like African Americans, were inherently alien and intrinsically inassimilable. There was also substantial immigration from Asia, and while southern and eastern Europeans also faced prejudice and resistance by the receiving populace, it was the arrival of, and threat of interracial relationships with, the Asian immigrants and their descendants that were most strongly opposed. The opportunity structures that led to an increased presence of Asians in the United States and subsequent opportunities for interracial relationships included economic aspirations, such the discovery of gold in the western United States and corresponding "gold rush"; the United States' desire to become a world power in the twentieth century; and changes in immigration policies.

This chapter has primarily considered the colonization and settlement of the northern, southern, and eastern regions of the United States. Yet much of the American experience is tied to the frontier. The areas west of the Mississippi River represented freedom, opportunity, and the prospect of riches. In 1848, gold was found in California, which led to a "gold rush," a massive migration both within the United States and from abroad. Among those who made the journey were ingot-seekers from Asia, primarily from China. Most of the Asian immigrants were young Chinese males, hoping to find work in the gold mines, earn money, and return to China within a few years. By the 1860s, there were more than 50,000 Chinese in the United States, primarily in California, and as their numbers grew, so did racist sentiment against them. Chinese were beaten, robbed, and murdered. They had little recourse, however, since an 1849 law had provided that "no Black, or mulatto person, or Indian, shall be allowed to give evidence in favor of, or against a white man"; the California Supreme Court ruled that the Chinese, as "non-whites," were included within this prohibition (Kitano 1991, 194).

Exacerbating anti-Chinese sentiment was that after the gold rush abated, rather than returning to China, the mostly male Chinese settled in the United States and, perhaps not surprisingly, began to look for potential partners and spouses. As the numbers of Chinese females were quite low, especially following the 1882 Chinese Exclusion Act, the men sought wives of other backgrounds (in 1890, there were only 3,868 Chinese women among 103,620 Chinese males in the United States). Laws barring "Mongolians" (as Chinese and other Asians were categorized) from marrying white Americans soon surfaced throughout the country.

After the Chinese Exclusion Act, immigration from other areas of Asia continued, primarily from Japan. The Japanese also came in search of jobs, primarily in the agricultural sectors in Hawai'i and California. In 1900, there were approximately 25,000 Japanese on the West Coast, and by 1920, more than 110,000. While culturally distinct from the Chinese, the Japanese were lumped together with them by most white Americans. The nativist attitudes and policies aimed at the Chinese were likewise refocused on the Japanese. Not unexpectedly, the first (*Issei*) generation of Japanese did not frequently intermarry. While President Theodore Roosevelt had made a "Gentleman's Agreement" with Japan restricting Japanese immigration in 1907, the agreement did not apply to Japanese women. Thus, Japanese males in the United States were able to have their wives join them, or to write to relatives to find them prospective wives in Japan.

The Immigration Act of 1924 (interestingly, passed in the same year as Virginia's Racial Integrity Act) set quotas that limited annual immigration from particular countries. The quota allocated immigration visas to 2 percent of the total number of foreign-born persons of each European nationality in the United States as of the 1890 national census, but almost completely excluded immigrants from Asia. The act included a provision barring entry by any alien who was ineligible for eventual American citizenship, and naturalization laws dating from 1790 excluded Asians from becoming citizens. The exclusion acts essentially halted immigration from China until their repeal in December 1943; in 1946, the right to immigrate and to acquire citizenship was extended to Filipinos and Asian Indians and to the Japanese and all others in 1952.

Not initially excluded by the Immigration Act of 1924, however, were immigrants from the Philippines. The United States had been watching very carefully as European nations had ventured into Africa and Asia in a scramble for empire. The United States, too, wanted to be perceived as a world power, and thus began looking beyond its borders as well. In 1898, the United States seized the Philippine archipelago in a war with the Spanish. The Filipinos became "nationals" from an American colony, and as such did not, for some three decades, face the same restrictions on immigration as did other Asians. Because they were American nationals and were associated with a new category of migrants—Malays—Filipinos could at first marry as they wished.

Depending upon the region of the country in which they lived, they intermarried frequently with white, Native-American, African-American, Latina, and Pacific-Islander women. During the 1930s, numerous state legislatures amended their antimiscegenation laws to include Malays.

Unfortunately, anti-Asian sentiment plagued the Filipino community. In the Philippines, Americans had viewed Filipinos as childlike and dependent—a notion that did not contribute to their acceptance in the United States, as Americans already felt Asians were "taking" jobs and other resources away from white Americans. Filipino males were stereotyped as dirty, unsophisticated, prone to commit crimes, and eager to mix and mate with white women. Nativists were particularly suspect of Filipino social clubs where men gathered; these clubs sponsored dances in which most of the female dance partners were white. Suspicion about Filipino men's motives often culminated in anti-Filipino protests and even violence: in 1930 in Watsonville, California, for example, 400 white men attacked a Filipino dance hall, beat many of the Filipino males, and shot one to death. Not surprisingly, Filipinos were soon added to the list of those who by law were not allowed to intermarry or even have sexual relations with whites. Sometimes grouped as "Mongolian," the "Malay" category also emerged to encompass Filipinos and was added to many anti-interracial laws (Barkan 2007, 274), such as the following 1912 Nevada Revised Law: "If any white person with any person shall live and cohabit with any black person, mulatto, Indian, or any person of the Malay or brown race or of the Mongolian or yellow race, in a state of fornication, such person so offending shall, on conviction thereof, be fined in any sum not exceeding five hundred dollars, and not less than one hundred dollars, or be imprisoned in the county jail not less than six months or more than one year, or both" (sec. 6517). Hostilities worsened until the Tydings-McDuffie Act of 1934 placed restrictions on Filipino immigration.

After World War II, Asians began to arrive in the United States again, and the demographics of the Asian immigrant population began to change. When World War II ended, thousands of American GIs were stationed in the newly defeated Japan, thousands more in Korea during the war of 1950–1953. Furthermore, while the United States promised to grant the Philippines their independence in 1946, the United States insisted on maintaining a military presence in the country, with its major bases at Subic Naval Base and Clark Air Force Base. The wars in Southeast Asia beginning in the 1960s led to the presence of troops in Thailand, Cambodia, and Vietnam over the next several decades as well. While abroad, the soldiers often met women who would become their girlfriends and wives in the service industries that sprang up around the American military bases. These industries were both ordinary (such as housekeeping and nursing) and gratuitous (such as bar dancing and prostitution).

Interpretations of Interracial Unions

Beginning with the War Brides Act of 1945, American GIs were allowed to marry and bring their wives back to the United States, and the McCarran-Walter (Immigration and Nationality Act) of 1952 overturned many of the United States' exclusionary policies that had banned immigrants from Asia. These opportunity structures reversed the trend of mostly male immigration from Asia to mostly female; between 1945 and 1952, for example, approximately 80 percent of Japanese immigrants were female, as were 70 percent of Korean immigrants. Filipinas, moreover, made up 71 percent of all immigrants from the Philippines between 1951 and 1960 (Singh 2010, 90).

The immigration of Asian women resulted in thousands of Asian-white and Asian-black (as well as Asian-Asian) offspring. The attitudes of white Americans toward interracial unions and marriages with immigrants from Asia are reflected in many antimiscegenation laws, such as those outlined above. For some time, they had also been reflected in the popular media of the time. Newspapers had often carried unflattering stories about Asian immigrants, and as with Native Americans and African Americans, popular literature also manifested the fears and anger of anti-Asian groups and individuals. In the 1930s, for example, writers and filmmakers created evil, malevolent Asian male characters, along the lines of Dr. Fu Manchu, "a diabolical genius bent on destroying Western civilization and compromising the virtue of

White womanhood" (Spickard 1989, 37). (Fu Manchu himself was created by British author Sax Rohmer, but a host of similar American characters soon followed.) Interracial relations between evil Fu Manchu–type male characters and white women were forbidden, lest they create hybrid degenerate offspring.

An alternative to the evil Fu Manchu emerged in the Charlie Chan character, popular throughout the 1930s and 1940s. While Charlie Chan was portrayed as a very intelligent detective (often spewing wise, cleverly worded proverbs), he was also "sexless, even effeminate" (Spickard 1989, 37). This stereotype of the smart yet definitely unsexy Asian male persisted for decades.

Asian and Asian-American females were usually typecast in one of two ways: one role was that of the docile, proper, subservient, self-sacrificing wife; the other was the exotic, erotic, sometimes oversexed (or at least, very eager to please), beautiful consort. Sometimes they were presented as a combination of both. Mixed-race ("Eurasian") women were deemed especially beautiful and sexy. Such female characters became particularly popular after World War II, when the American military presence in Asia was most pronounced. One of the best known is James Michener's *Tales of the South Pacific*—both the novel (first published in 1947) and its theatrical and screen productions—which takes place on an island occupied by the Americans battling the Japanese and in which interracial sexual relations and biracial children are introduced. It is perhaps not surprising that white women became major proponents of antimiscegenation laws during this time.

Consequences

The American military presence in countries around the globe is a controversial topic indeed. On the one hand, there is the strategic counsel, the direct combat assistance, and the economic boosts to members of the local population. On the other hand, this presence often brings with it an invasion of American culture, products, and ideas, and it is undeniable that service members often become the customer base for sexual recreation in the areas around military bases. In countries in which the majority of inhabitants are considered racially different from the American majority, this presence takes on an added dimension. In Asia, for example, the bars, clubs, and brothels around military bases "are ethnosexual sites where Western fantasies of Asian female sexuality meet material manifestations of Asian women, and where the marriage of geopolitics and racial cosmologies is consummated nightly" (Nagel 2003, 179). While certainly not all relationships between white military men and Asian women are based upon such fantasies, there is a certain "boys will be boys" attitude in the armed services—in many ways similar to the attitude toward white men who had sexual liaisons with Native Americans and African Americans—that seems to be tolerated, if not encouraged. The "exotic erotic" stereotype certainly played into Americans' behavior during the U.S. involvement in the Vietnam War.

The musical *Miss Saigon*, which has been performed on Broadway since 1991, tells the story of Chris, an American soldier in Vietnam. While there, he meets and begins a relationship with Kim, a young Vietnamese girl he meets in one of the many bars in Saigon. As in reality, however, Saigon falls, and Chris returns to the United States, leaving her, and, unbeknownst to him, their unborn child, behind. She is left to raise their multiracial child alone for years in a country that abhors "half-breed" children. Eventually, Chris finds out he has a child (named Tam) and goes to find them; but back in the United States, he has married an American woman, named Ellen. Upon finding this out, Kim commits suicide. Her hope is that Chris and Ellen will take Tam back to the United States to raise him.

Like the fictional Tam, by the end of the Vietnam War in 1975, more than 30,000 American-Vietnamese (sometimes called "Amerasian") children were living in Vietnam. Their experiences were "largely traumatic and dehumanizing" (Valverde 1992, 146). Left behind in a highly patriarchal culture without fathers (a Vietnamese proverb states that "a child without a father is like a house without a roof"), and sometimes abandoned by their disgraced mothers, Vietnamese Amerasians felt rootless and reviled. Those whose fathers were black Americans were particularly discriminated against, as the colorism described in this chapter exists within Asian communities as well. They were called *bui doi*, which means "dust of life," indicating their bleak circumstances. Some American fathers, like the fictional Chris, returned to Vietnam upon learning they had children with Vietnamese women. Others denied their relationships and rejected the children.

In 1980, Congress passed the Refugee Act of 1980, which opened different areas of the country to the resettlement of refugees from Cambodia, Vietnam, and Laos. As a result, tens of thousands of Southeast Asians arrived throughout the 1980s. In October 1982, Congress passed the Amerasian Act, which allowed children in Korea, Vietnam, Laos, Cambodia (Kampuchea), and Thailand born before October 22, 1982, and known to have been fathered by U.S. citizens to immigrate to the United States. However, their mothers were not allowed to immigrate with them; they had to sign "irrevocable releases." (One interpretation of this omission is that it reflects general attitudes toward Asian women as sexual objects to be used for pleasure by men who have no further accountability.) Furthermore, the Amerasians had to provide evidence of American paternity, such as marriage licenses, birth certificates, letters, or photos from their fathers. These documents, if they existed, were difficult to come by, and the application process was difficult to understand and tedious. Only a fraction of the many Amerasians actually immigrated. The December 1987 Amerasian Homecoming Act (also referred to as the Amerasian [Vietnam] Act) allowed more Amerasians to emigrate from Vietnam, with provisions that allowed immediate family members to accompany them but, unfortunately, did not adequately prepare them for their arrival. Moreover, some in Vietnam, seeing opportunities to get to the United States, pretended to be the parents or relatives of the Amerasian children.

Married for seven months, a woman from Vietnam and her husband, from the U.S., sit outside their home in Houston in 2010. They are part of a trend of inter-ethnic marriage. (AP Photo/Michael Stravato)

"[I]ronically, the 'dust of life' (*bui doi*) became valuable commodities to be prized as the 'gold children' (*con van*)" (Valverde 1992, 153).

The consequences for Asian multiracial children in the United States have varied. Some have been embraced by their fathers or by adoptive parents. Some have been verbally abused and discriminated against because it is assumed that their mothers were necessarily prostitutes, sustaining one of the stereotypes about Asian women. Furthermore, acknowledging the children is to acknowledge the behavior of American men abroad, for it is one thing to close one's eyes to a situation and quite another to disclose it publicly. Others wish to distance themselves from Amerasians because, as relatively new Americans (large numbers of refugees from Southeast Asia began arriving in the 1970s), they feel disgraced by their association with "bar girls," and feel that such association will prevent Southeast Asians in general from being fully accepted as Americans.

This segment is best summarized in the words of Joanne Nagel: "The drama of sex and war is not restricted to combat theatres. The post–World War II period with its economic competition and superpower geopolitical rivalry produced a massive military-sexual complex to feed its large-scale manpower's equally large-scale sexual appetites" (Nagel 2003, 193).

LaRaza Cosmica: Hispanic/Latino Americans

Opportunity Structures

While colonial-era English and French explorers focused their efforts in eastern and northern areas of the New World, and postrevolutionary Americans later moved westward to fulfill their destiny of expanding American frontiers all the way to the Pacific Ocean, their Spanish counterparts flourished in the south and southwest, including (but not limited to) modern-day New Mexico, Texas, Florida, California, and Mexico, as well as the Caribbean, including Cuba and Puerto Rico, and *mesoamerica*, or Central America. The Spanish mixed rather openly with the indigenous populations they encountered, without legal

proscriptions. It was noted, above, that a Spanish law passed in 1514 explicitly permitted intermarriage of Spanish colonists with indigenous natives. This is not to say that the Spanish considered the native peoples to be their equals; certainly not, as evidenced by the fact that they enslaved many of them. They also imported slaves, mostly Spanish Muslims (Arabs, Berbers, and Moors) and *ladinos*, blacks who had been slaves in Spain or other Spanish colonies prior to arrival in newly settled areas. These various groups also mixed with the indigenous populations and colonists, and, as a result, the Spanish-settled societies were (and remain) multiracial, with "elaborate racial taxonomies" that did not correspond to, or fit in with, the binary "one-drop" system of the country that would come to annex many of them.

This section provides a brief history of the opportunity structures that brought Mexicans and Puerto Ricans to the United States, where they are now the two largest "Hispanic" groups in the United States as identified by the 2000 U.S. census. As such, it is intended to provide a snapshot and not a complete picture of Hispanics. However, it does provide an example of the experiences of both Mexican Hispanics and what have been called Caribbean Hispanics. Moreover, in addition to being the largest Hispanic populations in the United States, both of their histories as peoples who have intermixed and intermarried for centuries makes them compelling examples of the complexities of Hispanic/Latino identity.

Mexican Americans

In 1821, Mexico, which at the time included large areas of California, Texas, New Mexico, and Arizona, declared its independence from Spain. Following this declaration, Mexicans (a national designation that collectively included "pure" Spaniards, indigenous natives, and persons of mixed heritage, or *mestizos*) offered *norteamericanos* (North Americans) land and livestock to establish settlements in the south and southwest. The populations of *norteamericanos* thereby increased significantly. Despite the Mexicans' generosity, however, within two decades, *norteamericanos* in parts of Texas and California (independently of each other) challenged Mexican authority in the regions and declared their autonomy from Mexico. These actions led to war between the United States and Mexico in 1846, concluding with the defeat of Mexican military forces in 1848. Through the Treaty of Guadalupe Hidalgo, signed in 1848, Mexico ceded much of its northern territory (today the U.S. Southwest). Nonetheless, the Mexican-ancestry populations of these areas remained high, and migration across the newly formed American borders with Mexico continued in both directions. Several factors would soon cause immigration into the United States to increase. First, in 1910, revolution in Mexico pushed thousands of Mexicans to flee spreading violence and social chaos.

Second, since much of the Asian labor flow had been staunched by the Chinese Exclusion Act of 1882, the Gentleman's Agreement of 1907, and the Immigration Act of 1924, American employers were in search of another source of inexpensive labor. Initially, they readily welcomed Mexican immigrants to fill such jobs. As has been evident in the twenty-first century as well, the state of the American economy has generally been the primary barometer for the degree to which Mexican immigrants have been welcomed or shunned in this country. For example, during the Great Depression of the 1930s, when jobs were scarce, Mexicans came to be seen as interlopers whose objectives were to take those jobs from "real" Americans. As a result, the United States established a repatriation program that sent approximately 1.0 to 1.5 million Mexicans back to Mexico. During the recession after the Korean War, the government launched "Operation Wetback" ("wetback" is a derogatory slang term for Mexican immigrants), which apprehended and deported perhaps as many as one million persons in 1954–1955.

When President Lyndon Johnson signed the Immigration and Nationality Act in 1965, he did not expect it to have the impact that it did. As mentioned, the central purpose of the act was to reunite families; as such, it was responsible for a tremendous surge in immigration in the last third of the twentieth century. The unintended result of the act was that it created an opportunity structure for a strong immigration flow from countries in Asia and Latin America.

Traditionally, the Hispanic family is a close-knit group and the most important social unit, with the term *familia* usually representing more than the nuclear family. Individuals within the *familia* have a moral responsibility to aid other members of the family—hence the journey of individuals to the United States in search of employment to raise money to send back home. As many U.S. citizens and permanent residents of Mexican heritage were already in the United States, the law offered opportunities for them to further help their families by sponsoring them. The surge in migration of Mexicans made them much more visible, and also led to a resurgence of the nativist fear of the "browning" of America.

Puerto Ricans

In addition to acquiring the Philippines in the Spanish-American War that ended in 1898, the United States also took control of Puerto Rico. As in Mexico, the Spanish had mixed with the indigenous peoples there and also, as in Mexico, had brought African slaves with them. Moreover, Chinese labor was introduced to Puerto Rico in the nineteenth century, and while they were less likely to socialize and intermarry, some interracial mixing did occur. Moreover, there were also significant populations of French and Italians there, and more recently, Cubans. Thus the people of Puerto Rico are racially mixed as well. The United States was not willing to relinquish such a strategically important and economically viable asset, although in 1917, the Jones Act made Puerto Ricans U.S. citizens. In 1952, the island became completely self-governing as the Commonwealth of Puerto Rico while maintaining voluntary association with the United States.

Migration of Puerto Ricans to the United States began in the nineteenth century, with many traveling not to Florida or Texas but to New York City. The numbers of migrants increased significantly after the Jones Act, and by 1930, more than 50,000 Puerto Ricans lived on the U.S. mainland, mostly in East Harlem, which became known as Spanish Harlem. Another exodus occurred during the economic boom that occurred after World War II, and, according to the U.S. census, by 1960, Puerto Ricans numbered nearly

900,000; by 1970, nearly 1.5 million (including both first and second generations); and by 2000, 3.4 million. Some estimates suggest that more than half of all Puerto Ricans live outside of Puerto Rico, mostly on the mainland and in Hawai'i.

The Hispanic population as a whole has grown faster than the total U.S. population in recent decades and now comprises the largest nonwhite minority group. In 2000, almost 13 percent of the population reported a Hispanic origin, for a total Hispanic population of 35,238,481. In addition to Mexicans and Puerto Ricans, there are also Hispanics from Central and South America as well as other Caribbean countries, including the Dominican Republic and Cuba. The U.S. Census Bureau projects that by 2020, the Hispanic population will be almost one-sixth (17 percent) of the total population (Ramirez 2004, 1).

Interpretations of Interracial Unions

The United States has struggled with how to identify immigrants from Mexico, Puerto Rico, Latin America, and South America for some time. If it could not be determined what "race" someone was, how could it be determined whether or not a relationship (an informal union or formal marriage) was interracial? After the Mexican-American War, for example, there was great debate at the 1849 California Constitutional Convention over how to designate the (racial) status of Mexicans in the soon-to-be state. It was determined that Mexicans would be deemed "white" for legal purposes, a status denied to Native Americans, Asian Americans, and African Americans. As a result, Mexicans were exempt from some nineteenth-century miscegenation laws: between 1860 and 1870, for example, approximately 35 percent of Mexican-American marriages in Los Angeles were with "Anglos." Some historians assert that Mexican Americans were perceived as much closer culturally to European-American immigrants, based upon their mixed European ancestry, use of a Romance language (Spanish) as the national language, large-scale conversion to Catholicism, and reports of advanced ancient societies such as the Mayans.

The complex histories of Hispanics' home countries have led to various complex ethno-racial

taxonomy structures. While an exhaustive listing of the various descriptive terms cannot be included here, some of the most commonly used are: *mestizo* (mixed), *indio* (bronze-colored or with indigenous features), *blanco* (white), *cafe con leche* (skin the color of coffee with milk), *moreno* (dark-skinned), *negro* (black), and *mulato* (mixed white and black). The terms vary from country to country, from region to region within countries, and from individual to individual. This further confuses the binary American taxonomy: for example, some Hispanics are mixed with African slaves and/or their descendants; however, given that there may be only slight phenotypical distinctions that would indicate this ancestry (which might or might not be evident in their Spanish-language designations), are they then "black" in the United States, in keeping with the American "one-drop" rule? This confusion is likewise evident in the attempts of the U.S. Census Bureau to categorize Mexican Americans; in 1950 and 1960, they were placed into a vague category of "Persons of Spanish Mother Tongue"; in 1970, into "Persons of Spanish Surname and Spanish Mother Tongue"; and since 1980, they have comprised the largest percentage of the "Hispanic" ancestry category. (They and other respondents self-identify.)

It is clear that, legal definitions notwithstanding, the Anglo-American majority has not considered Hispanics to be social equals. This does not mean, however, that when multicultural territories such as Puerto Rico became part of the United States, white Americans did not mix, mate, and/or marry with the residents. As Nagel comments, "The American colonial gaze and the behavior of American men toward colonized women suggests that the United States took the lead of its European cousins" (2003, 154).

Yet perhaps because Puerto Rico was now a part of the United States, and its peoples were under the protection of the United States, the view toward Puerto Ricans, especially Puerto Rican females, was slightly different than it had been toward Native American and especially African women. While both men and women in Puerto Rico were viewed as highly sensual "exotic erotics," Puerto Rican women were also viewed as somewhat innocent. They were not "savage" like Africans or some Native Americans; furthermore, since most were Catholic as a result of Spanish missionary efforts, they were alternatively viewed as virtuous.

A telling example of this twofold white-American view of Puerto Ricans appeared in Turnbull White's book entitled *Our New Possessions*, written in 1898. The captions and images contained in the book were typical of turn-of-the-century travel books in which Puerto Rico was described as an unfamiliar yet welcoming place, and Puerto Rican women as "comely damsel[s] embracing American ways and welcoming American travelers." The new U.S. territory *and* its people are depicted as "sexually exotic, but safe, wild, but tame, exotic enough to arouse but familiar enough to reassure the eager, but anxious traveler" (Nagel 2003, 155).

A more recent example of the dual view surfaced in *West Side Story*, which first appeared as a stage musical in 1957 and as a film in 1961. Essentially a twentieth-century Romeo and Juliet, *West Side Story* tells of two rival gangs in New York City: the Sharks, a Puerto Rican gang, and the Jets, an Anglo-American gang. Tony, the leader of the Jets, falls in love with Maria, the younger sister of Bernardo, the leader of the Sharks, who is portrayed as a stereotypical hot-tempered and fight-prone Latino. Maria (whose name, not unintentionally, is the same as *La Virgien Maria*, mother of Jesus in the Catholic/Christian tradition) is portrayed as innocent and naive, drawn in by her love of a tough yet kind-hearted American. In contrast, another female character, Anita, who is Bernardo's girlfriend, is depicted as highly sexual as well as boisterous and sharp-tongued. Anita warns Maria about Tony's intentions, telling her to "stick with her own kind." On one hand, the story ends tragically, with both bloodshed and the message that perhaps the differences between the two cultures are insurmountable; on the other hand, Tony and Maria were willing to try to overcome their differences, and perhaps represent hope for such interracial/intercultural relationships.

More often than not, however, interracial relationships between whites and Hispanics/Latinos have caused uneasiness, particularly among those who feel that Hispanics are "taking over" the United States.

Americans' tendency to group Mexicans, Puerto Ricans, Cubans, Chileans, Argentineans, etc., together as "Hispanics" and to conflate Hispanic U.S. citizens and permanent residents with illegal immigrants based upon supposed ethno-racial similarities has led to the belief that Hispanic/Latino Americans are not "true" Americans. Rather, they are believed to be a negative influence: "the public airwaves are filled with concerned voices about the impact that a non-English dominant, Catholic, non-white, largely poor population will have on 'American' identity" (Alcoff 2006, 227). Furthermore, the economic recession that began with the financial crisis of 2007 has pushed many Americans (of all races) to apply for public assistance, albeit unemployment benefits or welfare. The belief that illegal immigrants are consuming these benefits that are meant for "true" Americans is quite pervasive, and has led to increased resentment of Hispanics.

Consequences

One of the paradoxical consequences of the increased immigration of Mexicans, Central Americans, South Americans, and Caribbean Hispanics to the United States is that despite the increasing diversity of national (and ethno-racial) backgrounds, the perception of these groups by most Americans tends to amalgamate them into one, enormous "Hispanic" or "Latino/Latina" grouping. On one hand, since Americans' obsessions with race and racial boundaries have caused so much detriment, perhaps any move toward connecting communities is encouraging. On the other hand, refusal to acknowledge distinctions lends itself to stereotyping, sweeping judgments, and purist ideologies.

The sensibilities to ethnic or ancestral multiplicity by those who have become known as Hispanic or Latino Americans have unquestionably influenced their attitudes toward interracial relationships and marriages. According to a study by the Pew Research Center, for example, white-Hispanic couples accounted for 41 percent of all interethnic marriages in 2008 (Passel et al. 2010, 1).

This is not to say that there is no discrimination in Latino cultures. Lillian Comas-Diaz writes of *racismo*, a racialized concept based upon social class:

"Regardless of color, the higher the person's social class, the whiter the person is perceived to be," and "people can change their color when they change their socioeconomic class" (Comas-Diaz 1996, 172). According to Comas-Diaz, there is the tendency within Hispanic cultures to want to *adelantar o mejorar la raza* (literally, to improve the race). She, of course, does not mean that one's physical skin color can change, although she comments that many persons of color attempt to change theirs to satisfy societal beliefs about beauty. Rather, when a person of color meets or exceeds expectations about being productive, respectable members of society—expectations highly valued by whites—he or she can shift whites' stereotypical perceptions about the racial group of which he or she is a part.

And yet, despite Comas-Diaz's misgivings, it is perhaps serendipitous that Hispanics are the fastest-growing segment of the population in the United States. While Hispanics' taxonomies are imperfect, they do transcend binary thinking and acknowledge that individuals need not be pigeonholed via a white-versus-nonwhite dichotomy. As the numbers of nonbinary thinkers grow, they may persuade American society to adopt systems that yield to diversity, rather than the other way around. It is not only the existence of intermarriage and multiracial/multiethnic children that is important, but also their acknowledgment. David Hollinger comments that "a critical mass of acknowledged mixed-race people heightens the credibility of an ideal according to which individuals decide how tightly or loosely they wish to affiliate with one or more communities of descent" (2000, 165).

Given the neoconservatism of the twenty-first century and the seeming backlash against diversity in modern times, it may not seem likely that the United States will soon entertain the notion of *la raza cosmica* (the global/universal race); however, the breaking down of boundaries is still an admirable aspiration.

Conclusion

On June 12, 1967, in the landmark case *Loving v. Commonwealth of Virginia*, a unanimous ruling by the U.S. Supreme Court struck down Virginia's antimiscegenation statutes and overturned the laws against interracial marriages in the 15 states that had retained them. While *Loving* certainly marks a watershed moment in interracial relations (indeed, June 12 is celebrated by some as "Loving Day"), noting at the end of this chapter, rather than at the beginning, is deliberate.

According to the U.S. Census Bureau, nearly 15 percent (14.6, or nearly 280,000) of all new marriages in the United States in 2008 were between spouses of different races. According to the Pew Research Center, analysis of the 2008 data showed that 9 percent of white, 16 percent of black, 26 percent of Hispanic, and 31 percent of Asian newlywed individuals (within the 12 months before the survey) married someone of a different racial or ethnic group (Passel et al. 2010, 1–2). While these percentages are certainly higher than any other census on record, the analysis seems to suggest that interracial unions and marriages are a new phenomenon, something that has occurred only since *Loving*. But as seen here, this is not the case. People have always mixed; rather, it is the opportunity structures and interpretations of interracial unions that have varied. Throughout American history, interracial unions have been forbidden and permitted, criminalized and legalized, but they, and the offspring of these unions, have always existed. As one notable author explains: "Individuals can have a portfolio of ethnic identities, some of which are more or less salient in various situations and vis-à-vis various audiences. As settings and spectators change, the socially defined array of ethnic options open to us changes: white, Irish, Catholic, black, Nigerian, Muslim, Indian, Navajo. A person's ethnicity is, thus, a matter of structure and power: which ethnic categories are available in a society to be sorted into, and who gets to do the sorting" (Nagel 2003, 42).

Bibliography

Alcoff, Linda Martin. 2006. *Visible Identities: Race, Gender and the Self*. New York: Oxford University Press.

Barkan, Elliott Robert. 2007. *From All Points: America's Immigrant West, 1870s–1952*. Bloomington: Indiana University Press.

Carver, Jonathan. 1778. *Travels through the Interior Parts of North-America, in the Years 1766, 1767 and 1768*. Excerpted from *American History Told by Contemporaries*, Vol. II, 334–36, *Building of the Republic, 1899*, edited by A. B. Hart. New York: MacMillan. http://www.shsu.edu/~his_ncp/Ind1768.html (accessed May 30, 2010).

Comas-Diaz, Lillian. 1996. "LatiNegra: Mental Health Issues of African Latinas." In *The Multiracial Experience: Racial Boundaries as the New Frontier*, edited by Maria P. P. Root, 167–90. Thousand Oaks, CA: Sage Publications.

Cruz, Barbara C., and Michael J. Berson. 2001. "The American Melting Pot? Miscegenation Laws in the United States." *OAH Magazine of History* 15, no. 4 (Summer). Bloomington, IN: Organization of American Historians.

Daniel, G. Reginald. 1992. "Passers and Pluralists: Subverting the Racial Divide." In *Racially Mixed People in America*, edited by Maria P. P. Root, 91–107. Newbury Park, CA: Sage Publications.

Gutierrez, Ramon. 1991. *When Jesus Came, the Corn Mothers Went Away: Marriage, Sexuality, and Power in New Mexico, 1500–1846*. Stanford, CA: Stanford University Press.

Hollinger, David. 2000. *Postethnic America: Beyond Multiculturalism*. Rev. ed. New York: Basic Books.

Jacobs, Margaret D. 2002. "The Eastmans and the Luhans: Interracial Marriage between White Women and Native American Men, 1875–1935." *Frontiers* 23, no. 3: 29–54.

Kalmijn, Matthijs. 1998. "Intermarriage and Homogamy: Causes, Patterns, Trends." *Annual Review of Sociology* 24: 395-421

Kantor, Jodi. 2009. "A Portrait of Change: Nation's Many Faces in Extended First Family." *New York Times*, January 21, Section A, Final Edition, 1.

Kitano, Harry H. L. 1991. *Race Relations*. Englewood Cliffs, NJ: Prentice-Hall.

Lee, Sharon M., and Barry Edmonston. 2005. "New Marriages, New Families: U.S. Racial and Hispanic Intermarriage." *Population Bulletin* 60, no. 2. Washington, DC: Population Reference Bureau.

Nagel, Joanne. 2003. *Race, Ethnicity, and Sexuality: Intimate Intersections, Forbidden Frontiers*. New York: Oxford University Press.

Passel, Jeffrey S., Wendy Wang, and Paul Taylor. 2010. "Marrying Out: One-in-Seven New U.S. Marriages in Interracial or Interethnic." *Pew Research Center Social and Demographic Trends Report*. Washington, DC: Pew Research Center Publications.

Ramirez, Roberto R. 2004. *We the People: Hispanics in the United States*. U.S. Census Special Reports. Washington, DC: U.S. Bureau of the Census.

Root, Maria P. P., ed. 1992. *Racially Mixed People in America*. Newbury Park, CA: Sage Publications.

Russell, Kathy, Midge Wilson, and Ronald Hall. 1992. *The Color Complex: The Politics of Skin Color Among African Americans*. New York: Anchor Books.

Singh, Jaideep. 2010. "War Brides and War Brides Act (1945)." In *Asian American History and Culture: An Encyclopedia*, edited by Huping Ling and Allan Austin, 90–91. Armonk, NY: M. E. Sharpe.

Spickard, Paul R. 1989. *Mixed Blood: Intermarriage and Ethnic Identity in Twentieth-Century America*. Madison: University of Wisconsin Press.

Spickard, Paul R. 2010. "Obama Nation? Race, Multiraciality, and American Identity." Keynote address, Mixed Race in the Age of Obama Conference, Center for the Study of Race, Politics and Culture. University of Chicago, March 5.

U.S. Bureau of the Census. 2001. "The Two or More Races Population: 2000." Census 2000 brief (November). Washington, DC: U.S. Bureau of the Census.

U.S. Mint. 2010. "Sacagawea Golden Dollar Coin." *Coins and Medals*. Washington, DC: U.S. Department of the Treasury. http://www.usmint.gov/mint_programs/golden_dollar_coin/index.cfm?action=sacAbout (accessed May 31, 2010).

Valverde, Kieu-Linh Caroline. 1992. "From Dust to Gold: The Vietnamese Amerasian Experience." In *Racially Mixed People in America*, edited Maria P. P. Root, 144–61. Newbury Park, CA: Sage Publications.

Muslim Society: Life and Integration in the United States, Pre- and Post-9/11

Jackleen M. Salem

Muslims are one of the largest-growing populations in the United States. They have been part of American history since the arrival of the first Muslim slaves who were kidnapped from their homes and transported with other Africans in the transatlantic slave trade, dating back to the fifteenth century. They began to immigrate in the late nineteenth and early twentieth centuries in the Great Migration of the period. Later, President Lyndon B. Johnson's Immigration Act of 1965 would open the gates for large numbers of immigrants from around the world. By the late 1990s, the presence of Muslims in the United States became more prominent in the news media due to political events in the Middle East. But September 11, 2001, would cast a spotlight on Muslims globally and especially in the United States. The terrorism committed on the World Trade Center, the Pentagon, and United Flight 93, which crashed in Shanksville, Pennsylvania, were one of the most horrific crimes of terrorism in the history of mankind. Of the 2,977 victims, the total number of all those innocently killed on September 11, 32 were Muslims.

The events of this day would change life for all Americans, but especially for Muslim Americans. Although the attention to their communities had already begun prior to the catastrophe of 9/11, this event brought an unparalleled level of scrutiny. Everyone wanted to know more about Muslims, Islam, and the communities in their midst. The U.S. government oriented its focus on the Muslims living amongst them by imposing measures that curtailed many of their civil liberties. The USA Patriot Act of 2001 made changes to the U.S. immigration system, financial reporting, and criminal law. It authorized government officials to search homes and businesses without informing the owners. Court orders were no longer needed for wiretaps as well as for accessing e-mails and phone records. Some Muslims in the United States have been detained indefinitely, while others had their homes searched or they were harassed at work. Airports and airlines have been a continued source of racial profiling, with various incidents of Muslims or those thought to be Muslim being specifically targeted. For example, a Secret Service agent named Walid Shater, who was on the detail of President George W. Bush in 2002, was prevented from boarding an American Airlines flight. Communities of Muslims have been interviewed in the government's attempt to assess ties to terrorism. Many Muslims became victims of this new legislation and faced unprecedented challenges to their civil liberties. They entered a whole new era of identity negotiation in terms of American culture, society, and law.

The life of Muslims in the United States during the twenty-first century has grown along the same patterns as other immigrant groups through various levels of assimilation—identificational, educational, occupational, residential, second-language attainment, and intermarriage. Although many Muslims have followed along those patterns to varying degrees, some Muslims still hold strong with their religious identity and have worked to develop organizations and institutions that intertwine their beliefs as Muslims with their identity as Americans. Muslims of various ethnic backgrounds work together towards common goals of helping people to comprehend Islam and Muslims but also providing assistance when global disasters strike—the tsunami of 2004, earthquakes in Haiti and Pakistan—and national issues—Hurricane Katrina, presidential elections, homelessness, poverty, immigration issues, abuses in civil liberties, and other societal issues important to Americans.

Shi'ite and Sunni Muslims have been marked by sectarian violence and religious division in the Middle East and beyond, but they have been making strides in the United States toward working together as Muslims. They have also intermarried with other Americans—Muslims and non-Muslims, Shi'ites and Sunnis, and Arabs and Indians. Another component of vital importance is the role and position of Muslim women. Muslim women defy the stereotype often imposed on them as submissive and passive members of their community by being active individuals of society through family, work, social and economic development. Muslims in the United States are a blend of various ethnicities that seek to carve out their own niche as Muslims and Americans that in some cases still struggle with the push and pull of the cultural norms of their parents, their American identity, and their religion.

Population of Muslims in the United States

The exact number of Muslims in the United States is a debated issue because there are no official ways to tally their numbers. The U.S. Census Bureau does not require its participants to state their religious orientation, nor do mosques and other Islamic organizations take a count of the people who attend their events. In 1959, the Federation of Islamic Associations in America estimated there to be 1.2 million Muslims. The *World Almanac 2001* estimates 5.8 million Muslims in the United States. Researchers at the Hartford Institute for Religious Research believed there to be 6–7 million Muslims. The *2005 Britannica Book of the Year* suggested 4.7 million Muslims. The Pew Research Center concluded that there were 1.4 million Muslims over the age of 18 and 850,000 under the age of 18, for a total of 2.35 million Muslims in the United States. Thus, the numbers are "guestimates" at best, inexact calculations ranging from 2 million to 7 million.

The ethnic makeup of these Muslims in the United States can be divided into the following

groups: South-Central Asian (Indian, Pakistani, and Bangladeshi), 33 percent; African American, 30 percent; Arab (Lebanese, Palestinians, Egyptians, Syrians, Jordanians, Saudi Arabians, and Yemenis), 25 percent; African, 3 percent; Southeast Asia, 2 percent; European, 2 percent; and Iranians, converts, and others, 5 percent. According to the Pew Survey on Muslim Americans in 2007, nearly 65 percent of Muslims in the United States are immigrants and come from 68 different countries. The majority of these immigrants arrived after 1990—33 percent during the 1990s and 28 percent during the first decade of the twenty-first century. In the Pew Survey on Muslim Americans, Muslims cite a variety of motives for coming: 26 percent migrated for education, 24 percent for economic reasons, 24 percent for family, and 20 percent because of the political instability in their home countries. In addition, 35 percent of the Muslim population was born in the United States as second- and third-generation Muslims.

The majority of Muslims in America settled in or near major cities, such as: New York City; Chicago; Los Angeles; Detroit; Houston; Philadelphia; Boston; Dallas; Washington, D.C.; Atlanta; Minneapolis–St. Paul; and Tampa. There are large concentrations of Arab Muslims of Lebanese and Palestinian descent—Shia and Sunni—in Dearborn, Michigan, Iranians in Los Angeles, Sudanese in Minnesota, South Asians—Indians and Pakistanis—in New York City and Chicago, and Turks and Egyptians in New Jersey. There are also pockets of Muslims in smaller cities throughout the United States, such as Cortland, New York; Muncie, Indiana; Winona, Minnesota; Edmond, Oklahoma; and Panama City, Florida. In addition, there are towns with very old Muslim populations, with third- and fourth-generation Muslims, such as Cedar Rapids, Iowa; Lackawanna, New York; Gary, Indiana; Chicago, Illinois; and Dearborn, Michigan.

The majority of American mosques are Sunni, which means they follow the *sunnah* or teachings of the Prophet Muhammad. But, there are also many other important sects of Islam practiced in the United States, including Shiism. The Shia split from Sunni Islam occurred early in Islamic history, when the untimely murder of the third caliph, Uthman ibn Affan, led to a challenge to the authority of

Ali (died in 661 AD)—the fourth caliph in Islamic history, first cousin to the Prophet Muhammad, and married to his daughter, Fatima. The governor of Damascus, Muawiya—a cousin of Uthman—was upset that Ali refused to punish the murderers of Uthman. It caused a pronounced split in the Muslim community and the supporters of Ali were known as *Shi'atu Ali*, which translates as the "party of Ali."

By the eighth century, Shia ideology had developed into a legal framework that believed in the Imamate, which designated the leadership in the Shia community to the imam, who had to have four specific qualifications: descended from the Prophet Muhammad, possessed perfect judgment, was appointed by God, and was a bearer of divine knowledge. Today, there are three major groups of Shia Islam in the United States—the Twelvers, Nizari Ismailis, and Bohra Ismailis—and they number roughly 1.5 million. The Twelver Shiites first arrived in the late nineteenth century as part of the first great wave of migration to the United States from the area under the Ottoman Empire known as Greater Syria, which today includes Syria, Lebanon, Jordan, Israel, Palestine, and parts of Turkey and Iraq. Shiites have migrated for a variety of reasons, but most especially because of the political instability in the Middle East at the time, especially in areas with high Shia populations such as Iran and Iraq. Today, there are Shiites from all parts of the world, including: Lebanon, Iran, Iraq, India, East Africa, Bahrain, and other parts of the Muslim world. The Dearborn/Detroit Shia community is the largest in the United States, with approximately 75,000 members. There are also communities of Shiites in Los Angeles, New York City, Minneapolis, Miami, Seattle, and Orlando.

The relationship between Sunnis and Shiites has been affected by political, social, and religious events overseas. On both Sunni and Shia sides, there is mistrust, skepticism, and fear. In general, Shiites and Sunnis have separate institutions. Shiism is viewed by orthodox Sunnis as heretical because of their ideas concerning Caliph Ali and the Imamate. Shiites distrust Sunnis because of the political and religious persecution they experienced over the centuries in the Middle East. Despite this, Shias and Sunnis are learning to work together in the United States.

The diversity of the Muslim community forces its members to work with people from different sects and ethnic backgrounds. There are many documented cases of Shiites and Sunnis working together for the broader Muslim-American community. For example, the leader of the Islamic Center of America in Dearborn, Michigan, Imam Muhammad J. Chirri was a Shiite from Lebanon who worked alongside Sunnis in the United States to organize and build the Islamic community. In 1959, in an effort to bridge the divide between Sunnis and Shiites worldwide, he also met with the Grand Sheik, Imam Mahmoud Shaltut, of Al Azhar University in Cairo, Egypt, a bastion of Sunni thought since the twelfth century. Imam Shaltut issued a fatwa (religious injunction) that declared that Shiite beliefs were a valid school of thought. This was an important achievement in attempting to unite Muslims globally. In addition, some conferences are now attended by both Sunni and Shia Muslims. *In 2006, Denver held a dialogue between Sunnis and Shi'ites in order to dispel the sectarian conflict between them.* Shia and Sunni Muslims have also united on various topics concerning Muslims, such as supporting candidates for president, senator, or Congress. They have also united locally to support candidates for school boards, mayors, and other municipal positions and to foster cooperation with those officials.

Mosques in America

Traditionally, mosque, or *masjid* as it is referred to in Arabic, is a place where people congregate each day to perform the five prayers prescribed to all Muslims. *Imam* is technically the person who leads the prayer. The imam is not a priest and cannot intercede on behalf of Muslims with their Lord. He is educated in the recitation, writing of the Qur'an, and other Islamic sciences. In many cases, he has even memorized the whole Qur'an. According to the teachings of Islam, he is supposed to be chosen from the best people in the community. In other parts of the world where Muslims constitute the majority in their societies, such as Indonesia, Syria, Jordan, Saudi Arabia, Senegal, Morocco, Algeria, Libya, Egypt, Turkey, and Albania, the purpose of the mosque is performing the five daily prayers, reciting the Qur'an (Holy Book of Islam), celebrating the two Muslim religious holidays of Eid al Fitr and Eid al-Adhu, funeral services, wedding events, and classes on religion, history, sewing, English, fitness, law, and more.

But the role of the mosque has taken on a new meaning for Muslim men and women in the United States. It has become the place where you pray, hold Qur'an competitions, have Ramadan iftars (dinner when you break your fast), seek marriage counseling, search for financial assistance, and hold classes and lectures on religion, politics, and society. It also sponsors community picnics and community pantry (donates food to people in the community in need), and raises funds for various organizations in their local area and nationally. These local and national organizations serve a variety of different purposes—as social work agencies (dealing with the elderly, immigrants, and domestic abuse), global relief agencies, Muslim Legal Fund of America, other mosques, schools, and Islamic organizations. It is estimated that 70 percent of the mosques in the United States give help to those under financial difficulties. It depends on the location and size of the mosque. Some are able to assist their local community, while others are able to branch out. American mosques in the twenty-first century also donate to such causes as the Indian Ocean tsunami of 2004; Hurricane Katrina; earthquakes in Turkey in 1999, China in 2008, and Haiti in 2010; and other worldwide disasters.

Muslims living overseas have many different organizations attending to their needs as a community—from governmental to social. But, when Muslims first arrived in the United States, they were a minority in a Christian majority. There were no organizations to address their needs as a community. The traditional role of the imam has morphed into much more than just the leader of the prayer in the United States. Sometimes, he is also considered a *sheik* (a person of great religious knowledge). He not only leads the prayer, but he advises and councils the youth, couples, and lectures on Islam and related topics. The imam in the United States serves as a spiritual and social leader. However, in the mosque, the imam or sheik is not the only one making decisions on behalf of the mosque. Most mosques have an executive committee or board of directors, made up of men and

women, who make all final decisions related to the mosque as an institution, including making the choice of imam for a mosque. This executive committee or board of directors is elected by the mosque's members or constituents. They usually consist of men and women living in the community, such as lawyers, teachers, businessmen, doctors, and other professionals.

The mosque was one of the first institutions that Muslims built. As of 2000, there were 1,209 mosques in the United States and four-fifths of them were in metropolitan areas, either in the cities or in their suburbs. As of 2010, there are closer to an estimated 1,900 mosques in the United States. However, most mosques were established only recently—30 percent were started in the 1990s, and 32 percent opened in the 1980s. Today, the mosque remains strong as a place where both men and women come to get support, pray, and join in activities with other Muslims. The number of people attending or participating in mosque functions has increased by more than 75 percent between 1995 and 2000.

Ethnicity of individuals attending mosque in the United States can be broken down into three categories: 33 percent are South Asian, 30 percent are African American, and 25 percent are Arab. But this depends on location. Most mosques are ethnically diverse, but 7 percent are attended by only one ethnic group. The average attendance for *juma*, the Friday congregation prayer, in 2000 was 292; and this was a 94 percent increase from 1994 when the average number was 150. But anywhere from 4,000 to 5,000 Muslims attend the mosque for Friday prayer. Only 15 percent of mosques are facing any kind of financial issues. The function of the mosque has altered in the United States for a variety of reason—Muslims have different needs in their new environment. Another important note is that the involvement and participation of women in the American mosque has increased in the past 15 years. The involvement of women in the mosque varies in the United States more than in many other Muslim countries due to the social, cultural, economic, and political factors inherent in those societies.

In addition, more than 20 percent of all mosques have full-time schools for the Muslim children in the community. In their efforts to preserve their religious and cultural identity, Muslims have sought to establish weekend and full-time schools. As of 2000, there were 300 full-time Islamic schools around the United States. Weekend schools teach the Qur'an, the life of the Prophet Muhammad, the other important histories about the other revered prophets in Islam—Jesus, Moses, Solomon, Noah, Adam, and Abraham—and the basics of Islam. The full-time Islamic schools have an Islamic curriculum, but they also teach other traditional subjects such as math, science, history, art, and more. The National Association of Islamic Schools estimates that there are 300 such schools in the United States today. Most of these schools are in their early stages and still in the accreditation process or learning how to run and support a private school. Many students who complete their education in these schools eventually move on to reputable universities and become professionals. One research study found that among Muslim students in Southern California (in Islamic or secular schools), 87 percent of the students wanted to become lawyers, doctors, engineers, and other professionals that require a higher level of education. There are also many Islamic schools run by the Muslim American Society that was headed by Imam Warith Deen Muhammad, the son of the Nation of Islam's leader Elijah Muhammad.

In addition to Sunni mosques, there are also Shia mosques and centers throughout the United States. For example, the Islamic Center of America in Dearborn, Michigan, is the biggest Shia mosque in the country. The mosque was founded in 1963 by Imam Muhammad J. Chirri, who came at the urging of the Muslims in Detroit because they needed religious guidance for their community. Today, it predominantly serves the Shia community in the greater Detroit area. Other Shia mosques and centers are located throughout California, New York, New Jersey, Pennsylvania, Texas, Illinois, and Georgia.

Prominent Muslim Institutions and Organizations

The first national Muslim organization in the United States began to be formed as early as 1952 when Abdullah Igram, a businessman from Cedar Rapids, Iowa, contacted other mosque leaders throughout

Muslims pray at the Islamic Center of America mosque in Dearborn, Michigan, the largest Shi'a mosque in the United States. (AP Photo/Paul Sancya)

the United States about bringing together all the mosques and centers under one umbrella organization (Ba-Yunus and Kone 2006, 46). In 1954, the Federation of Islamic Associations of North America and Canada (FIAA) was established to unite and preserve the identity of Muslims in North America. Their mission was to educate Muslims and non-Muslims about Islam and connect them with other Muslims, but also to address their needs. The FIAA held an annual convention in various cities such as, Chicago, Detroit, and Michigan City, bringing Muslims from all over the United States and Canada. In 1959, over 1,000 people attended the organization's ninth annual convention in Michigan City, Indiana (Ba-Yunus and Kone 2006, 47). Although the FIAA tried and wanted to be inclusive of all Muslims, it remained predominantly an Arab-Muslim association, and with the development of other national organizations, it eventually weakened and lost support.

The next major national Muslim organization to form was the Muslim Students Association (MSA) of the United States and Canada. After World War II, various educational programs and opportunities were created that allowed foreign students to apply to study at U.S. universities (Ba-Yunus and Kone 2006, 48). Muslim students started arriving at large university campuses under the F-1 visa category, which was created for foreign students to stay in the United States as long as they were studying at an educational institution seeking a college/university degree. By the late 1950s and early 1960s, there were many Turkish, Arab, Iranian, Asian, Pakistani, and Indian Muslim students throughout the United States at various schools. The university became a place where Muslims from all parts of the world could interact with each other and with non-Muslims as well. The Civil Rights Act of 1964 and the Immigration and Nationality Act of 1965 removed the restrictive quotas of the Johnson-Reed Act of 1924 and increased the number of categories and individuals allowed to enter the United States. Muslim students on campuses began to organize in the late 1950s and early 1960s in order to provide a prayer place for the Friday sermon and address other needs of Muslims at universities. In 1963, a group of Muslim students at the University of Illinois at Urbana-Champaign invited all other Muslim student organizations in the United States to join them in a conference to help organize all Muslim students. The final result of the meeting was the creation of the Muslim Students Association. It held its first convention in 1963 and elected a Shia from Iran as its first president. The MSA represents and respects Muslims of all religious sects. Every year thereafter, the MSA convention was attended by increasing numbers, and it brought together the most educated Muslims and professionals—making it the most important and vibrant Muslim institution in the United States. The 1990s saw another great influx of Muslims arriving in the United States—brothers, sisters, and relatives of the first generation. But it also saw the coming of age of the second-generation American Muslims. This changed the nature of the MSA from being a predominantly immigrant-exclusive institution to one in which the majority of the members were American-born Muslims. This reinvigorated the MSA's activism and expansion throughout the 1990s.

The MSA mission is to organize and address the needs of Muslim students and their activities in American society. It works on issues such as homelessness, education, violence, Islamophobia, spirituality, and other concerns pertaining to Americans and Muslims. Today, there are over 200 chapters of the MSA established at various universities and colleges throughout the United States and Canada (Cesari 2007, 342). The MSA also spawned the creation of other organizations, such as the North American Islamic Trust (NAIT), American Trust Publications, Association of Muslim Scientists and Engineers (AMSE), the Islamic Medical Association (IMA), and the largest organization to represent Muslims in the United States—the Islamic Society of North America.

A decade after the establishment of the MSA, Muslims in the United States began to settle into family and professional life. They would need an organization to represent them and their needs as families and larger communities. In 1981, the MSA would help found the Islamic Society of North America (ISNA) in Plainfield, Indiana. The mission of ISNA is to represent Muslims of all sects and their organizations in building a life for Muslims in the United States. It is an umbrella organization that has 300 associations and centers connected to it (Cesari 2007, 342). It aims to address supports the social and educational needs of Muslims as well as to provide outreach to other religious communities throughout the United States. In addition, it raises funds for national and international disasters, such as the earthquakes, tsunamis, and hurricanes. ISNA also assists Muslims in marriage services, *shahada* (declaration of faith in Islam), and counseling. It supplies other aid, such as: literature on Islam, *zakat* (charity), and the Speaker's Bureau, which helps provide professional speakers on Islam. In 2002, almost 50,000 people attended the conference in Washington, D.C. In 2006, roughly 35,000 Muslims attended the annual conference held in Chicago. It also has its own publication—*Islamic Horizons*—which covers issues and information for Muslims in the United States. Each year, the ISNA conference aims to address the most pressing matters confronting Muslims today. Although it serves to represent all Muslims, African-American Muslims have felt that their concerns and realities are not always addressed by the organization. But this has changed as ISNA heads into the twenty-first century with its first female president, Professor Ingrid Matteson of Hartford Seminary. African Americans have been integrated into the organization and their needs are gradually being addressed. In addition, ISNA is also focusing on the role of women and the involvement in Muslim institutions and affairs with its support of publications, such as, "Women Friendly Mosques and Community Centers: Working Together to Reclaim our Heritage," which seeks to remind people that Islam gives women equal opportunities to participate in the public sphere. ISNA was the first American-Muslim organization to speak out against terrorism and the violent acts perpetrated on September 11, 2001.

Due to the increasing needs of Muslims, other organizations have emerged to address their needs, including the Islamic Circle of North America (ICNA) and the Muslim American Society (MAS). ICNA was founded in 1971 for the education and spiritual development of Muslims. It also works to connect the U.S. public to Islam and the improvement of American society through outreach, youth groups, and social service. It does many interfaith dialogues and has partnerships in many other religious communities throughout the United States. Although begun by Muslims of South Asian descent, ICNA is inclusive of all ethnicities and aims to secure a place for Islam and Muslims in America. It has established various projects, including ICNA Relief, Young Muslims, 877-Why Islam, the National Shura Council, Muslim Savings and Investment, and other branches designed to attend to the basics of Muslim life; and it works with other organizations, such as the Islamic Society of North America, Muslim American Society (MAS), Council for American-Islamic Relations (CAIR), American Muslim Society, Muslim Public Affairs Council, and North American Islamic Trust, to achieve its end.

MAS was established in 1993 with the goal of helping Muslims to better themselves and to work to improve their society by equipping them with the

Islamic knowledge they need to make a social and political difference. Their mission is "To move people to strive for God consciousness, liberty, and justice, and to convey Islam with the utmost clarity." MAS's activities can be divided into the following categories: its youth program, Freedom Foundation—which works with social, educational, and political forums that include diversity training, and outreach. For example, it has trained over 1,500 federal, state, and local law enforcement agents about Islam to improve their understanding of and to better deal with Muslims. They helped the victims of Hurricane Katrina and annually have a meat drive to support homeless shelters and other needy organizations. Based in Falls Church, Virginia, it also works with interfaith groups to clarify the meaning of Islam. MAS has over 40 chapters in the United States and works alongside other national organizations such as ICNA, ISNA, and the MSA.

In addition to the spectrum of affiliated organizations and diverse activities, the ICNA vehemently condemned the attacks of September 11, 2001. After the attacks, ICNA worked with CAIR to educate Muslim Americans about their civil rights. ICNA, along with other 144 Islamic organizations in the United States, condemned any kind of terrorism in 2005 by signing a fatwa by the Fiqh Council of North America. They have an annual convention, which is done in collaboration with the Muslim American Society's convention; it had over 10,000 attendees in 2005.

The Council on American-Islamic Relations (CAIR) was founded in 1994 in Washington, D.C., in order to address the prominent anti-Muslim and anti-Arab stereotypes in the government and the media—books, newspapers, television, movies, advertisements, and more. According to CAIR's website, their mission is to promote an accurate understanding of Islam and communication between Muslims and American society in general, to safeguard civil rights, and to develop alliances that support justice and understanding. They also support justice internationally, such the protests of Egyptians in January 2011 and their demands for freedom. It also condemned church attacks in Nigeria and Egypt in 2011. They strive to help American Muslims be model citizens who participate and contribute to their society. CAIR seeks to educate Muslims about their legal rights and supports the belief that Islam is compatible with their identity as American citizens.

CAIR is a nonprofit organization that was established by Omar Ahmad and Nihad Awad, both immigrants from Jordan. Ahmad has a BS and MS in computer engineering, while Awad studied civil engineering at the University of Minnesota. Awad is CAIR's national executive director and has met government officials such as Condoleezza Rice and Colin Powell in order to advocate for Muslims in the United States. Today, CAIR has 32 chapters throughout the United States. Among their most important achievements was in 1998 and 1999, when they successfully persuaded Nike to redesign a logo with the Arabic word for God—Allah—written on one of their shoes. They also support claimants against discrimination in the workplace, airplanes, and other public facilities. They have documented the civil rights abuses of Muslims since 1996. CAIR works with many other Muslim and non-Muslim organizations such as the American Civil Liberties Union.

The American Society of Muslims, one of the largest and oldest Muslim organizations in the United States, actually has its roots in another famous organization—the Nation of Islam (NOI). At the death of the Nation of Islam's leader, Elijah Muhammad, his eldest son, Wallace Deen Muhammad, had been named as successor. Despite his doctrinal disagreements with his son, it was understood from early on that Warith Dean would be the chosen successor of the NOI because Elijah Muhammad had indicated that he was W. D. Fard's choice. Wallace Deen Muhammad, who changed his name to Warith Deen Muhammad, had converted to traditional Sunni Islam in between 1960 and 1963 while in prison for refusing to serve in the U.S. Army. Warith Deen used his time in jail to better comprehend the teachings of the Qur'an and Islam. He had studied orthodox Sunni Islam in Egypt and tried to challenge his father regarding many of the teachings of the NOI. He had a close relationship with Malcolm X, who also had converted to Sunni Islam after his pilgrimage to Mecca, Saudi Arabia in 1964.

Warith Deen had been excommunicated by his father from the organization five times for refusing to accept the divinity of Fard or his father as a prophet of God, which contradicts the major tenets of Islam. He finally returned to the NOI in 1974. When his father died in 1975, Warith Deen became leader and openly rejected the teachings of his father that were considered heresy by Sunni Muslims and aimed to reform the movement from within by embracing mainstream Sunni Islam. He dropped the black separatist aim of the organization and preferred the title of "imam" to any other. But, he pushed on with his father's message of self-improvement and betterment of African Americans. However, not everyone agreed with Imam Warith Deen's move to make the Nation of Islam follow orthodox Islam. In 1977, Minister Louis Farrakhan, a onetime disciple of Malcolm X and top official in the Nation of Islam, disagreed and splintered off with his own group of NOI followers. They continued on with the original teachings of Elijah Muhammad.

The American Society of Muslims has gone through a variety of name changes, from the Nation of Islam to the World Community of Al-Islam in the West in 1976, and then in 1980 it became the American Muslim Mission until 1985 when it changed to the Ministry of Imam W. D. Mohammad. Its name would alter yet again in 1997 to the Muslim American Society until it reached its current evolution in the form of the American Society of Muslims (ASM) in 2002. The formal newspaper for the NOI was *Muhammad Speaks*, but that changed to the *Muslim Journal* in 1981. Warith Deen also helped to established over 40 Sister Clara Muhammad Schools throughout the United States. Mohammad's American Society of Muslims is the largest and oldest indigenous Muslim group of its kind. At its height, Warith Deen's movement had 2.5 million followers. His mission and aim of his organization became the building of a community open to all Muslims based on the highest Islamic principles.

AMS has been active in establishing relations with Muslims from all parts of the world, including building partnerships with other Muslim, Christian, and Jewish institutions. Imam Warith Deen has met with various political and religious leaders throughout the world. In 1975, he met with Egypt's president Anwar Sadat and in 1976 with Sheik Sultan Bin

Mohammad al-Qasmini, the head of Sharjah, one of the emirates of the United Arab Emirates. His organization received $16 million from Sheik Sultan al-Qasmini for their expansion of the Clara Muhammad Schools. In 1993, Imam Warith Dean was the first Muslim to lead the prayer on the U.S. Senate floor. He was also invited to the Vatican in 1996 to convene with Pope John Paul II. In addition, Imam Warith Deen spoke regularly at the Islamic Society of North America's yearly convention. He resigned from the American Society of Muslims in 2003 but continued on with his work in the Muslim community and interfaith dialogue until his death on September 9, 2008, at the age of 74.

In addition to these organizations, there is also a new crop of educationally based institutions that seek to educate Muslim Americans about Islam. Traditionally, when Muslims have sought to learn Arabic, understand the Qur'an, or study the Islamic sciences, they have gone to institutions like Al-Azhar University in Cairo, Egypt, or to renowned Islamic scholars throughout the Muslim world. Many Muslims in the United States still seek Islamic knowledge by traveling to these places; however, they are starting to have other options within the United States. For example, the Zaytuna Institute in San Francisco, California, was founded in 1996 by Hamza Yusuf, a convert to Islam in 1977 who was formerly known as Mark Hanson. The institute initially sought to address the lack of teachers and schools available to students of Islam in the United States by providing access to teachers trained at reputable universities in the Middle East and among the best scholars. It seeks to intimately acquaint its students with centuries-old learning about Islam and get American Muslims to become intellectually engaged with Islam. The institute converted into Zaytuna College in 2009. It was founded by Hamza Yusuf, Zaid Shakir, and Dr. Hatem Bazian. The mission of the new college is to become the first accredited Muslim college specializing in a four-year education in the Islamic sciences and producing Muslim-American scholars.

There are also other organizations, such as the Nawawi Foundation based in Chicago, Illinois. The Nawawi Foundation was founded in 2000 in order to provide relevant authentic Islamic teachings, based on genuine scholarship, to the generations of Muslims indigenous to and growing up in the United States. The scholar-in-residence is Dr. Umar Faruq Abd-Allah, a convert to Islam in 1970 with a PhD from the University of Chicago in Islamic studies and also classically trained in the Islamic sciences. Under Dr. Abd-Allah, Nawawi Foundation has focused on understanding the American Muslim cultural experience within the parameters of Islam. It has provided classes without charge, on a donation basis, for people in the greater Chicago area on such topics as: the "Principal Imams and their Schools" in 2005, "Famous Women in Islam" in 2004, "Exploring the Ottoman Legacy" in 2004, "Gender and Islamic Law" in 2003, and the "Legacy of Muslim Spain" in 2001. They also provide weekend retreats throughout the United States on specific issues like, "Ethnic Jihad: The Struggles of Muslims in America," which was held in Santa Clara, California; and "The Cultural Imperative: Our Islamic Identity in the Modern World," held in Washington, D.C. It also focuses its attention on traveling to various countries to study the great cultural and religious experience of Muslims globally—how they integrate into their societies, maintain their own religiosity, and express that religious sense. The Nawawi Foundation has traveled to China, Morocco, Spain, Saudi Arabia, Turkey, and other countries in exploration of the Muslim presence.

They have also included other scholars, such as Dr. Ingrid Matteson of the Hartford Seminary, Dr. Sherman Jackson of the University of Michigan, and Dr. TJ Winters of the University of Cambridge, on these journeys to intellectually enrich the experiences of their participants. The Nawawi Foundation has collaborated with a variety of scholars and organizations nationally and internationally. The popularity of the organization has increased progressively as many Muslims in the United States identify with their message and are interested in the educational options they provide. In addition, many of the individuals involved with Nawawi helped to establish the Mohammad Webb Foundation, which seeks to "promote the practice of Islam while embracing the positive aspects of American life and culture. It seeks to provide facilities and programs that offer guidance and create a spiritually uplifting atmosphere in which the community may prosper within our pluralistic society while maintaining its core beliefs and values." It offers programs for children, young adults, and adults on Qur'an, *sunnah*, parenting, exercise, skiing, camping, community support, and other social and religious issues pertaining to Muslims in the United States.

Besides these Sunni organizations, there are also Shia institutions around the United States. The Twelver Shiites established the Universal Muslim Association of America (UMAA) in 2003. It encourages the political participation of Muslim in American society and addresses stereotypes and other misconceptions about Muslims. Another large institution that serves as an umbrella organization for all other Shia groups in the United States and Canada is the North American Shi'a Ithna 'Ashari Muslim Communities (NASIMCO), which was established in 1980. There are 10,000 members of NASIMCO which helps organize events for its constituents. There is also the Islamic Information Center (IIC), established in Washington, D.C., in 2003. It works on promulgating a positive image of Islam and Muslims. There are also publishing companies, such as the Tahrike Tarsile Quran (TTQ), which was established in 1978 for the purpose of printing the Qur'an.

Muslim Women in the United States

The earliest Muslim women in the United States came in the late nineteenth and early twentieth centuries as part of the largest wave of immigration to the United States. The majority followed their husbands who had come before them, but many also came independently in search of better economic opportunities and political stability for them and their families. Although the early immigrants were mostly Arab, today Muslim women in the United States come from all ethnic backgrounds. They are all American, but they also have Arab, Indian, European, Pakistani, Iranian, African, Latin American, and other Middle Eastern and Asian backgrounds. A significant number of Muslim women are also American converts to Islam. According to the survey *Muslim Americans: A National Portrait*, conducted in 2009 by the Muslim West Facts Project (a partnership between Gallup

and the Coexist Foundation), 42 percent of American-Muslim women have a college degree or higher. This makes them more educated than American-Muslim men, only 39 percent of whom have a college degree or higher. They also work, and fully half of American-Muslim women earn the equivalent of men. Of the Muslims in the United States earning $5,000 or more, 30 percent of the men are earning at least that much, as do 25 percent of working women.

In addition, women and men are about the same in their weekly attendance to the mosque, with 40 percent of American-Muslim women and 42 percent of American-Muslim men saying they attend once a

A mother and child listen to an Islamic prayer led by Amina Wadud, who led a mixed-gender Muslim service at Synod House at the Cathedral of St. John the Divine, an Episcopal church in Manhattan, New York, 2005. (AP Photo/Gregory Bull)

week. This is in contrast to Muslim countries, where the majority of the attendees of the mosque are men. American-Muslim women are among the most educated religious women in the United States, second only to Jewish women. They work in all professions, from lawyers to doctors, to filmmakers and environmentalists. Among the Muslim women in the United States, 35 percent are in the following professions: engineering, medicine, law, stockbroking, teaching, music, nursing, accounting, pharmacy, banking, computer engineering, art, science, and marketing.

Muslim women in the twenty-first century are very active in American society and within Muslim communities. They have established a number of organizations, and the following is only a description of some of the ones available nationally. KARA-MAH: Muslim Women Lawyers for Human Rights educates Muslim women on legal issues. Rahima Foundation works to provide charitable support for Muslim women and their families. Sisters in Islam addresses the reinterpretation of Muslim women's rights in Islamic law. The North American Council for Muslim Women (NACMW), based in northern Virginia, seeks to provide Muslims with a clear understanding of women's place in Islam. It works in legislation, advocacy, education, and policy. The Muslim Women's League, based in Los Angeles, actively engages in practicing and living according to Islamic principles, which in turn gives women the right to live and participate in society equally. It provides spiritual retreats for women, supports other organizations with similar goals, offers educational forums for and about Muslim women, and publishes articles that put forward the perspective of Muslim women. Furthermore, the Association of Muslim Women in America (AMWA) aims to represent Muslim women in various disciplines and fields. It seeks to help women in what it deems the most pressing issues—social services, gender equality in the workplace and society, and their social and economic development. Islamic organizations have also increased the participation of women and their candidacy for leadership positions.

There are many challenges facing Muslim women in the United States today. Among the most prominent is their battle against the persistent negative stereotypes of Muslim women found in Western society and manifested in the media through newspapers, television, movies, literature, and other venues. There is often much confusion over the cultural expectations of Muslim women in their respective societies and the mandates of Islam. What culture dictates is separate from what Islamic doctrines dictate, though they may seem intimately intertwined. For example, in Egypt, female circumcision occurs among segments of the population but is not part of Islamic religious traditions. In Afghanistan, women are limited in their educational and work opportunities because of the politics and culture of the region. In Saudi Arabia, women are legally not allowed to drive, and this law reflects culture, not religion. According to Islamic precepts, knowledge and education for men and women is of the utmost importance. Muslim women in the United States seek to rectify these misperceptions and prove that Muslim women are multifaceted and multidimensional. Their versatility can be demonstrated in the issue of *hijab*—the headscarf adorned by some Muslim women. It is often considered that *hijab* is a sign of male hegemony or coercion. But most Muslim women in the United States would strongly disagree with such an interpretation. Although the majority of Muslim women do not cover their hair, the wearing of *hijab* has become more popular among women, especially young women on campuses and in high schools. At whichever point in their life they are, Muslim women who wear *hijab* find it to be liberating because they are making a choice about their faith and how they want to reflect their piety and personal choice in the modesty of their dress.

Marriage and Muslims

Marriage among Muslims in the United States has metamorphosed over the last two decades. Initially, when Muslim immigrants arrived, they chose to marry someone of their ethnic and cultural background, whether they were from Egypt, Turkey, Lebanon, Iran, India, or another part of the world. Arabs did not just marry other Arabs. It was not enough that they spoke a common language, even if there was a different dialect. There are many cultural and regional differences among Egyptians,

Palestinians, Syrians, and other Arab and Muslim groups. In essence, Egyptians preferred marrying Egyptians, and this applied to all the various ethnic groups who were Muslim. With the second large wave of Muslim immigrants to arrive, after President Lyndon B. Johnson's Immigration Act in 1965, the community was growing, but it was still small. Early immigrants met their spouses through family and friends. When Muslim families could not find someone in their community for their son or daughter, they went back home. This occurred because many immigrants were culturally and/or religiously conservative and wanted someone with the same background. Muslim women in the United States were housewives, but some also were employed with their husbands or worked independently. Muslim men and women also married American men and women who were not Muslim. Throughout the 1980s and 1990s, as the community developed, immigrant Muslims were able to marry second-generation women and men who had grown up in the United States.

In the twenty-first century, the situation for Muslims and marriage has continued to grow and transform within the United States. According to *Muslim Americans: A National Portrait*, 49 percent of Muslim-American women and 53 percent of Muslim-American men are married. Today, Palestinians, Egyptians, Iranians, Turks, and other groups still marry persons from their own ethnic backgrounds, but the numbers of Muslims marrying interculturally has significantly increased. African-American Muslims are marrying Arabs; and Egyptians are marrying Syrians. Cross-cultural ties have developed among the second generation of Muslims. Islam encourages men and women to marry Muslims of other ethnic backgrounds. Having matured in the United States, various Muslim ethnic groups now have more in common culturally because they identify themselves as Muslims and Americans. They may still identify with their Syrian, Turkish, Lebanese, Indian, Palestinian, Iranian, or Egyptian culture, but they now share more with the children of other Muslim immigrant groups whom they may have gone to school with or grown up with in America.

According to a 2007 survey done by the Pew Research Center titled "Muslim Americans: Middleclass and Mostly Mainstream," 72 percent of Muslims polled say that religion is very important in their life. Of that number, only 23 percent were committed to the five daily prayers and attending the mosque weekly. For Muslims who choose to practice their faith, their relationship patterns do not conform to the traditional dating practices in American culture. They believe marrying a Muslim is important and necessary because they want to maintain their beliefs and pass them on to their children. There is no casual dating in Islam, and a serious relationship between a man and woman must be for the end purpose of marriage. For example, Muslims who have been raised in the United States sometimes meet their spouse at school, work, matrimonial sites, conventions, or through a friend or family. Once they meet, they decide whether they are compatible by talking to one another extensively. This may take up to a month or over a number of years; it is up to each individual to decide how long they need. They may then choose to get engaged and get married. Furthermore, Muslim-American women who are married often juggle career and family, like women in many parts of the world. The 2009 Gallup poll on Muslim Americans describes one in three Muslim-American women as having professional jobs.

There has also been an increase in the numbers of Muslim men and women marrying American non-Muslim men and women. This has occurred for a variety of reasons. First, there are Muslims who identify themselves as such only nominally and are not interested in maintaining the cultural traditions or religious beliefs of their parents, either because they identify more with their American heritage or because they were not raised practicing Islam. Of the Muslim Americans surveyed by the Pew Research Center, 26 percent of them do not practice their faith regularly and do not believe it to be an important part of their lives. For them, there is no necessity in marrying a Muslim, and they may choose to follow American dating patterns. In addition, 51 percent of Muslim Americans find themselves somewhere between the practicing Muslims and those who do not follow their faith at all. Also, different sects of Islam—Sunni and Shiite—are intermarrying. The religious differences between these two groups, although to a certain extent still practiced here, are more prominent overseas. There has also been an increase in divorce among Muslim Americans, with the recent Gallup poll in 2009 now putting it at 10 percent. However, family is an important component of Muslim life. According to the same poll, in comparison to other religious groups, such as Protestants, Catholics, Mormons, and Jews, Muslims have the largest households, with 3.81 people.

Muslims and Education

For these growing Muslim families in the United States, educational institutions have sprouted in order to provide them additional support. The first kind of schools started by the Muslim community was weekend schools. They are still offered on a Saturday or Sunday, from the morning until the afternoon in a mosque or school. The curriculum consists primarily of Arabic, Qur'an, *sunnah* (sayings and practices of the Prophet Muhammad), and Islamic history classes. These weekend schools are meant to supplement the education received in public schools. Many Muslim-American parents believe it is imperative for their children to also learn the Arabic language and understand the Qur'an to comprehend the teachings of Islam. Weekend schools have been in existence since the 1950s. With the development of full-time Islamic schools, some parents still utilize the weekend schools, while others have chosen to send their children to these new schools.

The first Islamic schools were called the Islamic University and started by Elijah Muhammad, the leader of the Nation of Islam, in the 1930s. They were geared solely toward educating his followers in urban cities such as Detroit, Chicago, and New York City. In 1975, under the leadership of his son, Imam Warith Deen, the name and mission of these schools changed. Imam Warith Deen renamed the Clara Muhammad Schools (after his mother) and reoriented them toward embracing Sunni orthodox Islam. Today, there are 60 such schools. By the 1980s and 1990s, Muslim immigrants and their children began to establish more Islamic schools. They often started out small, only going from elementary to junior high; but with time, they moved to include high schools as well. These

private schools have tuition costs ranging from $2,000 to $8,000. Today, there are 235 Islamic schools in the United States, and more are being built as the need and demand for these schools grows. Islamic schools focus their attention on the same subjects covered in public schools, such as math, science, English, history, gym, and those mandated by the state and various accreditation agencies. They also cover Arabic, Islamic studies, and Qur'an. These schools are religiously oriented, and consequently, students congregate to perform the obligatory prayers and have *Eid* celebrations.

These schools also have sports and academic teams and compete locally and nationally. They interact with other schools in their areas, either by inviting them to Ramadan or *Eid* festivities or by showing their solidarity in local and national events that affect all Americans—such as the terrorist attacks of September 11, 2001. They are predominantly Sunni in orientation, but they admit children of all ethnic and religious backgrounds. The following ethnic groups of Muslims make up the majority of the school population: Pakistanis, Indians, Egyptians, Palestinians, Syrians, and Jordanians, with pockets of African Americans, American converts to Islam, Moroccans, Libyans, Algerians, Sudanese, and other Muslim groups depending on the area. These Muslim schools can now be found in large metropolitan areas, including New York City, Los Angeles, Chicago, and other areas throughout the United States.

The Future of Muslims in America

Although Muslims have moved toward having their own voice by establishing their own institutions and organizations, they are now living in the aftermath of 9/11 and the hysteria, fear, political instability, and religious extremism associated with Islam. After decades of living in the United States, many Muslims believed they had moved past stereotypes, media biases, and misunderstanding about Islam and Muslims. But, after 9/11, Muslims in the United States came onto the center stage and faced a new age of identity and societal negotiations. The image and attitude toward Muslims in the United States has increasingly become worse since 9/11. According to a *Time* poll in 2010, 46 percent of Americans believe Islam encourages violence, while only 37 percent of Americans actually know a Muslim (Ghosh 2010, 19) In 2008, during President Barack Obama's campaign, national news coverage gained momentum when Obama was accused of being a Muslim. Although he had repeatedly declared his faith as Christianity, questions began to arise from the conservative right that Obama was a secret Muslim. This created a controversy in the media, with individuals making all sorts of anti-Islamic comments. This situation illustrated the negative perception of Muslims in the United States. A year later, on November 5, 2009, Fort Hood was the site of a massacre when Nidal Malik Hassan shot and killed 13 people and wounded 29 others. It was an act of terrorism that resulted from his psychological instability. The following year, in May 2010, Faisal Shahzad was arrested for leaving a car with explosives in Times Square. These incidents, alongside the political turbulence and instability in the Middle East, have gradually increased the negative perception of Islam and Muslims in the United States. Although these people are terrorists and do not represent Islam, their actions have increased the Islamophobic attitude towards Muslims

This Islamophobia has come to manifest itself in another sector of American life. With the increase of the Muslim population in the twenty-first century, the growing need and demand for more mosques has become an eminent issue. Muslims across the nation have raised funds for the building of mosques to address the community needs. However, since 2000, a trend of hostility and resistance has ensued at city council meetings over attempts to build mosques. Americans of various communities protest and spew insults at Muslims at city council meetings as they try to explain why a mosque is unacceptable in their community. In all these forums, an important correlation is always made by the individuals that Islam equals hatred and violence. But, for the hundreds of thousands of Muslims living in the United States and the billion living elsewhere in the world, their faith represents and literally means peace.

A prominent example of this occurred in 2000 and received national attention in the *New York Times* and *Chicago Tribune* when Al-Salam Mosque signed a contract to purchase the Reformed Church of Palos Heights, Illinois. No one in the Muslim community

of Chicago anticipated the response from the residents of Palos Heights because the property had been up for sale for two years. During the city council meeting to discuss local issues, residents appeared at the meeting and made insulting, ignorant, and insensitive statements about Islam and Muslims—clearly associating Islam with violence. The mayor of Palos Heights, Dean Koldenhoven, felt embarrassed by the expressions of anti-Muslim sentiment and opposed blocking the purchase of the mosque as unconstitutional and bigoted. The city council eventually agreed to pay Al-Salam Mosque $200,000 to withdraw from their contract. In 2002, former mayor Koldenhoven was awarded, by the Kennedy Library Foundation, the John F. Kennedy Profile in Courage Award, next to the former secretary-general of the United Nations and Nobel Peace Prize winner Kofi Annan.

This is not the only such incident of American opposition to mosque building. In 2010 in Sheboygan County, in the city of Wilson, Wisconsin, Dr. Mansoor Mirza had purchased a property and planned to open a mosque near Oostburg. As a resident of the city, Dr. Mirza did not anticipate opposition from this quiet population of 3,200 because he had served everyone regardless of race or creed as a doctor in the local hospital for five years. But, when he attended the meeting of the city's planning commission, residents started throwing in objections and insults, claiming that Muslims kill their children and teach hate, and that there were jihadi camps throughout the United States. Although none of these claims could be substantiated, the mosque continued to face opposition when local pastors started to campaign against it.

The most well-known opposition to date of the building of a mosque in the United States began in May 2010 and is recognized as the Park 51 project, otherwise known as the Ground Zero Mosque of New York City. Park 51 was conceived by Imam Feisul Rauf and his wife Daisy Khan, but also by the owner and developer, Sharif El-Gamal. Imam Feisul has been the leader of his own mosque two blocks away for 30 years, but with the community of Muslims growing in Manhattan, a larger space was needed to meet their needs. He had traveled abroad as a representative of the Bush and Obama administrations to spread a positive message about the United States in the Middle

East. Initially, El-Gamal intended the space to be solely a mosque, but eventually it expanded based on community needs to be a mosque and community center for Muslims that would provide cultural exhibitions, a culinary school, a space for recreation and fitness, a restaurant, educational programs, a 500-seat auditorium, a library, a reading room, an art studio, and a memorial to the victims of 9/11.

The controversy over Park 51 began when right-wing conservative Pamela Geller began blogging on her site, Atlas Shrugs, about it, setting up protests, and dubbing it the Ground Zero Mosque. The land for the project is actually two blocks away from the area designated as Ground Zero, an area known for its liquor stores and strip clubs. Geller made it a national issue because she asserts that it was an insult to the memory of the 9/11 victims (32 of whom were Muslim) to put a mosque on Ground Zero, and that it was an issue to which all Americans should take offense. The controversy became heated throughout the United States in the summer and fall of 2010, with national and international coverage of the issue. However, all along, the city commission had approved the plan, almost unanimously four times, even with the media frenzy surrounding it. In addition, Mayor Michael Bloomberg advocated the constitutional rights guaranteed under the First Amendment, freedom of religious expression, and he openly supported the mosque.

In 2010, six mosques across the United States faced similar controversies. These facts illustrate that, while some Muslims in the United States may be generations old or indigenous, the perception of Muslims is very negative. According to a *Time* poll in 2010, 28 percent of voting-age Americans believe that Muslims should not be allowed to sit on the Supreme Court, and one-third think they should not be allowed to run for president. Islamophobia took a turn for the worse in 2010 as acts of violence perpetrated by Muslims continued to be associated with Islam and Muslims in general. While there may be hostility toward Muslims, 55 percent of Americans polled believe that most Muslims love the United States. At present, the future of Muslims in the United States is unclear; but what is certain is that their numbers are growing, and so are their needs. Muslims will continue to strive in their daily lives to be better Americans, as some continue

to practice their faith and others define themselves as nominal Muslims. Islam has been and will continue to be part of the American experience.

Bibliography

Altman, Alex. 2010. "TIME Poll: Majority Oppose Mosque, Many Distrust Muslims." *Time*, August 19.

Bagby, Ihsan, Paul M. Perl, and Bryan T. Froehle. 2001. "The Mosque in America: A National Portrait." Washington, DC: Council on American-Islamic Relations, April 26.

Ba-Yunus, Ilyas, and Kassim Kone. 2006. *Muslims in the United States.* Westport, CT: Greenwood Press.

Cesari, Jocelyne, ed. 2007. *Encyclopedia of Islam in the United States*, 2 vols. Westport, CT: Greenwood Press.

Council on American Islamic Relations. 2011. http://www.cair.com (accessed October 23, 2011).

Gallup and the Coexist Foundation, 2009. *Muslim Americans: A National Portrait.* The Muslim West Facts Project.

Ghanea Bassiri, Kambiz. 2010. *A History of Islam in America.* New York: Cambridge University Press.

Ghosh, Bobby. 2010. "Islamophobia: Does America have a Muslim Problem?" *Time*, August 19.

"Ground Zero Mosque." 2010. *60 Minutes*, September 26.

Haddad, Yvonne Y., and Jane I. Smith, ed. 1994. *Muslim Communities in North America.* Albany: State University of New York Press.

Haddad, Yvonne Y., Jane I. Smith, and Kathleen M. Moore. 2006. *Muslim Women in America.* New York: Oxford University Press.

Islamic Society of North America. http://www.isna.net (accessed October 23, 2011).

Muslim Americans: Middle Class and Mostly Mainstream. 2007. Pew Research Center, May 22.

Nawawi Foundation. 2010. http://www.nawawi.org/index.html (accessed October 23, 2011).

Nyang, Sulayman S. 1999. *Islam in the United States of America.* Chicago: ABC International Group.

Smith, Jane I. 2010. *Islam in America.* New York: Columbia University Press.

The Daily Lives of Immigrants

Charles E. Orser Jr.

Archaeology in North America has always been about immigration in some fashion. For example, the pre-Columbian Moundbuilders have been viewed as either an unknown people whose name was lost to history or a historically known culture like the Phoenicians, the Egyptians, or the Lost Tribes of Israel. In any case, the Moundbuilders have always been thought of as immigrants to North America. With the development of a much more scientific archaeology, beginning in the late eighteenth century, archaeologists still agreed that the first humans on the continent were probably immigrants, having traveled across the Bering land bridge from Siberia. These unintentional immigrants were probably chasing mammoths and other large game animals. The Bering land bridge theory has been archaeological orthodoxy for decades, but since the late 1990s, some archaeologists have begun to dispute the contention that the Bering route was the only avenue into North America. Some have suggested that the first immigrants may have arrived by boat from Asia or perhaps may even have come from Europe. These views are currently controversial, even though all archaeologists agree that some form of immigration brought the earliest Americans to the continent.

When we think about an archaeology directed specifically toward the study of immigration into the United States, however, we are more aptly drawn to historical archaeology, which relies on a combination of excavated finds, written records, and other sources of information, including oral testimony, to investigate the material conditions of daily life during the past 500 years. In the United States, the earliest historical archaeology was practiced by historical architects and other specialists who examined the buildings and ruins they were charged with reconstructing or restoring, mostly for the purposes of heritage tourism. For the most part, these buildings and properties were associated with the nation's most prominent and influential individuals and families. Thus, the attention of early historical archaeologists was drawn to places like Valley Forge, Mount Vernon, Monticello, and Colonial Williamsburg rather than to the thousands of places in which immigrants established homes and communities throughout the United States. Beginning in the late 1960s, however, a generation of younger archaeologists, influenced by the development of social history and the rise of ethnic awareness, began to investigate the homes of men and women lesser known in history. They turned their attention to enslaved African Americans, hardscrabble tenant farmers, frontier shopkeepers, and the residents of the nation's most crowded urban centers. By analyzing artifacts and soil deposits, as well as floral and faunal remains found at past habitation sites and other places, archaeologists of recent history have been able to provide new information about past daily life. Their research has fleshed out much about the daily lives of American immigrants. To increase the social relevance of their research, historical archaeologists also increasingly collaborate with members of descendant and indigenous communities. The new emphasis on collaboration is providing a much deeper understanding of daily life in the United States.

At the beginning of the twenty-first century, historical archaeologists in the United States overwhelmingly concentrate upon the daily lives of the men and women who built the country's institutions and infrastructure rather than merely on the properties and possessions of prominent families. Included in this corpus of study is the archaeology of the thousands of immigrants who came to the United States since the nation's earliest development. This chapter introduces a few of the archaeological projects that have concentrated on immigrants in the United States.

Colonial Days to 1870

Historical archaeologists have compiled a huge body of literature about the earliest influx of Europeans into the Western Hemisphere. Much of the early archaeology of America's famous families focused specifically on colonial history. Many Americans may equate "colonial archaeology" solely with the excavation of English settlements along the East Coast, a mainstay of much archaeology. Archaeologists indeed have made many important discoveries at notable sites—in particular at Jamestown, Virginia—but they have also conducted both small- and large-scale analyses of Dutch, French, Spanish, and Russian villages, forts, outposts, and missions in the United States as well as in other parts of the colonial world. These researches have significantly enhanced our knowledge of the material culture of colonial immigrants—the very objects the people used on a daily basis—as well as providing new insights about the ways in which they incorporated the material culture, eating habits, and housing of the indigenous peoples they encountered and in many cases lived among. The process of acculturation and accommodation was complex, multifaceted, and mutable, demonstrating that the United States has been a multicultural society from the very beginning.

One long-term investigation has focused on the colonial Spanish city of St. Augustine, Florida, one of the first archaeological projects undertaken in the United States to concentrate specifically on the nature of immigrant life in America as well as on the cultural transformations experienced by the people who lived there.

The Spanish founded St. Augustine in 1565–1566 in an effort to check the influence of the French along the southeast coast. The impetus for the town's development was based purely on interstate rivalry. Precious metals were unknown in the area; no large cultures of Native Americans lived nearby who could become trading partners or religious converts; and the area's sandy soils were not conducive to European-style agriculture. The town's first residents— about 700 soldiers and sailors—struggled through a series of natural disasters and a devastating attack by the English. The town survived, and before long, Franciscan priests arrived in what was by then largely a Hispanic town in design. But the cultural character of this New World settlement persisted as it grew, and by the eighteenth century, St. Augustine had expanded in extent and population. Its residents included Spaniards, *criollos* (people of Spanish descent born in the New World), Africans, and Native Americans. Archaeologists excavated finds from about 200 undisturbed deposits that included thousands of artifacts and animal bones. These materials showed that the historical impression of sixteenth-century life in St. Augustine was accurate: it was often a bleak place where the residents struggled to survive.

One of the most important archaeological discoveries was the high percentage of Native-American pottery in the Spanish deposits. As was common at the time, the city's Spanish settlers used a variety of European earthenware and Asian porcelain dishes. Sixteenth-century European and Chinese potters marketed these ceramic wares around the world, and archaeologists find them in almost every colonial site. But the early residents of St. Augustine also used vessels of indigenous manufacture. This unglazed Indian pottery, technically termed "San Marcos pottery," was present in St. Augustine in a shape that archaeologists also frequently find at nearby Native-American villages: the round-bottomed pot. A few of the shards, however, exhibit the flat bottoms typical of dinner plates. The discovery of even small numbers of flat-bottomed vessels of Indian manufacture provides early evidence of cultural exchange, because it appears that Indian potters made some vessels to mimic European forms. Their very presence provides undeniable testimony for the complex nature of cultural interaction and exchange when immigrants come into contact with indigenous people.

One explanation for the use of Native-American pottery in Spanish homes may be that it was simply the result of intermarriage between Spanish military men and Indian women. Commonsense suggests that Native women who prepared meals probably used vessels with which they were familiar and which they had readily available. The absence of Spanish women in the settlement "introduced new elements into the kitchen and foodways activities of the Hispanic colonial households" (Deagan 1983, 267–68). As a result, Spanish soldiers and sailors slowly adopted hybrid cultural practices that were unique to the New World. In particular, out of necessity, the Spaniards also adopted many of the eating habits of the natives. For example, since the soils of Florida would not support growing wheat, oats, and barley—the crops known to the Spanish—they were forced to consume the traditional native triad of maize, beans, and squash, as well as a variety of nuts, fruits, and greens that were entirely new to them. They also ate the seafood native to the coastal waters. The study of the excavated food remains provides important evidence that the Spanish settlers were not dependent on imported foods, and makes a strong case for cultural change and adaptation during the immigration process. Accordingly, the process of intermarriage and thus descent—*mestizaje*—constitutes the beginning of Hispanic-American culture in what would become the United States.

Findings among Spanish sites in New Mexico demonstrate the variability of the immigrant experience during colonial times, even among people of the same national origin. The differences largely result because of the diverse contacts that colonial settlers had with the native peoples they encountered and because of the environments in which they lived.

In the sixteenth- and seventeenth-century American Southwest, many of the cultures lived in pueblos and practiced subsistence practices that were suited to the harsh environment. Clothing was one area in which Spanish settlers adapted to local conditions. Spanish and Indian men initially dressed in dissimilar fashion, but their styles became more similar as the Spanish adopted their impractical clothes for cotton garments and as Indian men were increasingly encouraged to wear trousers. Spanish men generally abandoned the finery they wore in Spain and central Mexico and adopted cotton, cow- and sheep-hide clothing. Clothing differences between immigrant and native women, however, remained distinct.

Even given the local differences, overall similarities did exist between Spanish colonial immigrants wherever they settled. As in Spanish Florida, the settlers in New Mexico used a mixture of European ceramics and Indian-made pottery. They used native pottery for the same reason as in Florida: the pots were made by local Indian women, many of whom lived in Hispanic domestic situations. And, as was also true in the East, Spanish settlers in the West adopted the native foods of the region. But, Spanish immigrants also brought with them innovations. These included the plow, animal power, and irrigation, foreign tools that would help to ensure their survival in a harsh and unfamiliar environment.

Despite the cultural introductions, Hispanic culture did not fully develop in the Southwest until the eighteenth century "after the successful Pueblo Revolt [1680], when Spanish-descended immigrants began coming to New Mexico in greater numbers and Pueblo population had been reduced by European-borne disease" (Rothschild 2003, 223–24). The culture, however, was a hybrid mixture of Spanish and Indian elements as each culture learned from one another and adopted specific practices and material culture.

Numerous historical archaeologists have investigated the major immigrant populations of the colonial era, and most of their research explains the ways in which the in-migrating groups interacted with and were changed by native peoples. Occasionally, archaeologists will examine a case that is wholly unique, where the desire was to remain as culturally distinct as possible. One such instance involved immigrants from the Appenzell region of Switzerland, who settled in South Carolina in the eighteenth century.

In 1737, a group of Swiss immigrants settled along the Savannah River in western South Carolina across from the future site of Augusta, Georgia. The British colonial government had organized a series of townships on the frontier with the intention of settling white Europeans who could simultaneously strengthen the militia, provide a buffer between the more developed region along the coast and the Native Americans of the interior, and serve as a racial counterbalance to the growing population of enslaved Africans in the colony. The Appenzellers were one of the groups who chose to settle on this frontier, along with English, Scottish, Welsh, and Irish groups.

The Appenzellers generally sought to retain their ethnic cohesion by practicing an insular strategy.

They desired to live in isolated places that were mountainous, both because they reminded them of home and because they thought them especially healthy. These locales were environments where they believed they could reconstruct their traditional village life in the New World. Excavation showed that they laid out their farmsteads in the traditional *Streuhof* manner, and they built their houses in the *Blockbau* style. In the *Streuhof* pattern used in Switzerland the buildings were dispersed across the landscape rather than being placed close together. The *Blockbau* style of building incorporated square log houses set on horizontal sills placed on the ground, with their gables facing forward. The buildings had wattle-and-daub—stick and mud—chimneys, and the lack of nails in the archaeological deposits indicated that the builders used notched-log construction. The continuation of the *Streuhof* and the *Blockbau* traditions in the South Carolina frontier "made for a distinct, visible symbol of ethnicity" for the immigrant Appenzellers (Penner 1997, 286). The Appenzellers in essence physically recreated an old-world settlement on the American frontier.

One might easily equate the urge to retain traditional building styles and settlement designs with a general urge to be conservative in all practices, including economics; but the excavated finds at the Appenzeller sites indicated that their possessions bore no appreciable differences from those of nearby English families. In other words, inside the old-world houses, the residents used the same artifacts that were prevalent throughout English South Carolina and throughout much of the English-influenced world. The percentages of ceramics and wine bottles, as well as objects associated with furniture, arms, and clothing, were all found to be relatively equal between Appenzeller and English sites in the area. However, the Appenzeller sites clearly stood out in their low numbers of iron framing nails compared to the English sites. But, like their English neighbors, they used small nails for roofing.

The similarity in the artifacts used by Appenzeller and English settlers indicates the way in which material culture can appear to provide a homogeneity. As a practical matter, people purchase what is available to them, and South Carolina was an English colony when the Appenzellers settled there. Therefore, similarities between the material cultures of the two populations are understandable and unsurprising. What makes immigrant populations different are the ways in which they continue to practice cultural traditions in adaptive ways. Unable to obtain the kinds of material objects they used in the Old World, Appenzellers simply began to use what was available to them in South Carolina, even while they continued to practice traditional ways of building their homes and designing their settlements. They could use the same building materials as their non-Swiss neighbors—the logs, framing timbers, and shingles—but in ways that mirrored their old environs as much as possible. Meanwhile, in their quest to maintain a mono-ethnic community, the Appenzellers employed a settlement pattern that promoted separation and insularity, and they continued using a High German dialect that kept them distinct from the surrounding English population, even if the artifacts of the two groups were indistinguishable.

Africans in the New World constitute one group of immigrants, albeit unwilling immigrants, whom archaeologists have studied in depth. Research of enslaved life in America—the lives lived from sundown to sunup and largely absent from much contemporary observation—has provided unique information about many segments of daily life, from dietary patterns to artifact possession. In many specific cases, archaeologists have corrected or enhanced the historical record, showing, for example, that the quality of the slaves' housing was not always as sturdy as planters often noted. Archaeological research also documents that many of the enslaved dug pits under their cabins in an effort to hide as many of their personal possessions as possible. The discovery of hidden storage pits highlights an important aspect of the enslavement: Non-African observers did not know (or at least did not report) everything that occurred inside the communities of the enslaved.

One of the most enlightening areas has involved the study of African religions in the United States in the colonial, antebellum, and postbellum eras. Many of the enslaved were Christians or Muslims upon their arrival in the Americas, and many still practiced the religions their ancestors had observed for generations.

Reconstructed colonial vessels. The initials MHD are etched into this shard and likely stand for Maria Henrietta Drayton who resided at Drayton Hall from around 1780–1840. The artifact shows how African crafts and skill sets were transferred to the Low Country where they were further influenced by European and Native cultures. (Carter C. Hudgins/Courtesy Drayton Hall, a site of the National Trust for Historic Preservation)

Some had already merged their traditional religions with Christianity or Islam, and others constructed entirely new religious forms from the admixture of two or more traditions. There is, nonetheless, abundant evidence for the continued practice of traditional belief systems among enslaved Africans in the United States. Beginning in the late 1970s, archaeologists excavating at plantation sites throughout the American South began to notice the presence of cosmological signs (usually a simple "X") scratched onto the bases of handmade pottery and on metal spoons. They have been able to use ethnographic information to link these signs with cultures in present-day Central Africa.

At the same time, archaeologists excavating at sites associated with enslaved Africans have begun to find discrete groups of artifacts that they interpret as relating to ritual practice. Seemingly mundane objects like buttons, straight pins, crystals, marbles, and pieces of broken ceramics, when put together in a "ritual cache" or "spirit bundle," were thought to have healing or protective powers. People of African heritage could bury these bundles under earthen floors or place them under floorboards, believing that they had thus protected the space from malevolent influence.

The practice of making spirit bundles was widespread and long-lived. Archaeologists have found them in seventeenth-century deposits in Dutch New York as well as in eighteenth-century English Maryland and elsewhere along the eastern shore. The existence of these caches provides evidence for the continuance of African beliefs in North America, and the materials incorporated within them show the complex meanings that people can attach to artifacts that may initially appear to have different functions altogether. The hidden meaning of the pins, marbles, and buttons can be discerned only when they are viewed collectively and when the interpreter adopts a perspective that is sensitive to African spiritual traditions.

Magic, of course, was not confined to Africans in the New World, as many European cultures also created a significant place for magical beliefs in their daily habits. While investigating a German-American property in Virginia containing an extant log house, an archaeologist discovered a small clay figure of a human skull. Only about three-fourths of an inch in size, the back of the skull exhibited an incised X, and inside the spaces created between the arms of the X were the inscribed initials R, H, S, and D. Many explanations for this odd find can be proposed—gaming piece, toy, idle manufacture—but the object does bear resemblance to European charms relating to the crucifixion of Christ. The discovery of such a find appears to be extremely rare; but, in truth, archaeologists have not paid adequate attention to the continuation of European beliefs in America to know the full extent of the practice.

When considering the archaeology of immigration before 1870, no project has more significance than that conducted at the infamous Five Points area of Lower Manhattan. Modern readers may be familiar with the Five Points largely through the writings of Jacob Riis and the famous visit by Charles Dickens, as well as the wildly inaccurate movie *The Gangs of New York*. In the 1990s, however, the area entered archaeological history by becoming an excavation site in a place that most people would not immediately consider to be a viable location for a large-scale archaeological investigation. The U.S. General Services Administration planned to construct a new courthouse in the area, and federal regulations require that an archaeological assessment must occur before the ground surface is irreparably disturbed. When archaeologists began excavating in the triangular area that stretched from Pearl Street to Worth Street—where the courthouse was to be situated—they unearthed 850,000 artifacts. This area was at the heart of the old Five Points, immediately adjacent to the intersection of streets that gave the place its name. Privies, cisterns, and other subterranean features yielded artifacts that allowed archaeologists to reconstruct daily life in the neighborhood's tenements. A wide range of nineteenth-century immigrants—the families of Jewish tailors, German shoemakers, and Irish day laborers as well as tavern keepers and prostitutes—were responsible for having deposited the artifacts.

Archaeologists were interested in how the different immigrant groups in the neighborhood negotiated their identities when faced with American patriotism, national identity, and nativism. Archaeologists reasoned that because the largely Anglo-Saxon power elite who controlled New York City held different attitudes about the various immigrant groups who arrived on the city's docks, the different peoples probably adopted varying strategies for survival, inclusion, and cultural and personal expression. Among the thousands of artifacts they discovered, the archaeologists decided that one class of artifacts—clay smoking pipes—might provide a window on the complex social issues involved in the negotiation of immigrant identity.

White clay smoking pipes of the seventeenth, eighteenth, and nineteenth centuries have small bowls and long, thin stems. Many people know these as "church warden pipes." Researchers have learned that they can discern the manufacturing dates of pipes from the size of the hole through the stem (the bore) if they have a large enough sample. They also know that pipe makers changed the size, shape, and angle of the bowl over time, and they know how to date these changes. But pipe makers also decorated their delicate products with evocative emblems, portraits, and letters they hoped would appeal to consumers. By the nineteenth century, the short-stemmed, white clay pipe (called the "dudeen" in Ireland and the "cuttie" in the United States) became especially associated with Irish immigrants (both male and female) and with members of the working class in general. And, since many urban saloons were enmeshed in the political culture of the era, it is no surprise that pipe makers decorated many of their clay pipes with patriotic and political images. Using these little objects, smokers could subtly profess their affiliations, beliefs, and attitudes.

Archaeologists discovered pipes decorated with patriotic images, including the American eagle and 13 stars. Other pipes carried images, such as shamrocks, that were designed to appeal to both Irish and Irish-sympathizing consumers who opposed the anti-immigrant messages of the Know-Nothings. Archaeologists excavating at the Boott Mills in Lowell, Massachusetts, found similar pipes. There, excavated clay pipes were marked with images having resonance with Irish immigrants, such as the image of Wolf Tone, the famous Irish patriot. Such findings add support for the idea that smoking pipes, though small and seemingly insignificant, are "a communicative element" in society (Cook 1989, 229). Studies of mundane artifacts—like the simple clay smoking pipe—demonstrate that immigrants, like other Americans, employed artifacts in subtle ways to demonstrate their collectivity and their common fate as immigrants at the same time that they proclaimed their distinct allegiances and affiliations.

In another study of the Five Points, forensic anthropologists examined the skeletal remains of two neonates and a fetus associated with a brothel. The brothel had been located in the basement of a tenement, and the remains were found inside the associated privy. The analysts were unable to determine whether the remains were the result of stillbirth, infant abandonment, or infanticide. In any case, the discovery of the remains in an outhouse directed archaeologists to investigate the social and legal attitudes toward infanticide, abortion, and prostitution in pre–Civil War America, research that highlighted the difficult choices immigrant women often faced.

Some of the artifact types provide information about the preferences of different immigrant groups. For example, an analysis of the glass condiment bottles from 22 distinct deposits in the Five Points project area show that German Americans tended to use more mustard than non-Germans. Irish immigrants preferred more sauces than either German or Jewish immigrants, and Jewish immigrants used much more olive oil than other immigrant groups in the area. Eating habits tend to be some of the most conservative elements of people's cultural lives, so it is perhaps not surprising that these differences occur. The archaeological research provides tangible evidence for the past practices of different immigrant groups.

Indeed, a study of the medicine bottles from the Five Points indicates that Irish immigrants spent more money on cures than did German and Polish immigrants. The Irish tended to purchase treatments for ailments related to the manual labor many of them performed. The deposits related to German and Polish immigrants, unlike those associated with the Irish, contained substantial quantities of blackberry or raspberry, substances "highly regarded as a virtual medicinal panacea throughout the 19th century, both by professional medical practitioners and in folk medicine" (Bonasera and Raymer 2001, 61).

Other studies conducted with the Five Points artifacts highlight the decisions immigrants made when purchasing mundane objects, such as ceramics. An analysis of the 601 separate ceramic dishes present in two deposits in the backyard of a tenement reveal that the immigrant tenement dwellers had access to a wide variation in wares and decorations. Mid-nineteenth-century immigrants in the Five Points, just like many New Yorkers, commonly purchased the starkly white dishes that were then replacing the more decorated printed wares. They also bought dishes that were printed with important messages and pictures. One excavated child's cup is printed with "John," and another cup carries the image of Father Theobald Mathew, the leader of an Irish alcohol abstinence movement who had visited New York City in 1849.

Perhaps not surprisingly, the wares used in the tenements were generally of lower price than those used in the middle-class homes of New York. But, the values of the wares in the tenements tended to more closely match those of rural New York residents who lived further away from the urban marketplace. Moreover, a close examination of the ceramic dishes from the Five Points deposits indicates that the immigrants in the tenements spent a significant portion of their incomes to purchase objects that could perform many functions. In addition to their use in food preparation and consumption, ceramic objects could make a home look more fashionable while they also communicated subtle messages about the residents' attitudes and aspirations. In a related view, and perhaps not surprisingly, the immigrants in the Five Points tended to eat cuts of meats that were less expensive than those found in middle-class New York homes. The bones left by one Jewish family indicate that they predominantly consumed beef and little mutton. The presence of little pork, few bones from the loins and hind shanks of cows, and the discovery of lead seals from kosher poultry indicate that this family regularly ate kosher meals.

One of the most significant, overall outcomes of the Five Points archaeological project is that the archaeological remains help to dispel the idea that the Five Points was a monolithic section of Manhattan characterized by universal debauchery, dishonesty, and vice. Nineteenth-century writers and social reformers, intent on foregrounding the poverty in the area, tended to overlook—or perhaps did not see—that the immigrant families had not completely sunk into ennui by the conditions around them. Instead, the evidence demonstrates the diversity of action in the area, and the ability of immigrant families to create the best lives they could within the parameters of their environments.

1870–1940

Archaeological research specifically directed to the immigrant experience in the United States, though certainly conducted at sites dating to before 1870, is somewhat more visible in the 1870–1940 period, specifically in studies of the late nineteenth century. The Five Points project, which also included the excavation of post-1870 deposits, is one exception because an equal number of its features date to before 1870. The influx of immigrants to the United States after 1870 probably accounts for the greater archaeological awareness of immigration as a topic of study in the later era.

The study of Chinese immigrant sites constitutes one of the major topics of interest to American historical archaeologists, particularly, though not exclusively, in the American West. The University of Idaho, whose archaeologists have been leaders in the excavation of Chinese immigration sites, maintains the Asian American Comparative Collection. This repository holds images, documents, and a huge collection of artifacts of many descriptions.

The history of the discrimination and legal strictures imposed upon the Chinese across America has meant that archaeologists have lately tended to concentrate on the role of material culture in the construction of ethnic maintenance by Chinese immigrants. When archaeologists first began to investigate Chinese immigrant life in the United States, they tended to look for discrete material markers of Chinese ethnicity. For example, many facilely associated the remains of opium pipes with Chinese immigrants, believing that these objects symbolized Chinese ethnicity. At one time, archaeologists tended to associate artifacts decorated with shamrocks solely with the presence of Irish immigrants. Of course, such

characterizations are far too simplistic. Archaeologists currently investigating Chinese immigrant life have come to accept that the material dimensions of past daily life were as complex as any other social dimension. In addition, archaeologists of Asian America have begun to think more critically about the role that discrimination played in past daily life, because these realities affected the way the archaeological remains were distributed.

One mainstay of archaeological research—household-level analysis—is not necessarily applicable to the study of Chinese immigrant communities. Not all archaeological research, however, is amenable to household-level analysis. For example, discrete family deposits are impossible to segregate from the huge artifact collection recovered at the tenement yards in the Five Points. Yards and privies were communally used in high-density living areas, so the artifacts they contain were deposited by a diverse collection of now-unidentifiable individuals. At the same time, tenements witnessed a rapid turnover in residents as families moved in and out. Many immigrant Asian settlements in the United States had the same characteristics as urban tenements. As a result, archaeologists have found it more appropriate to focus on a larger analytical scale than the household, replacing the concept of personal ownership with "cultural ownership." The term "cultural ownership" is intended to mean that "a group might assert a claim on property—land, resources, objects, and intangibles such as 'tribal knowledge'—in situations where there may be little or no legal basis for such a claim" (Voss 2008, 46). In communal deposits, archaeologists cannot establish ownership beyond the group level. They can only assume that a collection of artifacts once belonged to a particular group.

Working with artifacts excavated from the Market Street Chinatown in San José, California, archaeologist Gina Michaels noticed that slightly over 1 percent of the porcelain vessels bore the evidence of hand-pecked Chinese symbols on their surfaces. Of the 12 marks that she could translate, she identified seven as individual or family names ("sir" or "dad"), and five as wishes or blessings ("peace" or "harmony"). The pecking of plates and bowls with symbols of good luck is still practiced in China, so the discovery of these vessels in San José provides evidence for long-term cultural continuity and the transnational nature of some cultural practices. These dishes also undermine the practice of considering a cultural group as composed of identical men and women. Individuals who lived in discrete communities and who were grouped together by the dominant society—in this case, as "the Chinese"—strived to create their own identity with regard to personal ownership. That archaeologists have found one or two similarly pecked ceramic vessels at other Chinatown sites in California suggests the widespread, if perhaps infrequent, nature of this practice.

Excavations at many sites associated with Chinese immigrants have shown, perhaps not surprisingly, that these individuals used a mixture of American and Asian artifacts. Excavation at a Chinese laundry site in Stockton, California, shows that Chinese immigrants used a variety of patent medicines, including tonics, liniments, and blood purifiers. In this instance, Chinese immigrants acted like thousands of Americans who regularly turned to patent medicines for relief at a time when professional medical care was either unavailable or suspect in its efficacy and safety. The archaeologists' discovery of small medicine vials and jars, some with the labels still intact, indicate that in addition to using store-bought patent cures, Chinese immigrants could also frequent Chinese-owned apothecaries. The use of traditional healing remedies appears as one element of life that distinguishes Chinese immigrants from their American neighbors. At Stockton, excavators unearthed an ordinary brown bottle inside of which they found the bones of five crows and the remnants of five herbs, three of which they could identify. Chinese herbalists commonly used crows in the preparation of medicines designed to ease the effects of spasms, breathing problems, epilepsy, headaches, and dizziness. They deemed the herbs in the bottle to be useful for easing insomnia, rheumatism, and arthritis, and for promoting blood circulation. The find of this bottle provides concrete evidence that Chinese herbalists adapted to the American flora and fauna when making otherwise traditional medicines. The cultural theory behind the medicines, however, remained unchanged.

The animal bones excavated from the laundry also provide information about the workers' diet.

Analysts determined that over 80 percent of the bones came from beef and pork. Cat bones were also present in the faunal collection. The archaeologists could not determine whether the laundry workers ate the animals, but the consumption of cats constitutes one element of the nineteenth-century stereotype used against Chinese immigrants.

Excavations in Los Angeles' Chinatown provide further information about the immigrant Chinese diet. This excavation yielded high percentages of fish and shellfish, but pork was the primary meat consumed, though much chicken was also eaten. Prominent in the collection were the feet of pigs, chickens, and ducks. Squirrels and cats were also present, although to a lesser extent. Saw marks on the excavated beef bones indicate that Chinese immigrants probably purchased the meat from established meat markets, but then used cleavers for secondary preparation. The lack of glass and tin containers in the Los Angeles deposits indicate that the immigrants in Chinatown purchased little of their diet from American markets and that they conducted little canning or home preservation.

Other archaeologists investigating the Chinese immigrant experience have documented how Chinese workers were forced out of various kinds of labor, like shrimp fishing, and how they found other workplace niches, such as seaweed harvesting. The examination of a house in San Luis Obispo County, California, owned by Wong How, reveals the simple nature of many houses built by Chinese immigrants seeking life on their own terms. Wong How had come to the United States in 1909 at age 14. He was able to enter as a U.S. citizen because his father had been born in San Francisco. He spoke Cantonese, but in 1910 claimed to be able to read, write, and speak English (even though he still required the use of an interpreter). Wong How dutifully registered for the draft in 1917 and 1919, but was refused because of poor health. He made many trips back to China, and in 1920, he married there. In the 1920s and 1930s, he listed his occupation as a seaweed gatherer.

Wong How's house, still standing in 2004, was a one-story, linear structure built with a patchwork of materials, including plywood and corrugated sheet metal, some of which he may have salvaged from another building. The exterior and interior show that Wong How made changes to the building to suit his needs. The artifacts collected from the site mirror those found on other Chinese immigrant sites: teapots, rice bowls, and porcelain spoons. Also present are Chinese stoneware food jars and a porcelain saucer made in England.

This examination of vernacular housing—houses made with cultural knowledge and following custom rather than being based on the designs and plans of formally trained architects—demonstrates the mixture of American and Asian building techniques and shows how some Chinese laborers sought physical isolation in a hostile world by creating separate, remote settlements. Such locales reveal how Chinese immigrants negotiated through their new, often hostile, environment using a combination of cultural continuity and adaptive change.

Archaeology in the American West, especially in the region's mining-related boomtowns, has created opportunities to investigate immigrant life. Excavations in Virginia City, Nevada, presented unique information about saloons operated by immigrants. The proprietors tended to establish saloons in the less desirable part of town, the area most frequented by itinerant miners, drifters, and prostitutes. Despite the area's poor reputation, excavation showed that the owners of the saloons outfitted the building's interior with glass decanters and crystal stemware. Decorative wall and ceiling treatments helped to create an ambiance of refinement and leisure for saloon patrons. One saloon owner even purchased linoleum, a new invention in flooring at the time. The presence of this now-familiar floor covering in a Western saloon deflates the stereotype that all saloons had hardwood floors that reverberated with the sound of cowboy boot heels and the jingle of spurs. Conversely, however, the discovery of bone dice, dominoes, poker chips, and a complete cribbage board reinforces the stereotype that saloons were places for leisure, game playing, and gambling.

In another realm, when the family of a residence can be determined with historical records, archaeologists can present deeply contextualized insights into past daily life. A rare opportunity was afforded by the material life of an Italian immigrant family that settled in Queens, New York, in the late nineteenth century. Italian immigrant Michael Peete disembarked in the United States in 1885. Like many others who sailed from southern and eastern Europe, he was virtually penniless at the time. And, like thousands of others, he soon found a series of unskilled, low-paying jobs that provided his sustenance. Because Peete was ambitious, he slowly acquired better-paying jobs, and before long, he started a business making artificial flowers. He became a naturalized citizen in the late 1890s, and by the first decade of the twentieth century, he was a successful real estate developer and community leader.

Excavation made possible an especially close examination of the 1903–1907 period. The unusually rich documentary record of the Peete family's experience—including Peete's autobiography—allowed archaeologists to understand that one of Peete's most important goals in the United States was to become Americanized as quickly as possible. In fact, a grand piano was one of the first things he purchased when he became financially sound. He even hired a young woman to teach him how to play this physical symbol of American refinement, sophistication, and belonging.

The archaeological excavation visibly demonstrates the material side of Peete's desire to become fully American. Some of the recovered artifacts—pieces of a mantel clock, a porcelain crucifix wall hanging, and a number of ceramic flower pot and glass vase shards—suggest that Peete added a parlor to his house around 1904. The parlor was the ultimate symbol of American domesticity, a belonging that perfectly complemented the grand piano. Other artifacts also demonstrate the Peetes' desire to conform to their American home. The discovery of poison, ammonia, and disinfectant bottles in the archaeological deposits shows that they had accepted the contemporary ideas of germ theory as well as the importance of cleanliness and hygiene that had been part of American life for many years.

But Peete's assimilation to American material culture was not total. Other archaeological evidence suggests that the Peete family strove, like many other immigrants, to retain some traditional cultural practices. For example, ceramic shards suggest that the family had the ability to set their dinner table in both American and Italian fashions. Like many genteel families, the Peetes owned three sets of dishes, two for everyday use and a more formal, porcelain set. They also owned several tea sets—the equipment absolutely necessary for the "proper" conduct of the tea ceremony—and a few vessels similar to Italian types in material, shape, and style.

Without a doubt, the Peete family, like thousands of immigrants, negotiated the assimilation process on their own terms as much as possible. Michael Peete sought to become Americanized quickly, but at the same time he did not wish to lose his Italian roots and cultural heritage. The archaeological research at the family's homesite helps to demonstrate the subtle roles that material objects can play in the complex process of belonging while attempting to remain distinct at the same time.

Post 1940

Little archaeological research has focused on immigrant life after 1940. The belief that "old is better" is long standing in archaeology, though the development and dramatic growth of historical archaeology has done much to dispel this thinking. One approach to archaeology that has done much to change attitudes, while also showing how archaeological research can help us to understand our own time, has been the development of "modern material culture" studies. Archaeologists who pursue this avenue of research seek to use archaeological methods to interpret the common and everyday materials that surround us. In other words, the focus is more on the role of artifacts in human life rather than a strict interest in any one aspect of history. Even so, however, some studies have a direct bearing on the archaeology of immigration.

One of the first and most significant archaeological projects to investigate the role of material culture in modern-day immigrant life is the University of Arizona's Garbage Project (sometimes grandly referred to as *Le Projet du Garbage*). This research effort was a wholly innovative project that sought to use archaeological field methods to examine modern-day garbage: its disposal patterns, rates of accumulation, and

preservation over time. Many archaeologists have stated over the years that all they really do is examine other people's garbage—the unwanted refuse of past generations—so the realization that archaeology could be used to understand present-day garbage perhaps follows logically. The timing of this project shows the relationship between archaeology and the concerns of society at large, because its development coincides with the rise of the worldwide ecology movement.

In addition to the many important findings of the project's archaeologists—including that hot dogs and guacamole dating to the 1950s remain perfectly intact in the nation's landfills—are their discoveries about the consumption habits of various immigrant groups. One study conducted by project members involved testing the classic hypothesis of ethnic assimilation: that immigrants seek to chart a middle course between full assimilation and the retention of traditional habits. To conduct this study, the analysts decided to concentrate on food consumption by examining seven food groups: meats and eggs, breads, cereals, coffee, soft drinks, alcohol, and convenience foods. Using garbage that they collected, they compared average daily household consumption in Tucson (Mexican American and Anglo-American) and Mexico City. Their findings allowed them to conclude that the practices of Mexican Americans did not fall midway between Anglo-American and Mexican habits. Regarding beef consumption, for example, the Mexican-American pattern far exceeded both the Anglo and the Mexican figures. The researchers learned that Mexican Americans were also greater consumers of tea, coffee, sugar-rich sodas, white bread, sugar-based breakfast cereals, and eggs than members of the other two groups. Whereas Anglo-American households tended to reduce their consumption of high-sugar and fatty foods—in their effort to eat in concert with the American health craze—Mexican-American habits were similar to those of Anglo-Americans in the 1960s.

Since it is likely that economics and class position play a role in dietary patterns—what foods a family can afford to purchase, what is available in the neighborhood or within the reach of public transportation, and so forth—the analysts decided to examine more than 1,000 refuse samples from Tucson; Milwaukee,

Wisconsin; and Marin County, California. Some correlations between income and diet were readily apparent. Mexican and American households tended to consume more dairy products, syrup, honey, and liquor as their incomes rose. Poorer consumers in the United States generally ate more canned vegetables than wealthier consumers, and wealthier Mexicans consumed six times the canned vegetables as Americans. This innovative archaeological research, which has many important ramifications for modern-day life, sheds further light on the relationship between material culture and the immigrant experience, and illustrates that the relationship remains complex through time.

In a more conventional study, an archaeologist investigated a neighborhood in a small town called Steptoe City, Nevada. A nearby, more substantial town was built in the early twentieth century as a company town dedicated to housing copper miners. Early in its existence, the miners were typically European immigrants, but after 1945, most of the labor force was Hispanic. A study of the still-extant buildings in the town showed that most were one- and two-room cabins with additions constructed from recycled materials. Oral testimony provided most of the historical context for the town because little written information was available. This information revealed that most outsiders tended to perceive the town much like middle- and upper-class New Yorkers had viewed the Five Points much earlier: as a place of ill repute, filled with dance halls and houses of prostitution. It was a place known for tar-paper shacks and a restless population. This research, though preliminary, demonstrates the kind of places that many immigrants first inhabited when they entered the United States. Such, marginal "shanty towns" in the American West thus may have functioned like the once-crowded tenements of the eastern cities.

The Archaeology of Immigration in America

American archaeology has always been about immigration to some extent, even if archaeologists have not actually created "an archaeology of immigration" as a definable field of study. With time and more field research, archaeologists accepted that immigrants indeed had been the first humans to live in North America, but that they were not Indo-Europeans. The first residents were immigrants from Eurasia and were the ancestors of the North American Indians. These were the original immigrants whom the first European immigrants encountered when they landed.

Archaeologists began their study of non-Indian history with the excavation of sites inhabited by European immigrants at well-known places. Their interpretations mostly told the story of the wealthiest and most prominent immigrants, and sometimes focused only on the earliest immigrants. Today, however, historical archaeologists throughout the United States are excavating sites inhabited not simply by colonial notables, but by immigrants from many nations. Their excavations are no longer limited to colonial history; increasingly, they reach the most recent decades.

By investigating the artifacts, soil deposits, and structures created and used in the past—and examining them in conjunction with historical sources of all kinds—historical archaeologists have been able to provide fresh perspectives on the immigrant experience in the United States. Each excavation yields new evidence for the ways in which immigrant individuals and communities adapted to life in the United States and illustrate the strategies they used to create the American culture we know today. Excavations reveal that immigrants used portable artifacts and non-portable objects, such as houses and neighborhoods, in various ways to create new lives. Individuals and families sometimes used artifacts in idiosyncratic ways, while in other instances, whole communities conformed to consistent patterns of activity. The research reveals that immigrant men and women (and even children) created identities in their new homes by using artifacts in creative and often-subtle ways. Archaeological research, despite its inherent local nature, provides special insights about the diversity of response and action among all American immigrants.

Bibliography
Bonasera, Michael C., and Leslie Raymer. 2001. "Good for What Ails You: Medicinal Use at Five Points." *Historical Archaeology* 35, no. 3: 49–64.

Cook, Lauren J. 1989. "Tobacco-Related Material and the Construction of Working-Class Culture." In *Interdisciplinary Investigations of the Boott Mills, Lowell, Massachusetts, Volume III: The Boarding House System as a Way of Life*, edited by Mary C. Beaudry and Stephen A. Mrozowski, 209–29. Boston: National Park Service.

Deagan, Kathleen. 1983. *Spanish St. Augustine: The Archaeology of a Colonial Creole Community*. New York: Academic Press.

Dixon, Kelly J. 2005. *Boomtown Saloons: Archaeology and History in Virginia City*. Reno: University of Nevada Press.

Fitts, Robert K. 2002. "Becoming American: The Archaeology of an Italian Immigrant." *Historical Archaeology* 36, no. 2: 1–17.

Goddard, Richard A. 2002. " 'Nothing but Tar Paper Shacks.' " *Historical Archaeology* 36, no. 3: 85–93.

Orser, Charles E., Jr. 2007. *The Archaeology of Race and Racialization in Historic America*. Gainesville: University Press of Florida.

Penner, Bruce R. 1997. "Old World Traditions, New World Landscapes: Ethnicity and Archaeology of Swiss-Appenzellers in the Colonial South Carolina Backcountry." *International Journal of Historical Archaeology* 1: 257–321.

Rathje, William L. 1977. "In Praise of Archaeology: Le Projet du Garbage." In *Historical Archaeology and the Importance of Material Things*, edited by Leland Ferguson, 36–42. California, PA: Society for Historical Archaeology.

Rothschild, Nan A. 2003. *Colonial Encounters in a Native American Landscape: The Spanish and Dutch in North America*. Washington, DC: Smithsonian Books.

Voss, Barbara L. 2008. "Between the Household and the World System: Social Collectivity and Community Agency in Overseas Chinese Archaeology." *Historical Archaeology* 42, no. 3: 37–52.

Voss, Barbara L., and Bryn Williams, eds. 2008. "The Archaeology of Chinese Immigrant and Chinese American Communities." *Historical Archaeology* 42, no. 3: 1–193.

Yamin, Rebecca, ed. 2000. *Tales of Five Points: Working-Class Life in Nineteenth-Century New York*. West Chester, PA: John Milner Associates.

Immigrant Literature and the Immigrant Experience

Priscilla Wald

The Immigrant as Stranger

Nothing better explains the powerful and imaginative hold that the immigrant has exerted on the American imagination than the German sociologist Georg Simmel's description of the stranger. That figure, he explained in a highly influential 1908 essay, could both crystallize and challenge a group's sense of itself. The stranger is not an inveterate wanderer, moving aimlessly from one community to another, but a *"potential wanderer"* who "has not quite overcome the freedom of coming and going." The stranger's relationship to the group with which he resides "is determined, essentially, by the fact that he has not belonged to it from the beginning, that he imports qualities into it, which do not and cannot stem from the group itself" (Simmel [1908] 1950, 402). The immigrant is the consummate stranger, marking an "elsewhere" from which the immigrant will always have come. Immigrant literature manifests a deep engagement with the implications of that strangeness.

Simmel's stranger offers insight not only into the characteristics around which a group coheres, but also into the processes of group formation. The figure shows how a sense of estrangement inflects all relationships, which happens when a sense of the uniqueness of the group gives way to a recognition of its common humanity. Within a small but definable group, one finds feelings of intimacy and a sense that certain common characteristics are shared. As the group expands, its members recognize the possibility of their commonality with others, and the knowledge of these possibilities permeates all relationships. The stranger, the immigrant, carries the reminder of such possibilities, a reminder that Simmel describes as permeating "shadows" or "mist" (Simmel [1908] 1950, 407).

It is for that reason that immigrants both express and are met with ambivalence, for they call attention to the distinctions between the native-born Americans and foreigners as well as to their unexpected commonalities. Accordingly, the stories immigrants tell about their transformations (or failed transformations) into Americans make visible the processes of socialization and the characteristics that distinguish "Americanism." As with Simmel's stranger, the immigrant challenges the uniqueness of a group—the characteristics that groups (here, a native population) believe distinguish them from other groups. Consequently, literature by and about immigrants bears witness to the "shadows" and the possibilities they foretell about the intrinsic mutability of the group—about, that is, the inevitability of change.

The Early Nation

Jedidiah Morse coined the word "immigrant" in his 1789 geography textbook, *American Geography*. His use of "immigrant" instead of the familiar "emigrant" registered a subtle shift in emphasis from identifying individuals with their place of origin to associating them with their destination. The first recorded use of the word coincided with the ratification of the U.S. Constitution, and while it did not refer specifically to would-be citizens of the nascent nation, Morse and others understood that such an entity needed more than bodies; it needed *American* bodies to constitute an *America* that was at once a destination and a political concept. Noah Webster famously called for an "America ... as independent in *literature* as she is in politics, as famous for *arts* as for *arms*" (Webster 1953, 4), and, along with Morse and other prominent educators, he argued that the classrooms were an important place to develop and articulate such an identity. There, the sons and daughters of the new nation could learn from such subjects as geography and history, orthography and poetry to see and think and even spell and speak like Americans.

No one more urgently embodied the need for such an articulation than the would-be immigrant who sought to assume the mantle of Americanism. It was crucial to Americanize newcomers quickly lest they challenge the precarious terms of the emergent national identity. What we might retroactively call nativist sentiments preceded the fledgling nation. Benjamin Franklin articulated a common sentiment when he wondered in 1751, "Why should Pennsylvania, founded by the *English*, become a Colony of *Aliens*, who will shortly be so numerous as to Germanize us instead of our Anglifying them, and will never adopt our Language or Customs, any more than they can acquire our Complexion?" (Franklin, quoted in Labaree 1959, 99). The imperative to distinguish between Americanism and Englishness amplified such sentiments, as it fueled efforts to define the contours of an Americanism that could turn immigrants into Americans.

The nation's authors heeded Webster's call. Following a cessation of immigration during the War of 1812, the first significant wave of immigration began in the 1820s, coinciding with an outpouring of historical fiction penned by such authors as Washington Irving, James Fenimore Cooper, Lydia Maria Child, Catherine Maria Sedgwick, and Nathaniel Hawthorne. Although their work has not typically been classified as "immigrant literature," immigrants and other strangers are central figures in many works by these writers, who sought to fashion an emerging national identity to complement the new political entity.

In their struggle to adapt to the distinctive culture of the new nation, for example, the female protagonists of Child's 1824 *Hobomok* and Sedgwick's 1827 *Hope Leslie*, both of whom come from England to settle in the colonies, dramatize the terms of that identity. Both novelists explain the motivation for their tales as responses to the many calls for a national literature featured in the nation's periodicals. The 22-year-old Lydia Maria Francis (not yet Child) adopts the

Author Lydia Maria Child wrote *An Appeal in Favor of That Class of Americans Called Africans* (1833), an early and important antislavery book. (Library of Congress)

persona of a male author who explains in the preface that such calls have planted in him the " 'desire to write a New England novel' " (Child [1824] 1986, 3) and then offers the story as the putatively discovered manuscript of an ancestor that manifests "the varying tints of domestic detail [that] are already concealed by the ivy which clusters around the tablets of our recent history" (Child [1824] 1986, 6). In the preface to *Hope Leslie*, Sedgwick offers her novel "to illustrate not the history, but the character of the times" (Sedgwick [1827] 1987, 3). Both novels depict a "national character" through anachronisms that superimpose the values of their moment onto their historical sketches of the colonies.

The fledgling nation needed a history that could turn a largely Anglo-American population into Americans, and a common strategy was to establish them as the ostensible natural heirs of an antiquated indigenous population. Such histories obscured, or at least justified, colonial violence, as exemplified in both novels, despite the authors' efforts to depict their heroines' grappling with the cultural biases and exclusions that were plaguing their early nineteenth-century moment. At a time when legal battles and violent eruptions were witnessed in the nation's efforts to disenfranchise tribal nations and destroy tribal culture, Child's Mary Conant and Sedgwick's Hope Leslie befriend indigenes, whose nobility they recognize, acknowledge the incompatibility of their cultures, and ultimately become "native" Americans by replacing the original inhabitants—with their blessing. Indigenous protagonists in both novels serve as agents of Americanization, and, in so doing, embody the intrinsic violence of that process.

The daughter and sole surviving child of a rigid Puritan patriarch who rejects her Royalist fiancé, Mary experiences life in the colonies as dreary and difficult. News of her fiancé's reputed death leaves her feeling desperate, and she impulsively marries Hobomok, a Wampanoag, who has befriended the community and fallen in love with Mary. Although Mary feels bound to Hobomok because of her wedding vows, his kindness, and, eventually, their child, when her fiancé turns up alive and still wanting to marry her, Hobomok removes the barrier by effecting his own removal " 'far off among some of the red men in the west,' " a benevolent version of the (violent) contemporary policy of "Indian Removal" (Child [1824] 1986, 139). The novel concludes with the English settlers all realizing their commonalities in contrast to the irreconcilable stranger, Hobomok. The new nation finds its analogue in the 1820s ideal of family, which turns the rigid Puritan patriarchs into benevolent fathers and can even assimilate Mary and Hobomok's son into the nation. His Americanization is complete, ironically, when he is sent to England to be educated—and thereby fully anglicized. An individual can be absorbed where a collective native presence cannot.

Sedgwick's Hope Leslie is similarly Americanized through her contact with indigenes. Hope and her sister, Faith, come to the colonies as orphans after their mother dies en route. They are taken in by their mother's erstwhile fiancé, William Fletcher, whose Puritanism had proved an insurmountable obstacle to

their marriage and occasioned his emigration. The Fletcher household includes Magawisca and Oneco, two Pequot children who had been captured in an English raid on their village while the men were away hunting. Seeking his children and vengeance, their father enlists several Mohawk companions to raid the house, where they kill Mrs. Fletcher and her children, with the exception of her oldest son, Everell, who, with Faith, is spared because of Magawisca's and Oneco's intervention, but who are nonetheless taken captive. The novel continues to build on the children's attachments across cultural barriers via intermarriage.

While the children's relationships seem to offer the promise of a peaceful, integrated nation, the novel underscores both their spiritual bonds and their cultures' uncrossable borders. On one hand, Magawisca and Hope appreciate the "mysterious" workings of fate that had led their mothers "from a far distance to rest together [in adjoining graves in an English cemetery]—their children connected in indissoluble bonds!" (Sedgwick [1827] 1987, 201). On the other hand, to Hope and Everell's plea at the end of the novel that Magawisca remain with them, the native responds that " 'the Indian and the white man can no more mingle and become one, than day and night' " (Sedgwick, 1987, 349). Faith, who has married Oneco, is absorbed into her Pequot family, and the spirited Hope is domesticated by her marriage to Everell; while Magawisca, like Hobomok, remains an irreconcilable stranger who presides over and enables the English settlers' transformation into Americans and who tacitly forgives their violence and confirms their right to the land. The two novels' reconstituted families represent an emerging immigrant ideal. Mary and Hope adapt to a new environment, as they demonstrate their fitness to embody and to reproduce "America." The "America" they embody is an ideal of inclusion and paternal benevolence, modeled on an idealized family that obscures not only the exclusions but also the violence of the assimilation process.

That violence is the subject of Nathaniel Hawthorne's depiction of the earliest articulations of a national identity viewed through the eyes of an idealistic stranger. "My Kinsman, Major Molineux" (1832) is set in the pre-Revolution colonies just as "the people" had begun to "look[,] with most jealous scrutiny to the exercise of power, which did not emanate from themselves" (Hawthorne [1832] 1982, 68). Robin, a youth from the country, sets out for the city and to meet his kinsman, Major Molineux, a British colonial governor, "respecting the future establishment of [him or his brother] in life" (Hawthorne [1832] 1982, 81). But he finds the world he encounters incomprehensible, dangerous, and disorienting, for he is continually met with mockery and threats when asking for directions to his kinsman's house. Nothing makes sense until he comes face to face with a tarred-and-feathered Major Molineux. Although horrified by the encounter, his incorporation into the violence of the scene is marked by his joining in the townspeople's laughter. The story represents the coercive as opposed to consensual dimensions of the Revolution and prompts readers to consider the violence that is both intrinsic to assimilation and at the heart of a national identity.

The struggles and estrangement recorded in the accounts of the immigrants who came in the decades in which Child, Sedgwick, and Hawthorne penned their tales to mark their experiences as closer to Robin's than to Mary's or Hope's. Economics rather than religion was the most significant motivating factor in the immigration of the antebellum period, and it came largely from Ireland and Germany, with Scandinavia and, on the West Coast, China, South America, and Mexico contributing significant numbers as well. Difficulties involving literacy, especially in English, access to publications, and leisure to write all contribute to a relative dearth of publications, but diaries and letters bear witness to the hardships and alienation that were common characteristics of an immigrant's life. While letters to family and friends back home often expressed amazement at American cities as well as the wide open spaces further west (where many settled with the intention of farming), they most typically record dismay and disappointment at the strangeness of the customs, the lack of community and law and order, and the sheer amount of hard work that it took just to survive. These accounts register a marked difference between the promise of this new land and daily life within its borders.

Mid-nineteenth-century Norwegian immigrant Gro Gudmundsrud Svendsen misses her native land and finds America wanting by comparison. She is troubled by the American women she encounters on her journey, finding them to be "the vainest women [she has] ever seen. . . . loaded down with golden trinkets. No moderation, no taste" (Svendsen 1950, 24). Once she is settled, she complains that "one must readjust oneself and learn everything all over again, even to the preparation of food. We are told that the women of America have much leisure time, but I haven't yet met any woman who thought it so! Here the mistress of the house must do all the work that the cook, the maid, and the housekeeper would do in an upper-class family at home. Moreover, she must do her work as well as these three together do it in Norway." Critical of the "shoddy and careless workmanship everywhere" (Svendsen 1950, 28–29), she cautions those considering immigration to bring their possessions with them since "everything Norwegian is of better quality than what can be bought" in America. Svendsen hoped eventually to return to her beloved Norway and is especially disappointed when her husband is "coaxed and threatened" until he finally becomes a citizen and angry that he must then fight in the Civil War (Svendsen 1950, 40, 65). While the change in customs and language barriers contributed to the hardship and sense of loneliness, American-born migrants reported similar feelings of disappointment and alienation.

Those immigrants who settled in the cities similarly experienced many of the same disappointments as their American-born counterparts. People who came to the city seeking more comfortable economic circumstances encountered urban violence; crime; dirty, low-paying, and dangerous jobs in factories; and squalid living conditions. The German immigrant and pioneering woman physician Marie Zakrzewska laments the fate of numerous women she had encountered who left their European homes for the cities of the United States with the promise of employment only to find degradation and exploitation. "Shame on society," she chastens, "that women are forced to surrender themselves to an abandoned life and to death when so many are enjoying wealth and luxury in extravagance!" (Zakrzewska 1924, 96–97). Assuring her readers that she is "no friend to communism in any form[,]" she advocates for greater access to education for women in America, immigrant and native-born alike, and notes that, while the fate of these women is not unique in the United States, it is a particular shame that "this great free nation . . . notwithstanding, lets its women starve" (Zakrzewska 1924, 97).

The novels of one of the most prolific immigrant writers in this period, Irish-born Mary Anne Sadlier, offers scathing critiques of the conditions of life for the working classes in the United States as well as the corrosiveness of a culture that values earthly over spiritual riches. Many of Sadlier's characters, such as the eponymous heroine of *Bessy Conway; or the Irish Girl in America* (1861), come to America for money, opportunities, or adventure, but most find only hardship and corruption. Bessy is scandalized by her fellow (immigrant) servants' lack of religious convictions and moral standards. An immigrant priest confirms her sense of the superiority of Irish culture, noting " 'the calm repose, so to speak, that pervades Irish life, the contentment which springs from true religion, and is altogether opposed to that feverish whirl of excitement in which people here are perpetually engaged: —honor seeking!—money-seeking!— office-seeking!—progress!—utility!' " (Sadlier [1861] 1863, 125).

On her return home to Ireland, Bessy warns her compatriots against the temptations of " 'dress and finery, and balls and dances,' " which corrupt " 'many a girl . . . that leaves home a simple country girl with the fear of God in her heart, and the blush of modesty on her cheek, [but] turns out very bad and very indifferent in America' " (Sadlier [1861] 1863, 295).

While *Hobomok* and *Hope Leslie* used the contrast with indigenes to underscore the similarities— and heal family rifts—between British Royalists and Puritans, Sadlier stresses the threat to Catholics posed by " 'Protestants and Jews, and everything that way' " (Sadlier [1861] 1863, 295) in the mobile, materialistic, and antitraditional American culture. One of her earliest novels—*The Blakes and the Flanagans: A Tale Illustrative of Irish Life in the United States* (1855)—contrasts two families to dramatize the dangers of giving in to American materialism. The Blakes are destroyed by intermingling with Protestants; while their cousins, the Flanagans, thrive by maintaining

their Catholicism. Sadlier finds even love an insufficient justification to renounce faith and homeland; the protagonist of a later novel, *Confessions of an Apostate* (1864), watches his family succumb to disaster and ultimately dies a lonely but repentant exemplar for the Irish community to which he returns after his sojourn to America, where he converted to Protestantism to marry the woman he loved.

Sadlier wrote against a backdrop of two related trends: anti-immigrant sentiment in the United States, evinced in the rise of nativist organizations as well as the proliferation of nativist sentiment, on one hand; and the rise of ethnic identities and organizations on the other. These trends fueled one another. Anxieties about labor competition, differences in customs, and, in some cases, religion underlay nativism and prompted the emergence of such organizations as the Know-Nothings. Nativist sentiment, in turn, galvanized a sense of cultural solidarity among groups that would have been divided along regional, class, or other lines in their natal lands. It helped, that is, to create nationally based hyphenated identities. As Sadlier's work attests, immigrant groups' prejudice against mainstream cultural influences and other immigrant groups evinced a vehemence that helped to strengthen the newly forged bonds of cultural nationalism within these immigrant groups.

The mid-nineteenth century witnessed the rise of a race science that further consolidated these new ethnic categories. The biological distinction of groups, such as "the Jews" or "the Irish" was a subject of debate, and immigrant writing increasingly recorded discrepancies between the professed democratic ideals of the nation versus its exclusionary policies and social practices. Those discrepancies found especially dramatic expression in writings by and about members of groups that, while not conventionally marked as "immigrants," were especially dehumanized by the contemporary race science. The tacit assumption that "immigration" implies some kind of choice on the part of the migrant is made more apparent by the groups that do not fall under that classification: notably, Africans, who were forcibly removed from their homes ("involuntary migrants") during the years of the Middle Passage; members of tribal nations who were "resettled" under the European colonizers' "Indian Removal" policies; and Mexicans who found themselves cultural outsiders in their homes when national borders shifted. Yet, the literary output of these groups significantly shaped American letters as it raised questions about the terms of American identity that complemented the challenges of the literature of marginalized immigrant groups.

The genre of the slave narrative in particular underscored the discrepancy between the "peculiar institution" and the ideals of the American republic embraced by immigrants; and it showed how enslaved persons were excluded not only from the rights and privileges of citizenship, but also from the fullest expression of humanity and, as a result, from access to a participatory American identity. The renowned orator and antislavery spokesman Frederick Douglass, for example, explains in his hard-hitting 1852 oration "What to the Slave is the Fourth of July" that such exclusions challenge the very meaning of an "America" that he declares to be "false to the past, false to the present, and . . . false to the future," as they manifest the slipperiness of the concept of an "American" (Douglass [1852] 1985, 369).

Late Nineteenth Century

The consolidation of the post–Civil War nation necessarily entailed a new iconography, and nothing more powerfully symbolized its professed ideals than the Statue of Liberty, designed by the French sculptor Frédéric Bartholdi and dedicated in October 1886. Instrumental to its iconographic status was the poem inscribed on a plaque at its base, which honors, "A mighty woman with a torch, whose flame / Is the imprisoned lightning, and her name / Mother of Exiles." The poet of "The New Colossus" was Emma Lazarus, a native-born American of Portuguese-Jewish descent, and into the mouth of this Mother she puts the words that would become the professed creed of the modern nation:

"Give me your tired, your poor,
Your huddled masses yearning to be free,
The wretched refuse of your teeming shore.
Send these, the homeless, tempest-tost to me,
I lift my lamp beside the golden door!" (Lazarus [1886] 1993, 457–58)

While economic hardship motivated the journey of many of the immigrants of this period, like the immigrants of the prewar period, others came to escape religious and political persecution, and their narratives record both their excitement on seeing the powerful symbol of American liberty for the first time and frequently their rapid disappointment soon thereafter when they encountered the realities of Ellis Island, or any other port of entry, and beyond.

Ironically, Lazarus herself expressed ambivalence about her natal land in her writings. Her experience of anti-Semitism led to her expression of her disappointment that "Even in free America, we have not yet succeeded everywhere and at all times in persuading the non-Jewish community to accept or reject us upon our personal merits, instead of condemning us as a race for the vices and follies of individual members. This species of injustice, from which we occasionally suffer, in common with some other races, is the inevitable consequence of our representing an unpopular minority in opposition to a dominant and numerically overwhelming majority" (Lazarus 1883, 608). Lazarus registered her ambivalence by both joining the nascent movement that would soon become known as Zionism in advocating a Jewish homeland in Palestine and continuing to believe in the democratic ideals she associated with the land of her birth. She puts both her critique of and her faith in her homeland into the mouths of the two protagonists of one of her two works of fiction, "The Eleventh Hour," which she published in *Scribner's* magazine in 1878.

When Sergius Azoff, a Romanian immigrant and artist, expresses his despair at both the corruption of America and the materialism that forestalls artistic expression and achievement, his American-born interlocutor, Dick Bayard, counsels patience, urging him to "discriminate between the vulgar noise of a venomous world of ignorant politicians and the grand, seldom-heard voice of the American people." Yet, while the story ends with Bayard's having persuaded Azoff not to commit suicide, as he had intended, Lazarus gives no particular reason to trust the perceptions of the "loyal-eyed American" over those of the "stately artist" (Lazarus 1878, 256).

The immigrants who arrived in unprecedented numbers between 1880 and 1920—when the percentage of the foreign-born reached as high as 14.7 (1880 and 1910 censuses) and of native-born children of mixed or foreign-born parents climbed from 16.5 to 21.5 percent of the total population—contributed to a rapidly changing demographic that stepped up debates surrounding immigration. Opponents of immigration often drew on the pronouncements of the nation's most prominent statistician, Francis Amasa Walker, who had earned his reputation at least partly through his innovation in the censuses of 1870 and 1880, which he superintended. Walker warned that the data collected in the census showed a tendency toward what he called "racial suicide," in which white middle- and upper-class people were having fewer children, while immigrants and other "non-white" ethnic or racial groups were reproducing themselves at much greater rates.

"Race suicide" became a watchword among groups advocating immigrant restriction, but even many of their opponents worried about perceived population discrepancies. Theodore Roosevelt famously drew on such pronouncements when he expressed concern about the reproduction of native-born, white Americans, as in an oft-cited letter from 1902, where he warned that "if the [native-born white] men of the nation are not anxious . . . to be fathers of families, and if the women do not recognize that the greatest thing for any woman is to be a good wife and mother, . . . that nation has cause to be alarmed about its future" (Roosevelt [1902] 1904, 510).

Efforts to define such terms as "Americanism" and "Americanization" proliferated in the mainstream media and scholarly journals, such as the *Forum* and the *American Journal of Sociology*. The need to reproduce a clearly defined "Americanism" prompted the prominent Harvard English professor Barrett Wendell, a founder of composition studies, to turn his attention to "American literature." Hoping that the idea of "American literature" would help to articulate the national identity of the emerging world power ("as independent in arts as in arms"), he penned *A Literary History of America* (1901) and offered the first American-literature classes at Harvard. Wendell believed in both great literature and the classroom as important sites of socialization, and his interest in articulating a reproducible (white) Americanism

informed his pedagogy—how as well as what he taught. In the classroom, American values were transmitted and Americans made. The stakes could hardly be higher. "Nationality is generally conceived to be a question of race, of descent, of blood," he wrote in the introduction to his *Literary History of America*, "and yet in human experience there is a circumstance perhaps more potent in binding men together than any physical tie. . . . In a strange, subtle way each language grows to associate with itself the ideals and the aspirations and the fate of those peoples with whose life it is inextricably intermingled" (Wendell 1901, 3). Learning to express oneself effectively and appropriately was, for Wendell, central to the development of character and, by extension, to the responsibilities of citizenship.

Through his wife, Wendell came in contact with the nascent science of bacteriology. Intrigued by theories of microbial transmission, he incorporated the metaphor of contagion liberally into his literary writings. He saw language and the values it embodied as contagious, and literary works as "carriers," for good or ill. Literary contagion was fundamentally institutional, the glue of national culture, and it underscored the need for experts who, through their reading practices and rhetorical strategies, could monitor this spread of culture and turn the literary "carrier" into a bearer of an appropriately communicable Americanism.

Wendell offered that Americanism—and its means of transmission—as an antidote against the influx of immigrants who threatened American culture with their corrupting language and ideas, just as medical practitioners and public health officials warned that the "flood," as it was commonly called, of southern and East European immigrants threatened public health with their strange diseases. It is not coincidence, in fact, that the first identified healthy carrier of disease, an Irish immigrant named Mary Mallon (and known more widely by her infamous epithet "Typhoid Mary"), became the focus of national attention, while other such (native-born) individuals, many of whom were responsible for more deaths from typhoid, remained anonymous. The amorphous conceptual threat that immigrants posed to "American identity" found vivid expression in the more comprehensible notion of health anxieties: as threats to the health of the national body politic.

Early Twentieth Century

Typically, the strongest opponents of the restrictionists shared with them a concern about the integrity of "America." But their solution was strong Americanization programs in the schools and settlement houses and other places where immigrants might gather. The progressive philosopher and educator John Dewey argued, in a 1902 speech at the annual meeting of the National Education Association, that "every public school" should do "something of the same sort of work that is now done by a settlement or two scattered at wide distances thru the city." It should be "a social clearing house . . . where ideas and beliefs may be exchanged, not merely in the arena of formal discussion—for argument alone breeds misunderstanding and fixes prejudice—but in ways where ideas are incarnated in human form and clothed with the winning grace of personal life" (Dewey 1902, 381). Americanism had to be reproduced ideologically as well as literally by American families, which served as both metaphor of and socializing agent for the nation.

Settlement workers set up houses in immigrant neighborhoods where immigrant families could learn both English and American values and gender roles: men could learn trades, while women could learn American cooking and housekeeping. *Putnam's Monthly and the Reader* described the "character factories" that were, as the subtitle of Day Allen Willey's "Americans in the Making" explained, "New England's Method of Assimilating the Alien." In these institutions, set up on the model of the four-year college, "the hundred and odd members of the student body are also members of one family. During the four years they become part of a household which as far as possible is patterned after the typical New England home. They become accustomed to opening the day with religious exercises. The young women assist in the preparation of the meals and the care of the buildings, and thus are taught the vocation of the American housewife, while the male students engage in gardening and do other work about the premises, by which they partly pay for their living expenses" (Willey 1909, 462–63).

The goal of these institutions, like the settlement houses in the major cities, was to address "the peril which threatens [the American] home" from "the number of foreigners yearly settling on Puritan soil" by teaching "young men and young women . . . to become apostles of Americanism among those of their own blood" (Willey 1909, 457, 462). The Americanizing importance of the family is evident as well in the Danish immigrant Jacob Riis's 1890 reformist journalistic account of immigrant ghettoes, *How the Other Half Lives*, when he recommends loosening the restriction of immigration legislated by the 1882 Chinese Exclusion Act, which sought to halt the immigration of a nationality that he labeled "in no sense a desirable element of the population," in order to promote Chinese families: "I would have the door opened wider—" Riis wrote, "for [the Chinese worker's] wife; make it a condition of his coming or staying that he bring his wife with him. Then, at least, he might not be what he now is and remains, a homeless stranger among us" (Riis [1890] 1971, 83).

Americanization was an important topic in immigrant fiction, which registers a range of responses from highly critical of America (reminiscent of Sadlier's novels) to celebratory, although always with the expression of some form of reservation. The process of assimilation was never free from the hint of violence, which, while not typically as explicit as the violence evident in the fiction of Child, Sedgwick, and Hawthorne, nonetheless entailed a self-denial that writers represented as some form of profound loss or death. The most iconic image of assimilation, as well as the work that most dramatically popularized it, expressed both the exuberant hopefulness and the violence inherent in the transformation that characterized the immigrant writing that proliferated in this period.

"America is God's Crucible," proclaims the protagonist of the British Jewish Israel Zangwill's 1908 play, *The Melting-Pot*, "where all the races of Europe are melting and re-forming . . . [T]he real American has not yet arrived. He is only in the Crucible . . . he will be the fusion of all races, the coming superman" (Zangwill [1908] 1914). The play premiered in Washington D.C.'s Columbia Theater for an audience that included an enthusiastic President Theodore Roosevelt. Although the image had been in use since the eighteenth century, the melting-pot quickly became the most familiar emblem of assimilation and the promise of a nation that the proponents of immigration argued would "fuse" the influx of new blood and talent into "the coming superman."

Yet, as both the alchemical emblem and Zangwill's play were hailed as unqualified celebrations of immigration and assimilation, critics seemed to overlook the violence and ambiguity implicit in both, as the protagonist's inability to suppress his past suggests. Like Lazarus, Zangwill was (ironically) a Zionist and, later, a Territorialist (supporter of a Jewish state wherever it may be located), and he never immigrated to the United States. His play followed the development of a romance between David Quixano, a Russian-Jewish immigrant, and Vera Revendal, a Russian Orthodox settlement worker. The murder of David's family in a notorious pogrom, in which he was himself wounded, prompts his immigration to the United States, where he comes to live with relatives. The anti-Semitic Vera is drawn to David's magical violin-playing and is subsequently won over by his passion and charisma as well as by the visionary symphony he is composing to capture the music of the melting-pot and the "new American" that is being forged there.

David's enchanting spirit casts its spell on everyone he meets—his belief in his adopted land is contagious—but he remains haunted by the memory of the Kishinev pogrom and falls prey to a dark depression when he is reminded of it by name or by the pain in his (violinist's) left shoulder, where he had suffered a bullet wound. His betrothal to Vera appears to offer a cure, but the crisis of the play turns on his discovery that her estranged father, who has come to America to dissuade her from marrying a Jew, is the same man whose face haunts David's darkest memory: a man he knows as the "butcher" of Kishinev, who oversaw the infamous pogrom.

The discovery ends his betrothal and threatens his powerful, sustaining vision of America, as he descends into a melancholy bordering on madness. The immigrants' enthusiastic reception of his symphony following its performance in the settlement house, however, restores David's faith in his vision of America and his determination to forget his past. Vera is skeptical of the possibility of such a

renunciation, and, when he implores her to renew their betrothal, she worries that she will remind him of her father and the pogrom; she is convinced that a repressed past will invariably return. The stage directions confirm her suspicions; she kisses him "as we Russians kiss at Easter—three kisses of peace," which the stage directions describe "as in ritual solemnity." David notes the irony of her choice of words, since "Easter was the date of the massacre," and assures her that he is nonetheless "at peace" (Zangwill [1908] 1914, 198). But rituals are for commemorating, not forgetting, and David's words show that while he may be "at peace," he has not forgotten the past.

While David's assurances follow the paradigm of assimilation with which the melting-pot is associated—he is exuberant in his celebration of "the glory of America, where all races and nations come to labour and look forward!"—Vera's skepticism, the stage directions, and even the images of both the churning crucible/melting-pot, which Zangwill describes as "roaring and bubbling ... stirring and seething," and "the great Alchemist," who "melts and fuses [the immigrants] with his purging flame," undermine an uncomplicated celebration of that vision (Zangwill [1908] 1914, 198–99). The process of transformation cannot be painless, and efforts to forget the past invite its uncanny return—for David, as for his real-life counterparts.

The Russian Jewish immigrant Mary Antin embraces, in her 1912 autobiographical account *The Promised Land*, the same ideal of absolute assimilation and forgetting that David expresses. Her odd analogy troubles her apparently unqualified exuberance when she assures her readers, "I am just as much out of the way as if I were dead, for I am absolutely other than the person whose story I have to tell" (Antin 1912, xi). Antin dramatizes that otherness through a use of pronouns that marks her complete alienation from her earlier self: "I could speak in the third person and not feel that I was masquerading. I can analyze my subject, I can reveal everything; for *she,* and not *I,* is my real heroine. My life I have still to live; her life ended when mine began" (Antin 1912, xi). Yet, the irrepressibility of the past is clear in her confession of her "long[ing] to forget." That longing is in fact painful, as she notes: "I think I have thoroughly assimilated my past—I have done its bidding—I want now to be of to-day. It is painful to be consciously of two worlds. The Wandering Jew in me seeks forgetfulness. I am not afraid to live on and on, if only I do not have to remember too much" (Antin 1912, xiv).

The Wandering Jew, as in Simmel's description of the wanderer, carries the reminder of past affiliations. Neither Antin nor the "group" into which she claims to be wholly assimilated (American) can ever forget her past. The Wandering Jew in her troubles those claims and provokes a consciousness of belonging to two worlds that Antin describes as "painful." While the exact source of that pain is unclear, it seems to emanate from that consciousness itself and from the injunction to forget. Antin cannot finally kill off her old self, much as she might long to, and the very confession of that longing undermines the thoroughness of the assimilation that she proclaims throughout her autobiography. Her language betrays her, as in her odd claim that she tells her tale, "like the Ancient Mariner . . . in order to be rid of it" (Antin 1912, xv). The eponymous character of Samuel Coleridge's *The Rime of the Ancient Mariner* relates his tale compulsively, as part of a cosmic punishment. Yet, not only does the telling of the tale afford him no relief, but he also imparts grief, if accompanied by wisdom, to his listeners.

Even the accounts of immigrants who belonged to groups that did not threaten to contribute to race suicide, such as that of the Danish Riis, were not entirely free of ambiguity. Having immigrated in 1870, Riis was part of the wave of Scandinavian immigration from the late nineteenth century through the early twentieth century that was motivated by largely economic factors (especially a shortage of land), but also religious intolerance and mandatory military service. While Scandinavian immigrants produced a body of literary works, Riis is unusual among them in publishing his works in English. In his autobiographical account *The Making of an American* (1901), Riis anticipates Antin in depicting his Americanization in the language of conversion. While recovering from a long illness in Denmark, Riis reports seeing "the flag of freedom" on a ship passing outside his window. Although he is "sick and discouraged," the glimpse of the flag seems miraculously to cure him.

He "thanked God, and, like unto the man sick of the palsy, arose . . . and went home, healed" (Riis [1901] 1928, 283). A shift in pronouns, again anticipating Antin's account, marks the conversion: "I have told the story of the making of an American. There remains to tell how I found out that he was made and finished at last." Whereas Antin uses the third person to describe her past self, Riis invokes it to signal his new *American* self. "I" and "he" do not, that is, refer to the past and present selves; rather, they coexist as though the Americanization has split him in two. The third person, the American, is a stranger whom "I," the storyteller, has to learn to recognize. This odd formulation signals the kind of estrangement, expressed through an apparent excessiveness and self-consciousness. Many later theorists of Americanization, such as Horace Kallen, would come to recognize those features as tell-tale characteristics of immigrant ambivalence—their marginality.

For many immigrant writers, that ambivalence found expression in familial struggle, as the protagonists are pulled between familial traditions, represented by a parent or spouse, and American or more Americanized peers. The eponymous protagonist of the Lithuanian Jewish Abraham Cahan's *Yekl* (1896) exemplifies this struggle. Economics motivated his immigration, and he vows to send for his wife and infant son as soon as he has earned enough money for them to live on. But Yekl's struggles begin with that promise, for he gives in to the temptations of life in America and finds himself spending his money on social events even while he chastises himself for doing so, until his father's death prompts the immigration of his young family. Yekl, who has renamed himself Jake and worked to become a "*regely* Yankee," is disgusted by his wife's "uncouth and un-American appearance": "She was naturally dark of complexion, and the nine or ten days spent at sea had covered her face with a deep bronze, which combined with her prominent cheek bones, inky little eyes, and, above all, the smooth black wig, to lend her resemblance to a squaw" (Cahan [1896] 1970, 34).

Cahan tells a story that he had surely witnessed numerous times, in which the unwitting processes of Americanization had put more than an ocean between spouses, siblings, or even parents and children.

Yekl/Jake ends up divorcing his wife and immediately becoming betrothed to a more Americanized fellow immigrant, Mamie. Yet, the novella ends ominously, with Jake's sense of entrapment, as he sits on a cable car with Mamie and her "emissary" en route to be married and feeling "painfully reluctant to part with his long-coveted freedom" (Cahan [1896] 1970, 89).

Variants of Yekl/Jake's struggle were common in autobiographical writings by immigrants and other cultural outsiders of this period. For Eurasian writer Edith Maud Eaton (Sui Sin Far), the sense of being between cultures that she had as an immigrant corresponds to her experience of growing up mixed race in England. She begins her autobiographical account, "Leaves from the Mental Portfolio of an Eurasian" (1909), with the memory of her frustrated attempt to communicate an early experience of cultural bias. Overhearing her nurse's gossip about Sui Sin Far's mother's nationality (she is Chinese), she tries to report the incident to her mother, but her effort earns her the epithet "storyteller" from her nurse and a slap from her mother. Storytelling for her is associated from that time on with the pain of a cultural outsider's observations about a world in which it is difficult to find her place.

Espousing intermarriage as the logical extension of the melting-pot, she concedes that her "mother's race is as prejudiced as [her] father's" and expresses her conviction that "[o]nly when the whole world becomes as one family will human beings be able to see clearly and hear distinctly" (Eaton 1909, 129). Racism, for her, is an inevitable outgrowth of racial difference that not only thwarts cross-cultural communication, but also impedes self-realization. Yet, despite her certainty "that some day a great part of the world will be Eurasian" (Eaton 1909, 129), her autobiographical narrative and many of her stories record the difficulties of bridging cultures, and she concludes "Leaves" with the hope that if she gives her "right hand to the Occidentals and [her] left to the Orientals, . . . between them they will not utterly destroy the insignificant 'connecting link' " (Eaton 1909, 132).

The anguish and perspectives evinced by Sui Sin Far and Yekl/Jake characterize the experience of a sociological type that University of Chicago sociologist Robert Park would identify as "marginal man." In his best-known essay, "Human Migration and the Marginal Man" (1928), the sociologist who pioneered the study of ethnicity and urban space in the United States builds on his former teacher Simmel's description of the stranger to describe the emergence of a "personality type" from the "relatively permanent" crisis that comes from the effort to live in two cultures (Park 1928, 893). Park, who was familiar with Cahan's work, saw the Jew who sought to escape the ghetto as the prototype, but by no means the only example, of this contemporary figure, who "may or may not be a mixed blood" but is in any case "an unstable character." Such figures were important to sociologists, he explained, because "it is in the mind of the marginal man—where the changes and fusions of culture are going on—that we can best study the processes of civilization and progress" (Park 1928, 881).

Park, who introduced the idea of human ecology into sociology, understood the social world as premised fundamentally on the biotic one. The relationship of the figure of "marginal man" to his (or her) surroundings was "symbiotic rather than social" (Park 1928, 887). Like Simmel's stranger, these figures were necessary to the ecology of the group. But he shared many immigrant writers' understanding of their sacrificial nature and recognized the anguish produced by the mental clash. Like Sui Sin Far, he believed that racial mixture would inevitably follow cultural contact—that it was humanity's certain horizon—although world war and global strife cast their shadows, and his work evinced increasing concern that the power of the racial tensions he sought to study could fuel global cataclysm before that horizon was reached (a vision that preceded the use of the atomic bomb, which Park did not live to see).

The German-Jewish philosopher Horace Kallen both shared Park's interest in the diversity of American culture and advocated "cultural pluralism" as a crucial premise of democracy. Kallen penned his oft-cited essay "Democracy versus the Melting-Pot," appeared in consecutive issues of the *Nation* in February 1915. It was a response to the publication of sociologist Edward Alsworth Ross's 1914 *The Old World in the New*, which cautioned about the danger contemporary immigration posed to the homogeneity of American culture and called for immigration restriction. In his essay, Kallen did not dispute the incompatibility of the new immigration with "that inward unanimity of action and outlook that make a national life," which Ross and other such critics decried. But he challenged the sociologist's understanding of American identity, calling the "ethnic dissimilarity" that so troubled Ross "one of the inevitable consequences of a democratic principle on which our theory of government is based" (Kallen 1915, 219).

Equally troubling to Kallen were the Americanization efforts of the settlement workers and other prophets of Americanization, including his friend John Dewey. Nothing better illustrated both the impossibility and the desirability of such "standardizing" efforts than the ambivalence that he identified in the work of the immigrant writers who most avidly embraced the ideal of Americanization, including Mary Antin and Jacob Riis, whose paeans to Americanization made them appear "more excessively and self-consciously American than Americans." Their claims defied belief for the popularizer of the term "cultural pluralism," who noted that they "protest too much, they are too self-conscious and self-centered, their 'Americanization' appears too much like an achievement, a *tour de force*, too little like a growth" (Kallen 1915, 193). That self-consciousness stemmed, he argued, from their inability to suppress the past; Kallen found nationality, unlike class, "inevitably intrinsic" (Kallen 1915, 194). Much like Zangwill, he celebrated the "federation or commonwealth of nationalities" that he saw emerging in the United States at the turn of the twentieth century; but unlike Zangwill, he championed not the grinding of the Crucible, but the healthy diversity of a democracy that recognized the productive messiness of heterogeneity (Kallen 1915, 219). "[N]o human being . . . is a mere mathematical unit of nature," Kallen intoned; "whatever else he changes, he cannot change his grandfather" (Kallen 1915, 194).

Kallen saw the ambivalence that he identified in the work of immigrant writers as intrinsic both to the experience of Americanization and to the idea of Americanism itself. The immigrants' work expresses "underneath the excellent writing, a dualism and the strain to overcome it" that corresponds to an analogous ambiguity in the mainstream American culture. The immigrant, like Simmel's stranger, is disturbing not so much in his or her difference from the group as in his or her similarity; the immigrant embodies the fundamental uncertainties and irresolution of the concept of America, which Kallen identifies precisely with the icon of the melting-pot. In contrast, Kallen offers the richness of mutual enhancement in place of conquest. He concludes his essay by invoking not the melting-pot of Zangwill's play, but the image with which it ends, a symphony in which " 'American civilization' may come to mean the perfection of the co-operative harmonies of 'European civilization,' the waste, the squalor, and the distress of Europe being eliminated—a multiplicity in a unity, an orchestration of mankind [in which] . . . each ethnic group is the natural instrument, its spirit and culture are its theme and melody, and the harmony and dissonances and discords of them all make the symphony of civilization" (Kallen 1915, 220).

Between the World Wars

Although the city was the most common setting of immigrant literature from the mid-nineteenth century to the mid-twentieth century, many immigrants moved westward in search of land. While the Norwegian writer Johan Bojer had documented the struggle of Norwegian settlers in the Dakotas in the late nineteenth century in his 1924 novel *Vor egen stemme* (*The Emigrants*, 1925), it was his countryman Ole Edvart Rølvaag, who had immigrated to the United States in 1896, who popularized that struggle in America with the publication of *Giants in the Earth*, an English translation of an earlier novel, in 1927. Rølvaag's prize-winning novel is among the best known of the immigrant works written in the author's native language, and it is characteristic of many of these works in its epic scope.

The novel follows Per Hansa and his family as they struggle to adjust to the isolation and harsh climate of the Dakotas. His wife Beret in particular cannot overcome her sense of foreboding in what seems to her to be a forsaken land. While Beret's laments, like those of her real-life counterpart Gro Gudmundsrud Svendsen, are similar to the complaints of American-born women pioneers, their distance from their homelands and their unfamiliarity with the English language and American culture exacerbates their sense of isolation. Beret descends temporarily into insanity as she tries to come to terms with the difficulty and loneliness of her life and eventually seeks stability through a devoutness that allows her to exert a small measure of control over the overwhelming uncertainties of her new life. While the novel ends bleakly, with Per Hansa's unnecessary death—he freezes to death in a severe winter storm, which he had braved because Beret insisted on his going in search of a minister to give communion to his dying friend Hans. And yet, the novel is part of a trilogy that follows the growth of the Norwegian-American community. *Giants in the Earth* celebrates the vision of cultural pluralism that Kallen had advocated.

Although set against a radically different backdrop, in the novels of the Polish-Jewish immigrant Anzia Yezierska, family struggles yield to productive marriages that similarly conform to assimilation processes advocated by settlement workers and character factories, and herald the possibility of the kind of harmony that Kallen imagined. These marriages are often preceded by marriages or other liaisons with more inappropriate spouses. A consistent theme in Yezierska's fiction involves non-Jewish-American men's attraction to fiery Jewish women who believe, in the words of a recurring character Shenah Pessah, that " 'the hunger to make [her]self a person . . . can't be crushed by nothing—nor nobody—the life higher!' " (Yezierska [1920] 1997, 42). Shenah's declaration typifies the sentiment of other female protagonists of Yezierska's 1920 short-story collection *Hungry Hearts* in its expression of a yearning to make use of the opportunities afforded by the United States. That yearning characteristically takes shape as a desire to create in some fashion, although in their struggle to understand it, they often begin by experiencing it through their love for an American male mentor, frequently a teacher (modeled, perhaps, on Yezierska's own love affair with her teacher, John Dewey), who is searching, as one such character puts it, for an antidote to his " 'age-long repressions' " (Yezierska [1920] 1997, 87). Those relationships generally prove incompatible and lead the way to the women's realization of their own potential and often to more suitable marriages.

The women in *Hungry Hearts* are prototypes for the female protagonists of Yezierska's novels, the 1923 *Salome of the Tenements* and the 1925 *Bread Givers*. In *Salome,* the protagonist, Sonya Vrunsky—whose marriage to the wealthy philanthropist John Manning suggests the marriage of Yezierska's friend and fellow eastern European Jewish immigrant Rose Pastor to well-known philanthropist Graham Stokes—discovers her incompatibility with a man who "was bound in with centuries of inhibitions that would take a cataclysmic love to break down" (Yezierska [1923] 1995, 36). Their love is based on a mutual fantasy that attests to the cultural preconceptions each has of the other. Manning's vision seems to emerge directly out of the pages of *The Melting-Pot*, as he proclaims that their marriage represents " 'the mingling of the races . . . The oriental mystery and the Anglo-Saxon clarity that will pioneer a new race of men.' " Sonya is suspicious of his vision and complains about his need to explain their "perfect" happiness "in high words from sociology books."

In turn, she resorts to a language that is similarly conventional, declaring, " 'I can't think. I only feel that we are for each other as the sun is for the earth. Races and classes and creeds, the religion of your people and my people melt like mist in our togetherness. . . . We are the sphinx—the eternal riddle of life—man and woman in love' " (Yezierska [1923] 1995, 108). They eventually divorce, and Sonya finds happiness and a genuine creative outlet both as and with a fashion designer, the Americanized Jew Jaky Solomon, better known by New York's Four Hundred as their most exclusive fashion designer, Jacques Hollins.

Similarly, Sara Smolinsky, the female protagonist of *Bread Givers* and youngest of four daughters of an Orthodox Jewish immigrant, struggles both with her conscience and against accusations leveled by her rigid and self-centered father that she is not an obedient and dutiful daughter. Eventually, she, like Sonya, finds both satisfaction and happiness in employment (she is a teacher) and with a more Americanized Jewish husband (the principal of her school). She works through her own ambivalence towards her Americanization in maternal terms, as she both proudly identifies and feels frustrated with her students, themselves children of immigrants. She initially falls in love with, and subsequently marries, the principal of her school, Hugo Seelig, because he is the only "one in [her] school who was what [she] had dreamed a teacher to be.... When he entered a classroom sunlight filled the place" (Yezierska [1925] 1975, 270).

Midcentury Viewpoints: Chicano and Japanese American

Many immigrant writers celebrated teaching as a process of becoming as well as creating Americans—within one's own ethnic group (as in Yezierska's novel), or across ethnic groups, as in the work of native-born Irish American Myra Kelly, who based her fictionalized accounts, such as *Little Citizens: The Humours of School Life* (1902), on her own experiences as a teacher on the Lower East Side. Such accounts conformed to the best version of the Americanization vision espoused by settlement

Mexican American author and scholar Américo Paredes. (University of Texas Libraries)

workers, educators like John Dewey, and politicians. But that vision became increasingly clouded, as the events of the century belied the optimism of either Kallen's or Zangwill's orchestral visions. The Chicano author Américo Paredes depicted the classroom as an important site of ideological transmission and violence, in which the protagonist of his novel *George Washington Gómez* (written in the late 1930s), although growing up on the land of his ancestors, "was gently prodded toward complete Americanization" (Paredes [1930s] 1990, 148), a process that includes "thinking in English" and learning to "feel infinitely dirty if he forgets to brush his teeth in the morning" (Paredes 1990, 149).

Paredes's protagonist, Guálinto, registers cultural fusion: his father insists on the "American" name of "Jorge Wachinton," hoping his son will do great things for his country, although he is called Guálinto because of his grandmother's mishearing of the name. The novel recounts Guálinto's struggles with the biases of a school system and other institutions in a racist border town and chronicles his coming to consciousness about the nature of his education, including his recognition that his history books tell a slanted story. Despite his valiant efforts to challenge the biases of his history lessons, however, Guálinto eventually becomes the "marginal man." Moving away from his home, he assimilates to the best of his ability, marrying an Anglo woman, serving in the armed forces in counterintelligence, and vowing to raise a child who does not need to learn Spanish. The novel ends with his temporary return to his hometown, where he has been assigned to "border security" (Paredes 1990, 299): the double-consciousness that he has experienced growing up has trained him to become, as his uncle points out, "a spy."

While Paredes dramatizes the impact of Guálinto's transformation, the psychological anguish of the marginal man is nowhere more fully explored than in the Japanese American John Okada's 1957 *No-No Boy*. It chronicles Ichiro Yamada's homecoming, after serving a prison term for having refused to serve in the U.S. Army and to swear unqualified allegiance to the United States during World War II. One among the fictional and autobiographical responses to Japanese internment by such authors as Toshio

Mori, Jeanne Wakatsuki Houston, Hisaye Yamamoto, Monica Sone, and the Canadian Joy Kogawa, Okada's novel explores the shock of discovering one's statelessness and the impossibility of responding adequately to that discovery. All of these works chronicle the experience of living through an intrinsic dehumanization that Okada describes bitterly in the preface to the novel: "when the Japanese bombs fell on Pearl Harbor . . . the Japanese in the U.S. became, by virtue of their ineradicable brownness and the slant eyes which, upon close inspection, will seldom appear slanty, animals of a different breed" (Okada [1957] 1979, iii).

Ichiro, like Simmel's stranger, is disturbing in his familiarity rather than his difference. In a marvelous twist, Okada marks the ordinariness of the experience of estrangement through the figure of a stranger in a hotel room who awakens from the "period between each night and day when one dies for a few hours, neither dreaming nor thinking nor tossing nor hating nor loving, but dying for a little while because life progresses in just such a way." Experiencing a "fleeting sound of lonely panic" and a "momentary terror," the stranger is relieved when "he remembers that he is away from home and smiles smugly as he tells himself that home is there waiting for him forever." That Ichiro has no such home comes as no surprise to the reader, but the contrast is starker: "For Ichiro, there was no intervening span of death to still his great unrest through the darkness of night" (Okada [1957] 1979, 39). Ichiro is cursed, like the ancient mariner, to wander through the dreamscape of a never-ending nightmare, embodying the countless stories of irresolution, ambivalence, and violence that no one wants to hear.

The only hope offered in Okada's novel is ambiguous at best. When Gary, a no-no boy like Ichiro, expresses gratitude for an imprisonment that he claims turned him into an artist, Ichiro is dubious. He finds it suspect when Gary celebrates a transformation that has turned "old friends" into "strangers," confessing " 'I've no one to talk to and no desire to talk, for I have nothing to say except what comes out of my paint tubes and brushes.' " But Gary's eyes betray none of "the fear and loneliness and bitterness that ought to have been there"; Ichiro instead sees "only the placidness reflected in the soft, gentle smile" (Okada [1957] 1979, 224).

If Gary has learned to channel his estrangement productively into artistic vision, however, the gruesome death of Ichiro's other fellow no-no boy, Freddie, with which the novel ends, is a reminder of its danger. One thinks of Sui Sin Far, of connecting links and the hope they will not be torn asunder before the nation catches up to the vision of its immigrant artists.

Coda

With the constant migrations and multiple challenges to the nation form that characterize late capital, it is not surprising that literature by and about immigrants has proliferated and that the figure of the stranger and the experience of estrangement have become dominant themes of literature and other arts generally in the more than half a century following the original publication (in Japan) of Okada's novel. The themes find cultural expression across genres, media, and forms as diverse as the many movements that fall promiscuously under the heading of "postmodernism" as well as in the contemporaneous emergence of the genre of science fiction. Estrangement becomes, as in Okada's novel, the occasion for cultural insight and artistic production.

While a shrinking globe and increasingly permeable boundaries make it ever more difficult to generalize about "immigrant literature" or its close cousins, "ethnic literature" and, more recently, "transnational literature," many contemporary writers have translated their experiences of multiple locations—and dislocations—into formal and thematic experimentation. The rapid decolonization in the 1960s and 1970s as well as changes in immigration policy resulted in a particular spike in immigrants from Asia, for example, whose literary output included some especially haunting and beautiful formal experiments that emerged from writers' meditations on the ways in which events resonate among and across locations. The work of such writers as Korean American Theresa Hak Kyung Cha, Chinese American John Yau, Filipina American Jessica Hagedorn, Indian American Amitav Ghosh, Burmese American Wendy Law-Yone, Vietnamese Americans Monique Truong, Linh Dinh, and Lê Thi Diem Thúy, Japanese American Karen Tei Yamashita, and numerous others translate the uncanny experience of estrangement into literary experiments that challenge the fundamental terms of classifications such as "genre" and "immigrant."

The category of "immigrant" and the classification of "immigrant" (and "ethnic") groups, as I have suggested throughout this chapter, emerges through its engagement with the unstable term "American." Characteristically, the production of and mainstream America's interest in "immigrant" (and "ethnic") literature surges when world events result in new categories of "dangerous strangers." Such a surge is evident, for example, following the events of September 11, 2001, by a heightened interest in literature by immigrants of Arab descent. Yet, what writers as diverse as Jordanian-Lebanese American Laila Halaby, Iraqi American Diana Abu-Jaber, Syrian American Mohja Kahf, Lebanese Americans Rabih Alameddine and Etel Adnan, and Palestinian American Suheir Hammad have most in common is the lens through which an American literary establishment is currently reading and classifying them.

Nothing better illustrates a continuing—and anxious—investment in the idea of the dangerous stranger, however, than the controversial legislation known as the Arizona Senate Bill 1070, which required aliens in Arizona to register with the U.S. government and to carry documentation of their registration with them at all times. Although the bill passed the Arizona State Legislature in 2010, its most controversial aspects were soon blocked by a U.S. district judge so that the law remained in limbo until June 2012, when the U.S. Supreme Court presented its decisions on S.B. 1070. The Court upheld Arizona's right to ask for documentation of legal residence, if a person were stopped for breaking the law, but it struck down the requirement of carrying documentation at all times and other key provisions. Other states, however, including Alabama, have since passed similar anti-illegal immigrant legislation, and it remains unclear what their legislative status will be. Nonetheless, the passage of these bills has resulted in violations of privacy and policies of harassment that may rival the worst chapters in the history of the nation. Simmel's exploration of the causes of estrangement, as well as the literature that has recorded its effects, offers important insight into the nature of this legislation as a symptom not just of urban

alienation, but also of the alien as an embodied projection of the threat of social and geopolitical change. Throughout American history, literature by and about immigrants has told the story of the sources and consequences of the anxieties that attend estrangement. With Sui Sin Far, we might hope that a deeper understanding of that story might at this time facilitate its conscious revision in the current moment.

Bibliography

Antin, Mary. 1912. *The Promised Land*. Boston: Houghton Mifflin Company.

Cahan, Abraham. 1970. *Yekl and the Imported Bridegroom and Other Stories of Yiddish New York* (1896, *Yekl*; 1898, stories). New York: Dover Publications, Inc.

Child, Lydia Maria. (1824) 1986. *Hobomok and Other Writings on Indians*, edited by Carolyn L. Karcher. New Brunswick, NJ: Rutgers University Press.

Dewey, John. 1902. "The School as Social Center." *Journal of the Proceedings and Addresses of the National Education Association. Forty-First Annual Meeting. 1902.* 373–83.

Douglass, Frederick. (1852) 1985. "What to the Slave is the Fourth of July." In *Frederick Douglass Papers*, vol. 2. Edited by John Blassingame. New Haven, CT: Yale University Press.

Douglass, Frederick. 1999. *Narrative of the Life of Frederick Douglass, an American Slave*. In *The Frederick Douglass Papers*, vol. 1, series 2, *Autobiographical Writings*. Edited by John W. Blassingame, John R. McKivigan, and Peter P. Hinks. New Haven, CT: Yale University Press.

Eaton, Edith Maud (Sui Sin Far). 1909. "Leaves from the Mental Portfolio of an Eurasian." *Independent* 66 (January 21): 125–32.

Franklin, Benjamin. 1959–1999. "Observations Concerning the Increase of Mankind, Peopling of Countries, etc." In *The Papers of Benjamin Franklin*, 35 vols., edited by Leonard W. Labaree, vol. 4, 225–34. New Haven, CT: Yale University Press. http://www.ditext.com/franklin/observations.html.

Hawthorne, Nathaniel. 1982. "My Kinsman, Major Molineux." In *Hawthorne: Tales and Sketches*. New York: Library of America.

Higham, John. 1984. *Send These to Me: Immigrants in Urban America*. Rev. ed. Baltimore: Johns Hopkins University Press.

Kallen, Horace. 1915. "Democracy versus the Melting-Pot." *Nation* 100, 2509–91 (February 18 and 25): 190–94, 217–20.

Lazarus, Emma. 1878. "The Eleventh Hour." *Scribner's* 16 (July): 242–56.

Lazarus, Emma. 1883. "The Jewish Problem." *Century* 25 (February): 602–11.

Lazarus, Emma. (1883) 1993. "The New Colossus," 457–58. New York: Library of America.

Lincoln, Abraham. 1953. "The Gettysburg Address" [1863]. In *Collected Works of Abraham Lincoln*, 8 vols., edited by Roy P. Basler, vol. 7, 23. New Brunswick, NJ: Rutgers University.

Okada, John. (1957) 1979. *No-No Boy*. Seattle: University of Washington Press.

Paredes, Américo. 1990. *George Washington Gómez: A Mexicotexan Novel*. Houston, TX: Arte Publico Press.

Park, Robert E. 1928. "Human Migration and the Marginal Man." *American Journal of Sociology* 33, no. 6 (May): 881–93.

Riis, Jacob. (1890) 1971. *How the Other Half Lives*. New York: Dover.

Riis, Jacob. (1901) 1928. *The Making of an American*. New York: Macmillan.

Rølvaag, Ole Edvart. 1927. *Giants in the Earth: A Saga of the Prairie*. Translated by Lincoln Colcord and the author. New York: Perennial Library, Harper and Row Publishers.

Roosevelt, Theodore. 1904. Letter to Mrs. Bessie Van Vorst, October 18, 1902. In *Works: Presidential Addresses and State Papers*, part 2, vol. 14, Statesman ed., 508–10. New York: Review of Reviews Co.

Sadlier, Mrs. J.[Mary Anne]. (1861) 1863. *Bessy Conway; or the Irish Girl in America*. New York: D and J Sadlier and Co.

Sedgwick, Catharine Maria. (1827) 1987. *Hope Leslie*. Edited by Mary Kelley. New Brunswick, NJ: Rutgers University Press.

Simmel, Georg. 1950. "The Stranger." In *The Sociology of Georg Simmel*, translated and edited by Kurt H. Wolff, 402–8. New York: Free Press.

Svendsen, Gro Gudmundsrud. 1950. *Frontier Mother: The Letters of Gro Svendsen*. Translated and edited by Pauline Farseth and Theodore C. Blegen. Northfield, MN: Norwegian-American Historical Association.

Wald, Priscilla. 1995. *Constituting Americans: Cultural Anxiety and Narrative Form*. Durham, NC: Duke University Press.

Wald, Priscilla. 1998. *Contagious: Cultures, Carriers, and the Outbreak Narrative*. Durham, NC: Duke University Press.

Wald, Priscilla. 2001. "Immigration and Assimilation in Nineteenth-Century U.S. Women's Narratives." In *The Cambridge Companion to 19th-Century American Women's Writing*, edited by Dale Bauer and Philip Gould, 176–99. Cambridge: Cambridge University Press.

Wald, Priscilla. 2003. "The East European Immigrants: Of Crucibles and Grandfathers." In *The Cambridge Companion to Jewish American Literature*, edited by Michael Kramer and Hana Wirth Nesher, 50–69. Cambridge: Cambridge University Press.

Webster, Noah. 1953. *Letters of Noah Webster*. Edited by Harry R. Warfel. New York: Library Publications.

Wendell, Barrett. 1901. *A Literary History of America*. New York: Charles Scribner's Sons.

Willey, Day Allen. 1909. "Americans in the Making: New England's Method of Assimilating the Alien." *Putnam's Monthly and the Reader* 5: 456–63.

Yezierska, Anzia. (1920) 1997. *Hungry Hearts*. New York: Penguin.

Yezierska, Anzia. (1923) 1995. *Salome of the Tenements*. Urbana and Chicago: University of Illinois Press.

Yezierska, Anzia. (1925) 1975. *Bread Givers*. New York: Persea Books.

Zakrzewska, Marie E. 1924. *A Woman's Quest: The Life of Marie E. Zakrzewska, M.D.* Edited by Agnes C. Vietor. New York: D. Appleton and Co.

Zangwill, Israel. (1909, 1914) 1921. *The Melting-Pot*. New York: The Macmillan Company; New York: The American Jewish Book Company. http://www.gutenberg.org/files/23893/23893-h/23893-h.htm (Project Gutenberg).

Cultural Impact of American Immigrants

Padma Rangaswamy

The impact of immigrants and ethnic populations on American culture has varied over the course of American history, depending on the tides of immigration and the capacity of American society to absorb new influences. From the Pilgrims and fur traders of the earliest days to the university students and entrepreneurs of the twenty-first century, immigrants have shaped and been shaped by American culture in a dynamic process of continuous transformation, thanks to the American capacity to integrate new immigrants while allowing them to continue to identify with their ethnic origins.

American culture has thus evolved into a distinct set of values, ideals, and traditions that have emerged from centuries of struggle to maintain freedom, unity, and independence. Many Europeans, such as from Spain, Portugal, England, and France, gradually introduced the ideas and ideals of Christianity, democracy, and civil liberties on which American culture is founded, especially the English. Building on their own traditions, they also brought with them the basic economic concepts of competition, entrepreneurship, and free markets that serve as pillars of American society and which were steadily expanded and refined by Americans. For centuries economic growth and vast opportunities have had the power to draw new immigrants to achieve the "American dream."

Millions more immigrants from Europe and Africa entered in the seventeenth and eighteenth centuries, and each population left its mark on components of American culture, some quite profoundly so, notably those who were brought to America forcibly from Africa as slaves. These "involuntary immigrants" influenced American popular culture so profoundly that their contribution, especially in music, sports, and entertainment, is often taken for granted as part of Americana and their source not always acknowledged. Another ethnic group whose contribution to American culture is often overlooked is that of indigenous Native Americans. Strictly speaking, they are not an immigrant group, but there are many elements of American culture that evolved from them, including the foods associated with that most American of holiday traditions, the Thanksgiving feast (their contribution of foods, not the holiday itself). The nineteenth and twentieth centuries brought new immigrants from all parts of the globe, who continued to modify and enrich American culture in myriad ways manifested in every field of human endeavor, including language, literature, arts, entertainment, sports, food, festivals, as well as vast economic endeavors, technological innovations, and innovative models of enterprise.

By the dawn of the twenty-first century, American culture had also permeated the principal population centers of the globe, thanks mainly to the development of an information and communication technology revolution from the telegraph to the radio, the cinema, and television, to the Internet, Wi-Fi, and Facebook. Many, many innovations were launched in America (in whole or in part) and many, many had immigrants doing the launching, playing significant roles in myriad phases of these communications and media revolutions.

But American culture is not simply a layering of one immigrant group's culture over another's. Indeed, its dynamism comes from the tension between the established culture of earlier arriving groups and the new culture of later arrivals, tellingly called "aliens" in American legislative terminology. This resistance has repeatedly caused cultural conflict, sometimes violent, making it apparent that not only do immigrants influence American culture, but American culture itself influences immigration patterns. Because of American ambivalence about immigration, and the restrictions placed on it over the years, only some immigrant groups have attained the critical mass required to have a significant impact. However, even smaller groups that have sought incorporation into mainstream American society and forgotten the beliefs and customs of their homelands have played a significant role in shaping American culture through the contributions of individual immigrants and their descendants.

One could ask "What is American culture?" and come up with as many variations in the answer as befitting the question "What is an American?" Indeed, is there any one inclusive and identifiable American culture? The answer is complicated further by the fact that, while there are many elements of American culture that apply to the American population as a whole, there are also many subcultures based on regional and racial differences, economic conditions, and religious attitudes. These variations, which can be attributed in large part to the composition of immigrants who settled in these areas, become more significant when they spread to larger communities and enter mainstream American culture.

Furthermore, immigrants themselves have subcultures that go beyond or cut across national boundaries. Thus, immigrants from India may emphasize their Gujarati or Punjabi identity far more than their pan-Indian identity, while the Chinese may value their Chinese ethnicity more than the fact that they may have come here as immigrants from Taiwan or Vietnam or Malaysia. Ancient histories and rapid mobility have contributed in such complex ways to immigrant identities that it is not always possible to know when and where a particular aspect of an immigrant culture is most powerfully manifested and has influenced American culture most significantly. Add to this the complication of mixed racial, ethnic, and national identities created by intermarriages among immigrants and their descendants, and traditional boundaries become even more blurred. It is a miracle and a tribute to the fundamental nature of culture, and immigrant cultures in particular, that they can still be recognized and celebrated in the American mosaic.

Language

If Americans have managed to attain any measure of unity in the presence of so much diversity in their midst, they surely owe it to the fact that most of them speak the same language—as their principal or secondary one. The 2000 census showed that 82 percent of Americans are English speakers, while all other languages combined account for 18 percent of U.S. population usage. English became the dominant language during the colonial period because the majority of immigrants at the time were of English origin, and government, laws, and other institutions were all in English. Legend has it that German almost became the official language of the United States when the Continental Congress voted on the issue back in 1775, but the measure lost by one vote. Whether the story is true or not, language has always been a political and emotional issue. Americans have generally discouraged bilingualism, fearing immigrants who speak in other languages and at times attacking those languages and their speakers. Though there is no law declaring English the "official" language of the United States, the 1906 Naturalization Act (and subsequent citizenship requirements) mandated the use of English for those seeking citizenship. During World War I, nativists reacted violently to the use of languages other than English in public and used racist theories of eugenics and Social Darwinism to denounce immigrants as racially inferior, illiterate, and even lazy.

English continues to be jealously guarded against those ethnic groups who are often accused of subverting American national unity by speaking in their native tongue. In the 1980s and 1990s, many states, such as Florida, Colorado, and Arizona, feeling threatened by the rise of non-English-speaking groups, passed "English-only" laws. Immigrants are encouraged to learn English in order to succeed in their new homeland. ESL (English as a Second Language) classes are offered in schools with large immigrant populations, and a mandatory civics and literacy test in English for new immigrants seeking citizenship ensures that English will continue to be accessible to new groups and one of the key criteria for full citizenship.

The United States is the second-largest Spanish-speaking country in the world (10 percent of the population is Spanish-speaking), after Mexico, but the American attitude toward Spanish is largely dependent on the status and influence of American Latinos. Increasing publicity over illegal immigration from Mexico at the turn of the twenty-first century raised protectionist fears of being overwhelmed by Spanish-speaking groups (The term "Hispanic" is not a coherent identity, and includes Spanish speakers with diverse origins, from Cuba, Puerto Rico, Mexico, the Dominican Republic, and other South American and Central American states). There are also some widely spoken variants called Chicano English, and Spanglish, which is a form of Spanish that incorporates words freely from English and is an expression of bicultural identity. American English, in turn, has adapted many Spanish words from early exploration that had to do with plant and animal life, ranch life, housing, food and drink, mining, and clothing. Such words as mesquite, marijuana, poncho, canyon, adobe, coyote, patio, etc., trace their Spanish/Native American origins to this time period. Nearly half of the names of American states are derived from Native-American languages.

African Americans developed a distinctive, nonstandard form of English (perhaps made deliberately incomprehensible to whites) called by some "Ebonics." In the 1990s, there were activists who sought to give certain African-American language patterns the status of a separate language rather than it being labeled merely nonstandard or just "bad English." However, the desire to belong won over the desire to be distinct, and Ebonics soon lost its importance as a defining feature of African-American culture.

Other languages besides English and Spanish do thrive in the United States, especially when significant numbers of non-English-speaking immigrants flock to ethnic enclaves and create their own world, isolated from mainstream America. For example, Chinatowns in New York and San Francisco, dating back to the California Gold Rush and the building of the transcontinental railroad, have some of the largest concentrations of Chinese Americans in the United States. Here, Cantonese and Mandarin are spoken freely.

These languages are at the core of a complete support system built for new Chinese immigrants to help them get over homesickness and survive in the United States. Fujianese and Taiwanese are among the more extensively used Chinese dialects.

Other immigrant groups at various times have created their own Little Italy, Germantown, Indiatown, Korea town, Little Tokyo, or "Polonia" where the homeland language was spoken and helped sustain distinct cultures before they spread across to the larger communities. The evolution of American English, as distinct from English spoken in the United Kingdom and other parts of the world, owes much to the contribution of immigrants and ethnic groups. With second and third generations of immigrants, many of the institutions that began with native languages shifted to English, thus ensuring the dominance of English in the United States. Meanwhile, from Native Americans come words such as toboggan and tomahawk, moccasin and totem. The vocabulary of food is especially dependent on immigrant culture, which has contributed such words as hamburger, pizza, enchiladas, tacos, tamales, pierogi, kabob, and kosher to American English. In the late twentieth century, a whole new vocabulary developed around computer technology, fueled by the innovations of immigrant entrepreneurs. Words including online, chat rooms, e-mail, and web pages have become commonplace within a year or two of their introduction and spread rapidly around the world. The American stream of English thus continues to evolve and change, staying vibrant and alive with the contributions of immigrants—groups and individuals.

Literature

Some common themes run through all immigrant literature, regardless of which era they were written in and by which immigrant group. For instance, narratives of departure from the homeland, loss of identity, struggles to make good in the United States, and the pains and pleasures of immigrant success and failure are present throughout, as are issues of language, culture, and place. But the literature of some groups, such as African Americans, resonate more with problems of slavery and racism, freedom and equality (which were long denied to them), while Latino-American and Asian-American literature deals more with dilemmas of being caught between two worlds and not being accepted as Americans.

The pioneers, settlers, and adventurers who came from Europe in the sixteenth century told stories of the immigrant experience and the lure of America's promise through pamphlets, letters, diaries, and religious writings. American literature across the centuries includes the intimate personal stories and autobiographical accounts of immigrant settlers (mostly Europeans) who braved the harsh winters of the upper Midwest to settle farmland, or, later on, those who went on wagon trails to settle as far as California, Oregon, and elsewhere along the Pacific Coast. These letters provide invaluable firsthand testimony and add the voices of ordinary immigrants to more erudite accounts of American character and culture. Meanwhile, immigrants who came from Asia—mainly China, Japan, Korea, and India—and settled in many locations along the Pacific Coast were writing home in their native languages and creating their own record of life in the United States. Unfortunately, only a small fraction of these accounts have been preserved or translated as part of American literature—but more so since the greater legitimation of ethnic diversity and ethnic heritages beginning in World War II and accelerating since the 1960s.

African American culture fostered a rich tradition of oral literature, including spirituals, religious sermons, and blues, all born out of the field experience of slaves. In the late eighteenth and first half of the nineteenth centuries, writers of African descent were already creating a distinct literature, astounding audiences in Europe and the United States with the eloquence of their slave narratives. Writers such as poet Phillis Wheatley, Olaudah Equiana, Frederick Douglass, and the Anglo-American novelist Harriet Beecher Stowe (*Uncle Tom's Cabin*) wrote poignantly of the slavery experience and argued passionately for liberation. During the first three decades of the twentieth century, 40,000 African Caribbeans settled in Harlem. Many were Spanish- or French-speaking, but they also included English speakers from Jamaica, Trinidad, and other British colonies. Among them was Jamaican Marcus Garvey, who spearheaded the first black mass nationalist movement in New York, called the Universal Negro Improvement Association, urging African Americans to be proud of their ancestral homeland and to celebrate a pan-African identity. His poems, editorials, and speeches inspired other black nationalist movements, including the Nation of Islam and the Rastafari movement, which hails him as a prophet. Another surge of immigration from the Caribbean (especially Haiti, Jamaica, and the Dominican Republic) and continental Africa (mainly Nigeria, Guinea, Ghana, and Senegal) occurred between 1970 and 2000, when the proportion of foreign-born among blacks in the United States rose from 1.3 percent to 7.8 percent. These new immigrants redefined American race relations by sometimes emphasizing their solidarity with the native African Americans and at other times retaining their ethnic distinctiveness.

In the nineteenth century, the settling of America in the agricultural and industrial sectors by immigrants from Europe inspired novelists to write of their hardships and triumphs. The novels of Ole Edvart Rølvaag (1876–1931), *Giants in the Earth* and *Peder Victorious*, received international acclaim for their account of pioneer life in the Dakota prairies in the 1870s. Starting off as a fisherman in his native Norway, Rølvaag worked as a farmhand in South Dakota and went on to become a celebrated author and professor, working all his life to preserve the Norwegian heritage and culture in the Northwest. On the urban front, clusters of immigrants from eastern and southern Europe, spurred by rapid industrialization, settled in crowded cities and gave rise to another major theme in American literature, the building of urban America. An excellent example of literature about this period is the American working-class novel *Out of This Furnace* (1941) by Thomas Bell. Set in Braddock, Pennsylvania, a steel town just south of Pittsburgh, it tells the story of three generations of Bell's Slovak ancestors, starting with their migration in 1880 from Austria-Hungary to the United States and ending with World War II. The novel provides insights into the daily lives of new immigrants and also explores larger themes of exploitation of workers in the steel mills, and the rise of trade unionism in the United States. The sorry plight of immigrants inspired other works that have become classics of American literature, such as *The Jungle* (1906) by Upton Sinclair, which highlighted the corruption of American industrial capitalism and the harsh poverty and slum-like living conditions of Lithuanian workers in the meatpacking industry.

A distinctly Jewish-American literature also started to flourish in the late nineteenth century as Jewish intellectuals sought refuge in the United States from a hostile Europe. Abraham Cahan (1860–1951) fled from his native Lithuania to New York City and propagated his socialist ideas among working-class Jews through his Yiddish periodicals. His English novels depicted ghetto life in New York, and his best-known work is in the form of a fictional autobiography, *The Rise of David Levinsky*. Other Jewish-American writers of the twentieth century who received critical acclaim include Henry Roth (for his 1934 novel *Call It Sleep*), Bernard Malamud (the son of Russian-Jewish immigrants who was renowned for his short stories and whose baseball novel *The Natural* was made into a movie), Chaim Potok (born to Polish immigrants and influenced deeply by his Jewish theological background) and Saul Bellow (a Chicago icon whose insightful portraits of Jewish life and identity won him the Nobel Prize for Literature in 1976). Other Jewish-American literary giants include Phillip Roth, Isaac Bashevis Singer, and Norman Mailer, all of whose works explore the tensions between Jewish traditions and American identity, the dilemmas of rootlessness and isolation, and the emptiness of urban life. Jewish immigrants and their children had a massive impact on American literature as novelists, journalists, essayists, poets, and playwrights and their contributions are well recognized through the number of book awards and Pulitzer Prizes bestowed on them.

The twentieth century also saw many first-generation Italian Americans distinguish themselves in the world of letters as poets, playwrights, and novelists. John Ciardi, born in 1916 to Italian immigrants, wrote an acclaimed English translation of Dante's *Divine Comedy*, became a poet in his own right, and taught at Harvard and Rutgers Universities. Don DeLillo, brought up by his immigrant parents in an Italian-American neighborhood in the Bronx, wrote novels that dealt with themes as diverse as television, sports, the Cold War, and industrial disaster. Among his more notable works are *Americana*, *White Noise*, *Libra*, *Mao 11*, *Underworld*, and *Falling Man*. Pietro di Donato, son of an Italian construction worker and himself a bricklayer, achieved fame with *Christ in Concrete* (1939), one of the few proletarian novels written by a blue-collar worker. Lawrence Ferlinghetti, poet and activist of the 1950s Beat Generation, cofounded the publishing house City Lights and is best known for his collection of poems, *A Coney Island of the Mind*. Gregory Corso was another prominent Italian-American poet of this generation. Jerre Mangione (1909–1998) wrote of the Italian-American experience of negotiating the world between two cultures. His first book, *Mount Allegro* (1943), and his later *An Ethnic At Large* (1978), explore the evolution of his immigrant identity from a child of Sicilian immigrants to an American. His last book, which he coauthored with Ben Morreale, is a monumental social history titled: *La Storia: Five Centuries of the Italian American Experience*. Gay Talese (b. 1932), son of an Italian-immigrant tailor, is a prolific writer of sports and politics and one of the founders of the 1960s "New Journalism," which incorporates fictional elements (dialogue, scene description, and shifting points of view) into news writing. Among his many best-sellers are *Honor Thy Father*, the story of crime boss Joe Bonanno and his son Bill; and *Unto the Sons*, a largely autobiographical book about his Italian heritage.

Frances Winwar (1900–1985), one of the few female Italian-American writers born in Italy, became a biographer of poets and statesmen, including nineteenth-century literary figures and heroes such as Napoleon and Joan of Arc. She also built a reputation as a book reviewer, translator, and novelist. Perhaps the most famous Italian-American writer of all is Mario Puzo (1920–1999), whose most celebrated work *The Godfather* (published in 1969) had a deep impact on American society through its film adaptation. Puzo was born into a poor immigrant family in New York's infamous Hell's Kitchen neighborhood. While working as a freelance journalist, he collected Mafia anecdotes, which he turned into the runaway international best seller about crime, corruption, violence, and honor.

He went on to write screenplays for Hollywood (*Earthquake, Superman, The Godfather—Parts 1, 2, and 3*) and more mafia novels (*The Sicilian, The Last Don,* and *Omerta*).

Irish immigrant writers of the nineteenth century tended to specialize in two kinds of literature—satirical propaganda and parody, or sentimental and didactic novels. Finley Peter Dunne (1867–1936), who was born to Irish immigrants in Chicago, wrote satirical columns in which he freely criticized the nation through the voice of the opinionated, first-generation Irish-American bar owner Mr. Dooley. Mary Anne Sadlier (1820–1903) wrote sentimental novels, short stories, and religious catechisms for Irish immigrants in the United States and Canada. The Irish-American experience continued to be a major theme in American literature in the twentieth century, finding its most tragic renderings in the plays of the towering dramatist Eugene O'Neill, *A Moon for the Misbegotten* and *Long Day's Journey into Night.* His other works, *Desire under the Elms* and *Mourning Becomes Electra* are classics of American literature and represent attempts to bring elements of Greek tragedy into an American setting. Likewise receiving much acclaim was James Farrell's *Studs Lonigan* trilogy and Frank McCourt's Pulitzer Prize–winning *Angela's Ashes* and *'Tis.*

The period encompassing the two world wars was a time of great hostility toward immigration, and the immigrant literature of this time reflects this attitude of hatred and suspicion, especially toward nationals of "enemy" countries, specifically Germany and Japan. Cartoon images of Germans in newspapers and books—for example, *Desert Exile: The Uprooting of a Japanese American Family* by Yoshiko Uchida (1982)—document the stresses and strains suffered by these ethnic groups due to the xenophobia of the government and the people. Michi Weglyn uncovered important documents regarding the incarceration in American concentration camps, in *Years of Infamy* (1976). Other powerful first-person accounts on this same topic include *The Kikuchi Diary* by Charles Kikuchi and Jeanne Wakatsuki Houston's *Farewell to Manzanar.*

The comparative prosperity of the United States after World War II and the passage of the Immigration and Naturalization Act of 1965 brought new groups of immigrants from Asia and Latin America. The emphasis of their literature was not so much on physical conditions as the challenges of assimilation into mainstream America, and the conflict caused by the pull of dual identities. Other common themes are those of generation gaps between older immigrant parents and their younger, American-born children as well as tensions between established Americanized immigrants and newer arrivals.

Chinese authors, such as Maxine Hong Kingston (*The Woman Warrior*, 1976) and Amy Tan (*The Joy Luck Club*, 1989), criticized the sexism and patriarchy of their homeland culture through the voices of their American-born female protagonists. The Indian-American writers Bharati Mukherjee (*Wife*, 1975) and Chitra Banerjee Divakaruni (*Arranged Marriages*, 1995) also explored similar themes. Jhumpa Lahiri, another Indian-American writer, wrote of immigrants and their children making complex adjustments between old-world traditions and the challenging demands of new cultures and relationships in the United States. She is best known for her novel *The Namesake* (2004), which, like many other Asian-American books, was successfully made into a movie.

A Latino literature also developed around the 1960s that evolved in subsequent decades around themes of identity, cultural conflict, and gender. One of the most successful writers of this genre was Sandra Cisneros, whose story of a Mexican-American girl coming of age in Chicago (*House on Mango Street*, 1984) made her one of the best-selling Hispanic authors in the United States. Esmeralda Santiago's *When I Was Puerto Rican* (1994) provides insights into what it is like to be an American and yet a foreigner in New York City, an experience shared by many other immigrant groups across the United States. *Pocho*, by Jose Antonio Villarreal, is another classic for young readers that captures the conflict felt by Mexican Americans as they are torn between loyalty toward ethnic traditions and the lure of American ideas. Intensely powerful was Victor Villaseñor's family history *Rain of Gold* (1991).

American immigrant literature soon evolved into a post-ethnic period, when writers shifted focus to second- and third-generation immigrants. And the works did not emanate solely from the principal groups, for two French-Canadian Americans produced works that altered American literature: Grace Metalious's novel *Peyton Place* (1956) and Jack Kerouac's *On the Road* (1957). They went beyond issues of ethnic identity and explored what it meant to be American in a multiracial, multicultural America.

Arts and Entertainment

The contribution of immigrants to the artistic and cultural diversity of the United States is remarkable not so much for what they imported from the homeland as for what they did to help create new art forms that are uniquely American. For instance, immigrant music has been preserved and promoted in the United States by communities and organizations, but there are also instances of outstanding individuals who have made their mark on the American music scene through their unique talents.

Music

Almost all the musical forms that the United States can lay claim to having their roots in African-American history and culture. Blues and ragtime, hymns and spirituals had their origins in the African oral musical traditions, which were nurtured during slavery to tell stories and ease the suffering. Many distinct elements of African-American music combined with European influence to form jazz, and the 1920s became known as the Jazz Age. Aided by the technological innovations of radio and phonographs, jazz spread overseas as well. Rock 'n' roll, soul and R&B (rhythm and blues) developed in the mid-twentieth century as distinct American genres.

The Ashkenazi Jews who came from eastern Europe in the early twentieth century brought klezmer music they could dance to, while immigrants from Germany, Slovenia, and Poland popularized the polka. The brass-band tradition in the United States has its roots in the immigrant communities of England and Ireland. After the 1960s, many Irish artists immigrated to the United States. The band Green Fields of America was founded by Mick Maloney in 1977 to bring together immigrant and American-born Irish musicians. It contained many Irish Americans who achieved international fame, such as Susan McKeown, Seamus Egan, Eileen Ivers, and Jerry O'Sullivan. The Riverdance company also made enormous contributions to the spread of Irish music and dance among a wide American audience.

Individual immigrants made their mark in the world of classical and pop music. Examples in the classical field include Itzhak Perlman, the Israeli-born violinist; Yehudi Menuhin, violinist and conductor born to Russian-Jewish parents; symphony conductor Zubin Mehta, of Indian origin; and composer Yo-Yo Ma, born in Paris to Chinese parents. All are outstanding in their fields. Pop music in the second half of the twentieth century had many icons of Italian ancestry, including Tony Bennett, Perry Como, Dean Martin, Connie Francis, and Frank Sinatra, the Oscar-, Emmy-, and Grammy-winning legend. The variety of immigrant contributions to music is such that it both encompasses and goes beyond group categorizations.

Entertainment

Americans are known to work hard and play hard, and entertainment is more than fun and games; it is serious, money-making business. It is also a reflection of how Americans see themselves and others, others being new immigrants in their midst. The first organized form of entertainment in the United States came with the minstrel shows of the 1830s, which presented African Americans as caricatures for ridicule to larger white audiences. They also enabled new Jewish and Irish immigrants to "blacken" their faces to show that they were not black but indeed "white" and were thus an instrument of assimilation.

Throughout the 1850s and 1860s, the most popular forms of entertainment in frontier settlements and urban centers were vaudeville variety shows. Actors, jugglers, comedians, tumblers, dancers, all performed in a medium that allowed them to represent their heritage and skills they had acquired in the old country while becoming an active part of mainstream popular culture. With the advent of the silent movies in the early nineteenth century and television in midcentury,

World Champion Irish dancer, Sinead McCafferty, center left, and Conor Hayes, right, perform as the Riverdance troupe at Radio City Music Hall in New York, 2005. (AP Photo/Adam Rountree)

the big names of vaudeville, such as Will Rogers, a Cherokee cowboy, and Bob Hope and Charlie Chaplin, both English-born comedians, went on to become famous movie and TV stars,

The evolution of dance in American popular culture is also a tale of strong ethnic influences. In the eighteenth and nineteenth centuries, the United States still looked to Europe for refinement; but by the early twentieth century, home-grown American dance forms, such as the Charleston, the Jitterbug, and the Shuffle, were spreading across Europe as fun and fashionable. Tap-dancing, which is a combination of African and European influences, became hugely popular through the movie musicals of the 1950s and 1960s. Music, dialogue, performance, and dance all came together on Broadway to define American

theater entertainment at its best. From the early 1900s, Broadway has served as the platform showcasing the talents of immigrant actors and producers, singers and dancers. Jewish music composers, notably Irving Berlin and George Gershwin, wrote songs for Broadway musicals and revues that have been re-recorded throughout the twentieth century by countless singers, as did Leonard Bernstein with *West Side Story* and Richard Rogers and Oscar Hammerstein with *Oklahoma! Carousel*, *South Pacific*, and *The Sound of Music*. Other long-running musicals, such as *Fiddler on the Roof*, engaged the American public in the saga of immigrant families struggling to assimilate.

As immigrants from Asia and Latin America poured into the United States after 1965, dance, music, and popular entertainment became even more free-flowing and vibrant. Many fusion forms that combine genres and cultures emerged. Americans were introduced to the music of India through the sitar maestro Ravi Shankar, tabla virtuoso Zakir Hussein, and sarod player Ali Akbar Khan. In the 1970s and 1980s, immigrants from Jamaica imported reggae, Latin, and Afro-Caribbean rhythms and nurtured them in the streets of New York before they became popular throughout the United States. Jamaican immigrant DJ Kool Herc is credited as the inventor of the hip-hop genre of music, while second-generation Jamaican Busta Rhymes is an important figure in gangsta rap, a subgenre that reflects the violent lifestyles of inner-city black youth.

Radio, Television, and Film

Since its earliest days, radio has been used by immigrants to stay in touch with their homeland and communicate in their own language, with the original radio and then television networks cobbled together or vastly expanded by two Jewish immigrants—David Sarnoff (NBC) and William S. Paley (CBS). Radio stations in Spanish, Polish, Urdu, Russian, Italian, and other languages have since that time proliferated in response to immigrant needs wherever they gathered in sufficiently large numbers. In 2009, there were nearly 500 Spanish radio stations in the United States, and online radio channels offered free Internet radio in scores of languages, making ethnic media a powerful force in marketing and advertising.

Thanks to satellite TV, programs from all over the world can be streamed live into American homes. For instance, immigrants from South Asia watch television channels broadcast in India in any of several regional languages, the most popular ones being Hindi, Gujarati, Tamil, Malayalam, and Telugu. Because these channels are carried by providers such as Comcast and AT&T, they are available to mainstream subscribers as well. This is merely an example of how globalization of the media has enabled immigrants and corporate interests from the home country to influence American culture.

As with so many other aspects of culture, ethnic entertainment begins with a small niche culture before it merges into mainstream America. Because of their long and established history in the United States, both Spanish-language and black-oriented programs have appeal far beyond their ethnic audiences. A rapid increase in Spanish-language TV programming made Univision, the fifth-largest U.S. television network, and helped expand its rival Telemundo to all the major Spanish-speaking areas of the United States, including Miami, New York, and San Diego.

The diversity of the American population in the second half of the twentieth century was clearly visible in the increasingly diverse ethnicity of radio and television personalities. CNN personalities, such as Rick Sanchez (born to Cuban exiles in Florida) and Sanjay Gupta (raised in a Detroit suburb by his Indian engineer parents) are just two examples of hundreds of TV talk show hosts and media personalities who are either immigrants or children of immigrants appearing on American television on a daily basis. Such visibility made it easier to integrate immigrant elements into American popular culture.

At the same time, the emergence of immigrant stereotypes on television shows, especially the character of Apu, the Indian convenience store owner in *The Simpsons*, or the Arab terrorist in TV dramas, kept alive the American tradition of hostility toward new immigrants. On the other hand, in 2010, a major network ran repeated comic commercials involving two Asian Indian men promoting an inexpensive cellular phone service.

The biggest growth factor in entertainment has been Hollywood, the home of the American film industry. When it started in the early 1900s in the form of nickelodeons or storefront theaters, many Jewish immigrants found employment in the business, but the more ambitious among them soon switched to the production side. The biggest names amongst Hollywood producers were all Jews born in Hungary, Austria, Poland, or Russia—Samuel Goldwyn, William Fox, Adolph Zukor, Louis B. Mayer, and the Warner Brothers. Many of them began their careers in the garment industry and experienced failure before taking a gamble with the movies. The Jewish dominance in Hollywood continued well into the turn of the twenty-first century. Studio heads and top studio executives are frequently still Jewish, as are some of the most acclaimed directors, notably Steven Spielberg and Woody Allen.

Hollywood films have, for the most part, held a mirror up to society, though they have also influenced the way people think by being selective in their choice of themes and how they have chosen to portray immigrants. While the virtues of immigrants, namely hard work, family values, religiosity, and thrift, have been extolled by media and politicians, immigrants have also been portrayed as dangerous villains out to destabilize American values. Gangster movies in the 1930s, notably *Public Enemies* and *Scarface*, portrayed Jewish, Irish, and Italian immigrants as ruthless criminals and helped to stereotype these groups. But even while they engendered fear, these characters fascinated Americans who admired their meteoric climb to notoriety and fortune. These films also gave immigrant actors opportunities to enter the industry.

Other immigrants of this era created their own opportunities. Rudolph Valentino became a sex symbol on the silver screen and built a reputation as the Latin lover boy, while English-born Charlie Chaplin (cofounder of United Artists) became a comic legend and one of the most influential figures of the silent-movie era. Foreign-born actors continue to make it big in Hollywood. Antonio Banderas, Penelope Cruz, and Arnold Schwarzenegger are examples of successful actors who keep the American dream alive for millions of aspirants throughout the world.

Asian Americans of the post-1965 era have cried foul at being shut out of the Hollywood scene; however, many made their mark not as actors, but as directors. Ang Lee and M. Night Shyamalan directed movies that were critically acclaimed and made box-office history, and their movies went beyond ethnicity to deal with social and cultural themes of broad interest to Americans.

Sports

Sports in the United States is far more than a cultural institution. Avid fans who worship at the shrines of baseball, football, basketball, and ice hockey have elevated these games to the status of a religion and turned them into thriving commercial enterprises.

Organized sports have been tied to the rise of cities from the times of rapid industrialization and immigration in the middle of the nineteenth century. Sports gave immigrants a sense of community and helped release them from the tensions of back-breaking, low-wage work in crowded conditions. The success of individual immigrants was a source of inspiration to others who dreamed of achieving the same heights of fame and fortune. Sports also provided many ethnic groups with an opportunity to re-create the familiar games of their homeland and cling to their cultural traits, e.g. the festivals of German-American clubs in Philadelphia and New York, the Scottish Highland games in New Jersey and Michigan, and the Ukrainian holiday celebrations in the Midwest all featured sports as played in the home country.

Baseball

Professional baseball started in 1869 and reigned supreme as the United States' most popular game through the 1960s. Its precursor is said to be the British game of rounders. The number of foreign players, especially Irish and German, gradually increased, and with the rise in immigration in the early twentieth century, the game provided a path to immigrant assimilation and acceptance in American society. The career of Joe DiMaggio, born to Italian immigrants in 1914, is a classic example of an outstanding individual achieving legendary success in sports. He went on to become one of the greatest ball players of all time, winning awards and titles and being voted into the National Baseball Hall of Fame in 1955. Hank Greenberg, born to Romanian-Jewish parents in 1911, led the Detroit Tigers to an American League pennant victory in 1934. Both DiMaggio and Greenberg served in the U.S. Army during World War II, and when they returned to the sport, they found themselves in such an anti-immigrant environment, they preferred to downplay their immigrant heritage and project themselves as all-American. By this time, professional baseball had built a reputation for bigotry and discrimination by closing its doors to African Americans until Jackie Robinson broke the color line in 1947. Soon Hispanics joined the ranks

Hall of Famer Roberto Clemente of the Pittsburgh Pirates baseball team looks down a bat, May 1967. The Puerto Rican star died in 1972 in a plane crash on his way to assist earthquake survivors in Nicaragua. (AP Photo/J. Spencer Jones)

of talented baseball players. The most famous among them was Puerto Rican Roberto Clemente, who played with the Pittsburgh Pirates from 1955 to 1972 and became the first Hispanic to be inducted into the National Baseball Hall of Fame. In 1997, the number of Hispanic athletes in major league baseball was 24 percent. New York is the city to which immigrants flock for baseball opportunities, and the New York Yankees remains one of professional sports' greatest franchises with players from Cuba (Jose Contreras, 2003–2004, Orlando Hernandez, 1998–2003), Japan (Hideki Matsui, 2003–2009), and Panama (Mariano Rivera, 1995 and still playing as of 2012) contributing to its diversity.

The National Foundation for American Policy did a nationwide study on baseball and immigration and found that the impact of foreign-born players was at an all-time high of 23 percent, more than double the 10 percent figure in 1990. The Dominican Republic, with 81 players, topped the list of country of origin among active major leaguers, followed by Venezuela (45), Mexico (10), Canada (10), Japan (8), Panama (6), Cuba (4), South Korea (3), Colombia (2), and Taiwan (2). Foreign-born players help contribute to the increasing diversity of the fan base. In the 2008 season, 17 of the top-paid 50 players were Hispanic, and between 20 percent and 50 percent of the fans who flock to watch the Los Angeles Dodgers, the Miami Marlins, and the New York Mets are Hispanic fans.

The competitive nature of professional baseball and the desire of fans to see the most skilled players from any part of the world helped pass the Compete Act of 2006, which made it easier for baseball teams to get visas for foreign-born players. The trend in the early years of the twenty-first century was thus not to wait for immigrants to come to the United States, but to actively recruit them from abroad and turn them into immigrants or get them special visas to play in professional sports. For Hispanics from countries such as Cuba and the Dominican Republic, baseball was their escape from grinding poverty and political repression. It was their only chance to live the American dream and become the next Sammy Sosa or Manny Ramirez and to earn astronomical figures—the average salary for major league baseball players rose from $578,930 in 1990 to $2.87 million in 2006.

Football

Football is the sport that has been least penetrated by immigrants, partly because of its elitist origins and partly because it remains the one game that is not played in other parts of the world. The game had its beginnings in the late nineteenth century in prestigious colleges, such as Harvard and Princeton, and was reserved for Anglo-Saxon athletes. By the turn of the century, Ivy League football had changed into American football, which was a much more free-for-all, brutal, and, as its advocates described it, a "manly" version of the game. As more and more immigrants began to enter college, they made their way into the football rosters. Outside campus, many of the social and fraternal institutions that helped buttress immigrant identity for European immigrants also helped induct them into football. Individual immigrants who contributed to football include Norwegian-born coach Knute Rockne, who developed the Notre Dame Fighting Irish into a winning football team; Dick Butkus, of Lithuanian heritage, considered one of the greatest linebackers of all time; and Danish-born Morton Andersen, a football kicker and leading scorer in National Football League history, who was inducted into the New Orleans Saints' Hall of Fame in 2009.

Basketball

Basketball is said to have been invented in 1891 by a Canadian immigrant, a YMCA instructor. It quickly caught on in the cities, since all that was needed was a hard-surface court, a ball, and a basket, and did not call for open fields or expensive equipment. In the 1920s and 1930s, interethnic basketball games drew large crowds, as teams that were organized along racial or ethnic lines competed in immigrant neighborhoods. During this time, the Jews, Irish, and Italians dominated the game. After World War II, Jewish youths wanted nothing more than to travel around the country playing basketball; but in later decades, as they and other white immigrants moved away to the suburbs and went on to colleges and into professions, African Americans moved into the inner cities and took over the sport. The majority of players in professional basketball are African Americans from predominantly urban backgrounds. The popularity of basketball on college campuses has made it accessible to large student immigrant populations. Immigrants who have made a mark in basketball are Hakeem Olajuwon, born in Lagos, Nigeria, in 1963, who led the Houston Rockets to a National Basketball Association (NBA) title in 1994 and 1995; Jamaican-born Hall of Famer Patrick Ewing who played for the New York Knicks; and the sensational 7-foot-5 Chinese player Yao Ming, who popularized NBA basketball in China. Basketball remains the one homegrown American sport that started off as a game played by poor immigrant kids in tenements

and was transformed through the nineteenth and twentieth centuries in urban centers and college campuses and sports arenas into a truly global cultural phenomenon.

In the late 1990s, there was also a major push to recruit in war-torn Yugoslavia. Among the more famous of players from these countries are Tony Kukoc (Croatia), Vlade Divac (Serbia) and Vladimir Radmanovic (Bosnia-Herzegovina). At the college level, too, there was a vigorous recruiting effort to bring in players from these countries on sports scholarships and groom them young for professional basketball.

Ice Hockey

Though ice hockey is the fourth major professional sport in the United States (after football, basketball, and baseball) it is the national sport of Canada, where its preeminence has nearly overshadowed its presence in the United States. The game originated in Canada in the mid-1800s, and became professionalized in the early 1900s in the United States. The game remained at its most popular in the Great Lakes and New England regions, though in the late twentieth century, new teams in California and the South sprang up due to the aggressive expansion plans of the National Hockey League (NHL). Only 20 percent of the players were U.S.-born; more than 50 percent were Canadian and the remaining were Europeans—mostly from the Czech Republic, Russia, Sweden, and Finland. The status of ice hockey as an Olympic sport has drawn many NHL players (who have maintained their foreign nationalities) to represent their own countries at this event, even while they played for U.S. or Canadian teams during the regular season and helped popularize the sport for American fans.

Soccer

The history of soccer in the United states is an interesting example of how a sport can be imported by ethnic groups from southern and eastern Europe in a particular time period (early twentieth century) and be revived by other ethnic groups (Latinos and Asians) in a later time period (later twentieth century). It is also noteworthy that the sport moved from the inner city and predominantly immigrant enclaves to the predominantly white suburbs. It turned from a working-class sport to an upper-middle-class phenomenon where it earned the epithet "soccer moms" for those mothers who happily ferried their children back and forth from after-school soccer practice.

Soccer had its roots overseas but thrived among the immigrants who came to the United States after 1900 from southern and eastern Europe—Austria-Hungary, the Balkans, Italy, and Greece. They worked in factory jobs during the week and played soccer after work or on weekends, often in dirt lots next to the factories or on open grass fields. In their urban ethnic enclaves, they created soccer clubs, where they welcomed new immigrants from their homeland and helped them acclimate to the United States. These clubs grew in all the major cities along the East Coast and in the Midwest, and soccer thrived in America until immigration from southern and eastern Europe declined drastically after World War I.

The 1965 Immigration Act encouraged immigration from entirely different regions of the world, and many of the new immigrants came from Latin America, the Caribbean, and Asia, where soccer is a national passion. There was a dramatic increase in soccer clubs, with players from Mexico, El Salvador, and Korea forming new leagues in the suburbs. But unlike the ethnicized adult teams that drove the growth of soccer in the past, there was a proliferation of youth soccer leagues supported by parents and volunteer coaches. The Brazilian soccer star Pele, who came out of retirement in 1975 to play in New York, is credited with having sparked new public awareness and enthusiasm for the sport. However, the game is still considered a marginalized American sport, since it has not acquired the same status as football and baseball and continues to be considered "foreign." As long as the controlling authority behind the game is FIFA (Fédération Internationale de Football Association), it may be difficult for Americans to embrace the game fully; but with the increasing number of games on television, the influx of new immigrants and the game's popularity among the youth, soccer is poised to gain greater acceptance in the United States.

Other Sports

Another game that follows a pattern similar to soccer is cricket. Cricket is said to have flourished in the nineteenth century through cricket clubs in cities like Seattle and Philadelphia. But it declined in the twentieth century with the advent of baseball, until new immigrants from the former British colonies of South Asia and the Caribbean started immigrating in large numbers after 1965 and revived it. The game got a big boost in the 1980s and 1990s, when many cricket pitches began showing up next to baseball diamonds in local park districts. Soon cricket leagues were formed and tournaments were being played all along the Eastern seaboard and the Midwest, and in Florida, Texas, California, and the Pacific Northwest.

While team sports have always had the most widespread impact on American culture, individual sports have also played their role helping immigrants succeed in the United States. Immigrant contributions in the sphere of boxing are particularly significant. Working-class Jewish, Italian, and Irish immigrants of the later nineteenth and early twentieth centuries assimilated into American culture by their prowess at boxing and, in subsequent decades, it was African and Hispanic Americans who dominated the sport, with names such as Muhammad Ali and Oscar de La Hoya being among the most famous boxers of all time. Italian American Rocky Marciano was heavyweight champion of the world from 1952 to 1956, having won every major fight in his career.

Some practices that have been introduced by immigrants into the everyday life of Americans and gained the status of a sports form include martial arts and yoga. Martial arts gained in popularity in the 1970s and 1980s, thanks to the movies of Jackie Chen and Jet Li. The term "martial arts" generally refers to fighting arts, which originated in East Asia even though such traditions exist in Native American, European, African, and Latin American cultures as well. Judo, karate, and taekwondo became dissociated from their martial origins and crossed over into competitive sports. Classes are offered in almost all major cities, and while the students are mostly Americans, the instructors are often immigrants from the land of origin. Yoga, imported from India during the counterculture of the 1960s, grew in strength and survived into the twenty-first century as a healthy, stress-relieving exercise and a preventive for many routine ailments. In 2008, a study released by *Yoga Journal* showed that Americans spent nearly $5.7 billion a year on yoga classes and products, practicing it in sports clubs, ashrams, and meditation halls spread throughout the country.

Sports continues to hold a sacred place in American culture, for its entertainment value, for the opportunity it offers new immigrants to succeed, and for the way it inspires the competitive spirit in Americans. Immigration laws have been changed to accommodate individual sportspersons and athletes, and when immigrants have come in large enough numbers, they have invented, modified, and transformed the games, giving them a uniquely American flavor.

Food and Festivals

Americans love to celebrate over food, and linking food to festivals enables us to explore three different but related themes: the contribution of indigenous peoples to American cuisine and festive traditions; the regional differences in cuisine due to variations in settlement patterns of immigrants; and the impact of ethnic-heritage festivities on the evolution of a distinctly American cuisine.

American holidays and festivals may be broadly divided into two kinds—those that celebrate unity and seek to blur distinctions among Americans, and those that celebrate ethnic differences. Among the former are Valentine's Day, the Fourth of July celebrations, Labor Day, Thanksgiving Day, and Veterans Day. Even though Christmas is a religious observance, it is celebrated by many segments of society. But it also generated a separate ethnic pride among African Americans, who began celebrating Kwanzaa in 1966 as an alternative to Christmas and in recognition of their own African heritage. The Jews have Hanukkah, which is a relatively minor holiday in the Jewish calendar but is given greater importance in the United States as an alternative to Christmas. With the growing presence of Muslims and Hindus in the United States, the White House recognized Diwali and Eid as important festivals for significant numbers of Americans. Christmas, Kwanzaa, Hanukkah, and Diwali are all festivals of lights and, along with Eid, are accompanied by fasts and feasts that perpetuate the culinary traditions of the home countries for immigrants.

The Thanksgiving Feast

The development of American cuisine as a fusion of many cultures can be traced back to the historic peaceful encounter between the Pilgrims and Native Americans in Plymouth Colony. Thanks to the Native American Wampanoag tribe who helped the settlers when they were short of supplies in the winter and taught them how to catch eel and grow corn, the Pilgrim settlers survived to reap a successful harvest in 1621 and celebrated with a thanksgiving feast. It was not until 1863, in the middle of the American Civil War, that Abraham Lincoln proclaimed the last Thursday of November as the official national Thanksgiving Day and perpetuated a tradition to forge national unity among an increasingly diverse population. New immigrants, regardless of class or religion, are quick to adapt it as a rite to Americanization. Thanksgiving is next only to the Fourth of July as a celebration of American identity.

Regional Variations in American Cuisine

The subcultures of the United States are celebrated in their cuisine, and the distinctions are as much due to environmental and seasonal factors as to the influences of immigrants. The southern colonies had a more diverse diet than the northern ones, not only because they had more land available for farming, but because of the disparities between their immigrant populations. African Americans ate stews and porridges made of leafy vegetables and root crops, reminiscent of dishes popular in West Africa. As slaves, they were fed large quantities of cornmeal used in breads and indigenous vegetables such as sweet potatoes and beans and salted pork. Though some of the ingredients in their diet were discontinued after emancipation, African Americans continued to uphold much of their distinctive food tradition, and in the

1960s, southern African-American cooking came to be distinguished as "soul" food, when the word "soul" was used to define African-American culture

Other southern cuisine, not limited to the slave diet, includes fried chicken, grits, biscuits, and desserts such as pies and fruit cobblers, made with plenty of sugar, flour, milk, and eggs. These dishes trace their lineage to the British and Scots Irish who settled in the South as slave-owners. Another variation is in Creole or Cajun cuisine, which developed in Louisiana as a mixture of French and Caribbean influence and is renowned for its spicy, aromatic flavors.

As more and more southern and western states became integrated into the United States, a new southwestern cuisine developed that was influenced by native Americans, the ranch-style cooking of cowboys, and Mexicans who became part of the American population. This cuisine is distinguished by spicy, tangy barbecues, grilled meats and vegetables, and chili dishes made of tomatoes, beans, corn, and ground meats. Tacos, tortillas, tamales, and salsa entered mainstream American culture through this region.

California and the Pacific Northwest became home to immigrants pouring in from the eastern part of the country as well as from the western waters as early as the 1820s. Among the earliest Asian immigrant groups to come to the western U.S. shores were the Chinese who came during the Gold Rush. They prepared meals for the miners that were tasty combinations of textures, flavors, and spices, quite different from the bland meat and beans they were used to. Americans have developed a taste for the American version of Chinese cuisine that has led to a proliferation of Chinese restaurants in every major city and small town in the United States. The Japanese, too, brought their cuisine to the entire West Coast, eventually making the sushi bar as widespread as the Chinese takeout places in such cities as Seattle and San Francisco. The Italians are credited with having developed the wine industry in California, where wine-tasting tours and festivals have helped the industry grow to compete with the traditional wineries of Europe. And, of course, Italian immigrants introduced what is now a preeminent America staple—pizza—which is now as ubiquitous as Chinese food.

Immigrant Influences Are Everywhere

When does a dish stop being an immigrant import and become an American original? Take the case of the hot dog and hamburger, both based on traditional German dishes, or the pizza. There is no rival to the Coney Island hot dog or the Chicago-style pizza in Germany or Italy. Despite having their origins in other countries, these dishes have been so transformed by American adaptation and innovation that they are now considered authentic American dishes. It is safe to say that Italian, Mexican, and Chinese cuisine and items of German origin (plus their redefining what Americans could do for relaxation on Sundays) are so much a part of Americana that people no longer consider them foreign.

The popularity of foods introduced by immigrants depended on the size of the immigrant population and the regions in which they were concentrated. Thus, the late nineteenth century and early twentieth century saw the importation and acceptance of European foods from Germany, Italy, and Greece; while the post–World War II period saw Americans embracing many foods from Asian countries, including Thailand and Korea and later Vietnam, as immigrants from these countries made their way into the United States.

Since the time of their arrival in the United States and throughout the ebb and flow of immigration patterns, ethnic groups have celebrated their heritage through food fests, like the German Oktoberfests in the Midwest, or the Day of the Dead food festivals among Mexican Americans. Every major American city, including New York, Los Angeles, Miami, and Chicago, has ethnic restaurants, owned and operated by immigrants but patronized by the wider population, especially those who have traveled abroad and acquired a taste for such cuisine. Hotels, too, started offering ethnic cuisine when catering for weddings, banquets, and conventions in the immigrant communities. In the 1970s, it was hard to find a single major hotel willing to serve Indian food at a wedding in the Chicago area. By 2010, every major hotel chain (many of which were becoming Indian-owned, such as Sheraton, Westin, Marriott, Wyndham and Hilton), offered an Indian menu on a regular basis for large gatherings. Ethnic food aisles became common in large grocery chains, with fresh, frozen, and packaged foods for Jewish, Mexican, Indian, Chinese, and Thai making up the fastest-growing segments of this market. A quite recent addition has been the variety of Middle Eastern foods in markets and restaurants.

Media

The end of the twentieth century saw the development of a full-blown Internet culture whose main features were instant communication, worldwide reach, and easy access. For the price of a cell phone and an Internet subscription, one could be connected to anyone anywhere, anytime; and immigrants, especially the younger generation, took to this technology with unbridled enthusiasm. Indeed, they were responsible for leading this revolution and steering its progress through leaps and bounds—from the personal computer of the 1980s to the laptop of the 1990s to the iPhones and iPods of the twenty-first century. Those who stood at the forefront of this development were immigrant entrepreneurs and innovators, risk-takers and visionaries.

The role of immigrant entrepreneurs and scientists in U.S. technology development in the information age is well documented. In the decade 1999–2008, 3.87 million H-1B temporary workers of specialty occupations were admitted, while over 645,000 (E-class visas) priority workers, professionals, and those with advanced degrees (and nearly 90 percent of them already working in the United States) were having their status adjusted to legal permanent residents. In 2005, immigrants accounted for almost half the PhD scientists in the United States. More than half the graduates in U.S. universities in science and engineering were born overseas. A special permit—the H-1B visa—allowed U.S. companies to temporarily employ foreign workers in specialty occupations that could not be filled by native-born Americans and enabled them to seek permanent residency after six years of stay in the United States. Many immigrants from Europe and Asia who entered the United States on a H-1B visa went on to pioneer the Internet revolution.

A Duke University study in 2005 reported that immigrant-founded companies accounted for $52 billion in sales and 450,000 jobs. Foreign-born entrepreneurs were behind one in four technology startups between 1995 and 2005. Leading the pack were immigrants from India. Of an estimated 7,300 U.S. tech startups founded by immigrants, 26 percent had Indian founders, CEOs, presidents, or head researchers. In a survey of 2,054 high-tech companies nationwide, 25.3 percent had one or more founders who were immigrants—39 percent in California and 38 percent in New Jersey. Indeed, in California's Silicon Valley between 1980 and 1998, Chinese and Asian Indians were involved as founders of almost one-fourth of high-tech firms. Conversely, four-fifths of Chinese startup firms were located in California, while as much as 35 percent in Florida had one or more founders who were Cuban, Colombian, Brazilian, Venezuelan, and Guatemalan. In Massachusetts, 17 percent of high-tech firms were begun by Israelis; and in New Jersey, 47 percent were started by Asian Indians.

Among the leading lights who were Asian Indian immigrants are Sabeer Bhatia, the inventor of Hotmail; Vinod Khosla, co-founder of Sun Microsystems; and Vinod Dham, acclaimed father of the Intel Pentium processor. In fact, Indian immigrants founded more high-tech startups from 1995 to 2005 than people from the four next-largest sources—the United Kingdom, China, Taiwan, and Japan—combined. In addition, Duke University researchers also found that foreign-born inventors living in the United States without citizenship accounted for 24 percent of patent filings in 2004, compared with 7.3 percent in 1998. Moreover, by 2012, these developments have taken another twist, with young immigrants and 1.5ers as well as second-generation entrepreneurs accelerating a reverse flow (predominantly in sciences, engineering, and manufacturing and marketing of homeland-produced products. This current trend is now referred to as "brain circulation" to homelands and not simply brain drain from those homelands (Semple 2012, 1).

These phenomena underscore America's global reach aided by continuing flows of immigrant workers, business, and hi-tech leaders. For example, Indian and Chinese immigrants make up a large part of the workforce in such companies as Microsoft, Apple, Intel, and Google. They account for the surge in population of immigrants in the Pacific Northwest in the 1900s and 2000s. Many of the software engineers are recruited abroad, and once in the United States, are given free rein to innovate and create with ample resources. Google has grown to dominate the search-engine market by acquiring many companies started by immigrants or children of immigrants, such as YouTube (acquired for $1.65 billion from founders Steve Chen, Chad Hurley, and Jawed Karim). Besides creating enormous wealth for immigrant inventors and workers in the industry, these innovations have created a culture of sharing and collaboration through groups and forums; communication through blogs, videos, and events; and even fun and recreation through downloading of photos and music.

The role of immigrants in the era of Internet communications has been as both producers and consumers. Not only did they help invent and popularize digital communication in the United States, but they exposed millions of Americans to the ways in which that technology could be used to communicate around the globe. At the local level, they revitalized neighborhoods, bringing new productivity, competitiveness, and dynamism to American campuses and cities.

Conclusion

Looking back at American history, it is clear that immigrants were influential in the development of American popular culture, no matter what the circumstances of their immigration. From the western Europeans who settled the colonies, to the Scandinavians who settled the frontiers, from the Africans who worked the fields, to the southern and eastern Europeans who transformed American cities, from the Asians who laid the railroads to the Mexicans who worked the farms, they have helped foster an American national identity that is much more than the sum of its parts. They all came to change their own lives, not to shape America; but in the process of struggling to make it good, they forced America to change. Immigration has always excited controversy, and while the arguments against immigration have been loud and noisy from time to time, overall, immigrants have managed to create a positive impact through their contributions to popular culture. Their yearning to assimilate and be accepted as Americans has combined with their attachment to their home cultures and memories of their past to weave new threads in the fabric of American society.

The last decade of the twentieth century ranks as the period of highest immigration in U.S. history, and despite major setbacks to immigrants caused by negative backlash after the terror attack on American soil on September 11, 2001, the new century is poised to continue receiving new immigrants. It is impossible to predict where they will come from and with what talents, but one thing is for sure—they will continue to influence the way Americans live their everyday lives. They will determine what Americans eat, how they speak, write, play, and celebrate, and interact with the rest of the world. Most of all, they will keep stretching the boundaries of what it means to be an American. In the process of becoming American themselves, they will continue to transform the character of American society and culture.

Bibliography

Batchelor, Bob. 2008. *American Pop: Popular Culture Decade by Decade*. Westport, CT: Greenwood Press.

Ciment, James, ed. 2001. *Encyclopedia of American Immigration*, vol. 3. New York: M. E. Sharpe.

Fanning, Charles, 1990. *The Irish Voice in America: 250 Years of Irish-American Fiction*. Lexington: University Press of Kentucky.

Gems, Gerald R., and Gertrude Pfister, eds. 2009. *Understanding American Sports*. New York: Routledge.

Hirschman, Charles. 2006. "The Impact of Immigration on American Society: Looking Backward to the Future." http://borderbattles.ssrc.org/Hirschman.

Kirsch, George B., Othello Harris, and Claire Elaine Nolte, eds. 2000. *Encyclopedia of Ethnicity and Sports in the U.S.* Westport, CT: Greenwood Press.

Levinson, David, and Melvin Ember. 1997. *American Immigrant Cultures: Builders of a Nation.* New York: Simon and Schuster Macmillan.

Payant, Katherine B., ed. 1999. *The Immigrant Experience in North American Literature.* Westport, CT: Greenwood Press.

Rubin, Rachel, and Jeffrey Melnick. 2007. *Immigration and American Popular Culture: An Introduction.* New York: New York University Press.

Semple, Kirk. 2012. "Many U.S. Immigrants' Children Seek American Dream Abroad." *New York Times,* April 16, A1+.

Immigrants and Political Incorporation in the United States

Els de Graauw

Defining Immigrant Political Incorporation

Immigrant political incorporation refers to the process through which, over time, immigrants become part of the American political system. This is an intentionally general definition because the term *political* captures a wide range of activities. It includes legal citizenship, participation in the electoral process, and participation in more informal political acts such as petition-signing campaigns, demonstrations, and forms of organizational life. It also includes immigrants' direct participation in political institutions through both ethnic (or demographic) representation, which refers to a type of representation in which the characteristics of legislators (including their race, ethnicity, and socioeconomic background) proportionately reflect those of the population they represent; and policy (or substantive) representation, which refers to the adoption and implementation of public policies that reflect immigrants' unique needs and interests. *Incorporation* implies successful inclusion, but immigrants might very well fail to incorporate politically. *Nonincorporation* can happen because immigrants choose not to participate in politics or because they are intentionally excluded from the political arena.

Although scholars agree that immigrant political incorporation has many important outcomes, there are few systematic or theoretically concise analyses of the modes and trajectories of immigrants' incorporation into the American political system. Robert Dahl perhaps comes closest to providing a general model for immigrant political incorporation. His landmark book, *Who Governs?*—largely based on the experiences of successive waves of European immigrants to the city of New Haven, Connecticut—ties the political rise of immigrants to their socioeconomic assimilation and describes immigrants' political incorporation as proceeding in stages over roughly three generations. The first generation of immigrants is poor, has little to no political influence, and depends on elected officials from previously assimilated immigrant groups for both ethnic and policy representation. The second generation consists of native-born citizens, who are higher up on the socioeconomic ladder, participate in politics, and begin to challenge the political leaders they had previously depended on. Finally, the third generation has fully ascended into the middle class and helps elect co-ethnic representatives who produce policies responsive to their constituents' concerns. Here, immigrant political incorporation is viewed as a linear and cumulative process of four distinct stages that build on each other: (1) naturalized citizenship, (2) electoral participation, (3) ethnic representation, and (4) policy representation.

This early incorporation model emphasizes that generational depth is key to achieving full political incorporation. Today, it is accepted knowledge that political incorporation takes time, often a lot of time, and that full incorporation likely remains elusive for most first-generation immigrants. This model, however, also invites several amendments and criticisms, especially in light of scholarship on the political incorporation dynamics of immigrants today. For example, the model glosses over how ethnic, racial, and religious discrimination affects immigrants' political incorporation. Since a majority of today's newcomers are nonwhite and hail from Latin

America, Asia, the Caribbean, Africa, and the Middle East, it is important to consider the effect that discrimination in its various guises can have on their political incorporation. The model, furthermore, privileges electoral politics and assumes that immigrants can accomplish ethnic and policy representation only *after* they have made the trek to the voting booth. The linearity and cumulative nature of this model has been questioned by scholars who show that non-elected civil servants can represent the policy needs of first-generation immigrants *before* (rather than after) these immigrants become American citizens or exercise the right to vote. The model also assumes that first-generation immigrants largely are of low socioeconomic status and therefore serve as a poor guide to understanding the political incorporation of the substantial number of contemporary immigrants who arrive in the United States with considerable human and financial capital. While not ideal and perhaps too simple, Dahl's early framework nonetheless continues to resonate with many incorporation scholars and has remained largely intact as a description of the political incorporation process. It has in fact been revived in a number of studies that describe the political incorporation experiences of recent immigrants from Latin America and Asia.

In this chapter, I do not aim to present a generic, all-inclusive model of immigrant political incorporation. Many incorporation scholars, pointing to the complexity of incorporation dynamics, doubt such a meta-model can be created. Instead, I focus on six common indicators of political incorporation to show that incorporation dynamics have changed over time and continue to differ from one immigrant group to another. The indicators I concentrate on are: (1) *naturalization*, or immigrants' acquisition of American citizenship after birth; (2) *voting and partisanship*, or immigrants' participation in national elections and vote choice; (3) *ethnic representation*, or the election to political office of immigrants and their direct descendants; (4) *policy representation and non-representation*, or the adoption and implementation of public policies that address immigrant issues in either an inclusive or exclusive manner; (5) *civic engagement*, or immigrants' participation in various types of civic organizations (such as religious

institutions, labor unions, and other types of interest groups) in efforts to advance their political interests; and (6) *transnational political participation*, with a focus on immigrants' external voting, or political participation in the elections of their homelands. The chapter concludes with a brief discussion of key determinants of immigrants' political incorporation today.

Naturalization and Citizenship

American citizenship can be obtained in one of two ways: at birth, or through naturalization. U.S. citizenship can be attributed at birth when individuals are born on American soil (*jus soli*) or when they are born in a foreign country to parents with American citizenship (*jus sanguinis*). Foreign-born individuals without American parents can acquire U.S. citizenship only through naturalization, which refers to the legal but voluntary process by which an immigrant acquires U.S. citizenship after birth. Throughout its history, the United States has offered a home to millions of immigrants, and naturalization has played an important role in building the country's population and economy. Naturalization, however, is also an important indicator of immigrant political incorporation. Naturalization makes clear that immigrants identify with American society and confers the right to vote, thus signaling that immigrants are ready to actively participate in the political affairs of their adoptive country.

In the past, the United States placed race and national origins restrictions on citizenship. The Naturalization Act of 1790, the first law on naturalization, restricted naturalization to "free white persons" who had resided in the country for two years, effectively excluding slaves, free blacks, and Asians. The Naturalization Act of 1795 modified the residency requirement for naturalization to five years and the Naturalization Act of 1798, which was repealed in 1802, temporarily raised it to 14 years. Decades later, the Naturalization Act of 1870 ushered in the right to acquire American citizenship for persons of African nativity and African descent. However, the Chinese Exclusion Act of 1882 prohibited Chinese immigrants from acquiring American citizenship through naturalization, a ban that would be lifted only in 1943 when China became a U.S. ally in the war against Japan. However, Filipino and Asian Indian immigrants gained the right to naturalize in 1946 as a result of the Luce-Celler Act. Finally, the 1952 McCarran-Walter Act removed all remaining race and national origins restrictions as criteria for American citizenship.

There also were gender restrictions, and for a long time the acquisition of U.S. citizenship was centered on men. The Naturalization Act of 1790 applied to both white men and women, but only foreign-born women with a father (rather than mother) residing in the United States could acquire U.S. citizenship. The Naturalization Act of 1855 stipulated that women's naturalization was derivative and automatic: an immigrant woman automatically became a U.S. citizen upon marrying an American man or following the naturalization of her foreign-born husband. Further tying women's citizenship to that of their husbands, the Expatriation Act of 1907 specified that a woman, whether a naturalized or U.S.-born citizen, would lose her American citizenship if she married a foreign national, and she could regain her citizenship only if her husband naturalized (or if she petitioned for repatriation after divorce from or upon the death of her foreign-born husband). The Cable Act of 1922, enacted shortly after the Nineteenth Amendment to the U.S. Constitution gave women the franchise, ended both marital naturalization and expatriation (except for women married to Asian immigrants). The Cable Act gave women the ability to control their own nationality and introduced the practice still in effect today in which men and women need to apply for citizenship independently, even when they are married.

In contrast to the past, and despite certain restrictions that persist, the United States today has some of the most open and inclusive naturalization policies in the world. Currently, adult immigrants in the United States are eligible to naturalize after a minimum of five continuous years of legal permanent residence in the country (or three years if married to a U.S. citizen, one year for immigrants who serve in the U.S. military during peacetime, and no residency requirement for immigrants who have served honorably on active military duty during wartime on or after September 11, 2001). They must also demonstrate knowledge of both the English language and American history

and government. As of 2012, applicants for naturalization also needed to pay an application fee of $675 (including $80 biometric fee; total cost is up from $90 in 1991; immigrants serving in the U.S. military do not pay the fee), take an oath of allegiance, demonstrate good moral character, and renounce their previous citizenship. The United States does not de jure recognize or encourage dual citizenship but de facto tolerates it because an increasing number of source countries of U.S.-bound immigrants—including Mexico, the Philippines, El Salvador, and the Dominican Republic—do permit dual citizenship. Once naturalized, immigrants enjoy legal and political equality with the U.S. native-born population. Naturalized citizens can vote in American elections and have the right to carry a U.S. passport. They also enjoy eligibility for government-funded social services on par with native-born Americans and immigration benefits for family members. In addition, naturalized citizens are eligible to hold any public office in the country except that of president of the United States.

Despite a relatively low bar to naturalization, only a minority of contemporary immigrants in the United States are naturalized citizens. Between 2006 and 2008, an estimated 42.5 percent of the nation's 38 million foreign-born were naturalized. Relative to the U.S. national average, the naturalization rates were higher for immigrants from Europe (60.2 percent) and Asia (57.1 percent), but lower for Latin American immigrants (30.9 percent). The naturalization rate was low for Mexican immigrants in particular (21.9 percent). Immigrants from Africa had a naturalization rate approximating the national average (41.3 percent). Between 2006 and 2008, female immigrants (45.7 percent) were more likely to have naturalized than male immigrants (39.4 percent). Moreover, because it takes considerable time and effort to become a naturalized citizen (and because prospective citizens might incur a psychological toll from having to switch national allegiances), it is not surprising that immigrants who have spent more time in the United States are more likely to have naturalized than more recent arrivals. Between 2006 and 2008, 78.5 percent of immigrants who entered the country before 1980 had naturalized, compared to 58.8 percent of immigrants who entered during the 1980s, 35.2 percent of those

A woman from Kenya holds her niece before the start of a special naturalization ceremony for 118 new citizens at the U.S. Citizenship and Immigration Services office, July 2, 2010 in Irving, Texas. (AP Photo/Cody Duty)

who were admitted during the 1990s, and only 8.8 percent of immigrants admitted after 2000.

Naturalization, however, is not within reach for all. Under current law, the estimated 11.9 million undocumented, or "illegal," immigrants in the country today are ineligible for U.S. citizenship. Their access to citizenship figured prominently in the 2005–2007 congressional debates on comprehensive immigration reform. Questions about their legalization and ability to naturalize—either through a path of "earned citizenship" or an amnesty program akin to that enacted as part of the 1986 Immigration Reform and Control Act—likely will also take center stage in future debates about immigration reform. Immigrants can also have their citizenship revoked. Prior to 1967, when the U.S. Supreme Court declared it unconstitutional in the case of *Afroyim v. Rusk*, immigrants could be denaturalized involuntarily because they voted in a foreign election. Today, immigrants can still lose their U.S. citizenship as a result of

participating in a foreign election; becoming an elected official in a foreign country; serving in a foreign military; being convicted for treason against the United States; joining a subversive organization; or for deliberately lying during the naturalization process.

Voting and Partisanship

Voting is emblematic of political participation in a democracy, and immigrants' electoral participation therefore should figure centrally in discussions about their political incorporation. In general, access to the right to vote in the United States has followed a progressive and expansive trajectory. Religious and property prerequisites for voting were eliminated in the early nineteenth century. Blacks gained the right to vote in 1870, women in 1920, Native Americans in 1924 (although two-thirds already had the right to vote by 1924), and 18-year-olds in 1971. Poll taxes and literacy tests were outlawed as requirements for voting in 1964 and 1965, respectively. For immigrants, in contrast, the trend has been in the *opposite* direction, and their right to vote is *more restricted* today than it was in the past. Between the founding of the nation and 1926, as many as 40 states and federal territories allowed immigrants without U.S. citizenship to vote in local, state, and federal elections.

However, the great wave of immigration at the turn of the twentieth century stirred up strong nativist sentiments and brought on the first efforts to restrict the political participation of the newest immigrants. In 1804, for example, New York State enacted a citizenship requirement for voting partly in an effort to stop French immigrants from spreading radical ideas after the French Revolution. There also were efforts to disenfranchise Irish and German immigrants to protect the republic from the supposed Catholic danger. World War I and the Red Scare of 1917–1920 generated more hostility toward newcomers such as Greek, Italian, and Russian immigrants, and by 1926, Arkansas was the final state to outlaw noncitizen or alien voting. Today, voting in American elections is a right reserved to U.S. citizens, and the 1996 Illegal Immigration Reform and Immigrant Responsibility Act made noncitizen voting in federal and state elections a federal crime. Only a handful of municipalities, including Takoma Park (Maryland) and Chicago, currently allow noncitizens to vote in local elections.

Immigrants who arrived to the United States after liberalization of immigration policy in 1965 have had to contend with electoral hurdles of a different kind. Despite their legal right to vote, many naturalized immigrants have limited proficiency in English and consequently have encountered language barriers that effectively exclude them from the electoral process. In 1975, on the coattails of civil rights legislation that bans racial discrimination in voting practices, Congress enacted Section 203, an amendment to the Voting Rights Act of 1965. Section 203 requires election officials to provide bilingual voting assistance in localities where a single language-minority group is greater than 10,000 or 5 percent of the overall eligible-voter population. Section 203 only applies to persons of American Indian, Asian, Alaskan Native, or Spanish heritage, all groups with a documented history of exclusion from the political process in the United States. While originally intended as a temporary measure, Congress has renewed the provisions of Section 203 a number of times, most recently for 25 years in 2006. As of 2002, a total of 466 local jurisdictions in 31 states were covered by Section 203 and required to provide voting information and ballots in non-English languages, including Spanish and Chinese.

The Current Population Survey's data for the 2000–2008 national elections show that naturalized citizens in the United States, regardless of their ethnic or racial background, are less likely to take advantage of their right to participate in the electoral process than native-born non-Hispanic whites (see Table 1). The

Table 1. Reported Voter Registration and Voting among Native-Born and Naturalized Citizens in the United States, by Race and Hispanic Origin: 2000–2008

CPS (November Supplement)	White (not Hispanic)		Black		Asian and Pacific Islander		Hispanic (of any race)	
	Native-Born	Naturalized	Native-Born	Naturalized	Native-Born	Naturalized	Native-Born	Naturalized
2000 (Presidential Election)								
Total citizen population 18 yrs. and over	141,008,000	3,724,000	21,887,000	866,000	1,778,000	2,940,000	9,902,000	3,257,000
% Registered	71.8	63.4	67.7	60.3	53.5	51.7	57.2	57.7
% Voted	62	55.9	56.8	56.8	43.2	43.4	43.6	49.6
2002 (Congressional Election)								
Total citizen population 18 yrs. and over	143,592,000	3,579,000	21,782,000	1,130,000	2,259,000	3,749,000	11,734,000	3,868,000
% Registered	69.6	62.5	62.7	57.9	49.9	48.8	52.7	51.9
% Voted	49.2	45	42.4	40.2	32.3	30.5	29.5	33.4
2004 (Presidential Election)								
Total citizen population 18 yrs. and over	144,302,000	3,857,000	21,993,000	1,353,000	2,344,000	3,926,000	12,062,000	4,026,000
% Registered	75.3	68.2	69.1	61.8	47.1	54.6	57.1	60
% Voted	67.3	61.8	60.4	54.4	40.5	46.4	45.5	52.1
2006 (Congressional Election)								
Total citizen population 18 yrs. and over	145,729,000	4,032,000	22,862,000	1,366,000	2,460,000	4,154,000	12,923,000	4,392,000
% Registered	71.5	61.1	61.5	52.3	45	51.5	54.6	51.2
% Voted	51.8	43.5	41.4	35.1	30.7	33.5	31.6	34.3
2008 (Presidential Election)								
Total citizen population 18 yrs. and over	146,906,000	4,415,000	23,442,000	1,488,000	2,654,000	4,405,000	14,461,000	5,077,000
% Registered	73.8	62.9	70.1	63.4	51	57.8	59.3	59.8
% Voted	66.4	56.7	65	59.4	45	49.1	48.4	54.2

Source: Current Population Survey, 2000–2008.

effect of nativity is most pronounced during mid-term, or congressional, elections, when the gap in voter registration and voting rates between native-born and naturalized citizens is larger than it is during presidential election years. Overall, natural-ized citizens of Asian descent have the lowest regis-tration and voting rates across the five election years reported in Table 28.1, followed by Hispanics, blacks, and then whites. Also, white and black natu-ralized citizens are *less* likely to register and vote than their native-born co-ethnics. However, Hispanic immigrants have been *more* likely to register and vote than their native-born counterparts; and for Asian immigrants, this has been the case for elec-tions since 2004. Furthermore, over time, registration and voting rates during presidential elections have increased for naturalized citizens of all racial and ethnic backgrounds, and larger percentages of natu-ralized citizens voted during the presidential election of 2008 than did during the presidential election of 2000.

The growing size and potential political power of immigrant voters today has interested both the Democratic and Republican Parties in increasing their share of partisan identifiers among those new to the American political system. While the newest immi-grants tend not to associate with either major political party, longer-established immigrants who have acquired U.S. citizenship are more likely to articulate a party preference. Various surveys, including the Lat-ino National Political Survey of 1989–1990 and the Latino National Survey of 2006, show that Latino immigrants—with the notable exception of Cubans—have a propensity to affiliate with the Democratic Party, in large part due to the party's image of being more supportive of policies favoring ethnic and racial minorities. Latinos of Colombian, Dominican, Ecuado-rian, and Peruvian descent are especially likely to self-identify as Democrats. Cubans, however, have more consistently affiliated with the Republican Party. Compared with Latino immigrants, there is more parti-san variation among Asian and Pacific-Islander immigrant groups, and their partisan identification remains in flux. Data from the 2001 Pilot National Asian American Politics Survey show that Asian and Pacific Islanders in recent years have moved toward

the Democratic Party: 36 percent of survey respondents identified as Democrat, 14 percent as Republican, 13 percent as independent, and 38 percent either had no partisan preference, were unsure about it, or declined to state it. However, immigrants of South Asian, Korean, Filipino, and Japanese origins were more likely to identify as Democrat than did Chinese or Vietnamese immigrants.

Ethnic Representation

Ethnic representation, or the extent to which immi-grants and their offspring have won seats in legislative bodies of government, is another important measure of immigrants' political incorporation. One way to determine whether immigrants have achieved politi-cal incorporation is to evaluate whether their share of elected officials is proportionate to their share of the population. Ethnic representation is considered important by some because elected officials with backgrounds similar to their constituents can better understand and act on the concerns of their constitu-ents. Extending this logic, government representatives who are foreign-born or the direct descendants of immigrants are best able to address immigrants' unique needs and interests in the policy-making process. Throughout American history, however, immigrants and their offspring have been notably underrepresented in elective positions on all levels of government.

Yesteryear's urban machines enabled some early European immigrants to win powerful elected posi-tions in municipal politics. Irish immigrants, for example, long dominated the Democratic Party machines in such cities as New York City, Boston, Philadelphia, and Chicago. The Irish were able to maintain machine control by appealing to immigrant voters, whom they rewarded with goods, services, and patronage jobs in exchange for their loyalty in the voting booth. While early urban scholars have argued that Irish machine bosses facilitated the political incorporation of new immigrant groups into local party politics, later scholars have provided important revisions to these inclusive accounts. Some persuasively argue that machines in actuality were self-interested institutions. They mobilized immigrants when it helped them to gain power in a competitive political environment, but actively suppressed immigrants' votes if that preserved the status quo or the machine's privileged position. These revisionist accounts explain why later-arriving immigrants, such as Jews, Italians, Poles, and other immigrants from southern and eastern Europe, had a hard time winning leadership positions in machine cities and rarely saw tangible rewards from the machine system.

Regarding the issue of ethnic representation today, the 1965 Voting Rights Act (VRA) is of particular importance for the immigrants of color who dominate the current wave of newcomers. The VRA prohibits discrimination against blacks, Latinos, Asians, and Native Americans and prevents states and municipalities from engaging in practices that make it difficult for ethnic and racial minorities to elect candidates of their choice. As a result of the VRA, many state legislatures have consciously sought to create "majority-minority" congressional districts where ethno-racial minority groups constitute more than 50 percent of the voting-age population, with the aim of increasing minority representation in the U.S. House of Representatives. All in all, the VRA has increased the proportion of minority legislators nationwide. A database of minority elected officials serving in the House in 2006 reveals, for example, that three-quarters of black and Asian officials and *all* Latino officials were elected from districts covered by the VRA. The VRA has had a similarly positive, though slightly weaker, impact on minority representation for state- and municipal-level elective offices.

Despite a substantial and documented relationship between the VRA and the election of minority officials at all levels of government, immigrants and their offspring remain underrepresented in the national legislature in particular. The 111th Congress (2009–2011) counts a total of 80 elected officials (4 in the Senate, 76 in the House) from ethnic or racial minority groups: 43 blacks, 28 Latinos, 8 Asian and Pacific Islanders, and one Native American. This equals 15 percent of members of Congress, yet nonwhites in 2006–2008 constituted 34 percent of the U.S. population. Furthermore, only 8 out of

535 members in the 111th U.S. Congress are foreign-born, all serving in the House of Representatives. While the foreign-born currently constitute 12.5 percent of the U.S. population, they make up only 1.5 percent of members of Congress. It takes considerable time for first-generation immigrants to become citizens, vote, and run for and win political office, which helps explain why immigrants' share of elected officials lags behind their share of the population. The difficulty for minority candidates to win the crossover votes of whites and the high cost associated with running for federal office also contribute to the underrepresentation in the U.S. Congress of the foreign-born and their direct descendants.

Some municipal legislative bodies, which are more accessible to immigrants with political aspirations than the U.S. Congress, are ethnically more representative of the population. The foreign-born, for example, have notable representation on the city councils of gateway cities such as New York City, Los Angeles, Chicago, Houston, and San Francisco. However, immigrants' representation at the municipal level is also well below their share of these cities' populations (see Figures 1 and 2). Ethnic representation significantly improves, however, when we count city council members who are black or the direct descendants of immigrants from Asia and Latin America. San Francisco, in particular, stands out because ethnic and racial minorities were slightly *overrepresented* among the city's legislators in 2009. Although non-Hispanic whites remain overrepresented and Asians and Latinos have yet to gain a stronger foothold on the city councils of New York City, Los Angeles, Chicago, and Houston, these cities have come a long way in the last three decades (Asian and Pacific Islanders, though, dominate elected posts at all levels of government in the state of Hawai'i, including the city of Honolulu). There were no immigrant-origin council members in New York City at the end of the 1980s, for example; but today, legislators with Asian or Latino roots make up 24 percent of the city's 51-member council. Similarly, voters in Houston elected their first Mexican-American city councilor in 1979 and the first Asian American in 1993.

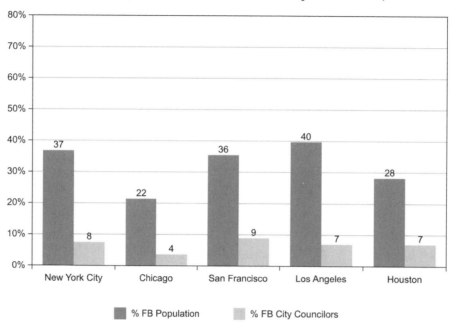

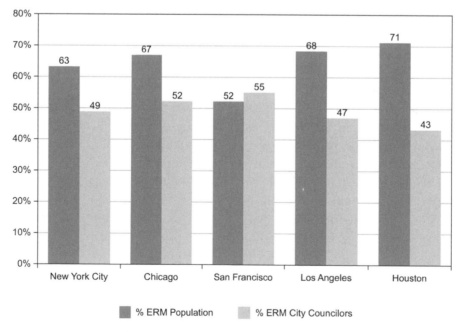

Figures 1 and 2.   Foreign-Born and Ethno-Racial Minority Representation on City Councils in Selected U.S. Gateway Cities. *Notes*: FB = foreign-born; ERM = ethno-racial minority. *Sources*: Population statistics for American cities are from the 2006–2008 American Community Survey, 3-year estimates; data for American city councils are for 2009 and, with the exception of New York City, they are the author's compilation of city council records available on the Internet; New York City data are from John Mollenkopf, with updates by the author.

Policy Representation and Non-Representation: Immigrant Inclusion and Exclusion

Not only is it important to know whether immigrants naturalize, vote, and win legislative seats, but it is equally important to consider whether their interests are reflected in the adoption and implementation of public policies. Given the difficulty in determining what immigrants want or what their collective political interests are, few studies have focused on policy representation as an indicator of immigrant political incorporation. Because immigrants are diverse in terms of their national origins, immigration status, and linguistic and socioeconomic backgrounds, their political interests are equally diverse. Immigrants, nonetheless, share certain unique needs and likely hold distinct views on a number of issues, including language policy, labor protections, drivers' licenses, and access to public services. These issues are all central to their lives, yet are of more tangential interest to most native-born Americans. While there are policies that address immigrants' needs and interests in an *inclusive* manner, throughout American history, there also have been notable attempts to single out the foreign-born for *exclusion* from important policy benefits. This section provides an overview of the most salient policies that affect immigrants in the areas of language and government benefits. Also discussed are more recent policy developments that specifically target undocumented immigrants.

Language

Most immigrants to the United States are not native speakers of English. As a result, language issues have figured prominently in public policy debates about immigrant integration. During much of the nineteenth century, the U.S. government officially tolerated languages other than English in the public sphere. At this time, bilingual education in public schools was explicitly authorized by law and publicly funded in many states. Also, federal government documents were routinely translated into French, German, Dutch, Swedish, and Spanish. This early bilingual and multilingual tradition came to an end at the opening of the twentieth century, when the wave of immigrants from southern and eastern Europe triggered patriotic and xenophobic feelings among the American public. Public support for "English only" grew and received another push from the Americanization movement, which insisted that national unity depended on cultural homogeneity and immigrants' adoption of the English language. American involvement in World War I further heightened anxieties about national loyalty, immigrant assimilation, and linguistic uniformity. It is during this time that various restrictive language policies were enacted. Congress, for example, enacted the English-language requirement for naturalization in 1906. Additionally, various states passed policies that made English the only language of instruction in schools and prohibited the teaching of German during wartime in particular. In 1923, Illinois even declared "American" the state's official language, a measure targeting British immigrants and other speakers of British English.

The new influx of non-English-speaking immigrants after the 1965 liberalization of immigration policy has brought renewed salience to language issues. The arrival of large numbers of Spanish-speaking immigrants in particular has reinvigorated debates over bilingual education, or the use of languages other than English for classroom instruction. In 1968, in the wake of the civil rights movement, Congress enacted the Bilingual Education Act (BEA) to provide federal funding to school programs to teach limited-English-proficient students in their native language. Since its enactment, BEA has been in the eye of stormy debates about whether the goal of bilingual education programs is to provide remedial or transitional English instruction only, or whether they also should support the maintenance of minority languages and cultures. After 34 years, federal policymakers allowed BEA to expire in 2001, when they replaced it with the English Language Acquisition Act (ELAA). Compared to BEA, ELAA signals a clear departure in federal support for native-language instruction. The act makes no mention of "bilingual education" and, with school performance measured in English-language proficiency alone, ELAA essentially limits classroom instruction to English.

Bilingual education programs have become especially controversial in certain states with large immigrant and Spanish-speaking populations. In California, the issue came to a head in 1998, when 61 percent of the state's voters approved Proposition 227, the "English for the Children" initiative, amid charges that bilingual school programs were ineffective and concerns that language diversity contributes to political disunity and the fragmentation of American culture. The California initiative was challenged in court, but eventually upheld by the federal Ninth Circuit Court of Appeals. Proposition 227—also referred to as the "Unz Initiative" after the software entrepreneur and millionaire Ron Unz, who subsidized the ballot campaign—virtually bans bilingual education from public schools and establishes a one-year sheltered-immersion program for all limited-English-proficient students. Following California's example, voters in Arizona and Massachusetts adopted similar Unz-funded initiatives in 2000 and 2002, respectively. However, in 2002, the voters of Colorado were the first to vote down a state ballot measure aimed at ending bilingual education.

Language issues have also surfaced in policy debates about immigrants' access to government information and public services. Even though 28 states today have policies on the books that declare English the official language of government, federal law nonetheless extends important language-access guarantees to immigrants with limited English proficiency. These federal language access provisions also trace their roots to the civil rights movement and the 1964 Civil Rights Act in particular. Title VI of the Civil Rights Act prohibits discrimination on the basis of race, color, or national origin in federally funded programs and activities and has allowed the federal government to intervene in language issues. Congress and the president have used Title VI to require administrative agencies at various levels of government to hire bilingual personnel and translate forms, notices, and applications for limited-English-proficient (LEP) students. To improve the implementation of Title VI, President Clinton issued Executive Order 13166, "Improving Access for Persons with Limited English Proficiency," in 2000. This order, reaffirmed by the Bush Administration in 2002, requires government agencies that receive federal funds to provide meaningful access to public services for LEP individuals, consistent with Title VI regulations. Since then, immigrant gateway cities such as San Francisco, Washington, D.C., and New York City have adopted their own, more expansive, language-access policies. In 2008, for example, Mayor Michael Bloomberg of New York City ordered city agencies to provide government information and public services in the city's six most prevalent non-English languages: Spanish, Chinese, Russian, Korean, Italian, and French Creole.

Public Benefits

The provision of government-funded benefits to immigrants has also figured prominently in public policy debates throughout American history. Federal immigration laws enacted around the turn of the twentieth century often defined poor immigrants—including "paupers," "beggars," and "vagrants"—as an excludable class. Early European immigrants who were able to enter the country and who needed assistance could not look to federal officials for help, as public support for the aged, the sick, widows, and orphans was largely a local responsibility at the time. Most early American cities had poor houses, but they often enforced residency requirements to prevent poor European immigrants from taking advantage of local poor laws and adding to cities' relief expenses. Due to their difficulty in accessing any type of public benefits, early immigrants turned to ethnic support networks, such as mutual-aid societies or fraternal orders, for employment assistance, burial funds, and direct relief for widows and orphans. By the early 1900s, mutual-aid societies, which were organized and run by immigrants themselves, provided more direct relief and social security programs to immigrants than any other type of institution. In 1920, an estimated one in three adult males was a member of a mutual-aid society. Well-known examples of mutual-aid societies included the Ancient Order of Hibernians, which started serving Irish immigrants in 1836, and the *L'Ordine Figli d'Italia* (the Order Sons of Italy), which dates from 1905 and was founded to provide welfare assistance and educational opportunities to Italian immigrants.

The American welfare system as we know it today came into being under New Deal legislation in the 1930s when the federal government assumed a greater responsibility in providing services, and again through policies enacted as part of the War on Poverty in the 1960s. Currently, the U.S. government funds a number of public benefits that constitute an important yet minimal safety net for American poor, elderly, and disabled. The major federal programs offer food stamps, Supplemental Security Income (SSI, a monthly income supplement to the aged, blind, and disabled), welfare assistance to indigent families (known as Temporary Aid to Needy Families, or TANF), and Medicaid (a federal/state-funded health insurance program for the poor).

Undocumented immigrants have never been eligible for federally funded public benefits other than emergency Medicaid. However, it was not until Congress enacted the 1996 Personal Responsibility and Work Opportunity Reconciliation Act (PRWORA), which made citizenship a criterion for receiving public benefits, that the federal government restricted legal immigrants' eligibility for federally funded public benefits. PRWORA denied food stamps, SSI, TANF, and Medicaid for a period of five years to legal immigrants who arrived *after* PRWORA was enacted on August 22, 1996 (so called "post-enactment immigrants"). PRWORA also limited the eligibility for federal public benefits for "pre-enactment immigrants," those who legally entered the country *on or before* August 22, 1996. Only refugees and legal immigrants with long work histories or military connections were exempted from PRWORA's five-year bar on federal assistance. PRWORA, furthermore, left it up to the states to decide whether they would use their own funding to cover immigrants who became ineligible for federal public benefits. Finally, PRWORA also raised the income sponsorship bar to 125 percent or more of the federal poverty level, making it harder for poorer families to sponsor family members for immigration to the United States. As of 2010, many of PRWORA's exclusionary provisions still stand, but some public benefits have been restored. Congress, for example, restored SSI payments to immigrants who were in the country before PRWORA was enacted, as well as food stamps to

immigrant children, disabled immigrants (regardless of date of entry into the country), and pre- and post-enactment immigrants who have been in the country for at least five years.

Public Policies Targeting Undocumented Immigrants

In recent years, policy debates about immigration have gravitated to the topic of undocumented immigration. Reacting to the public's heightened concern over the large number of undocumented immigrants currently residing in the country, policy makers at all levels of government have enacted a variety of exclusionary, or anti-immigrant, policies targeting undocumented immigrants in particular. While there are a few notable exceptions to this exclusionary trend, only a small number of municipalities have enacted policies that actually extend policy benefits to the undocumented.

The educational rights of undocumented children first surfaced as a policy issue in 1975, when the state of Texas revised its education laws to withhold state funding for the education of children who were not "legally admitted" into the United States. The Texas law also allowed local school districts to exclude undocumented school-age children from enrolling in their schools. In its 1982 *Plyler v. Doe* decision, however, the U.S. Supreme Court declared this law unconstitutional and ruled that undocumented children have a right to a free, public education—just like children who are U.S. citizens and legal permanent residents. As undocumented children have grown older and entered institutions of higher education, policy makers today find themselves considering the question of whether undocumented students should be allowed to pay in-state tuition, a lower rate of tuition that public colleges and universities charge the residents of their respective state, or even whether they may attend college at all. Since 2001, Congress has considered proposals for the DREAM Act, which would provide undocumented immigrants with five years of continuous residency in the United States and a U.S. high school diploma with the opportunity to legalize their status by attending college or joining the U.S. military. So far, DREAM Act proposals have failed to win enough congressional votes to become law.

Recent policies have also focused on restricting undocumented immigrants' access to the labor market and aspects of civic life. The federal government, for example, launched the E-Verify program in 1997, which is an Internet-based government program that, since 2009, federal contractors and subcontractors are required to use to verify that their employees have legal authorization to work in the United States (for all other employers, the use of E-Verify currently is voluntary). In 2002, undocumented workers also lost some labor protections as a result of the decision in *Hoffman Plastic Compounds Inc. v. NLRB* case, in which the U.S. Supreme Court denied undocumented workers the right to sue for back wages, even when the employer had used unfair labor practices to fire them. Additionally, the federal Real ID Act of May 2005 provided that undocumented immigrants could no longer obtain a state-issued driver's license, which commonly serves as identification for everything from interacting with local police, to using the public library, to opening a bank account. However, due to strong opposition, full implementation of the Real ID Act was postponed to May 2008, with a provision allowing states to seek an additional extension until May 2011.

When comprehensive immigration reform proposals failed to pass in Congress in 2005–2007, states and localities added their own anti-immigrant policies targeting the undocumented. In 2006, for example, the cities of Hazelton (Pennsylvania), Escondido (California), and Farmers Branch (Texas) adopted ordinances that bar undocumented immigrants from working and renting homes in the three cities. One year later, in 2007, the states of Arizona, Oklahoma, Tennessee, and West Virginia passed laws making it illegal for employers to hire undocumented workers. In April 2010, Arizona passed stringent legislation that made it a violation of *state* (and not just federal) law to be in the country without legal documentation and gave local police broad powers to stop and verify the immigration status of anyone they suspect of being undocumented. In June 2012, however, the Supreme Court struck down all but one of the provisions of the Arizona law, only allowing law enforcement officers to check the immigration status of anyone legally stopped for breaking the law. Additionally, various cities in the state of Virginia have used local zoning laws to discourage undocumented immigrants from settling in their communities. Many of these anti-immigrant state and local policies have been challenged and invalidated in court, yet they clearly signal policy makers' intent to exclude undocumented immigrants from policy representation.

Only a few municipalities have enacted immigrant-friendly laws that actually offer policy benefits to undocumented immigrants. Most notably, the cities of New Haven and San Francisco started issuing local ID cards in 2007 and 2009, respectively, with the goal of improving the civic integration of undocumented immigrants. Additionally, over 30 cities today—including many of the largest gateway cities—offer sanctuary to undocumented immigrants by refusing to collaborate with federal officials in the enforcement of U.S. immigration laws. It is worth noting, though, that formal laws do not always accurately reflect policy practice on the ground. Even when there is no official law mandating that benefits and services be extended to immigrants, it is still possible that undocumented immigrants enjoy policy benefits through a practice that scholars have termed "bureaucratic incorporation." This refers to actions by nonelected employees of government and public institutions, from libraries to business license departments to school administrators, to respond to the unique needs and interests of undocumented immigrants. These formal and informal policy responses that accommodate undocumented immigrants are, however, relatively few. By 2010, the trend clearly was one toward policy exclusion.

Immigrant Civic Engagement

It is also possible to learn about immigrant political incorporation by considering immigrants' civic engagement, which refers to their participation in communal activities through community-based organizations such as nonprofit organizations, religious institutions, and labor unions. There are two important reasons for considering immigrants' civic engagement. First, civic engagement provides access to aspects of public life even for immigrants who are legally excluded from the formal political process. Immigrants do not need to be citizens, or even legal residents, to participate in community organizations. Immigrants may also be more inclined to participate in civic affairs because they are afraid to participate in politics or because they perceive traditional politics to be dirty, corrupt, or confusing. Second, it is important to consider immigrants' civic engagement given the proven link between civic engagement on the one hand and formal political participation and policy influence on the other. For immigrants, civic engagement likely provides fertile grounds for later political incorporation by making them more aware of current events, increasing their sense of personal and collective efficacy, teaching skills useful for politics, and providing sites of mobilization around political or policy ends.

Immigrants arriving to the United States at the turn of the twentieth century participated in local civic life in a variety of ways. The large wave of Irish immigrants enabled the Catholic Church to become the largest religious denomination (with over nine million members) by the end of the nineteenth century, with significant political clout in such cities as New York City and Boston. Southern and eastern European immigrants in various East Coast cities, furthermore, formed the backbone of garment unions, including the International Ladies' Garment Workers' Union and the Amalgamated Clothing Workers of America. Jewish immigrants in particular participated in labor strikes to protest the poor working conditions in garment factories. The early immigrants from eastern Europe also created a host of mutual-aid societies, which encouraged members to acquire American citizenship and protested discrimination against their respective ethnic group. Notable examples include— as partially noted above—the Irish Ancient Order of Hibernians (founded in 1836), the Jewish B'nai B'rith (founded in 1843) and Free Sons of Israel (founded in 1849), the Mexican *Alianza Hispano-Americana* (founded in 1894), and the Order Sons of Italy (founded in 1905). Finally, early European immigrants also established a large number of ethnic newspapers that informed newcomers about American political news in their native language. In 1852, for example, there were 28 German-language newspapers in New York City alone, and there were 20 Yiddish dailies in the city by the end of the nineteenth century.

Contemporary immigrants continue to be active in the civic sphere. Post-1965 immigrants have not only introduced new faith traditions, but they are also revitalizing old ones. As result, in addition to Catholic and Protestant churches providing immigrants with an institutional point of entry into American political life, one can find Muslim mosques, Sikh gurdwaras, and, to a lesser extent, Jewish synagogues and Hindu and Buddhist temples that do so, too. After years of treating immigrants as a threat to the labor movement and in response to rapidly declining membership rates, unions today are likewise making efforts to organize and mobilize immigrants from Asia and Latin America, including undocumented immigrants, who work in the expanding service sector of the post-industrial economy.

The civic reach of labor unions into the immigrant community should not be overestimated, however. In 2004, for example, only about 10 percent of immigrant workers in the United States were members of unions (compared to 13 percent of native-born workers). Furthermore, the mutual-aid societies of the past have been succeeded by immigrant-serving nonprofit organizations. Often staffed and run by immigrants, these organizations provide essential social services to newcomers and advocate on immigrants' behalf in the public arena. Finally, ethnic media outlets continue to be important, and Latino immigrants are particularly well served by the Spanish-language media in the country. Today, there are more than 700 Spanish-language newspapers in print, close to 900 Spanish-language radio stations, and approximately 200 television stations that broadcast in Spanish. Consequently, Spanish-language media organizations have the national infrastructure to inform and educate millions of Latino immigrants on a host of political issues.

The immigration protests in the spring of 2006 also serve to illustrate that immigrants today continue to be active in the civic sphere. In Los Angeles, Chicago, and more than 100 other American cities, immigrants and their supporters marched the streets to protest the anti-immigrant legislation that Congress was considering at the time. In Los Angeles alone, an estimated 500,000 people took to the streets, and another 300,000 turned out in Chicago. Amounting to several million demonstrators nationwide, the 2006 immigration protests rivaled the size of the anti-war demonstrations of the Vietnam War era. The 2006

Students waving Mexican flags protest against the proposed Comprehensive Immigration Reform Act in Los Angeles in 2006. (AP/Wide World Photos)

demonstrations were not, as some have argued, spontaneous outbursts of frustration by immigration supporters. Rather, these demonstrations were orchestrated by immigrant organizations, labor unions, churches, and ethnic media outlets that organized public education campaigns, advocacy initiatives, and community mobilization efforts, often with the active involvement of Latino immigrants in particular.

Transnational Political Participation

In a rapidly globalizing world, the ties that immigrants in the United States have with their native countries can provide additional outlets for their civic and political energies. Over the last decade, there has

been a great deal of scholarly interest and research on transnational politics and the political engagement of immigrants in their countries of origin. Improved transportation and communication networks have made it easier for immigrants in the United States to engage in transnational politics, as have investments of sending states to create new opportunities for immigrants to maintain political ties with their native countries. During the 1990s, for example, more sending countries started offering dual citizenship to emigrants who acquired U.S. citizenship through naturalization. As of 2010, 16 of the top 25 countries of birth of the U.S. foreign-born population had such dual citizenship provisions (see Table 2).

Sending countries also have enacted provisions that allow for external, or out-of-country or expatriate, voting. External voting was uncommon until World War II, but today it is a global trend, with more than 100 countries worldwide permitting citizens living abroad to participate in the elections of their home countries. As of 2007, 17 of the top 25 countries of birth of the U.S. foreign-born population allowed external voting in one form or another (see Table 2). These countries have adopted external voting provisions for different reasons. The Dominican Republic and Mexico, for example, enacted external voting laws in 1997 and 2005, respectively, largely in response to lobbying pressures by organized groups of Dominican and Mexican immigrants in the United States. The Philippines, in contrast, adopted an external voting law in 2003 to recognize the role that Filipinos working abroad continue to play in nation building. The fact that immigrants in the United States remit millions of dollars back home every year (and Mexico, since 2002, has sought to leverage the remittances of Mexicans in the United States with its "3 x 1" government matching program) also helps explain why sending states have adopted external voting laws in an effort to secure emigrants' continued contributions to the home-country economy.

Despite the growing prevalence of external voting provisions, not many immigrants in the United States vote back home yet. For example, out of an estimated 4 million eligible voters, only 32,632 Mexican immigrants in the United States registered to vote, and only 28,335 cast a ballot during the 2006 Mexican

Table 2. Top 25 Countries of Birth of the U.S. Foreign-Born Population (2006–2008), Dual Citizenship (2010), and External Voting Rights (2007)

Country of Birth	Number	Percent of all Foreign Born	Dual Citizenship Allowed after U.S. Naturalization	Provisions for External Voting
Mexico	11,478,376	30.5%	✓	✓
Philippines	1,655,478	4.4%	✓	✓
China*	1,554,780	4.1%		
India	1,537,043	4.1%		✓
Vietnam	1,112,587	3.0%	✓	
El Salvador	1,078,643	2.9%	✓	
Korea	1,022,125	2.7%		
Cuba	958,832	2.5%		
Canada	834,478	2.2%	✓	✓
Dominican Republic	762,581	2.0%	✓	✓
Guatemala	720,852	1.9%		
United Kingdom	686,927	1.8%	✓	✓
Germany	639,161	1.7%		✓
Jamaica	622,748	1.7%	✓	
Colombia	596,511	1.6%	✓	✓
Haiti	522,681	1.4%		✓
Poland	487,996	1.3%	✓	✓
Honduras	428,543	1.1%		✓
Italy	411,469	1.1%	✓	✓
Ecuador	400,946	1.1%	✓	✓
Russia	398,413	1.1%	✓	✓
Peru	384,959	1.0%	✓	
Taiwan	347,801	0.9%	✓	✓
Japan	346,470	0.9%		✓
Brazil	339,771	0.9%	✓	✓

*China includes Hong Kong, not Taiwan.

Sources: 2006–2008 American Community Survey, 3-year estimates (for numbers on the foreign born) and Ellis et al. (2007, for data on external voting). Data on dual citizenship is author's compilation of various web sources.

presidential election, which was the first time that Mexicans could vote from abroad. Some argue that bureaucratic hurdles for voter registration and a prohibition on fund-raising and campaigning abroad explain these extremely low voter registration and turnout numbers. Likewise, data from the Central Electoral Board in the Dominican Republic show that only 37,905 Dominicans in the United States had registered to vote, of whom 26,818 actually cast ballots in the Dominican presidential election of 2004 (also the first time external voting was used). For the 2008 Dominican presidential election, however, voter registration among Dominicans in the United States nearly tripled (to 96,779) and turnout doubled (to 53,031). This, perhaps, suggests that a greater institutionalization of external voting practices in the future can result in more immigrants in the United States voting back home.

The primary focus of research on transnational politics, including scholarship on dual citizenship and external voting, has been on its impact on the sending country. Relatively little is known about how immigrants' transnational political participation affects their political incorporation in the United States, but we can identify two distinct hypotheses. Home-country political ties possibly divide immigrants' political attention and therefore can *dampen* their participation in American political affairs. Yet, it is also possible that transnational political activism has spill-over effects into the American political arena and consequently can *enhance* immigrants' political incorporation in the United States. Data are still limited, but early evidence suggests that Latin American immigrants from countries that allow dual citizenship average higher U.S. naturalization rates than Latino immigrants from countries that do not. Other data, however, suggest that Latin American immigrants who vote externally are less likely to envision permanent residency in the United States, thereby indirectly discouraging them from incorporating into American political life and possibly other aspects of American society as well.

Explaining Immigrant Political Incorporation

The focus of this chapter has been on specific incorporation outcomes, but it is important to emphasize that immigrant political incorporation is in fact a very dynamic process. Whether or not incorporation eventually happens is a function of a variety of factors at work simultaneously. In considering the many factors that facilitate and hinder the political incorporation of contemporary immigrants in the United States, it is useful to distinguish three sets of explanatory factors. First, there are *micro-level* factors that underscore the role of immigrants' individual characteristics, skills, and resources in the incorporation process. Second, factors that instead focus on the role of political institutions and the larger sociopolitical environment in the process of immigrant political incorporation can be referred to as *macro-level* factors. Finally, there are *meso-level* factors, which examine the mobilizing impact and mediating influence of civic institutions on immigrants' propensity to become active in American political affairs.

Much of the American scholarship on immigrant political incorporation focuses on immigrants' individual socioeconomic characteristics as key determinants of their political incorporation. This scholarship draws prominently on survey data and uses statistical analysis to measure the effect of a constellation of individual-level variables on the probability that immigrants participate in formal politics. More specifically, immigrants' age, gender, race, educational attainment, country of origin, income, language ability, homeownership, marital status, and length of stay in the United States are used to measure their

effect on immigrants' likelihood of naturalizing, registering to vote, developing partisanship, and casting a ballot on Election Day. To expand upon these sets of factors affecting incorporation, research shows that immigrants with more schooling, who are more proficient in English, who are married, who have spent more time in the United States, who are homeowners, etc., are more likely to acquire American citizenship through naturalization and participate in electoral politics than are immigrants who lack these resources and skills.

Another line of research considers institutional and contextual factors as macro-level explanations for immigrants' political incorporation. Examples of institutional and contextual factors include the availability of dual citizenship, the nature of the naturalization process, characteristics of the home country, government support for immigrant communities, election rules, home-country ties, and immigrants' perceptions of discrimination in American society. These macro-level variables do not affect the political incorporation of all immigrants or various immigrant groups in the same way, but the gist of established research is that immigrants who make decisions about political participation in contexts that facilitate participation—i.e., easy naturalization requirements, the availability of dual citizenship, less costly voter registration rules, no purging of nonvoters, more government support for immigrant communities, less experience with discrimination—are more likely to acquire citizenship and participate in electoral politics.

Only recently have scholars rediscovered the significance of meso-level structures in immigrants' political incorporation process. Meso-level structures consist of different types of local-level civic organizations that can mediate between the micro level of individuals and the macro level of larger political communities. These mediating institutions are especially important for noncitizen and poor immigrants who rarely wield power and political influence on their own in the U.S. political system. Meso-level organizations—including local political parties, churches, immigrant settlement houses, and ethnic mutual-aid societies—proved important in the past by providing the early immigrants from Europe with the skills, information, and motivation that facilitated their participation in various aspects of political life. Furthermore, settlement houses in gateway cities such as Chicago, Boston, and New York City also served as agents of political incorporation, particularly for poor and female immigrants. Settlement houses, such as the famed Hull House in Chicago, provided not only essential social services to immigrants, but also educated them about sanitation and labor issues, and they lobbied city officials for better labor conditions and more city services in immigrant neighborhoods.

Compared to the past, local party organizations in the United States today no longer mobilize immigrants' naturalization or their participation in the electoral process. Especially, party organizations in gateway cities (e.g., New York City and Los Angeles as well as Chicago and Boston) have been passive in helping contemporary immigrants from Asia, Latin America, and the Caribbean to acquire U.S. citizenship, register to vote, and become members of the parties' political clubs. Political parties' lack of interest in helping immigrants to incorporate politically is largely a result of the nonpartisan and noncompetitive nature of local elections today. Not needing the immigrant vote to win an election, local parties have little incentive to invest time and resources in reaching out to new voters. However, other civic institutions, and especially immigrant-serving nonprofit organizations, labor unions, and religious institutions, have become more active in the area of immigrant political incorporation in recent years. They provide immigrants, and especially immigrants of low socioeconomic status, opportunities to participate in both electoral and non-electoral political activities. In that capacity, nonprofits, unions, and churches form critical bridging institutions that connect contemporary immigrant communities with the larger political system in the United States.

Bibliography

Bloemraad, Irene, and Els de Graauw. 2012. "Immigrant Integration and Policy in the United States: A Loosely Stitched Patchwork." In *International Approaches: Integration and Inclusion*, edited by John Biles and James Frideres. Montréal: McGill–Queen's University Press.

Cordero-Guzmán, Héctor R., Nina Martin, Victoria Quiroz-Becerra, and Nik Theodore. 2008. "Voting with Their Feet: Nonprofit Organizations and Immigrant Mobilization." *American Behavior Scientist* 52, no. 4: 598–617.

Dahl, Robert. 1961. *Who Governs? Democracy and Power in an American City*. New Haven, CT: Yale University Press.

De Graauw, Els, and Caroline Andrew. 2011. "Immigrant Political Incorporation in American and Canadian Cities." In *Immigrant Geographies of American and Canadian Cities*, edited by Carlos Teixeira, Wei Li, and Audrey Kobayashi, 179–206. New York: Oxford University Press.

DeSipio, Louis. 2006. "Transnational Politics and Civic Engagement: Do Home-Country Political Ties Limit Latino Immigrant Pursuit of U.S. Civic Engagement and Naturalization?" In *Transforming Politics, Transforming America: The Political and Civic Incorporation of Immigrants in the United States*, edited by Taeku Lee, S. Karthick Ramakrishnan, and Ricardo Ramirez, 106–28. Charlottesville: University of Virginia Press.

Ellis, Andrew, Carlos Navarro, Isabel Morales, Maria Gatschew, and Nadja Braun. 2007. *Voting from Abroad: The IDEA International Handbook*. Stockholm and Mexico City: International Institute for Democracy and Electoral Assistance and the Federal Electoral Institute of Mexico.

Erie, Steven P. 1988. *Rainbow's End: Irish-Americans and the Dilemmas of Urban Machine Politics, 1840–1985*. Berkeley: University of California Press.

Hayduk, Ron. 2006. *Democracy for All: Restoring Immigrant Voting Rights in the United States*. New York: Routledge.

Jones-Correa, Michael. 2001. "Under Two Flags: Dual Nationality in Latin America and Its Consequences for Naturalization in the United States." *International Migration Review* 35, no. 4: 997–1029.

Jones-Correa, Michael. 2008. "Immigrant Incorporation in Suburbia: The Role of Bureaucratic Norms in Education." In *New Faces in New Places: The Changing Geography of American Immigration*, edited by Douglas S. Massey, 308–40. New York: Russell Sage Foundation Press.

Lien, Pei-te, Dianne M. Pinderhughes, Carol Hardy-Fanta, and Christine M. Sierra. 2007. "The Voting Rights Act and the Election of Nonwhite Officials." *PS: Political Science and Politics* 40, no. 3: 489–94.

Roig-Franzia, Manuel. 2006. "Mexican Presidential Rivals Both Claim Win in Tight Vote." *Washington Post*, July 3, A1.

U.S. Census Bureau. 2006–2008. American Community Survey: 3-Year Summary File.

Latinos and American Politics

Henry Flores

Who Are U.S. Latinos?

Latinos include all people living in the United States whose ancestors immigrated and continue to do so from various Spanish-speaking countries. The actual identifier chosen is one of personal preference, as some individuals identify as Latinos while others prefer the term Hispanic or refer to themselves preferring their national origin, such as Mexican, Honduran, Colombian, or Cuban.

Latino identity possesses two fundamental facets. It is a self-identifying term and, simultaneously, is a societally imposed term insofar as the U.S. government created the terms Hispanic (Latino and Latin American emerged separately) in an effort to make census data gathering more efficient. This unique aspect of Latinos, coupled with the national origin and racial identity of Latinos, can provide a complex identification web that oftentimes is confusing and politically and emotionally charged for some individuals and whole groups.

One of the most interesting discussions surrounding Latino identity is whether Spanish or Portuguese immigrants can be considered Latinos and whether non-Spanish-speaking Caribbean immigrants, for example Haitians or Guyanese, may be identified also as Latinos. The key element in Latino identity may simply be that all individuals regardless of how they identify themselves or how society identifies them root their identity in their mother or ancestral tongue—Spanish.

Historical Origins of Latinos

Latinos have been an essential thread in the North American social fabric since the first European settlers arrived on the continent. The earliest Latinos settled in parts of what are contemporary Florida and the greater southwestern United States. For example, the first Spanish settlers in Florida arrived in the middle of the sixteenth century and in New Mexico in the early part of the seventeenth century. By the time the United States became a nation, Latinos had explored and populated many regions of the South and Southwest United States, founding many towns and villages that are currently some of the fastest-growing cities and metropolises in the country, including Los Angeles and San Francisco, California; Phoenix, Arizona; and San Antonio, Texas.

Although the earliest Latino settlers were from Spain, they eventually intermarried with other European immigrants, and indigenous people and their descendants became more and more racially and ethnically hybridized. This is also the social formula governing Latino immigrants from all countries in the Americas who migrate to the United States. Whether the country of origin is Argentina, Guatemala, Mexico, or any other Latin American countries, most citizens of those countries trace their origins to the marriage between original explorers from Spain, other European countries, and indigenous people. For instance, in Argentina, there have been large migrations of Europeans from Italy, Germany, England, and Turkey who have intermarried with the descendants of the original Spanish settlers who earlier intermarried with indigenous people. In Mexico, one finds areas populated by descendants of immigrants from Poland, Russia, and Germany who intermarried with the native Mexican populations. Nevertheless, Mexicans pride themselves in their *mestizo* heritage, which was the marriage of Spanish and Indian cultures. As the children of the original Latin American settlers migrated to the United States, regardless of what historical era they entered the country, they became known as Latinos. The contemporary U.S. Latino population, therefore, by and large traces its roots to a mixture of Spanish, European, and indigenous origins. In some cases there is also an African influence among some national origin populations, such as in Mexico, Ecuador, Colombia, the Dominican Republic, and Cuba. Regardless, the characteristic that binds this very diverse group of people is that they find their cultural roots in countries where Spanish is and was the principal language.

Since the Spanish language is the principal facet of identity for Latinos in the United States, it raises an interesting issue that has occasionally incited debate or discussion among social scientists who study this population. The issue essentially revolves around whether descendants or immigrants from non-Spanish-speaking Latin American countries can be considered Latinos in the United States, notably Brazilians, Haitians, Guyanese, Trinidadians, and Jamaicans. Most scholars tend to separate these particular national origin groups from Latinos and simply treat them differently. Only a small group of scholars would include these Latin Americans under the overall Latino umbrella.

The earliest Latinos arrived in what is now the United States from Spain in the fifteenth and sixteenth centuries. These individuals were already well established economically and politically in the Southwest after the United States gained control of these lands. Mexicans in what was then northern Mexico were brought under the sovereignty of the United States as a result of the Treaty of Guadalupe Hidalgo that officially ended the Mexican-American War of 1846–1848. In defeat, Mexico ceded almost half of its land mass that today includes the states of California, New Mexico, Arizona, Nevada, Colorado, and parts of Utah, Wyoming, and Idaho. Texas had been annexed in December 1845, shortly before the beginning of the war. That was one of the actions on the part of the U.S. government that provoked the conflict initially. An essential element of the treaty, Article IX specifically, provided that all Mexican citizens who decided to stay within the new borders would become U.S. citizens. Although many Mexicans migrated

back to Mexico, the vast majorities stayed in the United States and were the forebears of contemporary Mexican Americans. The population of these early Mexicans has been bolstered by millions of immigrants that have arrived since then. Today, Mexican Americans comprise almost 65 percent of all Latinos in the United States.

Other Latino national origin groups became incorporated socially and politically into the United States through treaty or immigration. For instance, both Puerto Ricans and Cubans were brought under American control as the result of the Treaty of Paris in 1898 that ended the Spanish-American War; Spain ceded Puerto Rico, Cuba, Guam, and the Philippines as a consequence of losing the war. The Jones Act of 1917 granted Puerto Ricans U.S. citizenship. Consequently, Puerto Ricans are automatically born U.S. citizens and currently represent approximately 9.1 percent of all Latinos, the second-largest national origin group of Latinos. Since 1917, there has been continuous migration of Puerto Ricans to the mainland United States, with most settling in the vicinity of New York City, New Jersey, and Florida. Cuba and the Philippines gained their independence from the United States at later points in history.

Approximately 74 percent of all Latinos, then, are either of Mexican or Puerto Rican descent. The contemporary Mexican community is comprised of the descendants of either the original settlers in the southwestern United States who remained in their new country after the Mexican-American War of 1848, or immigrants who came into the United States subsequently. Two large immigration streams occurred in the twentieth century, one during the Mexican Revolution beginning in 1910, and the other during and after World War II. The first immigration stream was due to the political and economic turmoil surrounding the revolution, while the second was fueled by the manpower shortages caused in the United States by World War II. Even though there were repatriation efforts on the part of both governments after each conflict, many Mexican immigrants remained in the United States. Additionally, post–World War II America has witnessed the influx of millions more immigrants, both documented and undocumented, from Mexico. Most of these immigrants have settled throughout the United States but prominently in the states of California, Arizona, and Texas. Many recent Mexican immigrants have found homes in New York City and Chicago and throughout states in the southeastern and Midwestern United States. In fact, the fastest growing enclaves of Latinos, according to the 2000 census, were found in the southeastern parts of the country.

As pointed out earlier, only those immigrants from Spanish-speaking countries and their immediate offspring will be considered Latinos for purposes of this discussion, including immigrants from Cuba, Puerto Rico, the Dominican Republic, and most Central American and South American countries (with the exceptions noted above). Many of these immigrants left their countries to come to the United States for various political or economic reasons. The experiences of Cuban immigrants are an excellent example of this phenomenon. The first Cuban immigrants arrived in the United States shortly after the middle of the nineteenth century seeking their fortunes as musicians in New Orleans and cigar makers in the Tampa Bay and Ybor City areas of Florida. The Cuban population remained relatively small until the revolution of 1959, when Fidel Castro wrested control of the government from Fulgencio Batista. Since 1960, there have minimally been three waves of immigration from Cuba to the United States, with many settling in the Miami-Dade County area. Although the Cuban community in the United States only represents approximately 2 percent of all Latinos, they are heavily concentrated in the southern parts of Florida, where they have exercised a great deal of political influence, dominating most local elections and electing two members to the U.S. House of Representatives and one to the Senate.

Other Latinos have arrived in the United States from most countries in Central and South America, with the largest numbers arriving from El Salvador, the Dominican Republic, and Colombia. Interestingly enough, more immigrants arrive from all Central American as opposed to South American countries. Immigrants from Central and South America tend to settle around large urban areas, seeking work opportunities. As a result, one finds large communities of Dominicans in New York and Central Americans in Chicago, Los Angeles, and San Francisco. Regardless

of where the various Latino national origin groups settle, they are becoming more and more prominent politically in their new home cities and states and are touted by many in the media and political world as the next immigrant population that will play a significant role in American politics.

The Political History of Latinos in the United States

The political history of Latinos in the United States is as varied as the Latino population is diverse. Also, each group's political fortunes depended upon the historical circumstances under which they became incorporated into the political structure of the United States. The examples of the Mexican and Cuban Americans will serve as illustrations.

The Spaniards brought with them government as they settled throughout the southwest and parts of the southeast. These geographical areas already had experienced many years—in some areas, almost 150 years—of Spanish-imposed government by the time they came under U.S. control. For example, the Spanish Crown established primitive town or urban governments in St. Augustine, Florida, in 1565; Santa Fe, New Mexico, in 1608; El Paso, Texas, in 1659; San Antonio, Texas, in 1718; and San Diego, California, in 1769. After the Mexican War of Independence that ended in 1821, all of these cities became regional centers of the new Mexican Republic. Although many of the state and local governments were transferred to the Mexican government from the Spanish Crown, the laws governing the fundamental agricultural and pastoral economy remained relatively unchanged, as did the governing structures. Mexico ceded almost half of its landmass to the United States in two stages: the first occurring after the Texas War of Independence in 1836, the second after the Mexican-American War of 1846–1848. Texas was an independent republic from 1836 until 1845, when it was annexed by the United States and became a state.

The remainder of the ceded Mexican land was transferred to U.S. control at the end of the Mexican-American War under the provisions of the Treaty of Guadalupe Hidalgo of 1848 that finalized the transfer of what are now the states of California, New Mexico,

Arizona, Nevada, Colorado, and parts of Idaho, Wyoming, and Utah. As noted, Article IX of the treaty granted full citizenship to all Mexicans who chose to remain. Almost all of the lands that were ceded brought with them governing structures and their attendant laws that continued existing even after they fell under control of the U.S. government. As Anglos, non-Hispanic whites, moved into these various regions, they began taking control of local governments and displacing many of the local landowners through changing of property laws, "chicanery" or outright banditry. In some cases forced removal, a form of ethnic cleansing, was utilized to remove "Mexicans" from various towns in northeastern, central, and south central Texas. For example, after 1836, Mexican populations were removed forcibly from the towns of Victoria, Goliad, Austin, and San Antonio and forced south to Mexico or the communities along the Mexican border.

The political and economic dislocation of Mexicans in Texas has been chronicled by historians but is vividly exemplified by a brief look at how Mexicans fared in mayoral elections in San Antonio, Texas, between 1842 and 1983. During this almost 150-year time frame, there were no Latinos elected to the office of mayor in this city. In 1840, Juan Seguín was elected mayor and no other Mexican held that office until 1983, when Henry Cisneros ascended to that position. Seguín's tenure was marked with constant complaints by local Mexicans that they were being cheated, physically intimidated, and abused by Anglos. Eventually, Seguín was subjected to death threats, resulting in his departure to Mexico in 1842. Prior to 1842, San Antonio was governed almost exclusively by Mexicans, but after 1842 and not until 1889 were any Latinos elected to the governing commission of San Antonio. This official held office for only one term, and another Mexican was not elected to the commission until 1913. Through 1975, Latinos, although remaining by far a large segment of San Antonio's population, were unable to elect a mayor or any significant number of individuals to the city commission or council. This situation was not rectified until a 1975 lawsuit brought under the auspices of the Voting Rights Act required the city to change its representation and electoral systems from ones featuring at-large to a single-member district configuration. Since the imposition of single-member districts, San Antonio has elected three Latino mayors, and Latinos and women have made up a majority of the city council. The change in membership of the council has also resulted in major shifts in public policy positions, evident particularly in public works and the delivery of municipal services.

The displacement of Mexicans from the land and governing systems throughout the southwestern parts of Texas was replicated, with some variation, in every state in the southwestern United States. For instance, because the population of Mexicans represented a higher percentage of the population in New Mexico, the New Mexican *Mejicanos* were incorporated into what Montejano called a "peace structure," which was an understanding between conquerors and the conquered. In the case of New Mexico, California, and Texas this peace structure was a method whereby early Anglo settlers created alliances with the wealthy *Mexicano* landowners. The arrangement usually followed a pattern in which the Mexican landowners would control the lower-class *Mexicanos*, and in turn the Anglos would allow the *ricos* (wealthy ones) to retain their wealth. This relationship allowed Anglo lawyers, businessmen, and ranchers to gain control of a great deal of wealth. Eventually, poor New Mexicans revolted against the *ricos* and elected Latinos to the governorship—Ezequiel de Baca and Octaviano A. Larrazolo—and to the U.S. Senate—Larrazolo, Dennis Chavez, and Joseph Montoya. Chavez and Montoya in the twentieth century received the legacy of the revolt of the lower-class New Mexicans against the peace structure constructed by the "Santa Fe Ring" and *los ricos* during the nineteenth century.

In California and Arizona, land transfers almost completely wiped out the Latino upper classes, relegating them to the lowest levels of their respective states' social structures. Although, California, Arizona, and Texas have never elected Latinos to either governorships or to the U.S. Senate as of this writing, there have been some successes in the latter part of the twentieth century in which Latinos have won other political offices of significance in these states. For instance, Cruz Bustamante was elected lieutenant governor in California in 1998 and was spoken of as a potential

Los Angeles mayoral candidate Antonio Villaraigosa greets an African American supporter during a campaign stop, May 16, 2005. (David McNew/Getty Images)

gubernatorial candidate in that state, and Antonio Villaraigosa was elected mayor of Los Angeles in 2005. Both of these victories, however, were not accomplished solely with the support of Latino voters, but through the development of coalitions with liberal Anglos and the African-American communities. In the U.S. Congress, because of the manner in which representational districts are drawn during the decennial redistricting process, Latinos have won offices in California beginning with Ed Roybal (1962) and, more recently, the two Sanchez twin sisters, Laura and Linda.

Henry B. Gonzalez, elected in 1965, was the first of a long line of Latino congressmen elected throughout South Texas in the area of the state predominated by the Latino population. In Arizona, Raul Grijalva joined longtime Congressman Ed Pastor as the only

Latinos to be elected to the national legislature from that state. In every case, Latino electoral success has occurred most recently during the latter part of the twentieth century and is a reflection of the changing demographics of the states and the Latinos' ability to build coalitions with Anglos and African Americans.

Compounding the effects of the political and economic subjugation of Latinos in the Southwest were the social segregation and isolation ranging from the maintenance of separate schools, implementation of racial real estate covenants, job discrimination and racially based employment practices, and segregation in public and private accommodations. Examples of these were the establishment throughout various states of Mexican schools that were collocated sometimes on the same grounds as the "white" public schools. These schools were staffed by junior or emergency teachers and featured vocational training curricula in order to prepare children to enter the local labor forces as unskilled and skilled labor. Few, if any of the public schools offered college preparatory educational programs for Latino children until the latter half of the twentieth century in many parts of United States.

The educational segregation of Latinos has resulted in an undereducated population that contemporaneously lags far behind non-Hispanic whites. For example, it is estimated by some research organizations, such as the Intercultural Development Research Association (IDRA), that the high school dropout rate for Latinos in the state of Texas has remained between 40 and 45 percent since 1984. This lack of education has resulted in most Latinos working in lesser paying occupations and few entering and completing university- or professional-level education. The poor educational levels of Latinos have not only socioeconomic implications, but political ones as well. Every academic study conducted attempting to understand political participation has concluded that individuals possessing higher educational and income levels tend to participate politically—in particular, voting—more than those individuals lower on the social scale.

Racial covenants existed governing the transferring of land holdings among racial groups. For example in the northern parts of San Antonio, Texas real estate deeds stipulated that single-family dwellings could not be sold to "Mexicans or Negros." These covenants were the principal stepping-stones to the creation of racially segregated neighborhoods in this city. The covenants—coupled with real estate loan "redlining" practices (to exclude Mexicans and blacks from predominantly middle-class white neighborhoods) and the higher land values and the subsequent inability of Latinos to qualify for mortgages—eventually solidified the currently existing racial residential patterns in most cities throughout the United States that led to the creation of Latino ethnic enclaves.

The political history of national origin Latino groups other than Mexicans varies as well. For instance, the experiences of Cuban immigrants stand in stark contrast to those of Mexicans. As noted earlier, Cubans began arriving in the United States during the nineteenth century, seeking employment as musicians and cigar makers. The first substantial wave of Cuban immigrants arrived in the Miami-Dade County area after the Cuban Revolution of 1959. A substantial number of these individuals were large landowners and represented the wealthy classes of Cuba having their properties expropriated by the Castro government. Included in this first wave were also large numbers of the intelligentsia and professional classes. The second immigration wave came during the early 1980s and mostly represented working-class Cubans who also settled in South Florida. Cuban immigrants arrived in the United States under the relatively privileged immigration status of political-asylum seekers during the atmosphere surrounding the Cold War. As a result, this immigrant group received special treatment, politically and economically, from the American government and did not suffer the historical discriminatory treatment experienced by Mexicans.

Wealthy Cubans began dominating the South Florida economy almost immediately upon their arrival, eventually moving into the world of politics. Cubans became such a numerically superior presence in South Florida that they were able to elect a member to the U.S. Senate in 2005, Mel Martinez, and three members to the U.S. House of Representatives—Ileana Ros-Lehtinen and brothers Mario and Lincoln Díaz-Balart. Florida also has the distinction, however, of having elected the first Hispanic to Congress in 1822, José Mariano Hernandez, who served one term and was defeated attempting to win a seat in the Senate in 1845.

Where Mexican descendants are in a situation having to overcome several hundred years of discriminatory treatment, Cubans arrived and, given their privileged political position, comparatively quickly established themselves at the top of the South Florida social and economic structures. These contrasting histories are reflective of how these two national origin Latino groups have found their respective social place within American society.

The Social Status of Latinos in the United States

Attempting to understand where Latinos fit in the U.S. social system can be a daunting task given that the Bureau of the Census did not systematically gather data on this group until 1970. The Bureau's initial counting methodology for Latinos was crude and identified only individuals in that category who possessed what appeared as a Spanish surname in 1970. The methodology used by the Bureau in 2001, on the other hand, allowed for much more precision, because it provided an individual with a choice to identify him- or herself both racially and by national origin. Regardless, there have always been concerns among Latinos and their organizations that this group has been "undercounted" through misidentification for decades. The Bureau of the Census concedes that the "undercount" occurs and states that it has developed strategies in an effort to rectify this issue.

Generally, Latinos comprise more than 15 percent of the total population of the United States and, since 2000, have become the second-largest racial or ethnic population in the country, surpassing African Americans in 2003. The growth of the Latino community since 1970 has been dramatic. According to the U.S. Bureau of the Census, Latinos comprised 4.7 percent of the total population in 1970; 30 years later, this proportion had grown to 12.6 percent. By 2050, according to the Bureau's estimates, Latinos will comprise 24.4 percent of the total U.S. population. Over an 80-year period, the Latino population will have increased by 80.7 percent. To place this dramatic growth rate into perspective, it can be compared to the growth rates of both non-Hispanic whites and African Americans during the same time frame. Between 1970 through the projected year of 2050, the white non-Hispanic portion of the U.S. population decreases from 83.2 percent to 50.1 percent, while the black African-American population will grow from 11.1 percent to 14.6 percent. The Latino population went from being less than half the size of the African-American population to a projected growth of almost twice as large during the 80-year period covered by the Census Bureau report. Although the 2050 percentages are estimates, they are considered conservative estimates given that the Latino population has reached estimated growth projections in the past sooner than projections stated they would.

Even though Latinos are the largest racial and/or ethnic minority in the United States, they lag far behind the majority white non-Hispanic population in almost every category of socioeconomic attainment. For instance, the secondary or high school completion rate for Latinos is less than both non-Hispanic white and African-American students. The median income of Latinos, although rising three times faster than that of non-Hispanic whites, remains 40 percent less than the majority white population. These general demographic characteristics of the U.S. Latino community have implications for their political participatory patterns.

The rapid growth of Latinos between 1970 and 2010 has placed them at the top of the agenda for political strategists of both major political parties in the United States. The media initially noticed the arrival of Latinos on the political scene in the 1970s (*Time*, October 16, 1978) when they proclaimed it the decade of the Hispanics as they did again in 1990 and 2000. Yet every decade, Latinos have failed to influence politics in the manner in which pundits envisioned. In the general elections of 2008, both the Democratic and Republican Party presidential candidates courted Latinos for their votes. Some observers, principally Latino national organizations, such as the William C. Velasquez Institute (WCVI), National Council of La Raza (NCLR), and the National Association of Latino Elected Officials (NALEO), stated unequivocally that the Latino vote was behind President Obama's victory. These claims and the overtures of both parties were based upon several factors unique to the Latino electorate: their rapidly growing numbers and the particular states within which they reside. Those who argued that the Latino vote was not as important to the Democratic Party's victories in the presidency and Congress based their argument on still another characteristic of the Latino voter, their inability to vote in high percentages.

The two major American political parties sought the Latino vote due to their dramatic population increase and unique residential patterns. Both parties understand the political implications of Latinos becoming an increasingly larger share of the American voting public and the political implications of where they reside. Specifically, they reside throughout the heavily populated states of California, Texas, New York, and Florida, and they are concentrated in areas of Illinois, Arizona, New Jersey, New Mexico, Colorado, and

Massachusetts. These unique residential patterns reveal Latinos living in those states possessing the largest number of Electoral College votes. Prior to the 2008 presidential election, the WVCI, a Mexican-American think tank, estimated that 88 percent of the Latino population resided in states accounting for 267 of the 270 Electoral College votes required to elect the president. The WCVI indicated that the 2008 presidential election would be the first in which Latinos could influence the election of the president by providing the winning margin in closely contested states having large numbers of electoral votes. This conclusion was based on the assumption that Hispanics would vote overwhelmingly for one major political party or the other; as well, they would vote in numbers higher than ever before.

Although both parties have put forth vigorous efforts to seek out the support of increasing numbers of Latino voters, it appears that the Democratic Party has been more successful than its Republican counterpart. Why this is the case varies from one political observer to another, but in the final analysis, it appears that Latinos tend to support the Democratic Party and its candidates at all levels of the electoral structure due to their public policy compatibility. The Republican Party's positions on immigration, language policy, health, education, and voting rights appear to have alienated a great deal of the Latino electorate. According to all available estimates gleaned from surveys, exit polls, and telephone polls, regardless of their methodological limitations, it appears that at least since 1960, Latinos have supported the presidential candidates of the Democratic Party from between 53 percent in 1962 to more than 90 percent in 1976. The most recent general elections found that Latinos have consistently supported the Democratic Party's presidential candidates by more than 60 percent since 1984.

As noted by the media, more than 67 percent of registered Latinos voted for President Obama and another 30 percent supported Senator John McCain during the 2008 presidential election. President Obama appeared to reciprocate by appointing more Latinos to federal office, including nominating the first Latina to the Supreme Court, than any previous president. Fully 15 percent of President Obama's appointments to federal office during his first year in office were Latinos, mirroring their proportional representation in the general population.

The support levels in the 2008 general elections were the highest for a Democratic candidate and the lowest for a Republican candidate since 1972. Additionally, a review of exit polling data generated by the WCVI over the last three general elections revealed that the various Latino national subgroups voted quite differently. Normally, all Latino groups tend to support Democratic Party candidates with the exception of Cubans, who have historically been strong supporters of the Republican Party. The 2008 general election, however, saw the majority of Cubans deviate from this pattern by voting for Barack Obama. It should be noted that the dramatic change in the Cuban vote was driven by the youngest voting cohort, 18- to 24-year-olds, while the older cohorts remained loyal to the Republican Party. Whether this switch remains is unclear, except that it appears the movement is occurring among the youngest generation of Cuban voters, those born and educated in the United States who view the political world much differently than do the immigrants who arrived in 1959.

Support for Democratic Party presidential candidates among Mexican-descent Latinos has remained between 60 and 70 percent and among Puerto Ricans above 90 percent over the past 20 years. Data for immigrant voters of the other Latino national origin groups are difficult to acquire because of their small numbers. Although Latinos tend to be a personally conservative group of voters because their culture centers principally on the family, they tend to support liberal positions on education, health care, immigration, and the economy, partially explaining their support for Democratic Party candidates. The public opinion of Latinos, as reflected in polls conducted by the Pew Hispanic Center and WCVI, the two foremost collectors of data on Latino voting behavior and opinion, have revealed that Latinos are much like any other American voter. They tend to be concerned about the economy, employment, their children's education, and providing adequate health care for their families.

Latinos also have opinions that mirror the national attitudes toward various foreign policy issues facing the United States. For instance, in electronic polls conducted by WCVI subsequent to the 2008 general election, Latinos indicated that they were concerned first with the economy, then the war in Iraq, followed by such domestic social issues as health care and education. Media experts have occasionally spoken of Latinos as voters who will swing between both major parties, but their voting patterns appear relatively stable since the 1980s and appear to be settling in as a key Democratic Party constituent group when these types of data began being gathered by the WCVI.

An important research problem that must be overcome, then, in order to study the political participation of Latinos is to understand the generational differences among this population. Each national origin group appears to have differing voting patterns, and each generation within each group also votes differently. Although Latinos are treated as one homogeneous group by many researchers, they are not. As a result, a thorough understanding of this group's political participation patterns requires overcoming challenging research barriers. A methodological technique that would gather accurate data would have to navigate through the complex problem of racial/ethnic self-identification, gender, immigration, citizenship, national origin, and generational differences. Regardless, most of the research concerning the political participation of Latinos is of recent vintage, initially focusing on Mexicans because of their numbers. As methodologies were refined, population numbers rose, and the diversity of the Latino population in the United States became evident in their behavioral and participatory patterns.

Until the early 1970s, there were few efforts to register Latino voters; however, since then, there have been increased attempts to insure that Latinos register and vote often. As a result, much of the participation data for Latinos indicate that both registration and voting participation have been increasing steadily over the last four decades. For instance, Latino registration increased approximately 81 percent between 1972 and 2008, while their voting participation rate increased almost 74 percent during the same time frame. The overall Latino vote share, the percentage that Latino votes represent of the overall turnout, rose from 2.5 percent to approximately 7.4 percent over

the same reporting period. Essentially, 60 percent of eligible Latinos are registered to vote, and approximately 80 percent of registered Latinos voted in the 2008 general election. More Latinos are registering and voting in every election. Typically, the voting participation rates for Latinos in off-year elections reflect those of the general population; in other words, they are lower on the average, where approximately 32 percent of registered Latinos cast their votes.

Regardless of the increased Latino turnout rates in recent presidential elections, they are still much too low. Latinos represent no more that 6 percent of the national electorate with only 57.3 percent of eligible Latinos registering and barely 50 percent of those registered casting ballots. As a result, regardless of the growth of the Latino population and the machinations of both major political parties, neither has translated into either substantially greater turnout or increased political influence at the national political level. Latino political influence, however, is pronounced at local and state levels varying from city to city and from state to state. Why Latinos lack political influence and have low voter turnout and varying influence only in certain regions of the United States is best explained through a discussion of the forces that drive and inhibit Latino political participation.

Latinos and the Social Dynamics of Political Participation

A partial explanation for low voter turnout among Latinos may be found in the dynamics of the American electoral system that underlie the fundamental reasons why voters, vote. These dynamics may be categorized variously but generally include the openness of the political structure to Latinos, the general political culture of American society, and the effects of institutional variables that tend to suppress the vote in the United States generally.

Political participation generally is considered a two-way interactive activity. In other words, political participation is an action on the part of a person as well as an action encouraged and enhanced by the governing institutions of a given society. Political participation can run the gamut of everything from gathering in large groups spontaneously to voice political opinions in the media or public place, to casting a ballot in any number of ways, to vociferously expounding one's opinion to public officials during official meetings, and even to covering one's automobile or vehicle of conveyance with stickers supporting some political candidate or cause.

In liberal democracies, such as in the United States, where voting is the private choice of the individual, turnout rates for voting can range from the high-80th percentiles at the national, presidential levels, where the elections enjoy great notoriety and receive a large volume of media coverage and interest; to the single-digit percentiles in school or special district elections where the candidates are relatively unknown and the issues shrouded in complexity. Basically, voting turnout is dependent upon a broad multiplicity of variables interacting simultaneously during any given election all affecting the individual voter.

This particular dynamic of the American political system, in which the actual participation is the private purview of the individual, may actually act as a depressive variable on Latino participation for various reasons. In many instances, until the last two recent elections, there have not been concerted efforts by either of the two major political parties to reach out and encourage Latinos to vote. As a result, there lacks a basic ethos of voting in most Latino communities. In short, Latinos have not been encouraged to vote by many, particularly American national institutions, such as the public school system.

In many cases, there have been instances alleging violations of the federal Voting Rights Act of 1965, including gerrymandering, literacy testing, the unannounced changing of polling places, outright forceful intimidation of voters at polling places, and insufficient Election Day infrastructure support on the part of election officials. The federal courts have overturned many of these legal prohibitions after the fact—in other words, local officials make the corrections after the election has occurred and after the case has been adjudicated, rendering silent the voices of Latino voters. Still other facets of this characteristic include the lack of media exposure of candidates and issues in the Latino communities through local Spanish-speaking media outlets. In mid-2012, Florida's election division attempted to purge the voter rolls of non-citizen voters, but the U.S. Department of Justice

stopped it, based on it possibly violating both the Voting Rights Act of 1965 and the 1993 National Voter Registration act. Opponents of the purge maintained that it too often resulted in wrongly removing legal voters, especially from Latino and other immigrant groups.

Another layer affecting political participation is that of the political culture. American political culture has placed barriers against Latino political participation, many of which are based in racial stereotypes engrained in the American consciousness and eventually finding their way into the socialization process. Many of these stereotypes were founded in the pure racism that dictated social relations between racial and ethnic groups during the greater part of the nineteenth and early twentieth centuries. In the Southwest, one way in which racism was manifested in public policy was the segregation of Latino children into "Mexican schools" at both the elementary and secondary educational levels, a practice that existed as late as 1967 or 1968.

President Lyndon Baines Johnson started his public career as a schoolteacher in Cotulla, Texas, and his experiences reflected the lack of resources troubling these schools because it was assumed that Mexican children were not worth the investment since school officials believed the children were destined to work in the fields or become common laborers when they reached their late teens. Johnson's experiences were an essential motivator for the eventual passage of the Civil Rights Acts of 1964 and the Voting Rights Act of 1965. Similar conditions confronted Latinos throughout the Southwest and served as a tracking system that significantly contributed to Latinos becoming embedded at the lowest levels of the American ladder.

The general neglect of Latinos in the educational system eventually found its way throughout the entire social system and was reflected particularly in the lack of available political stimuli targeted to Latinos and the subsequent diminution of Latinos throughout the electoral process. This includes the failure of the national media to create political news and advertising designed to attract Latino voters; the failure of local and state governments to encourage Latinos to exercise their franchise; and the failure of political candidates of both major political parties to target Latinos as possible key constituents.

In the end, the failure of the American political system to reach out and integrate Latinos into the

A Latina voter leaves a polling station in Hollywood, California, during the United States midterm elections November, 2002. (Hector Mata/AFP/Getty Images)

country's political community contributed to the overall low voter turnout among Latinos generally. Although many Latino organizations sprang up to fill this need—such as the Southwest Voter Registration and Education Project (SWVREP), the National Council of La Raza (NCLR), the National Association of Latino Elected and Appointed Officials (NALEO), the Mexican American Legal Defense and Educational Fund (MALDEF), GI Forum, and the League of United Latin American Citizens (LULAC)—their combined efforts were not, nor have they been, enough to increase voter turnout among Latinos. The efforts on the part of these organizations, however, have gone far toward publicizing the political existence of Latinos nationwide. Nevertheless, the overall political culture of the United States has been slow to respond to these efforts for a broad array of reasons, one of the most important being the paradigm of race that dominates

national discourse tending to obscure the political reality facing Latinos.

American political culture's racial paradigm dominating political discourse is principally a dichotomous one of black versus white. Because of their unique cultural heritage, Latinos do not fit this dual-race model. The black/white discourse confuses the national dialogue over racism and confuses not just policy makers, but even Latinos resulting in some identifying as white, others black, others Indian or indigenous and still others as *mestizo* (mixed race). For decades, this confusing perception has made it difficult for Latinos to be covered by laws, programs, and political strategies.

For example, prior to a landmark Supreme Court decision, *Hernandez v. Texas* (1954), Latinos had always been included under the "White" persons' category by the Census Bureau and categorized as such by many local authorities. At the same time that Latinos, specifically Mexicans, were being counted as white, they were being treated as a separate people and suffered segregation and discrimination in many areas of public life simply because they were Mexicans. The Supreme Court in *Hernandez* ruled that Mexican Americans were a separate group of individuals under the law because they had been treated as such in Texas by authorities. The court specifically cited the "Mexican schools," segregated eating facilities (restaurants), and even separate public restrooms that were set up during the original trial as prime examples of this treatment. The court did not speak to Latinos as a separate race or as an ethnic group, only that they had been identified as "Mexicans" and, as such, treated differently in many areas of public accommodations, thus requiring the protection of the Fourteenth Amendment.

When they spoke of racial discrimination in their opinion, the U.S. Supreme Court recognized the "two-class theory" of race that predominated then in social science circles. The concept referred to the notion that all race relations in the United States centered on the relations of "two classes of people," whites and blacks. The justices pointed out that although the theory explained American race relations generally, it did not exclude discrimination of groups that fell outside the parameters of the theory, specifically citing "Mexicans" as one of the excluded groups that could be covered by the theory. The court was keeping within its tradition of ruling on the law only and not acting as social science investigators. (Even though this case was heard and decided in 1954, social scientists have yet to take up the challenge of expanding the "two-class theory" in the literature.)

The benign neglect and separate treatment of Latinos were not the only contributing factors to the prevention or dilution of the political participation of Latinos. Throughout the American political system there were concerted efforts by groups, individuals, and local and state governments to diminish the opportunities for Latinos to influence politics; and in some isolated areas, this behavior is still ongoing. For instance, although since ruled unconstitutional, some states instituted poll taxes and literacy tests as prerequisites to voting. Texas even instituted what came to be known as the "white primary" declaring the political party primaries as private events open only to party members in order to prevent either African Americans or Latinos from participating in party nominations

The decennial redistricting processes of many states in the southwestern United States have been legal battlegrounds for Latino organizations who feel that congressional, state assembly, and state senatorial district lines have been gerrymandered, preventing Latino voters from having the opportunity to elect a candidate of their choice to any of these offices. This is often accomplished through drawing representational lines through Latino neighborhoods effectively dividing the community into adjoining districts and then completing the districts with majority nonwhite Hispanic individuals, as happened in Laredo, Texas during the 2001 congressional redistricting process (*LULAC, et al. v. Rick Perry, et al.* [2006]).

At the extreme end of the activities designed to diminish the Latino vote are efforts at intimidation that occur at polls in various jurisdictions. For instance, instances have been chronicled in which individuals dressed to look like members of the U.S. Office of Immigration and Customs Enforcement (ICE) stood at voting booths informing Latino voters that it is a federal offense for a noncitizen to vote. This behavior tends to scare Latino voters away from the polls. In another type of intimidating behavior, polling judges have simply told Latino and African-American voters that they have lost the right to vote because the Voting Rights Act has been ruled unconstitutional. Finally, police officers have been used in still other jurisdictions to establish roadblocks on streets leading to polls, turning away both Latino and African-American voters. These and other types of intimidating activities have been recorded as occurring as recently as the presidential election of 2000.

For instance, in Florida during the 2000 general elections, the courts found in a voting rights lawsuit, *NAACP, et al. v. Katherine Harris, et al.* (2001), that a broad array of voting administration methods in various county jurisdictions throughout the state of Florida inhibited the vote. Some of these actions by county elections officials included not having enough voting machines available for precincts with large numbers of voters; not having the ability to check the voter registration of eligible voters; not having a sufficient number of election judges to manage high volumes of voter turnout; the inappropriate purging of eligible voters from registration rolls; not making available affidavits to appropriate voters; and, in several cases, simply using the police to intimidate some voters. These sorts of activities, however, are the obvious and marginally legal or illegal means that have traditionally been used to diminish the Latino vote and their subsequent political influence.

The American political system itself through the manner in which candidates are selected, the normal registration process, and the general manner in which elections are conducted tend to diminish the vote of not only Latinos, but also of the general population. The vote-dilution effects coupled with the vote-dilution methods utilized against Latinos throughout their voting history may eventually turn Latino voters into classical underachievers.

The Political Structure, Social Integration, and Latinos

Although Latinos have been an important element in the equation of American political culture since the middle of the nineteenth century, they have found it difficult to discover a welcoming atmosphere within this particular society. Latinos have suffered similar discrimination at all levels of American society as other racial and ethnic groups did upon their arrival in the United States. The discrimination that Latinos have suffered is unique, yet similar, to that suffered by African Americans throughout history. It is similar because, fundamentally, it is racial discrimination, and Latinos have been separated and segregated in the same manner as African Americans simply because they were considered different from white non-Hispanics. An example of this treatment, the "Mexican schools," was discussed earlier.

Latinos, however, were and still are discriminated against for speaking Spanish in the workplace and at schools and public meetings; in parts of the Southwest, certain types of employment are seen as the sole purview of Latinos even among professional occupations such as lawyers, doctors, and teachers; and certain behaviors or physical conditions, such as overindulgence of alcohol, adultery, spousal abuse, laziness,

and obesity, are still seen as endemic to Latinos. These latter perceptions have led to the creation and maintenance of stereotypes that were and are used as justifications to discriminate against Latinos in almost every walk of life and at every level of employment.

Latino stereotypes have been the driving forces behind both formal and informal exclusion from public arenas that, in turn, yielded many of the legal protections that grew out of the Civil Rights Act of 1964. Of all the civil rights acts, the most important law in relation to the political participation of Latinos by far has been the Voting Rights Act (VRA) of 1965. The three sections of this law that have propelled Latinos into political power, or at least electoral office, have been Sections 2, 5, and 203. Sections 2 and 5 of the VRA protect the sanctity of the polling place and protect the redistricting process from the overutilization of race as a rationale for the drawing of federal, state, local, and special governmental representational districts. These two sections of the VRA alone have been credited for the increased numbers of Latino elected officials since 1970. Section 203, known as the language provision, simply guarantees that election materials and accommodations be made available for any language group that makes up more than 5 percent of the population in any one jurisdiction.

The most powerful of all three sections is Section 5, or pre-clearance provision, that requires any jurisdiction subject to this provision seeking preclearance—permission, if you will—from the Department of Justice before they can even do something as mundane as moving the location of a polling place. Section 5 is seen by MALDEF as "protective" or "preventive" legislation that has enforcement power, while Sections 2 and 203 must require the deliberation of the federal courts before any enforcement can occur. As a result, Section 5 can prevent discriminatory behavior before it occurs, while Sections 2 and 203 must wait until discrimination occurs and lawsuits filed, and then they must run the risk of an unfavorable ruling from the bench.

Access to the halls of political power for Latinos has always been difficult to obtain, and often it has come only after either federal civil suits or massive political demonstrations. For instance, the already-cited *Hernandez* case brought to light the differential treatment of Latinos by political jurisdictions in jury selection and general treatment in many areas of public accommodations. Prior to this, the courts ruled in *Mendez v. Westminster* (1947) that segregated schools for Latino children were unconstitutional. The opinion in *Mendez v. Westminster*, however, was limited only to the jurisdiction of the Ninth Circuit Court of Appeals and not across the entire United States. As a result, schools in Texas and other parts of the United States outside the jurisdiction of the Ninth Circuit remained segregated until the passage of the Civil Rights Acts in 1964. The court also found in *White v. Regester* (1972) that the at-large representational systems used by the state of Texas to elect its members to both the state assembly and senate was unconstitutional. *White v. Regester* opened the doors for the election of increasing numbers of Latinos to those bodies.

So many Latinos have been elected in the California, New York, New Mexico, and Texas state assemblies that they have been responsible for leadership transformations in all of these chambers. Additionally, the Voting Rights Act has been credited by NALEO for being responsible for increasing the number of Latinos on city councils, school boards, and special districts throughout the nation. NALEO estimates that since 1996, the number of Latinos elected to any public office in the United States has increased by 37 percent, from 3,743 to 5,129 in 2007. Increases in Latinos on municipal bodies are exemplified by the New York City Council where nine of the 51 council members are Latinos (chiefly Dominicans or Puerto Ricans). Latinos have been elected in Michigan, North Dakota, Georgia, Kentucky, and Alaska, areas where Latinos have not traditionally migrated to but are beginning to do so. Regardless, Latinos have still found it difficult to influence the national political leadership of both major parties on policies that would directly benefit their community.

Even though there has been considerable political reform allowing Latinos to achieve a certain degree of electoral success, there still remain institutional barriers at all societal levels that must be overcome in order for Latinos to gain full political integration. For instance, in the United States, political participation is not as emphasized during the educational

experiences of most citizens as it is in other liberal democracies, notably Mexico and Australia. Although this situation weighs heavily on all U.S. citizens, it affects Latinos equally or worse given the poor quality of education they already receive in public schools. Not only are Latinos subject to a minimalist approach to civic education, but they are liable to miss it altogether given their high dropout rates.

Paradoxically, a number of structural considerations that are designed to maximize voter participation and input in some jurisdictions actually tend to diminish the vote. For instance, the state of Texas requires separate elections for every type and level of jurisdiction from the state to local utility districts. This has resulted in various county jurisdictions having more than one election per week in some years, which, in turn, has resulted in voter confusion as to location of polling places, candidates, issues, and voter fatigue. Voters participating in the 1998 Democratic Party primary for the 20th Congressional District of Texas, an overwhelmingly Latino district in the heart of San Antonio, indicated that they thought they had already voted in an election when, in fact, the election had not yet been held; other voters thought they were voting for the father of the actual candidate, and still other voters did not even know an election was taking place on the particular date. This proliferation of elections was designed to place more power in the hands of voters but in actuality has resulted in the opposite effect, not the least being voter fatigue.

For Latinos, political participation serves as an important social integrating mechanism. In the United States, it serves as both a signal on the part of the group seeking integration, in this case Latinos, and the political system's willingness to accept the group by allowing them to participate in the political process. For some groups seeking political integration, the manner of participation may reflect differing stages of acceptance. For instance, when the group first becomes large enough to put forth a position on a public policy issue, that group's first foray into the participatory realm may be to utilize street demonstrations or some other nontraditional participatory technique to set forth their position on policy issues. As the group grows in size and influence, it may begin taking on the traditional methods of political participation to put forth their agenda. So, the group seeking integration may move from the "streets" to the voting booths and the halls of the lobby to influence the political structure as that group achieves more sophisticated levels of political maturity and acceptance.

This political participatory evolutionary process certainly was the case of many immigrant groups, such as the Irish and Italians at the turn of the twentieth century, as well as African Americans and Latinos from the 1960s to the present. Each group began achieving their place in the American political mainstream through demonstrations, in some cases marred by violence; and as they became integrated into American society and the political process, which included gaining the franchise, these groups began to utilize the more traditionally accepted political participatory methods to propel their agendas through the policy process.

During the late 1950s through the early 1970s the African-American community utilized many nontraditional participatory techniques to publicize their need for legal protections in many areas of public accommodations such as education, voting, use of public facilities, and so forth. Beginning in the early 1960s, African Americans began voting in larger and larger numbers and became an essential block of support for Democratic Party candidates. The Democratic Party candidates who found themselves elected with the support of African-American voters began to champion various types of civil rights laws favoring African Americans. Once these laws were enacted, African Americans employed other traditionally accepted participatory techniques such as lobbying to ensure the protection of these laws, particularly the Voting Rights Act of 1965, from being overturned or substantially weakened every time the law was considered for renewal.

Latinos resorted to street demonstrations to publicize their position on immigration laws culminating with massive demonstrations in 2006. The demonstrations provided the imagery needed for many Latino organizations to utilize lobbying and "get out the vote" strategies in support of the Obama campaign in 2008. The Democratic Party now operates under the assumption that both Latinos and African Americans comprise essential blocks of their voter support and are courted by politicians of that party. In turn, elected Democratic Party officials champion the positions on certain public policy issues, including immigration reform that Latinos espouse. At the local political level, the "streets to lobby" phenomenon has been evidenced in the activities of community organizations that have changed their political tactics reflecting this tactical shift. The best examples of these organizations are those founded by Ernesto Cortes first in San Antonio, Texas (Communities Organized for Public Services), El Paso, Texas (EPISO), and Los Angeles (United Neighborhood Organization). These organizations are based in the Latino communities of their respective cities and lobby city hall on public works and educational projects pertinent to their neighborhoods. They have proven quite effective because of their abilities to command large segments of voters who can determine the fortunes of city council members, state legislators, and mayors.

Political participation and its relationship to the social and political integration of groups into a society is an essential element underlying the development of societies throughout history. Without the integration of new groups, societies cannot flourish and continue their existence. A particular society generally becomes tolerant of the ways of immigrants, including their language, allowing integration to occur. Even though integration is never a smooth occurrence, oftentimes marred by instances of discrimination and lack of acceptance, eventually immigrants achieve integration to various degrees in that society. As noted earlier, integration is a two-way interaction between the group seeking integration and the society to which it wishes to belong. The group seeking integration must conform to societal norms and accepted methods of political participation, while society must take steps to ensure that the group seeking integration is made to feel welcome.

Conclusion

Political participation, particularly voting, serves as a signal to an entire population that the individual exercising this act is a fully integrated person in that society. The example of Latino political participation places this last observation in this context because their increasing levels of participation signal that they are becoming more and more integrated into American political society. The example also indicates the importance of political participation, because it magnifies the potential ability of new immigrant or emergent groups to influence the election of the highest position in the U.S. government. Also just as clearly is that the increasing influence of Latinos portends the changing face of political leadership in the United States. Essentially, shifts in patterns of political participation may mark shifts in governmental control, resulting in changes in laws, relations with other states, and so forth. In short, a dramatic shift in political participation patterns can mark dramatic shifts in the political direction of the ship of state of any society.

Bibliography

Almond, Gabriel and Verba, Sidney. 1954. *The Civic Culture.* Princeton, NJ: Princeton University Press.

Bucks, Brian. K., et al. 2006. *Recent Changes in U.S. Family Finances: Evidence from the 2001 and 2004 Survey of Consumer Finances.* Federal Reserve Bulletin. Washington, DC: U.S. Government Printing Office.

Chua, Amy. 2009. *Day of Empire: How Hyperpowers Rise to Global Dominance—and Why They Fall.* Norwell, MA: Ander Press.

Davidson, Chandler. 1990. *Race and Class in Texas Politics.* Princeton, NJ: Princeton University Press.

Doppelt, Jack C., and Shearer, Ellen. 1999. *Nonvoters: America's No-Shows.* London: Sage Publications Inc.

Galindo, Aina. 2007. *Inequality in Political Participation: Contemporary Patterns in European Countries.* Paper 07'01. Center for the Study of Democracy. Irvine: University of California, Irvine.

Garcia, F. Chris, and Gabriel Sanchez. 2007. *Hispanics and the US Political System: Moving into the Mainstream.* Upper Saddle River, NJ: Pearson/Prentice Hall.

Gonzalez, Antonio, and Steven Ochoa. 2009. *The Latino Vote in 2008: Trends and Characteristics.* Los Angeles, CA: William C. Velasquez Institute.

Grebler, Leo, Joan Moore, and Ralph Guzman. 1970. *The Mexican American People: The Nation's Second Largest Minority.* New York: Free Press.

"It's Your Turn in the Sun." 1978. *Time*, October 16, 48–61.

Milbrath, Lester W. 1965. *Political Participation: How and Why Do People Get Involved in Politics?* Chicago: Rand McNally and Co.

Montejano, David. 1984. *Anglos and Mexicans in the Making of Texas, 1836–1986.* Austin: University of Texas Press.

NALEO. 1974–2007. *National Directory of Latino Elected Officials, 1974–2007.* Washington, DC: Educational Fund.

NALEO. 2009. *2008 Latino Election Handbook.* Los Angeles: NALEO Educational Fund.

Patterson, Thomas E. 2002. *The Vanishing Voter.* New York: Alfred A. Knopf.

Pew Research Center for the People and the Press and the Pew Internet and American Life Project. 2008. *Internet's Broader Role in Campaign 2008: Social Networking and Online Videos Take Off.*

Suárez-Orozco, Marcelo M. and Mariela. M. Páez. 2002. *Latinos Remaking America.* Berkeley: University of California Press.

U.S. Department of Commerce. Bureau of the Census. *1970, 1980, 1990, 2000, Current Population Series P-20.* Washington, DC: U.S. Government Printing Office.

U.S. Department of Commerce. Bureau of the Census. 1976–2000. *Voting and Registration in the Election of November 19xx.* Current Population Survey. Washington, D.C.: U.S. Government Printing Office.

U.S. Department of Commerce. Bureau of the Census. 2005–2007. *American Community Survey 3-Year Estimates.* Washington, DC: U.S. Government Printing Office.

Voting Rights Act, 42 U.S.C. § 1973 *et seq.* (2000).

Cases Cited in Essay

Hernandez v. Texas, 347 U.S. 475 (1954)

League of United Latin American Citizens, et al. v. Rick Perry, Governor of the State of Texas, et al., 548 U.S. 399 (2006).

NAACP, et al. v. Katherine Harris, et al., Case No. 01-CIV-120-GOLD

Mendez v. Westminster, 64 F.Supp. 544 (C.D. Cal. 1946), *affd.*, 161 F.2d. 774 (9th Cir. 1947) (*en banc*).

White v. Regester, 412 U.S. 755 (1973).

The Second Generation

Philip Kasinitz and Jessica Sperling

The economic, social, political, and cultural incorporation of new racial and ethnic groups into a society is among the most important long-term issues raised by human migration. It is also the source of much of the political tension and controversy around the issue of immigration in many receiving societies. Yet, in many ways, incorporation is not strictly or even primarily an "immigrant" issue. It often has at least as much to do with the immigrant's children—the second generation—and the position they hold in the host societies. This chapter discusses a variety of features about the second generation. It begins by discussing definitional issues about the second generation, past and present, and follows with an overview of the contemporary second generation and its social mobility. Finally, to provide a clearer view of how context determines second-generation outcomes, it discusses international and comparative research on the second generation.

The Second Generation: Definitions and Meanings in Flux

What is the second generation? The use of the term "second generation" has changed over time, and these shifts reflect changes in how we think about immigration. In the early twentieth century, many popular and scholarly commentators, as well as many in the immigrant communities, used the term "*first*-generation *American*" to describe people born in the United States to foreign-born parents. Although this usage has generally fallen out of favor among social scientists, it remains common in everyday speech. Following U.S. Census Bureau practice, such people are also referred to as being of "Foreign Stock."

While some popular commentators continue to use the term "first-generation Americans" or "new Americans," it has become more common to refer to persons with immigrant parents as "*second*-generation *immigrants*" since the revival of social scientific interest in the topic in the 1980s—although, of course, such people are not, in fact, immigrants at all. The older usage emphasizes assimilation and conveys the idea that birthplace fundamentally alters one's relationship to the host society. The latter places the emphasis on the continuity between the immigrants and their American-born children as both being part of the same community. Both, however, imply that something changes when a person is born in a nation different from that in which their parents were born—a very American idea that is clearly embedded in the American legal system and its tradition of birthright citizenship. This stands in contrast to ethnically based concepts of citizenship seen in much of the world, in which a person is considered a member of the social and political community of one's ancestors regardless of where one was born.

Further complicating matters is the fact that the term "generation" is used in at least three distinct, albeit interrelated, ways in the social scientific literature. The first is "generation" in the sense of an age cohort—that is, people of approximately the same age who experience the same historical events and at roughly the same points in their individual development. This is the sense of "generation" we use when we speak of the "greatest generation" or the "baby boom generation." A second meaning of "generation," one favored by anthropologists, refers to position in a kinship system and the relationship of individuals to parents in the generation above or children in the generation below. Finally, in studies of immigration, particularly in the United States, the term "generation" is used as a measure of distance from the "old country." Thus, we usually speak of people who move to the United States from another society as adults as being "first-generation" immigrants, their American-born children as the "second generation" and their children, in turn, the "third generation."

In more recent years, the numbering system has become increasingly complex. Ruben Rumbaut introduced the term "1.5 generation," referring to people born abroad but who emigrated as children and were largely raised in the host country. The 1990s and 2000s have seen more and more attention paid to the unique situation of people in that intermediate position, with special attention to how their role in the family is shaped by the timing of immigration. This attention brought on further refinement, and references the "1.25 generation" (people who immigrated as teenagers) and the "1.75 generation" (people who were born abroad but who immigrated as toddlers) soon followed.

Assimilation and Generational Status: Past and Present

For the large wave of southern and eastern European immigrants to the United States that began around 1880 and ended in the mid-1920s, these three meanings of "generation" were closely intertwined. Since immigration significantly diminished after 1924, by the mid-1930s, even in the most "ethnic" of American communities and neighborhoods, most children were American-born. Many, in some cases most, of their parents were immigrants. As this generation aged together in mid-twentieth-century America, they experienced an unusual confluence of the "historical cohort," "kinship," and "distance from the old country" meanings of generation that had often blurred the distinction between the three. Being the children of immigrants (and the parents of the third generation) and experiencing the unique historical events of the mid-twentieth century in young adulthood, they were linked. To some extent, they created a distinct "second-generation" identity, both in the minds of

the children of immigrants and in American popular culture. And while the experience of the second generation in western Europe and South America (which were also receiving large numbers of immigrants during this period) was sometimes quite different, many of the concepts born out of the American experience came to be used to describe the situations there, as well.

American observers of the late-nineteenth- and early-twentieth-century immigrants to the United States tended to assume that the assimilation of the second and third generations was both desirable and inevitable. Writing at the height of American self-confidence, they saw assimilation as closely tied to upward mobility and often wrote as if assimilation, acculturation, and upward mobility were virtually the same thing. While they disagreed on whether immigrants would drop immigrant values in favor of Anglo-Saxon ways or develop some hybrid instead ("Anglo-conformity" versus "melting pot" models of assimilation), they assumed that immigrants would achieve upward mobility by embracing the main elements of the culture of the dominant society. Whatever the psychic toll the shedding of old cultural identities might cause, substantial upward mobility would be the reward. William Lloyd Warner and Leo Srole's (1945) study of ethnic groups in *Yankee City* remains perhaps the most complete discussion of the identity and experience of the second generation of this historical period. Warner and Srole describe a generational march of the ethnic groups from initial poverty amidst residential and occupational segregation to residential, occupational, and identity integration and Americanization. This orderly pattern of mobility has come to be called the "straight line" model of assimilation: "Each consecutive ethnic generation pushes progressively farther out of the bottom level and into each of the successive layers above. That the class index of an ethnic group is related to the length of its settlement in the city is a manifestation of the continuous advance achieved in the hierarchy of each new generation" (Warner and Srole 1945, 72).

Warner and Srole further suggest that the forces that promote assimilation will also affect the relations between the first and second generations. Often, they argue, immigrant parents will try to socialize their children into the values and beliefs of their homelands. Yet as soon as the child enters into independent social relations outside the home, they begin to reorient themselves toward the host society. Schools, peer relations, modes of play, and the mass media all promote host-society ways of doing things. Indeed, often the second-generation child ends up leading the rest of the family in adapting to the New World. This process, Warner and Srole argue, often turns the traditional parent-child relationship on its head. The child, who has more access to knowledge about American society, teaches the parents, and this role reversal often leads to conflict.

There is, no doubt, much truth to these observations. However, looking back with the advantage of more than half a century of historical knowledge, we can also clearly see the weaknesses of this approach. Warner and Srole assumed that immigrant children would be absorbed into a single, unified, individualistic, middle-class "American culture." They ignored the diversity among natives and the ways in which immigrants were being assimilated into distinct segments of American society. They downplayed the possibility that immigrants might improve their prospects for upward mobility by *retaining* their immigrant culture. The model also discounted the ways in which immigrants, in the words of researchers Richard Alba and Victor Nee, "remade the American mainstream" and gradually brought the immigrant world and American world closer together. The model also takes it for granted that "American" culture has a higher status than the immigrant culture. As Warner and Srole note, while the children of immigrants may be caught between two social systems, "in any judgments of rank, the American social system, being the most vigorous and having also the dominance of host status, is affirmed the higher." As such, the child could be expected to identify with it (Warner and Srole 1945, 145).

Further, as early as 1938, Marcus Lee Hansen had observed distinct differences in attitudes toward ethnic identity between this second generation and their third-generation children. The second generation, Hansen argued, was anxious to assimilate. In many cases, they seek to distance themselves from their parents' foreignness. As Leonard Covello, a leading educator in New York's Italian-American community during the mid-twentieth century, famously recalled of his own second-generation childhood: "we were becoming Americans by learning how to be ashamed of our parents" (quoted in Iorizzo and Mondello 1980, 118). Yet Hansen suggests that the third generation may become sentimentally invested in ethnicity, which may go part of the way toward the mass resurgence in interest in ethnic origins among white Americans in the early 1970s).

For today's immigrants and their second-generation children, the situation is markedly different. Post-1965 immigrants to the United States (as well as their contemporaries in western Europe) often live in communities in which ethnicity is often replenished by a continuous stream of new immigrants. With this continuing immigrant influx, new first-generation immigrants in many communities today are often younger than third-generation adults. Second- and third-generation young people share neighborhoods, classrooms, and workplaces with recent immigrants their own age. "Old country" ways and identities are thus less associated with chronological age than in the past. Further, new immigrants may bring to the ethnic communities more up-to-date versions of the sending society's culture. The situation is also complicated by the greater degree of transnationalism and back-and-forth migration among contemporary immigrants. Some second-generation members, while born in the United States, have spent considerable time in their parents' homelands while growing up, and many recent immigrants are coming from communities where a large number of returned migrants have already challenged traditional ways.

Contemporary immigrant communities vary in the degree to which they emphasize distance from the old country versus chronological age when thinking about generational divides. Among Japanese Americans and Korean Americans, there are clear linguistic designations for people born abroad, those born in the United States of immigrant parents, and those whose parents were American-born: "Issei," "Nisei," and "Sansei" in Japanese; "Ilsae," "Yisae," and "Sansae" in Korean. Within their communities, these groups are thought of as having different attributes and different relationships to the sending and host societies. Korean Americans also use the term "iljeom osae," which is literally translated as the "1.5 generation." Within the Korean community, this generation is often seen as having the greatest difficulty in adjustment, a fact which is a cause for concern among community leaders.

Among other contemporary immigrant groups, generational distinctions seem less precise and less clear. Among Cuban Americans, there is considerable consciousness of generational and historical differences between the "exile generation" and those born in the United States as well as anticipation of what it will mean for the community when the former passes from the scene. Mexican Americans make distinctions between those born in the United States and those in Mexico and distinguish both from the descendants of populations who lived in the Southwest when it was still part of Mexico. Indeed, the terms used for Mexican-descended people of different political stripes and in different parts of the country ("Hispano," "Chicano," "Mexican American," "La Raza," etc.) have implications for the importance of American birth in shaping identity. Moreover, the long and complex history of Mexican immigration makes it difficult to disentangle the impact of chronological age from the number of generations in the United States in shaping generational identity. Dominicans and Puerto Ricans have also developed terms to refer to the American (usually New York)-born members of the community—"Dominican Yorks" and "Newyoricans." Yet the high level of back-and-forth migration, changes in home communities, and the importance of a distinctive youth culture mean that these terms are often as much about age cohort as actual birthplace.

The Contemporary Second Generation and Social Mobility

By 2000, approximately 10 percent of the American population was "second generation" in the sense that they were born in the United States and have at least one foreign-born parent. In many American cities, the combination of the second and 1.5 generations now outnumber the immigrants. The second generation now makes up more than a quarter of the nation's Hispanic and Asian populations. The fact that so much of the second generation is of non-European origin and considered "nonwhite" stands in sharp contrast to earlier periods, and the growth of this population thus raises questions about the future of race relations and about their social mobility in the United States.

Possibilities of Downward Mobility

These differences in the historical experience of past and present "second generations" has led to much speculation as to whether models of "assimilation" developed to describe the situation of earlier European immigrants to America still make sense in the United States or elsewhere. Many social scientists have been skeptical about whether the most recent wave of second-generation immigrants can expect to be upwardly mobile in the United States. In 1992, sociologist Herbert Gans inverted the usual "straight line" model of assimilation by proposing what he termed the "second generation decline." Gans outlined multiple ways in which the post-1965 second generation could do worse than their parents. Children who refused to accept the low level, poorly paid jobs of their parents could face a difficult bind. In adulthood, some members of the second generation, especially those whose parents did not themselves escape poverty, will end up in persistent poverty; they will be reluctant to work at immigrant wages and hours like their parents, but they will also lack the job opportunities and skills and connections to do better. Thus, by having the same reactions toward these low-level jobs as poor young native whites, blacks, and Hispanics, they might risk sliding into persistent poverty. Indeed, some may "become American" by adopting negative attitudes toward school, opportunity, hard work, and the "American dream."

Alejandro Portes and Min Zhou greatly expanded on these notions by proposing the idea of segmented assimilation—perhaps the single most influential concept in the contemporary study of the second generation. The segmented assimilation model argues that the varying modes of incorporation of the first generation endow the second generation with differing amounts of cultural and social capital in the form of ethnic jobs, networks, and values and exposes it to differing opportunities. This in turn exerts differential pulls and pushes on the allegiances of the second generation. Second-generation youth with strong ties to American minorities, whose parents lack the ability to provide them with jobs or to protect them from the influence the native poor may develop an "adversarial stance" toward the dominant white society similar to that of American minorities. These youth may become skeptical about the possibility of upward mobility and the value of education. Like Gans, Portes and his colleagues concluded that second-generation young people who cast their lot with American minority groups will experience downward social mobility, in part because high levels of discrimination will preclude the option of joining the white mainstream, even if they are highly acculturated. Joining the native circles to which they have access may be a ticket to permanent subordination and disadvantage.

Of course, the idea that assimilation has its costs and that children of immigrants may become the "wrong kind" of Americans is not new. As early as 1906, the *Outlook* magazine warned against rushing Italian children into the "streetiness" and "cheap Americanism," which "so overwhelms Italian youngsters in the cities" (quoted in Kahn 1987, 244). Even the notion that a dense "ethnic enclave" can provide a bulwark against the worst effects of the American street, a case made forcefully by Zhou and Bankston in the modern era, is foreshadowed by studies of juvenile delinquency among boys and sexual promiscuity among girls in New York's Jewish community in the early twentieth century that resulted directly from overly rapid Americanization.

Yet in earlier times, these skeptical perspectives were in the minority among intellectuals, social scientists, and in the immigrant communities themselves. Today, in contrast, such skeptical perspectives have gained wide traction in both research and the popular press. Researchers have highlighted certain characteristics of the modern era that might limit the possibility of upward mobility relative to previous eras. This includes rising inequality, a purported hourglass economy—limiting middle-income employment and upward career growth—and continued racial stereotyping and racial division in economic outcomes (which matters, given the nonwhite racial makeup of modern immigrants). Since the early 1990s, many have speculated that contemporary American culture and society might actually undermine the ability of the second generation to acclimate to the array of cultural changes and expectations they will confront.

Evidence of Upward Mobility

Despite these concerns of downward mobility, as more of the contemporary second generation has come of age and begun to join the labor force, data have generally not supported the more dire predictions of second-generation downward mobility. Different strains of research have compared the outcomes and achievement of the second generation relative to one of three groups: to their immigrant parents, to their native peers, and to the second generation of the past era. The first comparison indicates success from an intergenerational perspective; the second shows whether children of immigrants are performing better than the population that would have been solely present without the immigrant migration; and the third provides a temporal perspective on second-generation mobility.

Research has reached a clear consensus on the intergenerational question, and children of immigrants almost universally perform better than their parents. Parents often come from areas where low levels of education are common, and poor economic migrants often come from rural areas and have even lower levels of education than many in their home country. Thus, simply growing up in the United States, where completing high school (and, for some, attending college) is a general expectation and is widely available to all, gives these children a significant advantage. Of course, it is also true that the educational requirements of the mainstream U.S. job market are also generally higher than those in their parents' homelands. Immigrants also often come to the United States to create better opportunities for their children, so they will push their children to achieve more than they were able to in their sending countries. Large-scale research also finds that the second generation often even outperforms their native peers. These studies show that on most indicators of social and economic achievement, Asian and European second-generation immigrants often outperform the children of native whites.

Black and Latino second-generation members, while on average trailing behind native whites, are doing significantly better than members of native minority groups. Moreover, holding constant for parental earnings and other measures of socioeconomic status places black and Latino second-generation achievement at an equal level to native whites. These studies indicate that, while downward mobility is a factor in some immigrant groups, modest but significant gains between the first and second generations are far more typical.

In a historically comparative perspective, other explicit comparisons of both groups have shown concerns about second-generation decline to be overwrought. In some respects, children of immigrants today face troubles akin to, but no worse than, children of immigrants in the earlier era of mass immigration. For instance, some have claimed that an oppositional culture, hostile to educational achievement and drawing on the rebellious youth culture of American minority groups, is developing among today's second generation. However, this issue was often raised in the past regarding certain groups—most notably second-generation Italian Americans—who in the end actually achieved substantial upward mobility.

If today's second generation is developing such an "oppositional" stance, it is really not inconsistent with past experience and not necessarily an indication of intergenerational downward mobility. Some have also claimed the earlier groups had the benefit of being racially white, while today's second generation largely consists of racial minorities. However, these authors note that groups considered white today were considered racially distinct in the past (e.g., Irish). There are also ways in which today's second generation may actually be *better off* than the earlier group. In the previous era, limitations to educational advancement for certain groups was institutionalized and often socially accepted (e.g., university quotas for Jews), but today such action is seen as both illegitimate and illegal. Generally speaking, the prevailing political and cultural American context is more accepting of immigrant and minority groups than in the early and mid-twentieth century, and this creates a more accommodating environment for children of immigrants today. Moreover, more of today's second

generation comes from families with high or mid-level socioeconomic background than in the past, which undoubtedly has aided the educational and economic progress of their children.

Explanations for Upward Mobility

Such educational success can be explained by a variety of factors. For instance, cultural organization and strong ethnic communities can lead to economic opportunity through "selective acculturation," a term developed by Portes and collaborators (e.g., Zhou and Rumbaut). Portes and Zhou focus on how strong kinship ties among the Chinese, or the religious affiliations of the Koreans, constitute social capital that increases the ability of the first generation to instill loyalty and obedience in their children. Simultaneously, this ethnic community limits the second generations' ties to American minorities, thereby decreasing their likelihood of downward assimilation.

When these groups resist acculturation into the broader American culture, or allow their children to acculturate only selectively while retaining strong ties to the ethnic community, they paradoxically provide their children with better means to get ahead. Even some earlier researchers advocated strong ethnic ties and building social capital as avenues for combating psychological dislocation. Covello, who, while growing up, felt ashamed of his parents, would later, as the principal of an East Harlem high school, introduce the teaching of Italian as a means of preserving ethnic heritage and keeping assimilation partially at bay. Yet, when the second generation is successful, that success does not always seem tied to connections with the ethnic enclaves of their parents. Such enclaves have served as safety nets for the least successful members of the second generation but are rarely springboards to second-generation upward mobility once that second generation reaches adulthood. Consequently, among the most economically successful immigrant groups, such as Korean Americans, the second generation is usually anxious to avoid both economic and geographic ethnic enclaves.

Besides selective acculturation, a number of other factors, may support the second generation's educational success. The "immigrant optimism" proposition finds that immigrant parents hold higher hopes and expectations for their children than do native parents, and this holds positive implications for second-generation outcomes. Research also finds that the second generation views education as a means of escaping poverty rather than simply a vehicle for personal fulfillment, and this may provide an internal push for educational success, in addition to the parents' desires. Despite concerns about the development of oppositional culture, respondents in a large-scale study of the second generation in New York City conducted from 1999 to 2002 did not see doing well in school as "acting white"—an indication that these youth did not develop an adversarial stance to mainstream measures of success. For example, despite concern that immigrant children's exposure to non-English languages limit their English-language acquisition and educational success, research on the second generation definitively shows that the second generation is fluent in English. In fact, they often prefer English to their parents' mother tongue and are more fluent in English than any non-English language.

Consequences of Upward Mobility

Whereas the benefits of educational success have a clear impact on the socioeconomic success of the second generation, they also have a potential significance in broader realms. Specifically, Richard Alba has contended that such upward mobility for ethnic minorities holds implications for the placement and salience of ethnic and racial boundaries. Certain conditions that allow for the relaxing or redrawing of ethno-racial boundaries include the availability of non-zero-sum mobility in work and education, in which immigrant-descent gain does not come at the expense of the native population and may enhance the capacity to turn this economic advance into closer social relations with the majority group. This framework explains the entry of descendants of Jewish and Italian immigrants—who were seen as racially distinct and inferior in the early twentieth century—into the mainstream. The postwar era saw a shift to a mass education system that promoted ideas of meritocracy, increasing investment in public universities (some of which rose to elite status), and a general national economic expansion. Together, these factors have created an environment in which the gains by children of immigrants would not come at the expense of their native peers. Consequently, such children of immigrants were able to obtain mainstream jobs alongside native peers.

By obtaining this education and employment, and through the resultant move up the economic ladder, children of immigrants have been increasingly able to interact with children of nonimmigrants in school, employment, and neighborhoods. As a result, the ethnic background of children of immigrants has become a decreasingly salient marker of social difference. This era also saw the disproving of the biological basis of race, the expansion of a human rights discourse, and the civil rights movement—all of which contributed to the idea that minorities have the same moral worth as majority groups and, further, contributed to the decreasing social importance of ethnic boundaries. Given these factors, descendants of turn-of-the-century immigrants were able to relax, blur, or even eliminate barriers between their ethnic group and the mainstream.

This possibility of ethno-racial boundary change is not limited to previous eras. In fact, a key necessity for such change—the possibility of non-zero-sum mobility—may emerge again in the twenty-first century. Though many have presented pessimistic views of an increasingly hourglass economy, such concerns do not take into account a major impending demographic transition, namely the aging of the baby-boom generation and their impending retirement. As this generation retires, it leaves open a large number of available occupational positions, and especially high-level positions. This creates an opportunity for the contemporary second generation to find positions in the workforce without crowding out native youth. Just as in the past, the possibility of ethno-racial mixing at the top rung of the occupational ladder could lead to greater blurring of the salience of these ethno-racial boundaries in the workplace and potentially in the general public. We cannot yet say with certainty what glass ceilings even relatively successful groups may face in the future, but there is a chance that upward mobility today may change society's future perspective on ethno-racial boundaries.

Living between Two Worlds: Challenges and Benefits

Despite the second generation's overall success in schooling, they do face certain challenges that their American peers do not. Such challenges often relate to the second generation's position as both American and ethnic; they live both within and between American society and their parents' native culture. This situation is particularly problematic for groups for whom incorporation into American society means, in effect becoming part of a stigmatized ethnic or racial minority group, and for groups (most notably Mexicans and Central Americans) among whom the second generation remains far less well off than their white American peers, despite substantial upward mobility relative to the very low educational levels and incomes of many of their parents.

One point of contention across the generations has to do with parental expectations for their children. Immigrant parents feel they have made sacrifices so that their children will get ahead in America, and if the children do not succeed or make educational or occupational choices at odds with parental expectations, then tensions—and conflicts—can result. Many immigrant cultures also place a high value on deference to parents, so if children begin to assert independence and make their own decisions based on American norms they have seen, further conflicts may arise. Another common source of conflict between immigrant parents and their second-generation children are issues of cultural difference relating to dating and marriage. Immigrant children may face strong parental pressure to date and marry within the ethnic group. A large-scale second-generation study reports that among the children of immigrants, in almost every

At a middle school in Texas, Marisol attends a computer class taught by one of her favorite teachers. Marisol, a bright student, may yet have to drop out of school and work to help the family survive. (Janet Jarman/Corbis)

group, a majority—usually a large majority—reject the notion that it is important to marry within the group, a view they acknowledge is often not shared by their parents.

A number of immigrant cultures see the parents as playing a significant role in the choice of their child's dating partner. Therefore, when children feel they should choose their own dating partners (a common modern American cultural norm), conflict may develop. An extreme case in which immigrant norms are "out of sync" with those of the dominant American culture is arranged marriage, a common practice in many South Asian and Middle Eastern sending societies. Arranged marriages, needless to say, conflict sharply with the emphasis on romantic love and fulfilling one's own particular destiny so conspicuous in American youth culture. Of course, conflicts over arranged marriages are increasingly common in many of the immigrants' countries of origin as well. Yet, in the United States, children may be encouraged to reject traditional arranged marriages by the mainstream society's culture and, in some cases, its legal institutions as well.

In addition to cultural conflicts, familial tensions and stress may also emerge from logistical and legal repercussions of the second generation's in-between status. First, children are often used as translators, interpreters, and general cultural intermediaries for non-English-speaking parents. While parents may feel they have no choice but to place their children in this situation, it may provide undue stress for these children by requiring them to deal with their parents' adult responsibilities, such as bill payments and medical issues. By placing high levels of responsibility and power over family matters on the children, this can invert the typical parent-child power dynamic. Second, different legal statuses within a family can also complicate relations between parents and children. If a child was brought to the United States as a young child (so, technically, 1.25 or 1.5 generation) without state authorization, he or she becomes an undocumented immigrant, with little access to public benefits. However, if the mother gives birth to younger siblings while in the United States, these siblings are American citizens, which makes them eligible for health care and other state services. If older

undocumented siblings see that parents are more willing to provide younger siblings with certain care (e.g., medical care) but do not understand why, or if they believe parents otherwise favor these younger siblings based on the resources their legal status provide, undocumented children may develop strained feelings toward their parents.

Intergenerational strains and conflicts can be seen in arenas outside of the family as well. Studies of religious congregations indicate that members of the second generation may segregate themselves from the immigrant generation in these settings because they feel estranged from the ethnic ambiance; and in some religious institutions, members of the second generation resent being denied access to meaningful authority roles. In political organizations and community groups, the second generation, particularly those with an American college education, may have a different perspective on ethnic group identity as well as a different style of political expression than do those whose early political experience was in another society. Nicole Marwell's work on Dominican activists indicates a far greater influence of the American civil rights movement on both the style and substance of political expression among the second, as compared to the first, generation, as well as a greater willingness to work closely with other Latinos and African Americans. Similarly, Yen Lee Espiritu's study of "pan ethnicity" among Asian Americans notes a greater pan-ethnic consciousness of "Asian" (as opposed to "Chinese," "Korean," or "Vietnamese") identity among the second generation.

Despite these challenges associated with second-generation status, there are certain ways in which the cultural in-between status of the second generation does offer advantages. For one, the second generation tends to live with their immigrant parents longer than their third-plus generation American peers. Indeed, multigenerational households are more common among immigrant groups than among natives in the United States today. For most middle-class Americans, it has become normative to leave the parental home before age 20 to pursue higher education, join the armed forces, or to simply "strike out" on one's own. Young adults who return to their parents' home in their 20s are labeled "boomerang kids" or "ILYAS" ("incompletely launched young adults"). They are seen as somehow unsuccessful, and their rising numbers are considered a social problem.

By contrast, in many immigrant families, young people are seen as making the transition to adulthood not by leaving the parental household, but rather by beginning to make financial contributions to it. Whatever its emotional costs, it is a considerable financial advantage, particularly in high-cost housing markets such as New York and Los Angeles, where many immigrants are concentrated. It may partially explain why working-class immigrants in those metropolitan areas are more likely to own homes than natives of the same age and income level. It may also be advantageous in terms of obtaining education credentials, for it allows children to avoid needing to earn their own income for rent. In this sense, some second-generation individuals feel they benefit by living within and between two cultures. They are able to take advantage of exposure to American customs and social system (e.g., acquiring English-language skills, accessing free K–12 education) but they may also benefit from continued embeddedness in their parents' cultural norms (e.g., living with family beyond high school).

The Second Generation in an International Perspective

Research on the second generation has been spearheaded and established in the American context. However, toward the end of the twentieth century and the beginning of the twenty-first century, researchers began focusing increasing attention on the second generation in Europe. Because Europe, like the United States, saw an increase in immigration around the middle of the twentieth century, modern Europe also contains a large second-generation cohort. Though European research on the second generation is still in its early stages at the time of this chapter's publication, existing findings offer intriguing insights into the second-generation experience. In particular, these comparative views help identify ways in which institutional structures, such as educational systems, and cultural contexts, such as histories of immigration and racial diversity, affect second-generation experiences and outcomes.

Studies of the experiences of children of immigrants in schools in Europe, when compared with similar studies in the United States and elsewhere within the continent, provide key indicators of how different systems of schooling can drastically affect student outcomes. One significant factor is student tracking, in which students are placed in different educational systems, or "tracks," depending on their supposed academic ability. In places where students are tracked early and where it is difficult to move into a higher track (i.e., in Germany), children of immigrants seem to suffer lower educational outcomes. In contrast, children of immigrants seem to benefit from educational programs that do not use such strict tracking systems (e.g., France and the United States) or track students at a later age (e.g., Netherlands). In addition, different educational systems vary widely in the degree to which parents are expected to be involved in their children's education. Where high involvement is expected (e.g., Germany), immigrant parents' limited knowledge of host-country language and educational norms may negatively affect their children, whereas children of immigrants will have little disadvantage relative to native children if the state expects minimal parental involvement. School funding can also affect the second generation's educational outcomes, and there are significant differences between the American and European outcomes on this measure.

In the United States, schools are locally funded, so schools in poorer communities have fewer financial resources. Because many immigrant families live in poorer areas, children of immigrants may be detrimentally affected by this funding scheme. In contrast, many European systems fund schools through the state or national level, giving equal resources to all schools. In fact, in some locations (e.g., France), additional resources are provided to poorer areas. Other relevant factors include the level of residential segregation between immigrant and native families, the availability of private schools, and language support for children of immigrants in schools.

Just as comparative American-European studies have helped identify key features of educational contexts that affect second-generation outcomes, studies focused on membership, social boundaries, and identity have helped identify key features of societal contexts that shape second-generation outcomes. One study focuses on the salience of boundaries for second-generation Mexicans in the United States, Maghrebians in France, and Turks in Germany. In the European case, it finds that religion is the most salient difference (Maghrebians and Turks are mostly Muslim, while France and Germany are predominantly Christian), and it presents a bright boundary (i.e., the dividing line between groups is clearly defined) between immigrants and natives. In the United States, however, race is the main significant difference between Mexicans and natives; yet in contemporary America, race, historically the nation's central social cleavage, has become more of what Alba (2005, 20) terms a "blurred" boundary rather than a bright boundary. The principal immigrant/native distinction in Europe, where large-scale migration is a relatively recent phenomenon, is thus clear and durable; in contrast, the principal immigrant/native distinction in the United States (at least for Mexicans and/or Latinos in general) may be becoming more flexible in the post–civil rights era.

The issue of race is more problematic for the children of black immigrants, since the black/white divide in the United States, in contrast to the Hispanic/white divide, remains far less fluid. One study examines racial meaning amongst second-generation Caribbean immigrants in New York and London and it finds that the existence of a native minority population plays a significant role. In New York, with its large African-American populations, Caribbeans find they have less social contact with whites but they can claim American identity by claiming an African-American identity. In London, the lack of a native African-American population leads to a lesser social divide between the Caribbean second generation and whites; yet this lack of native black population also means that the Caribbean second generation is less able to claim British identity. Thus, the historical existence of a long-term visible minority in the United States (something that is generally not the case in Europe, save the Roma population) permits this second-generation group to claim membership in the majority society through association with a long-standing minority.

Conclusion

Since the 1990s, research on the modern second generation has taken great strides, and it will surely continue to develop in future years. Within the realm of immigration research, and the broader social science world, the study of the second generation takes on great significance at multiple levels. At the most basic level, it provides us with a deeper understanding of a growing subset of the general population, and it adds to our understanding of the immigrant experience. Given that the second generation will have to play an increasing role in society as the current cohort comes of age and as new second generations are produced through continued migration, studying this population also provides indications of how society may transform over time. Finally, by examining the ways in which the second generation is—or is not—incorporated into the larger society, and by comparing this incorporation between locations, we can understand key features of our social context that might have otherwise remained invisible.

Bibliography

Alba, Richard. 2005. "Bright vs. Blurred Boundaries: Second Generation Assimilation and Exclusion in France, Germany, and the United States." *Ethnic and Racial Studies* 28, no. 1: 20–49.

Alba, Richard. 2009. *Blurring the Color Line: The New Chance for a More Integrated America.* Cambridge, MA: Harvard University Press.

Alba, Richard, and Victor Nee. 2003. *Remaking the American Mainstream: Assimilation and Contemporary Immigration.* Cambridge, MA: Harvard University Press.

Espiritu, Yen Le. 1992. *Asian American Panethnicity: Bridging Institutions and Identities.* Philadelphia: Temple University Press.

Foner, Nancy. 2012. "Black Identities and the Second Generation: Afro-Caribbeans in Britain and the United States." In *New Dimensions of Diversity: The Second Generation in Comparative Perspective,* edited by Richard Alba and Mary Waters, 251–68. New York: New York University Press.

Foner, Nancy, and Philip Kasinitz. 2007. "The Second Generation." In *The New Americans: A Guide of Immigration since 1965*, edited by Mary C. Waters and Reed Ueda, 270–82. Cambridge, MA: Harvard University Press.

Gans, Herbert. 1992. "Second-Generation Decline: Scenarios for the Economic and Ethnic Futures of the Post-1965 American Immigrants." *Ethnic and Racial Studies* 15, no. 2: 173–92.

Hansen, Marcus Lee. 1938. "The Problem of the Third-Generation Immigrant." In *American Immigrants and Their Generations: Studies and Commentaries on the Hansen Thesis after Fifty Years*, edited by Peter Kivisto and Dag Blanck, 191–216. Urbana: University of Illinois Press.

Holdaway, Jennifer, Maurice Crul, and Catrin Roberts. 2009. "Cross-National Comparison of Provision and Outcomes for the Education of the Second Generation." In *Educating Immigrant Youth: Pathways to Employment and Citizenship in International Perspective*, edited by M. Crul, J. Holdaway, and C. Roberts. Special Issue Teachers College Records.

Iorizzo, Luciano, and Salvatore Mondello. 1980. *The Italian Americans: Third Edition*. Amherst, NY: Cambria Press.

Jimenez, Tomas. 2010. *Replenished Ethnicity: Mexican Americans, Immigration, and Identity*. Berkeley: University of California Press.

Kahn, Bonnie. 1987. *Cosmopolitan Culture: The Gilt-Edged Dream of a Tolerant City*. New York: Atheneum.

Kao, G., and Tienda, M. 1995. "Optimism and Achievement: The Educational Performance of Immigrant Youth." *Social Science Quarterly* 76, no. 1: 1–19.

Kasinitz, Philip, John H. Mollenkopf, Mary C. Waters, and Jennifer Holdaway. 2008. *Inheriting the City: Children of Immigrants Come of Age*. Cambridge, MA: Harvard University Press.

Landesman, Alter. 1969. *Brownsville: The Birth, Development, and Passing of a Jewish Community in New York*. New York: Bloch Publishing Co.

Mannheim, Karl. 1936. *Ideology and Utopia*. London: Routledge.

Marwell, Nicole P. 2004. "Ethnic and Post-Ethnic Politics in New York City: The Dominican Second Generation." In *Becoming New Yorkers: Ethnographies of the New Second Generation*, edited by Philip Kasinitz, Mary Waters, and John Mollenkopf, 257–84. New York: Russell Sage Foundation.

Novak, Michael. 1995. *Unmeltable Ethnics: Politics and Culture in American Life*. New York: Transaction Publishers.

Portes, Alejandro, and Min Zhou. 1993. "The New Second Generation: Segmented Assimilation and Its Variants." *Annals of the American Academy of Political and Social Science* 530, no. 1: 74–96.

Portes, Alejandro, and Ruben Rumbaut. 2001. *Legacies: The Story of the Immigrant Second Generation*. Berkeley: University of California Press.

Prell, Riv-Ellen. 1999. *Fighting to Become Americans: Jews, Gender, and the Anxiety of Assimilation*. Boston: Beacon Press.

Rumbaut, Ruben. 1997. "Ties That Bind: Immigration and Immigrant Families in the US." In *Immigration and the Family; Research and Policy on US Immigrants*, edited by Alan Booth, Ann C. Crouter, and Nancy Landale, 3–45. Mahway, NJ: Lawrence Erlbaum Associates.

Smith, Robert C. 2006. Mexican *New York: Transnational Lives of New Immigrants*. Berkeley: University of California Press.

Telles, Edward E., and Vilma Ortiz. 2008. *Generations of Exclusion: Mexican Americans, Assimilation and Race*. New York: Russell Sage Foundation.

Warner, William Lloyd, and Leo Srole. 1945. *The Social Systems of American Ethnic Groups*. New Haven, CT: Yale University Press.

Zhou, M., and C. L. Bankston. 1998. *Growing Up American: How Vietnamese Children Adapt to Life in the United States*. New York: Russell Sage Foundation.

Selected Bibliography

Elliott Robert Barkan

Alba, Richard, and Victor Nee. 2003. *Remaking the American Mainstream: Assimilation and Contemporary Immigration.* Cambridge, MA: Harvard University Press.

Barkan, Elliott Robert. 1995. *And Still They Come: Immigrants and American Society, 1920s – 1952.* Wheeling, IL: Harlan Davidson.

Barkan, Elliott Robert. 2007. *From All Points Due West: America's Immigrant West, 1870s – 1952.* Bloomington, IN: Indiana University Press.

Barkan, Elliott Robert, ed. 2007. *Immigration, Incorporation, and Transnationalism.* New Brunswick, NJ: Transaction.

Barkan, Elliott Robert. 2007. *Making It in America: A Sourcebook on Eminent Ethnic Americans.* Santa Barbara, CA: ABC-CLIO.

Barkan, Elliott Robert, ed. 1999. *A Nation of Peoples: A Sourcebook on America's Multicultural Heritage.* Westport, CT: Greenwood Press.

Barkan, Elliott Robert, Hasia Diner, and Alan M. Kraut, eds. 2008. *From Arrival to Incorporation: Migrants to the U.S. in a Global Era.* New York: New York University Press.

Barkan, Elliott Robert, and Michael LeMay, eds. 1999. *U.S. Immigration and Naturalization Laws and Issues: A Documentary History.* Westport, CT: Greenwood Press.

Binder, Frederick M., and David M. Reimers. 1995. *'All the Nations Under Heaven': An Ethnic and Racial History of New York City.* New York: Columbia University Press.

Dinnerstein, Leonard, and David M. Reimers. 1999. *Ethnic Americans: A History of Immigration.* 4th ed. New York: Columbian University Press.

Durand, Jorge, and Douglas S. Massey, eds. 2004. *Crossing the Border: Research from the Mexican Migration Project.* New York: Russell Sage.

Emmons, M. David. *2010. Beyond the American Pale: The Irish in the West, 1845–1910.* Norman, OK: University of Oklahoma Press.

Farley, Reynolds. 1996. *The New American Reality: Who We Are, How We Got Here, Where We Are Going.* New York: Russell Sage.

Foner, Nancy. 2000. *From Ellis Island to JFK: New York's Two Great Waves of Immigration.* New York: Russell Sage.

Gerstle, Gary. 2001. *American Crucible: Race and Nation in the Twentieth Century.* Princeton, NJ: Princeton University Press.

Gerstle, Gary, and John Mollenkopf, eds. 2001. *E Pluribus Unum? Contemporary and Historical Perspectives on Immigrant Political Incorporation.* New York: Russell Sage.

Glenn, Evelyn Nakano. 2002. *Unequal Freedom: How Race and Gender Shaped American Citizenship and Labor.* Cambridge, MA: Harvard University Press.

Hertzberg, Arthur. 1989. *The Jews in America: Four Centuries of an Uneasy Encounter.* New York: Touchstone Books.

Higham, Carol L., and William H. Katerberg. 2009. *Conquests and Consequences? The American West from Frontier to Region.* Wheeling, IL: Harlan Davidson

Hing, Bill Ong. 2004. *Defining America through Immigration Policy.* Philadelphia Temple University Press.

Hintzen, Percy C. 2001. *West Indian in the West: Self-Representation in an Immigrant Community.* New York: New York University Press

Kanstroom, Daniel. 2007. *Deportation Nation: Outsiders in American History.* Cambridge, MA: Harvard University.

King, Desmond. 2000. *Making Americans: Immigration, Race and the Origins of the Diverse Democracy.* Cambridge, MA: Harvard University Press.

Kivisto, Peter. 1995. *Americans All: Race and Ethnic Relations in Historical, Structural, and Comparative Perspectives. Belmont. CA: Wadsworth Publishing Comp.*

Kivisto, Peter, ed. 2005. *Incorporating Diversity: Rethinking Assimilation in a Multicultural Age.* Boulder, CO: Paradigm.

Lee, Erika. 2003. *At America's Gates: Chinese Immigration during the Exclusion Era, 1880–1943.* Chapel Hill: University of North Carolina Press.

Lee, J.J., and Marion R. Casey, eds. 2006. *Making the Irish American: History and Heritage of the Irish in the United States.* New York: New York University Press.

Leonard, Karen Isaksen. 2003. *Muslims in the United States: The State of Research.* Russell Sage.

Min, Pyong Gap. 2000. *Mass Migration to the United States: Classical and Contemporary Periods.* Walnut Creek, CA: Alta Mira Press

Ngai, Mae M. 2004. *Impossible Subjects: Illegal Immigrants and the Making of Modern America.* Princeton, NJ: Princeton University Press.

Reimers, David M. 2005. *Other Immigrant: The Global Origins of the American People.* New York: New York University Press.

Reimers, David M. 1998. *Unwelcome Strangers: American Identity and the Turn against Immigration.* New York: Columbia University Press.

Schneider, Dorothee. 2011. *Crossing Borders: Migration and Citizenship in the Twentieth Century United States.* Cambridge: Harvard University Press.

Singer, Audrey, Susan W. Hardwick, and Caroline B. Brettell. 2008. *Twenty-First Century Gateways: Immigrant Incorporation in Suburban America.* Washington, DC: Brookings Institute.

Spikard, Paul. 1989. *Almost All Aliens: Immigration, Race, and Colonialism in American History and Identity.* New York: Routledge.

Spikard, Paul. 1989. *Mixed Blood: Intermarriage and Ethnic Identity in Twentieth Century America.*

Strum, Phillippa, and Danielle Tarantolo, etc. 2003. *Muslims in the United States.* Washington, DC: Woodrow Wilson Center.

Takaki, Ronald. 1993, 2008. *A Different Mirror: A History of Multicultural America.* Rev. ed. Boston: Little, Brown, and Co.

Waters, Mary C., and Reed Ueda, eds. 2007. *The New Americans: A Guide to Immigration since 1965.* Cambridge: Harvard University Press.

Zhou, Min, and James V. Gatewood. 2007. *Contemporary Asian America: A Multidisciplinary Reader.* 2nd ed. New York: New York University Press.

Zolberg, Aristde R. 2006. *A Nation by Design: Migration Policy in the Fashioning of America.* New York: Russell Sage.

Zúñiga, Victor, and Rubén Hernández-León, eds. 2005. *New Destinations: Mexican Immigration in the United States.* New York: Russell Sage.

About the Editor and Contributors

Editor

Elliott Robert Barkan, PhD, professor emeritus, was, for 40 years, a professor of history and ethnic studies, California State University, San Bernardino. His principal publications include *And Still They Come: Immigrants and American Society, 1920–1990s* (1995); *Asian and Pacific Islander Migration to the United States: A Model of New Global Patterns* (Praeger, 1992); *A Nation of Peoples: A Sourcebook on America's Multi-cultural Heritage* (editor; Greenwood, 1999); *U.S. Immigration and Naturalization Laws and Issues* (coeditor; Greenwood, 1999); *Making It In America: A Sourcebook on Eminent Ethnic Americans* (editor; ABC-CLIO, 2001); and *From All Points: America's Immigrant West, 1870s–1952* (2007).

Contributors

The following have contributed chapters to *Immigrants in American History*. Their specializations and affiliations are listed.

June Granatir Alexander
Slavic Migration
University of Cincinnati, Ohio

James P. Allen
Ethnic and Race Group Distributions
Emeritus, California State University, Northridge

Peter T. Alter
Archivist
Chicago History Museum, Illinois

Ramona Fruja Amthor
Social Foundations of Education (Multiculturalism and Immigration)
Bucknell University, Lewisburg, Pennsylvania

Donald Howard Avery
Canadian Immigration Policy, Canadian Border Issues, Refugee Intellectuals
Emeritus, and Adjunct Research Professor
University of Western Ontario, London, Ontario, Canada

Anny Bakalian
Middle Eastern Americans
Graduate Center, City University of New York

Robert Eric Barde
U.S. Immigration History, Nineteenth and Twentieth Centuries
University of California, Berkeley

H. Arnold Barton
History of Scandinavia and Scandinavians in North America
Emeritus, Southern Illinois University, Carbondale

James M. Bergquist
German Americans and Historiography of Immigration
Emeritus, Villanova University, Villanova, Pennsylvania

Dag Blanck
Swedish-American History, Transnational Swedish-American Relations
Uppsala University, Sweden; and Augustana College, Rock Island, Illinois

About the Editor and Contributors

Carl Bon Tempo
History of U.S. Refugee Affairs and History of
Human Rights
University at Albany, State University of New York

Mehdi Bozorgmehr
Middle Eastern Americans
Graduate Center, City University of New York

Susan Roth Breitzer
American Jewish History, Immigration History
Campbell University, Fort Bragg Army Extension,
North Carolina

Caroline B. Brettell
Anthropology of Migration; and Gender and
Migration
Southern Methodist University, Dallas, Texas

Jørn Brøndal
U.S. Ethnic, Racial, and Political History
Center for American Studies
University of Southern Denmark, Odense

Norma Stoltz Chinchilla
Central American Immigration to the U.S.; Immigrant
Family Separation; Latin American Feminism
California State University, Long Beach

Jessica Cooperman
Modern Jewish History
Muhlenberg College, Allentown, Pennsylvania

Els de Graauw
Immigration, Civic and Political Participation; Urban
Politics; Public Policy
Baruch College, City University of New York

Linda C. Delgado
Latinos in the U.S.
State University of New York, New Paltz

Barlow Der-Mugrdechian
Armenian Literature and Armenian Studies
California State University, Fresno

Harriet Orcutt Duleep
Economics and Immigration
College of William and Mary, Williamsburg, Virginia

Meaghan Dwyer-Ryan
U.S. Immigration and Ethnicity, Irish-American and
Jewish-American History
Eastern Connecticut State University, Willimantic

Keith P. Dyrud
East Slavic Immigration to the U.S.
Independent Scholar, St. Paul, Minnesota

Rebecca Edwards
Community and Social Psychology
University of Massachusetts, Lowell

David M. Emmons
Irish America, Labor, Immigration
University of Montana, Missoula

Brett Jonathan Esaki
Religious Studies
University of California, Santa Barbara

Judith Fai-Podlipnik
Hungarian History and the Holocaust
Holocaust Educational Foundation, Independent
Scholar, Kenosha, Wisconsin

Henry Flores
Dean, Grad school, St. Mary's University, San
Antonio

Nancy Foner
Immigration to New York, to the U.S., Past and
Present; Comparisons of Immigration in Europe,
U.S., and Caribbean
Hunter College, Graduate Center, City College of
New York

Annick Foucrier
Centre de Recherches d'Histoire Nord America,
Paris, France

Samantha Friedman
Urban Sociology; Immigration; Housing
University at Albany, State University of New York

Christina Gerken
Sociology, University of South Bend, South Bend, IN

Solomon A. Getahun
Ethiopia/Horn of Africa, and African Diaspora
Central Michigan University, Mount Pleasant

Shannon Gleeson
Sociology, Demography, Labor, Immigration, Law
and Society
Latin American and Latino Studies,
University of California, Santa Cruz

Steven J. Gold
International Migration; Ethnic Economics; Ethnic
Communities
Michigan State University, East Lansing

Manuel G. Gonzales
Mexican-American History
Diablo Valley College, Pleasant Hill, California

April Gordon
African Studies
Winthrop University, Rock Hill, South Carolina

John J. Grabowski
Immigration and Public History
Case Western Reserve University, Cleveland, Ohio

Rudy P. Guevarra Jr.
Comparative Ethnic Studies; Asian, Pacific Islanders
Arizona State University, Tempe

Anita Olson Gustafson
Swedish Immigration
Presbyterian College, Clinton, South Carolina

Roland L. Guyotte
U.S. Immigration and Ethnic History
University of Minnesota, Morris

Marilyn Halter
History and Sociology of Immigration, Race and
Ethnicity, especially Immigrants of African Descent
Boston University

Robin Harper
Political Science
York College of City University of New York
Jamaica, New York

Angela Daley Hawk
Nineteenth Century U.S. West
University of California, Irvine

Joseph F. Healey
Sociology
Christopher News University, Christopher News, VA

Kimberly Kay Hoang
Gender, Globalization, Immigration, Ethnography
Rice University, Houston, Texas

Violet Showers Johnson
History of Race, Ethnicity, and Immigration in the
U.S.; History of African Diaspora
Agnes Scott College, Decatur, Georgia

Anna Karpathakis
Immigration, Greek Immigrants, Gender, Urban
History
Kingsborough Community College, Brooklyn,
New York

Philip Kasinitz
Sociology
Graduate Center, City University of New York

Matthew Kester
Oceana, U.S. West, Nineteenth and Twentieth
Centuries
Brigham Young University–Hawaii, Laie

Nazli Kibria
Sociology of Migration and Families
Boston University

Kwang Chung Kim
Immigration Studies
Emeritus, Western Illinois University, Macomb

Peter Kivisto
Immigrant Incorporation, Sociological Theory
Augustana College, Rock Island, Illinois

Matjaž Klemenčič
U.S. Immigration history, Indigenous and Immigrant
Groups in U.S. and Europe
University of Maribor, Ljubjana, Slovenia

Shira Miriam Kohn
Judaic Studies, New York University, NYC

Lisa Konczal
Immigration, Nicaraguans and Nicaragua, Global
Stratification
Barry University, Miami Shores, Florida

Auvo Kostiainen
History of Migration, Tourism, and Travel
University of Turku, Finland

Myron B. Kuropas
Ukrainian-American History, Ukrainian History, and
History of Education
Emeritus, Northern Illinois University

Peter Kwong
Asian-American Studies, Chinese History
Hunter College, City University of New York

Jonathan H. X. Lee
Asian-American Studies
San Francisco State University

James N. Leiker
American West
Johnson County Community College, Eudora, Kansas

Vivian Louie
Immigration and Education
Harvard Graduate School of Education

Odd S. Lovoll
Norwegians and Norwegian Immigration, 1940–
Present
Emeritus, University of Oslo and St. Olaf's College,
Northfield, Minnesota

Cherstin M. Lyon
Citizenship, Immigration, and Ethnic American History
California State University, San Bernardino

Jason MacDonald
Immigration
University of Southampton, England

Maxine L. Margolis
Anthropology, Brazilian Immigration
Emerita, University of Florida; Adjunct,
Columbia University Institute for Latin American
Studies

David C. Mauk
Norwegian and Scandinavian-American History
University of Oslo

Cecilia Menjívar
Social Networks, Gender, Family, Intergenerational
Relations, Religion, Central American Migration
Arizona State University, Tempe

Robert Mikkelsen
Labor, Migration, and Ethnic History
Østfold University College, Remmen, Norway

Elizabeth A. Miller
Sociology, Immigration
Graduate Center, City University of New York

Dušanka Miščević
Chinese History
Independent Scholar, New York, New York
Yuka Mizutani
International Area Studies; Native-American Studies
Center for Ainu and Indigenous Studies, Hokkaido
University, Japan

Mohsen M. Mobasher
International Migration, Iranians in Diaspora, Globalization, Middle East and Ethnic Relations
University of Houston Downtown

Suzanne Model
Sociology of Immigration
Emerita, University of Massachusetts, Amherst

Raymond A. Mohl
Race, Ethnicity, and Urbanization
University of Alabama at Birmingham

Katherine L. Moloney
Sociology, Housing, and Immigration
University at Albany, State University of New York

Roger L. Nichols
American Indian and Western-American History
University of Arizona, Tucson

Charles E. Orser Jr.
Historical Archaeology, Anthropology,
New York State Museum

Jennifer Osorio
Latin America
Young Research Library, University of California, Los Angeles

Dominic A. Pacyga
Immigration and Urban History
Colombia College, Chicago

Dennis R. Papazian
History
University of Michigan, Dearborn

Chang Gi Park
Health Economics
College of Nursing, University of Illinois at Chicago
Wayne Patterson
Modern East Asia History
St Norbert College, DePere, Wisconsin

Maritsa V. Poros
International Migration, Social Networks, Inequalities, Urban Studies
Graduate Center, City University
of New York

Barbara M. Posadas
U.S. Immigration and Ethnic History
Northern Illinois University, DeKalb

Matteo Pretelli
Independent Scholar, Florence, Italy

James S. Pula
Immigration and Polish Ethnicity
Purdue University

Bruno Ramirez
History of Migrations in the U.S. and
in Canada
University of Montréal

Padma Rangaswamy
South Asian–American and Immigration History
South Asian–American Policy and Research Institute, Chicago

David M. Reimers
American Immigration History
Emeritus, New York University

John D. Ribó
Comparative Literature—Latina/o Studies
University of North Carolina, Chapel Hill

Justin G. Riskus
Lithuanians in America
Independent Scholar, Hillside, Illinois

Emily Rosenbaum
Sociology
Fordham University, Bronx, New York
Ernesto Sagas
Ethnic Studies
Colorado State University

Jackleen M. Salem
Muslims in America, Immigration History, Race, and
Women's Issues
University of Wisconsin, Milwaukee

Marianne Sanua
American Jewish History
Florida Atlantic University, Boca Raton

Leo Schelbert
American and Swiss Migration History
Emeritus, University of Illinois at Chicago

Carol L. Schmid
Immigration in the U.S., Hispanics, Language
Politics
Guilford Technical Community College, Julian. North
Carolina

Robert Schoone-Jongen
Nineteenth-Century U.S. and Western European
Social History and Migrations
Calvin College, Grand Rapids, Michigan

Rankin Sherling
Irish Immigration
Queens University, Kingston, Ontario, Canada

Jana Sládková
Social and Community Psychology
University of Massachusetts, Lowell

Jessica Sperling
Immigration, Race, Ethnicity
Graduate Center, City University
of New York

Paul R. Spickard
Race and Immigration
University of California, Santa Barbara

Victoria Stone-Cadena
Indigenous Transnational Migration, Development,
and Social Movements
Graduate Center, City University of New York

Andris Straumanis
Historian of the Latvian Ethnic Press and Editor,
"Latvians Online"
University of Wisconsin, River Falls

Christine M. Su
Southeast Asian and Southeast Asian–American
Ethnic Identity; Cultures, Race, and Race Mixing in
Southeast Asian
Center for Southeast Asian Studies, Ohio University

Yukari Takai
Japanese Migration, French Canadian Migration,
Borders, Women and Work, and Pacific Northwest
Glendon College, York University, Toronto

David S. Torres-Rouff
U.S Nineteenth Century; Urban History; Race; Migration
Colorado College, Colorado Springs

William E. Van Vugt
British Migration
Calvin College, Grand Rapids, Michigan

Diane C. Vecchio
Immigration History
Furman University, Greenville, South Carolina

Priscilla Wald
American Literature and Culture
Duke University, Durham, North Carolina

Brian M. Walker
Irish Studies, Identity and Politics
School of Politics, Queens University, Belfast

Randy William Widdis
Historical Geography
University of Regina, Saskatchewan, Canada

K. Scott Wong
Asian-American History
Williams College, Massachusetts

Karen A. Woodrow-Lafield
Demography, International Migration, Sociology of
Citizenship
Population Research Center, University of Maryland

Donald R. Wright
Africa and African-American History
Emeritus, State University of New York, Cortland

Khalida P. Zaki
Social Demography of Southeast Asia, Muslim
Immigrants, Islam and Women and Family Issues
Michigan State University, East Lansing

Index

Mattson, Hans, 165, 169, 170, 632, 635
Matzoh making, 110
Maurer, Katharine, 1477
May, Cornelis Jacobsen, 59
Mayer, Louis B., 1865
Mayhew, Thomas, 1424
Mazewski, Aloysius, 1196
Mazour, Anatole, 593
Mazumdar, Akhay Kumar, 210
Mazzini Society, 447
Mazzoli, Romano, 1505
McAuley, Catherine, 1674
McAuliffe, Christa, 722
McCafferty, Sinead, 1864
McCain, Cindy, 1022
McCain, John, 1022, 1900
McCalla, Jocelyn (Johnny), 1394
McCann, Colum, 1018
McCarran, Pat, 1070–71, 1527
McCarran Internal Security Act, 1495
McCarran-Walter Act of 1952, 702,
    713–14, 759, 818–19, 1011, 1041,
    1058, 1071, 1376, 1441–42, 1493,
    1495, 1497, 1501, 1541–42, 1561,
    1563, 1776, 1877
McCarthy, Eugene J., 1016
McCarthy, Joseph, 1014, 1016,
    1044–45, 1494
McClatchy, V. S., 453
McCloskey, Frank, 1117
McCormack, John, 1016
McCourt, Frank, 1018, 1862
McCoy, Neal, 926
McDermott, Alice, 1018
McDonald, Alexander, 237
McDonald, Michael Patrick, 1018
McGrath, J. Howard, 1044, 1196
McHenry, James, 102
McKay, Claude, 668
McKay, James, 307
McKean, Thomas, 100
McKeown, Susan, 1863
McKinley, William, 434, 1488, 1554
McVeigh, Timothy, 1513–14
Meagher, Thomas Francis, 104
Meagher, Timothy, 1014
Meany, William George, 1016, 1494
Medellin Cartel, 832
Media images of Arabs, 1965–present,
    720–21, 1142, 1191, 1865
Medicaid, 1885
Medical profession, 736, 921
Medicine bottles, 1831

Medigovich, George, 599
Medill, Joseph, 378
Meehan, Marty, 1008
Megali Idea, 396
Mehmet, Bayram, 1344
Mehta, Zubin, 1863
Meili, Martin, 179
Melara, Julio, 984
Melchior, Lauritz, 878
Meletios, Bishop, 400–401
Mellon, Thomas, 434, 1023
Melnyk, Andrew, 1355
The Melting Pot (Zangwill), 1846–47
Melville, Herman, 52
Méndez, Olga, 1223
Mendez v. Westminster, 1906
Mendoza, Lydia, 1459
Menendez, Bob, 858
Menendez, Robert, 1519
Menéndez de Avilés, Pedro, 304
Menino, Thomas M., 1015, 1044
Mennonites, 66, 177, 179, 180, 249,
    385–87, 391, 393, 1688
Mensalvas, Chris, 919
Menuhin, Yehudi, 1863
Menzies, Gavin, 41
Mercier, Honoré, 260
Merrimac (ship), 170
Merveilleux, Charles Frédéric, 174
Mestrović, Ivan, 298
Meštrović, Joko, 527
Metalious, Grace, 800, 1863
Metcalfe, Victor H., 452
Methodists, 167, 316, 327
Métis, 1435
Metropolitan Opera, 298
Mexican-American War, 119, 128–31,
    1451, 1679, 1894
Mexican Farm Labor Program, 1733
Mexican Revolution, 509, 510, 1453
Mexicans and Mexican Americans
    as a conquered or coerced group,
        1608–10
    interracial unions, 1803–4
    Punjabi-Mexican marriages, 211–12
Mexicans and Mexican Americans, 1870
    to 1940, 507–19
    1870–1908, 507–9
    1908–1929, 509–10
    1930–1940, 516–17
    Americanization and segregation,
        513–14
    conclusion, 519

labor and community, 514–16
    migration and nativism, 513
    repatriation, 517
    second generation and beyond, 516
    struggle and innovation, 517–19
    transnationalism, 510–13
Mexicans and Mexican Americans,
    1940–present, 1119–32
    1940s–1960s, 1120–23
    1980s, 1123–24
    1990s, 1124–26
    2000 to the present, 1126–32
    introduction to, 1119–20
Mexicans and Mexican Americans, to
    1870, 119–32
    Mexican American War and aftermath,
        128–31
    Mexican period, 127–28
    Spanish period, 119–27
"Mexican schools," 1902, 1905
Mexicans in the Southwest, education
    and, 1764–65
Mexican War of Independence, 1895
Meyer, Adolf, 646
Meyer, Benjamin, 407
Meyer, Stephen, 1578
Meyer v. Nebraska, 1749
Mézières, Athanase de, 69
Miami, 308, 835–36, 851–53, 857,
    1474–75
Michael, Archbishop, 956
Michael Collins, 1020
Michaelius, Jonas, 59
Michel, Franz Ludwig, 177
Michel, Pras, 1393
Micheletti, Roberto, 977
Michener, James, 1801
Michigan, 63, 721
Micmacs, 1445–46. *See also* Aroostook
    Band of Micmacs
Micronesians, 1178–79
Middle-class dream, 1082–83
Middle Eastern and North African
    immigrants and Middle Eastern and
    North African Americans, 1940–
    present, 1135–44
    backlash and discrimination, 1142–43
    conclusion, 1143–44
    ethnic and religious identities,
        1141–42
    immigration patterns, 1136–38
    introduction to, 1135–36
    population and settlement, 1138–39

Mitropolsky, John, 587
Mladineo, Ivan, 298
Moberg, Vilhelm, 879
Mobility, socioeconomic
  downward mobility, possibility of,
    1914–15
  Hondurans and Honduran Americans,
    981–82
  Irish Catholics and Irish-Catholic
    Americans, 1013
  Jews and Jewish Americans, 466–67
  second generation and, 1914
  second generation Jewish Americans,
    466–67
  Slovaks and Slovak Americans,
    1268–70
  Slovenes and Slovene Americans,
    1279
  upward, 1915–17
  West Indians and West Indian (French-
    speaking) Americans, 1389–90
Moby Dick (Melville), 52
Moczygęba, Leopold, 148, 150
"Model Minority" myth, 477, 1062–63,
  1405–6
Modern Review, 213
Moe, Roger, 1171
Mohammad Webb Foundation, 1817–18
Mohawk Indians. *See* Akwesasne
  Mohawk
Moise, Pnina, 114
Mollenkopf, John, 1630
Monasticism, 957
Moncada, Guillermo, 302
Mondesir, Evenette, 1396
Monitor (ship), 170
Monk, Maria, 1750–51
Mont Allegro (Mangione), 1861
Montenegrins and Montenegrin
    Americans, 1870 to 1940, 521–28
  contacts with homeland, 527–28
  identity, 521–22
  immigrant life, 526–27
  immigrant organizations, 524–25
  settlement patterns, 522–24
Montenegrins and Montenegrin
    Americans, 1940–present, 1145–49
  conclusion, 1148–49
  emigration and settlement
    patterns, 1146
  introduction to, 1145–46
  social life and organizations, 1147–48
Montenegro, 229

Montgomery, David, 420
Montoya, Joseph, 1896
Moore, Annie, 1476
Moravians. *See* Czechs and Czech
  Americans
Morawska, Ewa, 550, 1626
Moreno, Catalina Sandino, 836
Morgenbladet, 133
Morgenthau, Henry, Jr., 1067
Mormons, 26, 1426–27
  Canadian, 249
  Danes and Danish Americans,
    325, 327
  Danish immigrants, 54–55
  Native Hawai'ians, Pacific Islanders,
    and Pacific Islander Americans,
    534–35
  Portuguese and Portuguese
    Americans, 564
  Swedes and Swedish Americans, 166
  Swiss and Swiss Americans, 643, 644
Morreale, Ben, 1861
Morris, Robert, 144
Morrison, Bruce, 1013, 1506
Morse, Jedidiah, 1839–40
Morse, Samuel B., 147
Mortara, Edgardo, 112
Mortensen, Enok, 330
Morton, Ferdinand Q., 670
Morton, John, 161
Morton, Samuel George, 1798
Mosadegh, Mohammad, 999
Mosques, 1811–13, 1822–23
"Mother of Immigrants" statue, 298
Motivations for migration
  Africans and African Americans from
    West Africa, 701–4
  Basques and Basque
    Americans, 220–21
  Brazilians and Brazilian
    Americans, 775–76
  British and British Americans, 789
  Burmese, 1298
  Cambodian, 1301
  Canadians (Anglo) and Anglo-
    Canadian Americans, 247–48
  Canadians (French) and
    French-Canadian
    Americans, 259–60
  Colombians and Colombian
    Americans, 829–30, 833
  Croats and Croatian Americans,
    842–43

Dominicans and Dominican
    Americans, 882–83
Dutch and Dutch Americans, 333–34
Estonians and Estonian
    Americans, 343
Guatemalans and Guatemalan
    Americans, 964–65
Hondurans and Honduran Americans,
    975–78
Irish Catholics and Irish-Catholic
    Americans, 88–89
Israelis and Israeli Americans,
    1031–32
Jews and Jewish Americans, 459–61
Laotian, 1306
Lithuanians and Lithuanian
    Americans, 487–89, 1099–1100
Mexicans and Mexican Americans,
    509, 1124, 1453
Middle Eastern and North African
    immigrants and Middle Eastern and
    North African Americans, 1136–37
Nicaraguans and Nicaraguan
    Americans, 1152
Norwegians and Norwegian
    Americans, 1165–66
Pacific Islanders and Pacific-Islander
    Americans, 1176
Poles and Polish Americans, 547–48
Puerto Ricans and Puerto Ricans on
    the mainland, 1216
Romanians and Romanian Americans,
    1227–28
Slovaks and Slovak Americans, 604
Slovenes and Slovene Americans, 614
Spanish and Spanish Americans,
    155–58, 624, 1315–16
Swedes and Swedish Americans, 629,
    1321–22
Swiss and Swiss Americans, 642–43
Thai, 1310–11
West Indians and West Indian
    (English-speaking) Americans,
    1377–78
See also Economic reasons for
    immigration; Political reasons for
    immigration; Religious reasons for
    immigration
Mountain West, 626
Mourra, Samir, 1396
Moynihan, Daniel P., 1016, 1624–25
Mrak, Ignacij, 613
Muesebach, John, 1430